STRETCH LIMIT   323 mm
SLACK   20 - 30 mm
T/P F 36 psi. (2.5) R 42 (2.9)

Kawasaki
Z750 & Z1000
Service and Repair Manual

by Matthew Coombs

(4762-336)

Models covered
ZR750-J. 748cc. 2004 to 2006
ZR750-L. 748cc. 2007 to 2008
ZR750-M (ABS). 748cc. 2007 to 2008
ZR1000-A. 953cc. 2003 to 2006
ZR1000-B. 953cc. 2007 to 2008
ZR1000-C (ABS). 953cc. 2007 to 2008

© Haynes Publishing 2008

ABCDE
FGHIJ
KLMNO
PQRST

A book in the Haynes Service and Repair Manual Series

ISBN 978 1 84425 762 1

British Library Cataloguing in Publication Data
A catalogue record for this book is available from the British Library.

Library of Congress Control Number 2008920631

Printed in the USA

Haynes Publishing
Sparkford, Yeovil, Somerset BA22 7JJ, England

Haynes North America, Inc
861 Lawrence Drive, Newbury Park, California 91320, USA

Haynes Publishing Nordiska AB
Box 1504, 751 45 Uppsala, Sweden

Contents

LIVING WITH YOUR KAWASAKI Z750/1000

Introduction

Pre-ride checks

MAINTENANCE

Routine maintenance and servicing

Contents

REPAIRS AND OVERHAUL

Engine, transmission and associated systems

Chassis components

Electrical system

Wiring diagrams

REFERENCE

Index

Kawasaki
The Green Meanies

by Julian Ryder

Kawasaki Heavy Industries

Kawasaki is a company of contradictions. It is the smallest of the big four Japanese manufacturers but the biggest company, it was the last of the four to make and market motorcycles yet it owns the oldest name in the Japanese industry, and it was the first to set up a factory in the USA. Kawasaki Heavy Industries, of which the motorcycle operation is but a small component, is a massive company with its heritage firmly in the old heavy industries like shipbuilding and railways; nowadays it is as much involved in aerospace as in motorcycles.

In fact it may be because of this that Kawasaki's motorcycles have always been quirky, you get the impression that they are designed by a small group of enthusiasts who are given an admirably free hand. More realistically, it may be that Kawasaki's designers have experience with techniques and materials from other engineering disciplines. Either way, Kawasaki have managed to be the factory who surprise us more than the rest. Quite often, they do this by totally ignoring a market segment the others are scrabbling over, but more often they hit us with pure, undiluted performance.

The origins of the company, and its name, go back to 1878 when Shozo Kawasaki set up a dockyard in Tokyo. By the late 1930s, the company was making its own steel in massive steelworks and manufacturing railway locos and rolling stock. In the run up to war, the Kawasaki Aircraft Company was set up in 1937 and it was this arm of the now giant operation that would look to motorcycle engine manufacture in post-war Japan.

They bought their high-technology experience to bear first on engines which were sold on to a number of manufacturers as original equipment. Both two- and four-stroke units were made, a 58 cc and 148 cc OHC unit. One of the customer companies was Meihatsu Heavy Industries, another company within the Kawasaki group, which in 1961 was shaken up and renamed Kawasaki Auto Sales. At the same time, the Akashi factory which was to be Kawasaki's main production facility until the Kobe earthquake of 1995, was opened.

Shortly afterwards, Kawasaki took over the ailing Meguro company, Japan's oldest motorcycle maker, thus instantly obtaining a range of bigger bikes which were marketed as Kawasaki-Meguros. The following year, the first bike to be made and sold as a Kawasaki was produced, a 125 cc single called the B8 and in 1963 a motocross version, the B8M appeared.

Model development

Kawasaki's first appearance on a road-race circuit came in 1965 with a batch of disc-valve 125 twins. They were no match for the opposition from Japan in the shape of Suzuki and Yamaha or for the fading force of the factory MZs from East Germany. Only after the other Japanese factories had pulled out of the class did Kawasaki win, with British rider Dave Simmonds becoming World 125 GP Champion in 1969 on a bike that looked astonishingly similar to the original racer. That same year Kawasaki reorganised once again, this time merging three companies to form Kawasaki Heavy Industries. One of the new organisation's objectives was to take motorcycle production forward and exploit markets outside Japan.

KHI achieved that target immediately and set out their stall for the future with the astonishing and frightening H1. This three-cylinder air-cooled 500 cc two-stroke was arguably the first modern pure performance bike to hit the market. It hypnotised a whole generation of motorcyclists who'd never before encountered such a ferocious, wheelie inducing power band or such shattering straight-line speed allied to questionable handling. And as for the 750 cc version ...

The triples perfectly suited the late '60s, fitting in well with the student demonstrations of 1968 and the anti-establishment ethos of the Summer of Love. Unfortunately, the oil crisis would put an end to the thirsty strokers but Kawasaki had another high-performance ace up their corporate sleeve. Or rather they thought they did.

The 1968 Tokyo Show saw probably the single most significant new motorcycle ever made unveiled: the Honda CB750. At Kawasaki it caused a major shock, for they also had a 750 cc four, code-named New

The three cylinder two-stroke 750

The first Superbike, Kawasaki's 900 cc Z1

no major difference between that first Z1 and the air-cooled GPz range. Add water-cooling and you have the GPZ900, which in turn metamorphosed into the GPZ1000RX and then the ZX-10 and the ZZ-R1100. Indeed, the last three models share the same 58 mm stroke. The bikes are obviously very different but it's difficult to put your finger on exactly why.

Other models have remained effectively untouched for over a decade: the KH and KE single-cylinder air-cooled two-stroke learner bikes, the GT550 and 750 shaft-drive hacks favoured by big city despatch riders and the GPz305 being prime examples. It's only when they step outside the performance field that Kawasakis seems less sure. Their first factory customs were dire, you simply got the impression that the team that designed them didn't have their heart in the job. Only when the Classic range appeared in 1995 did they get it right.

Racing success

Kawasaki also have a more focused approach to racing than the other factories. The policy has always been to race the road bikes and with just a couple of exceptions that's what they've done. Even Simmonds' championship winner bore a strong resemblance to the twins they were selling in the late '60s and racing versions of the 500 and 750 cc triples were also sold as over-the-counter racers, the H1R and H2R. The 500 was in the forefront of the two-stroke assault on MV Agusta but wasn't a Grand Prix

York Steak, almost ready to roll and it was a double, rather than single, overhead cam motor. Bravely, they took the decision to go ahead - but with the motor taken out to 900 cc. The result was the Z1, unveiled at the 1972 Cologne Show. It was a bike straight out of the same mould as the H1, scare stories spread about unmanageable power, dubious straight-line stability and frightening handling, none of which stopped the sales graph

rocketing upwards and led to the coining of the term 'superbike'. While rising fuel prices cut short development of the big two-strokes, the Z1 went on to found a dynasty, indeed its genes can still be detected in Kawasaki's latest products like the ZZ-R1100 (Ninja ZX-11).

This is another characteristic of the way Kawasaki operates. Models quite often have very long lives, or gradually evolve. There is

One of the two-stroke engined KH and KE range - the KE100B

The GT750 - a favourite hack for despatch riders

The high-performance ZXR750

winner. It was the 750 that made the impact and carried the factory's image in F750 racing against the Suzuki triples and Yamaha fours.

The factory's decision to use green, usually regarded as an unlucky colour in sport, meant its bikes and personnel stood out and the phrase 'Green Meanies' fitted them perfectly. The Z1 motor soon became a full 1000 cc and powered Kawasaki's assault in F1 racing, notably in endurance which Kawasaki saw as being most closely related to its road bikes.

That didn't stop them dominating 250 and 350 cc GPs with a tandem twin two-stroke in the late '70s and early '80s, but their path-breaking monocoque 500 while a race winner never won a world title. When Superbike arrived, Kawasaki's road 750s weren't as track-friendly as the opposition's out-and-out race replicas. This makes Scott Russell's World title on the ZXR750 in 1993 even more praiseworthy, for the homologation bike, the ZXR750RR, was much heavier and much more of a road bike than the Italian and Japanese competition.

The company's Supersport 600 contenders have similarly been more sports-tourers than race-replicas, yet they too have been competitive on the track. Indeed, the flagship bike, the ZZ-R1100, is most definitely a sports tourer capable of carrying two people and their luggage at high speed in comfort all day and then doing it again the next day. Try that on one of the race replicas and you'll be in need of a course of treatment from a chiropractor.

Through doing it their way Kawasaki developed a brand loyalty for their performance bikes that kept the Z1's derivatives in production until the mid-'80s and turned the bike into a classic in its model life. You could even argue that the Z1 lives on in the shape of the 1100 Zephyr's GPz1100-derived motor. And that's another Kawasaki invention, the retro bike. But when you look at what many commentators refer to as the retro boom, especially in Japan, you find that it is no such thing. It is the Zephyr boom. Just another example of Japan's most surprising motorcycle manufacturer getting it right again.

Back to The Future

It took Kawasaki a long time to get the whole naked-bike idea, which is ironic given that it is the spirit of the original Z1, specifically Eddie Lawson's Superbike, that roadtesters always evoke when trying to define what the class is about. Do not confuse this sort of bike with the pastiche of earlier designs usually labelled as 'retro', and realised by putting a modern motor in a twin-shock steel-tube chassis. Kawasaki did that years ago and called it the Zephyr, then tried and failed to update the concept with the ZR-7.

Credit where credit's due, Suzuki invented this class of bike with the Bandit, taking an old motor, wrapping it in parts from the spares bin and putting it in a steel chassis. The result was much more than the sum of its parts.

Kawasaki have performed the same trick with the Z1000 but in a completely different way. They took the ZX-9 motor, bored it out, added fuel injection and dressed it up in a zoot suit. The result is an attitude-laden streetfighter of a motorcycle – check out the aggressive, hunched stance and the four exhaust pipes of the original model. Costs were, of course, kept down. The chassis was a steel 'diamond' reminiscent of the first GPZ900R Ninja, suspension was soggy with minimal adjustment, and brake calipers were

The 2004 ZR750-J1

The 2003 ZR1000-A1

The 2008 ZR750-L8

The 2007 ZR1000-B7

distinctly low-tech sliding designs, none of which matters a jot unless you want to run with the fast group at a track day. The race track is the only place that anyone has ever found serious fault with a Z1000, in real-world road riding this is a bike which does everything well, and not in the worthy manner of some all-rounders but with a wolfish grin on its face. It revs like a racer, sounds glorious, looks mean, and evokes the spirit of the original Z1 perfectly. The 2003 model was greeted by universal praise and remained substantially unaltered until the 2007 model had its frame revised – stiffness was reduced! – and a superb radial-mount braking system bolted on.

Kawasaki were just as clever, but in a totally different way, with the 750cc version. The bigger bike was competitive on price within its peer group without ever being cheap. The 750 came in at £2000 cheaper than the 1000 and hit the important $7000 price point in the US, again without seeming cheap (unless you looked too hard at the brakes). By shrinking the bores of the 1000cc motor, Kawasaki produced a 750cc naked middleweight that immediately stood out in a class comprised of 600s, most of which were starting to look a bit long in the tooth. Also, the Z750 was the only one in the class with fuel injection and, given its price, looked very much like the best value for money as well as not being built down to a price. Reconciling those two usually mutually exclusive is a very clever trick. As with its bigger brother, the more obvious evidence of penny-pinching in the 750's specification was addressed by the redesign for the 2007 model with a cast aluminium sub-frame incorporating engine mountings and swingarm pivot mated to bolt-on spars either side. Ancillary parts were also updated, although all this improvement did come at the price of increased weight, especially if you go for the ABS brakes option.

Another very clever trick is that despite their many common parts, the two machines are very different in character. The smaller Zed's fast but user-friendly motor is perfectly set-up for a newly-qualified or born-again biker. The big Zed, though, is, in the right hands, quite capable of showing just about any other bike on the road the way home. Which most definitely is in the spirit of the very first bikes to carry the Z1000 name.

Acknowledgements

Our thanks are due to V & J of Yeovil, Taylors of Crewkerne and Bridge of Exeter, who supplied the machines featured in the illustrations throughout this manual. We would also like to thank NGK Spark Plugs (UK) Ltd for supplying the colour spark plug condition photographs, the Avon Rubber Company for supplying information on tyre fitting and Draper Tools Ltd for some of the workshop tools shown.

Thanks are also due to Julian Ryder who wrote the introduction and to Kawasaki Motors Europe who supplied model photographs.

About this Manual

The aim of this manual is to help you get the best value from your motorcycle. It can do so in several ways. It can help you decide what work must be done, even if you choose to have it done by a dealer; it provides information and procedures for routine maintenance and servicing; and it offers diagnostic and repair procedures to follow when trouble occurs.

We hope you use the manual to tackle the work yourself. For many simpler jobs, doing it yourself may be quicker than arranging an appointment to get the motorcycle into a dealer and making the trips to leave it and pick it up. More importantly, a lot of money can be saved by avoiding the expense the shop must pass on to you to cover its labour and overhead costs. An added benefit is the sense of satisfaction and accomplishment that you feel after doing the job yourself.

References to the left or right side of the motorcycle assume you are sitting on the seat, facing forward.

We take great pride in the accuracy of information given in this manual, but motorcycle manufacturers make alterations and design changes during the production run of a particular motorcycle of which they do not inform us. No liability can be accepted by the authors or publishers for loss, damage or injury caused by any errors in, or omissions from, the information given.

Professional mechanics are trained in safe working procedures. However enthusiastic you may be about getting on with the job at hand, take the time to ensure that your safety is not put at risk. A moment's lack of attention can result in an accident, as can failure to observe simple precautions.

There will always be new ways of having accidents, and the following is not a comprehensive list of all dangers; it is intended rather to make you aware of the risks and to encourage a safe approach to all work you carry out on your bike.

Asbestos

● Certain friction, insulating, sealing and other products - such as brake pads, clutch linings, gaskets, etc. - contain asbestos. Extreme care must be taken to avoid inhalation of dust from such products since it is hazardous to health. If in doubt, assume that they do contain asbestos.

Fire

● Remember at all times that petrol is highly flammable. Never smoke or have any kind of naked flame around, when working on the vehicle. But the risk does not end there - a spark caused by an electrical short-circuit, by two metal surfaces contacting each other, by careless use of tools, or even by static

electricity built up in your body under certain conditions, can ignite petrol vapour, which in a confined space is highly explosive. Never use petrol as a cleaning solvent. Use an approved safety solvent.

● Always disconnect the battery earth terminal before working on any part of the fuel or electrical system, and never risk spilling fuel on to a hot engine or exhaust.

● It is recommended that a fire extinguisher of a type suitable for fuel and electrical fires is kept handy in the garage or workplace at all times. Never try to extinguish a fuel or electrical fire with water.

Fumes

● Certain fumes are highly toxic and can quickly cause unconsciousness and even death if inhaled to any extent. Petrol vapour comes into this category, as do the vapours from certain solvents such as trichloro-ethylene. Any draining or pouring of such volatile fluids should be done in a well ventilated area.

● When using cleaning fluids and solvents, read the instructions carefully. Never use materials from unmarked containers - they may give off poisonous vapours.

● Never run the engine of a motor vehicle in an enclosed space such as a garage. Exhaust fumes contain carbon monoxide which is extremely poisonous; if you need to run the

engine, always do so in the open air or at least have the rear of the vehicle outside the workplace.

The battery

● Never cause a spark, or allow a naked light near the vehicle's battery. It will normally be giving off a certain amount of hydrogen gas, which is highly explosive.

● Always disconnect the battery ground (earth) terminal before working on the fuel or electrical systems (except where noted).

Electricity

● When using an electric power tool, inspection light etc., always ensure that the appliance is correctly connected to its plug and that, where necessary, it is properly grounded (earthed). Do not use such appliances in damp conditions and, again, beware of creating a spark or applying excessive heat in the vicinity of fuel or fuel vapour. Also ensure that the appliances meet national safety standards.

● A severe electric shock can result from touching certain parts of the electrical system, such as the spark plug wires (HT leads), when the engine is running or being cranked, particularly if components are damp or the insulation is defective. Where an electronic ignition system is used, the secondary (HT) voltage is much higher and could prove fatal.

Remember...

✘ **Don't** start the engine without first ascertaining that the transmission is in neutral.

✘ **Don't** suddenly remove the pressure cap from a hot cooling system - cover it with a cloth and release the pressure gradually first, or you may get scalded by escaping coolant.

✘ **Don't** attempt to drain oil until you are sure it has cooled sufficiently to avoid scalding you.

✘ **Don't** grasp any part of the engine or exhaust system without first ascertaining that it is cool enough not to burn you.

✘ **Don't** allow brake fluid or antifreeze to contact the machine's paintwork or plastic components.

✘ **Don't** siphon toxic liquids such as fuel, hydraulic fluid or antifreeze by mouth, or allow them to remain on your skin.

✘ **Don't** inhale dust - it may be injurious to health (see Asbestos heading).

✘ **Don't** allow any spilled oil or grease to remain on the floor - wipe it up right away, before someone slips on it.

✘ **Don't** use ill-fitting spanners or other tools which may slip and cause injury.

✘ **Don't** lift a heavy component which may be beyond your capability - get assistance.

✘ **Don't** rush to finish a job or take unverified short cuts.

✘ **Don't** allow children or animals in or around an unattended vehicle.

✘ **Don't** inflate a tyre above the recommended pressure. Apart from overstressing the carcass, in extreme cases the tyre may blow off forcibly.

✔ **Do** ensure that the machine is supported securely at all times. This is especially important when the machine is blocked up to aid wheel or fork removal.

✔ **Do** take care when attempting to loosen a stubborn nut or bolt. It is generally better to pull on a spanner, rather than push, so that if you slip, you fall away from the machine rather than onto it.

✔ **Do** wear eye protection when using power tools such as drill, sander, bench grinder etc.

✔ **Do** use a barrier cream on your hands prior to undertaking dirty jobs - it will protect your skin from infection as well as making the dirt easier to remove afterwards; but make sure your hands aren't left slippery. Note that long-term contact with used engine oil can be a health hazard.

✔ **Do** keep loose clothing (cuffs, ties etc. and long hair) well out of the way of moving mechanical parts.

✔ **Do** remove rings, wristwatch etc., before working on the vehicle - especially the electrical system.

✔ **Do** keep your work area tidy - it is only too easy to fall over articles left lying around.

✔ **Do** exercise caution when compressing springs for removal or installation. Ensure that the tension is applied and released in a controlled manner, using suitable tools which preclude the possibility of the spring escaping violently.

✔ **Do** ensure that any lifting tackle used has a safe working load rating adequate for the job.

✔ **Do** get someone to check periodically that all is well, when working alone on the vehicle.

✔ **Do** carry out work in a logical sequence and check that everything is correctly assembled and tightened afterwards.

✔ **Do** remember that your vehicle's safety affects that of yourself and others. If in doubt on any point, get professional advice.

● If in spite of following these precautions, you are unfortunate enough to injure yourself, seek medical attention as soon as possible.

Frame and engine numbers

The frame number is stamped into the right-hand side of the steering head. The engine number is stamped into the upper crankcase half, just inboard of the clutch cover. Both of these numbers should be recorded and kept in a safe place so they can be given to law enforcement officials in the event of a theft. The VIN plate is on the outside of the right-hand frame beam. The throttle bodies also have an ID number stamped into them.

The frame and engine numbers should also be kept in a handy place (such as with your driving licence) so they are always available when purchasing or ordering parts for your machine.

The procedures in this manual identify models by their engine size (i.e. Z750 or Z1000) or by model code (e.g. ZR750-J2 or ZR1000-B7) as required.

Model	Year
ZR750-J1	2004
ZR750-J2	2005
ZR750-J6	2006
ZR750-L7	2007
ZR750-M7 (ABS)	2007
ZR750-L8	2008
ZR750-M8 (ABS)	2008
ZR1000-A1	2003
ZR1000-A2	2004
ZR1000-A3	2005
ZR1000-A6	2006
ZR1000-B7/C7	2007
ZR1000-B8/C8	2008

Buying spare parts

Once you have found all the identification numbers, record them for reference when buying parts. Since the manufacturers change specifications, parts and vendors (companies that manufacture various components on the machine), providing the ID numbers is the only way to be reasonably sure that you are buying the correct parts.

Whenever possible, take the worn part to the dealer so direct comparison with the new component can be made. Along the trail from the manufacturer to the parts shelf, there are numerous places that the part can end up with the wrong number or be listed incorrectly.

The two places to purchase new parts for your motorcycle – the franchised or main dealer and the parts/accessories store – differ in the type of parts they carry. While dealers can obtain every single genuine part for your motorcycle, the accessory store is usually limited to normal high wear items such as chains and sprockets, brake pads, spark plugs and cables, and to tune-up parts and various engine gaskets, etc. Rarely will an accessory outlet have major suspension components, camshafts, transmission gears, or engine cases.

Used parts can be obtained from breakers yards for roughly half the price of new ones, but you can't always be sure of what you're getting. Once again, take your worn part to the breaker for direct comparison, or when ordering by mail order make sure that you can return it if you are not happy.

Whether buying new, used or rebuilt parts, the best course is to deal directly with someone who specialises in your particular make.

The engine number is stamped into the upper crankcase half

The VIN plate is riveted to the frame behind the steering head

The frame number is stamped into the right-hand side of the steering head

Note: *These checks are outlined in the owner's manual and covers those items which Kawasaki advise be inspected before you ride the motorcycle.*

Coolant level

 Warning: DO NOT remove the radiator pressure cap to add coolant. Topping up is done via the coolant reservoir tank filler. DO NOT leave open containers of coolant about, as it is poisonous.

Before you start

✔ Make sure you have a supply of coolant available (a mixture of 50% distilled or soft water and 50% corrosion inhibited ethylene glycol anti-freeze is needed).
✔ Always check the coolant level when the engine is cold.
✔ Support the motorcycle upright on level ground.

✔ On ZR750-J and ZR1000-A models the coolant reservoir is behind the left-hand side panel, and the level lines are visible via the cut-out in the rear of the panel. If topping-up is necessary remove the side panel (see Chapter 7).
✔ On ZR750-L/M, and ZR1000-B/C models the coolant reservoir is behind the right-hand seat cowl – remove the rider's seat to check the level, and remove the seat cowl if topping-up is necessary (see Chapter 7).

Bike care

● Use only the specified coolant mixture. It is important that anti-freeze is used in the system all year round, and not just in the winter. Do not top the system up using only water, as the system will become too diluted.
● Do not overfill the reservoir. If the coolant is significantly above the F level line at any time, the surplus should be siphoned or drained off to prevent the possibility of it being expelled out of the overflow hose.
● If the coolant level falls steadily, check the system for leaks (see Chapter 1). If no leaks are found and the level continues to fall, it is recommended that the machine is taken to a Kawasaki dealer for a pressure test.

ZR750-J and ZR1000-A

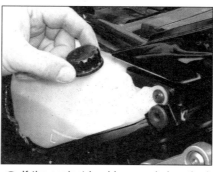
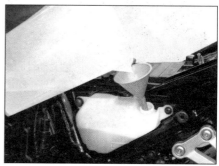

1 With the motorcycle vertical and level, the coolant level should lie between the F (FULL) and L (LOW) level lines (arrowed) marked on the side of the reservoir.

2 If the coolant level is on or below the L line, remove the side panel (see Chapter 7), then remove the reservoir filler cap.

3 Top the reservoir up with the recommended coolant mixture almost to the F level line, using a suitable funnel if required. Fit the cap securely.

ZR750-L/M and ZR1000-B/C

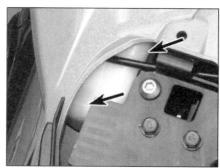

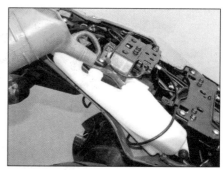

1 Remove the rider's seat (see Chapter 7). With the motorcycle vertical and level, the coolant level should lie between the F (FULL) and L (LOW) level lines (arrowed) marked on the side of the reservoir.

2 If the coolant level is on or below the L line, remove the seat cowl (see Chapter 7), then remove the reservoir filler cap.

3 Top the reservoir up with the recommended coolant mixture almost to the F level line, using a suitable funnel if required. Fit the cap securely.

Engine oil level

Before you start
✔ Support the motorcycle upright on level ground. If the engine has been run allow it to stand undisturbed for a few minutes to allow the oil level to stabilise.
✔ The oil level inspection window is located on the right-hand side of the engine in the bottom of the clutch cover. If necessary wipe the window so that it is clean.

The correct oil
● Modern, high-revving engines place great demands on their oil. It is very important that the correct oil for your bike is used.
● Always top up with a good quality motorcycle oil of the specified type and viscosity, that matches the type and viscosity of the oil already in the engine – do not use car oils and do not overfill the engine.
Caution: Do not use chemical additives or oils labelled "ENERGY CONSERVING". Such additives or oils could cause clutch slip.

Oil type	API grade SE, SF, SG, or API SH or SJ with JASO MA
Oil viscosity	SAE 10W/40

Bike care
● If you have to add oil frequently, check whether you have any oil leaks from the engine joints, oil seals and gaskets. If not, the engine could be burning oil, in which case there will be white smoke coming out of the exhaust (see *Fault Finding*).

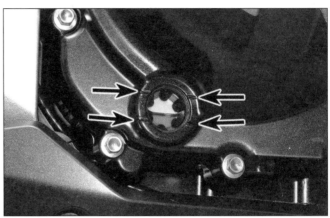

1 With the motorcycle vertical, the oil level should lie between the upper and lower level lines (arrowed).

2 If the level is on or below the lower line, unscrew the oil filler cap from the clutch cover.

3 Top up the engine with the recommended grade and type of oil almost up to the upper line on the inspection window. Do not overfill. On completion, make sure the filler cap is secure in the cover.

Legal and safety checks

Lighting and signalling
● Take a minute to check that the headlights, sidelights, tail light, brake light, licence plate light, instrument lights and turn signals all work correctly.
● Check that the horn sounds when the button is pressed.
● A working speedometer, graduated in mph, is a statutory requirement in the UK.

Safety
● Check that the throttle grip rotates smoothly when opened and snaps shut when released, in all steering positions. Also check for the correct amount of freeplay (see Chapter 1).
● Check that the brake lever and pedal, clutch lever and gearchange lever operate smoothly. Lubricate them at the specified intervals or when necessary (see Chapter 1).
● Check that the engine shuts off when the kill switch is operated. Check the starter interlock circuit (see Chapter 1).

● Check that sidestand return springs hold the stand up securely when retracted.

Fuel
● This may seem obvious, but check that you have enough fuel to complete your journey. If you notice signs of fuel leakage – rectify the cause immediately.
● Ensure you use the correct grade fuel – see Chapter 4 Specifications.

Brake fluid levels

> ⚠️ **Warning: Brake hydraulic fluid can harm your eyes and damage painted surfaces, so use extreme caution when handling and pouring it and cover surrounding surfaces with rag. Do not use fluid that has been standing open for some time, as it is hygroscopic (absorbs moisture from the air) which can cause a dangerous loss of braking effectiveness.**

Before you start:

✔ The front brake fluid reservoir is on the right-hand handlebar. The rear brake fluid reservoir is located below the side panel on the right-hand side.
✔ Make sure you have a supply of DOT 4 brake fluid.
✔ Wrap a rag around the reservoir being worked on to ensure that any spillage does not come into contact with painted surfaces.
✔ When checking the fluid in the front reservoir turn the handlebars so the reservoir is level.
✔ When checking the fluid in the rear reservoir support the motorcycle upright.

Bike care:

● The fluid in the front and rear brake fluid reservoirs will drop very gradually as the brake pads wear down. If the fluid level is low check the brake pads for wear (see Chapter 1), and

replace them with new ones if necessary (see Chapter 6). Do not top the reservoir(s) up until the new pads have been fitted, and then check to see if topping up is still necessary – this is because when the caliper pistons are pushed back to accommodate the extra thickness of the pads some fluid will be displaced back into the reservoir.
● If either fluid reservoir requires repeated topping-up there could be a leak somewhere in the system, which must be investigated immediately.
● Check for signs of fluid leakage from the hydraulic hoses and/or brake system components – if found, rectify immediately (see Chapter 6).
● Check the operation of both brakes before taking the machine on the road; if there is evidence of air in the system (spongy feel to lever or pedal), it must be bled (see Chapter 6).

REAR RESERVOIR – ALL MODELS

1 On ZR750-J and ZR1000-A models, the rear brake fluid level is visible through the front of the reservoir body – it must be between the UPPER and LOWER level lines (arrowed).

2 On ZR750-L/M and ZR1000-B/C models, the rear brake fluid level is visible through the back of the reservoir body – it must be between the UPPER and LOWER level lines (arrowed).

3 If the level is on or below the LOWER line, on ZR750-L/M and ZR1000-B/C models, slacken the reservoir cap clamp screw and displace the clamp. On ZR750-J and ZR1000-A models, remove the side panel (see Chapter 7).

4 Unscrew the cap and remove the diaphragm plate and diaphragm.

5 Top up with new clean DOT 4 hydraulic fluid, until the level is up to the UPPER line. Do not overfill and take care to avoid spills (see **Warning** above).

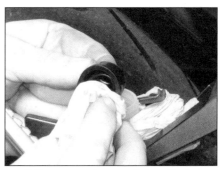

6 Wipe any moisture off the diaphragm with a tissue. Ensure that the diaphragm is correctly seated before installing the plate and cap. Refit the reservoir cap clamp or side panel, according to model.

FRONT RESERVOIR – ZR750-J AND ZR1000-A MODELS

1 The front brake fluid level is visible through the window in the reservoir body – it must be above the LOWER level line (arrowed).

2 If the level is on or below the LOWER line, undo the reservoir cover screws and remove the diaphragm plate and diaphragm.

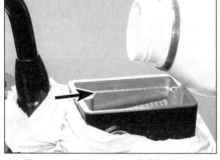

3 Top up with new clean DOT 4 hydraulic fluid, until the level is up to the upper level line on the inside of the reservoir (arrowed). Do not overfill and take care to avoid spills (see **Warning** above).

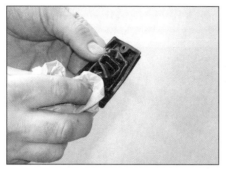

4 Wipe any moisture off the diaphragm with a tissue.

5 Ensure that the diaphragm is correctly seated before installing the plate and cover. Secure the cover with the screws.

FRONT RESERVOIR – ZR750-L/M AND ZR1000-B/C MODELS

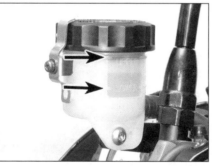

1 The front brake fluid level is visible through the reservoir body – it must be between the UPPER and LOWER level lines (arrowed).

2 If the level is on or below the LOWER line, undo the reservoir cap clamp screw and remove the clamp, then unscrew the cap and remove the diaphragm plate and diaphragm.

3 Top up with new clean DOT 4 hydraulic fluid, until the level is up to the UPPER line. Do not overfill and take care to avoid spills (see **Warning** above).

4 Wipe any moisture off the diaphragm with a tissue.

5 Ensure that the diaphragm is correctly seated before installing the plate and cap. Secure the cap with the clamp

Tyres

The correct pressures

● The tyres must be checked when **cold**, not immediately after riding. Note that incorrect tyre pressures will cause abnormal tread wear and unsafe handling. Very low tyre pressures may cause the tyre to slip on the rim or come off.

● Use an accurate pressure gauge. Spend as much as you can justify on a quality gauge.

● Proper air pressure will increase tyre life and provide maximum stability and ride comfort.

Front	Rear
36 psi (2.5 Bar)	42 psi (2.9 Bar)

Tyre care

● Check the tyres carefully for cuts, tears, embedded nails or other sharp objects and excessive wear. Operation of the motorcycle with excessively worn tyres is extremely hazardous, as traction and handling are directly affected.

● Check the condition of the tyre valve and ensure the dust cap is in place.

● Pick out any stones or nails which may have become embedded in the tyre tread. If left, they will eventually penetrate through the casing and cause a puncture.

● If tyre damage is apparent, or unexplained loss of pressure is experienced, seek the advice of a tyre fitting specialist without delay.

Tyre tread depth

● At the time of writing UK law requires that tread depth must be at least 1 mm over 3/4 of the tread breadth all the way around the tyre, with no bald patches. Many riders, however, consider 2 mm tread depth minimum to be a safer limit. Kawasaki recommend a minimum of 1 mm on the front and 2 mm on the rear for normal speeds, but note that German law requires a minimum of 1.6 mm for each tyre.

● Many tyres now incorporate wear indicators in the tread. Identify the location marking on the tyre sidewall (either an arrow, triangle, the letters TWI, or the manufacturer's logo) to locate the indicator bar and replace the tyre if the tread has worn down to the bar.

1 Remove the dust cap from the valve, and do not forget to fit the cap after checking the pressure.

2 Use an accurate gauge and make sure the tyres are cold.

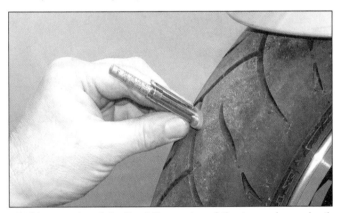

3 Measure tread depth at the centre of the tyre using a depth gauge.

4 Tyre tread wear indicator location marking (arrowed).

Suspension, steering and drive chain

Suspension and steering

● Check that the front and rear suspension operates smoothly without binding (see Chapter 1).

● Check that the suspension is adjusted as required (see Chapter 5).

● Check that the steering moves smoothly from lock-to-lock.

Drive chain

● Check that the chain isn't too loose or too tight, and adjust it if necessary (see Chapter 1).

● If the chain looks dry, lubricate it (see Chapter 1).

Model development

ZR750-J1H (2004) model

The 748cc engine uses an in-line four cylinder liquid-cooled unit. Drive to the double overhead camshafts which actuate the four valves per cylinder is by chain from the right-hand end of the crankshaft. The clutch is a conventional wet multi-plate unit and the gearbox is 6-speed. Drive to the rear wheel is by chain and sprockets.

Kawasaki's fuel injection system supplies fuel and air to the engine via Keihin 34 mm dual valve throttle bodies. An electronic engine management system controls both the injection system and the ignition system. The exhaust system is a four-into-one with the silencer mounted conventionally on the right-hand side.

The engine sits in a diamond-section steel frame which uses the engine as a stressed member. Front suspension is by conventional non-adjustable oil-damped 41 mm forks. Rear suspension is by a single shock absorber with adjustable spring pre-load and rebound damping, via a three-way rising rate linkage. The wheels are cast alloy.

The front brake system has two dual-piston sliding calipers, acting on floating discs. The rear brake system has a single piston sliding caliper acting on a conventional disc.

Available in, ebony, red and blue.

ZR750-J2H (2005) model

There were no significant changes from the J1 (2004) model.

Available in, silver, ebony and blue.

ZR750-J6F (2006) model

An immobiliser system has been added.

Available in silver, ebony and orange.

ZR750-L7F/M7F (2007) model

A host of changes were made for the 2007 model, most of them cosmetic.

Significant changes included the use of upside-down front forks with cartridge damper and adjustable for spring pre-load and rebound damping. The brake system features wavy front discs and there have been changes to the calipers and front master cylinder. The M7F had an anti-lock braking system (ABS). The cable actuated fast idle system for cold starting was replaced with an automatic system. A new instrument cluster was fitted. There was a new exhaust system incorporating a power valve and oxygen sensor.

Available in silver, ebony and green.

ZR750-L8F/M8F (2008) model

There were no significant changes from the 2007 L7/M7 models.

Available in ebony, blue and orange.

ZR1000-A1H (2003) model

The 953cc engine uses an in-line four cylinder liquid-cooled unit. Drive to the double overhead camshafts which actuate the four valves per cylinder is by chain from the right-hand end of the crankshaft. The clutch is a conventional wet multi-plate unit and the gearbox is 6-speed. Drive to the rear wheel is by chain and sprockets.

Kawasaki's fuel injection system supplies fuel and air to the engine via Keihin 38 mm dual valve throttle bodies. An electronic engine management system controls both the injection system and the ignition system. The exhaust system is a four-into-two-into-four design, with the silencers mounted conventionally on each side.

The engine sits in a diamond-section steel frame which uses the engine as a stressed member. Front suspension is by upside-down oil-damped 41 mm forks with cartridge dampers. The right-hand fork has adjustable rebound damping, and both forks have adjustable spring pre-load. Rear suspension is by a single shock absorber with adjustable spring pre-load and rebound damping, via a three-way rising rate linkage. The wheels are cast alloy.

The front brake system has two conventionally mounted opposed piston calipers, with four pistons per caliper acting on floating discs. The rear brake system has a single piston sliding caliper acting on a conventional disc.

Available in black, green and orange.

ZR1000-A2H (2004) model

There were no significant changes from the A1 (2003) model.

Available in red, black and orange.

ZR1000-A3H (2005) model

An immobiliser system was added.

Available in black, titanium and green.

ZR1000-A6F (2006) model

There were no significant changes from the A3H (2005) model.

Available in black, titanium and blue.

ZR1000-B7F/C7F (2007) model

A host of changes were made for the 2007 model, most of them cosmetic.

The brake system features wavy front discs and there have been changes to the calipers and front master cylinder. The front calipers were radially mounted and have a brake pad for each piston. The C7F model had anti-lock braking (ABS). There was a new swingarm. The cable actuated fast idle system for cold starting was been replaced with an automatic system. A new instrument cluster was fitted. There was a new exhaust system, incorporating a power valve and oxygen sensor.

Available in orange, black and blue.

ZR1000-B8F/C8F (2008) model

There were no significant changes from the 2007 B7/C7 models.

Available in black, white and green.

Bike spec

Dimensions and weights

ZR750-J modes

Overall length	.2080 mm
Overall width	.780 mm
Overall height	.1055 mm
Wheelbase	.1425 mm
Seat height	.815 mm
Ground clearance	.165 mm
Weight (dry)	.195 kg

ZR750-L/M models

Overall length	.2085 mm
Overall width	.805 mm
Overall height	.1100 mm
Wheelbase	.1440 mm
Seat height	.815 mm
Ground clearance	.155 mm
Weight (dry)	
L models	.203 kg
M models	.207 kg

ZR1000-A models

Overall length	.2080 mm
Overall width	.770 mm
Overall height	.1055 mm
Wheelbase	.1420 mm
Seat height	.820 mm
Ground clearance	.145 mm
Weight (dry)	.198 kg

ZR1000-B/C models

Overall length	.2090 mm
Overall width	.780 mm
Overall height	.1065 mm
Wheelbase	.1445 mm
Seat height	.820 mm
Ground clearance	.160 mm
Weight (dry)	
B models	.205 kg
C models	.209 kg

Engine

Type	Four-stroke in-line four
Capacity	
Z750	748 cc
Z1000	953 cc
Bore	
Z750	68.4 mm
Z1000	77.2 mm
Stroke – all engines	50.9 mm
Compression ratio	
Z750	11.3 to 1
Z1000	11.2 to 1
Cooling system.	Liquid cooled
Clutch	Wet multi-plate
Transmission.	Six-speed constant mesh
Final drive.	Chain and sprockets
Camshafts	DOHC, chain-driven
Fuel system	Keihin fuel injection
Ignition system	Computer-controlled digital transistorised with electronic advance

Chassis

Frame type	Diamond-section steel
Rake and Trail	
ZR750-J models.	24.5°, 104 mm
ZR750-L/M models.	24.5°, 103 mm
ZR1000-A models.	24°, 101 mm
ZR1000-B/C models.	24.5°, 103 mm
Fuel tank capacity (including reserve)	
ZR750-J and ZR1000-A models.	18.0 litres
ZR750-L/M and ZR1000-B/C models	18.5 litres
Front suspension	
ZR750-J models	
Type	41 mm oil-damped telescopic forks
Travel.	120 mm
Adjustment	None
ZR750-L/M models	
Type	41 mm oil-damped cartridge-type upside down telescopic forks
Travel.	120 mm
Adjustment	Spring pre-load and rebound damping
Z1000 models	
Type	41 mm oil-damped cartridge-type upside down telescopic forks
Travel.	120 mm
Adjustment	Spring pre-load and rebound damping (right-hand fork only on A1, A2, A3 and A6)
Rear suspension	
Type	Single shock absorber, rising rate linkage, aluminium swingarm
Travel (at rear wheel axle)	
Z750 models.	125 mm
ZR1000-A models.	138 mm
ZR1000-B/C models.	150 mm
Adjustment	Spring pre-load and rebound damping
Wheels	17 inch alloys
Tyres	
Z750	
Front	120/70-ZR17 (58W) Radial
Rear	180/55-ZR17 (73W) Radial
Z1000	
Front	120/70-ZR17 (58W) Radial
Rear	190/50-ZR17 (73W) Radial
Front brake	
Z750	Twin 300 mm floating discs with two piston sliding calipers
Z1000	Twin 300 mm floating discs with four piston calipers
Rear brake	Single 220 mm disc with single piston sliding caliper

Chapter 1
Routine maintenance and servicing

Contents

Degrees of difficulty

Easy, suitable for novice with little experience | **Fairly easy,** suitable for beginner with some experience | **Fairly difficult,** suitable for competent DIY mechanic | **Difficult,** suitable for experienced DIY mechanic | **Very difficult,** suitable for expert DIY or professional

Specifications

Engine

Cylinder numbering . . . . 1 to 4 from left to right
Firing order. 1-2-4-3
Spark plug type
  All Z750 and ZR1000-A models . . . . NGK CR9EK or ND U27ETR
  ZR1000-B/C models. . . . . NGK CR9EIA-9
Spark plug electrode gap
  All Z750 and ZR1000-A models . . . . 0.7 to 0.8 mm
  ZR1000-B/C models. . . . . 0.8 to 0.9 mm
Engine idle speed. . . . . 1100 ± 50 rpm
Valve clearances (COLD engine)
  Intake valves. . . . . 0.15 to 0.24 mm
  Exhaust valves . . . . 0.22 to 0.31 mm
Throttle body vacuum range at idle speed
  ZR750-J models. . . . . 215 to 235 mmHg
  ZR750-L/M models. . . . . 255 to 275 mmHg
  ZR1000-A models. . . . . 235 to 255 mmHg
  ZR1000-B/C models. . . . . 275 to 295 mmHg

Cycle parts

Drive chain slack
    ZR750-J models . . . . 25 to 30 mm
    ZR750-L/M models . . . . 30 to 40 mm
    ZR1000-A models . . . . 20 to 30 mm
    ZR1000-B/C models . . . . 25 to 30 mm
Drive chain 20-link length
    Standard . . . . 317.5 to 318.2 mm
    Stretch limit . . . . 323 mm
Clutch cable freeplay . . . . 2 to 3 mm
Throttle cable freeplay . . . . 2 to 3 mm
Fast idle cable freeplay . . . . 0 to 0.5 mm
Tyre pressures (cold) . . . . see *Pre-ride checks*
Brake pad lining minimum thickness . . . . 1 mm
Rear brake pedal position (see text)
    ZR750-J and ZR1000-A models . . . . about 47 mm
    ZR750-L/M and ZR1000-B/C models . . . . about 45 mm

Lubricants and fluids

Engine oil . . . . see *Pre-ride checks*
Engine oil capacity
    Oil change . . . . 3.1 litres
    Oil and filter change . . . . 3.3 litres
    Following engine overhaul – dry engine, new filter . . . . 3.8 litres
Coolant type . . . . 50% distilled or soft water, 50% corrosion inhibited ethylene glycol anti-freeze
Coolant capacity . . . . 2.9 litres
Brake fluid . . . . DOT 4
Drive chain . . . . Chain lubricant suitable for O-ring chains or SAE 80 or 90 gear oil
Steering head bearings . . . . Multi-purpose grease with EP2 rating
Swingarm pivot bearings . . . . Multi-purpose grease with EP2 rating
Suspension linkage bearings . . . . Multi-purpose grease with EP2 rating
Bearing seal lips . . . . Multi-purpose grease
Gearchange lever/rear brake pedal/footrest pivots . . . . Multi-purpose grease
Clutch lever pivot . . . . Multi-purpose grease
Sidestand pivot . . . . Multi-purpose grease
Throttle twistgrip . . . . Multi-purpose grease
Front brake lever pivot and piston tip . . . . Silicone grease
Cables . . . . Aerosol cable lubricant suitable for lined cables

Torque settings

Coolant drain bolt in cylinder block . . . . 10 Nm
Coolant drain bolt in water pump cover . . . . 11 Nm
Engine oil drain bolt . . . . 29 Nm
Engine oil filter
    ZR750-J and ZR1000-A models . . . . 31 Nm
    ZR750-L/M and ZR1000-B/C models . . . . 17 Nm
Fork clamp bolts (top yoke)
    ZR1000-A1 and A2 models . . . . 9 Nm
    ZR1000-A3 and A6 models . . . . 13 Nm
    All other models . . . . 20 Nm
Rear axle nut
    Z750 . . . . 108 Nm
    Z1000 . . . . 127 Nm
Spark plugs . . . . 13 Nm
Steering stem bolt . . . . 108 Nm
Timing rotor cover bolts . . . . 11 Nm

Note: *Perform the pre-ride inspection at every maintenance interval (in addition to the procedures listed). The intervals listed below are the intervals recommended by the manufacturer.*

Pre-ride

☐ See *'Pre-ride checks'* at the beginning of this manual.

After the initial 600 miles (1000 km)

Note: *This check is usually performed by a Kawasaki dealer after the first 600 miles (1000 km) from new. Thereafter, maintenance is carried out according to the following intervals of the schedule.*

Every 400 miles (600 km)

☐ Check, adjust, clean and lubricate the drive chain (Section 1)

Every 3750 miles (6000 km) or 6 months

☐ Check the drive chain and sprocket wear and chain stretch (Section 1)
☐ Check the brake pads for wear (Section 2)
☐ Check the brake system and brake light switch operation (Section 2)
☐ Check the EVAP (evaporative emission control) system (California models only) (Section 4)
☐ Check and adjust the clutch cable freeplay (Section 5)
☐ Check and adjust the throttle cables and fast idle cable (Section 6)
☐ Check the fuel system and hoses (Section 9)
☐ Check the spark plugs (Section 10)
☐ Check the air system (Section 13)
☐ Check and adjust the steering head bearings (Section 16)

Every 7500 miles (12,000 km) or 12 months

Carry out all the items under the 3750 mile (6000 km) check, plus the following:
☐ Check and adjust the engine idle speed (Section 7)
☐ Check throttle body synchronization (Section 8)
☐ Change the engine oil and fit a new filter (Section 11)
☐ Check the cooling system (Section 12)
☐ Check the sidestand and starter interlock circuit (Section 14)
☐ Check the front and rear suspension (Section 15)
☐ Re-grease the swingarm and suspension linkage bearings (Section 15)
☐ Check the condition of the wheels, wheel bearings and tyres (Section 17)
☐ Lubricate the clutch, gearchange and brake levers, brake pedal, sidestand pivot, and the clutch, throttle and choke cables (Section 18)
☐ Check the tightness of all nuts, bolts and fasteners (Section 19)
☐ Clean the air filter element (Section 20)

Every 15,000 miles (24,000 km)

Carry out all the items under the 7500 mile (12,000 km) check, plus the following:
☐ Check and adjust the valve clearances (Section 21)

Every 15,000 miles (24,000 km) or two years

Carry out all the items under the 7500 mile (12,000 km) check, plus the following:
☐ Change the brake fluid (Section 2)
☐ Change the coolant (Section 12)
☐ Re-grease the steering head bearings (Section 16)
☐ Fit a new air filter element (Section 20)

Every four years

☐ Fit new brake master cylinder and caliper seals (Section 2)

Non-scheduled maintenance

☐ Check the battery (Section 22)
☐ Change the front fork oil (Section 15)
☐ Fit new brake hoses (Section 2)
☐ Fit new cooling system hoses (Section 12)
☐ Fit new fuel system hoses (Section 9)

Note: *Perform the pre-ride inspection at every maintenance interval (in addition to the procedures listed). The intervals listed below are the intervals recommended by the manufacturer.*

Pre-ride
- [ ] See *'Pre-ride checks'* at the beginning of this manual.

After the initial 600 miles (1000 km)
Note: *This check is usually performed by a Kawasaki dealer after the first 600 miles (1000 km) from new. Thereafter, maintenance is carried out according to the following intervals of the schedule.*

Every 400 miles (600 km)
- [ ] Check, adjust, clean and lubricate the drive chain (Section 1)

Every 3750 miles (6000 km) or 6 months
- [ ] Check the drive chain and sprocket wear and chain stretch (Section 1)
- [ ] Check the brake pads for wear (Section 2)
- [ ] Check the brake system and brake light switch operation (Section 2)
- [ ] Check the exhaust valve cable (Section 3)
- [ ] Check the EVAP (evaporative emission control) system (California models only) (Section 4)

Every 7500 miles (12,000 km) or 12 months
Carry out all the items under the 3750 mile (6000 km) check, plus the following:
- [ ] Check and adjust the clutch cable freeplay (Section 5)
- [ ] Check and adjust the throttle cables and fast idle cable (Section 6)
- [ ] Check and adjust the engine idle speed (Section 7)
- [ ] Check throttle body synchronization (Section 8)
- [ ] Check the fuel system and hoses (Section 9)
- [ ] Fit new spark plugs (Section 10)
- [ ] Change the engine oil and fit a new filter (Section 11)
- [ ] Check the cooling system (Section 12)
- [ ] Check the air system (Section 13)
- [ ] Check the sidestand and starter interlock circuit (Section 14)
- [ ] Check the front and rear suspension (Section 15)
- [ ] Check and adjust the steering head bearings (Section 16)
- [ ] Check the condition of the wheels, wheel bearings and tyres (Section 17)
- [ ] Lubricate the clutch, gearchange and brake levers, brake pedal, sidestand pivot, and the clutch, throttle and choke cables (Section 18)
- [ ] Check the tightness of all nuts, bolts and fasteners (Section 19)

Every 11,250 miles (18,000 km)
- [ ] Clean the air filter element (Section 20)

Every 15,000 miles (24,000 km)
Carry out all the items under the 7500 mile (12,000 km) check, plus the following:
- [ ] Check and adjust the valve clearances – ZR750-J and all US, Canada and Australia models (Section 21)

Every 15,000 miles (24,000 km) or two years
Carry out all the items under the 7500 mile (12,000 km) check, plus the following:
- [ ] Change the brake fluid (Section 2)
- [ ] Re-grease the swingarm and suspension linkage bearings (Section 15)
- [ ] Re-grease the steering head bearings (Section 16)

Every 22,500 miles (36,000 km)
Carry out all the items under the 11,250 mile (18,000 km) checks, plus the following:
- [ ] Fit a new air filter element (Section 20)

Every 22,500 miles (36,000 km) or three years
Carry out all the items under the 11,250 mile (18,000 km) checks, plus the following:
- [ ] Change the coolant (Section 12)
- [ ] Fit new cooling system hoses (Section 12)

Every 26,000 miles (42,000 km)
- [ ] Check and adjust the valve clearances – ZR750-L/M and ZR1000-B/C models (Section 21)

Every 30,000 miles (48,000 km) or four years
Carry out all the items under the 15,000 mile (24,000 km) checks, plus the following:
- [ ] Fit new brake master cylinder and caliper seals (Section 2)
- [ ] Fit new brake hoses (Section 2)
- [ ] Fit new fuel system hoses (Section 9)

Non-scheduled maintenance
- [ ] Check the battery (Section 22)
- [ ] Change the front fork oil (Section 15)

ZR750-J left-hand side

1 Throttle cable in-line adjusters
2 Clutch cable upper adjuster
3 Cooling system pressure cap
4 Fast idle cable adjuster
5 Air filter
6 Spring preload adjuster
7 Coolant level inspection window
8 Coolant reservoir cap
9 Drive chain adjuster
10 Shock rebound damping adjuster
11 Coolant drain bolt
12 Engine oil drain bolt
13 Idle speed adjuster
14 Spark plugs
15 Fork oil seals

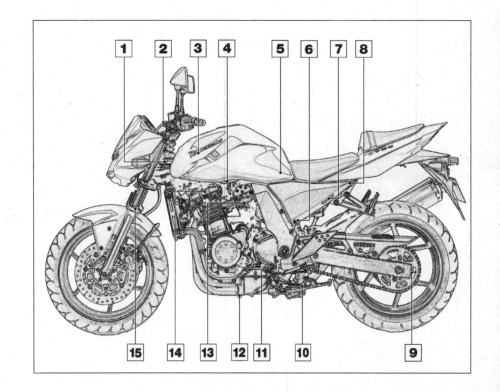

ZR750-J right-hand side

1 Rear brake fluid reservoir
2 Battery
3 Clutch cable lower adjuster
4 Spark plugs
5 Steering head bearing adjuster
6 Front brake fluid reservoir
7 Throttle cable upper adjuster
8 Fork oil seals
9 Engine oil filter
10 Engine oil level window
11 Engine oil filler
12 Rear brake light switch
13 Rear brake pedal height adjuster
14 Drive chain adjuster

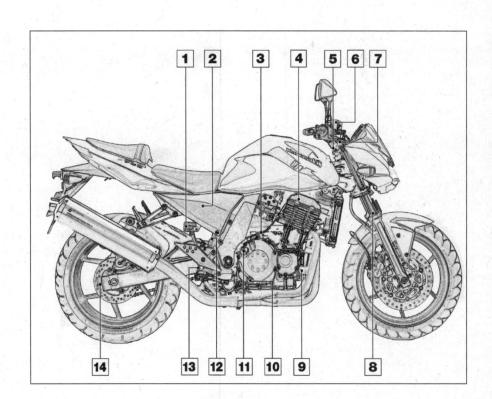

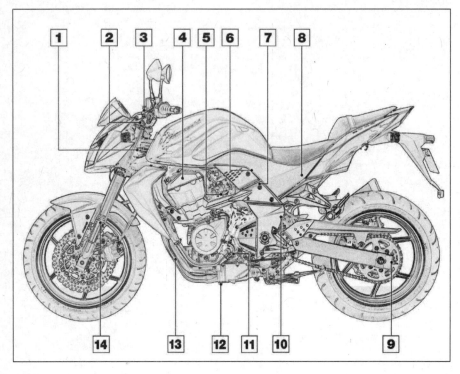

ZR750-L/M left-hand side

1 Throttle cable in-line adjusters
2 Front fork preload and rebound damping adjuster
3 Clutch cable upper adjuster
4 Spark plugs
5 Idle speed adjuster
6 Air filter
7 EVAP canister (California models)
8 Exhaust valve servo
9 Drive chain adjuster
10 Shock spring preload adjuster
11 Coolant drain bolt
12 Engine oil drain bolt
13 Engine oil filter
14 Fork oil seals

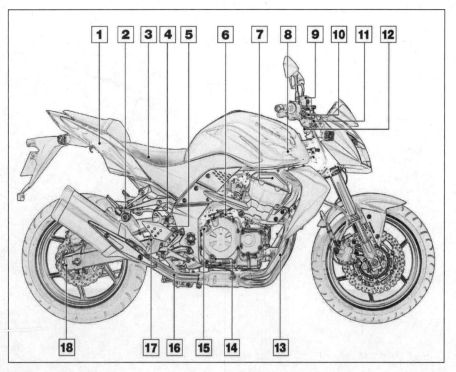

ZR750-L/M right-hand side

1 Coolant reservoir filler cap
2 Rear brake fluid reservoir
3 Battery
4 Exhaust servo cable adjusters
5 Rear brake light switch
6 Clutch cable lower adjuster
7 Spark plugs
8 Radiator pressure cap
9 Front brake fluid reservoir
10 Throttle cable upper adjuster
11 Front fork preload and damping adjusters
12 Steering head bearing adjuster
13 Engine oil filter
14 Engine oil level window
15 Engine oil filler cap
16 Shock rebound damping adjuster
17 Rear brake pedal height adjuster
18 Drive chain adjuster

ZR1000-A left-hand side

1 Throttle cable in-line adjusters
2 Front fork preload and rebound damping adjuster
3 Clutch cable upper adjuster
4 Cooling system pressure cap
5 EVAP canister (California models)
6 Air filter
7 Battery
8 Coolant level inspection window
9 Coolant filler cap
10 Drive chain adjuster
11 Shock spring preload adjuster
12 Coolant drain bolt
13 Idle speed adjuster
14 Spark plugs
15 Fork oil seals

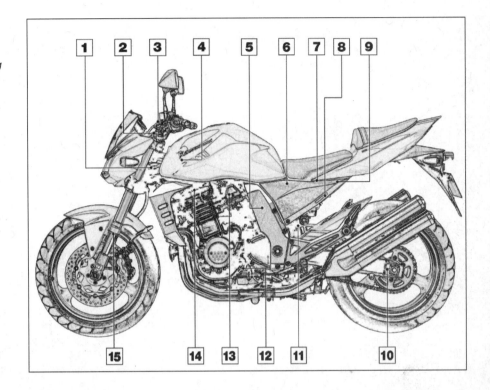

ZR1000-A right-hand side

1 Rear brake fluid reservoir
2 Clutch cable lower adjuster
3 Throttle cable upper adjuster
4 Steering head bearing adjuster
5 Front brake fluid reservoir
6 Fork preload and rebound damping adjuster
7 Radiator pressure cap
8 Fork seals
9 Engine oil filter
10 Engine oil drain bolt
11 Engine oil level window
12 Engine oil filler cap
13 Rear brake light switch
14 Shock rebound damping adjuster
15 Rear brake pedal height adjuster
16 Drive chain adjuster

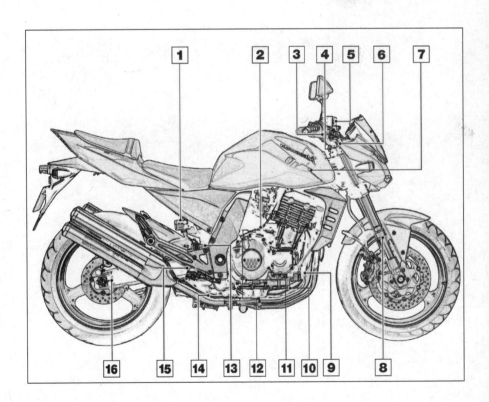

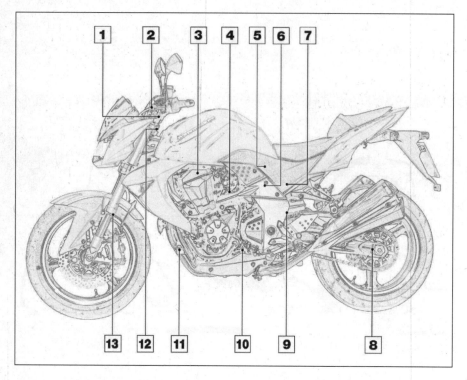

ZR1000-B/C left-hand side

1 Fork preload and damping adjuster
2 Clutch cable upper adjuster
3 Spark plugs
4 Idle speed adjuster
5 Air filter
6 EVAP canister (California models)
7 Exhaust valve servo
8 Drive chain adjuster
9 Shock spring preload adjuster
10 Coolant drain bolt
11 Engine oil filter
12 Steering head bearing adjuster
13 Fork oil seals

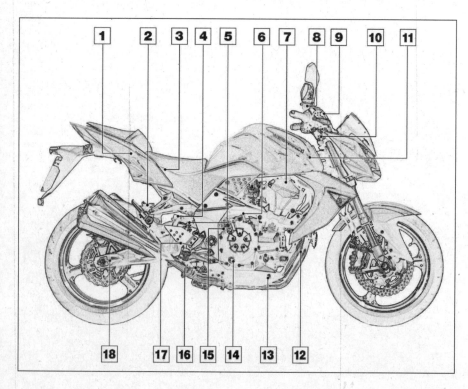

ZR1000-B/C right-hand side

1 Coolant reservoir filler cap
2 Rear brake fluid reservoir
3 Battery
4 Exhaust valve servo cable adjusters
5 Rear brake light switch
6 Clutch cable lower adjuster
7 Spark plugs
8 Front brake fluid reservoir
9 Throttle cable upper adjuster
10 Fork preload and damping adjuster
11 Radiator pressure cap
12 Engine oil filter
13 Engine oil drain bolt
14 Engine oil level window
15 Engine oil filler cap
16 Shock rebound damping adjuster
17 Rear brake pedal height adjuster
18 Drive chain adjuster

1 This Chapter is designed to help the home mechanic maintain his/her motorcycle for safety, economy, long life and peak performance.

2 Deciding where to start or plug into the routine maintenance schedule depends on several factors. If your motorcycle has been maintained according to the warranty standards and has just come out of warranty, start routine maintenance as it coincides with the next mileage or calendar interval. If you have owned the machine for some time but have never performed any maintenance on it, start at the nearest interval and include some additional procedures to ensure that nothing important is overlooked. If you have just had a major engine overhaul, then start the maintenance routine from the beginning. If you have a used machine and have no knowledge of its history or maintenance record, combine all the checks into one large service initially and then settle into the specified maintenance schedule.

3 Before beginning any maintenance or repair, the machine should be cleaned thoroughly, especially around the oil filter, spark plugs, valve cover, body panels, drive chain, suspension, wheels, etc. Cleaning will help ensure that dirt does not contaminate the engine and will allow you to detect wear and damage that could otherwise easily go unnoticed.

4 Certain maintenance information is sometimes printed on labels attached to the motorcycle. If the information on the labels differs from that included here, use the information on the label.

1   Drive chain and sprockets

Check chain slack

1 A neglected drive chain won't last long and will quickly damage the sprockets. Routine chain adjustment and lubrication isn't difficult and will ensure maximum chain and sprocket life.

2 To check the chain, place the bike on its sidestand and shift the transmission into neutral. Make sure the ignition switch is OFF.

3 Push up on the bottom run of the chain midway between the two sprockets and measure the slack, then compare your measurement to that listed in this Chapter's Specifications **(see illustration)**. Since the chain will rarely wear evenly, roll the bike forward so that another section of chain can be checked (having an assistant to do this makes the task a lot easier); do this several times to check the entire length of chain, and mark the tightest spot. As the chain stretches with wear, adjustment will periodically be necessary (see below).

Caution: Riding the bike with excess slack in the chain could lead to damage.

4 In some cases where lubrication has been neglected, corrosion and dirt may cause the links to bind and kink, which effectively shortens the chain's length and makes it tight **(see illustration)**. Thoroughly clean and work free any such links, then highlight them with a marker pen or paint. Take the bike for a ride.

5 After the bike has been ridden, repeat the measurement for slack in the highlighted area. If the chain has kinked again and is still tight, replace it with a new one (see Chapter 6). A rusty, kinked or worn chain will damage the sprockets and can damage transmission bearings. If in any doubt as to the condition of a chain, it is far better to install a new one than risk damage to other components and possibly yourself.

6 Check the entire length of the chain for damaged rollers, loose links and pins, and missing O-rings and replace it with a new one if necessary. **Note:** *Never install a new chain on old sprockets, and never use the old chain if you install new sprockets – replace the chain and sprockets as a set.*

7 Inspect the drive chain slider on the front of the swingarm for excessive wear and damage and replace it with a new one if necessary.

Adjust chain slack

8 Move the bike so that the chain is positioned with the tightest point at the centre of its bottom run, then put it on the sidestand.

9 Straighten and remove the split pin from the left-hand end of the axle on Z750 models, and from the right-hand end on Z1000 models **(see illustration)**. Discard it as a new one must be used. Slacken the rear axle nut.

10 On Z750 models slacken the locknut on each adjuster **(see illustration)**. Turn each adjuster nut evenly and a little at a time until the amount of freeplay specified at the beginning of the Chapter is obtained at the centre of the bottom run of the chain – if the chain was slack turn the nuts clockwise; if the chain was tight turn them anti-clockwise, then move the wheel forwards in the swingarm to take up the gap between the nuts and the adjuster plates.

11 On Z1000 models slacken the locknut on each adjuster bolt **(see illustration)**. Turn each adjuster bolt evenly and a little at a time until the amount of freeplay specified at the beginning of the Chapter is obtained at the centre of the bottom run of the chain – if the chain was slack turn the bolts anti-clockwise; if the chain was tight turn them clockwise, then move the wheel forwards in the swingarm to take up the gap between the adjustment marker blocks and the bolt heads.

1.3 Push up on the chain and measure the slack

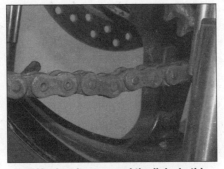

1.4 Neglect has caused the links in this chain to kink

1.9 Straighten and remove the split pin, then slacken the axle nut (arrowed)

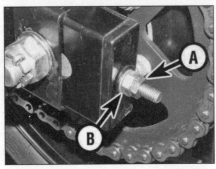

1.10 Adjuster locknut (A) and adjuster nut (B) – Z750

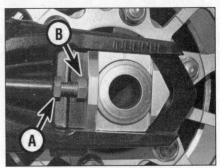

1.11 Adjuster locknut (A) and adjuster bolt (B) – Z1000

1.12a Adjustment marker (A) and alignment marks (B) – Z750

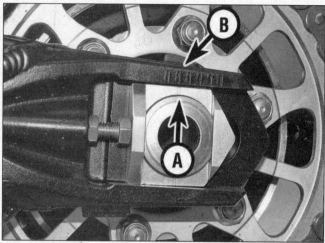

1.12b Adjustment marker (A) and alignment marks (B) – Z1000

12 Following adjustment, check that the index point on each chain adjustment marker is in the same position in relation to the marks on the swingarm **(see illustrations)**. It is important the alignment is the same on each side otherwise the rear wheel will be out of alignment with the front. Always make sure that the front edge of each marker is butted against the end of the adjuster bolt. If there is a difference in the positions, adjust one of them so that its position is exactly the same as the other. Check the chain freeplay again at its tightest point and readjust if necessary.

13 When adjustment is complete counter-hold the adjuster nuts or bolts (according to model) and tighten the locknuts **(see illustration 1.10 or 1.11)**. Tighten the axle nut to the torque setting specified at the beginning of the Chapter. Recheck the adjustment as above, then place the machine on an auxiliary stand and spin the wheel to make sure it runs freely.

14 Check the alignment of the hole in the end of the axle with the slots in the nut – they must align to allow the split pin to be fitted. If necessary tighten the nut further until the nearest slots align with the hole. If you go too far slacken the nut and tighten it again; do not tighten further to the second nearest slot. Fit a new split pin and bend it around the nut as shown **(see illustration)**.

Clean and lubricate the chain

15 If required, wash the chain using a dedicated aerosol cleaner that will not damage the O-rings, or in paraffin (kerosene), using a soft brush to work any dirt out if necessary. Wipe the cleaner off the chain and allow it to dry, using compressed air if available. If the chain is excessively dirty remove it from the machine and allow it to soak in the paraffin or solvent (see Chapter 6).
Caution: Don't use petrol (gasoline), an unsuitable solvent or other cleaning fluids which might damage the internal sealing properties of the chain. Don't use high-pressure water to clean the chain. The entire process shouldn't take longer than ten minutes, otherwise the O-rings could be damaged.

16 The best time to lubricate the chain is after the motorcycle has been ridden. When the chain is warm, the lubricant will penetrate the joints between the sideplates better than when cold. **Note:** *Kawasaki specifies SAE 80 or SAE 90 gear oil or an aerosol chain lube that it is suitable for O-ring chains; do not use any other chain lubricants – the solvents could damage the chain's sealing rings.* Apply the lubricant to the area where the sideplates overlap – not the middle of the rollers **(see illustration)**.

HAYNES HINT *Apply the lubricant to the top of the lower chain run, so centrifugal force will work the oil into the chain when the bike is moving. After applying the lubricant, let it soak in a few minutes before wiping off any excess.*

Warning: Take care not to get any lubricant on the tyres or brake system components. If any of the lubricant inadvertently contacts them, clean it off thoroughly using a suitable solvent or dedicated brake cleaner before riding the machine.

Check the drive chain stretch and sprocket wear

17 Remove the front sprocket cover (see Chapter 6). Check the teeth on the front sprocket and the rear sprocket for wear **(see illustration)**. If the sprocket teeth are worn excessively, replace the chain and both sprockets with a new set.

18 Measure the amount of chain stretch as follows:

1.14 Fit a new split pin through the holes and bend its ends round as shown

1.16 Apply the lubricant to the overlapping sections of the sideplates

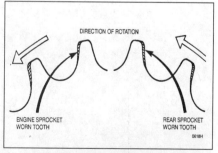

1.17 Check the sprockets in the areas indicated to see if they are worn excessively

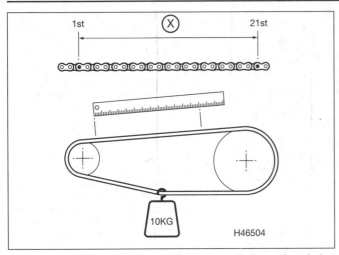

1.19 Measure a 20-link section (X) as shown to determine chain stretch

2.3a Flex the hoses and make sure they are not cracked or hardened

19 Obtain a 10 kg or 20 lb weight and hang it from the centre of the bottom run of the chain (see illustration). Measure along the top run the length of 20 links (from the centre of the 1st pin to the centre of the 21st pin) and compare the result to the stretch limit specified at the beginning of the Chapter. Rotate the rear wheel so that several sections of the chain can be measured, then calculate the average. If the chain stretch measurement exceeds the service limit the chain must be replaced with a new one (see Chapter 6). Note: Never fit a new chain onto old sprockets, and never use the old chain if you fit new sprockets – replace the chain and sprockets as a set.

2 Brake system

Brake system check

1 A routine general check of the brake system will ensure that any problems are discovered and remedied before the rider's safety is jeopardised.
2 Check the brake lever and pedal for loose fixings, improper or rough action, excessive play, bends, and other damage. Replace any damaged parts with new ones (see Chapter 5). Clean and lubricate the lever and pedal pivots if their action is stiff or rough (see Section 18).
3 Make sure all brake component fasteners are tight. Check the brake pads for wear (see below) and make sure the fluid level in the reservoirs is correct (see Pre-ride checks). Look for leaks at the hose connections and check for cracks in the hoses and unions (see illustration). On models with ABS remove the fuel tank (see Chapter 4) and check the brake pipes, the pipe joints and the ABS hydraulic unit for signs of fluid leakage and for any dents or cracks in the pipes (see illustration). If the lever or pedal is spongy, bleed the brakes (see Chapter 6).
4 Make sure the brake light operates when the front brake lever is pulled in. The front brake light switch, mounted on the underside of the master cylinder, is not adjustable. If it fails to operate properly, check it (see Chapter 8).
5 Make sure the brake light is activated after about 10 mm of pedal travel and just before the rear brake takes effect. If adjustment is necessary, hold the switch and turn the adjuster nut on the switch body until the brake light is activated when required (see illustration). The switch is mounted behind the rider's right-hand footrest bracket. If the brake light comes on too late or not at all, turn the nut clockwise (when looked at from the top) so the switch threads up out of the bracket. If the brake light comes on too soon or is permanently on, turn the nut anti-clockwise so the switch threads down into the bracket. If the switch doesn't operate the brake light, check it (see Chapter 8).
6 The front brake lever has a span adjuster which alters the distance of the lever from the

2.3b On models with ABS check the pipes and pipe joints for leakage

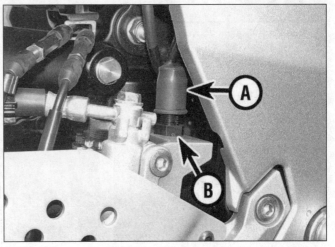

2.5 Hold the rear brake light switch body (A) and turn the adjuster ring (B) as required

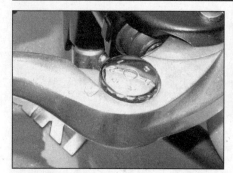

2.6a Front brake lever span adjuster

2.6b Push the lever forward when making adjustment

2.7a Make sure the height of the brake pedal is as specified or as required

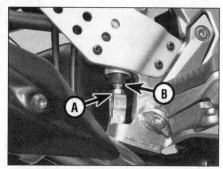

2.7b Slacken the locknut (A) and turn the pushrod using the hex (B) to adjust pedal height

2.8a Front brake pad wear indicator (arrowed) – Z750

2.8b Rear brake pad wear indicator (arrowed) – Z750

2.8c Front brake pad wear indicator (arrowed) – Z1000

2.8d Rear brake pad wear indicator (arrowed) – Z1000

handlebar **(see illustration)**. Each setting is identified by a number on the adjuster which aligns with the arrow or triangle on the lever. Push the lever away from the handlebar and turn the adjuster ring until the setting which best suits the rider is obtained **(see illustration)**. Setting 1 gives the maximum span and setting 5 or 6 (according to model) the minimum. Do not set the adjuster between the defined settings.

7 The position of the rear brake pedal (measured how far it is below a horizontal line taken from the top of the footrest) can be adjusted, either if it is not as specified at the beginning of the Chapter, or to suit the rider's preference **(see illustration)**. Slacken the clevis locknut on the master cylinder pushrod, then turn the pushrod using a spanner on the hex at the top of the rod until the pedal is at the desired height **(see illustration)**. Kawasaki give an alternative measurement for the brake pedal height – the distance between the bottom mounting bolt for the master cylinder and the clevis pin (measured centre-to-centre and parallel to the master cylinder centre line), that should be 69 to 71 mm. On completion tighten the locknut. Adjust the rear brake light switch after adjusting the pedal height (see Step 5).

Brake pad wear check

8 Each brake pad has wear indicators in the form of cut-outs in the friction material. The wear indicators should be plainly visible by looking at the edges of the friction material from the best vantage point, but note that an accumulation of road dirt and brake dust could make them difficult to see **(see illustrations)**.
9 If the indicators aren't visible, then the amount of friction material remaining should be, and it will be obvious when the pads need replacing. Kawasaki specify a minimum thickness of 1 mm for the friction material. **Note:** *Some after-market pads may use different indicators to those on the original equipment.*
10 If the pads are worn to the bottom of the cut-out on the front pads or to the beginning of it on the rear pads, or there is little friction material remaining, they must be replaced with new ones, though it is advisable to fit new pads before they become this worn.
11 If the pads are dirty or if you are in doubt as to the amount of friction material remaining, remove them for inspection (see Chapter 6). If the pads are excessively worn, check the brake discs (see Chapter 6).
12 Refer to Chapter 6 for details of pad removal and installation.

Brake fluid change

13 The brake fluid should be changed at the prescribed interval or whenever a master cylinder or caliper overhaul is carried out. Refer to Chapter 6, Section 11 for details. Ensure that all the old fluid is pumped from the hydraulic system and that the level in the fluid reservoir is checked and the brakes tested before riding the motorcycle.

Brake hoses

14 The hoses will deteriorate with age and should be replaced with new ones at the prescribed interval regardless of their apparent condition (see Chapter 6).

15 Always replace the banjo union sealing washers with new ones when fitting new hoses. Refill the system with new brake fluid and bleed the system as described in Chapter 6.

Brake caliper and master cylinder seals

16 Brake system seals will deteriorate with age and lose their effectiveness, leading to sticky operation of the brake master cylinders or the pistons in the brake calipers, or fluid loss. They should be replaced with new ones at the prescribed interval and particularly if fluid leakage or a sticking action is apparent.

17 Replace all the seals in each caliper and master cylinder as a set; master cylinder seals are supplied as a kit along with a new piston and spring (see Chapter 6).

3 Exhaust valve

Note: *The exhaust valve is only fitted on ZR750-L/M and ZR1000-B/C models.*

1 The system controls the flow of gases through the exhaust using a butterfly valve. The valve is actuated by cables from a servo motor that is controlled by the ECU.

2 Remove the left-hand side panel to access the servo (Chapter 7). Check that the pulley is in its original position as shown **(see illustration)**. Turn the ignition ON and check that the servo pulley rotates clockwise, then anti-clockwise, then clockwise again, so it

3.2 This is the original position of the pulley

ends up back in its original position. Turn the ignition OFF. If not, check the cables are not detached, seized or broken, and check the servo wiring connector.

3 Check there is no slack in the cables at the pulley. If there is, locate the adjusters above the rear brake master cylinder on the right-hand side of the bike **(see illustration)**. Pull the boots off the adjusters. Slacken the locknut on the valve opening cable adjuster (the rear of the two) and turn the adjuster away from the locknut until resistance is felt. Tighten the locknut. Repeat for the closing cable adjuster. Now turn the ignition ON so the pulley turns clockwise, then turn it OFF when the pulley is at its fully clockwise position, at which point the opening cable end should approximately align with the screw on the servo body as shown **(see illustration)**. Now repeat the adjustment on the opening cable adjuster to eliminate any slack. Now turn the ignition ON so the pulley completes its cycle by turning anti-clockwise then clockwise to its original position, then turn it OFF.

4 Refer to Chapter 4 if the cables cannot be adjusted or if the pulley is out of position when the valve is fully open or closed.

4 EVAP (Evaporative emission control) system (California models)

1 On ZR750-J and ZR1000-A models remove the rear seat and the left-hand frame cover (Chapter 7). On ZR750-L/M and ZR1000-B/C models remove the rider's seat and the right-hand side panel (Chapter 7).

2 Visually inspect all the system hoses between the fuel tank, the separator and the canister for kinks and splits and any other damage or deterioration. Make sure that the hoses are securely connected with a clamp on each end. Replace any hoses that are damaged or deteriorated.

3 Check the EVAP canister and the separator for cracks or other damage.

4 See Chapter 4 for further information on the system. Note that there is an information label and an emission control system hose routing label relating to the system.

5 Clutch

1 Check that the clutch lever operates smoothly and easily.

2 If the clutch lever operation is heavy or stiff, remove the cable (see Chapter 2) and lubricate it (see Section 18). If the cable is still stiff, replace it with a new one. Install the lubricated or new cable (see Chapter 2).

3 With the cable operating smoothly, check that it is correctly adjusted. Periodic adjustment is necessary to compensate for wear in the clutch plates and stretch of the cable. Pull lightly on the clutch lever until freeplay is taken up, then measure the gap between the inner front edge of the lever and

3.3a Exhaust valve cable adjusters (arrowed)

3.3b This is the fully clockwise position

5.3 Measure the gap between the lever and bracket as shown (arrowed)

5.4a On ZR750-J models slacken the locknut (arrowed)

5.4b Turn the adjuster in or out as required

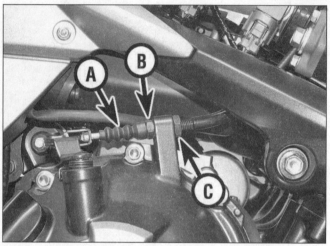

5.7 Rubber boot (A), rear nut (B) and front nut (C)

5.9 The angle between the arrows should be about 60°

the lever bracket **(see illustration)**. Check that the gap is as specified at the beginning of the Chapter.

4 If adjustment is required, this can be done first at the lever end of the cable. On ZR750-J models fully slacken the adjuster locknut **(see illustration)**. On all models turn the adjuster in or out until the specified amount of freeplay is obtained **(see illustration)**. To increase freeplay, thread the adjuster into the lever bracket. To reduce freeplay, thread the adjuster out of the bracket.

5 Make sure that the slot in the adjuster is not aligned with the slot in the lever bracket – these slots are to allow removal of the cable, and if they are all aligned while the bike is in use the cable could jump out. Also make sure the adjuster is not threaded too far out of the bracket so that it is only held by a few threads – this will leave it unstable and the threads could be damaged. On ZR750-J models tighten the locknut on completion.

6 If all the adjustment has been taken up at the lever, thread the adjuster into the bracket until 5 to 6 mm of thread is left exposed to give plenty of freeplay.

7 Now set the correct amount of freeplay using the adjuster on the clutch end of cable. The adjuster is set in a holder on the top of

the clutch cover on the right-hand side of the engine **(see illustration)**.

8 Draw the rubber boot back off the outer cable. Slacken the rear nut securing the cable in the holder. Grasp the cable and pull it towards the front of the bike until all freeplay in the release mechanism arm has been taken up, then thread the front nut down until it locates against the holder. Tighten the rear nut against the holder. Now reset the correct amount of freeplay using the lever adjuster (Steps 4 and 5).

9 Push the release mechanism arm forwards until freeplay is taken up and check that the angle between the arm and the cable is about 60° **(see illustration)**. If not the clutch plates could be worn and should be checked (Chapter 2).

6 Throttle and fast idle cables

Throttle cables

1 Make sure the throttle grip rotates smoothly and freely from fully closed to fully open with the front wheel turned at various angles. The grip should return automatically from fully open to fully closed when released.

2 If the throttle sticks, this is probably due to a cable fault. Remove the cables (see Chapter 4) and lubricate them (see Section 18). Check that the inner cables slide freely and easily in the outer cables. If not, replace the cables with new ones.

3 With the cables removed, make sure the throttle twistgrip rotates freely on the handlebar – dirt combined with a lack of lubrication can cause the action to be stiff. If necessary, unscrew the handlebar end-weight bolt, remove the weight and slide the twistgrip off the handlebar **(see illustration)**. Clean any old grease from the bar and the inside of the tube. Smear some new grease of the specified

6.3 Undo the screw (arrowed) to free the end-weight and twistgrip

6.4 Throttle cable freeplay is measured in terms of twistgrip rotation

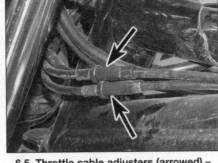

6.5 Throttle cable adjusters (arrowed) – Z750, ZR1000A

6.6 Throttle cable adjusters – ZR1000-B/C models

type onto the bar, then refit the twistgrip. Clean the threads of the end-weight bolt and apply a suitable non-permanent thread locking compound. Install the cables, making sure they are correctly routed (see Chapter 4). If this fails to improve the operation of the throttle, the cables must be replaced with new ones. Note that in very rare cases the fault could lie in the throttle bodies. Remove the air filter housing and check the action of the throttle pulley (see Chapter 4).

4 With the throttle operating smoothly, check for a small amount of freeplay in the cables, measured in terms of the amount of twistgrip rotation before the throttle opens, and compare the amount to that listed in this Chapter's Specifications **(see illustration)**. If it's incorrect, adjust the cables to correct it as follows.

5 On all Z750 models and ZR1000-A models loosen the locknut on the adjuster on the throttle opening cable where it leaves the switch housing, then turn the adjuster in or out until the specified amount of freeplay is obtained, then retighten the locknut. If the cable cannot be correctly adjusted, or if all the adjustment has been taken up, thread the adjuster all the way in so freeplay is at a maximum, then tighten the locknut. Now locate the adjusters in the middle of each cable between the frame and the fuel tank on

the left-hand side behind the steering head – remove the fuel tank for access if required (see Chapter 4) **(see illustration)**. Loosen the locknut on each adjuster and turn the adjusters in completely so there is plenty of freeplay. Now turn the throttle closing cable adjuster out until there is no freeplay with the throttle closed then retighten the locknut. Now turn the throttle opening cable adjuster out until the specified amount of freeplay is obtained, then retighten the locknut.

6 On ZR1000-B/C models loosen the locknut on each adjuster and turn the adjusters in completely so there is plenty of freeplay **(see illustration)**. Now turn the throttle closing cable adjuster out until there is no freeplay with the throttle closed then retighten the locknut. Now turn the throttle opening cable adjuster out until the specified amount of freeplay is obtained, then retighten the locknut.

Fast idle cable – ZR750-J and ZR1000-A models

7 With the fast idle lever on the handlebar held closed check that there is the specified amount of freeplay in the cable cam on the left-hand side of the throttle bodies **(see illustration)**. Zero freeplay is acceptable provided the cam is at its position of rest, i.e. it is not holding the link arm open. To adjust

freeplay remove the fuel tank (see Chapter 4). Loosen the locknut on the adjuster, then turn the adjuster in or out until the specified amount of freeplay is obtained at the cam, then retighten the locknut **(see illustration)**.

 Warning: Turn the handlebars all the way through their travel with the engine idling. Idle speed should not change. If it does, the cables may be routed incorrectly. Correct this condition before riding the bike.

7 Idle speed

1 The idle speed should be checked and adjusted before and after synchronising the throttle bodies and after checking the valve clearances, and when it is obviously too high or too low. Before adjusting the idle speed, check that the valve clearances were checked at the previous prescribed interval, the spark plugs are in good condition and the air filter is clean. Also, turn the handlebars from side-to-side and check the idle speed does not change. If it does, the throttle cables may not be adjusted or routed correctly, or may be worn out. This is a dangerous condition that

6.7a Check for freeplay at the cam (arrowed) . . .

6.7b . . . and if necessary reset it using the adjuster (arrowed)

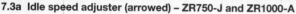

7.3a Idle speed adjuster (arrowed) – ZR750-J and ZR1000-A

7.3b Idle speed adjuster (arrowed) – ZR750-L/M and ZR1000-B/C

can cause loss of control of the bike. Be sure to correct this problem before proceeding.

2 The engine should be at normal operating temperature, which is usually reached after 10 to 15 minutes of stop-and-go riding. Place the motorcycle on its sidestand, and make sure the transmission is in neutral.

3 The idle speed adjuster is a knurled knob located on the left-hand end of the throttle bodies (see illustrations). With the engine running, turn the knob until the engine idles at the speed specified at the beginning of the Chapter. Turn the screw clockwise to increase idle speed, and anti-clockwise to decrease it.

4 Snap the throttle open and shut a few times, then recheck the idle speed. If necessary, repeat the adjustment procedure.

5 If a smooth, steady idle can't be achieved check the throttle body synchronisation, and re-check the valve clearances (see Sections 8 and 21).

8 Throttle body synchronisation

Warning: Petrol (gasoline) is extremely flammable, so take extra precautions when you work

on any part of the fuel system. Don't smoke or allow open flames or bare light bulbs near the work area, and don't work in a garage where a natural gas-type appliance is present. If you spill any fuel on your skin, rinse it off immediately with soap and water. When you perform any kind of work on the fuel system, wear safety glasses and have a fire extinguisher suitable for a Class B type fire (flammable liquids) on hand.

Warning: Do not allow exhaust gases to build up in the work area; either perform the check outside or use an exhaust gas extraction system.

Special tool: A set of four vacuum gauges or a manometer is necessary for this job.

1 Throttle body synchronisation ensures each throttle body passes the same amount of fuel/air mixture to each cylinder. This is done by measuring the vacuum produced in each cylinder. Throttle bodies that are out of synchronisation will result in increased fuel consumption, higher engine temperature, less than ideal throttle response and higher vibration levels. Before synchronising the throttle bodies, make sure that the idle speed is properly adjusted (Section 7) and that the valve clearances were checked at the previous prescribed interval (Section 21).

2 Start the engine and let it run until it reaches normal operating temperature, then shut it off. Support the machine upright on level ground using an auxiliary stand. Raise the fuel tank, keeping the wiring connectors connected, and making sure they don't get strained (see Chapter 4).

3 Remove the blanking cap or detach the hose from the **right-hand** vacuum take-off union on each throttle body, noting what fits where (see illustration). Plug the end(s) of the hose(s), where detached. Also detach the air system hose from the air filter housing, and plug its end and the union on the housing (see illustration). Connect the vacuum gauge hose ends to the exposed vacuum take-off unions. Make sure the No. 1 gauge is attached to the No. 1 (left-hand) throttle body, and so on.

4 Start the engine and let it idle, making sure the speed is still correct. If gauges are used, set their damping adjustment so that the needle flutter is just eliminated yet they can still respond to small changes in pressure.

5 The vacuum readings should all be the same and within the range specified at the beginning of the Chapter (see illustration).

6 If the vacuum readings are out of the specified range, first try to synchronise them by using the screw located in the

8.3a Expose the right-hand vacuum take-off point on each throttle body (arrowed)

8.3b Detach the air system hose from the air filter housing then plug the hose and its union

8.5 Checking throttle body synchronisation

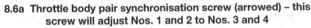

8.6a Throttle body pair synchronisation screw (arrowed) – this screw will adjust Nos. 1 and 2 to Nos. 3 and 4

8.6b Individual throttle body synchronisation air screws (arrowed)

centre between the throttle body pairs **(see illustration)**. If all four readings can be set within the range specified using this screw no further adjustment is necessary. If the difference between 1 and 2 or between 3 and 4 is greater than 20 mmHg, locate the air screws in the throttle bodies and adjust them as required by turning the appropriate air screw until the readings are the same and as specified **(see illustration)**.

7 When all the throttle bodies are synchronised, open and close the throttle quickly to settle the linkage, and recheck the gauge readings, readjusting if necessary.

8 When the adjustment is complete, adjust the idle speed (see Section 7). Remove the gauges and refit the blanking cap or reconnect the hose(s) as required according to your model. Now check the output voltage of the main throttle position sensor (see Chapter 4). Install the fuel tank (see Chapter 4).

9 Fuel system

⚠ **Warning: Petrol (gasoline) is extremely flammable, so take extra precautions when you work on any part of the fuel system. Don't smoke or allow open flames or bare light bulbs near the work area, and don't work in a garage where a natural gas-type appliance is present. If you spill any fuel on your skin, rinse it off immediately with soap and water. When you perform any kind of work on the fuel system, wear safety glasses and have a fire extinguisher suitable for a Class B type fire (flammable liquids) on hand.**

Check the fuel hoses, EVAP hoses and system components

1 Remove the fuel tank (see Chapter 4) and check the tank, the fuel hoses and unions,

the vacuum hoses, the air system hoses (see Section 13), and, on California models the EVAP system hoses (see Section 4), for signs of leaks, deterioration or damage. In particular check that there are no leaks from the fuel hoses or hose unions. Replace any hose that is cracked or deteriorated with a new one (see Chapter 4). Also check the crankcase breather hose **(see illustration)**.

2 If the joint between the fuel pump mounting plate and the tank is leaking, ensure the mounting bolts are tightened to the specified torque setting (see Chapter 4); if the leak persists, remove the pump and fit a new gasket (see Chapter 4).

3 Inspect the joints between the fuel rail, the injectors and the throttle bodies. If there are any leaks, remove the fuel rail and fit new seals and O-rings to the injectors (see Chapter 4).

Fuel filter

4 The filter is integral with the fuel pump, and is not available as a separate component. If after checking all other possibilities a blocked filter is the cause of fuel starvation a new pump assembly must be installed (see Chapter 4).

10 Spark plugs

Note: *The spark plug caps are integral with the ignition 'stick' coils. To avoid damaging the wiring, always disconnect the wiring connectors before removing the coils. Do not attempt to lever the coils off the plugs or pull them off with pliers. Do not drop the coils.*
Special tool: *A wire type feeler gauge is necessary for this job (see illustration 10.6b).*

All Z750 models and ZR1000-A models

1 Remove the ignition stick coils (Chapter 4).
2 Make sure your spark plug socket is the correct size before attempting to remove

9.1 Crankcase breather hose (arrowed)

the plugs – a suitable one is supplied in the motorcycle's tool kit which is stored under the passenger seat.

3 Using either the plug removing tool and spanner supplied in the bike's toolkit or a deep spark plug socket, unscrew and remove the plugs from the cylinder head **(see illustrations 10.11a and b)**. Lay each plug out in relation to its cylinder; if any plug shows up a problem it will then be easy to identify the troublesome cylinder.

4 Inspect the electrodes for wear. Both the centre and two side electrodes should have square edges and the side electrodes should be of uniform thickness. Look for excessive deposits and evidence of a cracked or chipped insulator around the centre electrode. Compare your spark plugs to the colour spark plug reading chart on the inside rear cover. Check the threads, the washer and the ceramic insulator body for cracks and other damage.

5 If the electrodes are not excessively worn, and if the deposits can be easily removed with a wire brush, and there are no cracks or chips visible in the insulator, the plugs can be re-used. If in doubt concerning the condition of the plugs, replace them with new ones, as the expense is minimal. Note that new spark plugs should be fitted at the prescribed service interval.

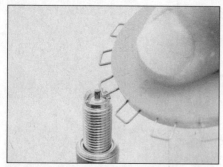

10.6a Using a wire type gauge to measure the spark plug electrode gap

10.6b Adjust each side electrode to create the correct gap

10.11a Unscrew the plug . . .

6 Before installing the plugs, make sure they are the correct type and heat range and check the gap between the electrodes **(see illustration)**. Compare the gap to that specified and adjust as necessary. If the gap must be adjusted, bend the side electrode and be very careful not to chip or crack the insulator nose **(see illustration)**. Make sure the sealing washer is in place on the plug before installing it.

7 Fit the plug into the end of the tool, then use the tool to insert the plug. Since the cylinder head is made of aluminium, which is soft and easily damaged, thread the plugs as far as possible into the head turning the tool by hand. Once the plugs are finger-tight, the job can be finished with a spanner on the tool supplied or a socket drive. If new plugs are being used, tighten them by 1/2 a turn after the washer has seated. If the old plugs are

being reused, tighten them by 1/8 to 1/4 turn after they have seated, or if a torque wrench can be applied, tighten the spark plugs to the torque setting specified at the beginning of the Chapter. Otherwise tighten them according the instructions on the box. Do not over-tighten them.

8 Install the ignition stick coils (Chapter 4).

HAYNES HiNT *As the plugs are quite recessed, slip a short length of hose over the end of the plug to use as a tool to thread it into place. The hose will grip the plug well enough to turn it, but will start to slip if the plug begins to cross-thread in the hole – this will prevent damaged threads.*

10.11b . . . and lift it out with the tool – the rubber insert should grip around the plug top

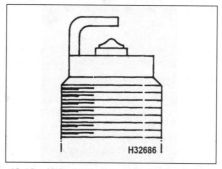

10.12a If the iridium centre electrode has rounded off the plug is worn

ZR1000-B/C models

9 Remove the ignition stick coils (Chapter 4).

10 Make sure your spark plug socket is the correct size before attempting to remove the plugs – a suitable one is supplied in the motorcycle's tool kit which is stored under the passenger seat.

11 Using either the plug removing tool and spanner supplied in the bike's toolkit or a deep spark plug socket, unscrew and remove the plugs from the cylinder head **(see illustrations)**. Lay each plug out in relation to its cylinder; if any plug shows up a problem it will then be easy to identify the troublesome cylinder.

12 Examine the pointed iridium-tipped centre electrode; if the tip has rounded off, the plug is worn **(see illustration)**. Measure the gap between the two electrodes with a wire type gauge only **(see illustrations)** – do not use blade type feeler gauges because the iridium tip might be damaged. The gap should be as given in the Specifications at the beginning of this chapter; if the electrodes have worn and the gap is wider than it should be, or for some reason the gap is narrower than it should be (if the plug has been dropped for instance) a new plug must be installed. Do not bend the outer electrode to adjust the gap.

13 Make sure the sealing washer is in place on the plug before installing it. Fit the plug into the end of the tool, then use the tool to insert the plug. Since the cylinder head is made of aluminium, which is soft and easily damaged, thread the plugs as far as possible into the head turning the tool by hand. Once the plugs are finger-tight, the job can be finished with a spanner on the tool supplied or a socket drive. If new plugs are being used, tighten them by 1/2 a turn after the washer has seated. If the old plugs are being reused, tighten them by 1/8 to 1/4 turn after they have seated, or if a torque wrench can be applied, tighten the spark plugs to the torque setting specified at the beginning of the Chapter. Otherwise tighten them according the instructions on the box. Do not over-tighten them.

14 Install the ignition stick coils (Chapter 4).

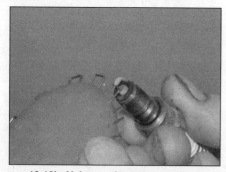

10.12b Using a wire type gauge . . .

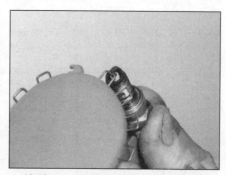

10.12c . . . to measure the spark plug electrode gap

HAYNES HiNT *Stripped plug threads in the cylinder head can be repaired with a Heli-Coil insert – see 'Tools and Workshop Tips' in the Reference section.*

11.3 Unscrew the oil filler cap to act as a vent . . .

11.4a . . . then unscrew the oil drain bolt . . .

11.4b . . . and allow the oil to completely drain

11.4c Some sealing washers need to be cut off

11.5 Use a new sealing washer and tighten the bolt to the specified torque

11 Engine oil and filter

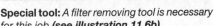

Special tool: *A filter removing tool is necessary for this job (see illustration 11.6b).*

 Warning: Be careful when draining the oil, as the exhaust pipes, the engine, and the oil itself can cause severe burns.

1 Consistent routine oil and filter changes are the single most important maintenance procedure you can perform. The oil not only lubricates the internal parts of the engine, transmission and clutch, but it also acts as a coolant, a cleaner, a sealant, and a protector. Because of these demands, the oil takes a terrific amount of abuse and should be replaced often with new oil of the recommended grade and type. The oil filter should be changed with every oil change.

2 Before changing the oil, warm up the engine so the oil will drain easily. Make sure the bike is on level ground. The oil drain plug is on the left-hand side of the sump on the bottom of the engine. The oil filter is on the front of the engine. On ZR1000-B/C models remove the left-hand sump cowl (see Chapter 7).

3 Position a clean drain tray below the engine. Unscrew the oil filler cap from the clutch cover to vent the crankcase and to act as a reminder that there is no oil in the engine **(see illustration)**.

4 Unscrew the oil drain bolt and allow the oil to flow into the drain tray **(see illustrations)**. Discard the sealing washer on the bolt and replace it with a new one – you may have to cut the old one off depending on the type used **(see illustration)**.

5 When the oil has completely drained, fit the bolt into the sump, using a new sealing washer if necessary, and tighten it to the torque setting specified at the beginning of the Chapter **(see illustration)**. Do not overtighten it as the threads in the sump are easily damaged.

6 Place the drain tray below the oil filter on the front of the engine. Unscrew the filter using a filter socket (one can be obtained with the new filter from Kawasaki dealers under part No. 57001-1249, or otherwise there are commercially available equivalents available from good accessory dealers), filter pliers, or a filter removing strap or a chain-wrench, and tip any residual oil into the drain tray **(see illustrations)**. The filter socket is the best tool

11.6a Fit the filter removing tool . . .

11.6b . . . then unscrew the filter . . .

11.6c . . . and allow the oil to drain

11.7a Smear clean oil onto the seal . . .

11.7b . . . then fit the filter and tighten it as described

11.8 Refill using the specified oil almost up to the upper level line

because it allows a means of tightening the new filter to the correct torque.

7 Smear clean engine oil or grease onto the rubber seal on the new filter and thread it onto the engine **(see illustrations)**. Tighten it to the specified torque setting, or by the number of turns specified on the filter itself or its packaging, using the filter socket **(see illustration)**. Note: *Do not use a strap or chain filter removing tool to tighten the filter as you will damage it, and do not tighten it by hand as it will not be tight enough.*

8 Refill the engine to the proper level using the recommended type and amount of oil (see *Pre-ride checks*) **(see illustration)**. With the motorcycle vertical, the oil level should lie between the upper and lower level lines on the inspection window (see *Pre-ride checks*). Check the condition of the O-ring on the filler cap and replace it with a new one if it is damaged or worn. Install the filler cap **(see illustration 11.3)**.

9 Start the engine and let it run for two or three minutes (make sure that the oil pressure light extinguishes after a few seconds). Shut it off, wait a few minutes, then check the oil level. If necessary, add more oil to bring the level close to the maximum line, but do not go above it.

10 Check around the drain plug and the oil filter for leaks. If there is a leak around the drain plug and a new washer wasn't used, then repeat the procedure using a new washer. Otherwise make sure the drain bolt is tightened to the specified torque. A leak around the filter probably means it is not tight

enough. On ZR1000-B/C models install the left-hand sump cowl (see Chapter 7).

11 The old oil drained from the engine cannot be re-used and should be disposed of properly. Check with your local refuse disposal company, disposal facility or environmental agency to see whether they will accept the used oil for recycling. Don't pour used oil into drains or onto the ground.

OIL CARE FOLLOW THE CODE

OIL BANK LINE
0800 66 33 66
www.oilbankline.org.uk

Note: It is antisocial and illegal to dump oil down the drain. To find the location of your local oil recycling bank, call this number free.

In the USA, note that any oil supplier must accept used oil for recycling.

HAYNES HiNT *Check the old oil carefully – if it is very metallic coloured, then the engine is experiencing wear from break-in (new engine) or from insufficient lubrication. If there are flakes or chips of metal in the oil, then something is drastically wrong internally and the engine will have to be disassembled for inspection and repair. If there are pieces of fibre-like material in the oil, the clutch is experiencing excessive wear and should be checked.*

12 Cooling system

Check

⚠ **Warning: The engine must be cool before beginning this procedure.**

1 Remove the fuel tank (see Chapter 4). On ZR1000-B/C models remove the left-hand sump cowl (see Chapter 7). Check the coolant level in the reservoir (see *Pre-ride checks*).

2 Check the entire cooling system for evidence of leaks. Examine each rubber coolant hose along its entire length. Look for cracks, abrasions and other damage. Squeeze each hose at various points to see whether they are dried out or hard **(see illustration)**. They should feel firm, yet pliable, and return to their original shape when released. If necessary, replace them with new ones (see Chapter 3).

3 Check each cooling system joint, the inlet and outlet unions on the back of the cylinder block and head respectively, and around the pump on the left-hand side of the engine. Make sure all hose clips are tight enough. If the pump is leaking around the cover, check that the bolts are tight. If they are, remove the cover and replace the O-ring with a new one (see Chapter 3). If it is leaking around the crankcase, remove the pump and replace the body O-ring with a new one (see Chapter 3). If the inlet or outlet unions are leaking replace their O-rings with new ones (Chapter 3).

4 To prevent leakage of coolant from the cooling system to the lubrication system and vice versa, two seals are fitted on the pump shaft. On the bottom of the pump housing there is a drain hole **(see illustration)**. If either seal fails, the drain allows the coolant or oil to escape and prevents them mixing. The seal on the water pump side is of the mechanical type which bears on the rear face of the impeller. The second seal, which is mounted behind the mechanical seal is of the normal feathered lip type. If on inspection the drain shows signs of leakage, remove the pump and replace the seals with new ones (see Chapter 3).

5 Check the radiator for leaks and other damage. Leaks in the radiator leave tell-tale scale deposits or coolant stains on the outside

12.2 Check all the coolant hoses as described

12.4 Check the pump drain hole (arrowed) for signs of leakage

12.7 Remove the pressure cap as described

12.12 Oil cooler (arrowed) shown with oil filter removed – ZR1000-B/C model type shown

of the core below the leak. If leaks are noted, remove the radiator (see Chapter 3) and have it repaired or replace it with a new one – do not use a liquid leak stopping compound to try to repair leaks.

6 Check the radiator fins for mud, dirt and insects, which may impede the flow of air through the radiator. If the fins are dirty, remove the radiator (see Chapter 3) and clean it using water or low pressure compressed air directed through the fins from the inner side of the radiator. If the fins are bent or distorted, straighten them carefully with a screwdriver. If airflow is restricted by bent or damaged fins over more than 20% of the radiator's surface area, replace the radiator with a new one.

> ⚠️ *Warning: Do not remove the pressure cap when the engine is hot. It is good practice to cover the cap with a heavy cloth and turn the cap slowly anti-clockwise. If you hear a hissing sound (indicating that there is still pressure in the system), wait until it stops, then continue turning the cap until it can be removed.*

7 Remove the pressure cap from the cooling system filler neck by turning it anti-clockwise until it reaches the stop. Now press down on the cap and continue turning it until it can be removed **(see illustration)**.

8 Check the condition of the coolant in the system. If it is rust-coloured or if accumulations

of scale are visible, drain, flush and refill the system with new coolant (see below). Check the cap seal for cracks and other damage. If in doubt about the pressure cap's condition, have it tested by a Kawasaki dealer or fit a new one.

9 Check the antifreeze content of the coolant with an antifreeze hydrometer. If the system has not been topped-up with the correct coolant mixture (see *Pre-ride checks*) the coolant will be too weak to offer adequate protection. If the hydrometer indicates a weak mixture, drain, flush and refill the system (see below).

10 Fit the cap by turning it clockwise until it reaches the first stop then push down on it and continue turning until it can turn no further. Start the engine and let it reach normal operating temperature, then check for leaks again. As the coolant temperature increases, the electric fan (mounted on the back of the radiator) should come on automatically and the temperature should begin to drop. If it does not, refer to Chapter 3 and check the fan and fan circuit carefully.

11 If the coolant level is consistently low, and no evidence of leaks can be found, have the entire system pressure checked by a Kawasaki dealer.

12 On Z1000 models check the oil cooler on the front of the engine for any signs of oil leakage between it and the engine **(see illustration)**. If there is leakage remove the

cooler and fit a new O-ring between it and the engine (see Chapter 2). Check that the coolant hoses are secure on the unions, and that there is no evidence of coolant leakage from the body of the cooler. If there is, the cooler is damaged and must be replaced with a new one.

Change the coolant

> ⚠️ *Warning: Allow the engine to cool completely before performing this maintenance operation. Also, don't allow anti-freeze to come into contact with your skin or the painted surfaces of the motorcycle. Rinse off spills immediately with plenty of water. Anti-freeze is highly toxic if ingested. Never leave anti-freeze lying around in an open container or in puddles on the floor; children and pets are attracted by its sweet smell and may drink it. Check with local authorities (councils) about disposing of anti-freeze. Many communities have collection centres which will see that anti-freeze is disposed of safely. Anti-freeze is also combustible, so don't store it near open flames.*

Draining

13 Support the motorcycle upright on a level surface using an auxiliary stand. Remove the fuel tank (see Chapter 4). On ZR1000-B/C models remove the left-hand sump cowl (See Chapter 7).

14 Remove the pressure cap from the top of the filler neck by covering it with a heavy cloth and turning it anti-clockwise until it reaches a stop **(see illustration 12.7)**. If you hear a hissing sound (indicating there is still pressure in the system), wait until it stops. Now press down on the cap and continue turning until it can be removed. Also remove the coolant reservoir cap.

15 Position a suitable container beneath the water pump on the left-hand side of the engine. Unscrew the drain bolt and allow the coolant to completely drain from the system **(see illustrations)**. Retain the old sealing washer for use during flushing.

12.15a Unscrew the drain bolt (arrowed) . . .

12.15b . . . and allow the coolant to drain

12.16 Unscrew the drain bolt (arrowed) and drain the cylinder jacket

12.17a Reservoir screws (arrowed) – ZR750-J and ZR1000-A

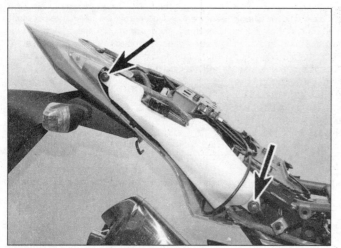

12.17b Reservoir screws (arrowed) – ZR750-L/M and ZR1000-B/C

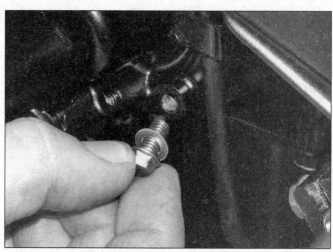

12.25 Use a new sealing washer on each drain bolt

16 Now position the container beneath the front of the engine on the left-hand side. Unscrew the cylinder drain bolt and allow the coolant to completely drain from the cylinder jacket **(see illustration)**. Retain the old sealing washer for use during flushing.

17 On ZR750-J and ZR1000-A models remove the left-hand side panel (see Chapter 7). On ZR750-L/M and ZR1000-B/C models remove the right-hand seat cowl (see Chapter 7). Undo the screws securing the reservoir, then undo the reservoir cap and drain the coolant into the container **(see illustrations)**. Refit the reservoir.

Flushing

18 Flush the system with clean tap water by inserting a hose in the filler neck. Allow the water to run through the system until it is clear and flows out cleanly. If the radiator is extremely corroded, remove it (see Chapter 3) and have it cleaned by a specialist. Also flush the reservoir, then fit the radiator overflow hose back onto the radiator filler neck.

19 Clean the drain holes in the water pump

and cylinder block then install the drain bolts using the old sealing washers **(see illustration 12.25)**.

20 Fill the cooling system with clean water mixed with a flushing compound **(see illustration 12.26)**. Make sure the flushing compound is compatible with aluminium components, and follow the manufacturer's instructions carefully. Fit the radiator cap.

21 Start the engine and allow it to reach normal operating temperature. Let it run for about ten minutes.

22 Stop the engine. Let it cool for a while, then cover the pressure cap with a heavy rag and turn it anti-clockwise to the first stop, releasing any pressure that may be present in the system. Once the hissing stops, push down on the cap and remove it completely.

23 Drain the system once again.

24 Fill the system with clean water and repeat Steps 21 to 23.

Refilling

25 Install the drain bolts using new sealing washers and tighten them to the torque

settings specified for your model at the beginning of the Chapter **(see illustration)**.

26 Fill the system to the base of the filler neck with the proper coolant mixture (see this Chapter's Specifications) **(see illustration)**. Note: *Pour the coolant in slowly to minimise the amount of air entering the system. Fill the reservoir to the F level line (see* Pre-ride checks*)*.

12.26 Fill the system and bleed it as described

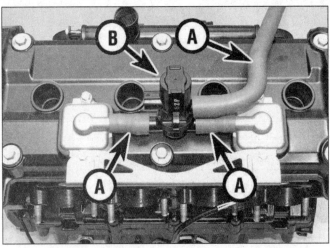

13.1a Check the air system hoses (A) as described. Air system control valve (B)

13.1b Control valve vacuum hose (arrowed) – ZR750-J and ZR1000-A

27 Start the engine and allow it to idle for 2 to 3 minutes. Tap the hoses to dislodge any trapped air. Flick the throttle twistgrip part open 3 or 4 times, so that the engine speed rises to approximately 4000 to 5000 rpm, then stop the engine. Any air trapped in the system should bleed back to the filler neck.

28 If necessary, top up the coolant level to the base of the filler neck, then fit the pressure cap. Also top up the coolant reservoir to the UPPER level line, then fit the cap.

29 Install the fuel tank (see Chapter 4). Start the engine and allow it to reach normal operating temperature, then shut it off. Remove the fuel tank. Let the engine cool then remove the pressure cap as described in Step 14. Check that the coolant level is still up to the base of the radiator filler neck. If it's low, add the specified mixture until it reaches the base of the filler neck. Refit the cap.

30 Check the coolant level in the reservoir and top up if necessary.

31 Check the system for leaks. Install the fuel tank (Chapter 4). On ZR1000-B/C models install the left-hand sump cowl (see Chapter 7).

32 Do not dispose of the old coolant by pouring it down the drain. Instead pour it into a heavy plastic container, cap it tightly and take it into an authorised disposal site or service station – see *Warning* above.

Hose renewal

33 The hoses will deteriorate with age and should be replaced with new ones at the specified interval regardless of their apparent condition (see Chapter 3).

13 Air system

1 The 'Clean Air System' is fitted to reduce the amount of unburned hydrocarbons released in the exhaust gases. The system consists of the control valve (mounted under the front of the air filter housing), the reed valves (fitted in the valve cover) and the hoses linking them **(see illustration)**. On ZR750-J and ZR1000-A models the control valve is actuated by vacuum sourced from the throttle bodies **(see illustration)**. On ZR750-L/M and ZR1000-B/C models it is actuated electrically by the ECU **(see illustration 13.3)**.

2 Under general running conditions the control valve is open allowing filtered air to be drawn through the reed valves and cylinder head passages and into the exhaust ports. The air mixes with the exhaust gases, causing any unburned particles of the fuel in the mixture to be burnt in the exhaust port/pipes.

This process changes a considerable amount of hydrocarbons and carbon monoxide into relatively harmless carbon dioxide and water. When the valve closes the air supply is cut off – this prevents exhaust popping when the throttle is closed with high engine revs. The reed valves in the valve cover are fitted to prevent the flow of exhaust gases back up the cylinder head passages and into the air filter housing.

3 The system is not adjustable and requires little maintenance. Remove the fuel tank to access and inspect the components (see Chapter 4). Check that the hoses are not kinked or pinched, are in good condition and are securely connected at each end **(see illustration 13.1a and b)**. Replace any hoses that are cracked, split or generally deteriorated with new ones. On ZR750-L/M and ZR1000-B/C models check the wiring connector is securely connected **(see illustration)**.

4 Refer to Chapter 4 for further information on the system and for checks if it is believed to be faulty.

14 Sidestand and starter interlock circuit

1 Check the stand springs for damage and distortion **(see illustration)**. The springs must be capable of retracting the stand fully and holding it retracted when the motorcycle is in use. If a spring is sagged or broken it must be replaced with a new one.

2 Lubricate the stand pivot regularly (see Section 18).

3 Check the stand and its mount for bends and cracks. Stands can often be repaired by welding.

4 Check the operation of the starter interlock circuit according to the conditions shown in the table overleaf for your model:

13.3 Control valve wiring connector (arrowed) – ZR750-L/M and ZR1000-B/C

14.1 Check the springs (arrowed) as described

ZR750-J and ZR1000-A

Sidestand	Gear position	Clutch lever	Engine start	Engine run
UP	NEUTRAL	RELEASED	STARTS	CONTINUES
UP	NEUTRAL	PULLED IN	STARTS	CONTINUES
UP	IN GEAR	RELEASED	DOESN'T START	CONTINUES
UP	IN GEAR	PULLED IN	STARTS	CONTINUES
DOWN	NEUTRAL	RELEASED	STARTS	CONTINUES
DOWN	NEUTRAL	PULLED IN	STARTS	CONTINUES
DOWN	IN GEAR	RELEASED	DOESN'T START	STOPS
DOWN	IN GEAR	PULLED IN	DOESN'T START	CONTINUES

ZR750-L/M and ZR1000-B/C

Sidestand	Gear position	Clutch lever	Engine start	Engine run
UP	NEUTRAL	RELEASED	STARTS	CONTINUES
UP	NEUTRAL	PULLED IN	STARTS	CONTINUES
UP	IN GEAR	RELEASED	DOESN'T START	CONTINUES
UP	IN GEAR	PULLED IN	STARTS	CONTINUES
DOWN	NEUTRAL	RELEASED	STARTS	CONTINUES
DOWN	NEUTRAL	PULLED IN	STARTS	CONTINUES
DOWN	IN GEAR	RELEASED	DOESN'T START	STOPS
DOWN	IN GEAR	PULLED IN	DOESN'T START	STOPS

5 If the circuit does not operate as described, check the sidestand switch, neutral switch and the clutch switch, and the circuit between them, then check the starter interlock circuit relay and diodes (see Chapter 8).

15 Suspension

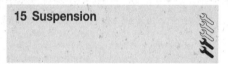

1 The suspension components must be maintained in top operating condition to ensure rider safety. Loose, worn or damaged suspension parts decrease the motorcycle's stability and control.

Front suspension check

2 While standing alongside the motorcycle, apply the front brake and push on the handlebars to compress the forks several times (see illustration). See if they move up-and-down smoothly without binding. If binding is felt, the forks should be disassembled and inspected (see Chapter 5).
3 Inspect the fork inner tubes for scratches, corrosion and pitting which will cause premature seal failure (see illustration) – if the damage is excessive, new tubes should be installed (see Chapter 5). Minor rust spots can be treated and cleaned up using a whetstone.
4 Inspect the fork inner tube just above or

below (according to model) the dust seal for signs of oil leakage, then carefully lever the seal up or down using a flat-bladed screwdriver and inspect the area around the fork seal. If leakage is evident, the seals must be replaced with new ones (see Chapter 5). If there is evidence of corrosion between the seal retaining ring and its groove in the fork outer tube spray the area with a penetrative lubricant, otherwise the ring will be difficult to remove if needed. Press the dust seal back into the fork outer tube on completion.
5 On ZR750-L/M and ZR1000-B/C models both forks are adjustable for spring pre-load and rebound damping and it is essential they

15.2 Compress the forks as described

15.3 Check the inner tubes for corrosion and signs of oil leakage (arrowed)

15.8 Compress the rear suspension as described

15.9 Checking for play in the swingarm bearings

are set the same. Refer to Chapter 5 and check the settings on each fork if in doubt.

6 Check the tightness of all suspension nuts and bolts to be sure none have worked loose, referring to the torque settings specified at the beginning of Chapter 5.

Rear suspension check

7 Inspect the rear shock absorber for fluid leakage and tightness of its mountings. If leakage is found, the shock must be replaced with a new one (see Chapter 5).

8 With the aid of an assistant to support the bike, compress the rear suspension several times **(see illustration)**. It should move up and down freely without binding. If any binding is felt, the worn or faulty component must be identified and checked (see Chapter 5). The problem could be due to either the shock absorber, the suspension linkage components or the swingarm components.

9 Support the motorcycle on an auxiliary stand so that the rear wheel is off the ground. Grab the swingarm and rock it from side-to-side – there should be no discernible movement at the rear **(see illustration)**. If there's a little movement or a slight clicking can be heard, inspect the tightness of all the swingarm and rear suspension mounting bolts and nuts, referring to the torque settings specified at the beginning of Chapter 5, and re-check for movement.

10 Next, grasp the top of the rear wheel and pull it upwards – there should be no discernible freeplay before the shock absorber begins to compress **(see illustration)**. Any freeplay felt in either check indicates worn bearings in the suspension linkage or swingarm, or worn shock absorber mountings. The worn components must be identified and replaced with new ones (see Chapter 5).

11 To make an accurate assessment of the swingarm bearings, remove the rear wheel (see Chapter 6) and the bolt securing the suspension linkage assembly to the swingarm (see Chapter 5). Grasp the rear of the swingarm with one hand and place your other hand at the junction of the swingarm and the frame. Try to move the rear of the swingarm from side-to-side. Any wear (play) in the bearings should be felt as movement between the swingarm and the frame at the front. If there is any play the swingarm will be felt to move forward and backward at the front (not from side-to-side). Next, move the swingarm up and down through its full travel. It should move freely, without any binding or rough spots. If there is any play in the swingarm or if it does not move freely, remove the bearings for inspection (see Chapter 5).

Front fork oil change

12 Although there is no set interval for changing the fork oil, note that the oil will degrade over a period of time and lose its damping qualities. Refer to Chapter 5, Sections 6 and 7 for details of front fork removal, oil draining and refilling. The forks do not need to be completely disassembled to change the oil.

Rear suspension bearing lubrication

13 Over time the grease in the bearings will be washed out or will harden allowing the ingress of dirt and water.

15.10 Checking for play in the rear shock mountings and suspension linkage bearings

14 On ZR1000-A1 and A2 models the swingarm and suspension linkage arm are equipped with grease nipples, allowing grease to be applied using a grease gun – do so until fresh grease can be seen to be squeezed out the side of the bearings.

15 On all other models the suspension linkage and the swingarm have no grease nipples and so they must be disassembled for the bearings to be cleaned and re-greased (see Chapter 5, Sections 12 and 14).

16 Steering head bearings

Freeplay check and adjustment

1 Steering head bearings can become dented, rough or loose during normal use of the machine. In extreme cases, worn or loose steering head bearings can cause steering wobble – a condition that is potentially dangerous.

Check

2 Raise the front wheel off the ground using an auxiliary stand placed under the engine – make sure it is the engine that takes the weight, not the exhaust system or any other component. Always make sure that the bike is properly supported and secure.

3 Point the front wheel straight-ahead and slowly move the handlebars from lock to lock. Any dents or roughness in the bearing races will be felt and if the bearings are too tight the bars will not move smoothly and freely. Again point the wheel straight-ahead, and tap the front of the wheel to one side. The wheel should 'fall' under its own weight to the limit of its lock, indicating that the bearings are not too tight (take into account the restriction that cables and wiring may have). Check for similar movement to the other side.

4 Next, grasp the bottom of the forks and

16.4 Checking for play in the steering head bearings

16.5 Unscrew the bolts (arrowed) to free the bracket

16.6 Slacken the fork clamp bolts (arrowed)

gently pull and push them forward and backward **(see illustration)**. Any looseness or freeplay in the steering head bearings will be felt as front-to-rear movement of the forks. If play is felt, adjust the bearings as described below.

 Make sure you are not mistaking any movement between the bike and stand, or between the stand and the ground, for freeplay in the bearings. Do not pull and push the forks too hard – a gentle movement is all that is needed. Freeplay between the fork tubes due to worn bushes can also be misinterpreted as steering head bearing play – do not confuse the two.

Adjustment

Special tool: *A suitably sized C-spanner is useful for this procedure **(see illustration 16.10)**.*

5 As a precaution, remove the fuel tank (see Chapter 4) – though not actually necessary, this will prevent the possibility of damage should a tool slip. Remove the fairing (see Chapter 7) and the instrument cluster (see Chapter 8). Unscrew the bolts securing the fairing bracket to the top yoke **(see illustration)**.

6 Displace the handlebars from the top yoke (see Chapter 5). Slacken the fork clamp bolts in the top yoke **(see illustration)**.

7 Remove the plug from the steering stem bolt **(see illustration)**. Unscrew the bolt and remove the washer **(see illustration)**.

8 Gently ease the top yoke up off the forks

and position it clear of the head bearings, using a rag to protect other components **(see illustration)**.

9 Bend the upward-pointing lockwasher tabs out of the notches in the locknut **(see illustration)**. Unscrew the locknut using either your fingers (it shouldn't be tight) or a C-spanner **(see illustration)**. Remove the lockwasher, noting how the downward-pointing tabs locate in the adjuster nut **(see illustration)**. Inspect the tabs for cracks or signs of fatigue. If there is any sign of damage, discard the lockwasher and use a new one; the old lockwasher can be re-used, but note that Kawasaki recommend using a new one as a matter of course.

10 Using a C-spanner, either loosen or tighten the adjuster nut slightly as required according to whether the bearings were too tight or too

16.7a Remove the plug ...

16.7b ... then unscrew the bolt and remove the washer ...

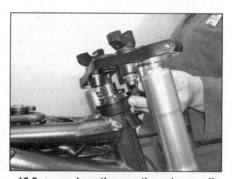

16.8 ... and gently ease the yoke up off the forks

16.9a Bend down the tabs securing the locknut ...

16.9b ... then unscrew the locknut ...

16.9c ... and remove the lockwasher

16.10 Adjust the bearings as described using a C-spanner

16.14 Bend the tabs up into the notches in the locknut

16.15a Fit the bolt with its washer . . .

loose **(see illustration)**. The object is to set the adjuster nut so that the bearings are under a very light loading, just enough to remove any freeplay, but not so much that the steering does not move freely from side-to-side as described in the check procedure above. Turn the nut only a little at a time, and after each adjustment repeat the checks outlined in Steps 3 and 4.

Caution: Take great care not to apply excessive pressure because this will cause premature failure of the bearings.

11 Turn the steering from lock to lock five times to settle the bearings, then recheck the adjustment.

12 If the bearings cannot be correctly adjusted, disassemble the steering head and check the bearings and races (see Chapter 5).

13 With the bearings correctly adjusted, fit the lockwasher, using a new one if the tabs are weakened or cracked, onto the adjuster nut and fit the downward-pointing tabs into the slots in the adjuster nut **(see illustration 16.9c)**.

14 Fit the locknut and tighten it finger-tight **(see illustration 16.9b)**. Tighten the locknut by a further two to four notches (or by about 90°) until the notches align with the remaining lockwasher tabs, making sure the adjuster nut

does not turn as well (though that is unlikely). Secure the locknut in position by bending up the horizontal tabs on the lockwasher into its notches **(see illustration)**.

15 Fit the top yoke onto the steering stem **(see illustration 16.8)**. Install the steering stem bolt with its washer and tighten it to the torque setting specified at the beginning of the Chapter **(see illustrations)**. Fit the plug into the bolt **(see illustration 16.7a)**. Tighten the fork clamp bolts to the specified torque **(see illustration 16.6)**.

16 Bolt the fairing bracket to the top yoke **(see illustration 16.5)**. Install the handlebars (see Chapter 5).

17 Check the bearing adjustment as described above and re-adjust if necessary.

18 Install the fuel tank (see Chapter 4), the instrument cluster (see Chapter 8), and the fairing (see Chapter 7).

Lubrication

19 Over a considerable time the grease in the bearings will be dispersed or will harden allowing the ingress of dirt and water.

20 The steering head should be disassembled periodically and the bearings cleaned and re-greased (see Chapter 5, Section 10).

17 Wheels, wheel bearings and tyres

Wheels

1 Cast wheels are virtually maintenance free, but they should be kept clean and checked periodically for cracks and other damage. Also check the wheel runout and alignment (see Chapter 6). Never attempt to repair damaged cast wheels; they must be renewed if damaged.

2 Check that the wheel balance weights are fixed firmly to the wheel rim. If you suspect that a weight has fallen off, have the wheel rebalanced by a motorcycle tyre specialist.

Wheel bearings

3 Wheel bearings will wear over a considerable mileage and should be checked periodically to avoid handling problems.

4 Support the motorcycle upright using an auxiliary stand so that the wheel being examined is off the ground. Check for any play in the bearings by pushing and pulling the wheel against the hub **(see illustration)**. Also rotate the wheel and check that it turns smoothly and without any grating noises.

16.15b . . . and tighten it to the specified torque

17.4 Checking for play in the wheel bearings

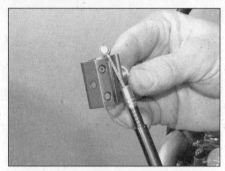

18.3a Fit the cable into the adapter . . .

18.3b . . . and tighten the screw to seal it in . . .

18.3c . . . then apply the lubricant using the nozzle provided inserted in the hole in the adapter

5 If any play is detected in the hub, or if the wheel does not rotate smoothly (and this is not due to brake or drive chain drag), the wheel should be removed and the bearings inspected for wear or damage (see Chapter 6).

Tyres

6 Check the tyre condition and tread depth thoroughly – see *Pre-ride checks*. Check the valve rubber for signs of damage or deterioration and have it renewed if necessary by a tyre fitting specialist. Also, make sure the valve stem cap is in place and tight.

18 Sidestand, lever pivot and cable lubrication

Pivot points

1 Since the controls, cables and various other components of a motorcycle are exposed to the elements, they should be checked and lubricated periodically to ensure safe and trouble-free operation.
2 The footrest pivots, clutch and brake lever pivots, brake pedal and gearchange lever pivots and linkage and sidestand pivot should be lubricated frequently. In order for the lubricant to be applied where it will do the most good, the component should be disassembled (see Chapter 5). The lubricant recommended by Kawasaki for each application is listed at the beginning of the Chapter. If an aerosol lubricant is used, it can be applied to the pivot joint gaps and will usually work its way

into the areas where friction occurs, so less disassembly of the component is needed (however it is always better to do so and clean off all corrosion, dirt and old lubricant first). If motor oil or light grease is being used, apply it sparingly as it may attract dirt (which could cause the controls to bind or wear at an accelerated rate).

Cables

Special tool: *A cable lubricating adapter is necessary for this procedure (see illustration 18.3c).*
3 To lubricate the cables, disconnect the relevant cable at its upper end, then lubricate it with a pressure adapter and aerosol lubricant cable lube **(see illustrations)**. See Chapter 4 for throttle cable, and where fitted fast idle cable, removal procedures, and Chapter 2 for the clutch cable.

19 Nuts and bolts

1 Since vibration of the machine tends to loosen fasteners, all nuts, bolts, screws, etc. should be periodically checked for proper tightness.
2 Pay particular attention to the following, referring to the relevant Chapter:
● Spark plugs
● Engine oil and coolant drain bolts
● Lever and pedal bolts
● Footrest and sidestand bolts
● Engine mounting bolts

● Shock absorber and suspension linkage bolts
● Swingarm pivot bolt, nut and locknut
● Handlebar clamp bolts
● Front fork clamp bolts (top and bottom yoke) and fork top bolts
● Steering stem bolt
● Front axle nut and axle clamp bolts
● Rear axle nut
● Front and rear sprocket nuts
● Brake caliper and master cylinder mounting bolts, brake caliper body bolts
● Brake hose banjo bolts and caliper bleed valves
● Brake disc bolts
● Exhaust system bolts/nuts
3 If a torque wrench is available, use it along with the torque settings given at the beginning of this and other Chapters.

20 Air filter

Caution: If the machine is continually ridden in wet or dusty conditions, the filter should be replaced more frequently.
1 Remove the fuel tank (see Chapter 4).
2 Unscrew the fuel tank bracket bolts and remove the bracket **(see illustration)**.
3 Undo the air filter cover screws and remove the cover **(see illustration)**. Remove the filter from the housing, noting how it fits **(see illustration)**.

20.2 Unscrew the bolts (arrowed) and remove the bracket

20.3a Undo the screws (arrowed) and remove the cover . . .

20.3b . . . then remove the filter

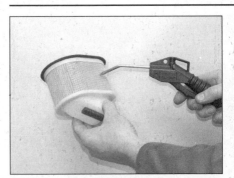

20.4 Direct the air in the opposite direction of normal flow

20.6 Locate the tab on the front end of the cover in the slot

20.7 Make sure the tank bracket is the correct way round

4 To clean the filter, tap it on a hard surface to dislodge any dirt and use compressed air to clear the element, directing the air in the opposite way to normal flow, i.e. from the outside **(see illustration)**. Do not use any solvents or cleaning agents on the element. Check the filter element for damage.

5 If the filter is damaged or ingrained with dirt that cannot be removed, or has reached the end of its service life according to the schedule, replace it with a new one.

6 Fit the filter into the housing, making sure it is properly seated **(see illustration 20.3b)**. Fit the cover, locating the tab in the slot, and tighten the screws **(see illustration)**.

7 Fit the fuel tank bracket and tighten the bolts **(see illustration)**.

8 Install the fuel tank (see Chapter 4).

21 Valve clearances

Special tool: A set of blade-type feeler gauges is necessary for this job **(see illustration 21.8)**.

Check

1 The engine must be completely cool for this maintenance procedure.

2 Remove the spark plugs (see Section 10). Remove the valve cover (see Chapter 2).

3 Make a chart or sketch of all valve positions so that a note of each clearance can be made against the relevant valve. The cylinders are numbered 1 to 4 from left to right. The intake valves are on the back of the cylinder head and the exhaust valves are on the front.

4 Unscrew the timing rotor cover bolts, noting the routing of the wiring and the position of the guides, and remove the cover **(see illustration)**. Discard the O-ring as a new one must be used.

5 To check the valve clearances the engine

21.4 Unscrew the bolts (arrowed) and remove the cover

must be turned so that the valves being checked are closed. The engine can be turned using a suitable spanner or a socket on the timing rotor bolt and turning it in a clockwise direction only **(see illustration 21.6a)**.

6 Turn the engine clockwise until the line next to the numbers 1 and 4 marked on the timing rotor points back and aligns with the crankcase mating surfaces, and so that the IN mark on the intake camshaft sprocket points back parallel to the top of the cylinder head, and the EX mark on the exhaust camshaft sprocket points forwards **(see illustrations)**. If the sprocket marks are upside down and

21.6a Turn the engine clockwise using the bolt . . .

21.6b . . . until the line next to the 1 and 4 aligns with the crankcase mating surfaces (arrowed) . . .

21.6c . . . and the sprocket marks are as shown

21.8 Insert the feeler gauge between the base of the cam lobe and the top of the follower as shown

21.12a Retrieve the shim (arrowed) from inside the follower . . .

facing the other way (i.e. 180° round from the desired position), rotate the engine clockwise one full turn (360°) until the line next to the 1 and 4 again aligns with the crankcase mating surfaces. The sprocket marks will now be facing correctly.

7 With the engine in this position the No. 4 cylinder is on its compression stroke and you can check the clearances on Nos. 4 and 2 cylinder intake valves and the Nos. 4 and 3 cylinder exhaust valves.

8 Insert a feeler gauge of the same thickness as the correct valve clearance (see Specifications) between the camshaft lobe and the follower of each valve and check that it is a firm sliding fit – you should feel a slight drag when the you pull the gauge out **(see illustration)**. If not, use the feeler gauges to obtain the exact clearance. Record the measured clearance on the chart.

9 Now rotate the engine 360° clockwise until the line next to the numbers 1 and 4 marked on the timing rotor again points back and aligns with the crankcase mating surfaces **(see illustrations 21.6a and b)**, and so that the IN mark on the intake camshaft sprocket points forwards parallel to the top of the cylinder head, and the EX mark on the exhaust camshaft sprocket points back, and both marks read upside down. With the engine in this position, the No. 1 cylinder is on its

compression stroke, and you can check the clearances on the Nos. 1 and 3 cylinder intake valves and the Nos. 1 and 2 cylinder exhaust valves.

10 When all clearances have been measured and charted, identify whether the clearance on any valve falls outside the specified range. If any do, the shim must be replaced with one of a thickness which will restore the correct clearance.

Adjustment

11 Shim replacement requires removal of the camshafts (see Chapter 2). Place rags over the spark plug holes and the cam chain tunnel to prevent a shim from dropping into the engine on removal. Work on one valve at a time to prevent the possibility of mixing up the followers, which must be returned to their original location. If you want to remove more than one shim and follower at a time, store them in a marked container or bag, denoting which cylinder and which valve the shim and follower are from, so that they do not get mixed up.

12 With the camshaft removed, lift out the cam follower of the valve in question using a magnet or the suction created by a valve lapping tool **(see illustration 21.16)**. Retrieve the shim from the inside the follower or pick it

out of the top of the valve spring retainer using either a magnet, a screwdriver with a dab of grease on it (the shim will stick to the grease), or a very small screwdriver and a pair of pliers **(see illustrations)**. Do not allow the shim to fall into the engine.

13 A size mark should be stamped on one face of the shim **(see illustration)**. If the mark is not visible measure the shim thickness using a micrometer **(see illustration)**. It is recommended that the shim is measured anyway to check whether it has worn.

14 Using the appropriate shim selection chart, find where the measured valve clearance and existing shim thickness values intersect and read off the shim size required **(see illustrations)**. Shims are available from 2.50 mm to 3.50 mm thick in increments of either 0.05 mm or 0.025 mm depending on size – consult your dealer. Note: *If the required replacement shim is greater than 3.50 mm (the largest available), the valve is probably not seating correctly due to a build-up of carbon deposits and should be checked and cleaned or resurfaced as required (see Chapter 2).*

15 Obtain the replacement shim, then lubricate it with molybdenum disulphide oil (a 50/50 mixture of molybdenum disulphide grease and engine oil) and fit it into the recess in the top of the valve spring retainer with the size mark facing up **(see illustration 21.12b)**.

21.12b . . . or from the top of the valve

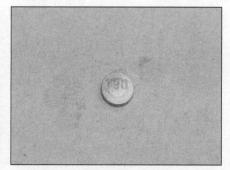

21.13a The shim size is marked on one face . . .

21.13b . . . but check the thickness of the shim using a micrometer

PART No. (92180-)	1014	1016	1018	1020	1022	1024	1026	1028	1030	1032	1034	1036	1038	1040	1042	1044	1046	1048	1050	1052	1054
PRESENT SHIM																					
MARK	50	55	60	65	70	75	80	85	90	95	00	05	10	15	20	25	30	35	40	45	50
THICKNESS (mm)	2.50	2.55	2.60	2.65	2.70	2.75	2.80	2.85	2.90	2.95	3.00	3.05	3.10	3.15	3.20	3.25	3.30	3.35	3.40	3.45	3.50
CLEARANCE																					
0.00 - 0.02	-	-	-	-	2.50	2.55	2.60	2.65	2.70	2.75	2.80	2.85	2.90	2.95	3.00	3.05	3.10	3.15	3.20	3.25	3.30
0.03 - 0.07	-	-	-	2.50	2.55	2.60	2.65	2.70	2.75	2.80	2.85	2.90	2.95	3.00	3.05	3.10	3.15	3.20	3.25	3.30	3.35
0.08 - 0.12	-	-	2.50	2.55	2.60	2.65	2.70	2.75	2.80	2.85	2.90	2.95	3.00	3.05	3.10	3.15	3.20	3.25	3.30	3.35	3.40
0.13 - 0.14	-	2.50	2.55	2.60	2.65	2.70	2.75	2.80	2.85	2.90	2.95	3.00	3.05	3.10	3.15	3.20	3.25	3.30	3.35	3.40	3.45
0.15 - 0.24	CORRECT INTAKE VALVE CLEARANCE																				
0.25 - 0.27	2.55	2.60	2.65	2.70	2.75	2.80	2.85	2.90	2.95	3.00	3.05	3.10	3.15	3.20	3.25	3.30	3.35	3.40	3.45	3.50	
0.28 - 0.32	2.60	2.65	2.70	2.75	2.80	2.85	2.90	2.95	3.00	3.05	3.10	3.15	3.20	3.25	3.30	3.35	3.40	3.45	3.50		
0.33 - 0.37	2.65	2.70	2.75	2.80	2.85	2.90	2.95	3.00	3.05	3.10	3.15	3.20	3.25	3.30	3.35	3.40	3.45	3.50			
0.38 - 0.42	2.70	2.75	2.80	2.85	2.90	2.95	3.00	3.05	3.10	3.15	3.20	3.25	3.30	3.35	3.40	3.45	3.50				
0.43 - 0.47	2.75	2.80	2.85	2.90	2.95	3.00	3.05	3.10	3.15	3.20	3.25	3.30	3.35	3.40	3.45	3.50					
0.48 - 0.52	2.80	2.85	2.90	2.95	3.00	3.05	3.10	3.15	3.20	3.25	3.30	3.35	3.40	3.45	3.50						
0.53 - 0.57	2.85	2.90	2.95	3.00	3.05	3.10	3.15	3.20	3.25	3.30	3.35	3.40	3.45	3.50							
0.58 - 0.62	2.90	2.95	3.00	3.05	3.10	3.15	3.20	3.25	3.30	3.35	3.40	3.45	3.50								
0.63 - 0.67	2.95	3.00	3.05	3.10	3.15	3.20	3.25	3.30	3.35	3.40	3.45	3.50									
0.68 - 0.72	3.00	3.05	3.10	3.15	3.20	3.25	3.30	3.35	3.40	3.45	3.50										
0.73 - 0.77	3.05	3.10	3.15	3.20	3.25	3.30	3.35	3.40	3.45	3.50											
0.78 - 0.82	3.10	3.15	3.20	3.25	3.30	3.35	3.40	3.45	3.50												
0.83 - 0.87	3.15	3.20	3.25	3.30	3.35	3.40	3.45	3.50													
0.88 - 0.92	3.20	3.25	3.30	3.35	3.40	3.45	3.50														
0.93 - 0.97	3.25	3.30	3.35	3.40	3.45	3.50															
0.98 - 1.02	3.30	3.35	3.40	3.45	3.50																
1.03 - 1.07	3.35	3.40	3.45	3.50																	
1.08 - 1.12	3.40	3.45	3.50																		
1.13 - 1.17	3.45	3.50																			
1.18 - 1.22	3.50																				

Example: Present shim is 2mm

Measured clearance is 0.4 mm

Replace 2 mm shim with 3.05mm shim

21.14a Shim selection chart – intake valves

PART No. (92180-)	1014	1016	1018	1020	1022	1024	1026	1028	1030	1032	1034	1036	1038	1040	1042	1044	1046	1048	1050	1052	1054
PRESENT SHIM																					
MARK	50	55	60	65	70	75	80	85	90	95	00	05	10	15	20	25	30	35	40	45	50
THICKNESS (mm)	2.50	2.55	2.60	2.65	2.70	2.75	2.80	2.85	2.90	2.95	3.00	3.05	3.10	3.15	3.20	3.25	3.30	3.35	3.40	3.45	3.50
CLEARANCE																					
0.00 - 0.04	-	-	-	-	-	2.50	2.55	2.60	2.65	2.70	2.75	2.80	2.85	2.90	2.95	3.00	3.05	3.10	3.15	3.20	3.25
0.05 - 0.09	-	-	-	-	2.50	2.55	2.60	2.65	2.70	2.75	2.80	2.85	2.90	2.95	3.00	3.05	3.10	3.15	3.20	3.25	3.30
0.10 - 0.14	-	-	-	2.50	2.55	2.60	2.65	2.70	2.75	2.80	2.85	2.90	2.95	3.00	3.05	3.10	3.15	3.20	3.25	3.30	3.35
0.15 - 0.19	-	-	2.50	2.55	2.60	2.65	2.70	2.75	2.80	2.85	2.90	2.95	3.00	3.05	3.10	3.15	3.20	3.25	3.30	3.35	3.40
0.20 - 0.21	-	2.50	2.55	2.60	2.65	2.70	2.75	2.80	2.85	2.90	2.95	3.00	3.05	3.10	3.15	3.20	3.25	3.30	3.35	3.40	3.45
0.22 - 0.31	CORRECT EXHAUST VALVE CLEARANCE																				
0.32 - 0.34	2.55	2.60	2.65	2.70	2.75	2.80	2.85	2.90	2.95	3.00	3.05	3.10	3.15	3.20	3.25	3.30	3.35	3.40	3.45	3.50	
0.35 - 0.39	2.60	2.65	2.70	2.75	2.80	2.85	2.90	2.95	3.00	3.05	3.10	3.15	3.20	3.25	3.30	3.35	3.40	3.45	3.50		
0.40 - 0.44	2.65	2.70	2.75	2.80	2.85	2.90	2.95	3.00	3.05	3.10	3.15	3.20	3.25	3.30	3.35	3.40	3.45	3.50			
0.45 - 0.49	2.70	2.75	2.80	2.85	2.90	2.95	3.00	3.05	3.10	3.15	3.20	3.25	3.30	3.35	3.40	3.45	3.50				
0.50 - 0.54	2.75	2.80	2.85	2.90	2.95	3.00	3.05	3.10	3.15	3.20	3.25	3.30	3.35	3.40	3.45	3.50					
0.55 - 0.59	2.80	2.85	2.90	2.95	3.00	3.05	3.10	3.15	3.20	3.25	3.30	3.35	3.40	3.45	3.50						
0.60 - 0.64	2.85	2.90	2.95	3.00	3.05	3.10	3.15	3.20	3.25	3.30	3.35	3.40	3.45	3.50							
0.65 - 0.69	2.90	2.95	3.00	3.05	3.10	3.15	3.20	3.25	3.30	3.35	3.40	3.45	3.50								
0.70 - 0.74	2.95	3.00	3.05	3.10	3.15	3.20	3.25	3.30	3.35	3.40	3.45	3.50									
0.75 - 0.79	3.00	3.05	3.10	3.15	3.20	3.25	3.30	3.35	3.40	3.45	3.50										
0.80 - 0.84	3.05	3.10	3.15	3.20	3.25	3.30	3.35	3.40	3.45	3.50											
0.85 - 0.89	3.10	3.15	3.20	3.25	3.30	3.35	3.40	3.45	3.50												
0.90 - 0.94	3.15	3.20	3.25	3.30	3.35	3.40	3.45	3.50													
0.95 - 0.99	3.20	3.25	3.30	3.35	3.40	3.45	3.50														
1.00 - 1.04	3.25	3.30	3.35	3.40	3.45	3.50															
1.05 - 1.09	3.30	3.35	3.40	3.45	3.50																
1.10 - 1.14	3.35	3.40	3.45	3.50																	
1.15 - 1.19	3.40	3.45	3.50																		
1.20 - 1.24	3.45	3.50																			
1.25 - 1.29	3.50																				

Example: Present shim is **3.00 mm**.

Measured clearance is **0.37 mm**.

Replace **3.00 mm** shim with **3.10 mm** shim.

21.14b Shim selection chart – exhaust valves

21.16 Fit the follower onto the valve

21.18a Smear some sealant as shown . . .

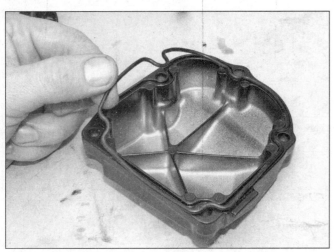
21.18b . . . then fit a new O-ring into the groove . . .

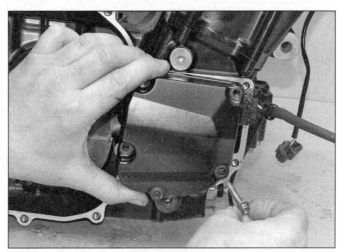
21.18c . . . and fit the cover

16 Check that the shim is correctly seated, then lubricate the follower with molybdenum disulphide oil and fit it onto the valve, making sure it fits squarely in its bore **(see illustration)**. Repeat the process for any other valves until the clearances are correct, then install the camshafts (see Chapter 2).

17 Rotate the crankshaft clockwise several turns to seat the new shim(s), then check the clearances again. Install the valve cover (see Chapter 2).

18 Smear sealant onto the crankcase mating surfaces with the timing rotor cover and the crankshaft position sensor wiring grommet **(see illustration)**. Install the timing rotor

cover using a new O-ring **(see illustrations)**. Make sure the wiring and guides are correctly positioned. Tighten the cover bolts to the torque setting specified at the beginning of the Chapter.

19 Install the spark plugs (Section 5). On completion, check and adjust the idle speed (see Section 7).

22 Battery

1 All models covered in this manual are

fitted with a sealed MF (maintenance free) battery. **Note:** *Do not attempt to remove the battery caps to check the electrolyte level or battery specific gravity. Removal will damage the caps, resulting in electrolyte leakage and battery damage. All that should be done is to check that the terminals are clean and tight and that the casing is not damaged or leaking. See Chapter 8 for details.*

2 If the machine is not in regular use, disconnect the battery and give it a refresher charge every month to six weeks (see Chapter 8).

Chapter 2
Engine, clutch and transmission

Contents

Degrees of difficulty

Easy, suitable for novice with little experience 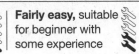	Fairly easy, suitable for beginner with some experience	Fairly difficult, suitable for competent DIY mechanic	Difficult, suitable for experienced DIY mechanic	Very difficult, suitable for expert DIY or professional 

Specifications

General

Type	Four-stroke in-line four
Capacity	
Z750	748 cc
Z1000	953 cc
Bore	
Z750	68.4 mm
Z1000	77.2 mm
Stroke	50.9 mm
Compression ratio	
Z750	11.3 to 1
Z1000	11.2 to 1
Cylinder numbering	1 to 4 from left to right
Firing order	1-2-4-3
Camshafts	DOHC, chain-driven
Clutch	Wet multi-plate
Transmission	Six-speed constant mesh
Final drive	Chain
Cooling system	Liquid cooled
Lubrication	Wet sump, trochoid pump

Camshafts and followers

Intake lobe height
  ZR750-J and ZR1000-A
    Standard . . . . 36.746 to 36.854 mm
    Service limit (min) . . . . 36.65 mm
  ZR750-L/M and ZR1000-B/C
    Standard . . . . 35.943 to 36.057 mm
    Service limit (min) . . . . 35.84 mm
Exhaust lobe height
  ZR750-J and ZR1000-A
    Standard . . . . 36.146 to 36.254 mm
    Service limit (min) . . . . 36.05 mm
  ZR750-L/M and ZR1000-B/C
    Standard . . . . 35.743 to 35.857 mm
    Service limit (min) . . . . 35.64 mm
Camshaft journal diameter
  Standard . . . . 23.950 to 23.972 mm
  Service limit (min) . . . . 23.92 mm
Camshaft holder bore diameter
  Standard . . . . 24.000 to 24.021 mm
  Service limit (min) . . . . 24.08 mm
Oil clearance
  Standard . . . . 0.028 to 0.071 mm
  Service limit (max) . . . . 0.16 mm
Runout
  Standard (max) . . . . 0.02 mm
  Service limit (max) . . . . 0.10 mm

Cylinder head

Warpage (max) . . . . 0.05 mm

Valves, guides and springs

Valve clearances . . . . see Chapter 1
Stem diameter
  Z750
    Intake valve
      Standard . . . . 3.975 to 3.990 mm
      Service limit (min) . . . . 3.96 mm
    Exhaust valve
      Standard . . . . 3.955 to 3.970 mm
      Service limit (min) . . . . 3.94 mm
  Z1000
    Intake valve
      Standard . . . . 4.475 to 4.490 mm
      Service limit (min) . . . . 4.46 mm
    Exhaust valve
      Standard . . . . 4.455 to 4.470 mm
      Service limit (min) . . . . 4.44 mm
Guide bore diameter – intake and exhaust valves
  Z750
    Standard . . . . 4.000 to 4.012 mm
    Service limit (max) . . . . 4.08 mm
  Z1000
    Standard . . . . 4.500 to 4.512 mm
    Service limit (max) . . . . 4.58 mm
Stem-to-guide clearance – wobble method (see Section 12)
  All Z750 models and ZR1000-A
    Intake valve
      Standard . . . . 0.03 to 0.12 mm
      Service limit . . . . 0.33 mm
    Exhaust valve
      Standard . . . . 0.10 to 0.18 mm
      Service limit . . . . 0.40 mm
  ZR1000-B/C models
    Intake valve
      Standard . . . . 0.03 to 0.10 mm
      Service limit . . . . 0.28 mm
    Exhaust valve
      Standard . . . . 0.09 to 0.15 mm
      Service limit . . . . 0.34 mm

Valves, guides and springs (continued)

Valve head thickness
  Z750
    Intake
      Standard . . . . 0.5 mm
      Service limit (min) . . . . 0.3 mm
    Exhaust
      Standard . . . . 1.0 mm
      Service limit (min) . . . . 0.5 mm
  Z1000
    Intake
      Standard . . . . 0.5 mm
      Service limit (min) . . . . 0.3 mm
    Exhaust
      Standard . . . . 0.8 mm
      Service limit (min) . . . . 0.4 mm
Seat width
  Z750
    Intake and exhaust . . . . 0.5 to 1.0 mm
  Z1000
    Intake . . . . 0.5 to 1.0 mm
    Exhaust . . . . 0.8 to 1.2 mm
Valve seating surface outer diameter
  Z750
    Intake valve . . . . 26.4 to 26.6 mm
    Exhaust valve . . . . 21.6 to 21.8 mm
  ZR1000-A
    Intake valve . . . . 29.4 to 29.6 mm
    Exhaust valve . . . . 25.2 to 25.4 mm
  ZR1000-B/C
    Intake valve . . . . 28.9 to 29.1 mm
    Exhaust valve . . . . 24.7 to 24.9 mm
Valve spring free length
  Z750
    Standard . . . . 40.7 mm
    Service limit (min) . . . . 38.9 mm
  Z1000
    Standard . . . . 38.98 mm
    Service limit (min) . . . . 37.4 mm
Stem runout
  Standard (max) . . . . 0.01 mm
  Service limit (max) . . . . 0.05 mm

Pistons

Piston diameter (measured 5 mm up from skirt, at 90° to piston pin axis)
  Z750
    Standard . . . . 68.345 to 68.360 mm
    Service limit (min) . . . . 68.21 mm
  Z1000
    Standard . . . . 77.174 to 77.184 mm
    Service limit (min) . . . . 77.02 mm
Piston-to-bore clearance
  Z750 . . . . 0.040 to 0.067 mm
  Z1000 . . . . 0.010 to 0.037 mm
Piston ring groove width
  Z750
    Top ring
      Standard . . . . 0.83 to 0.85 mm
      Service limit (max) . . . . 0.93 mm
    Second ring
      Standard . . . . 0.81 to 0.83 mm
      Service limit (max) . . . . 0.91 mm
  Z1000
    Top ring
      Standard . . . . 0.83 to 0.85 mm
      Service limit (max) . . . . 0.93 mm
    Second ring
      Standard . . . . 0.82 to 0.84 mm
      Service limit (max) . . . . 0.94 mm

Piston rings

Ring end gap (installed)
  ZR750-J
    Top ring
      Standard . . . . 0.30 to 0.40 mm
      Service limit (max) . . . . 0.70 mm
    Second ring
      Standard . . . . 0.45 to 0.55 mm
      Service limit (max) . . . . 0.80 mm
  ZR750-L/M
    Top ring
      Standard . . . . 0.30 to 0.40 mm
      Service limit (max) . . . . 0.70 mm
    Second ring
      Standard . . . . 0.45 to 0.55 mm
      Service limit (max) . . . . 0.90 mm
  Z1000
    Top ring
      Standard . . . . 0.20 to 0.30 mm
      Service limit (max) . . . . 0.60 mm
    Second ring
      Standard . . . . 0.35 to 0.50 mm
      Service limit (max) . . . . 0.80 mm
Ring-to-groove clearance
  ZR750-J
    Top ring
      Standard . . . . 0.04 to 0.08 mm
      Service limit (max) . . . . 0.18 mm
    Second ring
      Standard . . . . 0.02 to 0.06 mm
      Service limit (max) . . . . 0.16 mm
  ZR750-L/M
    Top ring
      Standard . . . . 0.04 to 0.07 mm
      Service limit (max) . . . . 0.17 mm
    Second ring
      Standard . . . . 0.02 to 0.05 mm
      Service limit (max) . . . . 0.15 mm
  Z1000
    Top ring
      Standard . . . . 0.04 to 0.08 mm
      Service limit (max) . . . . 0.18 mm
    Second ring
      Standard . . . . 0.03 to 0.07 mm
      Service limit (max) . . . . 0.17 mm
Ring thickness
  ZR750-J and all Z1000
    Top and second ring
      Standard . . . . 0.77 to 0.79 mm
      Service limit (max) . . . . 0.70 mm
  ZR750-L/M
    Top and second ring
      Standard . . . . 0.78 to 0.79 mm
      Service limit (max) . . . . 0.71 mm

Cylinder bores

Bore
  Z750
    Standard . . . . 68.400 to 68.412 mm
    Service limit (max) . . . . 68.50 mm
  Z1000
    Standard . . . . 77.194 to 77.206 mm
    Service limit (max) . . . . 77.30 mm
Warpage (max) . . . . 0.05 mm
Cylinder compression
  ZR750-J . . . . 161 to 230 psi (11.3 to 16.2 Bar) @ 300 rpm
  ZR750-L/M . . . . 137 to 196 psi (9.6 to 13.8 Bar) @ 265 rpm
  ZR1000-A . . . . 155 to 235 psi (10.9 to 16.5 Bar) @ 320 rpm
  ZR1000-B/C . . . . 150 to 214 psi (10.6 to 15.0 Bar) @ 270 rpm

Clutch

Friction plate thickness
    Standard . . . .   2.72 to 2.88 mm
    Service limit (min) . . . .   2.4 mm
Plate warpage (max)
    Standard . . . .   0.2 mm
    Service limit . . . .   0.3 mm
Spring free length
    Z750
        Standard . . . .   80.6 mm
        Service limit (min) . . . .   76.6 mm
    ZR1000-A
        Standard . . . .   75.42 mm
        Service limit (min) . . . .   71.8 mm
    ZR1000-B/C
        Standard . . . .   85.0 mm
        Service limit (min) . . . .   80.6 mm
Clutch plate assembly thickness
    Z750   . . . .   37.7 to 38.3 mm
    Z1000   . . . .   48.4 to 49.0 mm

Oil pump

Oil pressure (at main gallery, with engine warm)
    ZR750-J . . . .   37 to 46 psi (2.6 to 3.2 Bar) @ 4000 rpm, oil @ 90°C
    ZR750-L/M . . . .   21 to 33 psi (1.5 to 2.3 Bar) @ 4000 rpm, oil @ 90°C
    ZR1000-A . . . .   37 to 46 psi (2.6 to 3.2 Bar) @ 4000 rpm, oil @ 90°C
    ZR1000-B/C . . . .   21 to 33 psi (1.5 to 2.3 Bar) @ 4000 rpm, oil @ 90°C

Selector drum and forks

Selector fork end thickness
    Standard . . . .   5.9 to 6.0 mm
    Service limit (min) . . . .   5.8 mm
Gear groove width
    Standard . . . .   6.05 to 6.15 mm
    Service limit (max) . . . .   6.25 mm
Selector fork guide pin OD
    Standard . . . .   6.9 to 7.0 mm
    Service limit (min) . . . .   6.8 mm
Selector drum track width
    Standard . . . .   7.05 to 7.20 mm
    Service limit (max) . . . .   7.30 mm

Crankshaft and bearings

Crankshaft side clearance
    Standard . . . .   0.05 to 0.20 mm
    Service limit (max) . . . .   0.40 mm
Main bearing oil clearance
    Standard . . . .   0.020 to 0.044 mm
    Service limit (max) . . . .   0.07 mm
Main bearing journal diameter
    No mark on crank web . . . .   32.984 to 32.992 mm
    '1' mark on crank web . . . .   32.993 to 33.000 mm
    Service limit (min) . . . .   32.96 mm
Crankcase main bearing bore diameter
    '0' mark on crankcase . . . .   36.000 to 36.008 mm
    No mark on crankcase . . . .   36.009 to 36.016 mm
Connecting rod big-end journal (crankpin) diameter
    No mark on crank throw . . . .   34.984 to 34.992 mm
    '0' mark on crank throw . . . .   34.993 to 35.000 mm
    Service limit (min) . . . .   34.97 mm
Runout (max)
    Standard . . . .   0.02 mm
    Service limit . . . .   0.05 mm

Connecting rods

Big-end side clearance
    Standard. . . . . 0.13 to 0.38 mm
    Service limit (max) . . . . 0.58 mm
Big-end oil clearance
    Standard. . . . . 0.041 to 0.071 mm
    Service limit (max) . . . . 0.11 mm
Connecting rod big-end inside diameter
    No mark on side of rod. . . . . 38.000 to 38.008 mm
    '0' mark on side of rod . . . . 38.009 to 38.016 mm

Transmission

Gear ratios (no. of teeth)
  Z750
    Primary reduction . . . . 1.714 to 1 (84/49)
    Final reduction . . . . 2.867 to 1 (43/15)
    1st gear. . . . . 2.571 to 1 (36/14)
    2nd gear . . . . 1.941 to 1 (33/17)
    3rd gear. . . . . 1.555 to 1 (28/18)
    4th gear. . . . . 1.333 to 1 (28/21)
    5th gear. . . . . 1.200 to 1 (24/20)
    6th gear. . . . . 1.095 to 1 (23/21)
  ZR1000-A
    Primary reduction . . . . 1.714 to 1 (84/49)
    Final reduction . . . . 2.625 to 1 (42/16)
    1st gear. . . . . 2.571 to 1 (36/14)
    2nd gear . . . . 1.941 to 1 (33/17)
    3rd gear. . . . . 1.555 to 1 (28/18)
    4th gear. . . . . 1.333 to 1 (28/21)
    5th gear. . . . . 1.200 to 1 (24/20)
    6th gear. . . . . 1.095 to 1 (23/21)
  ZR1000-B/C
    Primary reduction . . . . 1.714 to 1 (84/49)
    Final reduction . . . . 2.667 to 1 (40/15)
    1st gear. . . . . 2.571 to 1 (36/14)
    2nd gear . . . . 1.882 to 1 (32/17)
    3rd gear. . . . . 1.555 to 1 (28/18)
    4th gear. . . . . 1.333 to 1 (28/21)
    5th gear. . . . . 1.200 to 1 (24/20)
    6th gear. . . . . 1.095 to 1 (23/21)

Torque settings

Cam chain tensioner blade and guide blade
    Tensioner blade pivot bolt . . . . 25 Nm
    Front guide blade upper bolt . . . . 25 Nm
    Front guide blade lower bolt. . . . . 12 Nm
Cam chain tensioner cap bolt
    ZR750-J . . . . 28 Nm
    ZR1000-A . . . . 28 Nm
    ZR750-L/M . . . . 20 Nm
    ZR1000-B/C . . . . 20 Nm
Cam chain tensioner mounting bolts . . . . 11 Nm
Camshaft holder bolts . . . . 12 Nm
Clutch cover bolts . . . . 11 Nm
Clutch nut. . . . . 135 Nm
Clutch spring bolts . . . . 9 Nm
Connecting rod bolt nuts
    New con-rod with attached new bolts and nuts . . . . 18 Nm +120°
    New con-rod with attached new bolts and separate new nuts . . . . . 20 Nm +120°
    Old con-rod with new bolts and new nuts . . . . 25 Nm +120°
    Old con-rod with new bolts and old nuts . . . . 24 Nm +120°
Coolant outlet pipe assembly bolts . . . . 11 Nm
Crankcase breather plate bolts . . . . 10 Nm
Crankcase bolts
    Crankshaft journal 9 mm bolts . . . . 42 Nm
    Lower crankcase 7 mm bolts . . . . 20 Nm
    Upper crankcase 8 mm bolts . . . . 27 Nm
    Upper crankcase 7 mm bolts . . . . 20 Nm
    Upper crankcase 6 mm bolts . . . . 12 Nm

Torque settings (continued)

Cylinder head 10 mm bolts
    Initial setting . . . . 20 Nm
    Final setting
        Used bolts. . . . . 40 Nm
        New bolts . . . . 54 Nm
Cylinder head 6 mm bolts . . . . 12 Nm
Engine mountings
    ZR750-J and ZR1000-A
        Adjuster bolt locknut. . . . . 49 Nm
        Front mounting bolts . . . . 44 Nm
        Front engine bracket bolts . . . . 44 Nm
        Rear engine bracket bolts. . . . . 25 Nm
        Rear mounting bolt nuts . . . . 44 Nm
    ZR750-L/M and ZR1000-B/C
        Lower rear mounting adjuster bolt locknut. . . . . 49 Nm
        Lower rear mounting bolt nut . . . . 44 Nm
        Rear engine bracket bolts. . . . . 25 Nm
        Upper rear mounting bolt nut . . . . 44 Nm
        Sub-frame bolts (each side) . . . . 25 Nm
        Front engine bracket bolts (each side) . . . . 44 Nm
        Middle engine mounting bolt (each side) . . . . 44 Nm
Gearchange shaft centralising spring locating pin. . . . . 29 Nm
Oil cooler bolt. . . . . 78 Nm
Oil gallery plug . . . . 20 Nm
Oil pipe retainer bolts (behind clutch). . . . . 13 Nm
Oil pressure relief valve . . . . 15 Nm
Oil sump bolts . . . . 11 Nm
Piston oil jet bolts (ZR750-L/M) . . . . 7 Nm
Selector drum bearing/fork shaft retainer plate
    Bolt . . . . 13 Nm
    Screw . . . . 6 Nm
Selector drum cam bolt . . . . 12 Nm
Starter clutch bolts. . . . . 12 Nm
Stopper arm bolt . . . . 12 Nm
Timing rotor cover bolts . . . . 11 Nm
Valve cover bolts . . . . 10 Nm

1 General information

The engine/transmission unit is a liquid-cooled in-line four cylinder. The sixteen valves are operated by double overhead camshafts which are chain driven off the right-hand end of the crankshaft.

The crankcase incorporates a wet sump, pressure-fed lubrication system which uses a dual rotor trochoidal oil pump that is gear-driven off the back of the clutch. The system has an oil strainer in the pick-up, a pressure relief valve in the feed from the pump to the filter, an oil filter, on Z1000 models an oil cooler, and an oil pressure switch off the main gallery.

The alternator is on the left-hand end of the crankshaft and the rotor carries the starter clutch. The water pump is on the left-hand side of the engine, and its driveshaft is keyed to the oil pump. The ignition timing triggers are on a rotor on the right-hand end of the crankshaft.

Power from the crankshaft is routed to the transmission via the clutch. The clutch is of the wet, multi-plate type and is gear-driven off the crankshaft. The clutch is operated by cable. The transmission is a six-speed constant-mesh unit. Final drive to the rear wheel is by chain and sprockets.

2 Component access

Operations possible with the engine in the frame

The components and assemblies listed below can be removed without having to remove the engine from the frame. If however, a number of areas require attention at the same time, removal of the engine is recommended.

Valve cover
Cam chain tensioner and blades
Camshafts
Cylinder head
Cylinder bock
Pistons
Clutch
Gearchange mechanism
Alternator/starter clutch
Oil filter and oil cooler
Oil sump, oil pump, oil strainer and oil pressure relief valve
Selector drum and forks (see **Note** *in Section 22)*
Starter motor
Timing rotor
Water pump

Operations requiring engine removal

It is necessary to remove the engine from the frame to gain access to the following components.

Crankshaft and bearings
Cam chain
Connecting rods and bearings
Transmission shafts

3 Engine wear assessment

Cylinder compression check

Special tool: *A compression gauge with adaptor to fit a 10 mm diameter x 1.0 mm pitch internal thread (use either the Kawasaki gauge and adapter (pt. Nos. 57001-221 and 57001-1317) or aftermarket versions) are needed. Depending on the outcome of the initial test, a squirt-type oil can may also be needed.*

Note: *The FI warning light will flash and a fault code will be shown with the ignition coils disconnected. This will cancel once the coils are reconnected.*

1 Poor engine performance may be caused by leaking valves, incorrect valve clearances, a leaking head gasket, or worn pistons, piston rings or cylinder walls. A cylinder compression check will highlight these conditions and can also indicate the presence of excessive carbon deposits in the cylinder head, and a leakdown test (for which special equipment is needed – consult a Kawasaki dealer) will pinpoint the actual cause(s) of the problem.

2 Start by making sure the valve clearances are correctly set (see Chapter 1).

3 Run the engine until it is at normal operating temperature. Stop the engine, then remove the ignition coils (see Chapter 4) and the spark plugs (see Chapter 1).

4 Fit the adaptor and gauge into the No. 1 cylinder spark plug hole.

5 With the ignition switch ON, the kill switch set to RUN, and the throttle held fully open, turn the engine over on the starter motor until the gauge reading has built up and stabilised.

6 Compare the reading on the gauge to the cylinder compression figure specified at the beginning of the Chapter (under Cylinder bore specifications). Repeat for the remaining cylinders.

7 If the reading is low, it could be due to worn cylinder bores, pistons or rings, failure of the head gasket, loose cylinder head bolts or worn valve seats. To determine which is the cause, pour a small quantity of engine oil

into the spark plug hole to seal the rings, then repeat the compression test. If the figures are noticeably higher the cause is a worn cylinder, piston or rings. If there is no change the cause is a leaking head gasket or worn valve seats.

8 If the reading is high there could be a build-up of carbon deposits in the combustion chamber. Remove the cylinder head and scrape all deposits off the piston and the cylinder head, and on installation fit a new gasket.

Engine oil pressure check

Special tool: *An oil pressure gauge and adapter (which screws into the main oil gallery) are needed; use either the Kawasaki gauge and adapter (pt. Nos. 57001-164 and 57001-1233) or aftermarket versions.*

9 If there is any doubt about the performance of the engine lubrication system an oil pressure check must be carried out. The check provides useful information about the state of wear of the engine.

10 The oil pressure warning light should come on when the ignition switch is turned ON and extinguish a few seconds after the engine is started. If the oil pressure light comes on whilst the engine is running, low oil pressure is indicated – stop the engine immediately and check the oil level (see *Pre-ride checks*). If the oil level is good an oil pressure check must be carried out.

11 You will need some rags to catch and mop up any residual oil that gets lost in between removing the plug and installing the gauge – place the bike on its sidestand so that the oil gathers at the other end of the gallery to reduce spillage.

12 On ZR1000-B/C models remove the right-hand sump cowl (see Chapter 7). Check the oil level (see *Pre-ride checks*). Warm the engine up to normal operating temperature then stop it.

13 Unscrew the oil gallery plug and screw the gauge adapter in its place **(see illustrations)**. Connect the oil pressure gauge to the adaptor.

14 Start the engine and briefly increase the engine speed to 4000 rpm whilst watching the gauge reading. The oil pressure should be similar to that given in the Specifications at the start of this Chapter.

15 If the pressure is significantly lower than the standard, either the pressure relief valve is stuck open, the oil pump or its drive mechanism is faulty, the oil strainer or filter is blocked, or there is other engine damage. Also make sure the correct grade oil is being used. Begin diagnosis by checking the oil filter, strainer and relief valve, then the oil pump (see Section 20). If those items check out okay, chances are the bearing oil clearances are excessive and the engine needs to be overhauled.

16 If the pressure is too high, either an oil passage is clogged, the relief valve is stuck closed or the wrong grade of oil is being used.

17 Stop the engine and unscrew the gauge and adapter from the crankcase.

 Warning: Be careful when removing the pressure gauge adapter as the exhaust pipes, the engine and the oil itself can cause severe burns.

18 Apply a suitable non-permanent thread locking compound to the gallery plug threads, then screw it into the engine and tighten it to the torque setting specified at the beginning of the Chapter. Check the oil level (see *Pre-ride checks*).

19 On ZR1000-B/C models install the right-hand sump cowl (See Chapter 7).

4 Engine removal and installation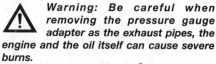

Caution: The engine is very heavy. Engine removal and installation should be carried out with the aid of at least one assistant; personal injury or damage could occur if the engine falls or is dropped.

Special tool: *A peg spanner is required to slacken and tighten the adjuster bolt locknuts and a hex key is required to slacken and tighten the adjuster bolts. If the Kawasaki combined service tool (Pt. No. 57001-1450), is not available, a suitable peg spanner can be fabricated out of an old socket (see Tool Tip) and a 20 mm bit or sump key can be obtained from a good tool supplier.*

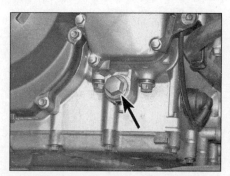

3.13a Unscrew the oil gallery plug (arrowed)

3.13b Oil pressure gauge, hose and adapter installed

Posts can be cut into a socket to create a peg spanner

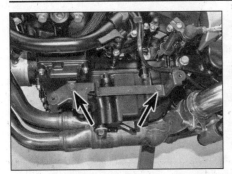

4.2 Unscrew the bolts (arrowed) and remove the bracket on each side

4.10 Release the heat shield clips (arrowed)

4.12 Make an alignment mark then unscrew the bolt (arrowed) and slide the arm off the shaft

Removal

All models

1 If possible support the bike upright using a paddock stand under the swingarm, making sure it is on level ground. Work can be made easier by raising the machine to a suitable working height on an hydraulic ramp or a suitable platform. Make sure the motorcycle is secure and will not topple over (also see *Tools and Workshop Tips* in the Reference section). Tie the front brake lever to the handlebar so the front wheel is locked.

2 Remove the side panels, frame covers and engine cowls as required according to model (see Chapter 7). On ZR1000-B/C models unscrew the sump cowl bracket bolts and remove the brackets **(see illustration)**.

3 If the engine is dirty, particularly around its mountings, wash it thoroughly. This will make work much easier and rule out the possibility of caked on lumps of dirt falling into some vital component.

4 Drain the engine oil and coolant (see Chapter 1). If required remove the oil filter (see Chapter 1).

5 Disconnect the negative (–ve) lead from the battery (see Chapter 8).

6 Remove the fuel tank (see Chapter 4). Remove the throttle bodies (see Chapter 4). Plug the engine intake manifolds with clean rag.

7 Refer to Section 18, Step 2 and detach the clutch cable from the engine. Position the cable clear.

8 Remove the radiator along with its hoses and pipe, noting their routing (see Chapter 3). Remove the thermostat housing along with the filler neck and hoses (see Chapter 3).

9 Remove the ignition coils and the coil wiring sub-loom (see Chapter 4). Remove the air system control valve and hoses (see Chapter 4).

10 On ZR750-L/M and ZR1000-B/C models release the trim clips securing the rubber heat shield to the bracket on the valve cover **(see illustration)**. If required release the upper trim clips as well and remove the shield.

11 Remove the exhaust system (see Chapter 4).

12 On ZR750-J and ZR1000-A models make an alignment mark where the slot in the gearchange linkage arm aligns with the shaft – on ZR750-L/M and ZR1000-B/C models there should already be a mark, but make your own if necessary **(see illustration)**. Unscrew the gearchange linkage arm pinch bolt and slide the arm off the shaft.

13 Remove the front sprocket (see Chapter 6). Slip the drive chain off the end of the output shaft **(see illustration)** – if not already done the chain must first be slipped off the rear sprocket to do this.

14 Working around the engine, disconnect the following wiring connectors: crankshaft position (CKP) sensor/oil pressure switch, camshaft position (CMP) sensor, speed sensor, neutral switch, alternator, sidestand switch, referring to Chapters 4 and 8 if required. Free the loom side of all wiring from any clips or ties to the engine, and free the sidestand switch wiring from the engine, and secure it clear, noting its routing. On ZR750-J and ZR1000-A models free the camshaft position (CMP) sensor connector from the bracket on the valve cover **(see illustration)**.

15 Either remove the starter motor, or just pull back the rubber cover on its terminal, unscrew the nut and disconnect the lead (see Chapter 8).

16 Detach the crankcase breather hose and remove it **(see illustration)**.

17 Unscrew the bolt securing the earth lead to the crankcase and detach the lead **(see illustration)** – if access is too restricted on ZR750-J and ZR1000-A models do this later (Step 24).

ZR750-J and ZR1000-A models

18 Position an hydraulic or mechanical

4.13 Slip the chain off the end of the shaft

4.14 Free the connector (arrowed) from its bracket on the valve cover

4.16 Remove the crankcase breather hose (arrowed)

4.17 Unscrew the bolt (arrowed) and detach the lead

4.19 Remove the bolt (arrowed) on each side

4.20 Unscrew the bolts (arrowed) and remove the bracket

jack under the engine with a block of wood between the jack head and sump **(see illustration 4.26)**. Make sure the jack is centrally positioned so the engine will not topple in any direction when the last mounting bolt is removed. Raise the jack to take the weight of the engine, but make sure it is not lifting the bike and taking the weight of that as well. The idea is to support the engine so that there is no pressure on any of the mounting bolts once they have been slackened, so they can be easily withdrawn. Note that it may be necessary to alter the position of the jack as some of the bolts are removed to relieve the stress transferred to the other bolts.

4.26 Place a jack under the engine

4.27b Unscrew the right-hand middle bolt . . .

19 Unscrew and withdraw the front mounting bolt on each side and remove the nuts, noting how they locate **(see illustration)**.
20 Unscrew the front engine bracket bolts, noting the washers, and remove the bracket, along with the baffle plate that locates between it and the frame on the left-hand side **(see illustration)**.
21 Unscrew the nut on the right-hand end of the upper and lower rear mounting bolts **(see illustration 4.29a)**. Unscrew the rear engine bracket bolts and remove the bracket **(see illustration 4.29b)**.
22 Check that the engine is properly supported by the jack. Check that all engine

4.27a Unscrew the left-hand middle bolt

4.27c . . . then unscrew the adjuster collar lockbolt

wiring, cables and hoses are disconnected, free and clear.
23 Unscrew the adjuster bolt locknut using the Kawasaki special tool or a suitable peg spanner **(see illustration 4.31a)**. Push the mounting bolt in slightly. Unscrew the adjuster bolt until the flange on the inner end just contacts the frame **(see illustration 4.31b)**.
24 The engine can now be removed from the frame (see **Caution** above). Withdraw the upper rear mounting bolt from the left-hand side **(see illustration 4.32a)**. Withdraw the lower rear mounting bolt from the left-hand side then carefully lower the jack slightly **(see illustration 4.32b)**. If access was too restricted earlier now unscrew the earth lead bolt and detach the lead **(see illustration 4.17)**. Fully lower the jack, then with the aid of an assistant remove the jack from under the engine and remove the engine.
25 Thread the adjuster bolt out of the frame **(see illustration 4.42b)**. If required, remove the upper rear engine mounting bolt damping rubbers **(see illustration 4.34a)** – lever them apart using a screwdriver between the inner ends.

ZR750-L/M and ZR1000-B/C models

26 Position an hydraulic or mechanical jack under the engine with a block of wood between the jack head and sump **(see illustration)**. Make sure the jack is centrally positioned so the engine will not topple in any direction when the last mounting bolt is removed. Raise the jack to take the weight of the engine, but make sure it is not lifting the bike and taking the weight of that as well. The idea is to support the engine so that there is no pressure on any of the mounting bolts once they have been slackened, so they can be easily withdrawn. Note that it may be necessary to alter the position of the jack as some of the bolts are removed to relieve the stress transferred to the other bolts.
27 Unscrew the middle engine mounting bolt on each side **(see illustrations)**. Unscrew the adjuster collar lockbolt on the right-hand middle mounting **(see illustration)**.

4.28a Unscrew the bolts (arrowed) and remove the sub-frame . . .

4.28b . . . then unscrew the bolts (arrowed) and remove the bracket

28 Unscrew the sub-frame bolts on each side, noting the washers, and remove the sub-frames **(see illustration)**. Unscrew the front engine bracket bolts on each side, noting the washers, and remove the brackets **(see illustration)**. Remove the nuts for the middle mounting bolts, noting how they fit **(see illustration)**.

29 Unscrew the nut on the right-hand end of the upper and lower rear mounting bolts **(see illustration)**. Unscrew the rear engine bracket bolts and remove the bracket **(see illustration)**.

30 Check that the engine is properly supported by the jack. Check that all engine wiring, cables and hoses are disconnected, free and clear.

31 Unscrew the adjuster bolt locknut on the right-hand end of the lower rear mounting bolt using the Kawasaki special tool or a suitable peg spanner **(see illustration)**. Push the mounting bolt in slightly. Unscrew the adjuster bolt until the flange on the inner end just contacts the frame **(see illustration)**.

32 The engine can now be removed from the frame (see **Caution** above). Withdraw the upper rear mounting bolt from the left-hand side **(see illustration)**. Withdraw the lower rear mounting bolt from the left-hand side then carefully begin to lower the jack **(see illustration)**. Fully lower the jack, then with the aid of an assistant remove the jack from under the engine and remove the engine.

4.28c Retrieve the middle engine mounting bolt nuts, noting how they locate

4.29a Unscrew the nuts from the rear mounting bolts

4.29b Unscrew the bolts (arrowed) and remove the bracket

4.31a Unscrew the locknut (arrowed) using a suitable peg spanner

4.31b Turn the adjuster bolt using a hex key or bit

4.32a Withdraw the upper bolt . . .

4.32b . . . then withdraw the lower bolt and remove the engine

4.34a Lubricate the rubbers and fit them into the mounts . . .

4.34b . . . using a drawbolt arrangement if required to ensure they are fully inserted

33 Thread the adjuster bolts out of the frame and sub-frame **(see illustrations 4.42b and a)**. If required remove the upper rear engine mounting bolt damping rubbers **(see illustration 4.34a)** – lever them apart using a screwdriver between the inner ends.

Installation

Note: *Smear copper grease onto the bolt shafts, not the threads, to prevent the possibility of them seizing in the engine or frame.*

ZR750-J and ZR1000-A models

34 Clean the threads of the adjuster bolt. Thread the adjuster bolt into the frame from the inside until the flange contacts the frame **(see illustration 4.42b)**. If removed fit the rubber dampers into the upper rear engine mountings using a lubricant to help them in **(see illustrations)** – make sure they are fully home (tap them in with a rubber mallet or use a drawbolt arrangement – refer to *Tools and Workshop Tips*) otherwise they will get in the way when fitting the engine back into the frame.

35 Manoeuvre the engine into position under the frame and lift it onto the jack **(see illustration 4.26)**. Raise the engine – before the engine is fully raised make sure that all

cables and wiring are correctly routed and do not get trapped, and connect the earth lead to the engine and secure it with the bolt. Further raise the engine to align all the mounting bolt holes. Note that it may be necessary to adjust the jack as some of the bolts are installed and tightened to realign the other bolt holes.

36 Insert the upper and lower rear mounting bolts from the left-hand side **(see illustrations 4.32a and b)**. Fit the rear engine bracket and lightly tighten the bolts **(see illustration 4.29b)**.

37 Locate the nut for the left-hand front mounting bolt in its holder then insert the bolt and tighten it to the torque setting specified at the beginning of the Chapter.

38 Push the lower rear mounting bolt in slightly, then turn the adjuster bolt until its flange contacts the engine **(see illustration 4.31b)** – it should only make a light contact so there is no clearance between them rather than pressing hard against it **(see illustration 4.47a)**. Thread the locknut onto the adjuster bolt **(see illustration 4.47b)**. Tighten the locknut to the specified torque using the Kawasaki special tool or the peg spanner as on removal **(see illustration 4.31a)**.

39 Tighten the rear engine bracket bolts to the specified torque setting **(see illustration 4.29b)**. Fit the nuts onto the upper and lower

rear bolts, then counter-hold the bolt heads and tighten the nuts in that order to the specified torque **(see illustration 4.29a)**.

40 Fit the front engine bracket, locating the baffle plate between it and the frame, and tighten its bolts finger-tight, not forgetting the washers **(see illustration 4.20)**.

41 Locate the nut for the right-hand front mounting bolt in its holder then insert the bolt and tighten it to the torque setting specified at the beginning of the Chapter. Now tighten the front engine bracket bolts to the specified torque.

ZR750-L/M and ZR1000-B/C models

42 Clean the threads of the adjuster bolts. Thread the shorter adjuster bolt into the sub-frame and the longer one into the main frame, inserting them from the inside and threading them in until the flanges make contact **(see illustrations)**. If removed fit the rubber dampers into the upper rear engine mountings using a lubricant to help them in **(see illustrations 4.34a and b)** – make sure they are fully home (tap them in with a rubber mallet or use a drawbolt arrangement – refer to *Tools and Workshop Tips*) otherwise they will get in the way when fitting the engine back into the frame.

43 Manoeuvre the engine into position under the frame and lift it onto the jack **(see illustration 4.26)**. Raise the engine – before the engine is fully raised make sure that all cables and wiring are correctly routed and do not get trapped. Further raise the engine to align all the mounting bolt holes. Note that it may be necessary to adjust the jack as some of the bolts are installed and tightened to realign the other bolt holes.

44 Insert the upper and lower rear mounting bolts from the left-hand side **(see illustrations 4.32a and b)**. Fit the rear engine bracket and lightly tighten the bolts **(see illustration 4.29b)**.

45 Locate the nuts for the middle mounting bolts in their holders **(see illustration 4.28c)**. Locate the left-hand front engine bracket then insert the bolts with their washers, and

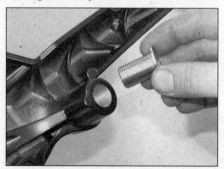

4.42a Thread the shorter bolt into the sub-frame . . .

4.42b . . . and the longer one into the main frame

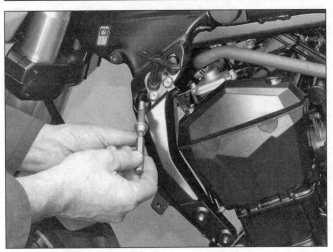
4.45a Fit the left-hand engine bracket . . .

4.45b . . . then fit the sub-frame

tighten them finger-tight (see illustration). Locate the left-hand sub-frame then insert the bolts with their washers and tighten them finger-tight (see illustration). Now tighten the bracket and sub-frame bolts to the torque settings specified at the beginning of the Chapter. Insert the left-hand middle mounting bolt, making sure the nut stays in place, and tighten it to the specified torque (see illustration 4.27a).

46 Tighten the rear engine bracket bolts to the specified torque (see illustration 4.29b).

47 Push the lower rear mounting bolt in slightly, then turn the adjuster bolt until its

flange contacts the engine (see illustration 4.31b) – it should only make a light contact so there is no clearance between them rather than pressing hard against it (see illustration). Thread the locknut onto the adjuster bolt (see illustration). Tighten the locknut to the specified torque using the Kawasaki special tool or the peg spanner as on removal (see illustration 4.31a).

48 Fit the nuts onto the upper and lower rear bolts, then counter-hold the bolt heads and tighten the nuts to the specified torque (see illustration 4.29a).

49 Locate the right-hand front engine bracket

then insert the bolts with their washers and tighten them finger-tight (see illustration). Locate the right-hand sub-frame then insert the bolts with their washers and tighten them finger-tight (see illustration). Insert the middle mounting bolt, making sure the nut stays in place, but do not thread the bolt into the nut – it is merely acting as a guide (see illustration). Now tighten the sub-frame rear bolts, then the front bolts, then the engine bracket bolts, to their specified torque settings. Remove the middle mounting bolt.

50 Turn the middle adjuster bolt until its flange contacts the engine – it should only make a light contact so there is no clearance between them rather than pressing hard against it. Thread the lockbolt into the adjuster bolt and tighten it to the specified torque (see illustration 4.27c). Refit the middle mounting bolt and tighten it to the specified torque (see illustration 4.27b).

All models

51 The remainder of the installation procedure is the reverse of removal, noting the following points:
● When fitting the gearchange linkage arm onto the gearchange shaft, align the slit in the arm with the mark on the shaft (see illustration 4.12).

4.47a Turn the adjuster bolt until the flange contacts the engine . . .

4.47b . . . then fit the locknut and tighten it

4.49a Fit the right-hand engine bracket . . .

4.49b . . . then fit the sub-frame

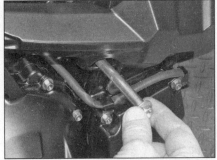
4.49c Temporarily insert the bolt as a guide

● Use new gaskets on the exhaust pipe connections.
● Make sure all wires, cables and hoses are correctly routed and connected, and secured by any clips or ties.
● Refill the engine with oil and coolant to the correct levels (see Chapter 1 and *Pre-ride checks*).
● Adjust the throttle and clutch cable freeplay (see Chapter 1).
● Adjust the drive chain (see Chapter 1).
● Start the engine and check that there are no oil or coolant leaks. Adjust the idle speed (see Chapter 1).

5 Engine overhaul information

1 Before beginning the engine overhaul, read through the related procedures to familiarise yourself with the scope and requirements of the job. Overhauling an engine is not all that difficult, but it is time consuming. Check on the availability of parts and make sure that any necessary special tools are obtained in advance.

2 Most work can be done with a decent set of typical workshop hand tools, although a number of precision measuring tools are required for inspecting parts to determine if they are worn.

3 To ensure maximum life and minimum trouble from a rebuilt engine, everything must be assembled with care in a spotlessly clean environment.

Disassembly

4 Before disassembling the engine, thoroughly clean and degrease its external surfaces. This will prevent contamination of the engine internals, and will also make the job a lot easier and cleaner. A high flash-point solvent, such as paraffin (kerosene) can be used, or better still, a proprietary engine degreaser such as Gunk. Use old paintbrushes and toothbrushes to work the solvent into the various recesses of the casings. Take care to exclude solvent or water from the electrical components and intake and exhaust ports.

 Warning: The use of petrol (gasoline) as a cleaning agent should be avoided because of the risk of fire.

5 When clean and dry, position the engine on the workbench, leaving suitable clear area for working. Gather a selection of small containers, plastic bags and some labels so that parts can be grouped together in an easily identifiable manner. Also get some paper and a pen so that notes can be taken. You will also need a supply of clean rag, which should be as absorbent as possible.

6 Before commencing work, read through the appropriate section so that some idea of the necessary procedure can be gained. When removing components note that great force is seldom required, unless specified (checking the specified torque setting of the particular bolt being removed will indicate how tight it is, and therefore how much force should be needed. In many cases, a component's reluctance to be removed is indicative of an incorrect approach or removal method – if in any doubt, re-check with the text.

7 When disassembling the engine, keep 'mated' parts that have been in contact with each other during engine operation together – i.e. cylinder bores, pistons and rings, connecting rods, valves, etc,). These 'mated' parts must not be mixed up and must be installed in their original location.

8 A complete engine strip should be done in the following general order with reference to the appropriate Sections.

Remove the valve cover
Remove the camshafts
Remove the cylinder head
Remove the cam chain blades
Remove the cylinder block and pistons
Remove the starter motor (see Chapter 8)
Remove the alternator/starter clutch (see Chapter 8)
Remove the clutch
Remove the gearchange mechanism
Remove the water pump and oil pump
Remove the oil sump
Remove the selector drum and forks
Separate the crankcase halves
Remove the crankshaft, connecting rods and cam chain
Remove the transmission shafts

Reassembly

9 Reassembly is accomplished by reversing the general disassembly sequence.

6 Oil cooler (Z1000)

Note: *The oil cooler is only fitted to Z1000 models. It can be removed with the engine in the frame. If the engine has been removed, ignore the steps which do not apply.*

Removal

1 The cooler is located on the front of the engine. Drain the engine oil and the coolant (see Chapter 1).
2 Remove the oil filter (Chapter 1).
3 Slacken the clamp securing each hose to the cooler and detach the hoses **(see illustration)**.
4 Unscrew the centre bolt, noting the washer **(see illustration)**. Remove the cooler, noting how the tabs on the cooler body locate on each side of the lug on the crankcase. Discard the O-ring as a new one must be used **(see illustration)**.
5 Check the cooler body for cracks and dents and any evidence of coolant leakage and replace it with a new one if necessary. Also check the hoses for splits, cracks, hardening and deterioration and fit new ones if required.

Installation

6 Installation is the reverse of removal, noting the following:
● Ensure the mating surfaces of the crankcase and the cooler are clean and dry.
● Use a new O-ring on the cooler body and smear it with grease. Make sure it seats in its groove *(see illustration 6.4b)*.
● Make sure the internal threads in the cooler are clean.
● Locate the tabs on the cooler body on each side of the lug on the crankcase *(see illustration 6.4a)*.
● Smear the cooler bolt threads with clean oil and tighten it to the torque setting specified at the beginning of the Chapter.

6.3 Slacken the clamp screws (arrowed) and detach the hoses (late model shown)

6.4a Unscrew the bolt and remove the cooler

6.4b Remove the O-ring and fit a new one on installation

7.2 Unscrew the front bolt (arrowed) to free the bracket on each side

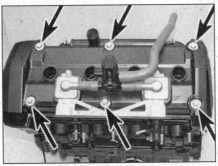

7.3a Unscrew the bolts (arrowed) . . .

7.3b . . . and remove the cover

● Make sure the coolant hoses are pressed fully onto their unions and are secured by the clamps (see illustration 6.3).
● Fit a new oil filter (Chapter 1).
● Fill the engine with oil to the correct level (see Chapter 1 and Pre-ride checks).
● Refill the cooling system (see Chapter 1).
● Run the engine and check that there are no leaks.

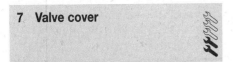

7 Valve cover

Note: *The valve cover can be removed with the engine in the frame. If the engine has been removed, ignore the steps which do not apply.*

Removal

1 Remove the fuel tank (see Chapter 4), the thermostat housing and hoses (see Chapter 3), the air suction control valve and hoses, and the ignition coils and the coil wiring sub-loom (see Chapter 4). Make sure all wiring is clear of the cover.
2 On ZR750-L/M and ZR1000-B/C models, if the engine is in the frame unscrew the front bolt on each reed valve cover to free the shield bracket (see illustration).
3 Unscrew the valve cover bolts and lift the cover off the cylinder head (see illustrations). If it is stuck, do not try to lever it off with a screwdriver. Tap it gently around the sides with a rubber hammer or block of wood to dislodge it. Note the washers for the bolts and remove them if they are loose (see illustration 7.10).
4 Remove the rubber gasket noting how it locates (see illustration 7.9). If it is in any way damaged, deformed or deteriorated, replace it with a new one.
5 Remove the spark plug bore gaskets and replace them with new ones if necessary (see illustration). Note the four dowels that link the air system passages between the valve cover and cylinder head and remove them for safekeeping if they are loose (which is unlikely), taking care not to drop them if they are not in the valve cover.

7.5 Remove the spark plug gaskets. Note the air passage dowels (arrowed)

6 If required, remove the air system reed valves (see Chapter 4).

Installation

7 If removed, install the air system reed valves (see Chapter 4). On ZR750-L/M and ZR1000-B/C models leave the bolts that secure the shield bracket loose (see illustration 7.2).
8 If removed, fit the air system dowels, and fit spark plug bore gaskets, making sure they locate around the rim (see illustration 7.5).
9 Clean all traces of old sealant from the cut-outs in the cylinder head and apply some fresh sealant (see illustration). Fit the valve cover gasket (see illustration).
10 Position the valve cover on the cylinder head, making sure the gasket stays in place (see illustration 7.3b). If removed, fit the washers onto the bolts or into the cover, using new ones if required, and making sure they

7.9b Make sure the gasket locates in the groove and stays there

7.9a Apply a sealant to the cutouts in the cylinder head

are installed with the metal side facing up (see illustration). Install the cover bolts and tighten them evenly and in a criss-cross sequence to the specified torque setting (see illustration 7.3a).
11 Install the remaining components in the reverse order of removal.

8 Cam chain tensioner

Note: *The cam chain tensioner can be removed with the engine in the frame. If the engine has been removed, ignore the steps which do not apply.*

⚠ *Warning: Do not turn the engine with the tensioner removed.*

7.10 Make sure the metal side of the washers faces up

8.1 Unscrew the cap bolt (arrowed) and
remove the washer, spring and rod

8.2a Unscrew the bolts . . .

8.2b . . . and withdraw the tensioner

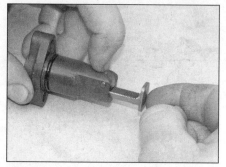

8.4 Release the stopper and make sure
the plunger moves smoothly and freely

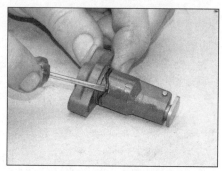

8.6 Fit a new O-ring into the groove

8 Refer to Section 9, Steps 2 and 3 and turn
the engine clockwise through two full turns to
set the tensioner.

9 Camshafts and followers

Note: *The camshafts can be removed with the
engine in the frame. Place clean rags over the
spark plug holes and the cam chain tunnel to
prevent any component from dropping into
the engine.*

Removal

1 Remove the spark plugs (see Chapter 1).
Remove the valve cover (see Section 7).
2 Unscrew the timing rotor cover bolts,
noting the routing of the wiring and the
position of the guides, and remove the cover
(see illustration). Discard the O-ring as a new
one must be used.
3 The engine must be turned so that the
Nos. 1 and 4 pistons are at TDC (top dead
centre), with No. 4 on its compression stroke.
Turn the engine using a suitable spanner or
socket on the timing rotor bolt and turning
it in a clockwise direction only until the line
next to the numbers 1 and 4 marked on the
timing rotor points back and aligns with
the crankcase mating surfaces, and the IN
and EX marks on the intake and exhaust

Removal

1 Unscrew the tensioner cap bolt and remove the
sealing washer, spring and rod **(see illustration)**.
Check the condition of the sealing washer and
replace it with a new one if necessary.
2 Unscrew the tensioner mounting bolts, then
withdraw the tensioner from the engine **(see
illustrations)**.
3 Remove and discard the O-ring as a
new one must be used on installation **(see
illustration 8.6)**. Do not attempt to dismantle
the tensioner.

Installation

4 Release the ratchet stopper and check
that the plunger moves smoothly in and out
of the tensioner **(see illustration)**. Ensure the

tensioner and cylinder block mating surfaces
are clean and dry.
5 Release the ratchet stopper and push the
plunger almost fully into the tensioner body
(see illustration 8.4).
6 Fit a new O-ring into the groove in the
tensioner body and smear it with grease
(see illustration). Install the tensioner with
the ratchet stopper facing up and tighten
the mounting bolts to the torque setting
specified at the beginning of the Chapter **(see
illustrations 8.2b and a)**.
7 Fit the sealing washer onto the cap bolt.
Fit the rod into the spring, then locate them
in the cap bolt and fit them into the tensioner,
and tighten the bolt to the specified torque
(see illustration). As you thread the cap bolt
inwards the plunger will be pushed out against
the tensioner blade.

8.7 Fit the cap bolt assembly into the tensioner

9.2 Unscrew the bolts (arrowed) and remove the cover

9.3a Turn the engine clockwise using the bolt . . .

9.3b . . . until the line next to the 1 and 4 aligns with the crankcase mating surfaces (arrowed) . . .

9.3c . . . and the camshaft sprocket marks are as shown

9.5a Remove the top cam chain guide . . .

9.5b . . . then lift the holders off

9.5c Remove the dowels (arrowed) if loose

camshaft sprockets respectively are as shown **(see illustrations)**. If the sprocket marks are not as shown, it means that No. 1 is on its compression stroke – rotate the engine clockwise one full turn (360°) until the line next to the 1 and 4 again aligns with the crankcase mating surfaces. The sprocket marks will now be facing correctly.

4 Remove the cam chain tensioner (see Section 8).

5 Unscrew the camshaft holder bolts, slackening them evenly and a very little at a time in a **reverse** of the tightening sequence shown **(see illustration 9.25d)**. Remove the bolts and top cam chain guide and lift off the holders, noting how they locate on the dowels **(see illustrations)**. Remove the dowels if they are loose and liable to drop out **(see illustration)**.

Caution: Make sure the holders lift up squarely and evenly and do not stick on a dowel or distort from some of the bolts being slackened more than the others as they or a camshaft could easily break.

6 If both camshafts are being removed, remove the intake camshaft first. Carefully lift each camshaft off the head and disengage the sprocket from the chain **(see illustrations 9.24a and 9.23a)**. The camshafts are marked for identification – the intake camshaft is marked IN and the exhaust camshaft is marked EX **(see illustration)**. If both camshafts have been removed allow the chain to drop down the tunnel – it can easily be hooked out. Place rags over the spark plug holes to prevent anything from dropping into the engine.

7 While the camshafts are out do not rotate the crankshaft unless necessary – the chain may bind between the crankshaft and case, which could damage these components. If you do need to turn the crankshaft hook the chain up hold taut as you do.

8 If the followers and shims are being removed from the cylinder head, obtain a container which is divided into sixteen compartments, and label each compartment with the location of a valve, i.e. intake or exhaust camshaft, left or right valve. If a container is not available, use labelled plastic bags (egg cartons also do very well!). Lift out each cam follower using a magnet or the suction created by a valve lapping tool **(see illustration 9.20)**. Retrieve the shim from the inside of the follower or pick it out of the top of the valve spring retainer using either a magnet, a screwdriver with a dab of grease on it (the shim will stick to the grease), or a very small screwdriver and a pair of pliers **(see illustrations)**. Do not allow the shim to fall into the engine.

9.6 Note the identity mark on each camshaft

9.8a Retrieve the shim (arrowed) from inside the follower . . .

9.8b . . . or from the top of the valve

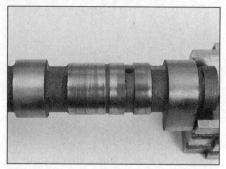

9.9 Check all related bearing surfaces as described

9.10 Measure the height of the camshaft lobes with a micrometer

9.20 Fit the shim into its recess then fit the follower onto the valve

Inspection

9 Inspect the bearing surfaces of the camshaft holders and cylinder head and the corresponding journals on the camshafts **(see illustration)**. Look for score marks, deep scratches and evidence of spalling (a pitted appearance). Check the oil passages for clogging.

10 Check the camshaft lobes for heat discoloration (blue appearance), score marks, chipped areas, flat spots and spalling. Measure the height of each lobe with a micrometer **(see illustration)** and compare the results to the minimum height listed in this Chapter's Specifications. If damage is noted or wear is excessive, the camshaft must be replaced with a new one.

11 Check the amount of camshaft runout by supporting each end on V-blocks, and measuring any runout using a dial gauge. If the runout exceeds the specified limit the camshaft must be replaced with a new one.

HAYNES HiNT *Refer to Tools and Workshop Tips in the Reference section for details of how to read a micrometer and dial gauge.*

12 Next, check the camshaft journal oil clearances, working on one camshaft at a time. In order to negate the probability of the camshaft rotating (due to the fact that some of the lobes will be depressing their valves) as the holder bolts are tightened down, which will disturb the Plastigauge and lead to a false measurement, the valves should be removed from the cylinder head – to do this the head must be removed from the engine (see Sections 11 and 12). Clean the camshaft and the bearing surfaces in the cylinder head and camshaft holder with a clean lint-free cloth, then lay the camshaft in its correct location in the cylinder head (see Step 6).

13 Cut some strips of Plastigauge and lay one piece on each journal, parallel with the camshaft centreline **(see illustration 25.14)**. Fit the holder and tighten the bolts as described in Step 25. While doing this, don't let the camshaft rotate, or the Plastigauge will be disturbed and you will have to start again.

14 Now unscrew the camshaft holder bolts as described in Step 5 and lift off the holder.

15 To determine the oil clearance, compare

the crushed Plastigauge (at its widest point) on each journal to the scale printed on the Plastigauge container **(see illustration 25.17)**. Compare the results to this Chapter's Specifications. If the oil clearance is greater than specified, measure the diameter of each camshaft journal and compare the results to the minimum listed in this Chapter's Specifications. If wear is excessive replace the camshaft with a new one and recheck the clearance. If the clearance is still too great, also replace the cylinder head and holders with new ones.

16 Except in cases of oil starvation, the cam chain should wear very little. If the chain has stretched excessively, which makes it difficult to maintain proper tension, or if it is stiff or the links are binding or kinking, replace it with a new one. Refer to Section 10 for replacement.

17 Check the sprockets for wear, cracks and other damage, and replace the camshafts with new ones if necessary. If the sprockets are worn, the cam chain is also worn, and so probably is the sprocket on the crankshaft. If severe wear is apparent, the entire engine should be disassembled for inspection.

18 Inspect the cam chain guides and tensioner blade (see Section 10).

19 Inspect the outer surface of each cam follower for evidence of scoring or other damage. If a follower is in poor condition, it is probable that the bore in the cylinder head in which it works is also damaged. Check for clearance between each follower and its bore. If any follower or bore is worn, out-of-round or tapered, replace the follower and/or cylinder head with a new one.

Installation

20 If removed, lubricate each shim and its follower with molybdenum disulphide oil (a 50/50 mixture of molybdenum disulphide grease and engine oil). Fit each shim into its recess in the top of the valve spring retainer with the size mark facing up, making sure it is correctly seated **(see illustration 9.8b)**. **Note:** *It is most important that the shims and followers are returned to their original valves otherwise the valve clearances will be inaccurate.* Install each follower, making sure it fits squarely in its bore **(see illustration)**.

21 Make sure the bearing surfaces on the camshafts and in the cylinder head are clean, then apply molybdenum disulphide oil (a 50/50 mixture of molybdenum disulphide grease and engine oil) to each of them. Also apply it to the camshaft journals and lobes. Make sure that none gets on the mating surfaces between the holder and the head, or in the bolt holes.

22 Check that the line next to the numbers 1 and 4 marked on the timing rotor points back and aligns with the crankcase mating surfaces **(see illustration 9.3b)**. If both camshafts have been removed, install the exhaust camshaft first, then the intake. Draw the cam chain up using a hook or magnet.

23 Lay the exhaust camshaft (marked EX) onto the head with the EX mark on the sprocket facing forward and level with the cylinder head top mating surface, fitting the cam chain around the sprocket as you install the camshaft, pulling up on the chain to remove all slack in the front run between the crankshaft and the camshaft **(see illustrations)**.

9.23a Install the exhaust camshaft as described . . .

9.23b . . . with the EX mark as shown, and fit the chain round the sprocket

9.24a Install the intake camshaft as described . . .

9.24b . . . with the IN mark as shown, and fit the chain round the sprocket

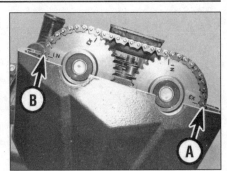

9.24c Count from the No. 1 pin (A) and make sure (B) is the 30th pin

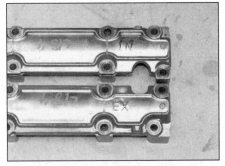

9.25a Note the identity mark on each camshaft holder

9.25b Locate the camshaft holders (arrowed) . . .

9.25c . . . then fit the bolts, the longer ones through the dowels

24 Lay the intake camshaft (marked IN) onto the head with the IN mark on the sprocket facing back and level with the cylinder head top mating surface, fitting the cam chain around the sprocket as you install the camshaft, pulling on it to remove all slack from between the two camshaft sprockets (see illustrations). Now count from the 1st pin that is in line with or just above the EX mark on the exhaust camshaft and make sure that the 30th pin is in line with the IN mark on the intake camshaft sprocket (see illustration). Any slack in the chain must lie in the rear run of the chain between the intake camshaft and the crankshaft so that it is later taken up by the tensioner.

25 Make sure the bearing surfaces in the camshaft holders are clean, then apply molybdenum disulphide oil (a 50/50 mixture of molybdenum disulphide grease and engine oil) to each of them. Make sure the camshaft holder dowels are installed (see illustration 9.5c). Lay the holders on the head – they are marked IN and EX to denote their position (IN on the intake side, EX on the exhaust side) (see illustrations). Install the bolts, not forgetting the top cam chain guide (see illustration 9.5a), and tighten them finger-tight – triangles on the holders mark the position for the longer bolts (2 per holder) that go into the dowelled holes (see illustration). Now tighten the bolts evenly and a little at a time in the numerical sequence shown until the dowels locate and the holder seats, making sure the holder is being pulled down squarely (see illustration). Now tighten them in the same sequence and in two stages to the torque setting specified at the beginning of the Chapter (set the first stage to half the final torque setting).

Caution: Whilst tightening the bolts, make sure the holders are being pulled evenly and squarely down and are not binding on the dowels or tilting to one side – if they do, adjust the relevant bolts until the holder is again square to the head. The holders or a camshaft is likely to break if the bolts are not tightened down evenly and squarely.

26 Use a piece of wooden dowel to press on the back of the cam chain tensioner blade via the tensioner bore in the cylinder block to ensure that any slack in the cam chain is taken up and transferred to the rear run of the chain (where it will later be taken up by the tensioner). At this point check that all the timing marks are still in **exact** alignment as described in Steps 3, 23 and 24. Note that it is easy to be slightly out (one tooth on the sprocket) without the marks appearing drastically out of alignment. If the marks are out, verify which camshaft is misaligned, then remove the wooden dowel. Displace the camshaft and disengage it from the chain, then move the camshaft round as required, refit the camshaft, and check the marks again, following correct bolt slackening and tightening procedures.

Caution: If the marks are not aligned exactly as described, the valve timing will be incorrect and the valves may strike the pistons, causing extensive damage to the engine.

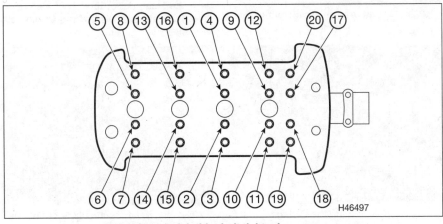

H46497

9.25d Camshaft holder bolt tightening sequence

9.29a Smear some sealant as shown . . .

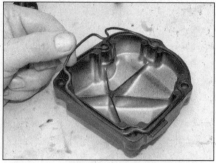

9.29b . . . then fit a new O-ring into the groove . . .

9.29c . . . and install the cover

27 Install the cam chain tensioner (see Section 8).
28 Turn the engine clockwise through two full turns and check again that all the timing marks still align (see Step 3). Check the valve

clearances and adjust them if necessary (see Chapter 1).
29 Smear sealant onto the crankcase mating surfaces with the timing rotor cover and the crankshaft position sensor wiring grommet

(see illustration). Install the timing rotor cover using a new O-ring (see illustrations). Make sure the wiring and guides are correctly positioned. Tighten the cover bolts to the torque setting specified at the beginning of the Chapter.
30 Install the valve cover (see Section 7). Install the spark plugs (see Chapter 1).

10.2a Unscrew the bolts (arrowed) . . .

10.2b . . . noting the collar . . .

10 Cam chain, tensioner blade and front guide blade

Note: The tensioner and guide blades can be removed with the engine in the frame. If the engine has been removed, ignore the steps which do not apply. To remove the cam chain the engine must be removed from the frame and the crankcases separated.

Removal

Tensioner and guide blades

1 Remove the camshafts (see Section 9).
2 Unscrew the front guide blade bolts, noting the collar with the lower bolt and the O-ring with the upper bolt, and draw the blade out of the top of the engine (see illustrations). Discard the O-ring as a new one must be used.
3 Unscrew the tensioner blade pivot bolt and draw the blade out of the top of the engine (see illustrations). Discard the O-ring as a new one must be used.

10.2c . . . and the O-ring . . .

10.2d . . . and draw the blade out of the engine

10.3a Unscrew the pivot bolt (arrowed) . . .

10.3b . . . noting the O-ring . . .

10.3c . . . and draw the blade out of the engine

10.5 Take the chain off the sprocket

11.5a Cylinder head 6 mm bolts (arrowed)

Cam chain

4 Remove the engine (see Section 4). Remove the crankshaft (see Section 25).
5 Slip the cam chain off the crankshaft sprocket **(see illustration)**.

Inspection
Tensioner and guide blades

6 Check the sliding surface and edges of the blades for excessive wear, deep grooves, cracking and other obvious damage, and replace them with new ones if necessary.

Cam chain

7 Check the chain for binding, kinks and any obvious damage and replace it with a new one if necessary. Check the camshaft and crankshaft sprocket teeth for wear and chipped teeth. Damage is unlikely, but if found the camshaft sprockets must be renewed; note that the crankshaft sprocket is integral with the crankshaft itself.

Installation

8 Installation of the chain and blades is the reverse of removal. Fit new O-rings smeared with grease with the tensioner blade pivot bolt and guide blade upper bolt **(see illustrations 10.3b and 10.2c)**. Tighten the bolts to the torque settings specified at the beginning of the Chapter.

11 Cylinder head removal and installation

Note: *The cylinder head can be removed with the engine in the frame. If the engine has been removed, ignore the steps which do not apply.*

Removal

1 Drain the coolant (see Chapter 3), then remove the throttle bodies and the exhaust downpipe assembly (see Chapter 4).
2 On ZR750-J and ZR1000-A models refer to Section 4, Steps 19 and 20, and remove the engine front mounting bolts and bracket.
3 Remove the camshafts, followers and shims (see Section 9).

4 Remove the cam chain tensioner blade and front guide blade (see Section 10). Remove the camshaft position (CMP) sensor (see Chapter 4).
5 The cylinder head is secured by two 6 mm bolts and ten 10 mm bolts with washers. First unscrew and remove the 6 mm bolts **(see illustration)**. Now unscrew and remove the 10 mm bolts, slackening them evenly and a little at a time in a **reverse** of the tightening sequence shown (i.e. working from the outside to the middle) until they are all loose **(see illustration)**.
6 Pull the cylinder head up off the block **(see illustration)**. If the head is stuck, tap around the joint faces with a soft-faced mallet. Do not attempt to free the head by inserting a screwdriver between the head and block mating surfaces – you'll damage them.
7 Remove the cylinder head gasket and discard it as a new one must be used. If they are loose, remove the dowels from the cylinder block or the underside of the cylinder head **(see illustration 11.11)**.

11.5b Cylinder head 10 mm bolts numbered in their TIGHTENING sequence

11.6 Carefully lift the head up off the block

11.11 Fit the dowels (arrowed) then lay the new gasket on the block

11.13a Make sure the washers are fitted and lubricated as described

8 Check the cylinder head gasket and the mating surfaces on the cylinder head and block for signs of leakage, which could indicate warpage. Refer to Section 12 and check the cylinder head gasket surface for warpage.

9 Clean all traces of old gasket material from the cylinder head and block. If a scraper is used, take care not to scratch or gouge the soft aluminium. Be careful not to let any of the gasket material fall into the cylinder bores or the oil and coolant passages.

Installation

10 Lubricate the cylinder bores with engine oil. If removed, fit the dowels into the cylinder block **(see illustration 11.11)**.

11 Ensure both cylinder head and crankcase mating surfaces are clean. Lay the new head gasket onto the block, locating it over the dowels and making sure all the holes are correctly aligned **(see illustration)**. Never reuse the old gasket.

12 Carefully fit the cylinder head onto the block, making sure it locates correctly onto the dowels **(see illustration 11.6)**.

13 Apply some molybdenum disulphide oil (a 50/50 mixture of molybdenum disulphide grease and engine oil) to both sides of the washers on the 10 mm bolts **(see illustration)**.

11.13b Fit the 6 mm bolts last

Install the 10 mm bolts and tighten them all finger-tight at first, then tighten them following the numerical sequence, first to the initial torque setting specified at the beginning of the Chapter, then to the final torque setting specified, noting the different settings for new and used bolts **(see illustration 11.5b)**. Now fit the 6 mm bolts and tighten them to the specified torque **(see illustration)**.

14 Install the remaining components in a reverse of the removal sequence, referring to the relevant Sections or Chapters (see Steps 1 to 4). On ZR750-J and ZR1000-A models refer to Section 4 and install the engine front bracket and mounting bolts, tightening the bolts to the specified torque settings.

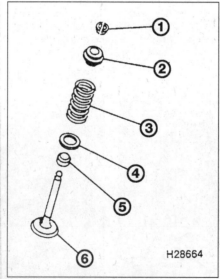

12.5 Valve components

1 Collets	5 Valve stem oil
2 Spring retainer	seal
3 Valve spring	6 Valve
4 Spring seat	

H28664

12 Cylinder head and valve overhaul

1 Because of the complex nature of this job and the special tools and equipment required, most owners leave servicing of the valves, valve seats and valve guides to a professional. However, you can make an initial assessment of whether the valves are seating correctly, and therefore sealing, by pouring a small amount of solvent into each of the valve ports. If the solvent leaks past any valve into the combustion chamber area the valve is not seating correctly and sealing.

2 With the correct tools (a valve spring compressor is essential – make sure it is suitable for motorcycle work), you can also remove the valves and associated components from the cylinder head, clean them and check them for wear to assess the extent of the work needed, and, unless seat cutting or guide replacement is required, grind in the valves and reassemble them in the head.

3 A dealer service department or specialist can replace the guides and re-cut the valve seats.

4 After the valve service has been performed, be sure to clean it very thoroughly before installation on the engine to remove any metal particles or abrasive grit that may still be present from the valve service operations. Use compressed air, if available, to blow out all the holes and passages.

Disassembly

5 Before proceeding, arrange to label and store the valves along with their related components in such a way that they can be returned to their original locations without getting mixed up **(see illustration)**. Either use the same container as the cam followers and shims are stored in (see Section 9), or obtain a separate container and label each compartment accordingly. Alternatively, labelled plastic bags will do just as well. If required unscrew the bolts securing

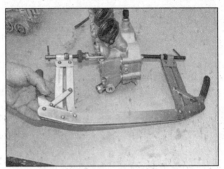

12.6a Compressing the valve springs using a valve spring compressor

12.6b Make sure the compressor locates correctly both on the top of the spring retainer . . .

12.6c . . . and on the bottom of the valve

12.7a Remove the collets . . .

12.7b . . . the spring retainer . . .

the coolant outlet pipe assembly and remove it. Discard the O-rings.

6 Compress the valve spring on the first valve with a spring compressor, making sure it is correctly located onto each end of the valve assembly (see illustration). On the top of the valve the adaptor needs to be about the same size as the spring retainer – if too big it will contact the follower bore and mark it (see Haynes Hint), and if too small it will be difficult to remove and install the collets (see illustration). On the underside of the head make sure the plate on the compressor only contacts the valve and not the soft aluminium of the head (see illustration) – if the plate is too big for the valve, use a spacer between them. Do not compress the spring any more than is absolutely necessary.

Caution: Take great care not to mark the cam follower bore with the spring compressor.

7 Remove the collets, using a magnet or a screwdriver with a dab of grease on it (see illustration). Carefully release the valve spring compressor and remove the spring retainer, noting which way up it fits, the spring and the valve (see illustrations). If the valve binds in the guide and won't pull through, push it back into the head and deburr the area around the collet groove with a very fine file or whetstone (see illustration).

8 Pull the valve stem seal off the top of the valve guide with pliers and discard it (the old seals should never be reused) (see illustration). Remove the spring seat noting

12.7c . . . the spring . . .

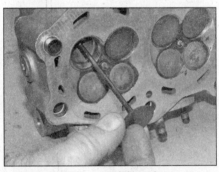

12.7d . . . and the valve

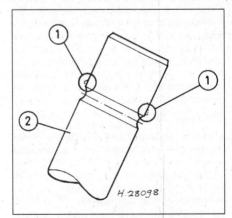

12.7e If the valve stem (2) won't pull through the guide, deburr the area above the collet groove (1)

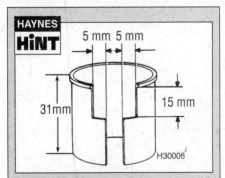

HAYNES HiNT

5 mm 5 mm

31mm

15 mm

H30006

Protect the follower bore in the cylinder head from scratches by the valve spring compressor by fabricating a shield from a 35 mm film canister cut as required.

12.8a Pull the seal off the valve stem . . .

12.8b . . . then remove the spring seat

12.15a Measure the seating surface diameter on the head (arrowed) . . .

12.15b . . . and the seat width on the valve (arrowed)

which way up it fits – using a magnet is the easiest way to remove it (see illustration).
9 Repeat the procedure for the remaining valves. Remember to keep the parts for each valve together so they can be reinstalled in the same location.
10 Clean the cylinder head with solvent and dry it thoroughly. Compressed air will speed the drying process and ensure that all holes and recessed areas are clean. Note: Do not use a wire brush mounted in a drill motor to clean the combustion chambers as the head material is soft and may be scratched or eroded away by the wire brush.
11 Clean all of the valve springs, collets, retainers and spring seats with solvent and dry them thoroughly. Do the parts from one valve

at a time so that no mixing of parts between valves occurs.
12 Remove any deposits that may have formed on the valve head using a scraper or a motorised wire brush. Again, make sure the valves do not get mixed up.

Inspection

13 Inspect the head very carefully for cracks and other damage. If cracks are found, a new head is required. Check the camshaft bearing surfaces for wear and evidence of seizure. Check the camshafts and holder for wear as well (see Section 9).
14 Using a precision straight-edge and a feeler gauge set to the warpage limit listed in the specifications at the beginning

of the Chapter, check the head gasket mating surface for warpage. Refer to Tools and Workshop Tips in the Reference section for details of how to use the straight-edge. If the head is warped beyond the limit specified at the beginning of this Chapter, consult a Kawasaki dealer or take it to a specialist repair shop for an opinion, though be prepared to have to buy a new one.
15 Examine the valve seats in the combustion chamber. If they are pitted, cracked or burned, the head will require work beyond the scope of the home mechanic. Measure the outer diameter of the seating surface and compare it to this Chapter's specifications (see illustration). Also measure the seat width on each valve and compare it to the Specifications (see illustration). If either exceeds the service limit, or if it varies around its circumference, overhaul is required.
16 Working on one valve and guide at a time clean the guide using a reamer to remove any carbon build-up – insert the reamer from the underside of the head and turn it clockwise only. Flush and clean the guide with solvent after reaming. Fit each valve in its guide in turn so that its face is above the seat. Mount a dial gauge against the side of the valve stem as close to the cylinder head as possible and measure the amount of side clearance (wobble) between the valve stem and its guide in two perpendicular directions (see illustration). If the side clearance exceeds the limit specified, remove the valve and measure the valve stem diameter (see illustration). Also measure the inside diameter of the guide with a small hole gauge and micrometer (see illustration). Measure the guides at each end and at the centre to determine if they are worn unevenly. Replace any component that is worn beyond its specifications with a new one. If the valve guide is within specifications, but is worn unevenly, it should be replaced.
17 Carefully inspect each valve face, stem and collet groove area for cracks, pits and burned spots (see illustration).
18 Rotate the valve and check for any obvious indication that it is bent, in which case it must be replaced with a new one. Using V-blocks and a dial gauge, measure the

12.16a Measure the amount of wobble using a dial gauge

12.16b Measure the valve stem diameter with a micrometer

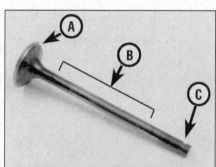

12.16c Measure the valve guide with a small bore gauge, then measure the bore gauge with a micrometer (arrowed)

12.17 Check the face (A), stem (B) and collet groove (C)

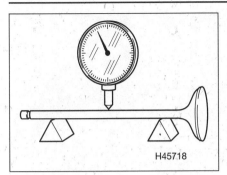

12.18 Check for any runout in the stem

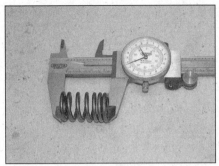

12.19 Measure the free length of the valve springs and check them for bend

12.23 Apply dabs of grinding paste round the valve face

valve stem runout and compare the results to the Specifications **(see illustration)**. If the measurement exceeds the service limit, replace the valve with a new one. Check the end of the stem for pitting and excessive wear. The presence of any of the above conditions indicates the need for valve servicing.

19 Check the end of each valve spring for wear and pitting. Measure the spring free length and compare it to the specifications **(see illustration)**. If any spring is shorter than specified it has sagged and must be replaced with a new one. Also place the spring upright on a flat surface and check it for bend by placing a ruler against it, or alternatively lay it against a set square **(see illustration 17.12b)**. If the bend in any spring is excessive, it must be replaced with a new one.

20 Check the spring seats, retainers and collets for obvious wear and cracks. Any questionable parts should not be reused, as extensive damage will occur in the event of failure during engine operation.

21 If the inspection indicates that no overhaul work is required, the valve components can be reinstalled in the head.

Reassembly

22 Unless a valve service has been performed, before installing the valves in the

head they should be ground in (lapped) to ensure a positive seal between the valves and seats. This procedure requires coarse and fine valve grinding compound and a valve grinding tool (either hand-held or drill driven – note that some drill-driven tools specify using only a fine grinding compound). If a grinding tool is not available, a piece of rubber or plastic hose can be slipped over the valve stem (after the valve has been installed in the guide) and used to turn the valve.

23 Apply a small amount of coarse grinding compound to the valve face **(see illustration)**. Smear some molybdenum disulphide oil (a 50/50 mixture of molybdenum disulphide grease and engine oil) to the valve stem, then slip the valve into the guide **(see illustration 12.7d)**. **Note:** *Make sure each valve is installed in its correct guide and be careful not to get any grinding compound on the valve stem.*

24 Attach the grinding tool to the valve and rotate the tool between the palms of your hands. Use a back-and-forth motion (as though rubbing your hands together) rather than a circular motion (i.e. so that the valve rotates alternately clockwise and anti-clockwise rather than in one direction only) **(see illustration)**. If a motorised tool is being used, take note of the correct drive speed for it – if your drill runs too fast and is not variable,

use a hand tool instead. Lift the valve off the seat and turn it at regular intervals to distribute the grinding compound properly. Continue the grinding procedure until the valve face and seat contact area is of uniform width, and unbroken around the entire circumference **(see illustration 12.15a and b)**.

25 Carefully remove the valve and wipe off all traces of grinding compound, making sure none gets in the guide. Use solvent to clean the valve and wipe the seat area thoroughly with a solvent soaked cloth.

26 Repeat the procedure with fine valve grinding compound, then use solvent to clean the valve and flush the guide, and wipe the seat area thoroughly with a solvent soaked cloth. Repeat the entire procedure for the remaining valves. On completion thoroughly clean the entire head again, then blow through all passages with compressed air. Make sure all traces of the grinding compound have been removed before assembling the head.

27 Working on one valve at a time, lay the spring seat in place in the cylinder head with its shouldered side facing up **(see illustration)**. As it is easy to cock the seat on the top of the valve guide, and then tricky to get it to sit properly, install it using a rod as a guide for it to slide down.

28 Coat the valve stem with molybdenum

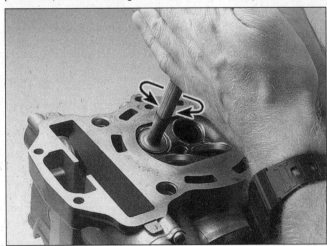

12.24 Rotate the valve grinding tool back and forth between the palms of your hands

12.27 Fit the spring seat using a rod to guide it if necessary

12.29a Fit a new valve stem seal . . .

12.29b . . . and press it squarely into place

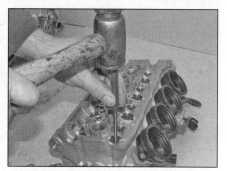

12.33 Seat the collets as described

disulphide oil (a 50/50 mixture of molybdenum disulphide grease and engine oil), then install it into its guide (see illustration 12.7d). Check that the valve moves up-and-down freely in the guide.

29 Fit a new valve stem seal over the top of the valve stem, which acts as a guide and prevents it getting cocked sideways, and onto the guide, using finger pressure, a stem seal fitting tool or an appropriate size deep socket, to push the seal squarely onto the end of the guide until it is felt to clip into place (see illustrations).

30 Next fit the spring, with its closer-wound coils facing down (see illustration 12.7c). Fit the spring retainer, with its shouldered side facing down so that it fits into the top of the springs (see illustration 12.7b).

31 Apply a small amount of grease to the collets to help hold them in place. Compress the valve spring with a spring compressor, making sure it is correctly located onto each end of the valve assembly (see Step 6) (see illustrations 12.6a, b and c). Do not compress the spring any more than is necessary to slip the collets into place. Locate each collet in turn into the groove in the valve stem using a screwdriver with a dab of grease on it (see illustration 12.7a). Carefully release the compressor, making sure the collets seat and lock in the retaining groove.

32 Repeat the procedure for the remaining valves. Remember to keep the parts for each valve together and separate from the other valves so they can be reinstalled in the same location.

33 Support the cylinder head on blocks so the valves can't contact the work surface, then tap the end of each valve stem lightly to seat the collets in their grooves (see illustration).

> **HAYNES HINT** *Check for proper sealing of the valves by pouring a small amount of solvent into each of the valve ports. If the solvent leaks past any valve into the combustion chamber the valve grinding operation on that valve should be repeated.*

34 After the cylinder head and camshafts have been installed, check the valve clearances and adjust as required (see Chapter 1). If removed, fit the coolant outlet pipe assembly using new O-rings smeared with grease. Apply a suitable thread locking compound to the bolts and tighten them to the torque setting specified at the beginning of the Chapter.

13 Cylinder block

Note: *The cylinder block can be removed with the engine in the frame. If the engine has been removed, ignore the steps which do not apply.*

Removal

1 On ZR750-L/M and ZR1000-B/C models refer to Section 4, Steps 27 and 28, and remove the engine's middle mounting bolts

and sub-frames – the engine front brackets can stay in place.

2 Remove the cylinder head (see Section 11).

3 Slacken the clamp screw securing the coolant hose to the inlet union on the back of the block and detach it, being prepared with a rag to catch any residual coolant (see illustration).

4 Pull the cylinder block up off the crankcase, supporting the pistons so the connecting rods do not knock against the crankcase (see illustration). If the block is stuck, tap around the joint faces with a soft-faced mallet. Do not attempt to free it by inserting a screwdriver between the block and crankcase mating surfaces – you'll damage them.

5 Remove the base gasket and discard it as a new one must be used. If they are loose, remove the dowels from the crankcase or the underside of the cylinder block (see illustration 13.13).

6 Stuff some clean rag around the connecting rods to protect and support them and the pistons and to prevent anything falling into the engine.

7 Clean all traces of old gasket material from the cylinder block and crankcase. If a scraper is used, take care not to scratch or gouge the soft aluminium. Be careful not to let any of the gasket material fall into the engine.

Inspection

Note: *Do not attempt to separate the cylinder liner from the cylinder block. The liner is made of aluminium and so great care must be taken not to scratch or gouge it.*

8 Check the cylinder walls carefully for scratches and score marks.

9 Using a precision straight-edge and a feeler gauge set to the warpage limit listed in the specifications at the beginning of the Chapter, check the block top surface for warpage. Take six measurements, one along each side and two diagonally across. If the block is warped beyond the limit specified at the beginning of this Chapter, consult a Kawasaki dealer or take it to a specialist repair shop for an opinion, though be prepared to have to buy a new one.

10 Using a telescoping bore gauge and a micrometer, check the dimensions of the cylinder to assess the amount of wear, taper

13.3 Slacken the clamp screw (arrowed) and detach the hose

13.4 Make sure the connecting rods do not fall against the crankcase

13.10a Measure the cylinder bore in the directions shown . . .

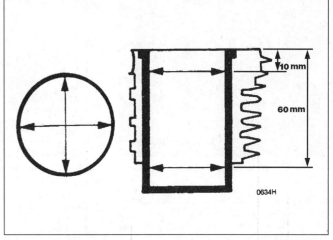

13.10b . . . using a telescoping gauge, then measure the gauge with a micrometer

13.13 Fit the dowels (arrowed) then lay the new gasket on the block

13.14 Fit two bolts as shown to act as guides

and ovality. Measure 10 mm and 60 mm from the top of the bore, both parallel to and across the crankshaft axis (see illustrations). Compare the results to the specifications at the beginning of the Chapter. If any cylinder is worn beyond the service limit, is oval or tapered, replace the block with a new one.

11 If the precision measuring tools are not available, take the cylinder block to a Kawasaki dealer or specialist motorcycle repair shop for assessment and advice.

Installation

12 Check that the mating surfaces of the cylinder block and crankcase are free from oil or pieces of old gasket.

13 If removed, fit the dowels into the crankcase and push them firmly home (see illustration). Remove the rags from around the pistons and the cam chain tunnel, taking care not to let the connecting rods fall against the crankcase, and lay the new base gasket in place, locating it over the dowels. The gasket can only fit one way, so if all the holes do not

line up properly it is the wrong way round. Never re-use the old gasket.

14 Fit two of the cylinder head bolts into two outer and diagonally opposite bolt holes in the block – these will act as guides to keep the block aligned as it is lowered (see illustration).

15 Ensure the piston ring end gaps are positioned correctly (see Section 15) (see illustration 15.12). If required, install piston ring clamps onto the pistons to ease their entry into the bores as the block is lowered. This is not essential as each cylinder has a good lead-in enabling the piston rings to be hand-fed into the bore. If possible, have an assistant to support the cylinder block while the piston rings are fed into the bore, or place equally sized wooden supports under the pistons to prevent the weight of the block pushing them down.

16 Rotate the crankshaft so that the centre pistons (Nos. 2 and 3) are at the top of their stroke. Lubricate the cylinder bores, pistons and piston rings with clean engine oil.

17 Hold the block above the pistons and

thread the two guide bolts into the holes – it is advisable to have an assistant to help do this. Carefully lower the block onto the centre pistons until the crowns fit into the bores, making sure they enter squarely and do not get cocked (see illustration).

18 Carefully compress and feed each ring into its bore as the block is lowered (see

13.17 Carefully lower the block onto the centre pistons . . .

13.18 . . . and feed the rings into the bore

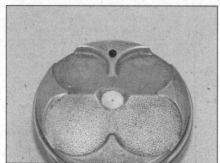

14.2 Note the mark on the piston which faces the front of the engine

14.3a Prise out the circlip using a suitable tool in the notch . . .

illustration). If necessary, use a soft mallet to gently tap the cylinder down, but do not use force if it appears to be stuck as the pistons and/or rings will be damaged.

19 When the centre pistons and rings are correctly located in the bores, carefully press the cylinder block down so that the outer piston crowns enter their bores, and feed the rings in the same way. When they have located press the block down onto the base gasket, making sure the dowels locate.

20 Hold the block down and turn the crankshaft to check that everything moves as it should. Remove the guide bolts.

21 Connect the coolant hose to its union and secure it with the clamp (see illustration 13.3).

22 Install the cylinder head (see Section 11).

23 On ZR750-L/M and ZR1000-B/C models refer to Section 4, Steps 27 and 28, and install the sub-frames and engine middle mounting bolts, tightening the bolts to the specified torque settings.

14 Pistons

Removal

1 Remove the cylinder block (see Section 13). Make sure there is plenty of rag stuffed around each connecting rod to prevent anything falling into the engine.

2 Before removing the piston from the connecting rod, use a sharp scriber or felt marker pen to write the cylinder identity on the crown of each piston (or on the inside of the skirt if the piston is dirty and going to be cleaned). Each piston crown should already be marked with a dot (though the mark is likely to be invisible until the piston is cleaned) and this mark faces the front of the engine (see illustration).

3 Carefully prise out the circlip on one side of the piston using needle-nose pliers or a small flat-bladed screwdriver inserted into the notch (see illustration). Push the piston pin out from the other side to free the piston from the connecting rod (see illustration). Remove the other circlip and discard them as new ones must be used. When the piston has been removed, slide its pin back into its bore so that related parts do not get mixed up.

 HAYNES HiNT *If a piston pin is a tight fit in the piston bosses, use a heat gun to expand the alloy piston sufficiently to release its grip on the pin. If the piston pin is particularly stubborn, extract it using a drawbolt tool, but be careful to protect the piston's working surfaces.*

4 Using your thumbs or a piston ring removal and installation tool, carefully remove the rings from the pistons (see illustrations 15.11, 15.10, 15.7c, b and a). Do not nick or gouge the pistons in the process. Carefully note which way up each ring fits and in which groove as they must be installed in their original positions if being reused. On Z750 models the upper surface of the top ring may be marked with the letter 1T at one end, and the second (middle) ring should be marked 2T On Z1000 models the upper surface of the top ring may be marked with the letter R at one end (but wasn't on the machine photographed), and the second (middle) ring should be marked RN (see illustration 15.9). The top and middle rings can also be identified by their different cross-section profiles.

5 Scrape all traces of carbon from the tops of the pistons. A hand-held wire brush or a piece of fine emery cloth can be used once most of the deposits have been scraped away. Do not, under any circumstances, use a wire brush mounted in a drill motor to remove deposits from the pistons; the piston material is soft and will be eroded away by the wire brush.

6 Use a piston ring groove cleaning tool to remove any carbon deposits from the ring grooves. If a tool is not available, a piece broken off an old ring will do the job. Be very careful to remove only the carbon deposits. Do not remove any metal and do not nick or gouge the sides of the ring grooves.

7 Once the deposits have been removed, clean the pistons with solvent and dry them thoroughly. If the identification mark previously made on the piston is cleaned off, be sure to re-mark it with the correct identity. Make sure the oil return holes below the oil ring groove are clear.

Inspection

8 Carefully inspect each piston for cracks around the skirt, at the pin bosses and at the ring lands. Normal piston wear appears as even, vertical wear on the thrust surfaces of the piston. If the skirt is scored or scuffed, the engine may have been suffering from overheating and/or abnormal combustion, which causes excessively high operating temperatures. Also check that the circlip grooves are not damaged.

9 A hole in the top of the piston, in one extreme, or burned areas around the edge of the piston crown, indicate that pre-ignition or knocking under load have occurred. If you find evidence of any problems the cause must be corrected or the damage will occur again (see *Fault Finding* in the Reference section).

10 Measure the piston ring-to-groove clearance by laying each piston ring in its groove and slipping a feeler gauge in beside it (see illustration). Make sure you have the correct ring for the groove (see Step 4). Check

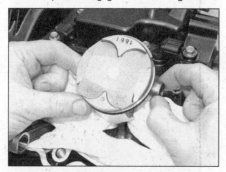

14.3b . . . then push out the pin and separate the piston from the rod

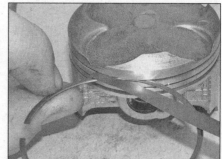

14.10 Measure the piston ring-to-groove clearance with a feeler gauge

14.11 Measure the piston diameter with a micrometer at the specified distance from the bottom of the skirt

14.12a Check for any play between the pin and its bore

14.12b Also check for freeplay between the pin and the small-end

14.16a Line the piston up with the rod and insert the pin . . .

the clearance at three or four locations around the groove. If the clearance is greater than specified, measure the thickness of each ring and the width of each groove and replace the components worn beyond their limits with new ones, though if wear like this is evident it is advisable to replace all pistons and rings as a complete new set.

11 Check the piston-to-bore clearance by measuring the bore (see Section 13), then measure the piston 5 mm up from the bottom of the skirt and at 90° to the piston pin axis **(see illustration)**. Make sure each piston is matched to its correct cylinder. Refer to the Specifications at the beginning of the Chapter and subtract the piston diameter from the bore diameter to obtain the clearance. If it is greater than the specified figure, the piston must be replaced with a new one (assuming the bore itself is within limits).

14.16b . . . then fit the circlip into its groove

12 Apply clean engine oil to the piston pin, insert it into the piston and check for any freeplay between the two **(see illustration)**. If the clearance is excessive, replace the components that are worn with new ones. Repeat the check between the pin and the connecting rod small-end **(see illustration)**.

Installation

13 Inspect and install the piston rings (see Section 15). Make sure there is plenty of rag stuffed around each connecting rod to prevent anything falling into the engine.
14 Lubricate the piston pin, the piston pin bore and the connecting rod small-end bore with molybdenum disulphide oil (a 50/50 mixture of molybdenum disulphide grease and clean engine oil).
15 When fitting the pistons onto the connecting rods make sure the dot on the

piston crown faces the front of the engine **(see illustration 14.2 and 14.3b)**.
16 Fit a *new* circlip into one side of the piston (do not reuse old circlips). Line up the piston on its correct connecting rod, and insert the piston pin from the other side **(see illustration)**. Secure the pin with the other *new* circlip **(see illustration)**. When fitting the circlips, compress them only just enough to fit them in the piston, and make sure they are properly seated in their grooves with the open end away from the removal notch.
17 Install the cylinder block (see Section 13).

15 Piston rings

Inspection

1 It is good practice to replace the piston rings with new ones when an engine is being overhauled. Before installing the new rings, check the end gaps with the rings installed in the bore, as follows.
2 Lay out each piston with its ring set and keep them together so the rings will be matched with the same piston and bore during the end gap measurement procedure and engine assembly. If the old rings are being reused, make sure they are matched with their correct piston and cylinder.
3 To measure the installed ring end gap, fit a top ring into its bore, setting it close to the bottom but above the lower limit of ring contact with the bore, and square it up with the bore walls by pushing it in with the top of the piston **(see illustration)**. Slip a feeler gauge between the ends of the ring and compare the measurement to the specifications at the beginning of the Chapter **(see illustration)**.
4 If the gap is larger or smaller than specified, double check to make sure that you have the correct rings before proceeding; excess end gap is not critical unless it exceeds the service limit.
5 If the service limit is exceeded with new rings, check the bore for wear (see Section 13). If the gap is too small, the ring ends may come in contact with each other during engine operation, which can cause serious damage.

15.3a Set the ring square in its bore using the piston . . .

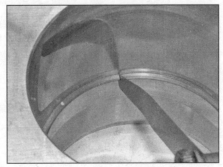

15.3b . . . and measure the end gap using a feeler gauge

15.7a Fit the oil ring expander in its groove . . .

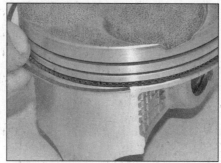

15.7b . . . then fit the lower side rail . . .

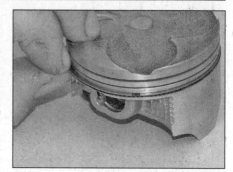

15.7c . . . and the upper side rail on each side of it

15.9 Note the marking and profile of each ring

15.10 Install the middle ring . . .

6 Repeat the procedure for the second ring, but not the three-piece oil control ring. Remember to keep the rings, pistons and bores matched up.

Installation

7 Install the oil control ring (lowest on the piston) first. It is composed of three separate components, namely the expander and the upper and lower side-rails. Slip the expander into the groove, making sure the ends butt against each other and do not overlap, then fit the lower side-rail (see illustrations). Do not use a piston ring installation tool on the side-rails as they may be damaged. Instead, place one end of the side-rail into the groove between the expander and the ring land. Hold it firmly in place and slide a finger around the piston while pushing the rail into the groove. Next, fit the upper side-rail in the same manner

(see illustration). Check that the ends of the expander have not overlapped.
8 After the three oil ring components have been installed, check to make sure that both the upper and lower side-rails can be turned smoothly in the ring groove.
9 On Z750 models the upper surface of the top ring may be marked with the letter 1T at one end, and the second (middle) ring should

be marked 2T On Z1000 models the upper surface of the top ring may be marked with the letter R at one end (but wasn't on the machine photographed), and the second (middle) ring should be marked RN (see illustration). The top and middle rings can also be identified by their different cross-section profiles.
10 Install the second (middle) ring next. Make sure that the identification letter near the end gap is facing up. Fit the ring into the middle groove in the piston (see illustration). Do not expand the ring any more than is necessary to slide it into place. To avoid breaking the ring, use a piston ring installation tool.
11 Finally, install the top ring in the same manner into the top groove in the piston (see illustration). Make sure the identification letter near the end gap (if shown) is facing up and that the chamfered edges of the ring are uppermost.
12 Once the rings are correctly installed, check they move freely without snagging and stagger their end gaps as shown (see illustration).

15.11 . . . and the top ring as described

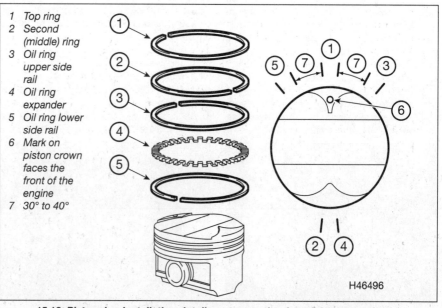

1 Top ring
2 Second (middle) ring
3 Oil ring upper side rail
4 Oil ring expander
5 Oil ring lower side rail
6 Mark on piston crown faces the front of the engine
7 30° to 40°

15.12 Piston ring installation details – stagger the ring end gaps as shown

16.1 The gear should rotate freely clockwise

16.3 Check the operation of the clutch as described

16 Starter clutch and gears

Note: *The starter clutch can be removed with the engine in the frame. If the engine has been removed, ignore the steps which do not apply.*

Check

1 The operation of the starter clutch can be checked while it is in situ. Remove the starter motor (see Chapter 8). Check that the idle/reduction gear is able to rotate freely clockwise as you look at it from the right-hand side via the starter motor aperture, but locks when rotated anti-clockwise **(see illustration)**. If not, the starter clutch is faulty and should be removed for inspection.

Removal

2 Remove the alternator rotor and the Woodruff key (see Chapter 8). Slide the starter driven gear off the end of the crankshaft **(see illustrations 16.11b)**.

Inspection

3 If separated, fit the starter driven gear into the clutch, rotating it anti-clockwise as you do to spread the rollers and allow the hub to enter. With the alternator rotor face down on a workbench, check that the starter driven gear rotates freely anti-clockwise and locks against the rotor clockwise **(see illustration)**. If it doesn't, the starter clutch should be dismantled for further investigation.

4 Withdraw the starter driven gear from the starter clutch, rotating it anti-clockwise as you do to free it from the starter clutch.

5 Check the condition of the sprags in the starter clutch and the external surface of the driven gear hub – if the sprags are damaged, marked or flattened at any point, the sprag

assembly must be replaced with a new one – see Steps 8 and 9 **(see illustration)**. If the hub is worn replace the driven gear with a new one.

6 Check the surface of the driven gear hub bush and the corresponding surface on the crankshaft **(see illustration)**.

7 Check the teeth of the reduction and idle gears and the corresponding teeth of the starter driven gear and starter motor drive shaft. Replace the gears and/or starter motor if worn or chipped teeth are discovered on related gears. Also check the idle/reduction gear shaft for damage, and check that the gear is not a loose fit on it. Check the gear shaft ends and the bores they run in for wear.

Disassembly and reassembly

8 To separate the starter clutch from the alternator rotor, counter-hold the rotor and unscrew the clutch housing bolts **(see**

16.5 Check the sprags (A) and the driven gear hub (B)

16.6 Check the bush (A) and the crankshaft (B)

16.8 Starter clutch bolts are on the inside of the rotor

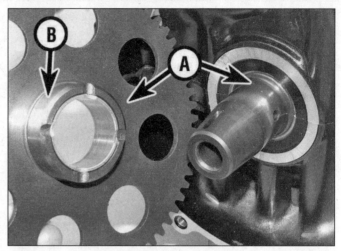

16.11a Smear molybdenum grease onto the crankshaft and gear face (A) and oil onto the hub (B)

illustration). Detach the clutch from the back of the alternator, then release the sprag assembly from the housing. Check the housing for damage and wear.

9 Fit the sprag assembly into the clutch housing locating the flange in the recess.

10 Clean the starter clutch housing bolts and apply a drop of locking compound to their threads. Fit the housing onto the back of the alternator rotor, then install the bolts and tighten them to the torque setting specified at the beginning of the Chapter **(see illustration 16.8)**.

Installation

11 Smear some molybdenum grease onto the inner flat section of the crankshaft (not the tapered section) and to the outer face of the gear where it seats on the clutch housing, and smear clean engine oil onto the outside of the starter driven gear hub where it contacts the sprags **(see illustration)**. Slide the driven gear onto the crankshaft **(see illustration)**.

12 Install the Woodruff key and alternator rotor (see Chapter 8).

17 Clutch

Note 1: *The clutch can be removed with the engine in the frame. If the engine has been removed, ignore the steps which don't apply.*

Note 2: *The clutch nut must be discarded and a new one used on installation – it is best to obtain the new nut in advance.*

Special tool: *A clutch centre holding tool will be required for this procedure (see Step 6).*

Removal

1 Drain the engine oil (see Chapter 1). On ZR1000-B/C models remove the right-hand sump cowl (see Chapter 7).

2 Refer to Section 18, Step 2 and detach the clutch cable from the engine. Position the cable clear.

3 Working evenly in a criss-cross pattern, unscrew the clutch cover bolts, on ZR1000-A models noting where the clutch cable holder locates and that the bolts are of different length **(see illustration)**. Remove the cover, turning the release lever arm back (anti-clockwise) as you do to disengage the shaft from the pull-rod. Be prepared to catch any residual oil. Remove the gasket and discard it – a new one must be used. Remove the two dowels from either the cover or the crankcase if they are loose.

4 Working in a criss-cross pattern, gradually slacken the clutch spring bolts until pressure is released **(see illustration)**. To prevent the assembly from turning, cover it with a rag and hold it securely – the bolts are not very

16.11b Slide the gear onto the shaft

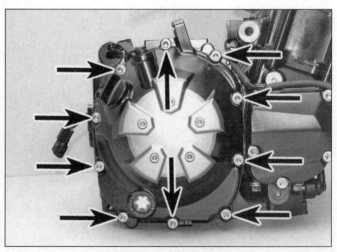

17.3 Clutch cover bolts (arrowed)

17.4a Unscrew the bolts (arrowed) and remove the springs . . .

17.4b . . . then remove the pressure plate – Z1000 shown

17.5 Remove the clutch plates, keeping them in order

tight. If available, have an assistant to hold the clutch while you unscrew the bolts. Remove the bolts, spring seats and springs, then remove the pressure plate **(see illustration)**. Remove the pull-rod from either the back of the pressure plate or the end of the shaft – on Z750 models note the thrust washer and spring on the rod and the ball bearing the pressure plate; on Z1000 models note the thrust washer and needle bearing on the rod **(see illustration 17.25a or b)**.

5 Remove the clutch friction and plain plates, hooking them out when necessary, noting how they fit and keeping them in order **(see illustration)**. Note how the tabs on the outer friction plate locate in the shallow slots in the housing, while the rest sit in the deep slots. Make sure you store the plates as a pack in the correct order. On ZR750-J1 and J2 to engine No. E026045, and on all Z1000

models, remove the anti-judder spring and spring seat, noting which way round they fit **(see illustrations 17.23b and a)**.

6 To remove the clutch nut, the input shaft must be locked. This can be done in several ways. If the engine is in the frame, engage 6th gear and have an assistant sit on the bike, holding the rear brake on hard with the rear tyre in firm contact with the ground. Alternatively, the Kawasaki service tool (Pt. No. 57001-1243) or a similar commercially available tool can be used to stop the clutch centre from turning whilst the nut is slackened **(see illustration)**. Unscrew the nut and remove the washer. Discard the nut as a new one must be used on installation.

7 Remove the clutch centre and the outer thrust washer from the shaft **(see illustrations 17.21b and a)**.

8 Ease out the clutch guide and needle

bearing from between the clutch housing and the input shaft – this can be done using a magnet, or more easily by threading a 4 mm bolt into one of the holes in the guide and using it to pull the guide out **(see illustration)**. Remove the clutch housing and the inner thrust washer, noting which way round it fits **(see illustrations)**.

Inspection

9 After an extended period of service the clutch friction plates will wear and promote clutch slip. Measure the thickness of each friction plate using a Vernier caliper **(see illustration)**. If any plate has worn to or beyond the service limits given in the Specifications at the beginning of the Chapter, or if any of the plates smell burnt or are glazed, the friction plates must be replaced with a new set.

10 The plain plates should not show any

17.6 Using a clutch holding tool while unscrewing the nut

17.8a Thread a bolt into the hole . . .

17.8b . . . then ease out the guide and bearing using the bolt as a puller . . .

17.8c . . . and remove the housing . . .

17.8d . . . and the thrust washer

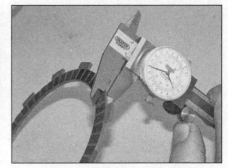

17.9 Measuring clutch friction plate thickness

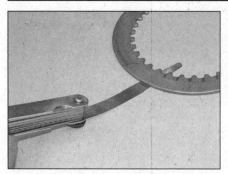

17.10 Check the plain plates for warpage

17.11 Measuring the assembled clutch plate pack thickness

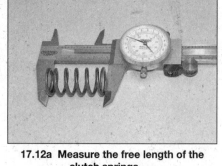

17.12a Measure the free length of the clutch springs . . .

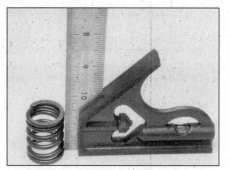

17.12b . . . and check them for bend

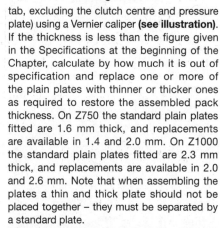

17.13a Check the friction plate tabs and housing slots . . .

signs of excess heating (bluing). Check for warpage using a flat surface and feeler gauges **(see illustration)**. If any plate exceeds the maximum permissible amount of warpage, or shows signs of bluing, all plain plates must be replaced with a new set.

11 Assemble the complete set of friction and plain plates (using new plates if new ones are needed) in the clutch centre (on ZR750-J1 and ZR750-J2 to engine No. E026045 and on all Z1000 models including the anti-judder spring seat and spring), then fit the pressure plate, making sure the castellations on its inner rim engage the slots in the clutch centre correctly (so there is no play between the plates), the springs, spring seats and bolts and tighten the bolts to the torque setting specified at the beginning of the Chapter. Measure the thickness of the complete plate pack (from the underside of the innermost friction plate tab to the outside of the outermost friction plate

tab, excluding the clutch centre and pressure plate) using a Vernier caliper **(see illustration)**. If the thickness is less than the figure given in the Specifications at the beginning of the Chapter, calculate by how much it is out of specification and replace one or more of the plain plates with thinner or thicker ones as required to restore the assembled pack thickness. On Z750 the standard plain plates fitted are 1.6 mm thick, and replacements are available in 1.4 and 2.0 mm. On Z1000 the standard plain plates fitted are 2.3 mm thick, and replacements are available in 2.0 and 2.6 mm. Note that when assembling the plates a thin and thick plate should not be placed together – they must be separated by a standard plate.

12 Measure the free length of each clutch spring using a Vernier caliper **(see illustration)**. Place each spring upright on a flat surface and check it for bend by placing

a ruler against it, or alternatively lay it against a set square **(see illustration)**. If any spring is below the minimum free length specified or if the bend in any spring is excessive, replace all the springs as a set. On ZR750-J1 and J2 to engine No. E026045, and on all Z1000 models, also check the anti-judder spring and spring seat for damage or distortion and replace them with new ones if necessary.

13 Inspect the friction plates and the clutch housing for burrs and indentations on the edges of the protruding tabs on the plates and/or the slots in the housing **(see illustration)**. Similarly check for wear between the inner teeth of the plain plates and the slots in the clutch centre **(see illustration)**. Wear of this nature will cause clutch drag and slow disengagement during gear changes as the plates will snag when the pressure plate is lifted. With care a small amount of wear can be corrected by dressing with a fine file, but if this is excessive the worn components should be replaced with new ones.

14 Inspect the needle roller bearing and the bearing surfaces in the clutch housing and on the clutch guide **(see illustration)**. If there are any signs of wear, pitting or other damage the affected parts must be replaced with new ones.

15 On Z750 models check the pressure plate and its bearing for signs of wear or damage and roughness. Check that the bearing outer race is a good fit in the centre of the plate, and that the inner race rotates freely without any rough spots. On Z1000 models check the needle bearing for wear and damage **(see illustration)**. On all models check the

17.13b . . . and the plain plate teeth and centre slots as described

17.14 Check the bearing and the bearing surfaces in the housing and on the guide

17.15a Check the needle bearing (arrowed)

17.15b Check for wear in the pull-rod end and the release lever shaft cut-out

17.16a Withdraw the shaft . . .

pull-rod end and the corresponding cut-out in the release lever shaft for signs of wear or damage **(see illustration)**. Replace any parts necessary with new ones.

16 Check the release mechanism in the clutch cover for a smooth action. If the action is stiff or rough, withdraw the shaft, noting how the return spring ends locate, and remove the

washer **(see illustration)**. Clean and check the oil seal and the two needle bearings in the cover **(see illustrations)**. The seal can be replaced by levering the old one out with a seal hook or screwdriver and pressing the new one in. Refer to *Tools and Workshop Tips* in the Reference Section for details of removing and installing needle bearings. Lubricate the

bearings with oil and the seal lips with grease before installing the shaft. Make sure the return spring ends locate correctly **(see illustration)**.
17 Check the teeth of the primary driven gear on the back of the clutch housing and the corresponding teeth of the primary drive gear on the crankshaft **(see illustration)**. Replace the clutch housing and/or crankshaft with a new one if worn or chipped teeth are discovered. Similarly check the oil pump drive and driven gear teeth.

Installation

18 Remove all traces of old gasket from the crankcase and clutch cover surfaces.
19 Slide the inner thrust washer onto the shaft with its stepped side facing in **(see illustration 17.8d)**.
20 Smear the inside and outside of the clutch guide, the inside of the clutch housing and the needle bearing with molybdenum disulphide oil (a 50/50 mixture of molybdenum disulphide grease and engine oil). Hold the clutch housing in place then slide the clutch guide and needle

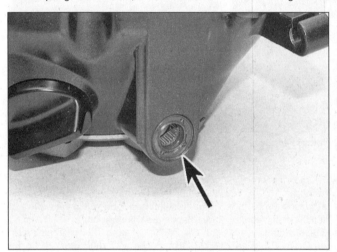

17.16b . . . and check the oil seal (arrowed) . . .

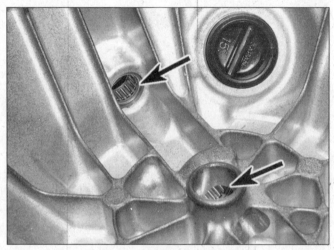

17.16c . . . and bearings (arrowed)

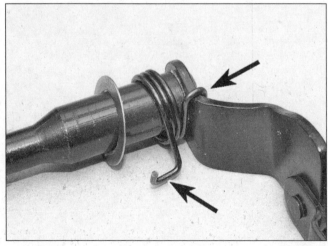

17.16d Make sure the spring ends (arrowed) locate correctly

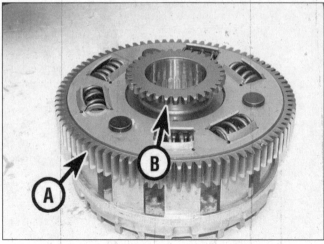

17.17 Primary drive gear (A), oil pump drive gear (B)

17.20a Locate the clutch housing then slide the bearing and guide into it

17.20b Check the teeth have meshed by turning the driven gear as described

17.21a Fit the outer thrust washer . . .

17.21b . . . and the clutch centre

17.22a Make sure the washer is the correct way round

bearing onto the shaft and into the centre of the housing **(see illustration)**. Make sure that the primary drive and driven gear teeth and the oil pump drive and driven gear teeth engage – turn the oil pump driven gear with your finger while pressing on the housing until the teeth are felt to engage and the housing moves in a bit further, then double-check by

making sure the gear can't turn independently of the housing **(see illustration)**.

21 Slide the outer thrust washer onto the shaft **(see illustration)**. Slide the clutch centre onto the shaft splines **(see illustration)**.

22 Fit the washer with its OUT SIDE mark facing out **(see illustration)**. Thread the new clutch nut onto the shaft and, using

the method employed on removal to lock the shaft (see Step 6), tighten the nut to the torque setting specified at the beginning of the Chapter **(see illustration)**.

23 On ZR750-J1 and J2 to engine No. E026045, and on all Z1000 models, fit the anti-judder spring seat into the clutch centre, then fit the spring so that its outer edge is

17.22b Fit the new clutch nut . . .

17.22c . . . and tighten it to the specified torque

17.23a Fit the anti-judder spring seat and spring . . .

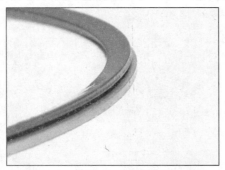

17.23b . . . so the spring's outer edge is raised off the seat

17.24a Fit a friction plate . . .

raised off the seat and facing outwards (see illustrations).

24 Coat each clutch plate with engine oil prior to installation, then build up the plates as follows: first fit a friction plate, on ZR750-J1 and J2 to engine No. E026045, and on all Z1000 models, making sure it seats around the spring and spring seat, then fit a plain plate, then alternate friction plates and plain plates until all are installed, and fit the outermost friction plate tabs into the shallow slots in the housing (see illustrations).

25 Lubricate the pull-rod bearing with oil and each end of the pull-rod with molybdenum grease. On Z750 models fit the thrust spring and washer onto the inner end of the rod, then fit the rod into the shaft (see illustration). On Z1000 models fit the needle bearing and thrust washer onto the outer end of the rod, then fit the rod into the shaft (see illustrations). Fit the pressure plate onto the clutch, aligning the dot on the plate with the line on the clutch centre rim, and engaging the castellations on its inner rim in the slots in the clutch centre (see illustration). Install the springs, spring seats and the bolts and tighten them evenly in a criss-cross sequence to the specified torque setting (see illustration). Counter-hold the clutch housing to prevent it turning when tightening the spring bolts.

26 Apply a smear of a suitable silicone sealant (ask your dealer) 10 to 15 mm each side of the crankcase joints on the mating surface with

17.24b . . . then fit a plain plate, then alternate between friction plates and plain plates

17.24c Locate the tabs on the outer friction plate into the shallow slots in the housing

17.25a Fit the thrust spring and washer onto the rod, then fit the rod into the shaft

17.25b Fit the needle bearing and washer onto the rod . . .

17.25c . . . then fit the rod into the shaft

17.25d Make sure the dot and line align and the castellations on the inner rim engage with those on the clutch centre

17.25e Fit the springs, seats and bolts

17.26a Apply the sealant around the crankcase joints

17.26b Fit the new gasket onto the dowels (arrowed)

17.26c Fit the cover making sure the release mechanism engages

18.1a On ZR750-J models slacken the locknut (arrowed)

28 Fill the engine with oil to the correct level (see Chapter 1 and *Pre-ride checks*). Adjust the clutch cable freeplay (see Chapter 1). On ZR1000-B/C models install the sump cowl (see Chapter 7).

18 Clutch cable

1 Start at the handlebar end of the cable. On ZR750-J models fully slacken the adjuster locknut **(see illustration)**. On all models thread the adjuster fully in **(see illustration)**. This provides freeplay in the cable and resets the adjuster to the beginning of its span.
2 Pull the rubber boot back off the threaded section of clutch cable set in the holder on the top of the clutch cover **(see illustration)**. Slacken the rear nut, then slip the cable out of the holder and free the end

the clutch cover **(see illustration)**. Fit the two dowels into the crankcase if removed. Fit a new gasket over the dowels **(see illustration)**. Install the cover, pulling the release lever arm back (anti-clockwise) as you do then moving it forward so that it engages behind the pull-rod end as you push the cover home on the dowels and shaft ends **(see illustration)**. Install the

bolts finger-tight, on ZR1000-A models not forgetting the clutch cable holder and making sure the different length bolts are correctly fitted, and tighten them evenly and a little at a time in a criss-cross pattern to the specified torque setting **(see illustration 17.3)**.
27 Refer to Section 18 and connect the clutch cable.

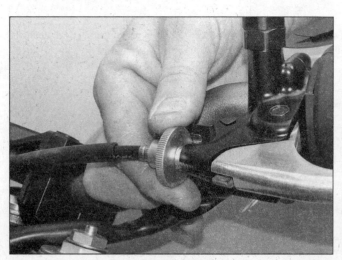

18.1b Turn the adjuster in

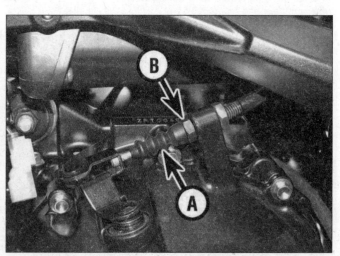

18.2a Pull back the boot (A) and slacken the nut (B) . . .

from the release lever, noting how it fits **(see illustrations)**.

3 At the handlebar end of the cable align the slot in the adjuster and locknut (where fitted) with that in the lever bracket, then pull the outer cable end from the socket in the adjuster and release the inner cable from the lever **(see illustrations)**. Remove the cable from the machine, noting its routing.

> **HAYNES HiNT**
> *Before removing the cable from the bike, tape the lower end of the new cable to the upper end of the old cable. Slowly pull the lower end of the old cable out, guiding the new cable down into position. Using this method will ensure the cable is routed correctly.*

4 Installation is the reverse of removal. Apply grease to the cable ends. Make sure the cable is correctly routed. Adjust the amount of clutch lever freeplay (see Chapter 1). On ZR750-J models tighten the locknut on completion.

19 Gearchange mechanism
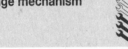

Note: *The gearchange mechanism can be removed with the engine in the frame. If the engine has been removed, ignore the steps which don't apply.*

Removal

1 Make sure the transmission is in neutral. Remove the clutch (see Section 17). Block the holes into the sump with clean rag to prevent anything falling in.

2 On ZR750-J and ZR1000-A models make an alignment mark where the slot in the gearchange linkage arm aligns with the shaft –

18.2b . . . then slip the cable out of the bracket . . .

18.2c . . . and detach the end from the lever

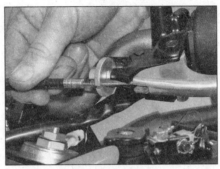

18.3a Align the slot and free the cable from the adjuster . . .

18.3b . . . and from the lever

on ZR750-L/M and ZR1000-B/C models there should already be a mark, but make your own if necessary **(see illustration 4.12)**. Unscrew the gearchange linkage arm pinch bolt and slide the arm off the shaft.

3 Wrap a single layer of thin insulating tape around the gearchange shaft splines to protect the oil seal lips as the shaft is removed.

4 Unscrew the oil pipe retainer bolts and remove the retainers, then grasp each end of the pipe and pull it out **(see illustration)**. Discard the O-rings as new ones should be used.

5 Note how the gearchange shaft centralising spring ends fit on each side of the locating pin in the casing, and how the pawls on the selector arm locate onto the pins on the end of the selector drum cam. Grasp the end of the shaft and withdraw the shaft/arm assembly **(see illustration)**.

6 To remove the stopper arm first remove the oil pump driven gear (see Section 20, Step 7). Note how the stopper arm spring ends locate and how the roller on the arm locates in the neutral detent on the selector drum cam. Unscrew the stopper arm bolt and remove the

19.4 Unscrew the bolts (arrowed) and remove the pipe

19.5 Withdraw the shaft/arm assembly, noting how it fits

19.6 Note how the spring ends locate, and how the roller sits in the neutral detent, then unscrew the bolt (arrowed) and remove the arm

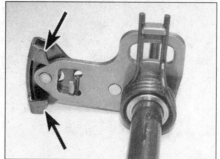

19.7a Check the selector arm pawls (arrowed) and the pins on the cam . . .

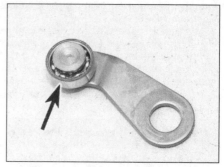

19.7b . . . and the stopper arm roller (arrowed) and the detents on the cam

arm with its collar and the spring, noting how they fit (see illustration).

Inspection

7 Check the selector arm for cracks, distortion and wear of its pawls, and check for any corresponding wear on the pins on the selector drum cam (see illustration). Also check the stopper arm roller and the detents in the cam for any wear or damage, and make sure the roller turns freely (see illustration). Replace any components that are worn or damaged with new ones. If required, remove the selector drum cam by counter-holding it and unscrewing the bolt in its centre (see illustration). Note the locating pin in the end of the drum and remove it for safekeeping

if required. On installation, locate the pin in the cut-out in the back of the cam. Apply a suitable non-permanent thread locking compound to the cam bolt and tighten it to the torque setting specified at the beginning of the Chapter.

8 Inspect the shaft centralising spring, the selector arm spring and the stopper arm return spring for fatigue, wear or damage (see illustrations). If any is found, they must be replaced with new ones. To replace the shaft spring, slide it off the shaft, noting how its ends locate and how it fits over the collar (see illustration 19.7a). Fit the new spring, locating the ends on each side of the tab. Also check that the centralising spring locating pin in the crankcase is securely tightened. If it is loose, remove it and apply a non-permanent thread locking compound to its threads, then tighten it to the specified torque. To replace

the selector arm spring note how its ends locate before unhooking it.

9 Check the gearchange shaft is straight and look for damage to the splines. If the shaft is bent you can attempt to straighten it, but if the splines are damaged the shaft must be replaced with a new one. Also check the condition of the shaft oil seal in the left-hand side of the crankcase. If it is damaged, deteriorated or shows signs of leakage it must be replaced with a new one – lever out the old seal with a seal hook or screwdriver (see illustration). With the seal removed, check the condition of the needle bearing, and replace that with a new one as well if necessary (see illustration) – refer to *Tools and Workshop Tips* for information on bearing removal and installation. Fit the new bearing and press or drive the new seal squarely into place using your fingers, a seal driver or suitable socket (see illustration).

19.7c Selector drum cam bolt (arrowed)

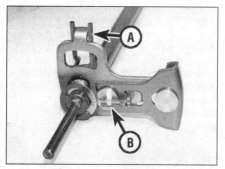

19.8a Check the centralising spring (A), the selector arm spring (B) . . .

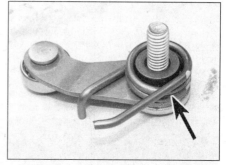

19.8b . . . and the stopper arm spring (arrowed)

19.9a Lever out the seal

19.9b Check the bearing (arrowed)

19.9c Press the new seal into its housing

19.10 Install the stopper arm and tighten the bolt

19.11 Make sure everything is correctly positioned

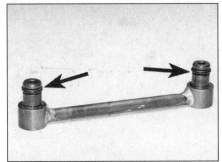

19.12a Fit a new O-ring (arrowed) onto each end of the pipe . . .

19.12b . . . then push the pipe into place . . .

19.12c . . . and secure it with the retainers and threadlocked bolts

14 Remove the insulating tape from around the gearchange shaft splines. Slide the gearchange linkage arm onto the shaft, aligning its slit with the mark made on the shaft **(see illustration 4.12)**. Install the pinch bolt and tighten it.

20 Oil pump

Note: *The oil pump can be removed with the engine in the frame. If the engine has been removed, ignore the steps which don't apply.*

Removal

Note: *When removing the rotors note which way round they fit, so that they can be returned to their original position on reassembly, thus ensuring that the mated surfaces between the two rotors continue to run together.*

1 Drain the engine oil and the coolant (see Chapter 1). Remove the water pump (see Chapter 3).

2 Slide the cover off the pump shaft **(see illustration)**. Note the locating pin on the inside of the cover and remove it for safekeeping if loose **(see illustration)**.

Installation

10 Fit the bolt through the stopper arm, then fit the collar and the return spring, making sure it is the correct way round **(see illustration 19.8b)**. Apply a suitable non-permanent thread locking compound to the bolt. Install the arm, locating the roller onto the neutral detent on the selector drum and making sure the spring ends are positioned correctly **(see illustration and 19.6)**. Tighten the bolt to the torque setting specified at the beginning of the Chapter. Install the oil pump driven gear (see Section 20, Step 7).

11 Check that the shaft centralising spring is properly positioned **(see illustration 19.7a)**. Apply some grease to the lips of the gearchange

shaft oil seal in the left-hand side of the crankcase. Slide the shaft into place and push it all the way through the case until the splined end comes out the other side **(see illustration 19.5)**. Locate the selector arm pawls onto the pins on the selector drum and the centralising spring ends onto each side of the locating pin in the crankcase **(see illustration)**.

12 Fit new O-rings smeared with grease onto the oil pipe and press it into place **(see illustrations)**. Apply a suitable non-permanent thread locking compound to the retainer bolts then fit the retainers and tighten the bolts to the specified torque **(see illustration)**.

13 Remove the rag that was blocking the sump, then install the clutch (see Section 17).

20.2a Remove the cover . . .

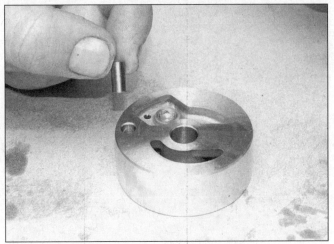

20.2b . . . and remove the locating pin

20.3a Draw the shaft and inner rotor out . . .

20.3b . . . then remove the outer rotor

20.5 Check for score marks as on this outer rotor

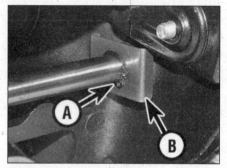

20.7a Release the circlip (A) and retrieve the shaped or plain washer (B, according to model) . . .

20.7b . . . and the plain washer (arrowed) . . .

20.7c . . . as you withdraw the gear and shaft

3 Withdraw the shaft and inner rotor **(see illustration)**. Remove the outer rotor from the pump housing **(see illustration)**. Slide the inner rotor up the pump shaft, then remove the drive pin and slide the inner rotor off **(see illustration 20.9)**.

Inspection

4 Clean all the components in solvent.
5 Inspect the pump rotors for scoring and wear. If any damage, scoring or uneven or excessive wear is evident, replace the rotors with a new pair **(see illustration)**.

6 To inspect the oil pump drive gear remove the clutch (Section 17) – the gear is on the back of the clutch housing. On all except ZR1000-A models the drive gear is integral with the clutch housing, so if the gear teeth are damaged fit a new housing.
7 To inspect the driven gear and drive shaft remove the clutch and the oil sump (Sections 17 and 21). To remove it release the circlip securing the shaft on the inside of the crankcase, then draw the gear and shaft out, retrieving the circlip and washer(s) as you do, where fitted noting how the shaped washer locates **(see illustrations)** – there are two plain washers on ZR750-J and ZR1000-A

models, one behind the circlip and one behind the gear, and one shaped washer behind the circlip and one plain washer behind the gear on ZR750-L/M and ZR1000-B/C models. On installation apply molybdenum disulphide oil (a 50/50 mixture of molybdenum disulphide grease and engine oil) to the bearing sections on the drive shaft, and make sure the plain washer(s) and shaped washer (where fitted) and circlip locate correctly – use a new circlip if the old one deformed on removal.

Installation

8 Coat the outer rotor with clean oil and fit it into the housing **(see illustration)**.

20.8 Slide the lubricated outer rotor into the housing

20.9 Fit the drive pin into the shaft and locate the inner rotor onto it

20.10a Align the shaft so it locates over the tab (arrowed) . . .

20.10b . . . and keep the rotor in position over the drive pin

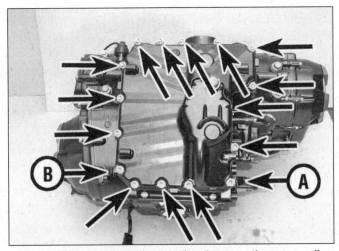

21.3 Unscrew the bolts (arrowed) and remove the sump – all models have the wiring clamp (A), models with an oxygen sensor also have the clamp (B)

21.5 Unscrew the relief valve

9 Fit the drive pin into its hole in the drive shaft, then slide the inner rotor onto the shaft so its cut-outs face the slotted inner end and locate over the pin **(see illustration)**. Coat the inner rotor with clean oil.

10 Fit the inner rotor into the outer rotor, aligning the slot in the end of the pump shaft

21.6 Ease the L-shaped pipe up out of its sockets

with the tab on the end of the drive shaft so they engage, and keeping a finger on the inner rotor so it does not get pushed back as the drive pin could then drop out **(see illustrations)**. Make sure the locating pin is on the inside of the cover, then fit the cover, locating the pin in its hole **(see illustrations 20.2b and a)**.

11 Install the water pump (Chapter 3). Replenish the engine oil and coolant (Chapter 1).

21 Oil sump, oil strainer and pressure relief valve

Note: *The oil sump, strainer and pressure relief valve can be removed with the engine in the frame. If the engine has been removed, ignore the steps which don't apply.*

Removal

1 On ZR1000-B/C models remove the sump

cowls (see Chapter 7). Drain the engine oil (see Chapter 1).

2 While the oil is draining, remove the exhaust downpipe assembly (see Chapter 4).

3 Unscrew the sump bolts, slackening them evenly in a criss-cross sequence to prevent distortion, and noting the position(s) of the wiring clamp(s) **(see illustration)**. Remove the sump and discard the gasket.

4 Pull the strainer out, noting how it locates **(see illustration 21.12b)**. Remove the rubber seal and discard it as a new one must be used **(see illustration 21.12a)**.

5 Unscrew the pressure relief valve **(see illustration)**.

6 If required (for removal of the selector drum and forks or crankcase separation) grasp the L-shaped oil pipe on the underside of the crankcase and ease it out of its three sockets simultaneously **(see illustration)**. Discard the O-rings as new ones should be used.

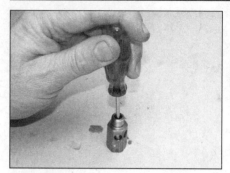

21.9 Push the plunger into the body and check that it moves smoothly

21.10 Fit a new O-ring onto each of the pipe nozzles (arrowed)

21.12a Lubricate the rubber seal and fit it into the crankcase . . .

Inspection

7 Remove all traces of gasket from the sump and crankcase mating surfaces, and clean the inside of the sump with solvent. Blow the sump dry with compressed air if available.

8 Clean the oil strainer in solvent and remove any debris caught in the mesh. If the strainer gauze is damaged, replace the strainer with a new one.

9 Push the relief valve plunger into the valve body and check that it moves smoothly and freely against spring pressure (see illustration). If not, replace the relief valve with a new one.

Installation

10 Fit new O-rings smeared with grease onto the L-shaped oil pipe nozzles (see illustration). Push the pipe into its sockets (see illustration 21.6).

11 Apply a smear of suitable locking compound to the threads of the pressure relief valve, making sure none gets near the oil passage. Fit the valve and tighten it to the torque setting specified at the beginning of the Chapter (see illustration 21.5).

12 Fit a new rubber seal smeared with clean oil into the strainer orifice in the crankcase

(see illustration). Do not fit it onto the strainer as it may distort when the strainer is fitted onto the pump. Fit the strainer, locating the tabs on either side of the crankcase rib (see illustration).

13 Lay a new gasket onto the sump (if the engine is in the frame) or onto the crankcase (if the engine has been removed and is upside down) (see illustration). Position the sump onto the crankcase. Fit the bolts with the wiring clamp(s) and tighten them finger-tight (see illustration 21.3). Now tighten the bolts evenly and a little at a time in a criss-cross pattern to the specified torque.

14 Install the exhaust (see Chapter 4).

15 Fill the engine with the correct type and quantity of oil as described in Chapter 1. Start the engine and check that there are no leaks around the sump.

16 On ZR1000-B/C models install the sump cowls (See Chapter 7).

22 Selector drum and forks

Note: The selector drum and forks can be

removed with the engine in the frame, though the procedure is considerably easier with the engine removed and placed upside-down on a bench – there is no need to separate the crankcase halves. If the engine has been removed, ignore the steps which don't apply.

Removal

1 The selector drum and forks are located in the lower crankcase half. For easiest access remove the engine (see Section 4) and rest it upside down, using blocks of wood to support it so that any projecting parts are not taking any excess weight.

2 Remove the gearchange mechanism (Section 19) and the oil sump, strainer and L-shaped oil pipe (Section 21).

3 Before removing the selector forks, note that each fork is marked with a 3-digit number that faces the right-hand side of the engine (see illustration 22.6). Mark the forks using a felt pen according to their location to aid identification on installation.

4 Unscrew the selector drum bearing/fork shaft retainer plate bolt and screw and remove

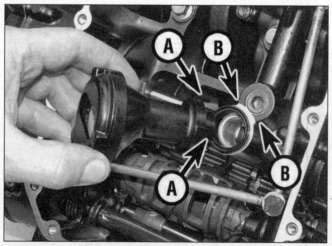

21.12b . . . then fit the strainer, locating the tabs (A) on each side (B)

21.13 Fit a new gasket

22.4 Undo the screw and the bolt (arrowed) and remove the plate

22.5 Withdraw the selector drum

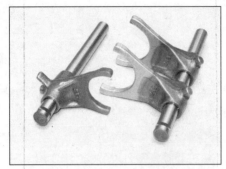

22.6 Keep the forks on the shafts in the correct order

the plate, noting how it fits **(see illustration)**.
5 Support the selector forks and withdraw the shafts from the casing **(see illustrations 22.16b and a)**. Pivot the fork guide pins out of the selector drum tracks, then withdraw the drum from the right-hand side of the engine **(see illustration)**.
6 Remove the forks **(see illustration 22.14a)**. Slide each one back onto its shaft to keep them in the correct order **(see illustration)**.

Inspection

7 Inspect the selector forks for any signs of wear or damage, especially around the fork ends where they engage with the groove in the pinion **(see illustration)**. Check that each fork fits correctly in its pinion groove. If the forks are in any way damaged they must be replaced with new ones.
8 Measure the thickness of the fork ends and the width of the groove in the relative pinion and compare the readings to the specifications. Replace the forks and/or gear pinions with new ones if they are worn beyond their specifications.
9 Check closely to see if the forks are bent. Check that the forks fit correctly on their shaft **(see illustration)**. They should move freely with a light fit but no appreciable freeplay. Check that the fork shaft holes in the casing are neither worn nor damaged.
10 Check each fork shaft is straight by rolling it along a flat surface. A bent rod will cause difficulty in selecting gears and make the

gearchange action heavy. Replace the shaft with a new one if it is bent.
11 Inspect the selector drum grooves and selector fork guide pins for signs of wear or damage **(see illustration)**. Measure the width of each groove and the diameter of the relative guide pin and compare the readings to the specifications. If either component shows signs of wear beyond their specifications or damage the fork(s) and/or drum must be replaced with new ones.
12 Check that the selector drum bearing rotates freely and has no sign of freeplay between it and the casing **(see illustration)**. To fit a new bearing, remove the selector drum cam by unscrewing the bolt in its centre – pass a rod through the drum to counter-hold it **(see illustration)**. Note the locating pin in the end of the drum and remove it for safekeeping if required. Remove the old bearing using a

puller if necessary and fit a new one (see *Tools and Workshop Tips* in the Reference Section if necessary). Install the selector drum cam, locating the pin in the cut-out in the back of the cam. Apply a suitable non-permanent thread locking compound to the cam bolt and tighten it to the torque setting specified at the beginning of the Chapter.

Installation

13 Prior to installation lubricate all moving and contacting surfaces (i.e. fork ends, pinion grooves, guide pins, selector drum grooves, fork shafts and bores) with molybdenum disulphide oil (a 50/50 mixture of molybdenum disulphide grease and engine oil).
14 Fit each selector fork into the groove in its related pinion – the outer forks are identical and locate in the pinions in the output shaft

22.7 Check the fork ends and pinion grooves

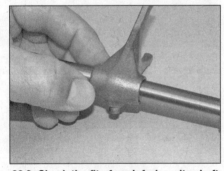

22.9 Check the fit of each fork on its shaft

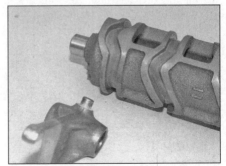

22.11 Check the guide pins and their grooves in the drum

22.12a Check the bearing (arrowed)

22.12b Counter-hold the drum and unscrew the bolt (arrowed)

22.14a Locate the outer forks in the output shaft and the centre fork in the input shaft . . .

22.14b . . . and position them as shown so they are clear of the drum

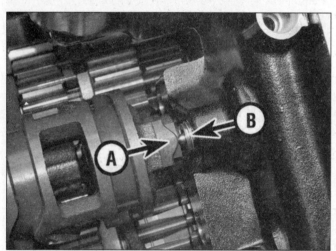

22.15 Position the drum so the raised neutral contact (A) is against the neutral switch plunger (B)

22.16a Slide the front shaft through the centre fork . . .

(see illustration). The smaller fork is the centre fork and locates in the pinion on the input shaft. Make sure they are the correct way round so the guide pins will locate in the selector drum tracks, but position them clear at the moment to allow the drum to be inserted (see illustration).

15 Slide the selector drum into position in

22.16b . . . and the rear shaft through the outer forks

the crankcase (see illustration 22.5). Make sure the drum end locates into its bore in the casing, and position it with the neutral contact against the neutral switch (see illustration).

16 Slide each fork shaft in turn into the crankcase with the groove for the retainer plate outermost, locating each selector fork's guide pin in its groove in the selector drum and

22.17 Manoeuvre the plate into position and locate it in the groove in each shaft

sliding the shaft through each fork and into its bore in the crankcase (see illustrations).

17 Clean the threads of the retainer plate bolt and screw then apply a suitable non-permanent thread locking compound. Fit the plate and tighten the bolt and screw to the torque settings specified at the beginning of the Chapter (see illustration).

18 Install the gearchange mechanism (Section 19) and the oil sump, strainer and L-shaped oil pipe (Section 21).

23 Crankcases

Note: *To separate the crankcase halves, the engine must be removed from the frame.*

Separation

1 To access the connecting rods, crankshaft, bearings and transmission shafts, the crankcase must be split into its two halves.

23.4 An example of a cardboard template to store crankcase bolts

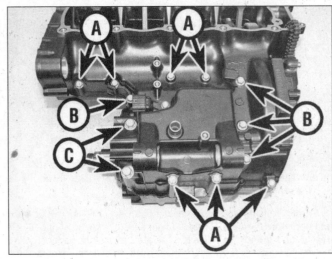

23.5 Upper crankcase 6 mm bolts (A), 7 mm bolts (B) and 8 mm bolts (C)

2 Before the crankcases can be separated the following components must be removed:
Valve cover (Section 7)
Camshafts (Section 9) – see Note
Cylinder head (Section 11) – see Note
Cylinder block (Section 13) – see Note
Pistons (Section 14) – see Note
Alternator (Chapter 8)
Starter clutch (Section 16)
Cam chain tensioner and guide blades (Section 10) – see Note
Clutch (Section 17)
Water pump (Chapter 3)
Gearchange mechanism (Section 19) – see Note
Oil cooler – Z1000 (Section 6)
Starter motor (Chapter 8) – see Note
Crankshaft position (CKP) sensor and timing rotor (Chapter 4)
Oil pump, if required (Section 20)
Oil sump, strainer and pressure relief valve (Section 21)
Selector drum and forks (Section 22) – see Note

Note: If the crankcases are being separated to inspect the crankshaft without removing it, the camshafts and top-end can remain in situ. To remove the crankshaft without removing the connecting rods and pistons, the camshafts must be removed but the head can stay. To inspect or remove the transmission shafts, the camshafts and cylinder head can remain in situ. However, if removal of the connecting rod assemblies is intended, full disassembly of the top-end is necessary to remove the pistons from the rods. The gearchange mechanism can remain in situ unless the selector drum and forks are being removed.

3 If not already done remove the engine's upper rear mounting bolt damping rubbers – lever them apart using a screwdriver between the inner ends (**see illustration 4.34a**).
4 Make a cardboard template punched with holes to match all the bolts in each crankcase half – as each crankcase bolt is removed, store it in its relative position in the template (**see illustration**). This will ensure all bolts and washers and any wiring clamps are installed in

the correct location on reassembly. Note that new copper sealing washers should be used on assembly where fitted, though keep the old ones with the bolts for the time being as a guide for reassembly.
5 Unscrew the seven 6 mm, the four 7 mm and the two 8 mm upper crankcase bolts in that order, evenly, a little at a time and in a criss-cross sequence until they are finger-tight, then remove them and fit them in the template, along with the wiring clamps (**see illustration**).
6 Turn the engine upside down.
7 Unscrew the six 7 mm bolts along the front evenly, a little at a time and working from the outside to the centre, until they are finger-tight, then remove them and fit them in the template (**see illustration**).
8 Now unscrew the ten crankshaft journal 9 mm bolts evenly, a little at a time and in a **reverse** of the tightening sequence shown and as cast into the crankcase adjacent to each bolt, i.e. starting from the outside and working to the centre, until they are finger-tight, then remove them (**see illustrations**).

23.7 Lower crankcase 7 mm bolts (arrowed)

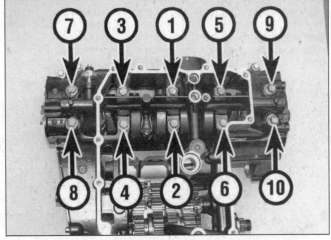

23.8a Crankshaft journal 9 mm bolts numbered in their TIGHTENING sequence

23.8b The sequence numbers are cast into the crankcase adjacent to each bolt

23.9 Carefully separate the crankcase halves

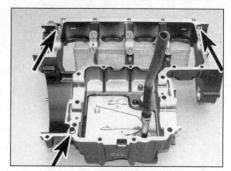

23.11 Remove the dowels (arrowed) if they are loose

9 Carefully lift the lower crankcase half off the upper half, using a soft-faced hammer to tap around the joint to initially separate the halves if necessary **(see illustration)**. **Note:** *If the halves do not separate easily, make sure all fasteners have been removed. Do not try and separate the halves by levering against the crankcase mating surfaces as they are easily scored and will leak oil in the future if damaged.* The lower crankcase half will come away with the selector drum and forks (unless they have been removed), leaving the crankshaft and transmission shafts in the upper crankcase half.

10 As required remove the crankshaft and connecting rods and the transmission shafts, and if not already done the selector drum and forks, speed sensor (ZR750-L/M and ZR1000-B/C models), neutral switch and oil pressure switch, referring to the relevant Sections of this Chapter, and to Chapter 8 for the speed sensor and oil pressure and neutral switches. If there are any other components or assemblies covered elsewhere that have not been removed as part of your stripdown procedure, for example the starter motor, remove these as well, referring to the relevant Chapter.

11 Remove the three locating dowels from the crankcase if they are loose (they could be in either crankcase half) **(see illustration)**.

12 If required, on ZR750-L/M models unscrew the two piston oil jet bolts and remove the jets **(see illustration)**. Discard their O-rings. If required unscrew the crankcase breather plate bolts and remove the plate **(see illustration)**.

13 Remove all traces of old sealant from the mating surfaces of the crankcases and those of the upper crankcase and the breather plate. Clean up minor damage to the surfaces with a fine sharpening stone or grindstone.

14 Clean the crankcases thoroughly with new solvent and dry them with compressed air. Blow out all oil passages with compressed air. Clean the inside of the oil level inspection window.

Caution: Be very careful not to nick or gouge the crankcase mating surfaces or oil leaks will result. Check both crankcase halves very carefully for cracks and other damage.

Inspection

15 Small cracks or holes in aluminium castings can be repaired with an epoxy resin adhesive as a temporary measure. Permanent repairs can only be done by argon-arc welding, and only a specialist in this process is in a position to advise on the economy or practical aspect of such a repair, although some of the low temperature kits such as Lumiweld are suitable for small repairs. If any damage is found that can't be repaired, replace the crankcase halves as a set.

16 Damaged threads can be reclaimed using a diamond section wire insert, for example of the Heli-Coil type (though there are other makes), which are easily fitted after drilling and re-tapping the affected thread.

17 Sheared studs or screws can usually be removed with extractors, which consist of a tapered, left-hand thread screw of very hard

steel. These are inserted into a pre-drilled hole in the stud, and usually succeed in dislodging the most stubborn stud or screw. If a stud has sheared above its bore line, it can be removed using a conventional stud extractor which avoids the need for drilling.

> **HAYNES HINT** *Refer to Tools and Workshop Tips for details of installing a thread insert and using screw extractors.*

Reassembly

18 On ZR750-L/M models fit new O-rings smeared with grease onto the two piston oil jets and fit them into the oil passages **(see illustration)**. Apply a suitable thread locking compound to the bolts and tighten them to the torque setting specified at the beginning of the Chapter.

19 Apply a 1 to 1.5 mm bead of suitable sealant (Three-Bond (TB1207B) or equivalent sealant) to the mating surface of the crankcase breather plate, then fit the plate. Apply a suitable thread locking compound to the bolts and tighten them to the torque setting specified for your model **(see illustration 23.12b)**.

20 If removed, fit the three locating dowels into the upper crankcase half **(see illustration 23.11)**.

21 Install all components and their bearings in place in the upper and lower crankcase halves (see Step 10). If the transmission shafts have not been removed, check the condition of the oil seal on the left-hand end of the

23.12a Piston oil jet bolts (arrowed)

23.12b Crankcase breather plate bolts (arrowed)

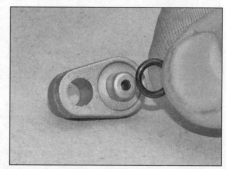

23.18 Fit new O-rings onto the oil jets

23.23a Apply the sealant . . .

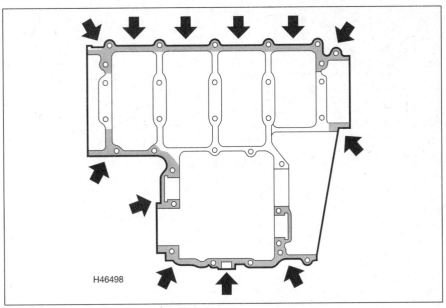
H46498

23.23b . . . to the area shown

output shaft and replace it with a new one if it is damaged or deteriorated or shows signs of leakage – it is highly advisable to fit a new one as a matter of course **(see illustration 27.4)**.

22 Generously lubricate the crankshaft and transmission shafts, particularly around the bearings, with clean engine oil, then use a rag soaked in high flash-point solvent to wipe over the mating surfaces of both crankcase halves to remove all traces of oil.

23 Apply and evenly spread a small amount of suitable sealant (Kawasaki-Bond 92104-1062 or equivalent RTV sealant) to the outer mating surface of the lower crankcase half as shown **(see illustrations)**.

Caution: Apply the sealant only to the shaded areas. Do not apply an excessive amount as it will ooze out when the case halves are assembled and may obstruct oil passages. Do not apply the sealant close to any of the bearing shells or surfaces, or oil passages.

24 Check again that all components are in position, particularly that the bearing shells are still correctly located in the lower crankcase half. Carefully fit the lower crankcase half down onto the upper crankcase half, making sure the dowels all locate correctly, and if installed the selector forks locate correctly in their pinion grooves **(see illustration 23.9)**.

25 Check that the lower crankcase half is correctly seated.

Caution: The crankcase halves should fit together without being forced. If the casings are not correctly seated, remove the lower crankcase half and investigate

23.26 Clean the bolts, fit new washers with the outer bolts, and lubricate them as described

the problem. Do not attempt to pull them together using the crankcase bolts as the casing will crack and be ruined.

26 Clean the ten crankshaft journal 9 mm bolts, then apply molybdenum disulphide oil (a 50/50 mixture of molybdenum disulphide grease and engine oil) under the heads and to the lower sides of the new copper washers with the outer bolts **(see illustration)**. Secure the bolts finger-tight at first, then tighten them evenly and a little at a time in the numerical sequence shown to the torque setting specified for your model at the beginning of the Chapter **(see illustrations 23.8a and b)**.

27 Clean the threads of the six 7 mm lower crankcase bolts and insert them in their original locations **(see illustration 23.7)**. Secure all bolts finger-tight at first, then tighten the 7 mm bolts, working from the centre outwards to the specified torque. Now tighten the 6 mm bolts to the specified torque settings.

28 Turn the engine over. Clean the threads of the two 8 mm bolts, the four 7 mm bolts and the seven 6 mm bolts and insert them in their original locations **(see illustration 23.5)**. Secure the bolts finger-tight at first, then tighten the 8 mm bolts first, then the 7 mm bolts and finally the 6 mm bolts, to the specified torque settings.

29 With all crankcase fasteners tightened, check that the crankshaft and transmission shafts rotate smoothly and easily. Check that the transmission shafts rotate freely and independently in neutral, then when installed rotate the selector drum by hand and select each gear in turn whilst rotating the output shaft as fast as possible – because of the positive neutral selector mechanism the output shaft has to turn fast enough to create enough centrifugal force for the steel balls to be flung out to free the 5th gear, otherwise it will remain locked to the shaft and you will not

be able to select gears properly. Check that all gears can be selected and that the shafts rotate freely in every gear. If there are any signs of undue stiffness, tight or rough spots, or of any other problem, the fault must be rectified before proceeding further.

30 Fit the rubber dampers into the upper rear engine mountings using a lubricant to help them in **(see illustrations 4.34a and b)** – make sure they are fully home (tap them in with a rubber mallet or use a drawbolt arrangement – refer to *Tools and Workshop Tips*) otherwise they will get in the way when fitting the engine back into the frame.

31 Install all other removed assemblies in a reverse of the sequence given in Step 2.

24 Connecting rod and main bearing information

1 Even though new main and connecting rod bearings are generally fitted during engine overhaul, the old bearings should be retained for close examination as they may reveal valuable information about the condition of the engine.

2 Bearing failure occurs mainly because of lack of lubrication, the presence of dirt or other foreign particles, overloading the engine and/or corrosion. Regardless of the cause of bearing failure, it must be corrected before the engine is reassembled to prevent it from happening again.

3 When examining the bearings, lay them out on a clean surface in the same general position as their location on the crankshaft journals. This will enable you to match any noted bearing problems with the corresponding crankshaft journal.

4 Dirt and other foreign particles get into the

engine in a variety of ways. They may be left in the engine during assembly or they may pass through filters or breathers, then get into the oil and from there into the bearings. Metal chips from machining operations and normal engine wear are often present. Abrasives are sometimes left in engine components after reconditioning operations, especially when parts are not thoroughly cleaned using the proper cleaning methods. Whatever the source, foreign objects often end up imbedded in the soft bearing material and are easily recognised. Large particles will not embed in the bearing and will score or gouge the bearing and journal. The best prevention for this cause of bearing failure is to clean all parts thoroughly and keep everything spotlessly clean during engine reassembly. Regular oil and filter changes are also recommended.

5 Lack of lubrication or lubrication breakdown has a number of interrelated causes. Excessive heat (which thins the oil), overloading (which squeezes the oil from the bearing face) and oil leakage or throw off (from excessive bearing clearances, worn oil pump or high engine speeds) all contribute to lubrication breakdown. Blocked oil passages will starve a bearing of lubrication and destroy it. When lack of lubrication is the cause of bearing failure, the bearing material is wiped or extruded from the steel backing of the bearing. Temperatures may increase to the point where the steel backing and the journal turn blue from overheating. Refer to *Tools and Workshop Tips* in the Reference section at the end of this manual for bearing fault finding.

6 Riding habits can have a definite effect on bearing life. Full throttle low, speed operation, or labouring the engine, puts very high loads on bearings, which tend to squeeze out the oil film. These loads cause the bearings to flex, which produces fine cracks in the bearing face (fatigue failure). Eventually the bearing material will loosen in pieces and tear away from the steel backing. Short trip riding leads to corrosion of bearings, as insufficient engine heat is produced to drive off the condensed water and corrosive gases produced. These products collect in the engine oil, forming acid and sludge. As the oil is carried to the engine bearings, the acid attacks and corrodes the bearing material.

7 Incorrect bearing installation during engine assembly will lead to bearing failure as well. Tight fitting bearings which leave insufficient bearing oil clearances result in oil starvation. Dirt or foreign particles trapped behind a bearing insert result in high spots on the bearing which lead to failure.

8 To avoid bearing problems, clean all parts thoroughly before reassembly, double check all bearing clearance measurements and lubricate the new bearings with clean engine oil during installation.

25 Crankshaft and main bearings

Note: *To remove the crankshaft the engine must be removed from the frame and the crankcase halves separated.*

Removal

1 Remove the engine from the frame (see Section 4) and separate the crankcase halves (see Section 23).

2 Before removing the crankshaft insert a feeler gauge between the crankshaft web and the No. 2 main bearing journal and check the side clearance **(see illustration)**. Compare the measurement with this Chapter's Specifications. If the clearance is excessive, replace the crankcase halves as a set.

3 If the crankshaft is being removed by itself and the top-end and pistons have not been removed, refer to Section 26 and detach the connecting rods, then push the rods and pistons up the bores so that the bottom ends are clear of the crankshaft, taking care to keep the rods clear of the cylinder liners.

4 Lift the crankshaft out of the upper crankcase half, along with the connecting rods if not detached, and the cam chain, taking care not to dislodge the main bearing shells **(see illustration)**. If required detach the connecting rods (see Section 26), and remove the cam chain.

5 If required remove the main bearing shells from the crankcase halves **(see illustration)**. Keep the shells in order – they must be returned to their original location.

Inspection

6 Clean the crankshaft with solvent, squirting it under pressure through all the oil passages. If available, blow the crank dry with compressed air, and also blow through the oil passages. Check the primary drive gear for wear or damage **(see illustration)**. If any of the main gear teeth are excessively worn, chipped or broken, the crankshaft must be replaced with a new one. If wear or damage is found, also inspect the primary driven gear on the back of the clutch housing (see Section 17). Also check the cam chain sprocket, and in relation to that the chain and the sprockets on the camshafts.

7 Refer to Section 24 and examine the main bearing shells. If they are scored, badly scuffed or appear to have been seized, new bearings must be installed. Always replace the main bearings as a set. If they are badly damaged, check the corresponding crankshaft journals. Evidence of extreme heat, such as discoloration, indicates that lubrication failure has occurred. Be sure to thoroughly check the oil pump and pressure relief valve as well as all oil holes and passages before reassembling the engine.

8 Give the crankshaft journals a close visual examination, paying particular attention where damaged bearings have been discovered. If the journals are scored or pitted in any way a new crankshaft will be required. Note that undersizes are not available, precluding the option of regrinding the crankshaft.

9 Place the crankshaft on V-blocks and check the runout at the main bearing journals using a dial gauge. Compare the reading to the maximum specified at the beginning of the

25.2 Check crankshaft side clearance using a feeler gauge

25.5 Remove the shells from their housings

25.4 Lift the crankshaft out of the crankcase

25.6 Check the primary drive gear (A) and the cam chain sprocket (B) for wear and damage

25.14 Lay a strip of Plastigauge along the centreline of each journal

25.17 Compare the width of the crushed Plastigauge with the scale provided

25.21 Measure the diameter of each main journal

Chapter. If the runout exceeds the limit, the crankshaft must be replaced with a new one.

Oil clearance check

10 Whether new bearing shells are being fitted or the original ones are being reused, the main bearing oil clearance should be checked before the engine is reassembled. Main bearing oil clearance is measured with a product known as Plastigauge.

11 Clean the backs of the bearing shells and the bearing housings in both crankcase halves.

12 Press the bearing shells into their correct locations. Make sure the tab on each shell engages in the notch in the casing **(see illustration 25.28a)**, and that the grooved shells are fitted to journals 1, 2 and 4 (left-to-right) **(see illustration 25.28b)**. Take care not to touch any shell's bearing surface with your fingers.

13 Ensure the shells and crankshaft are clean and dry. Lay the crankshaft in position in the upper crankcase **(see illustration 25.4)**. Install the three crankcase dowels if removed **(see illustration 23.11)**.

14 Cut five lengths of the appropriate size Plastigauge (they should be slightly shorter than the width of the crankshaft journals). Place a strand of Plastigauge on each (cleaned) journal, avoiding the oil hole **(see illustration)**. Make sure the crankshaft is not rotated.

15 Carefully fit the lower crankcase half onto the upper half **(see illustration 23.9)**. Check

that the lower half is correctly seated. **Note:** *Do not tighten the crankcase bolts if the casing is not correctly seated.* Clean the ten crankshaft journal 9 mm bolts, then apply molybdenum disulphide oil (a 50/50 mixture of molybdenum disulphide grease and engine oil) under the heads and to the lower sides of the copper washers (use the old ones) with the outer bolts **(see illustration 23.26)**. Secure the bolts finger-tight at first, then tighten them evenly and a little at a time in the numerical sequence shown to the torque setting specified for your model at the beginning of the Chapter **(see illustrations 23.8a and b)**.

16 Slacken the bolts evenly and a little at a time in a reverse of the tightening sequence, i.e. starting from the outside and working to the centre, until they are all finger-tight, then remove the bolts. Carefully lift off the lower crankcase half, making sure the Plastigauge is not disturbed.

17 Compare the width of the crushed Plastigauge on each crankshaft journal to the scale printed on the Plastigauge envelope to obtain the main bearing oil clearance **(see illustration)**. Compare the reading to the specifications at the beginning of the Chapter.

18 On completion carefully scrape away all traces of the Plastigauge material from the crankshaft journal and bearing shells; use a fingernail or other object which is unlikely to score them.

19 If the oil clearance falls into the specified range, no bearing replacement is required

(provided they are in good shape). If the clearance is between the maximum standard specification and the service limit, replace all the old bearing shells with new shells that have blue paint marks **(see illustration 25.26)**, then check the oil clearance once again.

20 The new clearance can slightly exceed the maximum standard clearance, but it must not be less than the minimum standard clearance.

21 If the clearance is greater than the service limit listed in this Chapter's Specifications, measure the diameter of the crankshaft journals with a micrometer and compare your findings with this Chapter's Specifications **(see illustration)**. Also, by measuring the diameter at a number of points around each journal's circumference, you'll be able to determine whether or not the journal is out-of-round. Take the measurement at each end of the journal, near the crank throws, to determine if the journal is tapered.

22 If any crank journal has worn down past the service limit, replace the crankshaft with a new one.

23 If the diameters of the journals aren't less than the service limit but differ from the original size according to the markings on the crankshaft in relation to the specifications given at the beginning of the Chapter, apply new marks with a hammer and punch, then select new bearing shells according to the new size marks (Steps 25 and 26).

24 Remove the main bearing shells and assemble the case halves (see Step 15). Using a telescoping gauge and a micrometer, measure the diameters of the main bearing bores, then compare the measurements with the marks on the upper case half. They should correspond.

Main bearing shell selection

25 Replacement bearing shells for the main bearings are supplied on a selected fit basis. Code marks and numbers stamped on the crankshaft and crankcase are used to identify the correct replacement bearings. The crankshaft main bearing journal size numbers are stamped on the crankshaft web adjacent to the journal and will be either unmarked or marked 1 **(see illustration)**. The corresponding main bearing housing size marks are stamped into the front of the upper

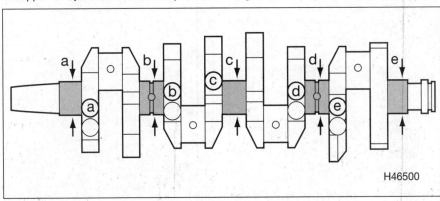

H46500

25.25a Circles denote location of main bearing journal markings. Letters indicate relevant journal

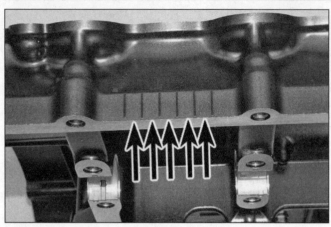

25.25b Main bearing housing mark locations (arrowed) – these are all unmarked

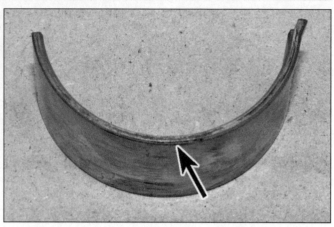

25.26 The colour code is marked on the side of the shell (arrowed)

crankcase half and will be either unmarked or marked O (see illustration). The left-hand mark corresponds to the left-hand housing, and the marks correspond consecutively from left to right.

26 A range of bearing shells is available. To select the correct bearing for a particular journal, use the table below and cross-refer the main bearing journal size mark (stamped on the crank web) with the main bearing housing size mark (stamped on the crankcase) to determine the colour code of the bearing required. The colour is marked on the side of the shell (see illustration). Note that the shells for journals 1, 2 and 4 (left-to-right) have an oil groove, while 3 and 5 don't – make sure you obtain the correct number of each type when ordering replacement shells.

Main bearing journal code	Main bearing housing code	Replacement bearing colour
1	O	Brown
1	None	Black
None	O	Black
None	None	Blue

Installation

27 Clean the backs of the bearing shells and the bearing cut-outs in both crankcase halves.

If new shells are being fitted, ensure that all traces of the protective grease are cleaned off using paraffin (kerosene). Wipe the shells and crankcase halves dry with a lint-free cloth. Make sure all the oil passages and holes are clear, and blow them through with compressed air if it is available.

28 Press the bearing shells into their correct locations. Make sure the tab on each shell engages in the notch in the casing (see illustration), and that the grooved shells are fitted to journals 1, 2 and 4 (left-to-right) (see illustration). Take care not to touch any shell's bearing surface with your fingers. Lubricate each shell with molybdenum disulphide oil (a 50/50 mixture of molybdenum disulphide grease and clean engine oil).

29 If detached fit the connecting rods onto the crankshaft (see Section 26). Fit the cam chain around the sprocket (see illustration 10.5).

30 Lubricate the crankshaft journals with molybdenum disulphide oil (a 50/50 mixture of molybdenum disulphide grease and clean engine oil). Lower the crankshaft into position in the upper crankcase, making sure all bearings remain in place (see illustration 25.4).

31 If the crankshaft was removed by itself and the top-end and pistons were not removed, carefully pull the connecting rods onto the crankpins, then refer to Section 26 and fit the caps onto the rods.

32 Check that the crankshaft rotates easily.

Check to make sure that all components have been returned to their original locations using the marks made on disassembly.

33 Reassemble the crankcase halves (see Section 23).

26 Connecting rods and bearings

Note 1: *To remove the connecting rods the engine must be removed from the frame and the crankcases separated.*
Note 2: *The connecting rod bolts can only be used in a running engine once, though they can be used when performing the oil clearance check. If new connecting rods are fitted they will come with nuts and bolts.*

Removal

1 Remove the engine from the frame (see Section 4) and separate the crankcase halves (see Section 23). Remove the crankshaft (Section 25).

2 Before removing the rods from the crankshaft, measure the side clearance (the gap between the connecting rod big-end and the crankshaft web) with a feeler gauge (see illustration). If the clearance is greater than the service limit listed in this Chapter's Specifications, replace the rods with new

25.28a Locate the tab on the bearing in the notch (arrowed)

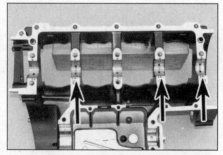

25.28b Make sure the grooved shells are correctly positioned (arrowed) – upper crankcase shown upside-down

26.2 Check connecting rod side clearance using a feeler gauge

26.3 Note the letter across the rod and cap, and note which way it faces

26.4a Unscrew the nuts (arrowed) . . .

26.4b . . . and detach the caps and rods

ones. If the clearance is still excessive, replace the crankshaft with a new one.

3 Using paint or a felt marker pen, mark the relevant cylinder identity across the cap-to-connecting rod join on one side and mark which side of the rod and cap faces the front of the engine to ensure that they are fitted the same way on reassembly. Note that the letter already across the rod and cap indicates rod weight – all rods should have the same letter for proper balance **(see illustration)**.

4 Unscrew the bearing cap nuts, separate the cap from the rod, then detach the rod from the crankshaft **(see illustrations)**. If the cap is stuck, tap on the ends of the rod bolts with a soft-faced hammer to free them. Unless an oil clearance check is being done remove the bolts from the rod and discard the nuts and bolts as new ones must be used **(see illustration)**.

Caution: The connecting rod bolts are designed to stretch when they are tightened. NEVER reuse the old bolts.

5 Keep the rod, cap, bolts (if they are to be used for an oil clearance check), and the bearing shells (if they are to be reused) together in their correct positions to ensure correct installation – fit the caps back onto the rods and finger-tighten the nuts to make sure.

Inspection

6 Check the connecting rods for cracks and other obvious damage.

7 If not already done (Section 14), apply clean engine oil to the piston pin, insert it into the connecting rod small-end and check for any

freeplay between the two **(see illustration 14.12b)**. If the clearance is excessive, replace the components that are worn with new ones.

8 Refer to Section 24 and examine the connecting rod bearing shells. If they are scored, badly scuffed, corroded, or appear to have seized, new shells must be installed. Remove them if required by pushing their centres out to the side then lifting them out **(see illustration)**. Always replace the shells in the connecting rods as a set. If they are badly damaged, check the corresponding crankpin. Evidence of extreme heat, such as discoloration, indicates that lubrication failure has occurred. Be sure to thoroughly check the oil pump and pressure relief valve as well as all oil holes and passages before reassembling the engine.

9 Have the rods checked for twist and bend by a Kawasaki dealer if you are in doubt about their straightness.

Oil clearance check

10 If the bearings and journals appear to be in good condition, check the oil clearances as follows:

11 Start with the rod for the number one cylinder. Wipe the bearing shells and the connecting rod and cap clean, using a lint-free cloth. Install the bearing shells in the connecting rod and cap. Make sure the tab on the bearing engages the notch in the rod or cap **(see illustration 26.24)**.

12 Wipe off the No. 1 crankpin with a lint-free cloth. Lay a strip of Plastigauge across the top of the crankpin, parallel with the axis **(see illustration 25.14)**.

13 Position the connecting rod on the bottom of the crankpin, then fit the cap **(see illustration 26.4b)**. Fit the nuts and tighten them to the torque setting specified in this Chapter's Specifications (for a used con-rod and old nuts), then tighten them further through 120° using a degree disc **(see illustrations 26.26b and c)**. Do not allow the connecting rod to rotate at all.

 HAYNES HiNT *If a degree disc is not available, the angle can be determined by using the points on the connecting rod cap nut. There are six points on the nut, so the angle between each point is 60°. Select one point as a reference and mark it with paint or a marker. Now select the second point clockwise from it and mark its position on the connecting rod cap. Tighten the nut – when the mark on the first point aligns with the mark made on the connecting rod cap, it will have turned through 120°.*

14 Unscrew the nuts and remove the connecting rod and cap, being very careful not to disturb the Plastigauge. Compare the width of the crushed Plastigauge to the scale printed in the Plastigauge envelope to determine the bearing oil clearance **(see illustration 25.17)**.

15 If the clearance is within the range listed in this Chapter's Specifications and the bearings are in perfect condition, they can be reused. If the clearance is between the maximum standard specification and the service limit, replace all the bearing shells with shells that have blue paint marks, then check the oil clearance once again **(see illustration 25.26)**.

16 The new clearance can slightly exceed the maximum standard clearance, but it must not be less than the minimum standard clearance.

17 If the clearance is greater than the service limit listed in this Chapter's Specifications, measure the diameter of the big-end journal (crankpin) on the crankshaft with a micrometer and compare your findings with this Chapter's

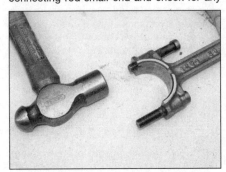

26.4c Knock the old bolts out and discard them

26.8 Remove the shells from the rod and cap

26.17 Measure the diameter of the big-end journal

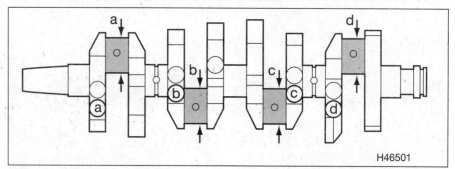

H46501

26.22 Circles denote big-end journal marking locations. Letters indicate relevant journal

Specifications **(see illustration)**. Also, by measuring the diameter at a number of points around the pin's circumference, you'll be able to determine whether or not it is out-of-round. Take the measurement at each end to determine if the journal is tapered.

18 If any crankpin has worn down past the service limit, replace the crankshaft with a new one.

19 If the diameters of the crankpins aren't less than the service limit but differ from the original size according to the markings on the crankshaft in relation to the specifications given at the beginning of the Chapter, apply new marks with a hammer and punch, then select new bearing shells according to the new size marks (Steps 22 and 23).

20 Remove the bearing shells from the connecting rod and cap, then assemble the cap to the rod. Tighten the nuts to the

torque and angle listed in this Chapter's Specifications.

21 Using a telescoping gauge and a micrometer, measure the inside diameter of the connecting rod big-end. The mark on the connecting rod (if any) should coincide with the measurement according to the specifications, but if it doesn't, make a new mark.

Bearing shell selection

22 Replacement bearing shells for the big-end bearings are supplied on a selected fit basis. Code marks stamped on the crankshaft and connecting rod are used to identify the correct replacement bearings. The big-end journal size marks are stamped on the crankshaft web adjacent to the journal and will be either unmarked or marked O **(see illustration)**. The connecting rod size mark is on the flat face of the connecting rod and cap and will be either

unmarked or marked with a circle around the weight mark **(see illustration 26.3)**.

23 A range of bearing shells is available. To select the correct bearings for a particular journal, use the table below and cross-refer the big-end journal size mark (stamped on the crank web) with the big-end housing size mark (stamped on the connecting rod) to determine the colour code of the bearing required. The colour is marked on the side of the shell **(see illustration 25.26)**.

Crankpin code	Connecting rod big-end code	Replacement bearing colour
O	None	Brown
None	None	Black
O	O	Black
None	O	Blue

Installation

24 Work on one rod at a time. Wipe off the bearing shells and connecting rod and cap. Fit the shells, using your hands only, making sure the tabs engage with the notches **(see illustration)**. Lubricate the shells with molybdenum disulphide oil (a 50/50 mixture of molybdenum disulphide grease and clean engine oil). Don't get any lubricant on the mating surfaces of the rod or cap.

25 Clean the new connecting rod bolts (and nuts if used) with solvent to remove the anti-rust coating then dry them using compressed air. Fit the bolts into the rod, aligning their flats so the head will seat in its cut-out; tap them lightly with a hammer if necessary to make sure they are correctly seated **(see illustrations)**. Assemble the connecting rod on its crankpin, making sure the previously applied matchmarks align and face the correct way (see Step 3) **(see illustration 26.4b)**. **Note:** *The letter present at the rod/ cap seam on one side of the connecting rod is a weight mark* **(see illustration 26.3)**. All rods should have the same letter on them to minimise vibration.

26 Apply a small amount of molybdenum disulphide oil to the threads of the bolts and the seating surface of the nuts. Fit the nuts and tighten them to the appropriate torque

26.24 Fit each shell into its housing making sure the tab locates in its notch (arrowed)

26.25a Fit the new bolts . . .

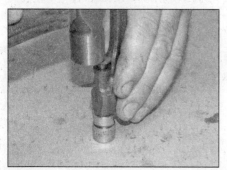

26.25b . . . and tap them into place, using a socket to support the rod and allow the bolt through . . .

26.25c . . . making sure the heads align correctly

26.26a Fit the nuts . . .

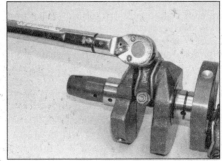

26.26b . . . and tighten them as described first to the specified torque . . .

26.26c . . . and then through the specified angle

setting listed in this Chapter's Specifications, then tighten them through the specified angle using a degree disc (see *Haynes Hint* above) **(see illustrations)**.

27 Turn the rod on the crankshaft. If it feels tight, tap on the cap with a hammer – this should relieve stress and free it up. If it doesn't, recheck the bearing clearance. Fit the other rods.

28 Install the crankshaft (see Section 25).

29 Reassemble the crankcase halves (see Section 23).

27 Transmission shaft removal and installation

Note: *To remove the transmission shafts the*

engine must be removed from the frame and the crankcases separated.

Removal

1 Remove the engine from the frame and separate the crankcase halves (see Section 23).

2 Lift the output shaft and input shaft out of the crankcase, noting their relative positions in the crankcase and how they fit together **(see illustrations)**. If they are stuck, use a soft-faced hammer and gently tap on the ends of the shafts to free them.

3 If required, remove the caged-ball bearing half-ring retainers and the needle bearing dowel pins from the upper crankcase half, noting how they fit **(see illustrations)**. If they are not in their slots or holes in the crankcase, remove them from the bearings themselves on the shafts.

4 Remove the oil seal from the left-hand end of the output shaft and discard it as a new one must be used **(see illustration)**.

5 If necessary, the input shaft and output shaft can be overhauled (see Section 28).

6 Referring to *Tools and Workshop Tips* in the Reference Section, check the bearings. Replace them with new ones if necessary.

Installation

7 Apply some grease to the lips of the new oil seal **(see illustration)**. Fit the seal onto the left-hand end of the output shaft **(see illustration 27.4)**.

8 If removed, fit the needle bearing dowels into their holes in the upper crankcase half, and fit the caged-ball bearing half-ring retainers into their slots **(see illustrations 27.3b and a)**.

9 Lower each shaft into position in the crankcase half **(see illustrations 27.2b**

27.2a Remove the output shaft . . .

27.2b . . . and the input shaft

27.3a Remove the retainers from their grooves . . .

27.3b . . . and the dowels from their holes

27.4 Remove the oil seal and discard it

27.7 Smear the lips of the seal with grease

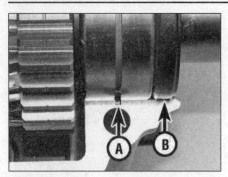

27.9 Make sure each ring (A) and the oil seal (B) seat correctly

and a) – make sure the hole in each needle bearing engages correctly with its dowel, and the groove in each caged-ball bearing engages correctly with the bearing half-ring retainer, and the oil seal seats correctly **(see illustration)**.

10 Make sure both transmission shafts are correctly seated and their related pinions are correctly engaged.
Caution: If the caged-ball bearing half-ring retainers or needle bearing dowel pins are not correctly engaged, the crankcase halves will not seat correctly.
11 Position the gears in the neutral position and check the shafts are free to rotate easily and independently (i.e. the input shaft can turn whilst the output shaft is held stationary) before proceeding further.
12 Reassemble the crankcase halves (see Section 23).

28 Transmission shaft overhaul

1 Remove the transmission shafts from

the crankcase (see Section 27). Always disassemble the transmission shafts separately to avoid mixing up the components **(see illustrations)**.

> **HAYNES HiNT** *When disassembling the transmission shafts, place the parts on a long rod or thread a wire through them to keep them in order and facing the proper direction.*

Input shaft
Disassembly

2 Remove the needle bearing outer race, then remove the snap-ring from the end of the shaft and slide the bearing off **(see illustrations 28.21d, b and a)**.
3 Slide the thrust washer and the 2nd gear

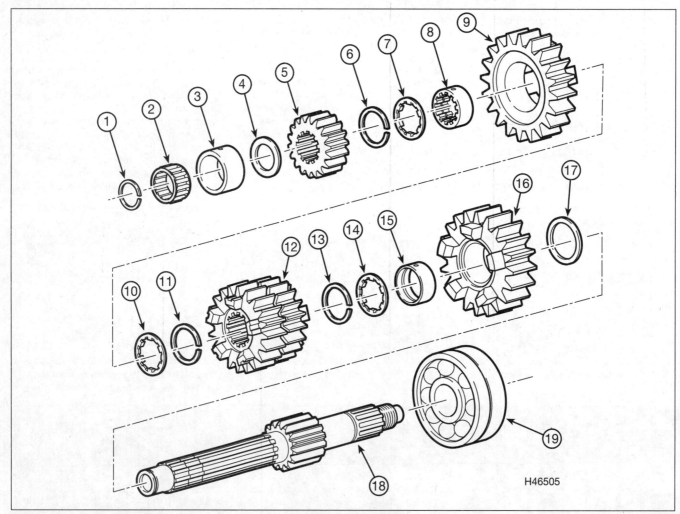

28.1a Transmission input shaft components

1 Snap ring	6 Circlip	11 Circlip	15 5th gear pinion bush
2 Needle bearing	7 Splined washer	12 Combined 3rd/4th gear	16 5th gear pinion
3 Outer race	8 6th gear pinion splined bush	pinion	17 Thrust washer
4 Thrust washer	9 6th gear pinion	13 Circlip	18 Input shaft/1st gear pinion
5 2nd gear pinion	10 Splined washer	14 Splined washer	19 Ball bearing

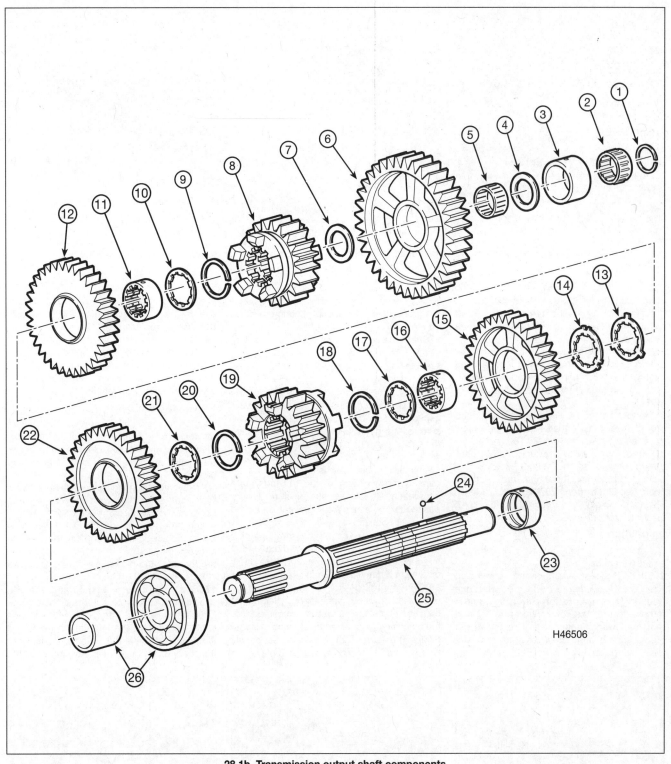

28.1b Transmission output shaft components

1 Snap ring	8 5th gear pinion	15 4th gear pinion	21 Splined washer
2 Needle bearing	9 Circlip	16 4th gear pinion splined	22 2nd gear pinion
3 Outer race	10 Splined washer	bush	23 2nd gear pinion bush
4 Thrust washer	11 3rd gear pinion splined bush	17 Splined washer	24 Steel balls
5 Needle bearing	12 3rd gear pinion	18 Circlip	25 Output shaft
6 1st gear pinion	13 Tabbed lockwasher	19 6th gear pinion	26 Ball bearing and
7 Thrust washer	14 Slotted washer	20 Circlip	spacer

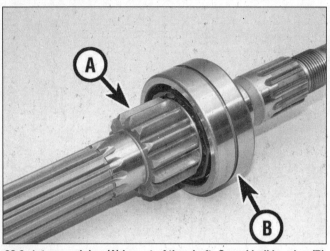

28.6 1st gear pinion (A) is part of the shaft. Caged ball bearing (B)

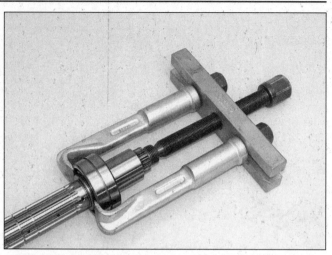

28.8 Using a puller to remove a bearing from the output shaft

pinion off the left-hand end of the shaft – note which way around the pinion is fitted by marking its outer face **(see illustrations 28.20b and a)**.

4 Remove the circlip securing the 6th gear pinion then slide the splined washer, the pinion, its splined bush and the splined washer off the shaft **(see illustrations 28.19e, d, c, b and a)**.

5 Remove the circlip securing the combined 3rd/4th gear pinion, then slide the pinion off the shaft **(see illustrations 28.18b and a)**.

6 Remove the circlip securing the 5th gear pinion, then slide the splined washer, the pinion, its bush and the thrust washer off the shaft **(see illustrations 28.17e, d, c, b and a)**. The 1st gear pinion is integral with the shaft **(see illustration)**.

Inspection

7 Wash all of the components in clean solvent and dry them off.

8 Check the caged-ball bearing, referring to *Tools and Workshop Tips* in the Reference Section **(see illustration 28.6)**. If required remove it from the shaft using a puller and replace it with a new one – if removing the output shaft bearing draw the spacer off with the bearing **(see illustration)**. Drive the new

bearing on using a suitable bearing driver – the groove in the input shaft bearing must be on the outside.

9 Check the gear teeth for cracking, chipping, pitting and other obvious wear or damage. Any pinion that is damaged as such must be replaced with a new one.

10 Inspect the dogs and the dog holes in the gears for cracks, chips, and excessive wear especially in the form of rounded edges. Make sure mating gears engage properly. Replace the paired gears as a set if necessary.

11 Check for signs of scoring or bluing on the pinions, bushes and shaft. This could be caused by overheating due to inadequate lubrication. Check that all the oil holes and passages are clear. Replace any damaged pinions or bushes.

12 Check that each pinion moves freely on the shaft or its bush but without undue freeplay. Check that each bush moves freely on the shaft but without undue freeplay.

13 The shaft is unlikely to sustain damage unless the engine has seized, placing an unusually high loading on the transmission, or the machine has covered a very high mileage. Check the surface of the shaft, especially where a pinion turns on it, and replace the

shaft if it has scored or picked up, or if there are any cracks. Damage of any kind can only be cured by replacement.

14 Check the washers and circlips and replace any that are bent or appear weakened or worn. Use new ones if in any doubt. Note that it is good practice to renew all circlips when overhauling gearshafts.

Reassembly

15 During reassembly, apply molybdenum disulphide oil (a 50/50 mixture of molybdenum disulphide grease and clean engine oil) to the mating surfaces of the shaft, pinions and bushes.

16 When installing the circlips, do not expand their ends any further than is necessary and position them with each end aligned with a spline **(see illustration 28.17f)**. Make sure the round edged side of the circlip faces the direction thrust so the sharp edged side takes the thrust of the pinion it seats against **(see illustration 28.31)**.

17 Slide the thrust washer and the 5th gear pinion bush onto the shaft, then fit the 5th gear pinion onto the bush with its dogs facing away from the integral 1st gear **(see illustrations)**. Slide the splined washer onto the shaft, then fit the circlip, making sure that

28.17a Slide the thrust washer . . .

28.17b . . . the 5th gear pinion bush . . .

28.17c . . . the 5th gear pinion . . .

28.17d . . . and the splined washer onto the shaft . . .

28.17e . . . and secure them with the circlip . . .

28.17f . . . making sure it locates properly in its groove

it locates correctly in the groove in the shaft **(see illustrations)**.

18 Slide the combined 3rd/4th gear pinion onto the shaft with the smaller 3rd gear pinion facing the 5th gear pinion, and aligning the oil holes **(see illustration)**. Fit the circlip, making

sure it is locates correctly in its groove in the shaft **(see illustrations)**.

19 Slide the splined washer onto the shaft, followed by the 6th gear pinion splined bush, aligning the oil hole in the bush with the hole in the shaft **(see illustrations)**. Slide the

6th gear pinion onto the bush, making sure its dogs face the 3rd/4th gear pinion **(see illustration)**. Slide the splined washer onto the shaft, then fit the circlip, making sure that it locates correctly in the groove in the shaft **(see illustrations)**.

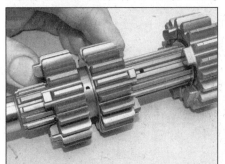

28.18a Slide the combined 3rd/4th gear pinion onto the shaft . . .

28.18b . . . and secure it with the circlip . . .

28.18c . . . making sure it locates properly in its groove

28.19a Slide the splined washer . . .

28.19b . . . the 6th gear pinion splined bush . . .

28.19c . . . the 6th gear pinion . . .

28.19d . . . and the splined washer onto the shaft . . .

28.19e . . . and secure them with the circlip . . .

28.19f . . . making sure it locates properly in its groove

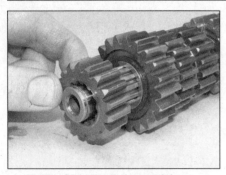

28.20a Slide the 2nd gear pinion . . .

28.20b . . . and the thrust washer onto the shaft

28.21a Slide the needle bearing on . . .

28.21b . . . then fit the snap ring . . .

28.21c . . . locating it in the groove

28.21d Fit the outer race over the bearing

20 Slide the 2nd gear pinion onto the end of the shaft with the mark made on removal facing out so it is the same way round **(see illustration)**. Fit the thrust washer **(see illustration)**.

21 Slide the needle bearing on, then fit the snap-ring into its groove **(see illustrations)**. Fit the outer race over the needle bearing **(see illustration)**.

22 Check that all components have been correctly installed **(see illustration)**.

Output shaft

Disassembly

23 Remove the needle bearing outer race, then remove the snap-ring from the end of the shaft and slide the bearing off **(see illustrations 28.38d, b and a)**.

24 Slide the thrust washer off the shaft, followed by the 1st gear pinion, the needle bearing and the thrust washer **(see illustrations 28.37d, c, b and a)**.

25 The fifth gear pinion has three steel balls

in it for the positive neutral finder mechanism. These lock fifth gear to the shaft unless it is spun rapidly enough to fling the balls outward. To remove fifth gear, place the shaft vertical with 5th gear uppermost, then spin the shaft by the 3rd gear pinion while pulling fifth gear up **(see illustration)**; it may take several tries to disengage fifth gear from the shaft, but it will slide off easily once it is disengaged – make sure it doesn't fly off the top of the shaft as you remove it as the steel balls will drop out. After fifth gear is removed, collect the

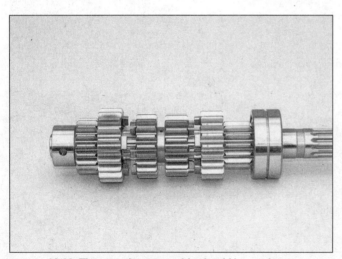

28.22 The complete assembly should be as shown

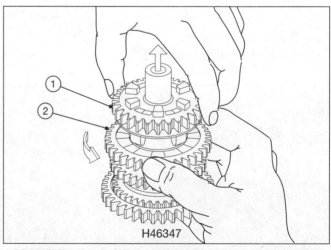

28.25 Pull up on the 5th gear pinion (1) whilst spinning the 3rd gear pinion (2)

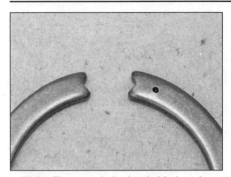

28.31 The rounded edged side is quite easy to distinguish, and here is marked by a punch

28.32a Slide the 2nd gear pinion bush . . .

28.32b . . . the 2nd gear pinion . . .

three steel balls from the slots inside it (see illustration 28.36a).

Caution: Don't pull the gear up too hard or fast – the balls will fly out of the gear.

26 Remove the circlip securing the 3rd gear pinion, then slide the splined washer, the pinion and its splined bush off the shaft (see illustrations 28.35d, c, b and a).

27 Slide the tabbed lockwasher off the shaft, noting how it engages the slotted washer, then turn the slotted washer to align the splines and slide it off (see illustrations 28.34f, e, and d). Slide the 4th gear pinion and its splined bush, followed by the splined washer, off the shaft (see illustrations 28.34c, b and a).

28 Remove the circlip securing the 6th gear pinion, then slide the pinion off the shaft (see illustrations 28.33b and a).

29 Remove the circlip securing the 2nd gear pinion, then slide the splined washer, the pinion and its bush off the shaft (see illustrations 28.32d, c, b and a).

Inspection

30 Refer to Steps 7 to 14 above.

Reassembly

31 During reassembly, apply molybdenum disulphide oil (a 50/50 mixture of molybdenum disulphide grease and clean engine oil) to the mating surfaces of the shaft, pinions and bushes. When installing the circlips, do not expand their ends any further than is necessary and position them with each end aligned with a spline (see illustration 28.32e). Make sure the round edged side of the circlip faces the direction thrust so the sharp edged

side takes the thrust of the pinion it seats against (see illustration).

32 Slide the 2nd gear pinion bush onto the shaft, then slide the 2nd gear pinion onto the bush with its shouldered side facing the bearing, followed by the splined washer (see illustrations). Fit the circlip, making sure it is locates correctly in its groove in the shaft (see illustrations).

33 Slide the 6th gear pinion onto the shaft with its selector fork groove facing away from the 2nd gear pinion, then fit the circlip, making sure it is locates correctly in its groove in the shaft (see illustrations).

34 Slide the splined washer and the 4th gear pinion splined bush onto the shaft, making sure the oil holes in the bush align with the hole in the shaft, then slide the 4th gear pinion

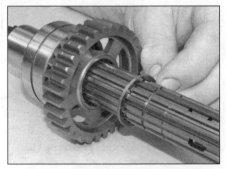

28.32c . . . and the splined washer onto the shaft . . .

28.32d . . . and secure them with the circlip . . .

28.32e . . . making sure it locates in the groove

28.33a Slide the 6th gear pinion onto the shaft . . .

28.33b . . . and secure it with the circlip . . .

28.33c . . . making sure it locates in the groove

28.34a Slide the splined washer . . .

28.34b . . . the 4th gear pinion splined bush . . .

28.34c . . . and the 4th gear pinion onto the shaft

28.34d Fit the slotted washer . . .

28.34e . . . then turn it so the splines lock in the groove

onto its bush with its open side facing the 6th gear pinion (see illustrations). Slide the slotted washer onto the shat then turn it in its groove to offset the splines (see illustrations). Slide the tabbed lockwasher onto the shaft and engage its tabs in the slots of the slotted washer (see illustration).

35 Slide the 3rd gear pinion splined bush onto the shaft, making sure the oil holes in the bush align with the hole in the shaft, then slide the 3rd gear pinion onto the bush with its recessed side facing away from the 4th gear pinion (see illustration). Slide the splined washer on, then fit the circlip, making sure it is locates correctly in its groove in the shaft (see illustrations).

28.34f Locate the tabs on the lockwasher into the slots

28.35a Slide the 3rd gear pinion bush . . .

28.35b . . . the 3rd gear pinion . . .

28.35c . . . and the splined washer onto the shaft . . .

28.35d . . . and secure them with the circlip . . .

28.35e . . . making sure it locates in the groove

28.36a Fit the steel balls into the holes . . .

28.36b . . . with the narrower outer ends

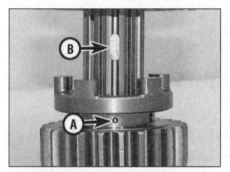

28.36c Place the 5th gear pinion on the bench as shown and fit the shaft into it making sure the splines with the balls (A) align with the slots (B) in the shaft . . .

28.36d . . . then pull the gear up onto the shaft

28.36e Make sure the balls have locked the pinion as described

36 Lubricate the positive neutral finder mechanism balls with engine oil – don't use grease as it will impair the action of the mechanism. Fit the balls into the holes with the narrow outer ends in the 5th gear pinion (see illustrations). Place the 5th gear pinion onto the bench with its selector fork groove facing up. Place the end of the output shaft down into the gear and hold the shaft vertical – the spline grooves in the gear that contain the holes with the balls must align with the slots in the shaft spline grooves (see illustration). Lift the gear up the shaft until it is in place, then tilt the shaft horizontal and turn it slowly, then check that the pinion cannot slide off (see illustrations).

37 Slide the thrust washer and the 1st gear pinion needle bearing onto the shaft, then slide the pinion onto the bearing with its more recessed side facing the 5th gear pinion (see illustration). Fit the thrust washer (see illustration).

28.37a Slide the thrust washer . . .

28.37b . . . the needle bearing . . .

28.37c . . . the 1st gear pinion . . .

28.37d . . . and the thrust washer onto the shaft

28.38a Slide the needle bearing on . . .

28.38b . . . then fit the snap ring . . .

28.38c . . . locating it in the groove

38 Slide the needle bearing on, then fit the snap-ring into its groove **(see illustrations)**. Fit the outer race over the needle bearing **(see illustration)**.
39 Check that all components have been correctly installed **(see illustration)**.

29 Running-in procedure

1 Make sure the engine oil and coolant levels are correct (see *Pre-ride checks*). Make sure there is fuel in the tank.
2 Turn the engine kill switch to the ON position and shift the gearbox into neutral. Turn the ignition ON.
3 Start the engine and allow it to run at a moderately fast idle until it reaches operating temperature.

 Warning: If the oil pressure warning light doesn't go off, or if it comes on while the engine is running, stop the engine immediately.

4 If a lubrication failure is suspected, stop the engine immediately and try to find the cause. If an engine is run without oil, even for a short period of time, severe damage will occur.

28.38d Fit the outer race over the bearing

5 Check carefully that there are no oil or coolant leaks and make sure the transmission and controls, especially the brakes, function properly before road testing the machine.
6 Treat the machine gently for the first few miles to make sure oil has circulated throughout the engine and any new parts installed have started to seat.
7 Upon completion of the road test, and after the engine has cooled down completely, recheck the valve clearances (see Chapter 1) and check the engine oil and coolant levels (see *Pre-ride checks*).

28.39 The assembled shaft should be as shown

8 If new pistons/rings, a new cylinder block or a new crankshaft have been fitted, the bike will have to be run in as when new. This means greater use of the transmission and a restraining hand on the throttle, keeping engine speed below 4000 rpm until at least 500 miles (800 km) have been covered. There's no point in keeping to any set speed limit – the main idea is to keep from labouring the engine. Between 500 and 1000 miles (800 and 1600 km) keep engine speeds below 6000 rpm. Experience is the best guide, since it's easy to tell when an engine is running freely.

Chapter 3
Cooling system

Contents

Degrees of difficulty

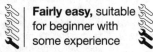

Easy, suitable for novice with little experience	**Fairly easy,** suitable for beginner with some experience	**Fairly difficult,** suitable for competent DIY mechanic	**Difficult,** suitable for experienced DIY mechanic	**Very difficult,** suitable for expert DIY or professional

Specifications

Coolant

Mixture type and capacity .... see Chapter 1

Cooling fan switch (ZR750-J and ZR1000-A)

Switch closes (fan ON)	93 to 103°C
Switch opens (fan OFF)	85 to 90°C
Resistance	
On	Less than 0.5 ohms
Off	More than 10 M-ohm

Temperature sensor

Temperature gauge function	
Resistance @ 50°C	170 to 250 ohms
Resistance @ 120°C	20 to 23 ohms

Thermostat

Opening temperature	58 to 62°C
Fully open	75°C
Valve lift	8 mm (min)

Radiator

Cap valve opening pressure	13 to 18 psi (0.95 to 1.25 Bar)

Torque settings

Coolant outlet pipe assembly bolts	11 Nm
Cooling fan thermo switch	18 Nm
Engine coolant temperature (ECT) sensor	25 Nm
Water pump cover bolts	11 Nm
Water pump impeller bolt	10 Nm
Water pump inlet and outlet pipe bolts	11 Nm

1 General information

The cooling system uses a water/anti-freeze coolant to carry away excess heat from the engine and maintain as constant a temperature as possible. The cylinders are surrounded by a water jacket from which the heated coolant is circulated by thermo-syphonic action in conjunction with a water pump, which is driven by the oil pump. The hot coolant passes upwards to the thermostat and through to the radiator. The coolant then flows across the core of the radiator, then to the water pump and back to the engine where the cycle is repeated.

A thermostat is fitted in the system to prevent the coolant flowing through the radiator when the engine is cold, therefore accelerating the speed at which the engine reaches normal operating temperature. A dual circuit sensor (containing the temperature gauge sensor and the ECT (engine coolant temperature) sensor) mounted in the thermostat housing transmits information to the temperature gauge on the instrument panel, and to the ECU (electronic control module). A cooling fan fitted to the back of the radiator aids cooling in extreme conditions by drawing extra air through. The fan motor is controlled by a thermo switch on ZR750-J and ZR1000-A models, and by a relay which receives a signal from the ECU which in turn receives information from the ECT sensor on ZR750-L/M and ZR1000-B/C models.

The complete cooling system is partially sealed and pressurised, the pressure being controlled by a valve contained in the spring-loaded radiator cap. By pressurising the coolant the boiling point is raised, preventing premature boiling in adverse conditions. The overflow pipe from the system is connected to a reservoir into which excess coolant is expelled under pressure. The discharged coolant automatically returns to the radiator by the vacuum created when the engine cools.

⚠️ **Warning: Do not remove the pressure cap from the radiator when the engine is hot. Scalding hot coolant and steam may be blown out under pressure, which could cause serious injury. When the engine has cooled, place a thick rag, such as a hand towel, over the pressure cap; slowly rotate the cap anti-clockwise to the first stop. This procedure allows any residual pressure to escape. When the steam has stopped escaping, press down on the cap while turning it anti-clockwise and remove it.**

Caution: Do not allow anti-freeze to come in contact with your skin or painted surfaces of the motorcycle. Rinse off any spills immediately with plenty of water. Anti-freeze is highly toxic if ingested. Never leave anti-freeze lying around in an open container or in puddles on the floor; children and pets are attracted by its sweet smell and may drink it. Check with the local authorities about disposing of used anti-freeze. Many communities will have collection centres which will see that anti-freeze is disposed of safely.

Caution: At all times use the specified type of anti-freeze, and always mix it with distilled water in the correct proportion. The anti-freeze contains corrosion inhibitors which are essential to avoid damage to the cooling system. A lack of these inhibitors could lead to a build-up of corrosion which would block the coolant passages, resulting in overheating and severe engine damage. Distilled water must be used as opposed to tap water to avoid a build-up of scale which would also block the passages.

2 Cooling fan and fan switch or relay

Cooling fan
Check

1 If the engine is overheating and the cooling fan isn't coming on, first check the fan fuse (see Chapter 8). If the fuse is good, check the thermo switch or relay (according to model) as described below.

2 To test the cooling fan motor, remove the fuel tank (see Chapter 4). Disconnect the fan wiring connector (black 2-pin) **(see illustrations)**. Note that on ZR750-L/M and ZR1000-B/C models you'll need to detach the reservoir hose – keep the hose above the level of the reservoir or it will drain. Using a 12 volt battery and two jumper wires with suitable connectors, connect the battery positive (+) lead to the blue wire terminal on the fan side of the wiring connector, and the battery negative (–) lead to the black wire terminal on the connector. Once connected the fan should operate. If it does not, and the wiring and connectors are all good, then the fan motor is faulty. Individual components are not available for the fan assembly.

3 If the fan works when connected to a battery, check for continuity in the blue/white wire between the loom side of the connector and the fan switch or relay according to model, and in the black/yellow wire to earth.

Replacement

⚠️ **Warning: The engine must be completely cool before carrying out this procedure.**

4 Remove the radiator (see Section 5).
5 Unscrew the fan bolts and detach the fan from the radiator **(see illustration)**.

2.2a Fan wiring connector (arrowed) – ZR750-J, ZR1000-A

2.2b On ZR750-L/M and ZR1000-B/C detach the reservoir hose and place it aside . . .

2.5 Unscrew the bolts (arrowed) and remove the fan assembly

2.2c . . . then lift and pull back the rubber boot (arrowed) . . .

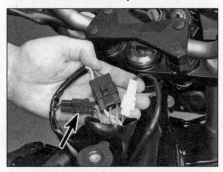

2.2d . . . to access the fan wiring connector (arrowed)

6 Installation is the reverse of removal.
7 Install the radiator (see Section 5).

Cooling fan thermo switch (ZR750-J and ZR1000-A models)

Check

8 If the engine is overheating and the cooling fan isn't coming on, first check the fan circuit fuse (see Chapter 8). If the fuse is blown, check the fan circuit for a short to earth (see *Wiring diagrams* at the end of Chapter 8).
9 If the fuse is good, disconnect the wiring connector from the fan switch on the radiator **(see illustration)**. Using a jumper wire connect between the terminals in the connector. The fan should come on. If it does, the fan switch is defective and must be replaced with a new one. If it does not come on, check for battery voltage at the blue/black wire terminal in the connector. If voltage is present, test the fan motor itself (see above). If there is no voltage, check the wiring and connectors for a fault or break.
10 If the fan is on the whole time, either the switch is defective and must be replaced with a new one, or there is a short in the switch wiring.
11 If the fan works but is suspected of cutting in at the wrong temperature, a more comprehensive test of the switch can be made as follows.
12 Remove the switch (see Steps 14 and 15). Fill a small heatproof container with coolant and place it on a stove. Connect the positive (+) probe of an ohmmeter to the blue/black terminal on the switch and the negative (–) probe to the blue/white terminal, and using some wire or other support suspend the switch in the coolant so that just the sensing portion and the threads are submerged **(see illustration)**. Also place a thermometer capable of reading temperatures up to 110°C in the coolant so that its bulb is close to the switch. **Note:** *None of the components should be allowed to directly touch the container.*
13 Initially the ohmmeter reading should be very high indicating that the switch is open (OFF). Heat the coolant, stirring it gently.

 Warning: This must be done very carefully to avoid the risk of personal injury.

When the temperature reaches around 93 to 103°C the meter reading should drop to around zero ohms, indicating that the switch has closed (ON). Now turn the heat off. As the temperature falls below 85 to 90°C the meter reading should show infinite (very high) resistance, indicating that the switch has opened (OFF). If the meter readings obtained are different, or they are obtained at different temperatures, then the switch is faulty and must be replaced with a new one.

Replacement

 Warning: The engine must be completely cool before carrying out this procedure.

14 Drain the cooling system (see Chapter 1).

2.9 Fan switch wiring connector (arrowed)

On Z1000 remove the left-hand radiator cowl.
15 Disconnect the wiring connector from the switch **(see illustration 2.9)**. Unscrew the switch and withdraw it from the radiator.
16 Install the switch and tighten it to the torque setting specified at the beginning of the Chapter. Take care not to overtighten it as the radiator could be damaged.
17 Reconnect the switch wiring and refill the cooling system (see Chapter 1). On Z1000 models fit the left-hand radiator cowl.

Cooling fan relay (ZR750-L/M and ZR1000-B/C)

Check

18 If the engine is overheating and the cooling fan isn't coming on, first check the fan fuse (see Chapter 8). If the fuse has blown, check the fan circuit for a short to earth (see *Wiring diagrams* at the end of Chapter 8).
19 If the fuse is good, remove the left-hand side of the seat cowling (see Chapter 7). Unscrew the passenger seat bracket bolts and displace the bracket **(see illustration)**.

2.19a Unscrew the bolts (arrowed) and displace the bracket

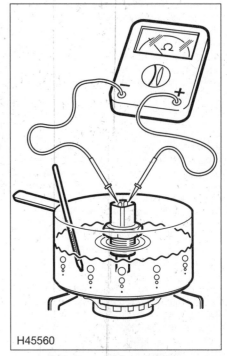

H45560

2.12 Fan switch test set-up

Draw the relay box out of its rubber holder and disconnect the wiring connectors **(see illustration)**.
20 Set a multimeter to the ohms x 1 scale and connect its probes to terminals 17 and 20 **(see illustration)**. There should be no continuity (infinite resistance). Using a fully-charged 12 volt battery and two insulated jumper wires, connect the positive (+) terminal of the battery to terminal 18 on the relay box,

2.19b Displace the relay box (arrowed) and disconnect the wiring connectors

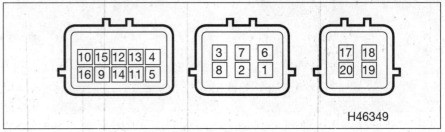

H46349

2.20 Relay box terminal identification

and the negative (–) terminal to terminal 19. At this point the multimeter should read 0 ohms (continuity). If this is the case the relay is proven good. If the relay still indicates no continuity (infinite resistance) across its terminals, it is faulty and the relay box must be replaced with a new one – individual relays are not available.

21 If the relay is good, check for battery voltage at the white and green wire terminals on the loom side of the wiring connector. If there is no voltage, check the wiring between the connector and the fuses for continuity, referring to the relevant wiring diagram at the end of Chapter 8. If voltage is present, check the blue/white wire between the relay and the fan wiring connector and the pink/blue wire between the connector and the ECU for continuity. If all is good test the fan motor (see above). If that is good the ECU or the ECT could be faulty (see Chapter 4).

22 If the fan operates all the time, test the relay (see above). If that is good, either the ECU or the ECT could be faulty.

23 If the fan works but is suspected of cutting in at the wrong temperature, check the ECT sensor (see Chapter 4).

Replacement

24 The relay is an integral part of the relay box – if it is faulty replace the box with a new one (see Step 19).

3 Temperature display and ECT sensor

Temperature and warning display

Check

1 The circuit consists of the sensor mounted in the thermostat housing and the display which is part of the instrument cluster LCD unit. When the ignition is first switched on all the digital display segments and modes should come on temporarily – this serves as an indication that the LCD is functioning correctly.

2 Under normal operating conditions, when the coolant temperature is below 40°C the display will show '- -'. When the temperature is between 40°C and 115°C the display will

3.8a Temperature sensor No. 2 terminal (arrowed)

show the actual temperature. Between 115°C and 120°C the display will start to flash. If this occurs stop the engine and check the coolant level in the reservoir (see *Pre-ride checks*). If the temperature goes above 120°C the display will flash 'HI'.

3 If the display is not working at all, check the instrument cluster power input (see Chapter 8). If the power lines are good, then either the printed circuit board (PCB) or the LCD display unit could be faulty.

4 If all other instrument displays function correctly, apart from the coolant display, or if you suspect that the coolant display is inaccurate, check the sensor (see below). If the sensor is good check the wiring between the sensor and the instrument cluster for continuity. If the wiring is good the display is faulty.

Replacement

5 The temperature display is part of the LCD unit in the instrument cluster PCB. If it is faulty, replace the PCB with a new one (see Chapter 8).

Engine coolant temperature (ECT) sensor

Check

6 Partially drain the coolant so it is below the level of the sensor mounted in the back of the thermostat housing (see Chapter 1).

7 Remove the sensor (see Steps 10 and 11 below).

8 Fill a small heatproof container with coolant and place it on a stove. Using an ohmmeter, connect the positive (+) probe of the meter to the No. 2 terminal on the sensor, and the negative (–) probe to the body of the sensor

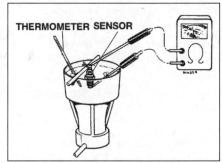

3.8b Temperature sensor test set-up

(see illustration). Using some wire or other support, suspend the sensor in the coolant so that just the sensing head up to the threads is submerged, and with the head a minimum of 40 mm above the bottom of the container. Also place a thermometer capable of reading temperatures up to 130°C in the coolant so that its bulb is close to the sensor (see illustration). **Note:** *None of the components should be allowed to directly touch the container.*

⚠ **Warning: This must be done very carefully to avoid the risk of personal injury.**

9 Begin to heat the coolant, stirring it gently. When the temperature reaches around 50°C the meter reading should be as specified at the beginning of the Chapter. When the temperature reaches around 120°C the meter reading should again be as specified at the beginning of the Chapter. If the meter readings obtained are different by a margin of 10% or more, then the sensor is faulty and must be replaced with a new one.

Replacement

⚠ **Warning: The engine must be completely cool before carrying out this procedure.**

10 Drain the cooling system (see Chapter 1). Remove the fuel tank (see Chapter 4). The sensor is mounted in the back of the thermostat housing.

11 Disconnect the sensor wiring connector **(see illustration)**. Unscrew the bolt securing the housing earth wire **(see illustration)**. Unscrew and remove the sensor **(see illustration)**. If fitted remove the sealing washer and discard it as a new one must be used.

3.11a Disconnect the wiring connector . . .

3.11b . . . then unscrew the bolt and detach the earth wire . . .

3.11c . . . so it doesn't get in the way while unscrewing the sensor (arrowed)

12 Install the sensor either using a new sealing washer if one was originally fitted, or using some suitable silicone sealant on the upper portion of the threads, and tighten it to the torque setting specified at the beginning of the Chapter. Connect the wiring.

13 Install the fuel tank (see Chapter 4). Refill the cooling system (see Chapter 1).

4 Thermostat and housing

1 The thermostat is automatic in operation and shouldn't require attention. In the event of a failure, the valve will probably jam open, in which case the engine will take much longer than normal to warm up. Conversely, if the valve jams shut, the coolant will be unable to circulate and the engine will overheat. Neither condition is acceptable, and the fault must be investigated promptly.

Removal

 Warning: The engine must be completely cool before carrying out this procedure.

2 Drain the coolant (see Chapter 1). Remove the fuel tank (see Chapter 4). On ZR750-L/M and all Z1000 models remove the right-hand radiator cowl (see Chapter 7).

3 Disconnect the ECT sensor wiring connector **(see illustration 3.11a)**. Unscrew the bolt securing the housing earth wire **(see illustration 3.11b)**. Unscrew the housing mounting bolt and detach the loom earth wires **(see illustration)**.

4 Detach the overflow hose from the filler neck **(see illustration 2.2b)**. Slacken the clamp and detach the hose from the outlet pipe on the back of the engine **(see illustration)**. Also detach the hose from the top of the radiator on the right-hand side **(see illustration 5.3a)**. Lift the thermostat housing away, noting the routing of the hoses and clutch cable **(see illustration)**.

5 Undo the cover screws, remove the bracket, detach the cover from the housing, and remove the thermostat **(see illustrations)**. Discard the O-ring as a new one must be used.

4.3 Unscrew the bolt and detach the earth connector

4.4b Lift the thermostat housing and hoses away

Check

6 Examine the thermostat visually before carrying out the test. If it remains in the open position at room temperature, it should be replaced with a new one. Check the condition of the rubber seal around the thermostat and replace it with a new one if it is damaged, deformed or deteriorated.

7 Suspend the thermostat by a piece of wire in a container of cold water. Place a thermometer capable of reading temperatures up to 110°C in the water so that the bulb is close to the thermostat **(see illustration)**. Heat the water, noting the temperature when the thermostat opens, and compare the result with the specifications given at the beginning of the Chapter. Also check the amount the valve opens after it has

4.4a Slacken the clamp screws (arrowed) and detach the hoses from the outlet pipe

4.5a Undo the screws (arrowed) . . .

been heated for a few minutes and compare the measurement to the specifications. If the readings obtained differ from those given, the thermostat is faulty and must be replaced with a new one.

8 In the event of thermostat failure, as an emergency measure only, it can be removed and the machine used without it (this is better than leaving a permanently closed thermostat in, but if it is permanently open, you might as well leave it in). **Note:** *Take care when starting the engine from cold as it will take much longer than usual to warm up. Ensure that a new unit is installed as soon as possible.*

Installation

9 Fit a new O-ring smeared with grease into

4.5b . . . detach the cover . . .

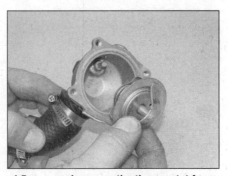

4.5c . . . and remove the thermostat from the housing

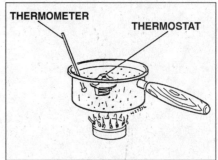

4.7 Thermostat testing set-up

4.9a Fit a new O-ring into the cover

4.9b Fit the mounting bracket on the left-hand side of the housing

5.3a Slacken the clamp screws (arrowed) and detach the hoses from the right-hand side of the radiator . . .

the groove in the cover **(see illustration)**. Fit the thermostat with the hole at the top and make sure it locates correctly **(see illustration 4.5c)**. Fit the cover and the bracket and tighten the screws **(see illustration)**.

10 Locate the thermostat housing, making sure the hoses are correctly routed **(see illustration 4.4c)**. Secure the hoses on their unions **(see illustrations 4.4b and a)**.

11 Fit the loom earth wires with the housing mounting bolt and secure the housing to the bracket **(see illustration 4.3)**. Connect the housing earth wire to the housing and tighten the bolt **(see illustration 3.11b)**. Connect the ECT wiring connector **(see illustration 3.11a)**.

12 Install the fuel tank (see Chapter 4). Refill the cooling system (see Chapter 1). On ZR750-L/M and all Z1000 models install the radiator cowl (see Chapter 7).

5 Radiator

Note: *If the radiator is being removed as part of the engine removal procedure, detach the hoses from their unions on the engine rather than on the radiator and remove the radiator with the hoses attached. Note the routing of the hoses.*

Removal

⚠ **Warning: The engine must be completely cool before carrying out this procedure.**

1 Drain the cooling system (see Chapter 1). Remove the fuel tank (see Chapter 4). On ZR750-L/M and all Z1000 models remove the radiator cowls (see Chapter 7).

2 Disconnect the fan motor wiring connector (black 2-pin) **(see illustration 2.2a or illustrations 2.2b, c and d)**. On ZR750-J and ZR1000-A models disconnect the fan switch wiring connector **(see illustration 2.9)**.

3 Slacken the clamps securing the hoses to the radiator and detach them **(see illustrations)**.

4 Unscrew the radiator mounting bolts and remove the radiator, taking care not to catch the fins on the bracket **(see illustrations)**.

5 Note the arrangement of the collars and rubber grommets in the radiator mounts **(see illustration 5.7)**. Replace the grommets with new ones if they are damaged, deformed or deteriorated.

6 If necessary, remove the cooling fan from the radiator (see Section 2). Check the radiator for signs of damage and clear any dirt or debris that might obstruct airflow and inhibit cooling. If the radiator fins are badly damaged or broken the radiator must be replaced with a new one.

Installation

7 Installation is the reverse of removal, noting the following.

● Make sure the rubber grommets are in place and the collars are correctly fitted in the grommets **(see illustration)**.

● Make sure that the fan, and on ZR750-J and ZR1000-A models the fan switch, wiring is correctly connected **(see illustrations 2.2a or d, and 2.9)**. Make sure all wiring is correctly routed and secured.

5.3b . . . and from the left-hand side

5.4a Unscrew the top bolt (arrowed) on each side . . .

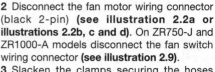

5.4b . . . and the bottom bolt (arrowed) . . .

5.4c . . . and carefully remove the radiator

5.7 Make sure the grommets are in good condition and the collars are fitted

6.2 Water pump drain hole (arrowed)

6.5 Slacken the clamp screw (arrowed) and detach the hose

6.6a Unscrew the bolt (arrowed) and detach the inlet pipe . . .

● Ensure the coolant hoses are in good condition (see Chapter 1), and are securely retained by their clamps, using new ones if necessary **(see illustrations 5.3a and b)**.
● On completion refill the cooling system as described in Chapter 1.

Pressure cap check

8 If problems such as overheating or loss of coolant occur, check the entire system as described in Chapter 1. The radiator cap opening pressure should be checked by a Kawasaki dealer with the special tester required to do the job. If the cap is defective, replace it with a new one.

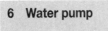

6 Water pump

Check

1 The water pump is located on the lower left-hand side of the engine. On ZR1000-B/C models remove the left-hand sump cowl (see Chapter 7). Visually check the area around the pump for signs of leakage.
2 To prevent leakage of water from the cooling system to the lubrication system and vice versa, two seals are fitted on the pump shaft. On the bottom of the pump housing there is a drain hole **(see illustration)**. If either seal fails, the drain allows the coolant or oil to escape and prevents them mixing.

3 The seal on the water pump side is of the mechanical type which bears on the rear face of the impeller. The second seal, which is mounted behind the mechanical seal, is of the normal feathered lip type. If on inspection the drain shows signs of leakage, remove the pump and dismantle it for inspection.

Removal

4 Drain the engine oil and coolant (see Chapter 1).
5 On Z1000 models slacken the clamp securing the oil cooler feed hose to the pump outlet pipe and detach the hose **(see illustration)**.
6 Unscrew the bolts securing the pump inlet and outlet pipes and pull the pipes out of the pump **(see illustrations)**. Discard the O-rings as new ones must be used.

6.6b . . . then unscrew the bolt (arrowed) and detach the outlet pipe

7 Release the wiring from the clamp. Unscrew the bolts and remove the cover **(see illustration)**. Remove the locating pins if they are loose **(see illustration 6.19b)**. Remove the O-ring and discard it as a new one must be used **(see illustration 6.19a)**.
8 Unscrew the impeller bolt, noting the washer **(see illustration)**. Keeping a finger pressed on the shaft end draw the impeller off – the shaft needs to stay in place otherwise you will draw the oil pump out with it.
9 Draw the seal housing off the pump shaft, again taking care not to draw the shaft out with it **(see illustration)**. Remove the O-ring and discard it as a new one must be used **(see illustration 6.17a)**. Remove the dowels if they are loose **(see illustration 6.17b)**.

Seal replacement

10 To remove the mechanical seal, a shaped

6.7a Release the wiring from the clamp (arrowed)

6.7b Unscrew the bolts (arrowed) and remove the cover

6.8 Counter-hold the impeller and unscrew the bolt (arrowed), then remove the impeller as described

6.9 Draw the housing off the shaft

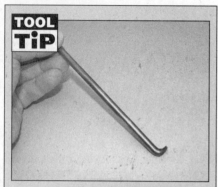

TOOL TIP

A drift can be easily made using a piece of steel rod – cut the rod to a suitable length, then heat one end red hot and hammer it flat, then cool it in water and dress it with a file as required. A local engineering or welding shop can do this for you cheaply.

drift is needed (see **Tool Tip**) – a standard punch does not work very well. Locate the shaped end of the drift against the inner face of the seal in the gap between the seals and drive it out **(see illustration)**. Discard it, as a new one must be fitted.

11 To remove the oil seal, first remove the mechanical seal (see Step 10). Tap the oil seal out from the inside or hook it out from the outside using a seal hook **(see illustration 6.13a)**. Note which way round the seal fits. Discard it, as a new one must be fitted.

6.14a **Use a socket that fits onto the rim . . .**

6.14c **. . . until the rim seats**

6.10 **Driving the mechanical seal out**

6.13b **. . . and drive it in until it seats . . .**

12 Clean any traces of sealant from around the mechanical seal seat with a suitable solvent.

13 Apply a smear of high temperature grease to the inner lips of the new oil seal.

6.14b **. . . to drive the seal into place . . .**

6.15a **Lever out the seal seat . . .**

6.13a **Fit the seal with the marked side facing out . . .**

6.13c **. . . so the drain hole (arrowed) is exposed**

Press or drive the seal into the body with the marked side facing out until it seats, at which point the drain hole is fully visible **(see illustrations)**.

14 Press or carefully drive the new mechanical seal into the pump body until its outer rim seats using a suitable sized socket or seal driver which bears only on the rim and not on the centre **(see illustrations)**.

15 The mechanical seal seat on the inner face of the impeller should come with the new mechanical seal – lever out the old seat and press the new one into place **(see illustrations)**.

Installation

16 Check for corrosion or a build-up of scale in the pump cover and on the impeller and clean them if necessary.

17 Fit a new O-ring into the groove on the

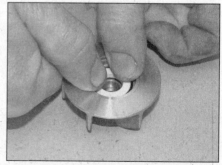

6.15b **. . . and press the new one in**

6.17a Fit a new O-ring into the groove and fit the dowels (arrowed) if removed . . .

6.17b . . . then fit the seal housing onto the engine

6.18 Fit the impeller and the bolt with its washer

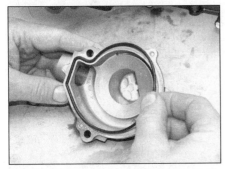

6.19a Fit a new O-ring into the groove

6.19b Fit the pins (arrowed) if removed . . .

6.19c . . . then fit the seal housing onto the dowels

inner face of the seal housing (see illustration). Make sure the dowels are installed. Fit the housing over the shaft and locate it onto the dowels (see illustration).

18 Apply coolant to the rubber seal and seat on the inner face of the impeller. Slide the impeller onto the shaft (see illustration). Fit the bolt with its washer and tighten it to the torque setting specified at the beginning of the Chapter.

19 Smear the new cover O-ring with grease and fit it into its groove in the cover (see illustration). Make sure the locating pins are installed (see illustration). Fit the cover onto the pump, making sure it locates on the

pins (see illustration). Fit the bolts, shorter one at the top, and not forgetting the wiring clamp with the rear bolt, and tighten them to the specified torque setting (see illustration 6.7b). Secure the wiring in the clamp (see illustration 6.7b).

20 Smear the new pipe O-rings with grease and fit them onto the pipes (see illustration). Fit the pipes into the pump, pushing them fully in (see illustration). Apply a suitable thread locking compound to the bolts and tighten them to the specified torque setting.

21 On Z1000 models fit the oil cooler hose onto the pipe and secure it with the clamp (see illustration 6.5).

22 Refill the engine oil and coolant to the correct levels (see Chapter 1 and *Pre-ride checks*). On ZR1000-B/C models install the left-hand sump cowl (see Chapter 7)

7 Coolant reservoir

1 On ZR750-J and ZR1000-A models remove the left-hand side panel (see Chapter 7). On ZR750-L/M and ZR1000-B/C models remove the right-hand seat cowl (see Chapter 7). Get a suitable container to drain the coolant into.

6.20a Fit a new O-ring into the groove in each pipe . . .

6.20b . . . then push the pipes in and fit the bolts

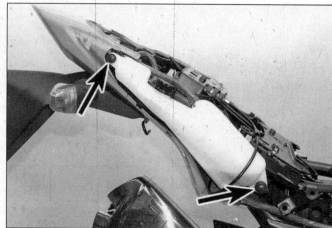

7.2a Reservoir mounting screws (arrowed) –
ZR750-J and ZR1000-A

7.2b Reservoir mounting screws (arrowed) –
ZR750-L/M and ZR1000-B/C

2 Undo the screws securing the reservoir, then undo the reservoir cap and drain the coolant into the container **(see illustrations)**.
3 Release the clamps and detach the hoses from the reservoir.
4 Installation is the reverse of removal. On completion refill the reservoir to the UPPER level line with the specified coolant mixture (see Chapter 1).

8 Coolant hoses and pipes

Removal

1 Before removing a hose or pipe, drain the coolant (see Chapter 1).
2 Use a screwdriver to slacken the larger-bore hose clamps, then slide them back along the hose and clear of the union spigot. The smaller-bore hoses are secured by spring clamps which can be expanded by squeezing their ears together with pliers.
Caution: The radiator unions are fragile. Do

not use excessive force when attempting to remove the hoses.
3 If a hose proves stubborn, release it by rotating it on its union before working it off. If all else fails, cut the hose with a sharp knife. Whilst this means replacing the hose with a new one, it is preferable to buying a new radiator.
4 The outlet pipe assembly on the cylinder head and the inlet and outlet pipes on the pump can be removed by unscrewing the bolts **(see illustration and 6.6a/b)**. The O-rings must be discarded and replaced with new ones **(see illustration 6.20a)**.

Installation

5 Slide the clamps onto the hose and then work the hose on to its union as far as the spigot where present.

 HAYNES HINT *If the hose is difficult to push on its union, soften it by soaking it in very hot water, or alternatively a little soapy water on the union can be used as a lubricant.*

8.4 Coolant outlet union bolts (arrowed)

6 Rotate the hose on its unions to settle it in position before sliding the clamps into place and tightening them securely.
7 Clean the threads of the pipe bolts to remove any old locking compound. Fit new O-rings smeared with grease. Apply a suitable thread locking compound to the bolts and tighten them to the torque setting specified at the beginning of the Chapter.
8 Refill the cooling system with fresh coolant (see Chapter 1).

Chapter 4
Engine management system

Contents

Degrees of difficulty

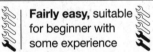

Easy, suitable for novice with little experience ⚹	**Fairly easy,** suitable for beginner with some experience ⚹	**Fairly difficult,** suitable for competent DIY mechanic ⚹	**Difficult,** suitable for experienced DIY mechanic ⚹	**Very difficult,** suitable for expert DIY or professional ⚹

Specifications

General information

Cylinder numbering	1 to 4 from left to right
Firing order	1-2-4-3
Spark plugs	see Chapter 1

Fuel

Z750 models and ZR1000-A	Unleaded. Minimum 91 RON
ZR1000-B/C models	Unleaded. Minimum 95 RON
Fuel tank capacity (including reserve)	
ZR750-J and ZR1000-A	18.0 litres
ZR750-L/M and ZR1000-B/C	18.5 litres

Fuel injection system

Idle speed	1100 ± 50 rpm
Throttle body vacuum range at idle speed	
ZR750-J	215 to 235 mmHg
ZR750-L/M	255 to 275 mmHg
ZR1000-A	235 to 255 mmHg
ZR1000-B/C	275 to 295 mmHg
Fuel pressure	
ZR750-J and ZR1000-A	
Ignition ON, fuel pump running	46 psi (3.2 Bar)
Ignition ON, fuel pump off, system pressurised	43 psi (3.0 Bar)
Engine idling	46 psi (3.2 Bar)
Minimum fuel flow rate	67 ml every 3 seconds
ZR750-L/M and ZR1000-B/C	
Engine idling	43 psi (3.0 Bar)
Minimum fuel flow rate	50 ml every 3 seconds

Engine management system sensors

Atmospheric pressure (AP) sensor
  Input voltage. . . . . 4.75 to 5.25 volts
  Output voltage . . . . 3.8 to 4.2 volts at standard atmospheric pressure
Camshaft position (CMP) sensor
  Resistance . . . . 400 to 460 ohms
  Minimum peak voltage output . . . . 0.2 volts
Crankshaft position (CKP) sensor
  Resistance . . . . 376 to 564 ohms
  Minimum peak voltage output . . . . 2.0 volts
Engine coolant temperature (ECT) sensor
  Output voltage . . . . 2.8 to 2.97 volts at 20°C (68°F)
  Resistance @ 20°C. . . . . 2.317 to 2.575 K-ohms
  Resistance @ 80°C. . . . . 0.31 to 0.33 K-ohms
  Resistance @ 110°C. . . . . 138.5 to 146.7 ohms
Fuel injector resistance. . . . . 11.7 to 12.3 ohms at 20°C (68°F)
Intake air pressure (IAP) sensor
  Input voltage. . . . . 4.75 to 5.25 volts
  Output voltage . . . . 3.8 to 4.2 volts at standard atmospheric pressure
Intake air temperature (IAT) sensor resistance
  ZR750-J and ZR1000-A
    At 20°C (68°F). . . . . 1.6 to 3.7 K-ohms
    At 80°C (176°F). . . . . 0.24 to 0.43 K-ohms
    Output voltage . . . . approx.2.25 to 2.5 volts at 20°C (68°F)
  ZR750-L/M and ZR1000-B/C
    At 20°C (68°F). . . . . 2.21 to 2.69 K-ohms
    At 80°C (176°F). . . . . approx. 0.322 K-ohms
    Output voltage . . . . approx.2.25 to 2.5 volts at 20°C (68°F)
Oxygen (O²) sensor
  Output voltage
    With air system blocked . . . . min 0.7 volts
    With air system open . . . . max. 0.2 volts
  Heater resistance . . . . 11.7 to 154.5 ohms at 20°C (68°F)
Secondary throttle position (STP) sensor
  Input voltage. . . . . 4.75 to 5.25 volts
  Output voltage . . . . approx. 0.5 to 3.8 volts as throttle is opened
  Resistance . . . . 4 to 6 K-ohms
Secondary throttle valve servo
  Resistance . . . . approx. 5.0 to 7.5 K-ohms
  Input voltage. . . . . 8.5 to 10.5 volts
Speed sensor
  ZR750-J and ZR1000-A
    Input voltage. . . . . 9 to 11 volts
    Output voltage . . . . 0.05 to 0.07 volts
  ZR750-L/M and ZR1000-B/C
    Input voltage. . . . . 4.75 to 5.25 volts
    Output voltage . . . . 0.05 to 0.09 volts
Throttle position (TP) sensor
  Input voltage. . . . . 4.75 to 5.25 volts
  Output voltage . . . . approx. 1.0 to 4.28 volts as throttle is opened
  Resistance . . . . 4 to 6 K-ohms
Tip-over (TO) sensor
  ZR750-J and ZR1000-A
    Input voltage. . . . . Battery voltage
    Output voltage
      Sensor upright . . . . 0.4 to 4.4 volts
      Sensor tilted . . . . 3.7 to 4.4 volts
  ZR750-L/M and ZR1000-B/C
    Input voltage. . . . . 4.75 to 5.25 volts
    Output voltage
      Sensor upright . . . . 0.65 to 1.35 volts
      Sensor tilted . . . . 3.55 to 4.45 volts

Exhaust valve

Input voltage. . . . . 4.75 to 5.25 volts
Output voltage . . . . 3.46 to 3.76 volts
Servo sensor resistance. . . . . 4 to 6 K-ohms
Servo actuator resistance. . . . . 5 to 200 ohms

Ignition timing

At idle . . . . 10° BTDC
Full advance
ZR750-J . . . . 37° BTDC @ 5800 rpm
ZR750-L/M . . . . 37° BTDC @ 5000 rpm
ZR1000-A . . . . 36° BTDC @ 7500 rpm
ZR1000-B/C . . . . 37.5° BTDC @ 5500 rpm

Ignition HT coils

Primary winding resistance . . . . 1.0 to 1.6 ohms
Secondary winding resistance . . . . 10.8 to 16.2 K-ohms
Initial voltage (see text) . . . . Battery voltage (approximately 12 volts)
Minimum peak voltage (see text) . . . . 88 volts

Immobiliser receiver

Receiver resistance . . . . 0.6 to 0.9 ohms

Torque settings

Camshaft position (CMP) sensor . . . . 12 Nm
Engine coolant temperature (ECT) sensor . . . . 25 Nm
Exhaust system
Header pipe nuts . . . . 17 Nm
Downpipe rear mounting bolt (ZR1000-B/C) . . . . 5 Nm
Silencer clamp bolt(s)
ZR750-J . . . . 17 Nm
ZR1000-A . . . . 17 Nm
ZR750-L/M . . . . 15 Nm
ZR1000-B/C
Left-hand silencer . . . . 17 Nm
Right-hand silencer . . . . 15 Nm
Silencer rear mounting bolt/nut
ZR750-J . . . . 30 Nm
All other models . . . . 34 Nm
Silencer front mounting bolt (ZR750-L/M) . . . . 5 Nm
LH silencer front mounting bolt (ZR1000-B/C) . . . . 25 Nm
Fuel level sensor bolts . . . . 6.9 Nm
Fuel pump bolts . . . . 10 Nm
Oxygen sensor . . . . 44 Nm
Timing rotor cover bolts . . . . 11 Nm
Timing rotor bolt . . . . 39 Nm

1 General information and precautions

Fuel system

The fuel supply system consists of the fuel tank, an integrated fuel pump, pressure regulator and filter, a level sensor, the fuel hoses, fuel rail, injectors, throttle bodies, and control cables. The fuel pump is switched on and off with the engine via a relay. The injection system supplies fuel and air to the engine via 38 mm throttle bodies. The injectors are operated by the Electronic Control Unit (ECU) using the information obtained from the various sensors it monitors (refer to Section 4 for more information on the operation of the fuel injection system).

All models have a six segment fuel gauge and low fuel warning incorporated in the instrument cluster LCD, actuated by a level sensor inside the fuel tank. When only one segment remains lit there is approximately 3 litres of fuel left on ZR1000-B/C models and 5 litres on all other models; when this segment starts to flash and the word FUEL flashes there are only 2.5 litres left on ZR1000-B/C and 4 litres on all other models.

An exhaust valve that controls the flow of gasses is fitted on ZR750-L/M and ZR1000-B/C models

Ignition system

The transistorised electronic ignition system is combined with the fuel injection system, both being controlled by the ECU (electronic control unit). The ignition system comprises a rotor, crankshaft position sensor (CKP sensor), electronic control unit (ECU), ignition coils and spark plugs.

The triggers on the rotor, which is fitted to the right-hand end of the crankshaft, generate signals in the CKP sensor as the crankshaft rotates. The CKP sensor sends those signals to the ECU which, in conjunction with information received from the throttle position and engine coolant temperature sensors, calculates the ignition timing and supplies the ignition coils with the power necessary to produce a spark at the plugs. There is no provision for checking or adjusting the ignition timing.

The system uses four HT coils, one for each cylinder. The coils are of the plug top type known as 'stick coils', with the coil windings being incorporated in the spark plug cap. This eliminates the need for HT leads and saves space.

The system incorporates a safety interlock circuit which will cut the ignition if the sidestand is extended whilst the engine is running and in gear. It also prevents the engine from being started if the sidestand is down and the engine is in gear. The engine can be started with the sidestand up when it is in gear as long as the clutch lever is pulled in.

Some models are fitted with an immobiliser system which will not allow the engine to be started unless the correct key is used.

Note: *Individual engine management system components can be checked but not repaired. If system troubles occur, and the faulty component can be isolated, the only cure for the problem in most cases is to replace the part with a new one. Keep in mind that most electronic parts, once purchased, cannot be returned. To avoid unnecessary expense, make very sure the faulty component has been positively identified before buying a new part.*

Precautions

⚠️ *Warning: Petrol (gasoline) is extremely flammable, so take extra precautions when you work on any part of the fuel system. Always remove the battery (see Chapter 8). Don't smoke or allow open flames or bare light bulbs near the work area, and don't work in a garage where a natural gas-type appliance is present. If you spill any fuel on your skin, rinse it off immediately with soap and water. When you perform any kind of work on the fuel system, wear safety glasses and have a fire extinguisher suitable for a class B type fire (flammable liquids) on hand.*

Residual pressure will remain in the fuel feed hoses and fuel rail assemblies after the motorcycle has been used. Before disconnecting any fuel hose, ensure the ignition is switched OFF then release fuel system pressure (see Section 2). It is vital that no dirt or debris is allowed to enter the fuel tank or the fuel rail assembly whilst the fuel hoses are disconnected. Any foreign matter in the fuel system components could result in injector damage or malfunction. Ensure the ignition is switched OFF before disconnecting or reconnecting any fuel injection system wiring connector. If a connector is disconnected or reconnected with the ignition switched ON, the electronic control unit (ECU) may be damaged.

Always perform service procedures in a well-ventilated area to prevent a build-up of fumes.

Never work in a building containing a gas appliance with a pilot light, or any other form of naked flame. Ensure that there are no naked light bulbs or any sources of flame or sparks nearby.

Do not smoke (or allow anyone else to smoke) while in the vicinity of petrol (gasoline) or of components containing it. Remember the possible presence of vapour from these sources and move well clear before smoking.

Check all electrical equipment belonging to the house, garage or workshop where work is being undertaken (see the **Safety first!** section of this manual). Remember that certain electrical appliances such as drills, cutters etc, create sparks in the normal course

2.1a Fuel pump and level sensor wiring connectors (arrowed) – ZR750-J, ZR1000-A

of operation and must not be used near petrol (gasoline) or any component containing it. Again, remember the possible presence of fumes before using electrical equipment.

Always mop up any spilt fuel and safely dispose of the rag used.

Any stored fuel that is drained off during servicing work must be kept in sealed containers that are suitable for holding petrol (gasoline), and clearly marked as such; the containers themselves should be kept in a safe place. Note that this last point applies equally to the fuel tank if it is removed from the machine; also remember to keep its filler cap closed at all times.

Read the **Safety first!** section of this manual carefully before starting work.

2 Fuel tank

⚠️ *Warning: Refer to the precautions given in Section 1 before starting work.*

Note: *Removing the tank involves a certain amount of unavoidable fuel spillage, which is obviously dangerous. Refer to the precautions given in Section 1 before starting work, and have plenty of rag to hand. Once the tank has been removed, rest it on some soft rag to prevent damaging the paintwork or hose unions. Try to time the removal procedure with a near empty tank, which makes it much easier to lift.*

2.1b Fuel pump and level sensor wiring connectors – ZR750-L/M, ZR1000-B/C

Raise

1 Make sure the fuel cap is secure. Remove the rider's seat (see Chapter 7). Find a piece of 4 x 2 inch wood, about eight inches long, and some rag. Disconnect the fuel pump and fuel level sensor wiring connectors **(see illustrations)**.

2 On ZR750-J and ZR1000-A models remove the right-hand frame cover (see Chapter 7).

3 On ZR750-L/M and ZR1000-B/C models remove the side panels (see Chapter 7).

4 Unscrew the tank mounting bolt, noting the collar **(see illustration)**. Lift the rear of the tank and draw the tank back so the front mounting cups clear the rubbers, then place the rag between the front of the tank and the frame and the wood between the rear of the tank and the frame, making sure it is secure **(see illustration)**.

Removal

5 Disconnect the battery negative (–) lead (see Chapter 8). Raise the tank as described above.

6 Place a rag under the fuel hose union either on the pump or on the back of the throttle bodies, depending on which hose joint the release clips are easiest for you to access – we found it best to disconnect the hose from the throttle body union on ZR750-J and ZR1000-A models and from the fuel pump union on ZR750-L/M and ZR1000-B/C models.

7 On ZR750-J and ZR1000-A models press in the tabs on the hose joint and pull it off the union, catching any residual fuel in the rag **(see illustration)**.

2.4a Unscrew the bolt and remove the collar

2.4b Displace and support the tank using rag and wood as shown

2.7 Press the tabs in to release the hose joint from the throttle body union

2.8 Press in the tabs and push the clip out then draw the hose joint off the fuel pump union

2.10a The tank drain/overflow hose routes through the guide along with the air filter housing drain hose and the coolant reservoir overflow hose (both shown)

8 On ZR750-L/M and ZR1000-B/C models press in the tabs on the hose joint clip and push the clip part-way out of the joint, then pull the joint off the union, catching any residual fuel in the rag **(see illustration)**.

9 On California models pull the two colour-coded EVAP system hoses off the unions on the back of the tank.

10 Draw the breather/overflow hose up from the left-hand side of the bike, noting its routing down to the guide between the swingarm and the shock absorber **(see illustration)**. Carefully lift the tank off the frame and remove it, bringing the hose with it **(see illustration)**.

11 Check all the tank rubbers for signs of damage or deterioration and replace them with new ones if necessary.

Installation

12 Installation is the reverse of removal, noting the following:

● Depending on how the tank has been stood and how full it is there is the possibility of fuel having made its way into the breather pipe which could spurt out of the union on the base when it is moved – be prepared with some rag for this. Once the tank is upright the pipe will fill itself with air.

● Make sure all mounting rubbers and collars are in place.

● On ZR750-J and ZR1000-A models press the fuel supply hose joint onto its union until it clicks into place **(see illustration 2.7)**.

● On ZR750-L/M and ZR1000-B/C models make sure the fuel supply hose joint clip is part-way out of the joint as on disconnection **(see illustration 2.8)**. Press the joint onto its union until it clicks into place, then press the clip into the joint until its tabs click into place.

● Make sure the fuel hose is secure by pulling and pushing the joint on the union – the hose should not come off, but there should be about 5 mm movement. If the joint does not slide, remove and refit it.

● Make sure the breather/overflow hose is correctly routed **(see illustration 2.10a)**.

● On California models connect the two EVAP system hoses to the back of the tank according to their colour coding.

● Connect the fuel pump and level sensor wiring connectors **(see illustration 2.1a or b)** and the battery negative (–) lead.

● Start the engine and check that there is no sign of fuel leakage.

Repair

13 All repairs to the fuel tank should be carried out by a professional who has experience in this critical and potentially dangerous work. Even after cleaning and flushing of the fuel system, explosive fumes can remain and ignite during repair of the tank.

14 If the fuel tank is removed from the bike, it should not be placed in an area where sparks or open flames could ignite the fumes coming out of the tank. Be especially careful inside garages where a natural gas-type appliance is located, because the pilot light could cause an explosion.

2.10b Lift the tank away bringing the breather/overflow hose with it

3 Fuel pressure check

Special Tool: A fuel pressure gauge is required for this procedure.

1 To check the fuel pressure, a suitable gauge, gauge adapter and hoses are needed. Kawasaki provides service tools (Pt. Nos. 57001-1593, 57001-1607 and 57001-125) for this purpose.

2 Raise the fuel tank, then disconnect the fuel hose from the both the pump union and the throttle body union (see Section 2). Use the hoses and adapter to connect the gauge between the fuel tank and the fuel rail **(see illustration)**.

3 Turn the ignition switch ON and check the pressure reading on the gauge as the pump runs for 3 seconds and pressurizes the system, then with the system pressurised when the pump has stopped. Start the engine and check the pressure with the engine idling. In each case the pressure should be as specified at the beginning of this Chapter.

4 Turn the ignition OFF and disconnect the gauge and adapters. Use a rag to catch any residual fuel as before. Connect the fuel hose (see Section 2).

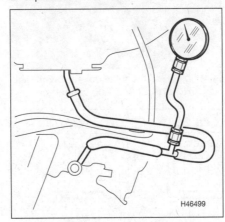

H46499

3.2 Fuel pressure gauge and hose set-up

5 If the pressure is too low, check for a leak in the fuel supply system, including the fuel rails and injectors. If there is no leakage the pick-up or filter in the pump could be blocked, or the pump could be faulty. Check the pump (Section 5).

6 If the pressure is too high, either the pressure regulator or the fuel pump check valve is faulty or the fuel hose or injector(s) is/are clogged. Check the pump, fuel hose and injectors.

4 Fuel pump relay

ZR750-J and ZR1000-A

1 Remove the seat cowlings (see Chapter 7).
2 Pull the relay off its mounting and disconnect the wiring connector **(see illustration)**. Using a multimeter or test light, check for continuity between terminals 3 and 4 on the relay **(see illustration)**. There should be no continuity. Now use jumper wires to connect the positive (+) terminal of a fully charged 12 volt battery to terminal 1 on the relay and the negative (–) battery terminal to relay terminal 2. There should now be continuity shown across terminals 3 and 4. If the relay fails either of the checks, replace it with a new one.
3 If the relay is good, check for battery voltage at the red and white/yellow wire terminals on the loom side of the wiring connector with the ignition and kill switch ON. If there is no voltage at either wire, check the circuit and its components, referring to the relevant wiring diagram at the end of Chapter 8. If voltage is present, check the wiring between the relay and the pump wiring connector and the ECU for continuity. If all is good the ECU could be faulty (see Section 10).

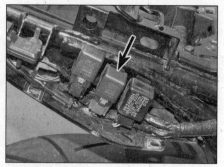

4.2a Fuel pump relay (arrowed)

ZR750-L/M and ZR1000-B/C

4 Remove the left-hand side of the seat cowling (see Chapter 7). Unscrew the passenger seat bracket bolts and displace the bracket **(see illustration)**. Displace the relay box and disconnect the wiring connectors **(see illustration)**.
5 Set a multimeter to the ohms x 1 scale and connect its probes to terminals 7 and 8 **(see illustration)**. There should be no continuity (infinite resistance). Using a fully-charged 12 volt battery and two insulated jumper wires, connect the positive (+) terminal of the battery to terminal 9, and the negative (–) terminal to terminal 10. At this point the multimeter should read 0 ohms (continuity). If this is the case the relay is proven good. If the relay still indicates no continuity (infinite resistance), it is faulty and the relay box must be replaced with a new one – individual relays are not available.
6 If the relay is good, check for battery voltage at the red wire terminal on the loom side of the wiring connector with the ignition and kill switch ON. If there is no voltage at the

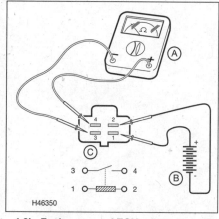

H46350

4.2b Fuel pump and ECU relay terminal identification and test set-up

A Multimeter or ohmmeter
B Battery
C Relay

red wire, check the ignition fuse and the kill switch and the wiring between them, referring to the relevant wiring diagram at the end of Chapter 8. If there is voltage at the red wire check the ECU fuse and the ECU relay. If all is good, check the wiring between the relay and the pump wiring connector and the ECU for continuity. If all is good the ECU could be faulty (see Section 10).

5 Fuel pump

Warning: Refer to the precautions given in Section 1 before starting work.

Check

1 The fuel pump is located inside the fuel tank. When the ignition is switched ON, it should be possible to hear the pump run for a few seconds until the system is up to pressure. If you can't hear anything, check the relay (see Section 4). If it is good, check the wiring, connectors and terminals for physical damage or loose or corroded connections and rectify as necessary (see the **Wiring Diagrams** at the end of Chapter 8). If the pump still will not run, proceed as follows.
2 On ZR750-J and ZR1000-A models remove the right-hand frame cover (see Chapter 7).
3 On ZR750-L/M and ZR1000-B/C models remove the right-hand side cover (see Chapter 7).
4 Ensure the ignition is switched OFF. Locate the fuel pump wiring connector **(see illustration 2.1a or b)**.
5 With the connector still connected, and using needle probes inserted into the pump side of the connector, connect the positive (+) lead of a voltmeter to the yellow/red wire terminal and the negative (–) lead to the black/white wire terminal. Switch the

4.4a Unscrew the bolts (arrowed) and displace the bracket

4.4b Displace the relay box (arrowed) and disconnect the wiring connectors

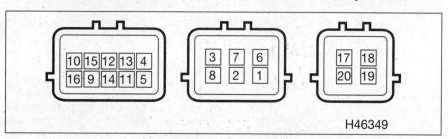

H46349

4.5 Relay box terminal identification

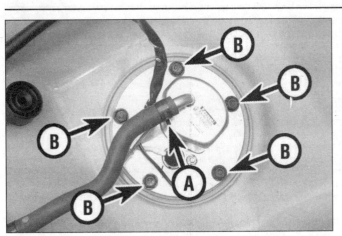

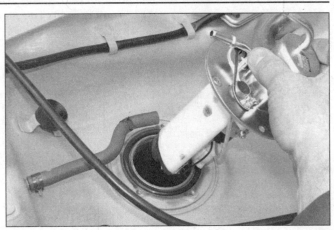

5.9 Release the clamp (A) and detach the fuel return hose. Fuel pump mounting bolts (B)

5.10 Withdraw the pump from the tank

ignition ON whilst noting the reading obtained on the meter.

6 If battery voltage is present for a few seconds, the fuel pump circuit is operating correctly and the fuel pump itself is faulty and must be replaced with a new one.

7 If no reading is obtained, check the white/red wire and connectors between the fuel tank and the pump relay for continuity using the wiring diagrams at the end of Chapter 8, and check for continuity to earth in the black/yellow wire. If continuity (zero resistance) is not present, locate the break in the wire or faulty connector and repair or replace as required. Make sure all the connectors are free from corrosion and are securely connected. Repair/replace the wiring as necessary and clean the connectors using electrical contact cleaner. If

this fails to reveal the fault, check the following components.

● Engine stop switch (see Chapter 8).
● ECU relay (see Section 10).
● Tip-over sensor (see Section 9).
● Electronic control unit (ECU) (see Section 10).

Removal

8 Remove the fuel tank (see Section 2), then place it upside down on some clean rag. If not already done when removing the tank detach the fuel supply hose from the pump.

9 Release the fuel return hose clamp and detach the hose from its union on the pump **(see illustration)**.

10 Unscrew the fuel pump mounting plate bolts **(see illustration 5.9)**. Carefully withdraw the

pump assembly from the tank **(see illustration)**. Remove the O-ring and discard it – a new one must be used on installation **(see illustration 5.12)**. The pump comes as a complete assembly and no individual components are available.

Installation

11 Make sure the wiring terminal screws and nuts are tight **(see illustrations)**.

12 Ensure the mounting plate and tank surfaces are clean and dry, then fit the new O-ring **(see illustration)**.

13 Carefully manoeuvre the pump assembly into the tank **(see illustration 5.10)** – make sure the fuel return hose union points to the back of the tank in line with the hose **(see illustration 5.9)**.

14 Apply a suitable non-permanent thread locking compound to the bolts and tighten them finger-tight. Now tighten them evenly and a little at a time in a criss-cross sequence to the torque setting specified at the beginning of the Chapter.

15 Fit the return hose onto its union and secure it with the clamp **(see illustration 5.9)**. Fit the fuel hose to the pump now if required, referring to Section 2 for details.

16 Install the fuel tank (see Section 2).

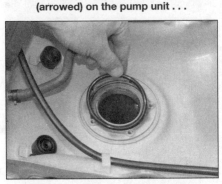

5.11a Make sure the screws and nuts (arrowed) on the pump unit . . .

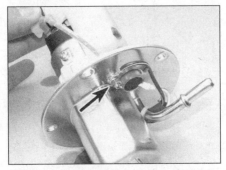

5.11b . . . and on the mounting plate are secure

6 Air filter housing

1 Remove the engine from the frame (see Chapter 2).

2 Disconnect the intake air temperature (IAT) sensor wiring connector **(see illustration 9.13)**. If required withdraw the sensor from the housing.

3 Make a note of the routing of the drain hose on the left-hand side of the housing **(see illustration 2.10a)**. Draw the housing forwards and remove it, bringing the drain hose with it **(see illustration)**.

4 If required detach the drain hose from the left-hand side of the housing and the crankcase breather hose from the front.

5 Installation is the reverse of removal.

5.12 Fit a new O-ring into the groove

6.3 Draw the housing out of the frame

7 Engine management system description

1 The engine management system consists of three main component groups, the fuel circuit, the ignition circuit and the electronic control circuit (see illustration).

2 The fuel circuit consists of the tank, integrated pump/filter/pressure regulator, throttle bodies and injectors. Fuel is pumped under pressure from the tank to the fuel rail, from which the individual injectors are fed. Operating pressure is maintained by the pressure regulator. The injectors spray pressurised fuel into the throttle bodies where it mixes with air and vaporises, before entering the cylinder where it is compressed and ignited.

3 The ignition circuit consists of the stick type ignition coils and the spark plugs.

4 The electronic control circuit consists of the electronic control unit (ECU), which operates and co-ordinates both the fuel injection and ignition systems, and the various sensors which provide the ECU with information on engine operating conditions.

5 The electronic control unit (ECU) monitors signals from the following sensors.
● Intake air temperature (IAT) sensor
● Intake air pressure (IAP) sensor
● Throttle position (TP) sensor
● Secondary throttle position (STP) sensor
● Camshaft position (CMP) sensor
● Crankshaft position (CKP) sensor
● Coolant temperature (ECT) sensor
● Atmospheric pressure (AP) sensor
● Tip-over (TO) sensor
● Oxygen (O^2) sensor (where fitted)

6 Based on the information it receives, the ECU calculates the appropriate ignition and fuel requirements of the engine. By varying the length of the electronic pulse it sends to each injector, the ECU controls the length of time the injectors are held open and thereby the amount of fuel that is supplied to the engine. Fuel supply varies according to the engine's needs for starting, warming-up, idling, cruising and acceleration.

7 On ZR750-J and ZR1000-A1 models, the FI warning light should come on briefly when the ignition is switched ON, then go out – this serves as a check that the circuit is working correctly. If the light comes on and stays on a fault has occurred. If the light does not come on at all check the instrument cluster (see Chapter 8).

8 On ZR750-L/M and ZR1000-B/C models all segments in the LCD display should come on briefly when the ignition is switched ON, then go out – this serves as a check that the circuit is working correctly. If the warning light and the FI letters in the display flash a fault has occurred. If the LCD display does not come on at all check the instrument cluster (see Chapter 8).

9 In the event of an abnormality in any of the sensor signals, the ECU will determine whether the engine can still be run safely. If it can, a back-up mode substitutes the sensor signal with a fixed signal, restricting performance but allowing the bike to be ridden home or to a dealer. In some cases the engine will continue to run after a fault has been registered, but once stopped the engine will not be able to be restarted. If the fault is serious, the fuel injection system will be shut down and the engine will not run.

10 After the engine has been stopped, the appropriate self-diagnostic fault code can be accessed. See Section 8 for fault diagnosis.

8 Engine management system fault diagnosis

ZR750-J and ZR1000-A

1 The self diagnosis system has three modes: user mode (the standard mode), in which the fuel injection system (FI) warning light will come on and stay on to warn the rider that a fault has occurred; dealer mode 1, in which the FI light will emit a series of flashes to denote the current fault code or codes; dealer mode 2 in which the FI light will emit a series of flashes to denote any past fault codes, thereby maintaining a history.

2 If the FI warning light comes on, enter dealer mode 1 as follows to read the fault code: remove the rider's seat (see Chapter 7). Identify the self diagnosis single female bullet connector (see illustration). Prepare an auxiliary lead with male bullet connector on one end and bare wire at the other. Turn the ignition ON. Connect the bare end of the auxiliary lead to the battery negative (-) terminal or lead end and keep it held there – the FI light should start to flash the fault code (see Step 4). Keep the lead earthed (grounded) until you have finished reading the fault code.

3 To read any previously stored fault codes, enter dealer mode 2 as follows: remove the rider's seat (see Chapter 7). Identify the self diagnosis single female bullet connector (see illustration 8.2). Prepare an auxiliary lead with male bullet connector on one end and bare wire at the other. Turn the ignition ON. Repeatedly connect and disconnect the

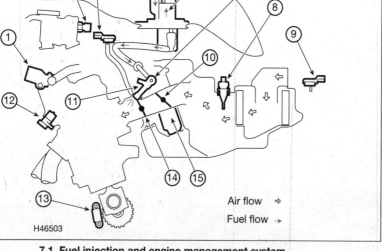

Air flow ⇨
Fuel flow →

H46503

7.1 Fuel injection and engine management system

1 Air system control valve
2 Engine coolant temperature (ECT) sensor
3 Intake air pressure (IAP) sensor
4 Fuel filter
5 Fuel pressure regulator
6 Fuel pump
7 Fuel rail
8 Intake air temperature (IAT) sensor
9 Atmospheric pressure (AP) sensor
10 Secondary throttle position (STP) sensor
11 Fuel injectors
12 Camshaft position (CMP) sensor
13 Crankshaft position (CKP) sensor
14 Throttle position (TP) sensor
15 Secondary throttle servo

8.2 Fault diagnosis connector

bare end of the auxiliary lead to the battery negative (-) terminal or lead five times or more within two seconds, then keep it held there – the FI light should start to flash if there are any previously stored fault codes (see Step 4). Keep the lead earthed (grounded) until you have finished reading the fault code(s). To enter dealer mode 2 from dealer mode 1, with the lead earthed (grounded) switch the ignition OFF, then ON again.

4 The FI warning light emits long (1 second) and short (0.5 second) flashes to give out the fault code. One or more long flashes are used to indicate the first digit of the fault code, and one or more short flashes are used to indicate the second digit (all codes are double digit). There is a 1.5 second gap between long (1 sec) flashes and a 0.5 second gap between the short (0.5 sec) flashes. For example, two long (1 sec) flashes followed by four short (0.5

sec) flashes indicates the fault code number 24. If there is more than one fault code, there will be a 3 second gap before the other codes are revealed (the codes will be revealed in numerical order, lowest to highest). Once all codes have been revealed, the ECU will continuously run through the code(s) stored in its memory, revealing each one in turn with a 3 second gap between them. The fault codes are shown in the table.

ZR750-J and ZR1000-A fault codes

Fault code	Faulty component – ECU response	Possible causes
11	Throttle position (TP) sensor – engine will continue to run but with reduced performance	Faulty wiring or wiring connector Faulty, damaged or improperly installed sensor Faulty ECU
12	Intake air pressure (IAP) sensor – engine will run	Faulty wiring or wiring connector Faulty, damaged or improperly installed sensor Detached, pinched or blocked hose Faulty ECU
13	Intake air temperature (IAT) sensor – engine will run, intake temperature signal fixed at 40°C	Faulty wiring or wiring connector Faulty, damaged or improperly installed sensor Faulty ECU
14	Engine coolant temperature (ECT) sensor – engine will run, coolant temperature signal fixed at 80°C	Faulty wiring or wiring connector Faulty, damaged or improperly installed sensor Faulty ECU
15	Atmospheric pressure (AP) sensor – engine will run, air pressure signal fixed at 760 mmHg	Faulty wiring or wiring connector Faulty sensor Faulty ECU
21	Crankshaft position (CKP) sensor – engine will not run	Faulty wiring or wiring connector Faulty, damaged or improperly installed sensor or timing rotor Faulty ECU
23	Camshaft positionn (CMP) sensor – engine will continue to run, ECU uses last good signal	Faulty wiring or wiring connector Faulty, damaged or improperly installed sensor Faulty ECU
24 and 25	Speed sensor – engine will run, no reading on instrument cluster, gear position signal fixed at 6th	Faulty wiring or wiring connector Faulty damaged or improperly installed sensor Faulty ECU
31	Tip-over (TO) sensor – engine will not run, fuel and ignition systems turned OFF	Machine overturned Faulty wiring or wiring connector Faulty damaged or improperly installed sensor Faulty ECU
32	Secondary throttle position (STP) sensor – engine will run, sensor signal and secondary throttle fixed fully open	Faulty wiring or wiring connector Faulty, damaged or improperly installed sensor Faulty ECU
35*	Immobiliser amplifier – engine will not run	Faulty wiring or wiring connector Faulty amplifier
36*	Ignition key – engine will not run	Faulty or unregistered key
51	No. 1 cylinder ignition coil – engine will run on other 3 cylinders, fuel supply to No. 1 cylinder cut	Faulty wiring or wiring connector Faulty or damaged ignition coil Faulty ECU
52	No. 2 cylinder ignition coil – engine will run on other 3 cylinders, fuel supply to No. 2 cylinder cut	Faulty wiring or wiring connector Faulty or damaged ignition coil Faulty ECU
53	No. 3 cylinder ignition coil – engine will run on other 3 cylinders, fuel supply to No. 3 cylinder cut	Faulty wiring or wiring connector Faulty or damaged ignition coil Faulty ECU
54	No. 4 cylinder ignition coil – engine will run on other 3 cylinders, fuel supply to No. 4 cylinder cut	Faulty wiring or wiring connector Faulty or damaged ignition coil Faulty ECU
62	Secondary throttle servo – engine will run, servo disabled	Faulty wiring or wiring connector Faulty, damaged or improperly installed servo Faulty ECU

* ZR750-J6 and ZR1000-A3 and A6 models with immobiliser only

5 To clear the stored fault codes first enter dealer mode 2 (see Step 3). With the lead kept earthed (grounded), pull the clutch lever in and hold it in for five seconds or more, then release it. Now repeatedly disconnect and connect the bare end of the auxiliary wire five times or more within two seconds, then keep it earthed for at least two seconds more. Remove the lead.

6 Once the code(s) has/have been revealed, identify the fault using the table above, then refer to Step 7 for checking procedures. To leave dealer mode remove the auxiliary lead from the connector and switch off the ignition.

7 The sensors can be checked using home equipment. If a fault appears, use the fault code table above to identify which component is faulty. First ensure that the relevant system wiring connectors are securely connected and free of corrosion – poor connections are the cause of the majority of problems. Also check the wiring itself for any obvious faults or breaks, and use a continuity tester to check the wiring between the component, its connectors and the ECU, referring to the wiring diagrams at the end of Chapter 8. Next refer to Section 9 for specific checks that can be made on that particular component (except codes 35 and 36 which are covered in Section 24, codes 51 to 54 in Section 22). It is also worth removing the sensor(s) in question (see Section 9) and checking that the sensing head is clean and not obstructed by anything. Where there is a vacuum hose to a sensor, make sure it is securely connected at both ends and has no cracks or splits. If this fails to locate and/or solve the problem, the motorcycle should be taken to a Kawasaki dealer for testing.

ZR750-L/M and ZR1000-B/C

8 The self diagnosis system has two modes: user mode (the standard mode), in which the warning light and the FI letters in the LCD display flash to warn the rider that a fault has occurred, and dealer mode, in which the LCD display shows the current fault code or codes.

9 If the warning light and the FI letters in the display flash, enter dealer mode as follows to read the fault code: turn the ignition switch ON and push the mode button on the top left of the instrument cluster to display the odometer. Now push the mode button again for more than 2 seconds – the fault code is shown on the LCD display. If there is more than one fault the codes are displayed sequentially in numerical order. Once all codes have been revealed, the ECU will continuously run through the code(s) stored in its memory, revealing each one in turn with a 3 second gap between them. The fault codes are shown in the table.

ZR750-L/M and ZR1000-B/C fault codes

Fault code	Faulty component – ECU response	Possible causes
11	Throttle position (TP) sensor – engine will continue to run but with reduced performance	Faulty wiring or wiring connector Faulty, damaged or improperly installed sensor Faulty ECU
12	Intake air pressure (IAP) sensor – engine will run	Faulty wiring or wiring connector Faulty, damaged or improperly installed sensor Detached, pinched or blocked hose Faulty ECU
13	Intake air temperature (IAT) sensor – engine will run, intake temperature signal fixed at 30°C	Faulty wiring or wiring connector Faulty, damaged or improperly installed sensor Faulty ECU
14	Engine coolant temperature (ECT) sensor – engine will run, coolant temperature signal fixed at 80°C or 120°C if fan is running	Faulty wiring or wiring connector Faulty, damaged or improperly installed sensor Faulty ECU
15	Atmospheric pressure (AP) sensor – engine will run, air pressure signal fixed at 760 mmHg	Faulty wiring or wiring connector Faulty sensor Faulty ECU
21	Crankshaft position (CKP) sensor – engine will not run	Faulty wiring or wiring connector Faulty, damaged or improperly installed sensor or timing rotor Faulty ECU
23	Camshaft position (CMP) sensor – engine will continue to run, ECU uses last good signal	Faulty wiring or wiring connector Faulty, damaged or improperly installed sensor Faulty ECU
24 and 25	Speed sensor – engine will run, no reading on instrument cluster, gear position signal fixed at 6th	Faulty wiring or wiring connector Faulty damaged or improperly installed speed sensor Faulty ECU
31	Tip-over (TO) sensor – engine will not run, fuel and ignition systems turned OFF	Machine overturned Faulty wiring or wiring connector Faulty damaged or improperly installed sensor Faulty ECU
32	Secondary throttle position (STP) sensor – engine will run, sensor signal and secondary throttle fixed fully open	Faulty wiring or wiring connector Faulty, damaged or improperly installed sensor Faulty ECU
33*	Oxygen (O^2) sensor not activated – engine will run, ECU stops feedback mode to sensor	Faulty wiring or wiring connector Faulty, damaged or improperly installed sensor Faulty ECU
34	Exhaust valve sensor – engine will run, valve fixed fully open	Faulty wiring or wiring connector Broken or detached cable(s) Faulty servo
35**	Immobiliser amplifier – engine will not run	Faulty wiring or wiring connector Faulty amplifier
36**	Ignition key – engine will not run	Faulty or unregistered key

Fault code	Faulty component – ECU response	Possible causes
39	ECU – if no signal is sent by the ECU to the instrument cluster for more than 30 seconds	Faulty wiring or wiring connector Faulty ECU Faulty instrument cluster
51	No. 1 cylinder ignition coil – engine will run on other 3 cylinders, fuel supply to No. 1 cylinder cut	Faulty wiring or wiring connector Faulty or damaged ignition coil Faulty ECU
52	No. 2 cylinder ignition coil – engine will run on other 3 cylinders, fuel supply to No. 2 cylinder cut	Faulty wiring or wiring connector Faulty or damaged ignition coil Faulty ECU
53	No. 3 cylinder ignition coil – engine will run on other 3 cylinders, fuel supply to No. 3 cylinder cut	Faulty wiring or wiring connector Faulty or damaged ignition coil Faulty ECU
54	No. 4 cylinder ignition coil – engine will run on other 3 cylinders, fuel supply to No. 4 cylinder cut	Faulty wiring or wiring connector Faulty or damaged ignition coil Faulty ECU
56	Cooling fan relay	Faulty wiring or wiring connector Faulty relay
62	Secondary throttle servo – engine will run, servo disabled	Faulty wiring or wiring connector Faulty, damaged or improperly installed servo Faulty ECU
63	Exhaust valve servo – engine will run, servo disabled	Faulty wiring or wiring connector Faulty, damaged or improperly installed servo Faulty ECU
64	Air system control valve	Faulty wiring or wiring connector Faulty valve Faulty ECU
67*	Oxygen (O^2) sensor heater – engine will run, ECU stops feedback mode to sensor	Faulty wiring or wiring connector Faulty, damaged or improperly installed sensor Faulty ECU
94*	Oxygen (O^2) sensor output voltage incorrect – engine will run, ECU stops feedback mode to sensor	Faulty wiring or wiring connector Faulty, damaged or improperly installed sensor Faulty ECU

* Only applicable to models with an oxygen sensor
** Only applicable to models with an immobiliser (see Section 24).

10 Once the code(s) has/have been revealed identify the fault using the table above, then refer to Step 11 for checking procedures. To leave dealer mode push the mode button for more than 2 seconds or turn the ignition OFF.

11 The sensors can be checked using home equipment. If a fault appears, use the fault code table above to identify which component is faulty. First ensure that the relevant system wiring connectors are securely connected and free of corrosion – poor connections are the cause of the majority of problems. Also check the wiring itself for any obvious faults or breaks, and use a continuity tester to check the wiring between the component, its connectors and the ECU, referring to the wiring diagrams at the end of Chapter 8. Next refer to Section 9 for specific checks that can be made on that particular component (except codes 35 and 36 which are covered in Section 24, codes 51 to 54 in Section 22, codes 34 and 63 in Section 16, and code 64 in Section 18). It is also worth removing the sensor(s) in question (see Section 9) and checking that the sensing head is clean and not obstructed by anything. Where there is a vacuum hose to a sensor, make sure it is securely connected at both ends and has no cracks or splits. If this fails to locate and/or solve the problem, the motorcycle should be taken to a Kawasaki dealer for testing.

9 Engine management system sensors

Caution: Ensure the ignition is switched OFF before disconnecting/reconnecting any fuel injection system wiring connectors. If a connector is disconnected/reconnected with the ignition switched ON the electronic control unit (ECU) could be damaged.

Throttle position (TP) sensor

Check

1 To check the sensor you need either needle probes for your meter that can be inserted into the back of the connector to contact the terminals with the connector connected, or the test harness (part No. 57001-1538) from Kawasaki that fits between the sensor and its wiring connector (see illustration).

2 Check the input voltage as follows: connect the positive (+) probe of a voltmeter to the blue wire terminal of the sensor wiring connector or the black wire terminal of the test harness, then connect the negative (–) lead to the brown/black wire terminal of the connector or the white wire terminal of the test harness. Turn the ignition switch ON and check that a voltage of 4.75 to 5.25 volts is present. If it isn't, there is a fault in one of the wires or the ECU – check the wires between the sensor connector and the ECU connector for continuity. If the wiring is good check the ECU (Section 10). If voltage was present follow Step 3.

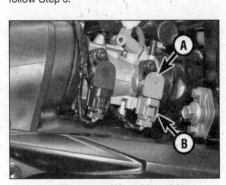

9.1 TP sensor (A) and its wiring connector (B)

9.6 IAP sensor (A) and its vacuum hose (B)

9.9 Disconnect the ECT wiring connector to access the IAP sensor below it

3 Check the output voltage as follows: first warm up the engine and make sure the idle speed is correct (see Chapter 1), then stop the engine. Connect the positive (+) probe of a voltmeter to the yellow/white wire terminal of the sensor wiring connector or the red wire terminal of the test harness, then connect the negative (–) lead to the brown/black wire terminal of the connector or the white wire terminal of the test harness. Turn the ignition switch ON and check that a voltage of around 1.02 volts is present with the throttle closed, and around 4.62 volts is present with the throttle fully open. If the voltage is as specified check the yellow/white wire between the sensor connector and the ECU connector for continuity. If the wiring is good check the ECU (Section 10). If the voltage is not as specified follow Step 4.

4 Check the sensor resistance as follows: disconnect the sensor wiring connector. Connect the positive (+) probe of an ohmmeter to the blue wire terminal on the sensor, then connect the negative (–) lead to the brown/black wire terminal. The resistance should be 4 to 6 K-ohms. If not, the sensor is faulty.

Removal and installation

5 The throttle sensor is an integral part of the throttle body assembly and is not available separately **(see illustration 9.1)**. If the sensor is faulty, a complete new throttle body assembly will have to be installed, though it is worth checking with a Kawasaki dealer to see if anything can be done to avoid this.

Intake air pressure (IAP) sensor

Check

6 To check the sensor you need either needle probes for your meter that can be inserted into the back of the connector to contact the terminals with the connector connected, or the test harness (part No. 57001-1561) from Kawasaki that fits between the sensor and its wiring connector. Remove the fuel tank to access the sensor (see Section 2). Disconnect the ECT sensor wiring connector to improve access **(see illustration 9.9)**. Make sure the all the vacuum hoses between the sensor and throttle bodies are securely connected and in good condition **(see illustration)**.

7 Check the input voltage as follows: connect the positive (+) probe of a voltmeter

to the blue wire terminal of the sensor wiring connector or the green wire terminal of the test harness, then connect the negative (–) lead to the brown/black wire terminal of the connector or the black wire terminal of the test harness. Turn the ignition switch ON and check that a voltage of 4.75 to 5.25 volts is present. If it isn't, there is a fault in one of the wires or the ECU – check the wires between the sensor connector and the ECU connector for continuity. If the wiring is good check the ECU (Section 10). If voltage was present follow Step 8.

8 Check the output voltage as follows: connect the positive (+) probe of a voltmeter to the yellow/blue wire terminal of the sensor wiring connector or the green/white wire terminal of the test harness, then connect the negative (–) lead to the brown/black wire terminal of the connector or the black wire terminal of the test harness. Turn the ignition switch ON and check that a voltage of around 3.8 to 4.2 volts is present at standard atmospheric pressure (higher readings will be obtained at higher pressures, and lower readings at lower pressures). If the voltage is as specified check the yellow/blue wire between the sensor connector and the ECU connector for continuity. If the wiring is good check the ECU (Section 10). If the voltage is not as specified the sensor is faulty.

Removal and installation

9 Remove the fuel tank (see Section 2). Disconnect the ECT sensor wiring connector **(see illustration)**.

10 On ZR750-J and ZR1000-A models undo

9.10 IAP sensor mounting bolt (arrowed) – ZR750-J, ZR1000-A

the bolt securing the sensor then detach the vacuum hose from the underside, disconnect the wiring connector and remove the sensor **(see illustration)**.

11 On ZR750-L/M and ZR1000-B/C models displace the sensor from its bracket then detach the vacuum hose from the underside, disconnect the wiring connector and remove the sensor **(see illustration 9.6)**.

12 Installation is the reverse of removal.

Intake air temperature (IAT) sensor

Check

13 To check the sensor you need either needle probes for your meter that can be inserted into the back of the connector to contact the terminals with the connector connected, or the test harness (part No. 57001-1700) from Kawasaki that fits between the sensor and its wiring connector. Remove the fuel tank (see Section 2). The sensor is mounted in the top of the air filter housing **(see illustration)**.

14 Check the output voltage as follows: connect the positive (+) probe of a voltmeter to the yellow wire terminal of the sensor wiring connector or the red wire terminal of the test harness, then connect the negative (–) lead to the brown/black wire terminal of the connector or the black wire terminal of the test harness. Turn the ignition switch ON and check that a voltage of 2.25 to 2.5 volts is present at 20°C (readings will vary with air temperature variation). If it isn't, there is a fault in one of the wires or the ECU – check the wires between the sensor connector and the ECU connector for continuity. If the wiring is good check the ECU (Section 10). If voltage was present follow Step 8.

15 Remove the sensor (See Step 17). Prepare a pan of oil on a cooker, and a thermometer. Connect an ohmmeter across the sensor terminals and suspend the sensor tip only in the liquid with the thermometer at the same level, making sure both are well away from the bottom of the container. Gradually heat the oil, stirring it give an even temperature, and measure the sensor resistance at 20°C (68°F) and 80°C (176°F). Compare the readings obtained to those given in the Specifications. If the resistance readings differ greatly from those specified, the sensor is probably faulty.

9.13 IAT sensor (arrowed)

9.19 ECT sensor (arrowed)

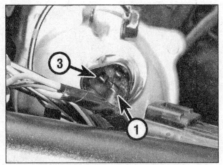

9.21 ECT sensor terminal identification (arrowed)

9.25a AP sensor (arrowed) – ZR750-J, ZR1000-A

Removal and installation

16 Remove the fuel tank (see Section 2).
17 Disconnect the IAT sensor wiring connector (see illustration 9.13). Pull the sensor out of the air filter housing.
18 Installation is the reverse of removal.

Engine coolant temperature (ECT) sensor

Note: *The sensor also operates the coolant temperature gauge (see Chapter 3).*

Check

19 To check the sensor you need either needle probes for your meter that can be inserted into the back of the connector to contact the terminals with the connector connected, or the test harness (part No. 57001-1700) from Kawasaki that fits between the sensor and its wiring connector. Remove the fuel tank (see Section 2). The sensor is mounted in the thermostat housing (see illustration).
20 Check the output voltage as follows: connect the positive (+) probe of a voltmeter to the orange wire terminal of the sensor wiring connector or the red wire terminal of the test harness, then connect the negative (–) lead to the brown/black wire terminal of the connector or the black wire terminal of the test harness. Turn the ignition switch ON and check that a voltage of 2.25 to 2.5 volts is present at 20°C (readings will vary with coolant temperature variation). If it isn't, there is a fault in one of the wires or the ECU – check the wires between the sensor connector and the ECU connector

for continuity. If the wiring is good check the ECU (Section 10). If voltage was present follow Step 21.
21 Refer to Chapter 3, Section 3, Steps 6 to 9 and check the resistance of the sensor, but connect the probes of the ohmmeter between the Nos. 1 and 3 terminals and check the resistances are as given at the beginning of this Chapter at the specified temperatures (see illustration).

Removal and installation

22 Refer to Chapter 3, Section 3, Steps 10 to 13.

Atmospheric pressure (AP) sensor

Check

23 The check for this sensor is the same as for the IAP sensor – refer to Steps 6 to 8, noting that when testing the output voltage the positive probe should be connected to the green/white wire terminal. See Steps 24 and 25 for sensor location.

Removal and installation

24 On ZR750-J and ZR1000-A models remove the seat cowling (see Chapter 7). On ZR750-L/M and ZR1000-B/C models remove the left-hand side of the seat cowling (see Chapter 7).
25 Displace the sensor from its mount then disconnect the wiring connector (see illustrations).
26 Installation is the reverse of removal.

Camshaft position (CMP) sensor

Check

27 Remove the fuel tank (see Section 2). Disconnect the sensor wiring connector (see illustrations).
28 Using an ohmmeter check for continuity between each terminal on the sensor side of the connector and earth (ground). If there is continuity in either case the camshaft position sensor is faulty. Measure the resistance of the sensor by connecting the meter, set to the ohms x 100 scale, to the terminals and compare the reading to that specified at the beginning of the chapter. If the value obtained differs greatly or is zero or infinity the sensor is faulty.
29 To check the peak voltage connect the positive (+) lead of a voltmeter and commercially available peak voltage adapter arrangement to the black wire terminal (ZR750-J and ZR1000-A) or the white/yellow wire terminal (ZR750-L/M and ZR1000-B/C) on the sensor side of the connector and the negative (–) lead to the yellow wire terminal. Turn the engine over on the starter motor and note the peak voltage reading obtained. If this reading is below the specified minimum for your model, the sensor is faulty.
30 If the sensor functions correctly then the fault must be in the wiring between the sensor and the ECU or in the ECU itself.

Removal

31 On ZR750-L/M and ZR1000-B/C models remove the radiator (see Chapter 3).

9.25b AP sensor (arrowed) – ZR750-L/M, ZR1000-B/C

9.27a CMP sensor wiring connector (arrowed) – ZR750-J, ZR1000-A

9.27b CMP sensor wiring connector – ZR750-L/M, ZR1000-B/C

9.33 Unscrew the bolt (arrowed) and remove the sensor

9.36a CKP sensor wiring connector (arrowed) – ZR750-L/M, ZR1000-B/C

32 Remove the fuel tank (see Section 2). Disconnect the sensor wiring connector **(see illustration 9.27a or b)**. Feed the wiring to the sensor, noting its routing.

33 Unscrew the bolt securing the sensor and draw it out of the head **(see illustration)**.

Installation

34 Clean the sensor. Smear the O-ring with oil or grease, then fit the sensor into the cylinder head and tighten the bolt to the torque setting specified at the beginning of the chapter **(see illustration 9.33)**.

35 Reconnect the wiring connector **(see illustration 9.27a or b)**. Install the fuel tank (see Section 2). On ZR750-L/M and ZR1000-B/C models install the radiator.

Crankshaft position (CKP) sensor

Check

36 Remove the right-hand frame cover (see Chapter 7). Trace the CKP sensor wiring from the timing rotor cover and disconnect it at the wiring connector - on ZR750-L/M and ZR1000-B/C models first free the connector from the bracket **(see illustrations)**. Perform the following checks.

37 Using an ohmmeter check for continuity between the black/yellow or yellow wire terminal (according to model) on the sensor side of the connector and earth (ground), and then between the black wire terminal and earth (ground). If there is continuity in either case the sensor is faulty. Measure the resistance of the sensor by connecting the meter, set to the ohms x 100 scale, to the same terminals and compare the reading to that specified at the beginning of the chapter. If the value obtained differs greatly or is zero or infinity the sensor is faulty.

38 To check the peak voltage connect the positive (+) lead of a voltmeter and commercially available peak voltage adapter arrangement to the black/yellow or yellow wire terminal (according to model) on the sensor side of the connector and the negative (–) lead to the black wire terminal. Turn the engine over on the starter motor and note the peak voltage reading obtained. If this reading is below the specified minimum for your model, the sensor is faulty.

39 If the sensor functions correctly then the fault must be in the wiring between the sensor and the ECU or in the ECU itself.

Removal

40 Remove the right-hand frame cover (see Chapter 7). Trace the CKP sensor wiring from the timing rotor cover and disconnect it at the wiring connector - on ZR750-L/M and ZR1000-B/C models first free the connector from the bracket **(see illustration 9.36a or b)**. Release the wiring from any clips and feed it back to the timing rotor cover, noting its routing. Pull the rubber boot off the oil pressure switch, undo the terminal screw and detach the wire **(see illustration)**.

41 Unscrew the timing rotor cover bolts, noting the routing of the wiring and the position of the guides, and remove the cover **(see illustration)**. Discard the O-ring as a new one must be used.

9.36b On ZR750-L/M and ZR1000-B/C models free the wiring connector from the bracket then disconnect it

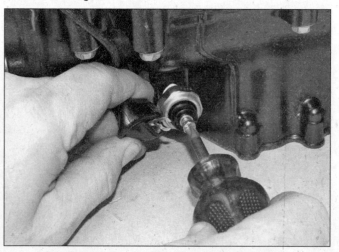

9.40 Detach the wire from the oil pressure switch

9.41 Unscrew the bolts (arrowed) and remove the cover

9.42a Free the wiring grommet . . .

42 Free the wiring grommet from the cut-out, then undo the sensor mounting bolts, and remove the sensor along with the wiring **(see illustrations)**.

Installation

43 Remove all traces of old sealant from the timing rotor cover, crankcase and wiring grommet.
44 Fit the sensor and tighten the bolts to the torque setting specified at the beginning of the chapter **(see illustration 9.42b)**.
45 Apply a smear of fresh sealant all round the grommet and to its cut-out and the crankcase joints on the cover mating surface **(see illustration)**. Fit the grommet into its cut-out **(see illustration 9.42a)**. Install the timing rotor cover using a new O-ring **(see illustrations)**. Make sure the wiring and guides are correctly positioned. Tighten the bolts to the torque setting specified at the beginning of the Chapter **(see illustration 9.41)**.
46 Route the wiring back to the connector and reconnect it **(see illustrations 9.36a or b)**. Fit the oil pressure switch wiring connector and rubber boot **(see illustration 9.40)**. Install the right-hand frame cover (see Chapter 7).

Speed sensor

47 See Chapter 8, Section 16.

Tip-over (TO) sensor

Check

48 To check the sensor you need either needle probes for your meter that can be inserted into the back of the connector to contact the terminals with the connector connected, or the test harness (part No. 57001-1700) from Kawasaki that fits between the sensor and its wiring connector. On ZR750-J and ZR1000-A models the sensor is mounted above the swingarm pivot **(see illustration)** – unscrew the sensor mounting bolts to access the wiring connector on the back. On ZR750-L/M and ZR1000-B/C models remove the rider's seat to access the sensor (see Chapter 7) **(see illustration)**.

9.42b . . . then unscrew the bolts and remove the sensor

9.45a Smear some sealant as shown . . .

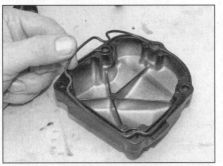

9.45b . . . then fit a new O-ring into the groove . . .

9.45c . . . and fit the cover

9.48a TO sensor (arrowed) – ZR750-J1, ZR1000-A

9.48b TO sensor (arrowed) – ZR750-L/M, ZR1000-B/C

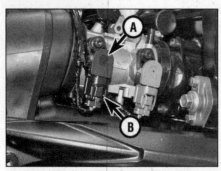

9.55 STP sensor (A) and its wiring connector (B)

9.57a Secondary throttle valves in closed position

9.57b Secondary throttle valves in open position

49 To check the input voltage connect the negative (–) lead of a voltmeter to the black/yellow (ZR750-J and ZR1000-A models) or brown/black (ZR750-L/M and ZR1000-B/C models) wire terminal of the connector (with the connector still connected) or to the red wire terminal of the test harness. Connect the voltmeter positive (+) lead to the white/yellow (ZR750-J and ZR1000-A models) or blue (ZR750-L/M and ZR1000-B/C models) wire terminal of the connector or to the black wire terminal of the test harness. Turn the ignition ON and check the input voltage is as specified at the beginning of the Chapter. Switch the ignition OFF. If it isn't, there is a fault in one of the wires or the ECU – check the wires between the sensor connector and the ECU connector for continuity. If the wiring is good check the ECU (Section 10). If voltage was present follow Step 50.

50 To check the output voltage displace the sensor from its mounting with the connector still connected (see Step 52 or 53). Connect the negative (–) lead of a voltmeter to the black/yellow (ZR750-J and ZR1000-A models) or brown/black (ZR750-L/M and ZR1000-B/C models) wire terminal of the connector (with the connector still connected), or to the black wire terminal of the test harness. Connect the voltmeter positive (+) lead to the yellow/green wire terminal of the connector or to the white wire terminal of the test harness. Hold the sensor upright (so the arrow on the sensor body points up) then switch the ignition ON and check that the output voltage is as specified at the beginning of the Chapter for your model. Slowly tilt the sensor to the left; once the sensor reaches an angle of approximately 60° the output voltage should change again as specified. Switch the ignition OFF and return the sensor to the horizontal, then switch the ignition back ON again and tilt the sensor to the right, checking the voltage again.

51 If the voltage readings are not as given, then it is likely the TO sensor is faulty.

Removal and installation

52 On ZR750-J and ZR1000-A models the sensor is mounted above the swingarm pivot. Unscrew the sensor mounting bolts

then disconnect the wiring connector and remove the sensor (see illustration 9.48a).

53 On ZR750-L/M and ZR1000-B/C models remove the rider's seat to access the sensor (see Chapter 7). Disconnect the sensor wiring connector then unscrew the bolts and remove the sensor (see illustration 9.48b).

54 Installation is the reverse of removal. Make sure the sensor is fitted with its UP arrow pointing upwards (see illustration 9.48a or b).

Secondary throttle position (STP) sensor

Check

55 To check the sensor you need either needle probes for your meter that can be inserted into the back of the connector to contact the terminals with the connector connected, or the test harness (part No. 57001-1538) from Kawasaki that fits between the sensor and its wiring connector (see illustration).

56 Check the input voltage as follows: connect the positive (+) probe of a voltmeter to the blue wire terminal of the sensor wiring connector or the black wire terminal of the test harness, then connect the negative (–) lead to the brown/black wire terminal of the connector or the white wire terminal of the test harness. Turn the ignition switch ON and check that a voltage of 4.75 to 5.25 volts is present. If it isn't, there is a fault in one of the wires or the ECU – check the wires between the sensor connector and the ECU connector for continuity. If the wiring is good check the ECU (Section 10). If voltage was present follow Step 57.

57 Check the output voltage as follows: first warm up the engine and make sure the idle speed is correct (see Chapter 1), then stop the engine. Connect the positive (+) probe of a voltmeter to the brown wire terminal of the sensor wiring connector or the red wire terminal of the test harness, then connect the negative (–) lead to the brown/black wire terminal of the connector or the white wire terminal of the test harness. Turn the ignition switch ON and check that a voltage of around

0.5 volts is present with the throttle closed, and around 3.8 volts is present with the throttle fully open – on ZR750-J and ZR1000-A models move the air filter housing back off the throttle bodies (see Section 11 – there is no need to disconnect any wiring or cables) and turn them by hand, and on ZR750-L/M and ZR1000-B/C models turn them using the lever on the left-hand side of the throttle bodies (see illustrations). If the voltage is as specified check the brown wire between the sensor connector and the ECU connector for continuity. If the wiring is good check the ECU (Section 10). If the voltage is not as specified follow Step 58.

58 Check the sensor resistance as follows: disconnect the sensor wiring connector. Connect the positive (+) probe of an ohmmeter to the blue wire terminal on the sensor, then connect the negative (–) lead to the brown/black wire terminal. The resistance should be 4 to 6 K-ohms. If not, the sensor is faulty.

Removal and installation

59 The secondary throttle sensor is an integral part of the throttle body assembly and is not available separately (see illustration 9.55). If the sensor is faulty, a complete new throttle body assembly will have to be installed, though it is worth checking with a Kawasaki dealer to see if anything can be done to avoid this.

Secondary throttle servo

Check

60 Turn the ignition ON and check that the secondary throttle valves (the rear set of valves in the throttle bodies) open and close – you should be able to hear them, and to see the secondary throttle shaft move, but if not move the air filter housing back off the throttle bodies (see Section 11 – there is no need to disconnect any wiring or cables), then repeat the check. If they don't move remove the throttle bodies and disconnect the servo wiring connector, then check the servo resistance first between the black/blue and pink/blue wire terminals on the servo, then between the green and white/blue wire

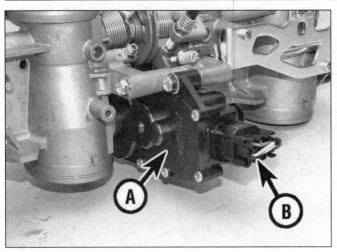

9.60 Secondary throttle servo (A) and its wiring connector (B)

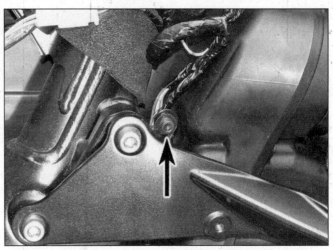

9.64 Unscrew the bolt (arrowed) and displace the bracket to access the sensor wiring connector

terminals **(see illustration)**. The resistance should be 5 to 7.5 ohms in each case. If not the sensor is faulty.

61 If the sensor is good the fault is in the wiring between the sensor connector and the ECU, or in the ECU itself (Section 10).

Removal and installation

62 The secondary throttle servo is an integral part of the throttle body assembly and is not available separately **(see illustration 9.60)**. If the servo is faulty, a complete new throttle body assembly will have to be installed, though it is worth checking with a Kawasaki dealer to see if anything can be done to avoid this.

Oxygen (O²)sensor

Fault code 33

63 To check the sensor you need either needle probes for your meter that can be inserted into the back of the connector to contact the terminals with the connector connected, or the test harness (part No. 57001-1682) from Kawasaki that fits between the sensor and its wiring connector.

64 Start the engine and run it until the cooling fan comes on, then switch it off. Remove the right-hand frame cover (see Chapter 7). Unscrew the wiring connector bracket bolt

9.70 Disconnect the sensor wiring connector

– the oxygen sensor wiring connector is the 4-pin connector **(see illustration)**.

65 Raise the fuel tank, making sure it is secure – the engine will be run with it in this position (see Section 2).

66 Detach the air system control valve hoses from the reed valve covers **(see illustration 18.7)**. Block the unions on the cover with a suitable plugs.

67 Check the output voltage as follows: connect the positive (+) probe of a voltmeter to the blue wire terminal of the sensor wiring connector or the blue/yellow wire terminal of the test harness, then connect the negative (–) lead to the white wire terminal of the connector or the brown/black wire terminal of the test harness. Start the engine and let it idle. The output voltage shown on the meter should be at least 0.7 volts. Now remove the plugs from the reed valve cover unions – the voltage should drop to a maximum of 0.2 volts. Stop the engine.

68 If the voltage is not as specified check the white/blue and brown/black wires between the sensor connector and the ECU connector for continuity. If the wiring is good replace the sensor with a new one. If the voltage reading was as specified check the ECU (see Section 10).

Fault code 67

69 Start the engine and run it until the cooling

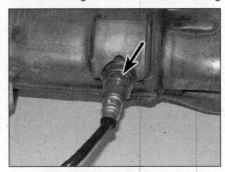

9.75 Oxygen sensor (arrowed)

fan comes on, then switch it off. Remove the right-hand frame cover (see Chapter 7). Unscrew the wiring connector bracket bolt – the oxygen sensor wiring connector is the 4-pin connector **(see illustration 9.64)**.

70 Disconnect the wiring connector **(see illustration)**. Measure the resistance of the sensor using an ohmmeter set to the ohms x 10 scale, across the two black wire terminals and compare the reading to that specified at the beginning of the chapter. If the value obtained differs greatly or is zero or infinity the sensor is faulty.

71 If the reading is good check for battery voltage at the light green wire terminal on the loom side of the connector with the ignition ON. If there is no voltage check the oxygen sensor heater fuse (see Chapter 8), and if that is good the light green wire between the sensor connector and the fuse for continuity. Next check the red wire between the sensor wiring connector and the ECU for continuity. If the wiring and fuse are good check the ECU (Section 10).

Fault code 94

72 Refer to Steps 63 to 67 and check the output voltage.

73 If the voltage is as specified check the ECU (Section 10). If the voltage is not as specified check the fuel pressure (Section 3) and the injectors (Section 12). If they are good replace the sensor with a new one.

Removal and installation

74 Remove the right-hand frame cover (see Section 2). On ZR1000-B/C models remove the right-hand sump cowl (see Chapter 7). Unscrew the wiring connector bracket bolt **(see illustration 9.64)**. Disconnect the oxygen sensor 4-pin wiring connector **(see illustration 9.70)**. Feed the wiring down to the sensor noting its routing and freeing it from its clamp.

75 Unscrew and remove the sensor **(see illustration)**. Take care not to drop the sensor, and keep the sensing portion on the bottom

10.5 Lift the relay unit to access the ECU below it

10.6 Remove the rubber holder off the ECU

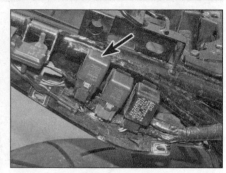

10.9 ECU relay (arrowed)

and the filter holes on the top free of dirt and dust.

76 Installation is the reverse of removal. If the correct tools are available tighten the sensor to the torque setting specified at the beginning of the Chapter.

10 Electronic control unit (ECU) and ECU relay

ECU

Check

1 Disconnect the ECU wiring connectors (see Steps 4 and 5 or 6). Visually inspect the connectors and the terminals in the ECU for dust and corrosion and clean them if necessary. Check for cracked or damaged connectors and bent or broken terminal pins and replace the main wiring harness or ECU with new ones if necessary.

2 It is not possible to check the inner workings of the ECU, only the power source and earth lines. Check for continuity between each of the three black/yellow wires and the battery negative terminal – there should be continuity (zero resistance) in each case. If not make sure the terminal on the battery is clean and tight, and if it is locate and repair or replace the broken wire or connector.

3 Check for battery voltage between the white/yellow wire and the battery negative (–) terminal – there should be no voltage with the ignition OFF and battery voltage with it ON. Check for battery voltage between the white/black wire and the battery negative (–) terminal – there should be battery voltage with the ignition OFF and ON. If there is no voltage where there should be, check the ECU fuse (see Chapter 8), then the ECU relay (see below). If they are good check the wiring and connectors between the ECU, the fuse and the relay for continuity.

Removal and installation

4 On ZR750-J and ZR1000-A models remove the rider's seat. On ZR750-L/M and ZR1000-B/C models remove the left-hand side of the seat cowling (see chapter 7). Make

sure the ignition is OFF, then disconnect the battery leads (see Chapter 8).

5 On ZR750-J and ZR1000-A models lift the relay unit off the ECU **(see illustration)**. Lift the ECU and disconnect its wiring connectors. Remove the rubber sleeve if required.

6 On ZR750-L/M and ZR1000-B/C models unscrew the passenger seat bracket bolts and displace the bracket. Lift the ECU and draw the relay box out of its rubber holder **(see illustrations 4.4a and b)**. Remove the rubber holder, then disconnect the ECU wiring connectors and remove the ECU **(see illustration)**. Note: *A metal security cage was fitted to the ECU on the bike photographed, and this has to be removed before the wiring can be disconnected – remove the foam padding from around the cage, then remove the bolts (drift them round carefully if they are the type that can be tightened but not loosened) and separate the cage halves.*

7 Installation is the reverse of removal. Do not forget to fit the rubber sleeve.

ECU relay

ZR750-J and ZR1000-A1

8 Remove the seat cowling (see Chapter 7).

9 Pull the relay off its mounting and disconnect the wiring connector **(see illustration)**. Using a multimeter or test light, check for continuity between terminals 3 and 4 on the relay **(see illustration 4.2b)**. There should be no continuity. Now use jumper wires to connect the positive (+) terminal of a fully charged 12 volt battery to terminal 1 on the relay and the negative (–) battery terminal to relay terminal 2. There should now be continuity shown across terminals 3 and 4. If the relay fails either of the checks, replace it with a new one.

10 If the relay is good, check for battery voltage at the brown and white/black wire terminals on the loom side of the wiring connector with the ignition ON. If there is no voltage at the brown wire, check the main fuse and the wiring, referring to the relevant wiring diagram at the end of Chapter 8. If there is no voltage at the white/black wire check the ECU fuse (if not already done). If voltage is present, check the white/yellow wire between the relay and the ECU, and the black/yellow wire to earth, for continuity. If all is good the ECU could be faulty.

ZR750-L/M and ZR1000-B/C

11 Remove the left-hand side of the seat cowling (see Chapter 7). Unscrew the passenger seat bracket bolts and displace the bracket **(see illustration 4.4a)**. Draw the relay box out of its rubber holder and disconnect the wiring connectors **(see illustration 4.4b)**.

12 Set a multimeter to the ohms x 1 scale and connect its probes to terminals 6 and 7 **(see illustration 4.5)**. There should be no continuity (infinite resistance). Using a fully-charged 12 volt battery and two insulated jumper wires, connect the positive (+) terminal of the battery to terminal 4, and the negative (–) terminal to terminal 5 on. At this point the multimeter should read 0 ohms (continuity). If this is the case the relay is proven good. If the relay still indicates no continuity (infinite resistance) across its terminals, it is faulty and the relay box must be replaced with a new one – individual relays are not available.

13 If the relay is good, check for battery voltage at the brown and white/black wire terminals on the loom side of the wiring connector with the ignition and kill switch ON. If there is no voltage at the brown wire, check the main fuse and the wiring, referring to the relevant wiring diagram at the end of Chapter 8. If there is no voltage at the white/black wire check the ECU fuse (if not already done). If voltage is present, check the wiring between the relay and the ECU, and the black/yellow wire to earth, for continuity. If all is good the ECU could be faulty.

11 Throttle bodies

⚠ *Warning: Refer to the precautions given in Section 1 before starting work.*

Removal

ZR750-J and ZR1000-A

1 Remove the fuel tank (Section 2). If you detached the fuel hose from the union on the pump, now detach it from the union on the throttle bodies and remove it, noting which way round it fits.

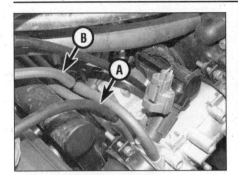

11.2 Disconnect the air system hose (A) and the IAP sensor hose (B)

11.3a Air filter housing bolt (arrowed)

11.3b Release the wiring from the clamp and move the connectors aside (arrowed)

2 Disconnect the air system hose from the air filter housing (see illustration 11.11). Disconnect the air system control valve vacuum hose and the IAP sensor vacuum hose (see illustration). On California models, disconnect the EVAP system vacuum hoses.
3 Remove the side panels (see chapter 7). Remove the coolant reservoir (see Chapter 3). On the right-hand side displace the starter relay and where fitted the immobiliser amplifier as required to access the air filter housing bolt (see illustration). On the left-hand side release the wiring clamp and move the connectors so they do not sit between the air filter housing and the frame (see illustration).
4 Disconnect the throttle body sub-loom wiring connector (see illustration).
5 Refer to Section 13 and detach the throttle cables at the twistgrip, and the fast idle cable at the lever and the throttle bodies.
6 Unscrew the bolt securing the air filter

housing on each side (see illustration 11.3a).
7 Loosen the clamp screws securing the air filter housing to the throttle bodies (see illustration 11.16a). Move the air filter housing back off the throttle bodies as far as it will go (see illustration 11.16b). Close the secondary throttle valves by hand so they are vertical.
8 Loosen the clamp screws securing the throttle bodies to the intake adapters (see illustration 11.17a). Move the clamps forwards out of their grooves. Ease the throttle bodies out of the adapters and draw them out to the left-hand side (see illustration 17.17b).
9 Unscrew the throttle cable retainer plate bolt and remove the plate, noting how it fits (see illustration 11.18a). Draw the throttle closing cable end out of the front holder in the bracket and detach the end from the upper socket in the pulley (see illustrations 11.18b and c). Draw the throttle opening cable end out of the rear holder in the bracket and detach the

end from the lower socket in the pulley (see illustrations 11.18d and e).

ZR750-L/M and ZR1000-B/C

10 Remove the fuel tank (Section 2). If you detached the fuel hose from the union on the pump, now detach it from the union on the throttle bodies and remove it, noting which way round it fits (see illustrations).
11 Disconnect the air system hose from the air filter housing (see illustration). Disconnect the IAP sensor vacuum hose (see illustration). On California models, disconnect the EVAP system vacuum hoses.
12 Remove the side panels and frame covers (see Chapter 7). On the right-hand side unscrew the wiring connector bracket bolt and pull the bracket down (see illustration 9.64). On the left-hand side draw the alternator wiring connector down so it does not sit between the air filter housing and the frame (see illustration).

11.4 Disconnect the wiring connector (arrowed)

11.10a Press the tabs in and push the joint clip up . . .

11.10b . . . and detach the fuel hose from the throttle body union

11.11a Detach the air system hose . . .

11.11b . . . and the IAP sensor vacuum hose

11.12 Move the wiring connector down out of the way (arrowed)

11.13a Disconnect the injector wiring connectors . . .

11.13b . . . the throttle sensor wiring connectors (arrowed) . . .

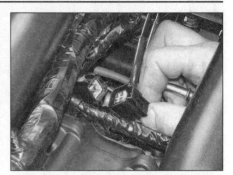

11.13c . . . and the secondary throttle servo wiring connector

11.15a Unscrew the air filter housing bolt (arrowed) . . .

11.15b . . . on each side (arrowed)

11.16a Slacken the clamp screws (arrowed) on each side . . .

11.16b . . . and move the throttle bodies back

13 Release the tie(s) securing the wiring to the fuel rail. Disconnect the wiring connectors from the fuel injectors, the throttle position sensors and the secondary throttle servo (see illustrations).

14 Refer to Section 13 and detach the throttle cables at the twistgrip.

15 Unscrew the bolt securing the air filter housing on each side (see illustrations).

16 Loosen the clamp screws securing the air filter housing to the throttle bodies (see illustration). Move the air filter housing back

off the throttle bodies as far as it will go (see illustration). Close the secondary throttle valves so they are vertical using the lever on the left-hand side (see illustrations 9.57a).

17 Loosen the clamp screws securing the throttle bodies to the intake adapters (see illustration). Move the clamps forwards out of their grooves. Ease the throttle bodies out of the adapters and draw them out to the left-hand side (see illustration).

18 Unscrew the throttle cable retainer plate bolt and remove the plate, noting how it fits

11.17a Slacken the clamp screws (arrowed) on each side . . .

11.17b . . . and carefully manoeuvre the throttle bodies out

11.18a Unscrew the bolt and remove the plate

11.18b Free the closing cable elbow from the holder . . .

11.18c . . . and the cable end from the cam

(see illustration). Draw the throttle closing cable elbow out of the front holder in the bracket and detach the cable end from the upper socket in the pulley **(see illustrations)**. Draw the throttle opening cable elbow out of the rear holder in the bracket and detach the end from the lower socket in the pulley **(see illustrations)**.
Caution: Do not snap the throttle cam/valves from fully open to fully closed once the cables have been disconnected because this can lead to engine idle speed problems.
Caution: Tape over or stuff clean rag into each cylinder head intake after removing

the throttle body assembly to prevent anything from falling in.
19 If the intake rubbers show signs of cracking or deterioration new ones must be fitted, along with new O-rings – first remove the throttle body clamps, then undo the intake rubber screws **(see illustrations)**. Also check the throttle body vacuum hoses and blanking caps for signs of damage or deterioration and replace them all with new ones if any are suspect **(see illustration)**.
Caution: The throttle body assembly must be treated as a complete unit. Do not loosen any nuts/bolts/screws other than as directed here or in the next Section

as they are pre-set at the factory to ensure correct operation. The only components on the assembly which are serviceable are the fuel rail(s) and injectors (see Section 12), the various vacuum hoses and the wiring.

Installation

20 Installation is the reverse of removal, noting the following:
● Connect the cables before installing the throttle bodies. Refer to Chapter 1 and adjust throttle cable freeplay after installing the throttle bodies.

11.18d Free the opening cable elbow from the holder . . .

11.18e . . . and the cable end from the cam

11.19a Remove the clamps, noting how they locate . . .

11.19b . . . then undo the intake rubber screws (arrowed)

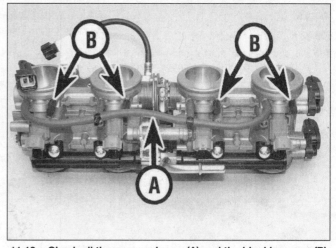

11.19c Check all the vacuum hoses (A) and the blanking caps (B) – varies according to model and country

11.20 Reconnect and secure the fuel hose

12.2 Measuring the resistance of an injector

12.6a Undo the screws (arrowed) . . .

● Remove the tape/plugs from the intakes. Make sure the clamp screws are at the top and pointing out, and that the clamps on the intake adapters are as far forwards as possible.
● Make sure the throttle bodies are fully engaged with the intake adapters on the cylinder head before tightening the clamps.
● Open the secondary throttle valves so they are in the horizontal position before locating the air filter housing – on ZR750-L/M and ZR1000-B/C models use the lever as shown (see illustration 9.57b).
● Make sure the air filter housing ducts locate correctly onto the throttle bodies.
● Refer to Section 2 if required and connect the fuel hose (see illustration).
● Make sure all hoses and wiring connectors are securely connected.
● Check the operation of the cables and adjust them as necessary (see Chapter 1).
● Check the engine idle speed and adjust as necessary (see Chapter 1).

12 Fuel rail and injectors

 Warning: Refer to the precautions given in Section 1 before starting work.

Check

1 If the engine runs, start it and allow it to idle. Check the operation of each injector in the throttle bodies using a sounding rod; an injector will emit a 'clicking' noise when functioning. If any injector is silent, either the injector or its wiring harness is faulty.

2 If the engine does not run, remove the fuel tank (Section 2). Disconnect the wiring connector from each injector (see illustration 11.13a). Connect an ohmmeter between the terminals of each injector in turn and measure the resistance (see illustration). Compare the reading for each injector to that given in the Specifications. If the resistance of any injector differs greatly from that specified a new injector should be installed.

3 If the injectors are good check for battery voltage at the white/red wire terminal in each wiring connector, with the connector connected (insert the needle probes into the back of the connector) and the fuel pump wiring connected. Turn the ignition switch ON - there should be voltage for three seconds. If there is no voltage, check the white/red wire to the fuel pump relay for continuity, then check the relay itself (Section 4). Also check for continuity in the wiring from each injector to the ECU. If the voltage does not drop to zero after three seconds, check the fuel pump relay. If all is good check the ECU, its fuse and relay (Section 10).

Removal

4 Remove the fuel tank (see Section 2). If you detached the fuel hose from the union on the pump, now detach it from the union on the throttle bodies and remove it, noting which way round it fits (see illustration 11.10). If

required, remove the throttle bodies (see Section 11) – this is not essential, but will make the job less fiddly.

5 Disconnect the wiring connector from each injector (see illustration 11.13a). Release the wiring from any clips or ties on the fuel rail.

6 Undo the fuel rail screws (see illustration). Carefully lift off the fuel rail assembly and injectors (see illustration). Remove the seals from the injectors, or from the injector seats in the throttle bodies (see illustration). Discard them as new ones must be used.

7 If required remove the injectors from the fuel rail (see illustration). Remove and discard the O-rings – they must be replaced with new ones.

8 If required separate each section of the fuel rail from the hose union, again discarding the O-rings.

Installation

9 Installation is the reverse of removal, noting the following:
● If the fuel rails were separated from the hose unions, fit new O-rings smeared with clean engine oil then press them together, making the O-rings stay located.
● If the injectors have been removed from their rail fit a new O-ring smeared with clean engine oil onto each one, locating it in the groove (see illustration 12.7). Ease each injector into the rail taking care not to damage the O-ring, aligning the wiring connector bridge between the tabs on each socket.
● Fit a new seal smeared with clean engine oil into each injector seat in the throttle

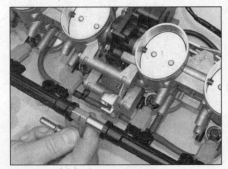

12.6b . . . and remove the fuel rail and injectors

12.6c Remove the seals and discard them

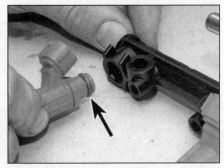

12.7 Remove each injector and discard the O-ring (arrowed)

bodies **(see illustration 12.6c)**. Fit the fuel rail assembly onto the throttle bodies, making sure each injector locates correctly and the seals stay in place **(see illustration 12.6b)**. Fit the fuel rail screws and tighten them **(see illustration 12.6a)**.
● Refer to Section 2 if required and connect the fuel hose to the fuel rail if detached at Step 4 **(see illustration 11.20)**.
● Make sure all wiring connectors are connected and the wiring is secured by any previously released clips or ties.
● Run the engine and check that the fuel system is working correctly before taking the machine out on the road.

13.2a Pull back the boot . . .

13.2b . . . then undo the screws (arrowed) . . .

13 Throttle cables and fast idle cable

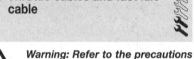

⚠ *Warning: Refer to the precautions given in Section 1 before proceeding.*

Throttle cables

Removal

1 Remove the fuel tank (see Section 2). Mark each cable according to its location.
2 On ZR1000-B/C models pull the rubber boot off the cable housing at the throttle pulley **(see illustration)**. Undo the housing screws and separate the halves **(see illustration)**. Detach the cable nipples from the pulley **(see illustration)**. Mark each cable to ensure it is connected correctly on installation.
3 On all other models refer to Chapter 1 and create maximum freeplay in the cables. Undo the switch housing screws and separate the halves. Detach the cables from the housing and the pulley.
4 Refer to Section 11 and displace the throttle bodies. This procedure involves detaching the cables; it is not possible to detach and fit them with the throttle bodies in place. Withdraw the cables from the frame noting their routing.

13.2c . . . and detach the housing . . .

13.2d . . . and the cables

Installation

5 Route the cables correctly between the handlebar and the throttle bodies. The cables must not interfere with any other component and should not be kinked or bent sharply.
6 Refer to Section 11 to connect the cables and install the throttle bodies.
7 On ZR1000-B/C models lubricate the cable ends with multi-purpose grease and fit them into the throttle pulley – fit the throttle closing cable under the handlebar and into the rear socket on the pulley **(see illustration)**. Fit the opening cable on top and into the front socket **(see illustration 13.2d)**. Fit the elbows into the housing then assemble the housing onto the

handlebar, making sure the pin in the bottom half locates in the hole, then fit the screws and tighten them **(see illustration)**. Fit the rubber boot.
8 On all other models lubricate the cable ends with multi-purpose grease and fit them into the housing and onto the pulley. Join the switch housing halves, locating the peg in the hole in the handlebar.
9 Operate the throttle to check that it opens and closes freely.
10 Check and adjust the throttle cable freeplay (see Chapter 1). Turn the handlebars back-and-forth to make sure the cable doesn't cause the steering to bind.

13.7a Fit the cable end into the rear socket then turn the throttle so the cable feeds round under the handlebar

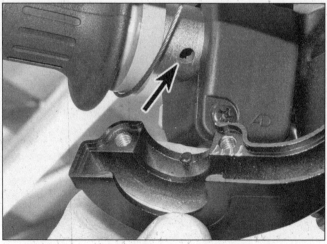
13.7b Locate the pin (arrowed) in the hole in the handlebar

13.14a Separate the housing halves . . .

13.14b . . . then detach the lever . . .

13.14c . . . and free the cable end

11 Install the fuel tank (see Section 2).
12 Start the engine and check that the idle speed does not rise as the handlebars are turned. If it does, the throttle cable is routed incorrectly. Correct the problem before riding the motorcycle.

Fast idle cable (ZR750-J and ZR1000-A models)
Removal

13 Remove the fuel tank (see Section 2).
14 Undo the left-hand switch housing screws and separate the halves **(see illustration)**. Remove the lever, noting how it fits, and detach the cable end **(see illustrations)**.
15 Free the cable elbow from its holder on the throttle bodies and detach the end from the lever **(see illustration)**.
16 Withdraw the cable from the frame noting its routing.

Installation

17 Route the cable correctly between the handlebar and the throttle bodies. The cable must not interfere with any other component and should not be kinked or bent sharply. Lubricate the cable ends with multi-purpose grease.
18 Fit the lower end of the cable into its socket in the lever then fit the elbow into its holder **(see illustration 13.15)**.

19 Fit the upper end of the cable into its socket in the lever, then fit the lever into the switch housing and join the halves, making sure the pin locates in the hole, and tighten the screws **(see illustrations 13.14c, b and a)**.
20 Operate the fast idle lever to check that it opens and closes freely.
21 Check and adjust the cable freeplay (see Chapter 1). Turn the handlebars back-and-forth to make sure the cable doesn't cause the steering to bind.
22 Install the fuel tank (see Section 2).
23 Start the engine and check that the idle speed does not rise as the handlebars are turned. If it does, the cable is routed incorrectly. Correct the problem before riding the motorcycle.

14 Fuel level sensor and display

> ⚠️ **Warning: Refer to the precautions given in Section 1 before starting work.**

Check

1 All models have a six segment fuel gauge and low fuel warning light incorporated in the instrument cluster LCD, actuated by a level

sensor inside the fuel tank. When only one segment remains lit there is approximately 3 litres of fuel left on ZR1000-B/C models, and 5 litres on all other models; when this segment starts to flash and the word FUEL flashes there are only 2.5 litres left on ZR1000-B/C models, and 4 litres on all other models. The level sensor on ZR750-J and ZR1000-A models incorporates a reserve switch.
2 If the system malfunctions raise the fuel tank (see Section 2). Check the wire(s) and connectors between the fuel tank and the instrument cluster for continuity using the wiring diagrams at the end of Chapter 8, and check for continuity to earth in the black/yellow wire. If continuity (zero resistance) is not present, locate the break in the wire or faulty connector and repair or replace as required. Make sure all the connectors are free from corrosion and are securely connected. If the wiring is good remove and inspect the sensor.

Removal

3 Remove the tank (see Section 2). Make sure the fuel cap is secure.
4 Turn the tank upside down and rest it on plenty of clean rag to soak up any fuel that may leak or spill and to protect the paintwork.
5 Release the sensor wiring from its clamps **(see illustration)**. Unscrew the bolts securing

13.15 Free the cable end from the lever (arrowed)

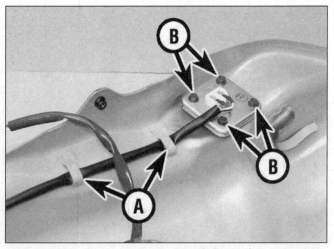

14.5 Free the wiring from the clamps (A), then unscrew the bolts (B) and withdraw the sensor

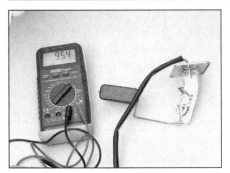

14.7a Check the resistance of the sensor in the empty position . . .

14.7b . . . then in the full position

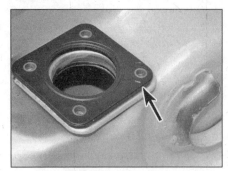

14.11 Make sure the ribbed corner (arrowed) is correctly positioned

the sensor base to the underside of the tank and manoeuvre the sensor out. Discard the gasket as a new one must be used on reassembly.

Inspection

6 Connect an ohmmeter between the white/ yellow and black/yellow wire terminals in the sensor connector.

7 With the sensor float in its lowest (empty) position the meter should show a resistance of between 90 and 100 ohms **(see illustration)**. Carefully raise the float to its highest (full) position – the meter should now show a resistance of between 9 and 13 ohms on ZR1000-B/C models from frame No. 017479-on, and between 4 and 10 ohms on all other models **(see illustration)**.

8 If no readings are obtained, or if they differ greatly from those specified, replace the sensor with a new one.

9 To check the reserve switch on ZR750-J and ZR1000-A models connect a continuity tester between the light blue and black/yellow wires on the sensor connector. There should be continuity. Now refit the sensor in the tank, and with fuel in the tank and the tank the correct way up repeat the test – there should be no continuity. The switch is part of the sensor, so if it doesn't behave as described replace the sensor with a new one.

10 If the tests show the sensor to be good, check the instrument cluster itself (see Chapter 8).

Installation

11 Fit the new seal onto the tank so the ribbed corner is positioned as shown **(see illustration)**.

12 Manoeuvre the sensor into the tank so that the wire on the base will point to the back of the tank **(see illustration)**. Apply a suitable thread locking compound to the bolts and install them finger-tight, then tighten them evenly and a little at a time in a criss-cross pattern to the torque setting specified at the beginning of this Chapter.

13 Secure the wiring in the clamps **(see illustration 14.5)**.

14 Install the fuel tank (see Section 2). Ensure there are no signs of fuel leakage around the sensor base.

15 Exhaust system

⚠️ **Warning: If the engine has been running the exhaust system will be very hot. Allow the system to cool before carrying out any work.**

14.12 Carefully fit the sensor into the tank

HAYNES HiNT *Exhaust system clamp bolts tend to become corroded and seized. It is advisable to spray them with WD40 or a similar product before attempting to slacken them.*

Silencer removal

ZR750-J and ZR1000-A

1 Slacken the silencer clamp bolt **(see illustration)**.

2 Unscrew the nut and remove the washer from the silencer mounting bolt **(see illustration)**. Withdraw the bolt, then ease the

15.1 Slacken the clamp bolt (arrowed)

15.2 Unscrew the nut (arrowed) and remove the washer

15.6a Silencer clamp bolt (arrowed) –
right-hand side, Z1000

15.6b Silencer clamp bolt (arrowed) –
left-hand side, Z1000

15.8a Silencer rear mounting bolt nut
(arrowed)

silencer back off the downpipe assembly and remove it.

3 If necessary remove the sealing ring from the silencer or downpipe assembly and replace it with a new one (see illustration 15.9).

4 Check the condition of the rubber dampers in the footrest bracket and replace them with new ones if necessary.

ZR750-L/M and ZR1000-B/C

5 Refer to Section 16 and detach the cables from the exhaust valve – this can be done after displacing the silencer from the downpipe assembly to improve access if required, but note that the silencer is quite heavy.

6 Slacken the silencer clamp bolt (see illustrations).

7 On ZR750-L/M models unscrew the nut and remove the washer from the silencer rear mounting bolt. Unscrew the front mounting

bolt, noting the washers. Withdraw the rear bolt, then ease the silencer back off the downpipe assembly and remove it (see illustration 15.8c).

8 On ZR1000-B/C models unscrew the nut and remove the washer from the silencer rear mounting bolt (see illustration). If removing the left-hand silencer unscrew the front mounting bolt, noting the washers (see illustration). Withdraw the rear bolt, then ease the silencer back off the downpipe assembly and remove it (see illustration).

9 If necessary remove the sealing ring from the silencer or downpipe assembly and replace it with a new one (see illustration).

10 Check the condition of the rubber dampers in the footrest bracket and replace them with new ones if necessary.

Downpipe assembly removal

11 On ZR750-L/M and all Z1000 models

remove the radiator cowls (see Chapter 7) and the horn (see Chapter 8).

12 Unscrew the radiator lower mounting bolt and move the bottom of the radiator forwards (see illustration). For best access and to negate the possibility of damage, remove the radiator (see Chapter 3).

13 On models with an oxygen sensor, refer to Section 9 and either disconnect the sensor wiring connector, or remove the sensor, as required.

14 On ZR1000-B/C models remove the left-hand silencer. Either slacken the clamp bolt on the right-hand silencer, or remove the silencer. Unscrew the mounting bolt at the back of the downpipe assembly, noting the washers (see illustration).

15 On all other models slacken the silencer clamp bolt(s). If required remove the silencer(s).

16 Unscrew the nuts securing the header pipes to the cylinder head (see illustration).

15.8b Silencer front mounting bolt –
left-hand side (arrowed)

15.8c Withdraw the bolt and remove the
silencer

15.9 Remove the sealing ring (arrowed) if
necessary and fit a new one

15.12 Unscrew the bolt (arrowed)

15.14 Unscrew the downpipe assembly
bolt (arrowed)

15.16 Unscrew the header pipe nuts
(arrowed)

15.17 Draw the flanges off the studs and remove the downpipes

17 Draw the flanges off the studs then manoeuvre the downpipe assembly down off the cylinder head and remove it **(see illustration)**.

18 Remove the sealing ring from each port in the cylinder head or from each pipe and discard them as new ones must be used **(see illustration 15.19)**.

Installation

19 Installation is the reverse of removal, noting the following:

● Fit a new sealing ring onto each header pipe **(see illustration)**.
● If necessary use a new sealing ring between the downpipe assembly and the silencer(s) **(see illustration 15.9)**.
● Apply a smear of copper grease to all nuts and bolts to prevent them from seizing up.
● When fitting the outer washers on the bolt for the front of the silencer on ZR750-L/M models and for the rear of the downpipe assembly on ZR1000-B/C models, fit the outer washer with its conical face pointing out.
● Leave all fasteners loose until the entire system has been installed, making alignment of the various sections easier.
● Tighten the downpipe nuts first, then the mounting bolt(s), then the clamp bolt(s), to the torque settings specified at the beginning of the Chapter.

● Where fitted do not forget to connect the exhaust valve cables (see Section 16), and to install the oxygen sensor if removed and connect its wiring (see Section 9).
● Run the engine up to normal temperature and check that there are no exhaust gas leaks. Allow the system to cool then recheck the torque setting on all nuts and bolts.

16 Exhaust valve

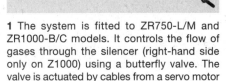

1 The system is fitted to ZR750-L/M and ZR1000-B/C models. It controls the flow of gases through the silencer (right-hand side only on Z1000) using a butterfly valve. The valve is actuated by cables from a servo motor that is controlled by the ECU.
2 Refer to Chapter 1, Section 3 for a functional check of the system.

Servo motor

Fault code 34 – servo actuator sensor

3 Remove the left-hand side panel (see Chapter 7).
4 Disconnect the servo's 3-pin wiring connector **(see illustration)**. Using an ohmmeter or multimeter set to the K-ohms scale check the resistance between the white and black wire terminals on the servo side of the connector. Compare the reading to that specified at the beginning of the Chapter and replace the servo with a new one if the reading differs.
5 To check the input voltage you need either needle probes for your meter that can be inserted into the back of the connector to contact the terminals with the connector connected, or the test harness (part No. 57001-1400) from Kawasaki that fits between the servo wiring connector sections. Connect the positive (+) probe of a voltmeter to the white wire terminal in the servo side of the

wiring connector or to the yellow/white wire terminal of the test harness, then connect the negative (–) lead to the black wire terminal in the connector or black/blue of the test harness. Turn the ignition switch ON and check that a voltage of around 4.75 to 5.25 volts is present. If not check the blue and brown/black wires between the loom side of the servo connector and the ECU for continuity. If that is good check the ECU (Section 10).
6 If the input voltage is good check the output voltage. Connect the positive (+) probe of a voltmeter to the yellow wire terminal in the servo side of the wiring connector or to the blue wire terminal of the test harness, then connect the negative (–) lead to the black wire terminal in the connector or black/blue of the test harness. Turn the ignition switch ON and wait until the servo pulley stops moving, and make sure it is in its original position. Check that a voltage of around 3.46 to 3.76 volts is present. If not check the blue and brown/black wires between the loom side of the servo connector and the ECU for continuity. If that is good check the ECU (Section 10).
7 If the wiring and ECU are good, but the pulley positions are not as they should be as described in Chapter 1, Section 3 yet the cables are correctly adjusted, replace the servo with a new one.

Fault code 63 – servo actuator

8 Remove the left-hand side panel (see Chapter 7).
9 Disconnect the servo's 2-pin wiring connector **(see illustration 16.4)**. Using an ohmmeter or multimeter set to the ohms scale check there is a resistance between the terminals on the servo side of the connector. The reading obtained may be 5 to 200 ohms or more – the important thing is that there is a resistance, and that a reading of either zero ohms or infinite resistance is not shown; if it is, replace the servo with a new one.
10 If the reading is good check the grey and green/red wires between the loom side of the

15.19 Fit a new sealing ring onto each pipe

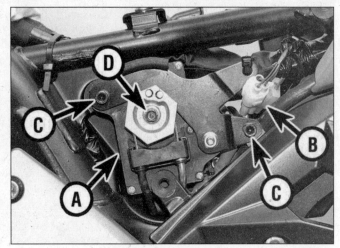

16.4 Exhaust valve servo (A), wiring connectors (B), mounting bolts (C), pulley bolt (D)

16.14a Release the cable clamp . . .

16.14b . . . then detach the cables from the holder . . .

16.14c . . . and the pulley

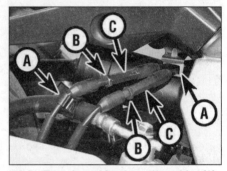

16.21 Free the cables from the guides (A). Cable adjuster locknuts (B) and adjusters (C)

servo connector and the ECU for continuity. If that is good check the ECU (Section 10).

Removal

11 Remove the left-hand side panel (see Chapter 7).

12 Pull the rubber boots off the exhaust valve cable adjusters **(see illustration 16.21)**. Fully slacken the adjuster locknuts then thread the adjusters fully in to give maximum freeplay.

13 Release the cable-tie on the bracket and disconnect the servo's wiring connectors **(see illustration 16.4)**.

14 Remove the cable clamp from the holder on the servo, noting how it fits **(see illustration)**. Free the outer cables from the holder and detach the cables from the pulley **(see illustrations)**.

15 Unscrew the servo mounting bracket bolts and remove the servo **(see illus-**

tration 16.4)**. Unscrew the bolt on the back, counter-holding the nut on the front, and separate the servo from the bracket. Note the arrangement of the collars and washers.

16 Counter-hold the pulley and unscrew its bolt, then detach the pulley – make sure the pulley does not turn as you unscrew the bolt as the servo could be damaged.

Installation

17 Installation is the reverse of removal, noting the following:
● If the pulley was removed, make sure you counter-hold it while tightening the bolt or the servo will be damaged.
● Make sure that the piece of trim is on the top of the servo bracket and the damper pad is on the back.
● Make sure the collars and washers are fitted.
● The cable with the dark elbow fits into the front of the servo and pulley **(see illustration 16.4)**.
● After installation turn the ignition ON and check the pulley rotates as it should (Chapter 1, Section 3).

Exhaust valve

Check

18 Detach the cables from the valve (see below).

19 Turn the valve pulley by hand. If it doesn't turn smoothly or has seized the silencer must be replaced with a new one.

Removal and installation

20 Remove the silencer and replace it with a new one (see Section 15).

Cable renewal

21 Remove the left-hand side panel (see Chapter 7). Mark each cable according to its location as a guide for fitting the new cables (the cable elbows are coloured differently at the servo end and shaped differently at the silencer end). Free the cables from the guides on the regulator/rectifier and brake hose **(see illustration)**.

22 Pull the rubber boots off the exhaust valve cable adjusters **(see illustration 16.21)**. Fully slacken the adjuster locknuts then note the positions of the adjusters (by counting the number of exposed threads) as a guide for installation. Thread the adjusters fully in to give maximum freeplay.

23 Unscrew the valve cover bolts and remove the cover **(see illustration)**. Slacken the locknuts securing the cables in the bracket, then free them and detach the ends from the valve pulley, noting which fits where (the cable elbows are shaped differently) **(see illustrations)**.

24 Remove the cable clamp from the holder on the servo, noting how it fits **(see illustration 16.14a)**. Free the outer cables from the holder and detach the cables from the pulley **(see illustrations 16.14b and c)**.

25 Withdraw the cables from the machine, noting the routing.

26 On installation lubricate the cable ends with multi-purpose grease. Make sure the cables are correctly routed. The cable with the dark elbow fits into the front of the servo and pulley **(see illustration 16.4)**. At the valve end the cable with the smaller radius curve sits

16.23a Unscrew the bolts (arrowed) and remove the cover

16.23b Free the cables from the bracket . . .

16.23c . . . and from the pulley

16.26 Fit the cables as shown

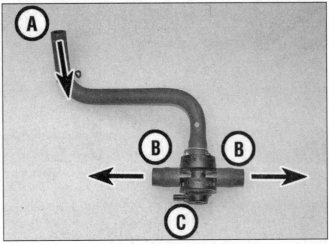

18.4 When blowing into hose (A) air should flow out of hoses (B). Vacuum hose union (C – ZR750-J, ZR1000-A)

above the larger one and goes to the top of the bracket on the silencer **(see illustration)**. Set the cables in the bracket on the silencer so there is 6 mm of the threaded section of each cable elbow (including that covered by the nut) protruding from the rear face of the bracket **(see illustration 16.23b)**. Now set the cable adjusters as noted on removal, then tighten the locknuts **(see illustration 16.21)**. Check the operation of the system (see Chapter 1) – if the servo pulley does not position itself as described the chances are the cables are not correctly set and are stopping the pulley from turning.

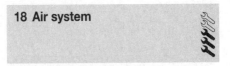

17 Fuel hoses

1 The fuel delivery, vacuum and air system hoses should be replaced with new ones at the first sign of deterioration. On California models, also replace the EVAP emission control system hoses.
2 Remove the fuel tank (see Section 2).
3 Disconnect the various non-fuel hoses from the throttle bodies and the air system control valve, noting the routing of each one and how it is secured. **Note:** *It is advisable to make a sketch of the hoses before removing them to ensure they are correctly installed.* Make sure each new hose is fully pushed onto its union. Use new clamps if necessary where fitted.
4 On ZR750-J and ZR1000-A models press in the tabs on the fuel hose joint and pull it off the union, catching any residual fuel in the rag **(see illustration 2.7)**. When fitting the hose, press the hose joint onto its union until it clicks into place.
5 On ZR750-L/M and ZR1000-B/C models press in the tabs on the fuel hose joint clip and push the clip part-way out of the joint, then pull the joint off the union, catching any residual fuel in the rag **(see illustrations 11.10a and b)**. When fitting the hose make sure

the hose joint clip is part-way out as on disconnection. Press the joint onto its union until it clicks into place, then press the clip into the joint until its tabs click into place **(see illustration 11.20)**.
6 Make sure the fuel hose is secure by pulling and pushing the joint on the union – the hose should not come off, but there should be about 5 mm movement. If the joint does not slide, remove and refit it.

18 Air system

General information

1 To reduce the amount of unburned hydrocarbons released in the exhaust gases, an air injection system is fitted. The system consists of the control valve (mounted under the front of the air filter housing), the reed valves (fitted in the valve cover) and the hoses linking them. On ZR750-J and ZR1000-A models the control valve is opened and closed by a vacuum sourced from the throttle bodies. On ZR750-L/M and ZR1000-B/C models the control valve is opened and closed electronically on a signal from the ECU.
2 Under normal running the control valve is open allowing filtered air to be drawn through the reed valves and cylinder head passages and into the exhaust ports. The air mixes with the exhaust gases, causing any unburned particles of fuel in the mixture to be burnt in the exhaust ports/pipes. This process changes a considerable amount of hydrocarbons and carbon monoxide into relatively harmless carbon dioxide and water. The reed valves in the valve cover are fitted to prevent the flow of exhaust gases back up the cylinder head passages and into the air filter housing. On ZR750-J and ZR1000-A models when the throttle is closed and manifold depression is sufficient to close the control valve, airflow

to the exhaust is cut off, preventing popping. On ZR750-L/M and ZR1000-B/C models the ECU determines when the same manifold depression occurs and the valve should be closed.

Testing

Control valve

3 Remove the valve from the motorcycle (see below).
4 Check the operation of the control valve by blowing through the air filter housing hose union; air should flow through the reed valve hose unions **(see illustration)**.
5 On ZR750-J and ZR1000-A models now apply suction to the small hose union (actual vacuum specified by Kawasaki is 310 to 370 mm Hg) - the valve should close and no air should flow through.
6 On ZR750-L/M and ZR1000-B/C models now apply battery voltage to the control valve connector terminals - the valve should close and no air should flow through. Also check the resistance of the valve by connecting an ohmmeter across the terminals – there should be 18 to 22 ohms **(see illustration)**.

Reed valves

7 Remove the fuel tank (see Section 2). Disconnect the hose from each reed valve

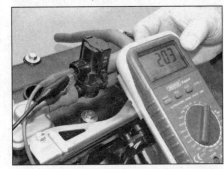

18.6 Check the resistance of the control valve

18.7 Detach the hose (arrowed) from the valve housing

18.10 Detach the vacuum hose (arrowed) from the valve housing

18.11 Disconnect the wiring connector (arrowed)

housing **(see illustration)**. Attach a clean auxiliary hose of the correct bore and about a foot long to one of the unions.

8 Check the valve by gently blowing and sucking on the auxiliary hose end. Air should flow through the hose only when blown down it and not when sucked back up. If this is not the case the reed valve is faulty, though it is worth removing it (see below) and cleaning it in case it is just sticking due to a build-up of muck. Check the other valve in the same way.

Component renewal

Control valve

9 Remove the fuel tank (see Section 2).
10 On ZR750-J and ZR1000-A models disconnect the control valve vacuum hose **(see illustration)**.

11 On ZR750-L/M and ZR1000-B/C models for best access remove the thermostat housing (see Chapter 3). Disconnect the control valve wiring connector **(see illustration)**.
12 Disconnect the air system hoses from each reed valve housing and from the air filter housing **(see illustrations 18.7 and 11.11a)**. Remove the control valve with its hoses attached. Detach the hoses if required.
13 Installation is the reverse of removal. On ZR750-J and ZR1000-A models fit the valve with the vacuum hose union to the left **(see illustration 18.10)**.

Reed valves

14 Remove the fuel tank (see Section 2).
15 On ZR750-J and ZR1000-A models disconnect the CMP sensor wiring connector and free the wiring from the clamp on the

left-hand housing **(see illustration 9.27a)**. Free the ignition coil sub-loom wiring connector from the right-hand housing **(see illustration)**.
16 On ZR750-L/M and ZR1000-B/C models for best access remove the thermostat housing (see Chapter 3). Free the ignition coil sub-loom wiring connector from the right-hand housing **(see illustration 18.15)**. Disconnect the control valve wiring connector **(see illustration 18.11)**.
17 Unscrew the bolts securing the reed valve cover, noting the wiring clamp/connector bracket(s)/shield bracket secured by the bolts according to model **(see illustration)**. Remove the cover, detaching it from the hose, then remove the reed valve, noting which way round it fits **(see illustration)**.
18 Installation is the reverse of removal. Make sure the reed valves and housings are clean and the valves are correctly fitted. Do not forget to secure the wiring clamp/connector bracket(s)/shield bracket according to model.

18.15 Free the wiring connector (arrowed) from the bracket

18.17a Unscrew the bolts (arrowed) . . .

18.17b . . . and remove the cover . . .

18.17c . . . and the reed valve

19 Evaporative emission control (EVAP) system

Note: *This system is fitted to California market models only.*

1 The evaporative emission control system (EVAP) is fitted to minimise the escape of fuel vapour into the atmosphere. The fuel tank is sealed and a charcoal canister collects the fuel vapours generated when the motorcycle is parked and stores them until they can be cleared from the canister, via the separator valve, to be burned by the engine during normal combustion. The separator valve (which controls the flow of the vapour according to whether the engine is running or not) is controlled by a vacuum sourced from the throttle bodies.
2 The storage canister and separator valve are maintenance-free and are designed to operate throughout the life of the motorcycle. Inspection and replacement of the hoses should be carried out according to the service schedule in Chapter 1.

21.2a Disconnect the wiring connector . . .

21.2b . . . and pull the coil off the spark plug

22.2 Unscrew the bolt, noting how it secures the earth wire cluster

20 Catalytic converter

General information

1 A catalytic converter is incorporated in the exhaust system to minimise the level of exhaust pollutants released into the atmosphere. ZR750-J and ZR1000-A models have an open-loop system with no feedback to the ECU. ZR750-L/M and ZR1000-B/C models have a closed-loop system where feedback to the ECU is enabled via an oxygen sensor.
2 The catalytic converter consists of a canister containing a fine mesh impregnated with a catalyst material, over which the hot exhaust gases pass. The catalyst speeds up the oxidation of harmful carbon monoxide, unburned hydrocarbons and soot, effectively reducing the quantity of harmful products released into the atmosphere via the exhaust gases.

Precautions

3 The catalytic converter is a reliable and simple device which needs no maintenance in itself, but there are some facts of which an owner should be aware if the converter is to function properly for its full service life.

● DO NOT use leaded or lead replacement petrol (gasoline) – the additives will coat the precious metals, reducing their converting efficiency and will eventually destroy the catalytic converter.
● Always keep the ignition and fuel systems well-maintained in accordance with the manufacturer's schedule – if the fuel/air mixture is suspected of being incorrect have it checked on an exhaust gas analyser.
● If the engine develops a misfire, do not ride the bike at all (or at least as little as possible) until the fault is cured.
● DO NOT use fuel or engine oil additives – these may contain substances harmful to the catalytic converter.
● DO NOT continue to use the bike if the engine burns oil to the extent of leaving a visible trail of blue smoke.
● Avoid bump-starting the bike unless absolutely necessary.

21 Ignition system check

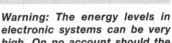

⚠ **Warning: The energy levels in electronic systems can be very high. On no account should the ignition be switched on whilst the plugs or coils are being held. Shocks from the HT circuit can be most unpleasant. Secondly, it is vital that the engine is not turned over or run with any of the coils detached from the plugs, and that the plugs are soundly earthed (grounded) when the system is checked for sparking. The ignition system components can be seriously damaged if the HT circuit becomes isolated.**

1 As no means of adjustment is available, any failure of the system can be traced to failure of a system component or a simple wiring fault. Of the two possibilities, the latter is by far the most likely. In the event of failure, check the system in a logical fashion, as described below.
2 Refer to Section 22 for details on accessing the individual ignition stick coils. Clean the area around each stick coil to prevent any dirt falling into the spark plug channels. Working on one coil at a time, disconnect the wiring connector **(see illustration)**. Pull the coil off the spark plug **(see illustration)**. Reconnect the wiring connector. Connect the coil to a new spark plug and lay the plug against the frame with the threads contacting it. If necessary, hold the spark plug with an insulated tool.

⚠ **Warning: Do not remove any of the spark plugs from the engine to perform this check – atomised fuel being pumped out of the open spark plug hole could ignite, causing severe injury! Make sure the plugs are securely held against the engine – if they are not earthed when the engine is turned over, the ECU could be damaged.**

3 Having observed the above precautions, check that the kill switch is in the RUN position and the transmission is in neutral, then turn the ignition switch ON and turn the engine over on the starter motor. If the system is in good condition a regular, fat blue spark should

be evident at the plug electrode. If the spark appears thin or yellowish, or is non-existent, further investigation is necessary. Turn the ignition OFF and repeat the check for each coil.
4 Ignition faults can be divided into two categories, namely those where the ignition system has failed completely, and those which are due to a partial failure. The likely faults are listed below, starting with the most probable source of failure. Work through the list systematically, referring to the subsequent sections for full details of the necessary checks and tests. **Note:** *Before checking the following items ensure that the battery is fully charged and that all fuses are in good condition.*

● Loose, corroded or damaged wiring connections, broken or shorted wiring between any of the component parts of the ignition system (see Chapter 8).
● Faulty spark plug, dirty, worn or corroded plug electrodes (see Chapter 1).
● Faulty ignition switch or engine kill switch (see Chapter 8).
● Faulty neutral, clutch or sidestand switch (see Chapter 8).
● Faulty crankshaft position (CKP) sensor (Sections 8 and 9) or damaged trigger on timing rotor (Section 23).
● Faulty ignition coil (Section 22).
● Faulty throttle position sensor (Sections 8 and 9).
● Faulty ECU or relay (Section 10).

5 If the above checks don't reveal the cause of the problem, have the ignition system tested by a Kawasaki dealer.

22 Ignition stick coils

Check

1 Remove the fuel tank (Section 2).
2 Clean the area around each stick coil to prevent any dirt falling into the spark plug channels. Access to the coils for cylinders 2 and 3 is restricted by the thermostat housing – unscrew its mounting bolt so it can be moved around to give clearance (see

22.4 To test the coil primary resistance, connect the multimeter leads between the connector socket terminals

22.5 To test the coil secondary resistance, connect the multimeter leads between the left-hand terminal and the spark plug socket

illustration). When removing No. 2 coil on ZR750-J and ZR1000-A models detach the CMP sensor wiring connector from its bracket **(see illustration 9.27a)**. When removing No. 2 coil on ZR750-L/M and ZR1000-B/C models detach the air control valve hose at one end and place it aside **(see illustration 11.11a)**. When removing No. 3 coil on all models detach the coil sub-loom wiring connector from its bracket **(see illustration 18.15)**. If required disconnect the connector and remove the sub-loom.

3 Check that the cylinder location is marked on the coil's wiring sleeve, then disconnect the coil wiring connector **(see illustration 21.2a)**. Pull the coil off the spark plug **(see illustration 21.2b)**.

4 To check the condition of the primary windings, set a multimeter to the ohms x 1 scale. Connect the positive (+) meter probe to the right-hand terminal in the coil socket and the negative (-) probe to the left-hand terminal and measure the resistance **(see illustration)**. If the reading obtained is not within the range given in the Specifications, it is likely that the coil is defective.

5 To check the resistance of the secondary windings, set the meter to the K-ohm scale. Connect the negative (–) meter probe to the left-hand terminal in the coil socket, and the positive (+) to the spark plug contact, using a steel rod or screwdriver as an extension if your probe is not long enough **(see illustration)**. If the reading obtained is not within the range given in the Specifications, it is likely that the coil is defective. To confirm this, it should be

tested as described below using the specified equipment, or by a Kawasaki dealer.

6 Kawasaki specify the peak voltage tester and harness adapter (Pt. Nos. 57001-1415 and -1449) along with an aftermarket digital multimeter, for a complete test. If this equipment is available, connect the harness adapter between the coil wiring connector and the coil itself. Connect the positive (+) lead of the voltmeter and peak voltage adapter arrangement to the white wire terminal on the harness adapter, and connect the negative (–) lead to the red wire terminal.

7 Connect the coil to a new spark plug and lay the plug on the frame with the threads contacting it. If necessary, hold the spark plug with an insulated tool. Check that the kill switch is in the RUN position and the transmission is in neutral, then turn the ignition switch ON. Note the initial voltage reading on the meter, then turn the engine over on the starter motor for 4 to 5 seconds and note the ignition coil peak voltage reading on the meter. Kawasaki specify to repeat the test five times. Once both readings have been noted, turn the ignition switch off and disconnect the meter.

8 If the initial voltage reading is not as specified or the peak voltage readings are lower than the specified minimum, and the coil resistances as tested above are good, then a fault is present somewhere else in the ignition system circuit (see Section 21); note that the peak voltage readings for each coil can be different but each one must exceed the specified minimum.

9 If the initial and peak voltage readings are as specified and the plug does not spark, then the coil is faulty and must be replaced with a new one; the coil is a sealed unit and cannot therefore be repaired.

Removal and installation

10 Remove the fuel tank (Section 2).
11 Refer to Step 2 for access to each coil.
12 Check that the cylinder location is marked on the coil's wiring sleeve, then disconnect the coil wiring connector **(see illustration 21.2a)**. Pull the coil off the spark plug **(see illustration 21.2b)**.
13 Installation is the reverse of removal.

23 Timing rotor

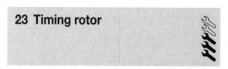

Removal

1 Unscrew the timing rotor cover bolts, noting the routing of the wiring and the position of the guides, and remove the cover **(see illustration 9.41)**. Discard the O-ring as a new one must be used.
2 Counter-hold the rotor using a suitable holding tool and unscrew the bolt **(see illustration)**.
3 Remove the rotor from the end of the crankshaft, noting how it locates.

Installation

4 Fit the rotor onto the end of the crankshaft, aligning the wide splines – it can only fit one way **(see illustration)**.
5 Fit the bolt, then counter-hold the rotor and tighten the bolt to the torque setting specified at the beginning of the Chapter **(see illustration)**.
6 Remove all traces of old sealant from the timing rotor cover, crankcase and wiring grommet. Apply a smear of fresh sealant to the grommet and the crankcase joints on the cover mating surface **(see illustration 9.45a)**.
7 Install the timing rotor cover using a new O-ring **(see illustrations 9.45b and c)**. Make sure the wiring and guides are correctly positioned **(see illustration 9.41)**. Tighten the cover bolts to the torque setting specified at the beginning of the Chapter.

23.2 Counter-hold the rotor using a suitable holding tool that locates into the holes in the rotor and unscrew the bolt

23.4 Align the wide splines and slide the rotor onto the shaft

23.5 Fit the bolt with its washer and tighten it to the specified torque

24 Immobiliser system

General information

1 An immobiliser system is fitted to ZR750-J6, ZR1000-A3, ZR1000-A6, ZR750-L7/M7, ZR750-L8, ZR1000-B7/C7, ZR1000-B8/C8 models sold in certain markets. Other models have facility in the wiring loom for connection of an immobiliser as optional equipment. The system will only allow the machine to be started if the correct registered key is used to turn the ignition ON. The system consists of a transponder which is part of the ignition key, a receiver which is fitted around the ignition switch, an amplifier and the ECU.

2 On ZR750-J6 and ZR1000-A3 and A6 models when the ignition is switched ON, the FI warning light comes on for two seconds and extinguishes when the ECU matches the code of the key being used with that stored in the ECU memory. If the key code signal is not recognised, the engine cannot be started and the FI light flashes. If there is a fault in the system, the FI warning light will flash. In either case refer to Section 8 to identify the fault code, then perform the checks given in this Section on the components as required.

3 On ZR750-L7/M7 and L8, and ZR1000-B7/C7 and B8/C8 models when the ignition is switched ON, the warning light and the key symbol in the LCD display come on briefly and extinguish when the ECU matches the code of the key being used with that stored in the ECU memory. If the key code signal is not recognised, the engine cannot be started and the light and symbol flash. If there is a fault in the system, the warning light and symbol will flash. In either case refer to Section 8 to identify the fault code, then perform the checks given in this Section on the components as required.

4 When the ignition is turned OFF the warning light flashes for a period of 24 hours before switching itself off, though the immobiliser system is still functional. To turn this flashing function off or on, press the mode and reset buttons on the instrument cluster down simultaneously for more than 2 seconds within 20 seconds of turning the ignition off. If the battery is low the flashing functions automatically switches off. If the battery is disconnected the flashing function is automatically set on when the battery is reconnected.

5 The ECU stores the codes for the registered master key (which has a red head) and up to five user keys (which have black heads). The master key should be kept in a safe place and not be used – if it is lost it is not possible to register any new user keys, so in the event they are also lost a new ECU must be installed. The user keys should be kept separately (i.e. not on the same key-ring) as the proximity of another key to the one being used in the switch can lead to the signal from it being jammed, and the bike will not start. The key has a built

24.7 Key registration wiring connector (arrowed) – ZR750-L/M and ZR1000-B/C

in transponder which can be damaged if the key is dropped or knocked, gets too hot, is too close to a magnetic object, or is submerged in water for too long. Always make sure you have at least one spare key. If a new key is obtained, it must be registered into the system before the bike can be started. For additional security if a key is lost it is best have the key registration invalidated in the ECU - take along your master key and a spare key.

Key registration procedure

With old ignition switch

Note: To do this you will need the Kawasaki special tool (Part No. 57001-1582) which is a wiring loom adapter that connects to a wiring connector under the seat. Otherwise registration must be carried at a Kawasaki dealer with the special tool.

6 Obtain a new key from a Kawasaki dealer, and have it cut to match the original key.

7 On ZR750-J6 and ZR1000-A3 and A6 models remove the rider's seat (see Chapter 7) – the connector is on the right-hand end of the junction box **(see illustration 10.5)**. On ZR750-L7/M7 and L8, and ZR1000-B7/C7 and B8/C8 models remove the pillion seat (see Chapter 7) – the connector is on the right-hand side **(see illustration)**. Remove the blanked side of the wiring connector and connect the special tool in its place.

8 Turn the ignition switch ON using the master key. The warning light in the instrument cluster should flash at 0.5 second intervals. If the light flashes at 0.2 second intervals check the immobiliser amplifier, and if it flashes at 0.3 second intervals the master key has not been recognised.

9 Turn the ignition OFF and remove the master key, placing it well away from the receiver – the light should flash at 0.5 second intervals, indicating that the system is in registration mode.

10 Within 15 seconds insert the new key into the switch and turn it ON. The light should now flash twice (for the first key being registered, three times for the second key, four times for the third key and so on for up to five keys) at 0.3 second intervals, then go out for 1 second, then repeat this pattern. This indicates that the system has registered the new key. If the light flashes continuously at 0.2 second intervals check the immobiliser amplifier (see below), if

it flashes at 0.3 second intervals the key has not been registered, if it flashes at 0.5 second intervals the key is already registered.

11 Turn the ignition OFF and remove the key – the FI light should flash at 0.5 second intervals, indicating that the system is still in registration mode. To register any other keys, repeat Step 8 within 15 seconds. After 15 seconds the system leaves registration mode.

12 On completion turn the ignition OFF, wait 15 seconds until the system is no longer in registration mode, then remove the special tool and fit the blank in its place.

13 Check that all registered keys can start the motorcycle.

With a new ignition switch

Note: To do this you will need the Kawasaki special tool (Part No. 57001-1582) which is a wiring loom adapter that connects to a wiring connector under the rider's seat. Otherwise registration must be carried at a Kawasaki dealer with the special tool.

14 Obtain a new switch, which comes with two new keys.

15 Remove the faulty switch (see Chapter 8), but retain the receiver to fit with the new switch.

16 On ZR750-J6 and ZR1000-A3 and A6 models remove the rider's seat (see Chapter 7) – the connector is on the right-hand end of the junction box **(see illustration 10.5)**. On ZR750-L7/M7 and L8, and ZR1000-B7/C7 and B8/C8 models remove the pillion seat (see Chapter 7) – the connector is on the right-hand side **(see illustration 24.7)**. Remove the blanked side of the wiring connector and connect the special tool in its place.

17 Connect the new ignition switch and the original receiver to their connectors, but keep them at least 15 cm apart. Place the master key next to the receiver.

18 Turn the new switch ON with one of the new keys. The warning light in the instrument cluster should flash at 0.5 second intervals. If the light flashes at 0.2 second intervals check the immobiliser amplifier, and if it flashes at 0.3 second intervals the master key has not been recognised.

19 Turn the ignition OFF and remove the new key. Within fifteen seconds fit the receiver onto the new switch. Insert the new key into the switch and turn it ON. The light should now flash twice (for the first key being registered, three times for the second key, four times for the third key and so on for up to five keys) at 0.3 second intervals, then go out for 1 second, then repeat this pattern. This indicates that the system has registered the new key. If the light flashes continuously at 0.2 second intervals check the immobiliser amplifier (see below), if it flashes at 0.3 second intervals the key has not been registered, if it flashes at 0.5 second intervals the key is already registered.

20 Turn the ignition OFF and remove the key – the light should flash at 0.5 second intervals, indicating that the system is still in registration mode. To register any other keys, repeat Step

24.33a On ZR750-L/M and ZR1000-B/C models detach the reservoir hose and place it aside ...

24.33b ... then lift and pull back the rubber boot (arrowed)

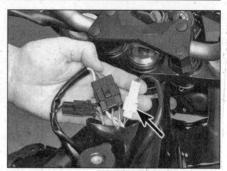

24.33c Receiver connector (arrowed)

17 within 15 seconds. After 15 seconds the system leaves registration mode.

21 On completion turn the ignition OFF, wait 15 seconds until the system is no longer in registration mode, then remove the special tool and fit the blank in its place.

22 Check that all registered keys can start the motorcycle.

With a new ECU (electronic control unit)

23 Obtain and install a new ECU (see Section 10).

24 Insert the master key into the switch and turn it ON. The warning light in the instrument cluster should flash once, then go out for 1 second, then repeat this pattern. This indicates that the system has registered the master key. If the light flashes continuously at 0.2 second intervals check the immobiliser amplifier (see below), if it flashes at 0.3 second intervals the key has not been registered.

25 Turn the ignition OFF and remove the master key. The immobiliser indicator light should flash at 0.5 second intervals.

26 Insert the first user key within 15 seconds and turn the ignition ON. The light should now flash twice (for the first user key being registered, three times for the second key, four times for the third key and so on for up to five keys) at 0.3 second intervals, then go out for 1 second, then repeat this pattern. This indicates that the system has registered the new key. If the light flashes continuously at 0.2 second intervals check the immobiliser amplifier (see below), if it flashes at 0.3 second intervals the key has not been registered, if it flashes at 0.5 second intervals the key is already registered.

27 Turn the ignition OFF and remove the key – the light should flash at 0.5 second intervals, indicating that the system is still in registration mode. To register any other keys, repeat Step 8 within 15 seconds. After 15 seconds the system leaves registration mode.

28 On completion turn the ignition OFF, wait 15 seconds until the system is no longer in registration mode.

29 Check that all registered keys can start the motorcycle.

Fault code 35

30 If fault code 35 is displayed (see Section 8), first check the receiver, then the amplifier (see below)

Fault code 36

31 If fault code 36 is displayed (see Section 8), either the transponder in the registered key being used has failed, or the key being used has not been registered. First try the key registration procedure above (Steps 6 to 13), and if the fault code still appears then replace the key with a new one and register it.

Receiver

Check

32 Remove the fuel tank (see Section 2).

33 Disconnect the receiver wiring connector (see illustrations) – on ZR750-L7/M7 and L8, and ZR1000-B7/C7 and B8/C8 keep the hose above the level of the reservoir or it will drain. Connect the probes of an ohmmeter to the terminals in the receiver side of the wiring connector and check the resistance. If it is not

as specified at the beginning of the Chapter replace the receiver with a new one.

Removal and installation

34 Remove the ignition switch (see Chapter 8).

35 Cut the cable-tie securing the receiver wiring. Undo the screws securing the receiver to the switch, then release the shroud from the tabs on the switch and remove the receiver and shroud (see illustration).

36 Fit a new receiver to the switch along with the shroud, making sure the wiring is routed down the channel. Install the switch (see Chapter 8).

Amplifier

Check

37 On ZR750-J6 and ZR1000-A3 and A6 models remove the right-hand side panel (see Chapter 7). On ZR750-L7/M7 and L8, and ZR1000-B7/C7 and B8/C8 models displace the fairing, leaving the wiring connected.

38 Check for battery voltage at the brown/white wire terminal in the amplifier connector with the connector connected and the ignition ON. Also check for continuity to earth in the black/yellow wire. Check for continuity in all the wiring and connectors, referring to the wiring diagrams in Chapter 8.

39 If all the wiring is good check the receiver. If that is good replace the amplifier with a new one.

Removal and installation

40 On ZR750-J6 and ZR1000-A3 and A6 models remove the right-hand side panel (see Chapter 7). Free the amplifier from its bracket and disconnect the wiring connector.

41 On ZR750-L7/M7 and L8 models remove the fairing (see Chapter 7). Unscrew the four bolts securing the fairing stay and brake hose holder and displace the stay. Unscrew the bolt and remove the holder, noting how it locates. Free the amplifier from its bracket and disconnect the wiring connector.

42 On ZR1000-B7/C7, ZR1000-B8/C8 models remove the fairing (see Chapter 7). Unscrew the amplifier holder and bracket bolts and remove the whole lot, noting how the holder locates (see illustration). Free the amplifier from its bracket and disconnect the wiring connector..

43 Installation is the reverse of removal.

24.35 Receiver screws (arrowed)

24.42 Immobiliser amplifier (arrowed)

Chapter 5
Frame and suspension

Contents

Degrees of difficulty

Easy, suitable for novice with little experience 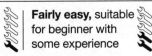	Fairly easy, suitable for beginner with some experience	Fairly difficult, suitable for competent DIY mechanic	Difficult, suitable for experienced DIY mechanic	Very difficult, suitable for expert DIY or professional

Specifications

Front forks

Fork oil type
- ZR750-J .... Kayaba KHL34-G10 or equivalent
- ZR750-L/M .... Kayaba 01 (KHL15-10) or equivalent SAE 5W
- All Z1000 models .... Showa SS08 or equivalent SAE 10W fork oil

Fork oil capacity (approx.)

At oil change
- ZR750-J1 and J2 .... 385 ml
- ZR750-J6 .... 390 ml
- ZR750-L/M
  - Right fork .... 400 ml
  - Left fork .... 410 ml
- ZR1000-A
  - Right fork .... 385 ml
  - Left fork .... 400 ml
- ZR1000-B/C .... 365 ml

At overhaul
- ZR750-J1 and J2 .... 452 ± 4 ml
- ZR750-J6 .... 457 ± 4 ml
- ZR750-L/M
  - Right fork .... 469 ± 4 ml
  - Left fork .... 485 ± 4 ml
- ZR1000-A
  - Right fork .... 450 ± 2.5 ml
  - Left fork .... 468 ± 2.5 ml
- ZR1000-B/C .... 430 ± 2.5 ml

Front forks (continued)

Fork oil level*
  ZR750-J1 and J2 .... 115 ± 2 mm
  ZR750-J6 .... 110 ± 2 mm
  ZR750-L/M
    Right fork .... 106 ± 2 mm
    Left fork .... 100 ± 2 mm
  ZR1000-A
    Right fork .... 62 ± 2 mm
    Left fork .... 47 ± 2 mm
  ZR1000-B/C .... 100 ± 2.5 ml
Fork spring free length (min)
  ZR750-J
    Standard .... 277.2 mm
    Service limit .... 272 mm
  ZR750-L/M
    Standard .... 260.6 mm
    Service limit .... 255 mm
  ZR1000-A
    Standard .... 282.7 mm
    Service limit .... 277 mm
  ZR1000-B/C
    Standard .... 272.0 mm
    Service limit .... 267 mm

Oil level is measured from the top of the tube with the fork spring removed and the leg fully compressed.

Torque settings

Clutch lever bracket clamp bolts .... 8 Nm
Footrest bracket bolts
  ZR750-J .... 34 Nm
  ZR750-L/M .... 25 Nm
  ZR1000-A .... 34 Nm
  ZR1000-B/C .... 25 Nm
Fork damper cartridge bolt
  ZR750-J .... 30 Nm
  ZR750-L/M .... 40 Nm
  ZR1000-A6 .... 20 Nm
  ZR1000-B/C .... 20 Nm
Fork top bolt
  ZR750-J .... 25 Nm
  ZR750-L/M .... 23 Nm
  ZR1000-A .... 35 Nm
  ZR1000-B/C .... 34 Nm
Fork top bolt locknut
  ZR750-L/M .... 15 Nm
  ZR1000-A .... 20 Nm
  ZR1000-B/C .... 19 Nm
Fork yoke clamp bolts
  ZR750-J
    Top yoke bolts .... 20 Nm
    Bottom yoke bolts .... 20 Nm
  ZR750-L/M
    Top yoke bolts .... 20 Nm
    Bottom yoke bolts .... 21 Nm
  ZR1000-A1
    Top yoke bolts .... 9 Nm
    Bottom yoke bolts .... 20 Nm
  ZR1000-A2, A3 and A6
    Top yoke bolts .... 13 Nm
    Bottom yoke bolts .... 29 Nm
  ZR1000-B/C
    Top yoke bolts .... 20 Nm
    Bottom yoke bolts
      Upper and lower bolts .... 25 Nm
      Middle bolts .... 17 Nm
Handlebar clamp bolts .... 25 Nm
Handlebar holder nuts .... 34 Nm
Shock absorber bolt nuts .... 34 Nm

Torque settings (continued)

Sidestand bracket bolts . . . . 49 Nm
Sidestand pivot bolt . . . . 44 Nm
Sidestand switch bolt . . . . 9 Nm
Steering head bearing adjuster nut
   Initial setting (pre-load)
      ZR750-J . . . . 39 Nm
      ZR750-L/M . . . . 55 Nm
      ZR1000-A . . . . 39 Nm
      ZR1000-B/C . . . . 55 Nm
   Final setting (with special tool) . . . . 27 Nm
Steering stem bolt . . . . 108 Nm
Suspension linkage arm-to-frame bolt nut . . . . 34 Nm
Suspension linkage rod bolt nuts . . . . 59 Nm
Swingarm pivot bolt locknut . . . . 98 Nm
Swingarm pivot bolt nut
   ZR1000-A . . . . 127 Nm
   All other models . . . . 108 Nm

1 General information

All models have a tubular steel frame which uses the engine as a stressed member.

Front suspension is by a pair of oil-damped telescopic forks. On ZR750-J the forks are conventionally mounted, have a conventional damper and are non-adjustable. On ZR750-L/M and ZR1000-A models the forks are upside-down, have a cartridge damper and are adjustable for spring pre-load on both forks and rebound damping on the right-hand fork. On ZR1000-B/C models the forks are upside-down, have a cartridge damper and are adjustable for spring pre-load and rebound damping on both forks.

At the rear, a box-section swingarm, made of steel on the Z750 and aluminium on the Z1000, acts on a single shock absorber via a three-way linkage. The swingarm pivots through the frame. The shock absorber is adjustable for spring pre-load and rebound damping.

2 Frame inspection and repair

1 The frame should not require attention unless accident damage has occurred. In most cases, fitting a new frame is the only satisfactory remedy for such damage. A few frame specialists have the jigs and other equipment necessary for straightening frames to the required standard of accuracy, but even then there is no simple way of assessing to what extent the frame may have been over stressed.

2 After a high mileage, examine the frame closely for signs of cracking or splitting at the welded joints. Loose engine mounting bolts can cause ovaling or fracturing of the mounting points. Minor damage can often be repaired by specialised welding, depending on the extent and nature of the damage.

3 Remember that a frame that is out of alignment will cause handling problems. If, as the result of an accident, misalignment is suspected, it will be necessary to strip the machine completely so the frame can be thoroughly checked by a specialist using a frame alignment jig.

3 Footrests, brake pedal and gearchange lever

Footrests

1 Front footrests: remove the E-clip from the bottom of the footrest pivot pin, then withdraw the pivot pin (see illustrations). Remove the footrest, noting the fitting of the return spring.

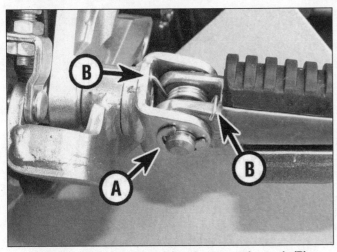

3.1a Front footrest E-clip (A) and return spring ends (B)

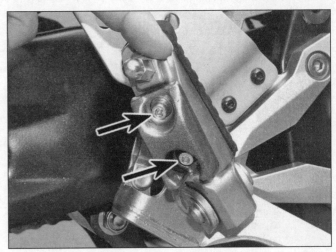

3.1b Undo the screws or bolts (arrowed) to remove the rubber

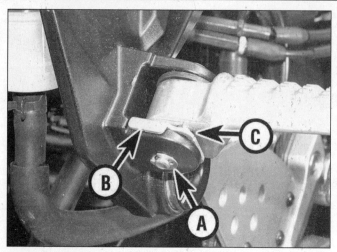

3.2 Rear footrest E-clip (A), detent plate (B) and ball (C)

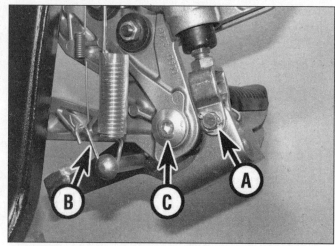

3.4 Remove the split pin (A) and withdraw the clevis pin, and unhook the springs (B), noting how they are joined. Footrest holder bolt (C)

If required undo the screws or bolts and separate the rubber from the peg – the rubber is available separately.

2 Rear footrests: remove the split pin and washer or E-clip (according to model) from the bottom of the footrest pivot pin, then withdraw the pivot pin **(see illustration)**. Remove the footrest, noting the fitting of the washer, detent plate, balls and springs, and take care not to let the ball(s) and spring(s) ping away when removing the footrest.

3 Installation is the reverse of removal. Apply a small amount of grease to the sliding surfaces of mated parts. Use new split pins where fitted, and use new E-clips if they are deformed.

Brake pedal

Removal

4 Remove the split pin from the clevis pin securing the brake pedal to the master cylinder pushrod, then withdraw the pin and detach

the pushrod from the pedal **(see illustration)**.
5 Unhook the brake pedal return spring from the hook on the pedal, noting how the brake light switch spring hooks onto it **(see illustration 3.4)**.
6 Unscrew the footrest bracket bolts and displace the bracket, taking care not to strain the hose and wiring **(see illustration)**.
7 Unscrew the footrest holder bolt and remove the footrest assembly and pedal, noting how they fit **(see illustration 3.4)**.

Installation

8 Installation is the reverse of removal, noting the following:
● Clean off any old grease and dirt. Apply grease to the pedal pivot.
● Make sure the footrest holder is angled correctly so the flat section locates against the lug on the inside of the bracket.
● Clean the threads of the footrest holder bolt and bracket bolts and apply a suitable non-permanent thread locking compound.

Tighten the footrest bracket bolts to the torque setting specified at the beginning of the Chapter for your model.
● Use a new split pin to secure the clevis pin. Do not forget to connect the springs **(see illustration 3.4)**.
● Check the operation of the rear brake light switch and check the rear brake pedal height (see Chapter 1).

Gearchange lever and linkage

Removal

9 Slacken the gearchange lever linkage rod locknuts, then unscrew the rod and separate it from the lever and the arm (the rod is reverse-threaded on one end and so will simultaneously unscrew from both lever and arm when turned in the one direction) **(see illustration)**. Note how far the rod is threaded into the lever and arm as this determines the height of the lever relative to the footrest.
10 Unscrew the footrest bracket bolts and

3.6 Unscrew the bolts (arrowed) and displace the bracket

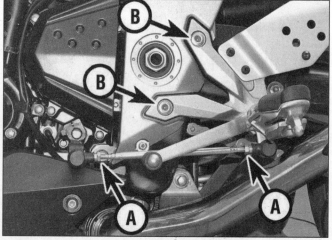

3.9 Slacken the locknuts (A) and thread the rod out. Footrest bracket bolts (B)

4.3a Unhook the springs (arrowed)

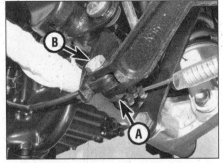

4.3b Unscrew the nut (A), then unscrew the bolt (B)

4.4 Stand bracket bolts (arrowed)

displace the bracket **(see illustration 3.9)**. Unscrew the footrest holder bolt and remove the footrest assembly and pedal, noting how they fit. Check the condition of the grease seal on each side of the lever and replace them with new ones if necessary.

Installation

11 Installation is the reverse of removal, noting the following:
● Clean off any old grease and dirt. Apply grease to the pivot.
● Make sure the footrest holder is angled correctly so the flat section locates against the lug on the inside of the bracket.
● Clean the threads of the footrest holder bolt and bracket bolts and apply a suitable non-permanent thread locking compound. Tighten the footrest bracket bolts to the torque setting specified at the beginning of the Chapter for your model.
● Adjust the gear lever height as required by screwing the linkage rod in or out of the lever and arm. Tighten the locknuts securely.

4 Sidestand

Removal

1 Support the bike on an auxiliary stand.
2 Displace the sidestand switch (see Chapter 8). There is no need to disconnect its wiring connector or remove it completely, just let it hang from its wiring.

3 Unhook the stand springs **(see illustration)**. Unscrew the nut from the pivot bolt **(see illustration)**. Unscrew the pivot bolt and remove the stand.
4 On ZR750-J models, if required unscrew the sidestand bracket bolts and remove the bracket **(see illustration)**.

Installation

5 Installation is the reverse of removal, noting the following:
● On ZR750-J models tighten the stand bracket bolts to the torque setting specified at the beginning of the Chapter.
● Clean off any old grease and dirt. Apply grease to the stand pivot and the post for the switch arm.
● Tighten the stand pivot bolt to the torque setting specified at the beginning of the Chapter, then fit the nut and tighten that.
● Clean the threads of the switch bolt and apply a suitable non-permanent thread locking compound. Tighten the switch bolt to the torque setting specified at the beginning of the Chapter.
● Fit the springs with the shorter ends hooked onto the post on the stand.

5 Handlebars and levers

Handlebar removal

Note: *The handlebars can be displaced from the top yoke for access to the steering stem*

nut without displacing or removing the master cylinder, cables or switch housings, though it is best to remove the mirrors – follow Steps 1 and 2 and 8 to 10 as required.
1 To avoid the possibility of damaging the fairing and fuel tank should anything not go quite according to plan, remove them (see Chapters 7 and 4), or at least cover them in plenty of rag.
2 Remove the mirrors (see Chapter 7).
3 Disconnect the front brake light switch and clutch switch wiring connectors **(see illustrations)**.
4 Undo each handlebar end-weight screw and remove the weight **(see illustration)**. Pull the throttle twistgrip off the right-hand end and remove the grip from the left-hand end. **Note:** *The grip will probably be stuck in place – it may be necessary to slit it with a sharp knife in order to remove it.*
5 Detach the throttle cables from the twistgrip (see Chapter 4). On ZR750-J and ZR1000-A models, detach the fast idle cable (see Chapter 4). If not already done when detaching the cables, displace the handlebar switch housing(s) (see Chapter 8) – there is no need to disconnect the main wiring connectors.
6 Displace the front brake master cylinder and position it clear of the handlebar, wrapping it in rag (see Chapter 6). Ensure no strain is placed on the hydraulic hoses and try to keep the reservoir upright to prevent air entering the system.
7 Unscrew the clutch lever bracket clamp bolts, noting the washers on ZR750-J

5.3a Disconnect the brake light switch wiring connector (arrowed) . . .

5.3b . . . and the clutch switch wiring connector (arrowed)

5.4 Handlebar end-weight screw (arrowed)

5.7 Unscrew the bolts (arrowed) and displace the clutch lever bracket

5.8 Remove the split pin (arrowed) from each side and slacken the nuts

5.9a Remove the blanking caps . . .

5.9b . . . then unscrew the bolts (arrowed) . . .

5.9c . . . lift off the clamp and remove the handlebars

models, and displace the lever/bracket/cable assembly, supporting it on some rag (see illustration).

8 If you are removing the handlebar holders from the yoke, remove the split pin from the bottom of each, then slacken the nuts slightly (see illustration).

9 Remove the blanking caps from the handlebar clamp bolts (see illustration). Unscrew the bolts and remove the clamp, then displace or remove the handlebars (see illustration) – if they are only being displaced rest them either in front of or behind the top yoke, on plenty of rag (see illustration).

10 If required unscrew the handlebar holder nuts on the underside of the top yoke and remove the washers, then remove the holders and rubber seats between each one and the yoke.

Handlebar installation

11 Installation is the reverse of removal, noting the following:
● Fit the rubber seat between each holder and the yoke. The holders are marked L and R according to which side they fit on. Only finger-tighten the holder nuts at this stage to allow the handlebars to properly align the holders.
● Make sure the clamp is the correct way round (see illustration 5.9c). Align the bars so they are central, with the punch mark on the back aligned with the left-hand holder/clamp mating surfaces (see illustration). Fit the bolts, then tighten the front ones first, then the rear, to the torque setting specified at the beginning of the Chapter – note that there should be a gap between the clamp and each holder at the back. If necessary now tighten the handlebar

holder nuts to the specified torque setting (see illustration 5.8) and fit new split pins.
● Refer to Chapter 6 for installation of the front brake master cylinder.
● Align the mating surfaces of the clutch lever bracket and clamp with the punch mark on the top of the handlebar. Fit the bolts, with their washers on ZR750-J models, then tighten the top one first, then the bottom, to the torque setting specified at the beginning of the Chapter – note that there should be a gap at the bottom (see illustration 5.7).
● Refer to Chapter 4 for installation of the throttle cables, and on ZR750-J and ZR1000-A models the fast idle cable. Refer to Chapter 8 for installation of the switch housings.
● If new grips are being fitted, secure them using a suitable adhesive.
● Check the operation of the throttle, clutch and brake levers, and the front brake light switch and clutch switch before riding the motorcycle.

Levers

12 To remove the front brake lever, undo the lever pivot screw locknut, then undo the pivot screw and remove the lever (see illustration).
13 To remove the clutch lever, on ZR750-J models, fully slacken the cable freeplay adjuster locknut, then thread the adjuster into the bracket to provide slack in the cable (see illustration). On all other models thread the adjuster into the bracket to provide slack in the cable (see illustration). Undo the lever pivot screw locknut,

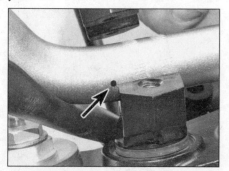

5.11 Align the punch mark (arrowed) with the clamp mating surfaces

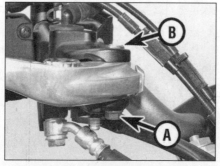

5.12 Undo the nut (A) then undo the pivot screw (B)

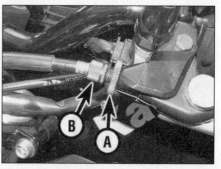

5.13a Slacken the locknut (A) then thread the adjuster in (B)

5.13b Thread the adjuster in

5.13c Unscrew the nut (arrowed)

Installation

6 Remove all traces of corrosion from the fork tube and the yokes. Slide the fork up through the bottom yoke and into the top yoke, making sure all cables, hoses and wiring are routed on the correct side of the fork **(see illustration 6.5b)**.

7 Set the amount of protrusion of the fork tube above the top yoke as noted on removal – on ZR750-J and ZR1000-A models the top of the fork tube should be flush with the upper surface of the yoke, leaving the top bolt rim above it. On ZR750-L/M and ZR1000-B/C models the top of the fork tube (where the tube meets the top bolt) should be 9 mm above the upper surface of the yoke **(see illustration 6.4b)**.

8 Tighten the fork clamp bolts in the bottom yoke evenly and a little at a time to the torque setting(s) specified at the beginning of the Chapter for your model **(see illustration 6.5a)**. If the fork has been dismantled or if the fork oil was changed, tighten the fork top bolt to the specified torque setting **(see illustration 6.4c)**. Now tighten the fork clamp bolt(s) in the top yoke to the specified torque **(see illustration 6.4a)**.

9 Install the front mudguard and the fairing (see Chapter 7), and the front wheel (see Chapter 6).

10 Check the operation of the front forks and brake before taking the machine out on the road.

then push up and withdraw the pivot screw and remove the lever, detaching the cable nipple as you do **(see illustration)**. Note the collar in the lever and remove it for safekeeping. On ZR750-J models note how the lever span adjuster, spring and lever locate together.

14 Installation is the reverse of removal, noting the following:

● When fitting the brake lever apply silicone grease to the contact area between the master cylinder pushrod tip and the brake lever, to the pivot screw and the contact areas between the lever and its bracket. Tighten the pivot screw lightly, then counter-hold it and tighten the locknut.

● When fitting the clutch lever apply silicone grease to the pivot screw and the contact areas between the lever and its bracket. Adjust clutch cable freeplay (see Chapter 1).

6 Fork removal and installation

Caution: *Although not strictly necessary, before removing the forks it is recommended that the fairing and fairing panels are removed (see Chapter 7). This will prevent accidental damage to the paintwork.*

Removal

1 Remove the fairing (see Chapter 7).
2 Remove the front wheel (see Chapter 6). Tie the front brake calipers and hoses back so that they are out of the way.

3 Remove the front mudguard (see Chapter 7). Note the routing of any cables, hoses and wiring around the forks.
4 Working on one fork at a time, slacken the fork clamp bolt(s) in the top yoke **(see illustration)**. Measure and note the amount of protrusion of the fork above the top yoke **(see illustration)**. If the fork is to be disassembled, or if the fork oil is being changed, slacken the fork top bolt at this stage **(see illustration)**.
5 Slacken the fork clamp bolts in the bottom yoke, and remove the fork by twisting it and pulling it downwards **(see illustrations)**.

 HAYNES HINT *If the fork legs are seized in the yokes, spray the area with penetrating oil and allow time for it to soak in before trying again.*

6.4a Top yoke fork clamp bolts (arrowed)

6.4b Note the amount of protrusion above the yoke . . .

6.4c . . . and slacken the fork top bolt if the fork is to be disassembled

6.5a Slacken the fork clamp bolts (arrowed) in the bottom yoke . . .

6.5b . . . then draw the fork down and out of the yokes

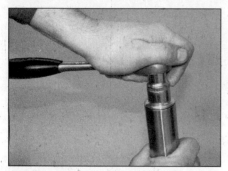

7.3 Unscrew the top bolt using a ratchet tool and keeping downward pressure on it

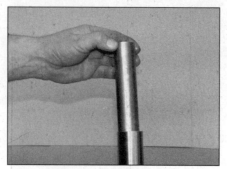

7.4a Remove the spacer . . .

7.4b . . . then hook out the washer and the spring

7 Fork oil change

1 After a high mileage the fork oil will deteriorate and its damping and lubrication qualities will be impaired. Always change the oil in both forks. Work on one fork at a time.
2 Remove the fork – make sure the top bolt is loosened while the leg is still clamped in the bottom yoke (see Section 6).

ZR750-J

3 Support the fork upright and unscrew the top bolt from the top of the inner tube, noting that it is under pressure from the spring – it is best to use a ratchet tool and to keep constant downward pressure on the top bolt while unscrewing it, or alternatively to hold the top bolt still using a ring spanner and to thread the inner tube off the bolt (see illustration). Slide the inner tube down into the outer tube (see illustration 8.1a).
4 Remove the spacer (see illustration). Hook out the spring and the washer, noting which way up the spring fits (see illustration).
5 Invert the fork leg over a suitable container and pump the inner tube to expel as much oil as possible (see illustration 7.31).
6 Support the leg and allow it to drain for several minutes. Wipe any excess oil off the spring and spacer. If the fork oil contains

metal particles inspect the fork components for signs of wear (see Section 8).
7 Slowly pour in the correct quantity and type of fork oil as specified at the beginning of this Chapter (see illustration 7.33). Pump the inner tube several times to circulate the oil and expel air. Secure the fork leg upright and allow it to stand for several minutes to allow all the air to escape.
8 Fully compress the inner tube into the outer tube and measure the oil level from the top (see illustration 7.34). Add or subtract oil until it is at the level specified at the beginning of this Chapter.
9 Fit the spring into the fork, followed by the washer and the spacer (see illustrations 7.4b and a).
10 Make sure the top bolt O-ring is in good condition then smear some fork oil onto it (see illustration). Fit the top bolt into the inner tube, compressing the spring as you do, and thread it in (making sure it does not cross-thread), keeping downward pressure on the spring, using a ratchet tool or by turning the tube while holding the bolt still as on removal (see illustration 7.3). Tighten the bolt to the specified torque setting after the fork leg has been installed and is securely clamped in the bottom yoke (see Section 6).
11 Install the fork (see Section 6).

ZR750-L/M

Special Tool: *A special holding tool is needed to disassemble the forks – see Step 13.*

12 Support the fork upright and unscrew the top bolt from the top of the outer tube (see illustration 7.27). Slide the outer tube down onto the inner tube.
13 With the aid of an assistant, pull up on the fork top bolt, then press down on the spacer to compress the spring and expose the locknut on the bottom of the top bolt. **Note:** *Kawasaki produces service tools (spacer holder Pt. No. 57001-1685 and stopper plate Pt. No. 57001-1374) to do this. Alternatively, use the set-up shown – the inner end of each handle locates in a hole in the spacer, and the slotted washer locates around the damper rod and under the locknut, so must be sized accordingly (see illustration 7.28a).* Insert the stopper plate or slotted washer under the locknut (see illustration 7.28b). Carefully release the pressure on the spacer and allow the plate or slotted washer to rest against the underside of the locknut under spring pressure.
14 Counter-hold the locknut and loosen the top bolt, then thread the top bolt assembly off the damper rod and remove it (see illustration 7.29a). On the right-hand fork withdraw the damping adjuster rod from inside the damper cartridge rod (see illustration). **Note:** *The top bolt assembly should not be disassembled.*
15 Compress the spacer and remove the plate or slotted washer, then carefully allow the spring to relax (see illustration). Remove the spacer, noting the shaped washer on its

7.10 Smear the O-ring (arrowed) with oil

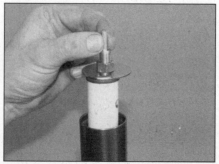

7.14 Withdraw the damping adjuster rod

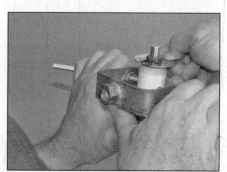

7.15a Remove the slotted washer . . .

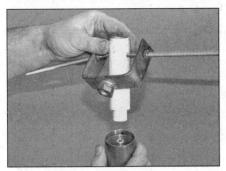

7.15b ... the spacer ...

7.15c ... and the spring

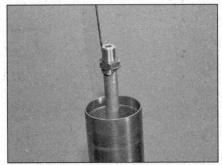

7.20a Draw the rod out and tie some wire round to hold it up ...

top **(see illustration)**. Withdraw the spring from the tube, noting which way up it fits **(see illustration)**.

16 Invert the fork leg over a suitable container and pump the fork and damper rod to expel as much oil as possible **(see illustration 7.31)**.

17 Support the leg and allow it to drain for several minutes, pumping it again. Wipe any excess oil off the spring and spacer. If the fork oil contains metal particles inspect the fork components for signs of wear (see Section 8).

18 Slowly pour in the correct quantity and type of fork oil as specified at the beginning of this Chapter **(see illustration 7.33)**. Draw the damper rod out of the fork using long-nosed pliers and pump the rod several times to expel air from the damper cartridge. Secure the fork leg upright and allow it to stand for several minutes to allow all the air to escape. Now pump the rod several times again – once all the air is expelled you should feel stiff resistance when pumping the rod. Take great care to ensure that all air is expelled from the damper cartridge at this stage.

19 Fully compress the fork and damper rod and measure the oil level from the top of the tube **(see illustration 7.34)**. Add or subtract oil until it is at the level specified at the beginning of this Chapter.

20 Install the spring with its tapered end upwards, sliding it over the damper rod **(see illustration 7.15c)**. Draw the rod out and fit a piece of thin wire around the rod under the locknut to help keep it extended **(see illustration)**. Fit the spacer **(see illustration)**, then fit the shaped washer on its top **(see illustration)**, sliding them over the wire or holding tool if being used.

21 Keeping the damper rod fully extended, press down on the spacer to compress the spring (see Step 13), then remove the wire and insert the stopper plate or slotted washer under the locknut **(see illustration)**.

22 On the right-hand fork fit the damping adjuster rod inside the damper rod **(see illustration 7.14)**. Make sure the locknut is threaded all the way down the damper rod so at least 12 mm of threads are exposed. On the left-hand fork make sure the locknut is threaded all the way down the damper rod so 25.5 mm of threads are exposed.

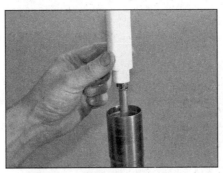

7.20b ... while fitting the spacer ...

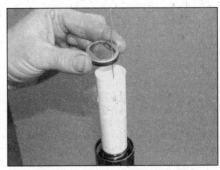

7.20c ... and the shaped washer

23 Make sure the top bolt O-ring is in good condition then smear some fork oil onto it. Fit the top bolt onto the damper rod and screw it all the way down to the locknut. Counter-hold the top bolt and tighten the locknut securely against it, to the specified torque if the correct tools are available **(see illustration 7.29a)**.

24 Press down on the spacer to compress the spring and remove the plate or slotted washer, then carefully release the spring pressure, making sure the spacer seats correctly against the pre-load adjuster flats **(see illustration 7.28b)**. Remove the holding tool.

25 Pull the outer tube all the way out of the inner tube and carefully screw the top bolt into the tube making sure it is not cross-threaded **(see illustration 7.27)**. Tighten the top bolt

to the specified torque when the fork leg has been installed and is securely clamped in the bottom yoke (see Section 6).

26 Install the fork (see Section 6).

Z1000 models

Special Tool: *A special holding tool is needed to disassemble the forks – see Step 28.*
Note: *Components for some model years may differ in appearance to the illustrations shown.*

27 Support the fork upright and unscrew the top bolt from the top of the outer tube **(see illustration)**. Slide the outer tube down onto the inner tube. Slide the rubber damper on the underside of the top bolt down the spacer below the holes.

28 With the aid of an assistant, pull up on

7.21 Compress the spring and fit the slotted washer under the locknut, and remove the wire

7.27 Thread the top bolt out of the tube

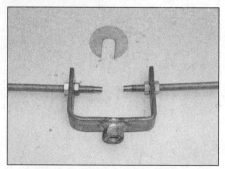

7.28a Using the home-made tools as shown or suitable equivalents . . .

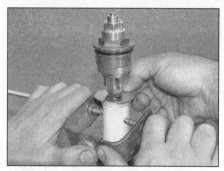

7.28b . . . compress the spring and fit the washer under the locknut

7.29a Counter-hold the locknut and thread the top bolt off . . .

the fork top bolt, then press down on the spacer to compress the spring and expose the locknut on the bottom of the top bolt. **Note:** *Kawasaki produces service tools to do this, but they may be expensive. Alternatively, use the set-up shown – the inner end of each handle locates in a hole in the spacer, and the slotted washer locates around the damper rod and under the locknut, so must be sized accordingly* **(see illustration).** Insert the stopper plate or slotted washer under the locknut **(see illustration).** Carefully release the pressure on the spacer and allow the plate or slotted washer to rest against the underside of the locknut under spring pressure.

29 Counter-hold the locknut and loosen the top bolt using a spanner on the base of the pre-load adjuster flats, then thread the top bolt assembly off the damper rod and remove it **(see illustration)** – the damping adjuster rod comes with it (right-hand fork only on ZR1000-A

models) **(see illustration). Note:** *The top bolt assembly should not be disassembled.*

30 Compress the spacer and remove the plate or slotted washer, then carefully allow the spring to relax. On ZR1000-A models remove the damper, the washer and the spacer, noting the shaped slider fitted in each end, and which way up it fits. On ZR1000-B/C models remove the damper and the spacer, noting the shaped slider fitted in its top. Withdraw the spring from the tube, noting which way up it fits **(see illustration 7.35b).**

31 Invert the fork leg over a suitable container and pump the fork and damper rod to expel as much oil as possible **(see illustration).**

32 Support the leg and allow it to drain for several minutes, pumping it again. Wipe any excess oil off the spring and spacer. If the fork oil contains metal particles inspect the fork components for signs of wear (see Section 8).

33 Slowly pour in the correct quantity and type of fork oil as specified at the beginning

of this Chapter **(see illustration).** Draw the damper rod out of the fork using long-nosed pliers and pump the rod several times to expel air from the damper cartridge. Secure the fork leg upright and allow it to stand for several minutes to allow all the air to escape. Now pump the rod several times again – once all the air is expelled you should feel stiff resistance when pumping the rod. Take great care to ensure that all air is expelled from the damper cartridge at this stage.

34 Fully compress the fork and damper rod and measure the oil level from the top of the tube **(see illustration).** Add or subtract oil until it is at the level specified at the beginning of this Chapter.

35 Draw the rod out and fit a piece of thin wire around the rod under the locknut to help keep it extended **(see illustration).** Install the spring with its tapered end upwards, sliding it over the damper rod **(see illustration).**

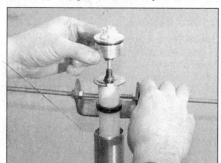

7.29b . . . bringing the damping adjuster rod out as well

7.31 Invert the fork over a container and tip the oil out then pump the tube and the rod to expel the rest

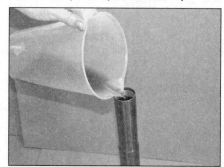

7.33 Pour the oil into the top of the tube and distribute and bleed it as described . . .

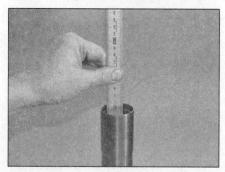

7.34 . . . then measure the level

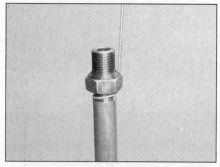

7.35a Draw the rod out and tie some wire round to hold it up . . .

7.35b . . . while fitting the spring

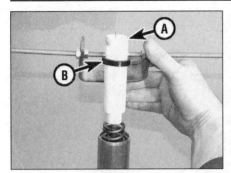

7.37 Fit the spacer with the slider (A) and the damper (B)

7.38 Compress the spring and fit the slotted washer under the locknut

7.40 Make sure the spacer seats correctly

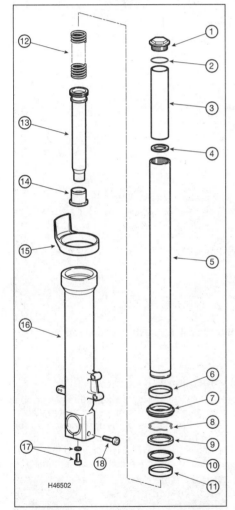

8.1a Front fork components – ZR750-J models

1 Fork top bolt
2 O-ring
3 Spacer
4 Washer
5 Inner tube
6 Bottom bush
7 Dust seal
8 Retaining clip
9 Oil seal
10 Washer

11 Top bush
12 Spring
13 Damper rod
14 Oil lock piece
15 Fork protector
16 Outer tube
17 Damper rod
    bolt and sealing
    washer
18 Axle clamp bolt

36 On ZR1000-A models make sure the shaped slider is fitted into each end of the spacer with the narrower inner rimmed one at the bottom, and note that if both forks have been disassembled the longer spacer is for the left-hand fork and the holes should be toward the bottom. Fit the spacer, locating the bottom end into the top of the spring, then fit the washer and the damper, sliding them all over the wire.

37 On ZR1000-B/C models make sure the shaped slider is fitted into the top of the spacer. Fit the spacer, locating the bottom end into the top of the spring, then fit the damper, sliding them all over the wire **(see illustration)**.

38 Keeping the damper rod fully extended, press down on the spacer to compress the spring (see Step 28), then remove the wire and insert the stopper plate or slotted washer under the locknut **(see illustration)**.

39 Make sure the top bolt O-ring is in good condition then smear some fork oil onto it. Fit the top bolt onto the damper rod, sliding the damping adjuster rod into the damper rod (right-hand fork only on ZR1000-A models), and screw it all the way down to the locknut **(see illustration 7.29b)**. Counter-hold the base of the pre-load adjuster using a spanner on the flats and tighten the locknut securely against it, to the specified torque if the correct tools are available **(see illustration 7.29a)**.

40 Press down on the spacer to compress the spring and remove the plate or slotted washer, then carefully release the spring pressure, making sure the spacer seats correctly against the underside of the top bolt assembly (see

illustration). Remove the holding tool. Slide the damper up against the top bolt.

41 Pull the outer tube all the way out of the inner tube and carefully screw the top bolt into the tube making sure it is not cross-threaded **(see illustration 7.27)**. Tighten the top bolt to the specified torque when the fork leg has been installed and is securely clamped in the bottom yoke (see Section 6).

42 Install the fork (see Section 6).

8 Fork overhaul

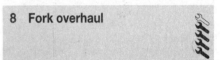

Note: *The fork bushes cannot be replaced with new ones. If upon inspection the bushes are found to be worn, new fork tubes will have to be fitted.*

ZR750-J1 and J2
Disassembly

1 Remove the fork; ensure that the top bolt is loosened while the leg is still clamped in the bottom yoke (see Section 6). Always dismantle the fork legs separately to avoid interchanging parts. Store all components in separate, clearly marked containers **(see illustration)**. Remove the fork protector from the top of the outer tube, noting how it locates **(see illustration)**. When dismantling the right-hand fork first remove the axle clamp bolt.

2 Before dismantling the fork leg, slacken the damper cartridge bolt in the bottom of the outer tube, then lightly re-tighten it to prevent oil coming out **(see illustration)**. If the bolt

8.1b Note how the tab (arrowed) on the fork protector locates

8.2 Slacken the damper rod bolt

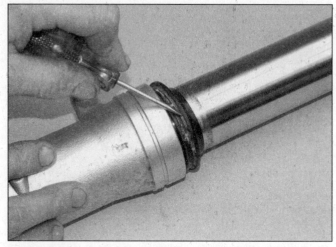

8.6 Prise out the dust seal using a flat-bladed screwdriver

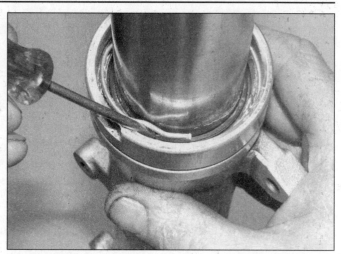

8.7 Prise out the retaining clip using a flat-bladed screwdriver

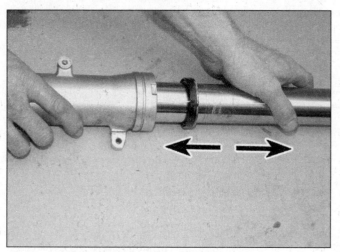

8.8a Repeatedly draw the tubes apart . . .

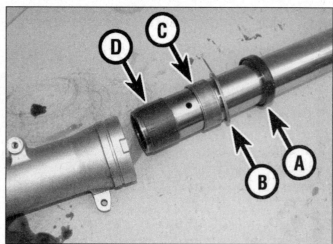

8.8b . . . to displace the oil seal (A), washer (B) and top bush (C). Bottom bush (D)

does not loosen, turn the leg upside down and compress the fork so that the spring exerts maximum pressure on the damper rod to prevent it turning, then try to loosen the bolt. If you still have no luck, and an air wrench is not available, carry on and use a holding tool as described in Step 4.

3 Refer to Section 7, Steps 3 to 6, and drain the fork oil.

4 Remove the previously loosened damper cartridge bolt and its sealing washer from the bottom of the outer tube. Discard the washer as a new one must be fitted on reassembly. If the damper cartridge bolt was impossible to slacken as described in Step 2, note that a Kawasaki service tool (Pt. Nos. 57001-183 and 57001-1057) is available to hold the damper rod in place while the bolt is unscrewed; the tool passes down the inner tube and engages the top of the damper rod.

5 Tip the damper rod out of the fork.

6 Carefully prise the dust seal from the top of the outer tube to gain access to the oil

seal retaining clip **(see illustration)**. Discard the dust seal as a new one must be fitted on reassembly.

7 Remove the retaining clip, taking care not to scratch the surface of the inner tube **(see illustration)**.

8 Grasp the inner tube in one hand and the outer tube in the other, then quickly and repeatedly draw the inner tube out until the oil seal, washer and top bush are displaced from the top of the outer tube by the bottom bush on the bottom of the inner tube **(see illustrations)**. Draw the oil seal, washer and top bush off the inner tube. Discard the oil seal as a new one must be fitted on reassembly.

9 Do not remove the bottom bush unless it is to be replaced with a new one. To remove it, spread its ends using a screwdriver to dislodge it from its seat and slide it off **(see illustration)**.

10 Tip the oil lock piece out of the outer tube.

Inspection

11 Clean all parts in a suitable solvent and blow them dry with compressed air, if available. Check the surface of the fork inner tube for score marks, scratches, pitting and flaking of the finish, and excessive or abnormal wear. Look for dents in the outer tubes and replace

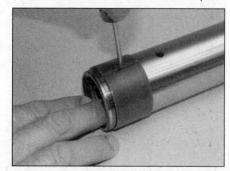

8.9 Remove the bottom bush by levering its ends apart

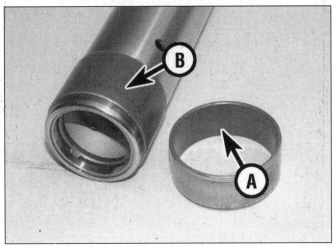

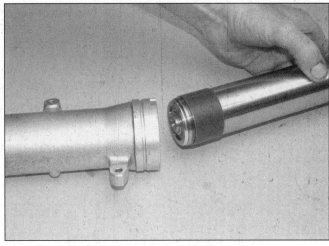

8.13 Check the inner surface (A) of the top bush and the outer surface (B) of the bottom bush

8.19 Slide the inner tube into the outer tube

the outer tubes in both forks with new ones if any are found.

12 Check the fork inner tubes for runout using V-blocks and a dial gauge. If the condition of either inner tube is suspect have it checked by a Kawasaki dealer or suspension specialist. Kawasaki provides no specifications for runout, but they do say tubes should not be straightened.

13 Inspect the inside surface of the outer tube and the working surface of each bush for score marks, scratches and signs of excessive wear (in which case the grey Teflon outer surface will have worn away to reveal the copper inner surface) **(see illustration)**. The bushes are available separately, and should be replaced with new ones if damaged or worn.

14 Check the fork oil seal seat for nicks, gouges and scratches. If damage is evident, leaks will occur. Also check the oil seal washer for damage or distortion and replace it with a new one if necessary.

15 Check the springs (both the main spring and the rebound spring on the damper rod) for cracks and other damage. Measure the main spring free length and compare the measurement to the specifications at the beginning of this Chapter **(see illustration 8.40)**. If the spring is defective or has sagged below the service limit, fit new springs in both forks. Never fit only one new spring.

16 Check the damper rod, and in particular the ring in its head, for damage and wear, and replace it with a new one if necessary (the ring is not available separately).

Reassembly

17 Make sure the bottom bush is correctly located in its recess in the bottom of the inner tube.

18 Insert the damper rod into the inner tube so its bottom end protrudes from the bottom of the tube. Fit the oil lock piece onto the bottom of the rod, then push them up into the bottom of the tube.

19 Lubricate the bottom bush and the inner

surface of the outer tube with the specified fork oil. Slide the inner tube into the outer tube and seat it at the bottom **(see illustration)**.

20 Fit a new sealing washer onto the damper cartridge bolt and apply a few drops of a suitable non-permanent thread locking compound. Fit the bolt into the bottom of the outer tube and thread it into the bottom of the damper rod and tighten it to the torque setting specified at the beginning of this Chapter. If the damper cartridge rotates inside the tube as you tighten the bolt, use the special tool (Step 4), or wait until the fork is fully reassembled and tighten it then (the pressure of the spring

on the cartridge should prevent it from turning, especially if you compress the fork – Step 25).

21 Lubricate the inner and outer surfaces of the top bush with the specified fork oil. Slide the bush down the inner tube and press it as far as possible into the top of the outer tube by hand, making sure it fits squarely **(see illustration)**. Slide the washer onto the top of the bush, then carefully drive the bush into place until it seats using a suitable drift or piece of tubing on the washer, using it as an interface to prevent damage to the upper rim of the bush **(see illustrations)**. Take care not to mark the inner tube when driving the bush

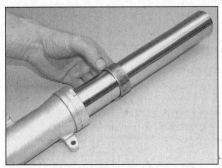

8.21a Slide the top bush into the outer tube . . .

8.21b . . . then rest the washer on top . . .

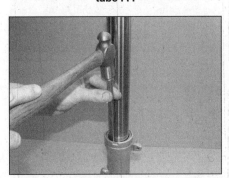

8.21c . . . to protect the bush as you drive it in

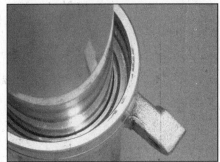

8.21d Make sure it has seated

8.22a Fit the oil seal . . .

8.22b . . . and drive it into the outer tube . . .

8.22c . . . until the groove (arrowed) is visible

8.23a Fit the retaining clip into the groove . . .

8.23b . . . then press the dust seal in

in. Remove the washer and make sure the bush has fully entered, in which case its upper rim will be flush with the oil seal seat. Refit the washer.

22 Lubricate the inner and outer surfaces of the new oil seal with the specified fork oil. Slide the seal, with its marked side facing up, down the inner tube and press it as far as possible into the top of the outer tube by hand, making sure it fits squarely (see illustration). Carefully drive the seal into place until it seats using a suitable drift or piece of tubing, or the special service tool (Pt. No. 57001-1288) (see illustration). Take care not to mark the inner tube when driving the bush in. Make sure the seal has fully entered, in which case the groove for the retaining ring will be fully exposed.

23 Fit the retaining clip, making sure it is correctly located in its groove (see illustration). Press the new dust seal into place (see illustration).

24 Refer to Section 7, Steps 7 to 10, and put new oil into the fork.

25 If the damper rod bolt requires tightening (see Step 20), place the fork upside down on the floor, using a rag to protect it, then have an assistant compress the fork so that maximum spring pressure is placed on the damper rod head while tightening the bolt to the specified torque setting.

26 Fit the axle clamp bolt in the bottom of the right-hand fork.

27 Fit the fork protector onto the top of the outer tube, making sure it is correctly

positioned and located (see illustration 8.1b).

28 Install the fork leg (see Section 6).

ZR750-L/M

Disassembly

29 Remove the fork; ensure that the top bolt is loosened while the leg is still clamped in the bottom yoke (see Section 6). Always dismantle the fork legs separately to avoid interchanging parts. Store all components in separate, clearly marked containers (see illustration). When dismantling the right-hand fork first remove the axle clamp bolt.

30 Before dismantling the fork leg, slacken the damper cartridge bolt in the bottom of the fork, then lightly re-tighten it to prevent oil coming out (see illustration 8.49). If the bolt does not loosen, turn the leg upside down and compress the fork so that the spring exerts maximum pressure on the damper cartridge assembly to prevent it turning, then try to loosen the bolt. If you still have no luck, and an air wrench is not available, carry on and obtain a holding tool as described in Step 32.

31 Refer to Section 7, Steps 12 to 17, and drain the fork oil.

32 Remove the previously loosened damper cartridge bolt and its sealing washer from the bottom of the inner tube. Discard the washer as a new one must be fitted on reassembly. If the damper cartridge bolt was impossible to slacken as described in Step 30, note that a Kawasaki service tool (Pt. No. 57001-1537) is available to hold the damper cartridge in place

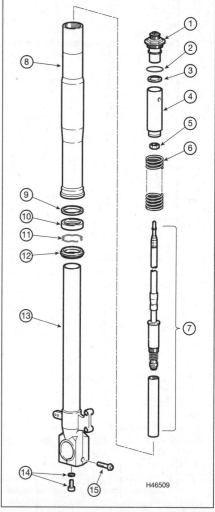

8.29 Front fork components – ZR750-L/M models

1 Fork top bolt	9 Washer
2 O-ring	10 Oil seal
3 Shaped washer	11 Retaining clip
4 Spacer	12 Dust seal
5 Locknut	13 Inner tube
6 Spring	14 Damper cartridge
7 Damper	bolt and sealing
cartridge	washer
8 Outer tube	15 Axle clamp bolt

8.35a Prise out the dust seal using a flat-bladed screwdriver

8.35b Prise out the retaining clip using a flat-bladed screwdriver

8.35c Fit the puller under the seal and expand . . .

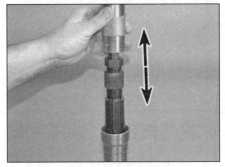

8.35d . . . then fit and operate the slide-hammer . . .

8.35e . . . and draw the seal out

8.35f Remove the washer

while the bolt is unscrewed; the tool passes down the fork tube, over the damper rod and engages the top of the cartridge body.

33 Withdraw the damper cartridge assembly from inside the fork tube.

34 Draw the inner and outer tubes apart **(see illustration 8.44a)**.

35 Carefully prise the dust seal from the bottom of the outer tube **(see illustration)**. Remove the retaining clip **(see illustration)**. Carefully prise out the oil seal using either a seal hook or an expanding internal puller with slide-hammer attachment, taking great care not to damage the rim of the tube, then remove the oil seal washer **(see illustrations)**. Discard the seals as new ones must be fitted on reassembly.

Inspection

36 Clean all parts in a suitable solvent and blow them dry with compressed air, if available.

Check the surface of the fork inner tube for score marks, scratches, pitting and flaking of the finish, and excessive or abnormal wear. Look for dents in the outer tubes and replace the outer tubes in both forks with new ones if any are found.

37 Check the fork inner tube for runout using V-blocks and a dial gauge. If the condition of either inner tube is suspect have it checked by a Kawasaki dealer or suspension specialist. Kawasaki provides no specifications for runout.

38 Inspect the inside surface of the outer tube, in particular the working surface of each bush, for score marks, scratches and signs of excessive wear **(see illustration)**. Replace the outer tube with a new one if necessary – the bushes are not available separately.

39 Check the fork oil seal seat for nicks, gouges and scratches. If damage is evident,

leaks will occur. Also check the oil seal washer for damage or distortion and replace it with a new one if necessary.

40 Check the spring for cracks and other damage. Measure the spring free length and compare the measurement to the specifications at the beginning of this Chapter **(see illustration)**. If the spring is defective or has sagged below the service limit, fit new springs in both forks. Never fit only one new spring.

41 Check the damper cartridge for damage and wear. Hold the cartridge and gently pump the rod in and out. If the rod does not move smoothly the damper must be replaced with a new one.

Reassembly

42 Fit the oil seal washer into the fork outer tube **(see illustration)**. Fit the new oil seal into the tube and tap it into place using a

8.38 Check the bushes in the tube for wear

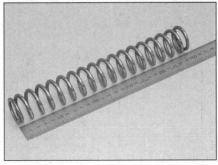

8.40 Measure the free length of the spring

8.42a Fit the oil seal washer . . .

8.42b . . . and the new seal . . .

8.42c . . . using a suitable driver or socket to drive it in

suitable seal driver or socket until it seats and the retaining clip groove is visible – if using a socket it should sit only on the hard outer rim of the seal and not on the spring rim on the top of the seal **(see illustrations)**. If necessary use the old seal as an interface between the socket and the new seal, especially if the socket is not the ideal size. Alternatively obtain the Kawasaki service tool (Pt. No. 57001-1288).

43 Fit the retaining clip, making sure it locates correctly in its groove **(see illustration)**. Lubricate the inner surfaces of the new seals and the outer surface of the inner tube with the specified fork oil. Slide the dust seal onto the inner tube, making sure it is the correct way up **(see illustration)**.

44 Carefully insert the inner tube fully into the outer tube **(see illustration)**. Press the dust seal into the outer tube **(see illustration)**.

45 Insert the damper cartridge assembly into the fork until it contacts the bottom of the inner tube. Fit a new sealing washer onto the damper cartridge bolt and apply a few drops of a suitable non-permanent thread locking compound, then fit the bolt into the bottom of the inner tube, thread it into the bottom of the damper cartridge and tighten it to the torque setting specified at the beginning of this Chapter. Note: *If the damper cartridge assembly rotates inside the tube, the Kawasaki service tool described in Step 32 can be used to hold the head of the cartridge body, or a suitable tool that will achieve the same result can be fabricated from a piece of tubing. Alternatively fit the slotted washer under the damper rod locknut and use it pull up on the rod which should help the bolt to tighten, or wait until the fork is fully reassembled and tighten it then (the pressure of the spring on the cartridge should prevent it from turning, especially if you compress the fork).*

46 Refer to Section 7, Steps 18 to 25, and put new oil into the fork.

47 Loosely fit the axle clamp bolt into the bottom of the right-hand fork. Install the fork leg (see Section 6). Check and adjust the fork settings as required (see Section 13).

Z1000 models

Disassembly

48 Remove the fork; ensure that the top bolt is loosened while the leg is still clamped in the bottom yoke (see Section 6). Always dismantle the fork legs separately to avoid interchanging parts and thus causing an accelerated rate of wear. Store all components in separate, clearly marked containers **(see illustrations)**. When dismantling the right-hand fork first remove the axle clamp bolt.

8.43a Fit the retaining clip . . .

8.43b . . . then fit the new dust seal onto the outer tube

8.44a Fit the inner tube into the outer tube . . .

8.44b . . . then press the dust seal into place

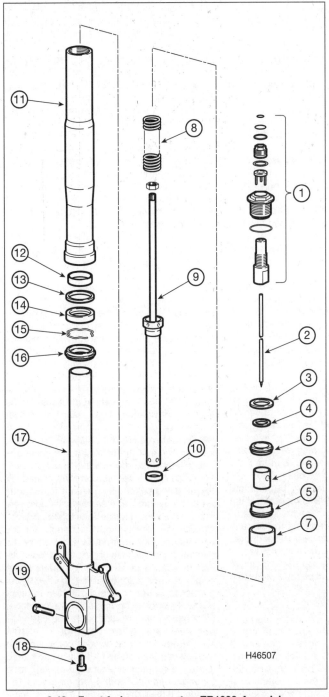

8.48a Front fork components – ZR1000-A models

1 Fork top bolt assembly
2 Damper rod
3 Rubber damper
4 Washer
5 Shaped slider
6 Spacer
7 Top bush
8 Spring
9 Damper cartridge with locknut
10 Damper cartridge seat

11 Outer tube
12 Bottom bush
13 Washer
14 Oil seal
15 Retaining clip
16 Dust seal
17 Inner tube
18 Damper cartridge bolt and
   sealing washer
19 Axle clamp bolt

8.48b Front fork components – ZR1000-B/C models

1 Fork top bolt body
2 O-ring
3 Rubber damper
4 Shaped slider
5 Spacer
6 Spring
7 Top bolt adjuster insert
8 Damping adjuster rod
9 Locknut
10 Damper cartridge
11 Damper cartridge seat

12 Outer tube
13 Bottom bush
14 Washer
15 Oil seal
16 Retaining clip
17 Dust seal
18 Inner tube
19 Damper cartridge bolt and
   sealing washer
20 Axle clamp bolt

H46507

H46508

8.49 Slacken the damper rod bolt

49 Lay the fork flat on the bench and hold it down then slacken the damper rod bolt in the base of the inner tube (see illustration). If the bolt does not loosen, turn the leg upside down and compress the fork so that the spring exerts maximum pressure on the damper cartridge assembly to prevent it turning, then try to loosen the bolt. If you still have no luck, use an air wrench.

50 Refer to Section 7, Steps 27 to 32 and drain the oil form the fork.

51 Remove the previously slackened damper cartridge bolt and its sealing washer from the bottom of the inner tube. Discard the sealing washer as a new one must be used on reassembly.

52 Withdraw the damper cartridge from inside the fork tube. If the seat is not on the bottom of the cartridge tip it out of the fork.

53 Carefully prise out the dust seal from the bottom of the outer tube (see illustration 8.6).

54 Prise out the retaining clip, taking care not to scratch the surface of the inner tube – slide the fork apart slightly to keep any accidental damage above the seal area (see illustration 8.7).

55 To separate the inner tube from the outer tube it is necessary to displace the bottom bush and oil seal. The top bush should not pass through the bottom bush, and this can be used to good effect. Grasp the inner tube in one hand and the outer tube in the other and compress them, then pull them apart so that the bottom bush strikes the top bush, doing so repeatedly until the top bush, washer and seal are tapped out (see illustrations 8.8a and b).

56 On ZR1000-A models remove the top bush from the inner tube by carefully levering its ends apart using a screwdriver (see illustration 8.9). On ZR1000-B/C models the top bush is part of the inner tube and is not available separately. On all models slide the bottom bush (prising its ends apart to expand it over the top bush on ZR1000-B/C models), the oil seal washer, the oil seal, the retaining clip and the dust seal off the inner tube, noting which way up they fit. Discard the oil seal and the dust seal as new ones must be used.

Inspection

57 Clean all parts in solvent and blow them dry with compressed air, if available. Check the fork inner tube for score marks, dents, pitting, scratches, flaking of the chrome finish

and excessive or abnormal wear. Fit new tubes if any are found. Check the fork seal seat for nicks, gouges and scratches. If damage is evident, leaks will occur. Also check the oil seal washer for damage or distortion and fit a new one if necessary.

58 Check the fork inner tube for runout using V-blocks and a dial gauge. If the condition of either inner tube is suspect have it checked by a Kawasaki dealer or suspension specialist. Kawasaki provides no specifications for runout.

 Warning: If the slider is bent or exceeds the runout limit, it should not be straightened; replace it with a new one.

59 Check the fork outer tube for dents and cracks. Check the fork seal seat and housing for nicks, gouges and scratches. If damage is evident, leaks will occur. Also check the oil seal washer for damage or distortion and fit a new one if necessary.

60 Check the spring for cracks and other damage. Measure the spring free length and compare the measurement to the specifications at the beginning of the Chapter (see illustration 8.40). If it is defective or sagged below the service limit, replace the springs in both forks with new ones. Never renew only one spring.

61 Examine the working surfaces of the two bushes (i.e. the outer surface of the top bush and the inner surface of the bottom bush); if the grey Teflon outer surface has been worn away to reveal the copper inner surface over more than 75% of the surface area, or if the bushes are scored or badly scuffed, they must be replaced with new ones – both are available on ZR1000-A models, but only the bottom bush on ZR1000-B/C models – if the top bush is worn a new inner tube is needed.

62 Check the damper cartridge for damage and wear. Holding the outside of the cartridge, pump the rod in and out. If any wear or damage is found, or if the rod does not move smoothly the damper must be replaced with a new one.

Reassembly

63 On ZR1000-A models wrap some insulating tape over the ridges on the end of the inner tube to protect the lips of the new oil seal as it is installed. Apply a smear of the specified clean fork oil to the lips of the dust seal and oil seal and the inner surface of the bottom bush, then slide the new dust seal, the retaining clip, the oil seal, and the oil seal washer onto the inner tube, making sure the dust seal is the correct way round and that the marked side of the oil seal faces the dust seal. Remove the insulating tape and slide the bottom bush on the tube, then fit the top bush into its recess.

64 On ZR1000-B/C models apply a smear of the specified clean fork oil to the lips of the dust seal and oil seal and the inner surface of the bottom bush, then slide the new dust seal, the retaining clip, the oil seal, and the oil seal

washer and the bottom bush onto the inner tube, making sure the dust seal is the correct way round and that the marked side of the oil seal faces the dust seal.

65 Apply a smear of the specified clean fork oil to the outer surface of each bush, then carefully insert the inner fully into the outer tube (see illustration 8.19).

66 Support the fork upside down, then press the bottom bush squarely into its recess in the outer tube as far as possible (see illustration 8.21a). Slide the oil seal washer on top of the bush, and keep the oil seal, the retaining clip and the dust seal out of the way by sliding them up the tube (see illustration 8.21b). If necessary, tape them to the tube to prevent them from falling down and interfering as the bush is driven into place.

67 Using either the special service tool (Pt. No. 57001-1288) or a suitable drift, carefully drive the bottom bush fully into its recess – the oil seal washer prevents damaging the edges of the bush (see illustration 8.21c). If using a drift, wrap tape around it and the fork tube to prevent scratching the chrome. Make sure the bush enters the recess squarely. It is best to make sure that the inner tube is withdrawn as much as possible from the outer tube so that any accidental scratching is confined to the area that does not affect the oil seal.

68 Lift the washer to check the bush is seated fully and squarely in its recess in the slider, then wipe the recess clean and re-seat the washer.

69 Drive the oil seal into place as described in Step 63 until the retaining clip groove is visible (see illustrations 8.22b and c).

70 Once the oil seal is correctly seated, fit the retaining clip, making sure it is correctly located in its groove, then press the dust seal into position (see illustrations 8.23a and b).

71 Lay the fork flat on the bench. Fit the damper cartridge seat onto the bottom of the damper cartridge, then slide the cartridge fully into the fork – on ZR1000-A models make sure the correct cartridge is being fitted to the correct fork, the one for the right-hand fork has a bigger head on the top of the cartridge. Fit a new sealing washer onto the cartridge bolt and apply a few drops of a suitable non-permanent thread locking compound. Fit the bolt into the bottom of the fork and thread it into the cartridge, tightening it to the torque setting specified at the beginning of the Chapter. If the damper cartridge rotates inside the tube as you tighten the bolt, wait until the fork is fully reassembled and tighten it then (the pressure of the spring on the cartridge will prevent it from turning).

72 Refer to Section 7, Steps 33 to 41 and fill the fork with oil and finish reassembly.

73 If the damper rod bolt requires tightening (see Step 67), place the fork upside down on the floor, using a rag to protect it, then have an assistant compress the fork so that maximum spring pressure is placed on the damper rod head while tightening the bolt to the specified torque setting.

9.2a Fairing bracket top bolt (arrowed – 1 of 2) ...

9.2b ... and bottom bolts (arrowed) ...

9.2c ... and brake hose holder bolt (arrowed) – ZR750-J and ZR1000-A

74 Loosely fit the axle clamp bolt into the bottom of the right-hand fork. Install the fork (see Section 6). Check and adjust the fork settings as required (see Section 13).

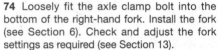

9 Steering stem

Removal

1 Remove the fairing (see Chapter 7), the instrument cluster (see Chapter 8), and the fuel tank (see Chapter 4). Remove the front forks (see Section 6). Displace the handlebars and support them clear of the top yoke on some rag, or alternatively remove them completely (Section 5).
2 Unscrew the bolts/nuts (according to model) securing the fairing bracket and front brake hose holder to the top and bottom yokes, then displace it and support it clear **(see illustrations)**.
3 If the top yoke is being removed from the bike rather than just being displaced, disconnect the ignition switch, and where fitted the immobiliser receiver, wiring connector(s) **(see illustrations)** – on ZR750-L/M and ZR1000-B/C models keep the hose above the level of the reservoir or it will drain. Release the wiring from any clips or ties and feed it through to the yoke, noting its routing.

9.2d Fairing bracket top bolts (arrowed) ...

9.2e ... and bottom bolts (arrowed) – ZR750-L/M and ZR1000-B/C

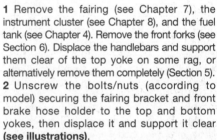

9.3a Ignition switch wiring connector (arrowed) – ZR750-J and ZR1000-A

9.3b On ZR750-L/M and ZR1000-B/C models detach the reservoir hose and place it aside ...

9.3c ... then lift and pull back the rubber boot (arrowed) ...

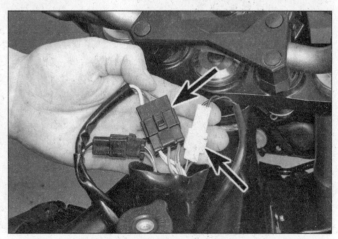

9.3d ... to access the ignition switch and immobiliser wiring connectors (arrowed)

9.4a Remove the plug . . .

9.4b . . . then unscrew the bolt and remove
the washer . . .

9.4c . . . and lift the top yoke off

4 Remove the plug from the steering stem bolt **(see illustration)**. Unscrew the bolt and remove the washer **(see illustration)**. Lift the top yoke up off the steering stem and position it clear, using a rag to protect the tank or other

components if it is only being displaced **(see illustration)**.
5 Bend the upward-pointing lockwasher tabs out of the notches in the locknut **(see illustration)**. Unscrew the locknut using

either your fingers (it shouldn't be tight) or a C-spanner located in one of the notches **(see illustration)**. Remove the lockwasher, noting how the downward-pointing tabs locate in the adjuster nut **(see illustration)**. Inspect the tabs for cracks or signs of fatigue. If there is any sign of damage, discard the lockwasher and use a new one; otherwise the old one can be re-used, but note that Kawasaki recommend using a new one.
6 Support the bottom yoke and unscrew the adjuster nut using a C-spanner, bringing the bearing cover with it **(see illustration)**. Gently lower the bottom yoke and steering stem out of the frame **(see illustration)**.
7 Remove the inner race and bearing from the top of the steering head **(see illustration)**. Remove the bearing from the base of the steering stem **(see illustration)**.
8 Remove all traces of old grease from the bearings and races and check them for wear or damage as described in Section 10. **Note:** *Do not attempt to remove the races from the steering head or the steering stem unless they are to be replaced with new ones (see Section 10).*

Installation

9 Smear a liberal quantity of multi-purpose grease onto the bearing races, and work some grease well into both the upper and lower bearings. Fit the lower bearing onto the steering stem **(see illustration 9.7b)**.
10 Carefully lift the steering stem/bottom yoke up through the steering head and support it there **(see illustration 9.6b)**. Fit the upper bearing and its inner race into the

9.5a Bend down the lockwasher tabs . . .

9.5b . . . then unscrew the locknut . . .

9.5c . . . and remove the lockwasher

9.6a Unscrew the adjuster nut and remove
the bearing cover . . .

9.6b . . . then draw the bottom yoke/
steering stem out of the steering head

9.7a Remove the upper bearing and inner
race . . .

9.7b . . . and the lower bearing

9.10a Fit the upper bearing and its inner race . . .

9.10b . . . then fit the bearing cover and thread the adjuster nut onto the stem

9.12 Tighten the adjuster nut as described

top of the steering head **(see illustration)**. Fit the bearing cover then thread the adjuster nut onto the steering stem **(see illustration)**.

11 If a suitable peg spanner (which can be made by cutting castellations into a suitably deep old socket) is available, tighten the adjuster nut to the initial torque setting specified at the beginning of the Chapter – this will apply a pre-load torque to the new bearings. Now slacken it until it just turns lightly, then tighten it to the final torque setting specified, noting that this setting can only be applied is using the Kawasaki steering stem nut wrench (Pt. No. 57001-1100). Ensure that the steering stem is able to move freely from lock-to-lock following adjustment – it is best to check and if necessary reset the bearing adjustment as described in Chapter 1 after the forks and front wheel and all other components have been installed (see Step 13).

12 If the tools described in Step 11 are not available, tighten the nut using a C-spanner so that bearing play is eliminated, but the steering stem is able to move freely from lock-to-lock **(see illustration)**.

Caution: Take great care not to apply excessive pressure because this will cause premature failure of the bearings.

13 Next temporarily install the forks and wheel as their leverage and inertia need to be taken into account. Now refer to the procedure in Chapter 1 for final tightening details. With the bearings correctly adjusted remove the wheel.

14 Fit the lockwasher, using a new one if the tabs are weakened or cracked, onto the adjuster nut and fit the downward-pointing tabs into the slots in the adjuster nut **(see illustration)**. Fit the locknut and tighten it finger-tight **(see illustration)**. Tighten the locknut by a further two notches (or by about 90°) until the notches align with the remaining

lockwasher tabs, making sure the adjuster nut does not turn as well (though that is unlikely). Secure the locknut in position by bending up the horizontal tabs on the lockwasher into its notches **(see illustration)**.

15 Fit the top yoke onto the steering stem **(see illustration)**. Fit the steering stem bolt with its washer **(see illustration 9.4b)**. Tighten the bolt to the torque setting specified at the beginning of the Chapter **(see illustration)**. Fit the plug **(see illustration 9.4a)**.

16 Set the fork height correctly in the yokes (see Section 6), then fit the remaining components in a reverse of the removal procedure, referring to the relevant Sections or Chapters. Do not forget to reconnect any wiring connectors.

17 Carry out a final check of the steering head bearing freeplay as described in Chapter 1, and if necessary re-adjust.

9.14a Fit the lockwasher . . .

9.14b . . . and the locknut

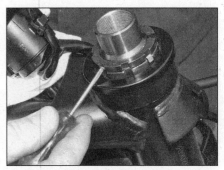

9.14c Bend the lockwasher tabs up into the notches in the lockwasher

9.15a Fit the top yoke onto the steering stem and forks . . .

9.15b . . . then fit the bolt with its washer . . .

9.15c . . . and tighten it to the specified torque

10.4a Drive the bearing races out with a brass drift . . .

10 Steering head bearings

Inspection

1 Remove the steering stem (see Section 9).
2 Remove all traces of old grease from the bearings and races and check them for wear or damage.
3 The races should be polished and free from indentations. Inspect the bearing balls for signs of wear, damage or discoloration, and examine the retainer cage for signs of cracks or splits. If there are any signs of wear on any of the above components both upper and lower bearing assemblies must be renewed as a set. Only remove the outer races in the steering head and the lower bearing inner

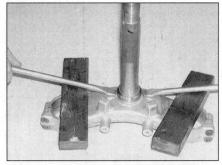

10.6a Remove the lower bearing race . . .

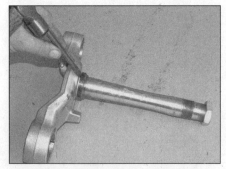

10.6b . . . using one of the methods described . . .

10.4b . . . locating it in the cut-outs where provided (arrowed)

race on the steering stem if they need to be replaced with new ones – do not reuse them once they have been removed.

Replacement

4 The outer races are an interference fit in the steering head – tap them from position using a suitable drift located on the rim of the race, using the recesses provided where present **(see illustrations)**. Tap firmly and evenly around each race to ensure that it is driven out squarely. Curve the end of the drift slightly to improve access if necessary.
5 Smear the new outer races with grease and press them into the head using a drawbolt arrangement **(see illustration)**, or alternatively (but less preferable) drive them in using a large diameter tubular drift. Ensure that the drawbolt washer or drift (as applicable) bears only on the outer edge of the race and does not contact the working surface. Alternatively, have the races installed by a Kawasaki dealer equipped with the bearing race installation tools.

HAYNES HiNT *Installation of new bearing outer races is made much easier if the races are left overnight in the freezer. This causes them to contract slightly making them a looser fit. Alternatively, use a freeze spray.*

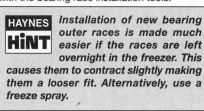

10.6c . . . or using a puller if necessary

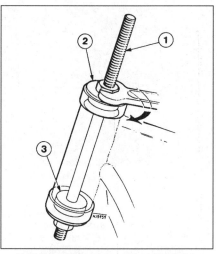

10.5 Drawbolt arrangement for fitting steering stem bearing races

1 Long bolt or threaded bar
2 Thick washer
3 Guide for lower race

6 Only remove the lower bearing inner race from the steering stem if a new one is being fitted. To remove the race, use two screwdrivers placed on opposite sides to work it free, using blocks of wood to improve leverage and protect the yoke, or tap under it using a cold chisel **(see illustrations)**. If the race is firmly in place it will be necessary to use a puller **(see illustration)**. Take the steering stem to a Kawasaki dealer if required.
7 Remove the dust seal (not fitted on ZR1000-A models) from the bottom of the stem and replace it with a new one. Smear the new one with grease, and smear some grease onto the stem above the seal to ease installation of the inner race.
8 Fit the new lower race onto the steering stem. Tap the new race into position using a length of tubing with an internal diameter slightly larger than the steering stem **(see illustration)**.
9 Install the steering stem (see Section 9).

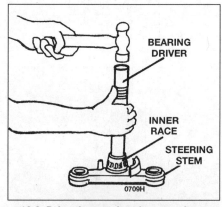

10.8 Drive the new bearing on using a suitable bearing driver or a length of pipe that bears only against the inner race and not against the rollers or cage

11.3 Unscrew the nut, withdraw the bolt and swing the rods down

11.4 Unscrew the nut, withdraw the bolt and swing the arm down

11.5 Disconnect the wiring connector (arrowed)

11 Rear shock absorber

Warning: Do not attempt to disassemble this shock absorber. It is nitrogen-charged under high pressure. Improper disassembly could result in serious injury. No individual components are available for it.

Removal

Note: *If you are removing the suspension linkage as well, do so first (see Section 12). The illustrations shown in this procedure are of a late Z1000 model – components on other models vary.*

1 On ZR750-J and ZR1000-A models remove the side panels (see Chapter 7). On ZR750-L/M and ZR1000-B/C models remove the frame covers (see Chapter 7).

2 Support the motorcycle so that no weight is transmitted through any part of the rear suspension – tie the front brake lever to the handlebar to ensure the bike can't roll forward. Position a support under the rear wheel or swingarm so that it does not drop when the shock absorber is removed, but also making sure that the weight of the machine is off the rear suspension so that the shock is not compressed.

3 Unscrew the nut and withdraw the bolt securing the linkgage rods to the swingarm

then swing the rods down **(see illustration)**.

4 Unscrew the nut and withdraw the bolt securing the bottom of the shock absorber to the linkage arm then swing the linkage arm down **(see illustration)**.

5 On ZR750-L/M and ZR1000-B/C models disconnect the regulator/rectifier wiring connector **(see illustration)**.

6 Unscrew the nut on the bolt securing the top of the shock absorber, then withdraw the bolt and manoeuvre the shock out **(see illustrations)**.

Inspection

7 Inspect the shock absorber for obvious physical damage and oil leakage, and the coil spring for looseness, cracks or signs of fatigue.

11.6a Unscrew the nut, then withdraw the bolt . . .

8 Check the bush in the top of the shock absorber and the mounting lugs on the bottom for wear or damage **(see illustration)**. On all except ZR1000-B/C models the bush is available separately so can be replaced with a new one.

9 No other parts (nuts and bolts excluded) are available for the shock absorber – if it is worn or damaged, it must be replaced with a new one or rebuilt by a suspension specialist.

10 On Z1000 models, before disposing of an old shock absorber, you should release the nitrogen gas from the reservoir. To do this, remove the cap from the valve on the reservoir, then point the valve away from you and anyone else (direct it into the ground) and depress the valve core **(see illustration)**. When all the pressure is released, remove the core of the valve using a valve core remover.

11.6b . . . and remove the shock absorber

11.8 Check the bush (arrowed) for wear

11.10 Remove the cap and press the valve core (arrowed) in to release the gas

12.6 Unscrew the nut, withdraw the bolt, and remove the rods

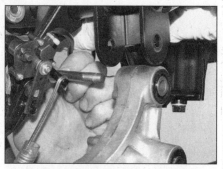

12.7 Unscrew the nut. withdraw the bolt, and remove the arm

12.8a Withdraw the spacers . . .

⚠️ *Warning: Be very careful when releasing the gas pressure – it is possible for fine debris particles to be released with it, and as the pressure is high these could damage your eyes if done carelessly. Always wear eye protection and point the valve well away.*

Installation

11 Installation is the reverse of removal, noting the following:

● Apply multi-purpose grease to the shock absorber pivots, linkage rod pivots and linkage arm pivots.
● On Z1000 install the shock absorber with the reservoir to the rear.
● Install the bolts from the right-hand side on ZR750-J and ZR1000-A models, and from the left on ZR750-L/M and ZR1000-B/C models. Install all nuts and bolts before tightening any of them.
● Counter-hold the bolts and tighten the nuts to the torque settings specified at the beginning of the Chapter.
● On ZR750-L/M and ZR1000-B/C models do not forget to reconnect the regulator/rectifier wiring connector **(see illustration 11.5)**.

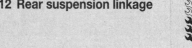

12 Rear suspension linkage

Removal

1 Support the motorcycle so that no weight is transmitted through any part of the rear suspension – tie the front brake lever to the handlebar to ensure the bike can't roll forward. Position a support under the rear wheel or swingarm so that it does not drop when the shock absorber is detached, but also making sure that the weight of the machine is off the rear suspension so that the shock is not compressed.
2 Remove the silencer(s) and/or sidestand as required according to model for access to the suspension linkage nuts and bolts.
3 Make a note of which side the bolts go in from, and so on which end the nuts are fitted – it varies from model to model, so do not go by the illustrations as your model may not be shown.

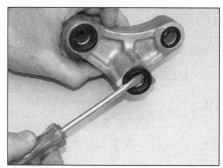

12.8b . . . then remove the seals . . .

4 Unscrew the nut and withdraw the bolt securing the linkage rods to the swingarm **(see illustration 11.3)**.
5 Unscrew the nut and withdraw the bolt securing the shock absorber to the linkage arm (see illustration 11.4).
6 Unscrew the nut and withdraw the bolt securing the linkage rods to the linkage arm and remove the rods, noting which way round they fit **(see illustration)**.
7 Unscrew the nut and withdraw bolt securing the linkage arm to the frame and remove the arm, noting which way round it fits **(see illustration)**.

Inspection

8 Withdraw the spacers from the linkage arm and from the linkage rod mount in the swingarm, then lever out the grease seals, noting what fits where – different sizes are

12.11a Check the bearings in the linkage arm . . .

12.8c . . . including those in the swingarm (shown removed)

used in each mount and so each must be returned to its original place, and though new seals must be fitted keep the old seals as a guide for installation of the new **(see illustrations)**.
9 Thoroughly clean all components, removing all traces of dirt, corrosion and grease.
10 Inspect all components closely, looking for obvious signs of wear such as heavy scoring, or for damage such as cracks or distortion. Slip each spacer back into its bearing(s) and check that there is not an excessive amount of freeplay between the two components. Replace worn or damaged components with new ones as required.
11 Check the condition of the bearings in the linkage arm and swingarm **(see illustrations)**. Refer to *Tools and Workshop Tips* (Section 5) in the Reference section for more information on bearings.

12.11b . . . and the swingarm

12 Worn bearings can be driven or drawn out of their bores, but note that removal will destroy them; new bearings should be obtained before work commences. Before removing the bearings measure their set depth (i.e. how much space is left for the grease seal) of each one using a Vernier caliper. The new bearings should be pressed or drawn into their bores rather than driven into position. In the absence of a press, a suitable drawbolt tool can be made up as described in *Tools and Workshop Tips* in the Reference section. When fitting the new bearings make sure the marked end faces out, with the correct gap (as measured before removal) between each end and the rim of the bore for the seal. Note that a Kawasaki dealer will have a set of bearing installation tools that will automatically set the bearings correctly, and if the components are taken loose and ready for assembly (i.e. clean) expense should not be excessive.

13 Lubricate the needle bearings, spacers and seals with molybdenum-disulphide grease.

14 Press the new seals into place in all the mounts, making sure each is in its correct place as noted on removal **(see illustration)** – on ZR750-L/M and ZR1000-B/C models the seals for the shock absorber mounting in the linkage arm are not shouldered and should be fitted with the marked side facing out **(see illustration 12.8b)**.

15 Fit the spacers into the bearing(s) **(see illustration 12.8a)**.

Installation

16 Installation is the reverse of removal, noting the following:

● Apply molybdenum-disulphide grease to the bearings, spacers and seals.

● Fit the linkage rods with the marked side facing out.

● Make sure the bolts are inserted from the correct side as noted on removal. Install all nuts and bolts before tightening any of them.

● Counter-hold the bolts and tighten the nuts to the torque settings specified at the beginning of the Chapter.

13 Suspension adjustment

ZR750-J

Forks

1 The front forks are not adjustable.

Shock absorber

2 The shock absorber is adjustable for spring pre-load and rebound damping.

3 Spring pre-load is adjusted by turning the adjuster ring on the top of the spring **(see illustration)**. Remove the rear mudguard to access the adjuster. Use a suitable C-spanner for adjustment (there should be one in the

12.14 Press the new seals into place

toolkit provided). There are seven settings, each identified by seats in the adjuster ring which locate under the tabs on the shock body. The lowest seat is the softest setting, and the fourth seat the standard.

4 Rebound damping adjustment is made by turning the adjuster knob on the bottom of the shock absorber **(see illustration)**. There are four settings, with number 1 providing the softest damping, and number 2 being the standard setting.

ZR750-L/M

Forks

5 The front forks are adjustable for spring pre-load on each fork and for rebound damping on the right-hand fork. Always make sure the pre-load on each fork is the same.

6 Spring pre-load is adjusted using a spanner on the adjuster flats **(see illustration)** – one should be provided in the toolkit. Turn the

13.3 Spring pre-load adjuster (arrowed) – ZR750-J

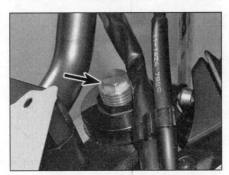

13.6 Spring pre-load adjuster (arrowed) – ZR750-L/M

adjuster clockwise to increase pre-load and anti-clockwise to decrease it. The amount of pre-load is indicated by the height of the adjuster above the top bolt hex (measured from the top of the top bolt to the top of the adjuster). The adjustment range is 4 to 19 mm, and the standard setting is 12 mm.

7 Rebound damping is adjusted using a screwdriver in the slot in the top of the damper rod protruding from the pre-load adjuster on the right-hand fork **(see illustration)**. Turn it clockwise to increase damping and anti-clockwise to decrease it. The amount of damping is measured by counting the number of clicks when turned anti-clockwise from the fully turned-in (clockwise) setting. The adjustment range is 11 clicks and the standard setting is 7 clicks out.

Shock absorber

8 The shock absorber is adjustable for spring pre-load and rebound damping.

9 Spring pre-load is adjusted by turning the adjuster ring on the top of the spring **(see illustration 13.3)**. Remove the rear mudguard to access the adjuster. Use a suitable C-spanner for adjustment (there should be one in the toolkit provided). There are seven settings, each identified by seats in the adjuster ring which locate under the tabs on the shock body. The lowest seat is the softest setting, and the fourth seat the standard.

10 Rebound damping adjustment is made by turning the adjuster screw on the bottom of the shock absorber on the right-hand side **(see illustration 13.22)**. Turn it clockwise to increase damping and anti-clockwise

13.4 Rebound damping adjuster (arrowed) – ZR750-J

13.7 Rebound damping adjuster (arrowed) – ZR750-L/M

to decrease it. The amount of damping is measured by counting the number of turns anti-clockwise from the fully turned-in (clockwise) setting. The adjustment range is 3 turns and the standard setting is 1 1/2 turns out.

ZR1000-A

Forks

11 The front forks are adjustable for spring pre-load on each fork and for rebound damping on the right-hand fork. Always make sure the pre-load on each fork is the same.
12 Spring pre-load is adjusted using a spanner on the adjuster flats **(see illustration 13.6)** – one should be provided in the toolkit. Turn the adjuster clockwise to increase pre-load and anti-clockwise to decrease it. The amount of pre-load is indicated by the height of the adjuster above the top bolt hex (measured from the top of the top bolt to the top of the adjuster). The adjustment range is 10 to 25 mm, and the standard setting is 19 mm.
13 Rebound damping is adjusted using a screwdriver in the slot in the top of the damper rod protruding from the pre-load adjuster on the right-hand fork **(see illustration 13.7)**. Turn it clockwise to increase damping and anti-clockwise to decrease it. The amount of damping is measured by counting the number of turns anti-clockwise from the fully turned-in (clockwise) setting. The adjustment range is about 2 turns and the standard setting is 1 turn out.

Shock absorber

14 The shock absorber is adjustable for spring pre-load and rebound damping. For pre-load adjustment remove the shock absorber (Section 11).
15 Spring pre-load is adjusted by slackening the adjuster locknut on the top of the spring, then turning the adjuster to alter the set length of the spring **(see illustrations 13.21a and b)**. Use a suitable C-spanner to do this (there may be one in toolkit provided). To reduce pre-load increase the length of the spring by threading the adjuster up the shock absorber (turning it anti-clockwise), and to increase pre-load compress the spring by threading the adjuster down the shock absorber (turning

13.18 Spring pre-load adjuster (arrowed) – ZR1000B/C

it clockwise). The adjustment range is a spring length of 193.4 to 183.4 mm, and the standard length is 188.4 mm.
16 Rebound damping adjustment is made by turning the adjuster screw on the bottom of the shock absorber on the right-hand side **(see illustration 13.22)**. Turn it clockwise to increase damping and anti-clockwise to decrease it. The amount of damping is measured by counting the number of turns anti-clockwise from the fully turned-in (clockwise) setting. The adjustment range is 3 to 4 turns and the standard setting is 1 turn out.

ZR1000-B/C

Forks

17 The front forks are adjustable for spring pre-load on each fork and for rebound damping on the right-hand fork. Always make sure the pre-load on each fork is set the same.
18 Spring pre-load is adjusted using a spanner on the adjuster flats **(see illustration)** – one should be provided in the toolkit. Turn the adjuster clockwise to increase pre-load and anti-clockwise to decrease it. The amount of pre-load is indicated by counting the number of turns clockwise from the fully turned-out (ant-clockwise) setting. The adjustment range is 15 turns, and the standard setting is 7 turns clockwise.
19 Rebound damping is adjusted using a screwdriver in the slot in the top of the damper rod protruding from the pre-load adjuster **(see illustration)**. Turn it clockwise to increase

13.19 Rebound damping adjuster (arrowed) – ZR1000B/C

damping and anti-clockwise to decrease it. The amount of damping is measured by counting the number of turns anti-clockwise from the fully turned-in (clockwise) setting. The adjustment range is 3 1/2 turns and the standard setting is 2 3/4 turns out.

Shock absorber

20 The shock absorber is adjustable for spring pre-load and rebound damping. For pre-load adjustment remove the shock absorber (Section 11).
21 Spring pre-load is adjusted by slackening the adjuster locknut on the top of the spring, then turning the adjuster to alter the set length of the spring **(see illustrations)**. Use a suitable C-spanner to do this (there may be one in toolkit provided). To reduce pre-load increase the length of the spring by threading the adjuster up the shock absorber (turning it anti-clockwise), and to increase pre-load compress the spring by threading the adjuster down the shock absorber (turning it clockwise). The adjustment range is a spring length of 195.5 to 185.5 mm, and the standard length is 190.5 mm.
22 Rebound damping adjustment is made by turning the adjuster screw on the bottom of the shock absorber on the right-hand side **(see illustration)**. Turn it clockwise to increase damping and anti-clockwise to decrease it. The amount of damping is measured by counting the number of turns anti-clockwise from the fully turned-in (clockwise) setting. The adjustment range is 3 turns and the standard setting is 1 1/4 turns out.

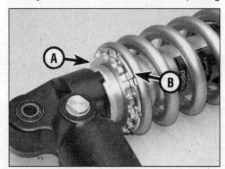

13.21a Slacken the locknut (A) and turn the adjuster (B) . . .

13.21b . . . to alter the set length of the spring – ZR1000B/C

13.22 Rebound damping adjuster (arrowed) – ZR1000B/C

14.3a Unscrew the bolts (arrowed) and remove the chainguard . . .

14.3b . . . then free the brake hose holder (A) and unscrew the bolt (B) and remove the mudguard

14.4a Unscrew the bolts (arrowed) . . .

14 Swingarm

Special Tool: *A peg spanner is needed to slacken and tighten the pivot bolt locknut (Step 6).*

Removal

1 Remove the frame covers (see Chapter 7).
2 Remove the rear wheel (see Chapter 6).
3 On ZR750-J and ZR1000-A models remove the chainguard and the mudguard from the swingarm, noting how they fit **(see illustrations)**.
4 On ZR750-L/M and ZR1000-B/C models, if required remove the chainguard, noting how it fits – this can also be done after removing the swingarm **(see illustrations)**.
5 Release the brake hose and on ABS models the wheel sensor wiring from the right-hand side of the swingarm as required according to model. Withdraw the three hoses from the guide on the inside of the arm – they are the fuel tank drain/overflow hose, the air filter housing drain hose and the coolant reservoir overflow hose **(see illustration)**.
6 Unscrew the locknut on the right-hand end of the pivot bolt using a suitable peg spanner (Kawasaki part no. 57001-1370 on ZR1000-A models, and 57001-1597 on all others, or equivalent - alternatively fabricate one by cutting castellations into an old socket of the correct size) **(see illustration)**.

14.4b . . . and remove the chainguard, noting how the holding clip locates

14.6 Unscrew the locknut using a peg spanner

7 Unscrew the nut on the left-hand end of the pivot bolt **(see illustration)**.
8 Unscrew the pivot bolt using a hex key, then

14.5 Withdraw the hoses (arrowed) from the guide

14.7 Unscrew the nut (arrowed)

withdraw it and manoeuvre the swingarm out of the frame **(see illustrations)**.
9 Remove the squared collar from the

14.8a Unscrew the pivot bolt . . .

14.8b . . . then withdraw it . . .

14.8c . . . and remove the swingarm

14.9a Remove the squared collar

14.9b Unscrew the bolt (arrowed) to remove the chain slider

14.13a Withdraw the sleeve . . .

14.13b . . . then lever the seal out from each side

right-hand side **(see illustration)**. On ZR1000-A models remove the rounded collar from the left-hand side. Remove the chain slider from the swingarm if necessary **(see illustration)**. If it is badly worn or damaged, it should be replaced with a new one. Clean, inspect and re-grease all pivot components (Steps 10 to 15).

Inspection

10 Thoroughly clean the swingarm, removing all traces of dirt, corrosion and grease.

11 Inspect the swingarm closely, looking for obvious signs of wear such as heavy scoring, and cracks or distortion due to accident damage. Any damaged or worn component must be replaced.

12 Check the swingarm pivot bolt is straight by rolling it on a flat surface such as a piece of plate glass (first wipe off all old grease and remove any corrosion using wire wool). Replace the pivot bolt with a new one if it is bent.

13 Withdraw the sleeve from the left-hand

side of the swingarm pivot **(see illustration)**. Lever the grease seal out from each side, noting which size fits where **(see illustration)**. New seals must be used, but keep the old ones laid out in order so the new seals can be matched for position.

14 Refer to *Tools and Workshop Tips* in the Reference section and check the bearings – there is a caged ball bearing and a needle bearing in the right-hand pivot, and one or two needle bearings (according to model) in the left-hand pivot. Clean them and inspect them for wear or damage. If the bearings do not run smoothly and freely or if there is excessive freeplay, they must be replaced with new ones – refer to the Reference Section for removal and installation methods. The bearings in the right-hand pivot are held by a circlip **(see illustration)**. The needle bearings must be replaced with new ones if removed – they cannot be reused. Before removing the bearings measure the set depth (i.e. how much space is left for the grease seal) of each one using a Vernier caliper. The new needle bearings should be pressed or drawn into their bores rather than driven into position. In the absence of a press, a suitable drawbolt tool can be made up as described in *Tools and Workshop Tips* in the Reference section. When fitting the new bearings make sure the marked end faces out, with the correct gap (as measured before removal) between each end and the rim of the bore for the seal. Note that a Kawasaki dealer will have a set of bearing installation tools that will automatically set the bearings correctly, and if the components are taken loose and ready for assembly (i.e. clean) expense should not be excessive.

15 Lubricate the bearings and grease seal lips with multi-purpose grease. Press the new seals into place, making sure they are fitted according to the layout of the old ones **(see illustration)**. Insert the sleeve **(see illustration 14.13a)**.

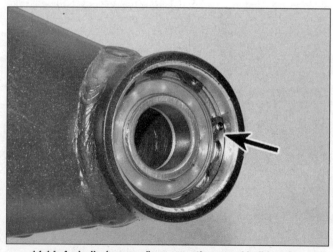

14.14 A circlip (arrowed) secures the caged ball bearing

14.15 Press the new seals into place

14.17a Locate the rear flat edge against the piece on the frame (arrowed)

14.17b Tighten the pivot bolt to the specified torque

Installation

16 If removed, fit the chain slider (see illustration 14.9b). Fit the squared collar into the seal on the right **(see illustration 14.9a)**. On ZR1000-A models fit the rounded collar into the left-hand side.

17 Offer up the swingarm, making sure the drive chain is looped over the front of the swingarm **(see illustration 14.8c)**, and locate the flat side of the collar on the right-hand side against the flat on the inside of the frame **(see illustration)**. Slide the pivot bolt through from the right-hand side and tighten it so there is no clearance between the squared collar and the frame **(see illustrations 14.8b and a)**. On ZR750-L/M and ZR1000-B/C models now slacken the pivot bolt, then tighten it to the torque setting specified at the beginning of the Chapter **(see illustration)**.

18 Thread the locknut onto the pivot bolt and tighten it to the torque setting specified at the beginning of the Chapter using the peg spanner as on removal, making sure the pivot bolt does not turn with it – it is advisable to make an alignment mark between it and the frame to make sure **(see illustrations)**.

19 Thread the nut onto the pivot bolt and tighten it to the torque setting specified at the beginning of the Chapter, counter-holding the pivot bolt head **(see illustration)**.

20 Make sure the swingarm moves up and down freely.

21 Install the remaining components in a reverse of the removal procedure (Steps 5 to 1).

22 Check and adjust the drive chain slack (see Chapter 1). Check the operation of the rear suspension and brake before taking the machine on the road.

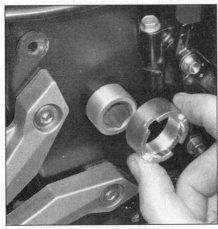

14.18a Thread the locknut on . . .

14.18b . . . and tighten it to the specified torque

14.19 Fit the nut and tighten it to the specified torque

Chapter 6
Brakes, wheels and final drive

Contents

Degrees of difficulty

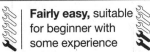

Easy, suitable for novice with little experience	**Fairly easy,** suitable for beginner with some experience	**Fairly difficult,** suitable for competent DIY mechanic	**Difficult,** suitable for experienced DIY mechanic	**Very difficult,** suitable for expert DIY or professional

Specifications

Front brakes

Brake fluid type	DOT 4
Disc thickness	
ZR750-J	
Standard	4.3 to 4.5 mm
Service limit	4.0 mm
ZR750-L/M	
Standard	4.3 to 4.7 mm
Service limit	4.0 mm
All Z1000 models	
Standard	5.8 to 6.2 mm
Service limit	5.5 mm
Disc maximum runout	0.3 mm

Rear brake

Brake fluid type	DOT 4
Disc thickness	
ZR750-J	
Standard	4.8 to 5.2 mm
Service limit	4.5 mm
ZR750-L/M	
Standard	5.8 to 6.2 mm
Service limit	5.5 mm
ZR1000-A	
Standard	4.8 to 5.2 mm
Service limit	4.5 mm
ZR1000-B/C	
Standard	5.8 to 6.2 mm
Service limit	5.5 mm
Disc maximum runout	0.3 mm

ABS system

Sensor air gap	0.7 to 0.9 mm

Wheels

Maximum wheel runout (front and rear)
    Axial (side-to-side) . . . . 1.0 mm
    Radial (out-of-round) . . . . 1.0 mm
Maximum axle runout (front and rear) . . . . 0.2 mm

Tyres

Tyre pressures . . . . see Pre-ride checks
Tyre sizes*
  Z750
    Front . . . . 120/70-ZR17 (58W) Radial
    Rear . . . . 180/55-ZR17 (73W) Radial
  Z1000
    Front . . . . 120/70-ZR17 (58W) Radial
    Rear . . . . 190/50-ZR17 (73W) Radial
*Refer to the owners handbook or the tyre information label on the swingarm for approved tyre brands.

Final drive

Drive chain slack and lubricant . . . . see Chapter 1
Drive chain
  ZR750-J
    Type . . . . Enuma EK520MVXL
    Length. . . . . 112 links
    Joining link staked ends diameter . . . . 5.6 to 6.0 mm
    Joining link plate width (outside-to-outside). . . . . 17.45 to 17.60 mm
  ZR750-L/M
    Type . . . . Enuma EK520MVXL1
    Length. . . . . 112 links
    Joining link staked ends diameter . . . . 5.7 to 6.0 mm
    Joining link plate width (outside-to-outside). . . . . 17.25 to 17.45 mm
  ZR1000-A
    Type . . . . Enuma EK525UVXL2
    Length. . . . . 112 links
    Joining link staked ends diameter . . . . 5.6 to 6.0 mm
    Joining link plate width (outside-to-outside). . . . . 19.85 to 20.00 mm
  ZR1000-B/C
    Type . . . . Enuma EK525UVXL3
    Length. . . . . 110 links
    Joining link staked ends diameter . . . . 5.6 to 6.0 mm
    Joining link plate width (outside-to-outside). . . . . 19.65 to 19.85 mm
Sprocket sizes
  Z750
    Front (engine) sprocket. . . . . 15 tooth
    Rear (wheel) sprocket. . . . . 43 tooth
  ZR1000-A
    Front (engine) sprocket. . . . . 16 tooth
    Rear (wheel) sprocket. . . . . 42 tooth
  ZR1000-B/C
    Front (engine) sprocket. . . . . 15 tooth
    Rear (wheel) sprocket. . . . . 40 tooth

Torque settings

Brake system bleed valves
  Calipers. . . . . 8 Nm
  Front master cylinder (ZR1000-B/C) . . . . 6 Nm
Brake disc bolts . . . . 27 Nm
Brake hose banjo bolts
  ZR1000-A . . . . 25 Nm
  All other models . . . . 34 Nm
Brake pipe joint nuts (ABS models) . . . . 18 Nm
Front axle
  Z750 models. . . . . 108 Nm
  Z1000 models. . . . . 127 Nm
Front axle clamp bolt
  ZR750-J . . . . 34 Nm
  All other models . . . . 20 Nm
Front brake caliper body joining bolts
  ZR1000-A . . . . 22 Nm
  ZR1000-B/C . . . . 27 Nm

Torque settings (continued)

Front brake caliper mounting bolts	
ZR750-J	34 Nm
ZR750-L/M	25 Nm
ZR1000-A	25 Nm
ZR1000-B/C	34 Nm
Front brake master cylinder clamp bolts	9 Nm
Front brake pad retaining pin(s)	17 Nm
Front sprocket cover bolts	10 Nm
Front sprocket nut	125 Nm
Rear axle nut	
Z750 models	108 Nm
Z1000 models	127 Nm
Rear brake caliper mounting bolt(s)	
ZR750-J and ZR1000-A	25 Nm
ZR750-L/M and ZR1000-B/C	22 Nm
Rear master cylinder mounting bolts	25 Nm
Rear sprocket nuts	59 Nm

1 General information

All models have hydraulically operated disc brakes, with twin discs at the front and a single disc at the rear. On Z750 models the front brake has twin piston sliding calipers, and the rear has a single piston sliding caliper. On Z1000 models the front brake has calipers with four opposed pistons, and the rear has a single piston sliding caliper.

The drive to the rear wheel is by chain and sprockets. The rear wheel hub incorporates a rubber 'cush-drive'.

All models are fitted with cast alloy wheels designed for tubeless tyres only.

Caution: Disc brake components rarely require disassembly. Do not disassemble components unless absolutely necessary. If an hydraulic brake hose is loosened or disconnected, the union sealing washers must be replaced with new ones and the system must be bled upon reassembly. Do not use solvents on internal brake components. Solvents will cause the seals to swell and distort. Use only clean DOT 4 brake fluid. Use care when working with brake fluid as it can injure your eyes and it will damage painted surfaces and plastic parts.

2 Front brake pads

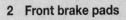

Warning: The dust created by the brake system may contain asbestos, which is harmful to your health. Never blow it out with compressed air and don't inhale any of it. An approved filtering mask should be worn when working on the brakes.

1 Work on one caliper at a time. **Note:** *Do not operate the brake lever while the pads are out of the caliper.*

2.2a Unscrew the bolts (arrowed) . . .

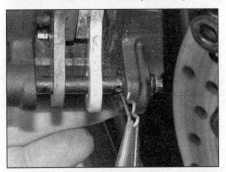

2.2c Remove the clip . . .

2 On ZR750-J models, unscrew the caliper mounting bolts and slide the caliper off the disc **(see illustrations)**. Remove the retaining clip from the pad pin **(see illustration)**.

2.2e Pivot the inner pad up then off the post . . .

2.2b . . . and slide the caliper off the disc

2.2d . . . then withdraw the pin

Withdraw the pad pin **(see illustration)**. Pivot the inner pad up and slide it off its post, then remove the outer pad, noting how it locates **(see illustrations)**.

2.2f . . . then remove the outer pad

2.4 Brake pad pin (A), caliper mounting bolts (B)

2.5a Slacken the brake pad retaining pins (arrowed)

3 On ZR750-L/M models, unscrew the pad pin plug, then slacken the pad pin. Unscrew the caliper mounting bolts and slide the caliper off the disc. Unscrew and withdraw the pad pin then remove the pads, noting how they locate.

4 On ZR1000-A models, slacken the pad pin **(see illustration)**. Unscrew the caliper mounting bolts and slide the caliper off the disc. Unscrew and remove the pad pin, then remove the pad spring and lift the pads from the caliper

5 On ZR1000-B/C models, slacken the pad retaining pins **(see illustration)**. Unscrew the

caliper mounting bolts and slide the caliper off the disc **(see illustrations)**. Work on one pair of pads at a time. Unscrew and remove the pad pin, then remove the pad spring and drop the pads from the caliper **(see illustrations)**.

6 Inspect the surface of each pad for contamination and check that the friction material has not worn beyond its service limit (see Chapter 1, Section 2) **(see illustration)**. If any pad is worn down to, or beyond, the service limit wear indicator (i.e. the wear indicator is no longer visible), is fouled with oil or grease, or heavily scored or damaged, fit a complete set of new pads. **Note:** *It is not*

possible to degrease the friction material; if the pads are contaminated in any way they must be replaced with new ones.

7 If the pads are in good condition clean them carefully, using a fine wire brush which is completely free of oil and grease to remove all traces of road dirt and corrosion. Using a pointed instrument, dig out any embedded particles of foreign matter. If required, spray with a dedicated brake cleaner to remove any dust.

8 Check the condition of the brake disc (see Section 4).

9 Remove all traces of corrosion from the pad pin(s) and check it/them for wear and damage.

2.5b Unscrew the bolts (arrowed) . . .

2.5c . . . and slide the caliper off the disc

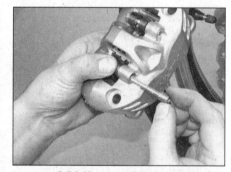

2.5d Unscrew the pin . . .

2.5e . . . and remove the spring . . .

2.5f . . . and the pads

2.6 Check the friction material for contamination and wear

10 On Z750 models slide the caliper off its bracket **(see illustration)**. Note the pad spring in the top of caliper and the pad guide on the caliper bracket and remove them if required for cleaning or replacement, noting how they fit **(see illustrations)**. Clean off all traces of corrosion and hardened grease from the slider pins and from their rubber boots. Check the slider pin boots for cracks and splits and replace them with new ones if necessary, making sure they locate correctly **(see illustration)**.

11 Clean around the exposed section of each piston to remove any dirt or debris that could cause the seals to be damaged. On ZR1000-B/C models block the gap between the fitted pair of pads with a suitable tool. If new pads are being fitted, now push the pistons all the way back into the caliper to create room for them; if the old pads are still serviceable push the pistons in a little way. To push the pistons back use finger pressure or a piece of wood as leverage, or place the old pads back in the caliper and use a metal bar or a screwdriver inserted between them (but take care not to damage the friction surface if the pads are being reused), or use grips and a piece of wood, with rag or card to protect the caliper body **(see illustration)**. On all except ZR1000-B/C models you can use a commercial piston-pushing tool **(see illustration)**. It may be necessary to remove the front brake fluid reservoir cap, plate and diaphragm and siphon out some fluid (see *Pre-ride checks*). If the pistons are difficult to push back, remove the bleed valve cap, then attach a length of clear hose to the bleed valve and place the open end in a suitable container, then open the valve and try again (see Section 11). Take great care not to draw any air into the system. If in doubt, bleed the brake afterwards.

12 If a piston appears seized, first block or hold the other piston(s) using wood or cable-ties, then apply the brake lever and check whether the piston in question moves at all. If it moves out but can't be pushed back in, it is likely there is some hidden corrosion stopping it. If it doesn't move at all, or to fully clean and inspect the pistons, overhaul the caliper (see Section 3).

2.10a Slide the caliper and bracket apart

2.10b Note the spring (arrowed) . . .

2.10c . . . and the guide (arrowed)

2.10d Check the condition of the rubber boots

13 On Z750 models, if removed fit the pad spring into the caliper and the guide onto the bracket **(see illustrations 2.10b and c)**. Apply some silicone grease to the slider pins and inside the boots. Slide the caliper onto the bracket **(see illustration 2.10a)**, making sure the boots locate correctly to provide a seal.

14 When fitting the pads into the caliper make sure the friction material on each pad faces the other.

15 On ZR750-J models fit the outer pad, making sure it locates correctly **(see illustration 2.2f)**. Slide the inner pad onto its post then pivot it down into the caliper **(see illustration 2.2e)**. Press both pads against the spring to align the holes, then insert the pad pin and secure it with the retaining clip **(see illustrations 2.2d and c)**. Slide the caliper onto the disc making sure the pads locate

correctly on each side **(see illustration 2.2b)**. Fit the caliper mounting bolts and tighten them to the torque setting specified at the beginning of the Chapter **(see illustration)**.

16 On ZR750-L/M models fit the pads into the caliper, making sure they locate correctly. Press both pads against the spring to align the holes, then insert the pad pin and tighten it finger-tight. Slide the caliper onto the disc making sure the pads locate correctly on each side. Fit the caliper mounting bolts and tighten them to the torque setting specified at the beginning of the Chapter. Tighten the pad pin to the specified torque, then fit the plug.

17 On ZR1000-A models smear some silicone grease onto the pad pin stopper ring. Fit the pads into the caliper. Fit the pad spring with its wider end at the lower end of the caliper. Slide the pad pin through the outer pad, over

2.11a On ZR1000-B/C models block one half of the caliper while pushing the pistons back in the other half

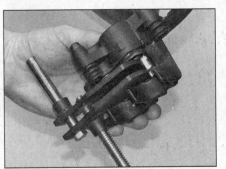

2.11b Using a proper tool to push the pistons in

2.15 Fit the bolts and tighten them to the specified torque – ZR750-J

2.18 Fit the bolts and tighten them to the specified torque – ZR1000-B/C

the spring leaf, through the inner pad and tighten it finger-tight. Slide the caliper onto the disc making sure the pads locate correctly on each side. Fit the caliper mounting bolts and tighten them to the torque setting specified at the beginning of the Chapter. Tighten the pad pin to the specified torque setting.

18 On ZR1000-B/C models fit the pads up into the caliper (**see illustration 2.5f**). Fit the pad spring with the wider sections at the upper end of the caliper (**see illustration 2.5e**). Insert the pad pin, then press down on the leaf and slide the pin all the way through and tighten it finger-tight (**see illustration 2.5d**). Repeat the procedure for the other pair of pads. Slide the caliper onto the disc making sure the pads locate correctly on each side of the disc (**see illustration 2.5c**). Fit the caliper mounting bolts and tighten them to the torque setting specified at the beginning of the Chapter (**see illustration**). Tighten the pad pins to the specified torque setting (**see illustration 2.5a**).

19 Repeat the procedure for the other caliper.

20 Operate the brake lever until the pads contact the disc. Check the level of fluid in the hydraulic reservoir and top-up if necessary (see *Pre-ride checks*).

21 Check the operation of the front brake before riding the motorcycle.

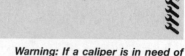

3 Front brake calipers

> **Warning: If a caliper is in need of overhaul all old brake fluid should be flushed from the system. Also, the dust created by the brake system may contain asbestos, which is harmful to your health. Never blow it out with compressed air and do not inhale any of it. An approved filtering mask should be worn when working on the brakes. Overhaul of the brake caliper must be done in a spotlessly clean work area to avoid contamination and possible failure of the brake hydraulic system components. Do not, under any circumstances, use petroleum-based solvents to clean brake parts. Use clean DOT 4 brake fluid, dedicated brake cleaner or denatured alcohol only, as described. To prevent damage from spilled brake fluid, always cover paintwork when working on the braking system.**

Removal

Note: *If the caliper is being overhauled (usually due to sticking pistons or fluid leaks) read through the entire procedure first, and make sure that you have obtained all the new parts required, and some new DOT 4 brake fluid.*

1 If the caliper is being completely removed or overhauled, unscrew the brake hose banjo bolt and detach the hose(s), noting how they align with the caliper (**see illustrations**). Wrap clingfilm around the banjo union and secure the hose in an upright position to minimise fluid loss, and wrap some rag or tissue around the caliper to catch the fluid inside. Discard the sealing washers, as new ones must be fitted on reassembly.

2 If the caliper is being overhauled, remove the brake pads (see Section 2).

3 If the caliper is just being displaced, unscrew the caliper mounting bolts and slide the caliper off the disc (**see illustrations 2.2a and b, 2.4, or 2.5b and c**). Secure it to the motorcycle with a cable-tie to avoid straining the brake hose. **Note:** *Do not operate the brake lever while either caliper is off the disc.*

Overhaul

4 Clean the exterior of the caliper with denatured alcohol or brake system cleaner. Have some clean rag ready to catch any spilled brake fluid.

5 On Z750 models, if not already done slide the caliper off its bracket, then remove the pad spring from the caliper (**see illustrations 2.10a and b**). Stuff thick rag or place a piece of wood between the pistons and the caliper body – it should be just thick enough to stop the pistons leaving the bores entirely. Apply compressed air gradually and progressively, starting with a fairly low pressure, to the fluid inlet on the caliper and allow the pistons to ease out of their bores. Make sure the pistons are displaced evenly, using a small piece of wood to block one while the other moves if necessary.

6 On Z1000 models, unscrew the caliper body joining bolts and separate the body halves, catching any residual fluid with the rag (**see illustration**). Remove the caliper body O-ring from whichever body half it is in and discard it – fit a new one on reassembly (**see illustration 3.16a**). Place one of the caliper halves piston-up on the bench. When working on the outer caliper half, make sure the bleed valve is tight, and find a suitable bolt to block the fluid inlet banjo bolt bore and thread it in. Get a wad of rag and hold it against the pistons as a cushion to protect your hand as the pistons are forced out. Apply compressed air gradually and progressively, starting with a fairly low pressure, to the fluid passage on the caliper joint and allow the pistons to ease out of their bores, controlling them with hand pressure and the rag (**see illustration**). Make sure the pistons are displaced evenly, using pressure to block one while the other moves

3.1a Brake hose banjo bolt (arrowed) – ZR750-J

3.1b Brake hose banjo bolt (arrowed) – ZR1000-B/C

3.6a Caliper body joining bolts (arrowed) – ZR1000-A

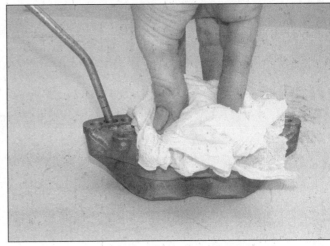

3.6b Apply compressed air to the fluid passage . . .

if necessary **(see illustration)**. Repeat the procedure for the other caliper half.

7 If a piston is stuck in its bore due to corrosion, the caliper should be replaced with a new one. Do not try to remove a piston by levering it out or by using pliers or other grips.

8 Mark each piston and the caliper body to ensure that the pistons can be matched to their original bores on reassembly.

9 Remove the dust seals and the piston seals from the piston bores using a soft wooden or plastic tool to avoid scratching the bores **(see illustration)**. Discard the seals as new ones must be fitted on reassembly.

10 Clean the pistons and bores with clean DOT 4 brake fluid. If compressed air is available, blow it through the fluid galleries in the caliper to ensure they are clear (make sure it is filtered and unlubricated).

Caution: Do not, under any circumstances, use a petroleum-based solvent to clean brake parts.

11 Inspect the caliper bores and pistons for signs of corrosion, nicks and burrs and loss of plating. If surface defects are present, the pistons and/or the caliper assembly must be replaced with new ones. If one caliper is in poor condition, the other front caliper and the master cylinder should also be checked.

12 Lubricate the new piston seals with clean brake fluid and fit them into their grooves in the caliper bores **(see illustrations)**. On ZR1000-A models note that there are two sizes of bore in each caliper and care must therefore be taken to ensure that the correct size seals are fitted to the correct bores – the same applies when fitting the new dust seals and pistons.

13 Lubricate the new dust seals with clean brake fluid and fit them into their grooves in the caliper bores **(see illustration)**.

14 Lubricate the pistons with clean brake fluid and fit them, closed-end first, into the caliper bores, taking care not to displace the seals **(see illustration)**. Using your thumbs,

3.6c . . . until the pistons are displaced

3.9 Remove the seals and discard them

3.12a Lubricate the new piston seals with brake fluid . . .

3.12b . . . then fit them into their grooves . . .

3.13 . . . followed by the new dust seals

3.14 Fit the pistons and push them all the way in

3.16a Fit the O-ring into its recess . . .

3.16b . . . then join the caliper halves . . .

3.16c . . . and tighten the bolts

push the pistons all the way in, making sure they enter the bore squarely.

15 On Z750 models, clean off all traces of corrosion and hardened grease from the slider pins and the rubber boots. Check the boots for cracks and splits and replace them with new ones if necessary, making sure they locate correctly **(see illustration 2.10d)**. Fit the pad spring into the caliper, and make sure the guide is on the bracket **(see illustrations 2.10b and c)**. Slide the caliper onto the bracket, making sure the boots locate correctly around the base of the pins to provide a seal **(see illustration 2.10a)**.

16 On Z1000 models, lubricate the new caliper body O-ring with clean DOT 4 brake fluid and fit it into the outer half of the caliper body **(see illustration)**. Join the two halves of the caliper body together, ensuring that the O-ring stays in place **(see illustration)**. Clean the threads of the caliper body joining bolts, then apply a suitable non-permanent thread locking compound and tighten them evenly to the torque setting specified at the beginning of the Chapter **(see illustration)**.

Installation

17 If removed, install the brake pads (see Section 2).

18 Slide the caliper onto the disc, making sure the pads fit over each side of the disc **(see illustration 2.2b or 2.5c)**.

19 Fit the caliper mounting bolts and tighten them to the torque setting specified at the beginning of the Chapter **(see illustration 2.15 or 2.18)**.

20 If removed, connect the brake hose(s) to the caliper using new sealing washers – you need three washers for the two hoses on the right-hand side **(see illustration 3.1a or b)**. Align the hose(s) correctly. Tighten the banjo bolt to the specified torque setting for your model.

21 Top up the hydraulic reservoir with DOT 4 brake fluid (see *Pre-ride checks*) and bleed the system as described in Section 11. Check that there are no fluid leaks and test the operation of the brake before riding the motorcycle.

4 Front brake discs

Inspection

1 Inspect the surface of the disc for score marks and other damage. Light scratches are normal after use and won't affect brake operation, but deep grooves and heavy score marks will reduce braking efficiency and accelerate pad wear. If a disc is badly grooved it must be replaced with a new one.

2 The disc must not be machined or allowed to wear down to a thickness less than the service limit listed in this Chapter's Specifications. The minimum thickness is also stamped on the disc **(see illustration)**. Check the thickness of the disc with a micrometer and replace it with a new one if necessary.

3 To check if the disc is warped, position the bike on an auxiliary stand with the front wheel raised off the ground. Mount a dial gauge to the fork leg, with the gauge plunger touching the surface of the disc about 10 mm from its outer edge **(see illustration)**. Rotate the wheel and watch the gauge needle, comparing the reading with the limit listed in the Specifications at the beginning of this Chapter. If the runout is greater than the service limit, check the wheel bearings for play (see Chapter 1). If the bearings are worn, install new ones (see Section 17) and repeat this check. If the disc runout is still excessive, a new pair of discs will have to be fitted.

Removal

4 Remove the wheel (see Section 15).
Caution: Don't lay the wheel down and allow it to rest on the disc – the disc could become warped. Set the wheel on wood blocks so the wheel rim supports the weight of the wheel.

5 If you are not replacing the disc with a new one, mark the relationship of the disc to the wheel, so it can be installed in the same position and on the same side as originally fitted. Unscrew the disc retaining bolts, loosening them evenly and a little at a time in a criss-cross pattern to avoid distorting the disc, then remove the disc – on ABS equipped models note the sensor rotor fitted on the outside of the disc **(see illustration)**. On all except ZR1000-A models remove the gasket and discard it – a new one must be used.

Installation

6 Before installing the disc, make sure there is no dirt or corrosion where the disc seats on the hub. If the disc does not sit flat when it is

4.2 The minimum thickness is marked on the disc

4.3 Checking disc runout with a dial gauge

4.5 The disc is secured by five bolts

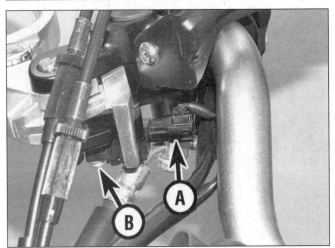

5.1 Disconnect the brake light switch connector (A). Switch mounting screw (B)

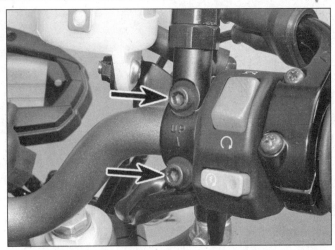

5.2 Unscrew the bolts (arrowed) and remove the master cylinder and its clamp

bolted down, it will appear to be warped when checked or when the front brake is used. On ABS models do the same where the sensor rotor seats on the disc.

7 On all except ZR1000-A models fit a new gasket onto the wheel, aligning the holes. Fit the disc on the wheel with its marked side facing out, aligning the previously applied matchmarks (if you're reinstalling the original disc), and making sure the arrow pints in the direction of normal rotation. On ABS models fit the sensor rotor onto the disc with marked side facing out, again aligning the holes.

8 Clean the threads of the disc mounting bolts, then apply a suitable non-permanent thread locking compound. Install the bolts and tighten them evenly and a little at a time in a criss-cross pattern to the torque setting specified at the beginning of this Chapter. Clean the disc using acetone or brake system cleaner. If a new disc has been installed, remove any protective coating from its working surfaces and fit new brake pads (see Section 15).

9 Install the front wheel (see Section 15).

10 Operate the brake lever several times to bring the pads into contact with the disc. Check the operation of the brake before riding the motorcycle.

5 Front brake master cylinder

Warning: If the brake master cylinder is in need of overhaul all old brake fluid should be flushed from the system. Overhaul of the brake master cylinder must be done in a spotlessly clean work area to avoid contamination and possible failure of the brake hydraulic system components. Do not, under any circumstances, use petroleum-based solvents to clean brake parts. Use clean DOT 4 brake fluid, dedicated brake cleaner or denatured alcohol only, as described. To prevent damage from spilled brake fluid, always cover paintwork when working on the braking system.

Note: If the master cylinder is being overhauled (usually due to sticking or poor action, or fluid leaks) read through the entire procedure first and make sure that you have obtained all the new parts required, including some new DOT 4 brake fluid.

Removal

1 Remove the mirror (see Chapter 8). Disconnect the brake light switch wiring connector(s) **(see illustration)**.

2 If the master cylinder is just being displaced from the handlebar, make sure the fluid reservoir cover or cap is secure. Unscrew the master cylinder clamp bolts and remove the back of the clamp, noting how it fits, then wrap the master cylinder and reservoir assembly in some rag and position it clear of the handlebar **(see illustration)**. Make sure no strain is placed on the hydraulic hose. Keep the reservoir upright to prevent air entering the system.

3 If the master cylinder is being overhauled, remove the brake lever (see Chapter 5).

4 Unscrew the brake hose banjo bolt and detach the hose, noting its alignment with the master cylinder **(see illustrations)**. Wrap clingfilm around the banjo union and secure the hose in an upright position to minimise fluid loss, and wrap some rag or tissue around the master cylinder to catch the fluid inside. Discard the sealing washers as new ones must be fitted on reassembly.

5 On ZR750-J and ZR1000-A models slacken

5.4a Brake hose banjo bolt (arrowed) – ZR750-J and ZR1000-A

5.4b Brake hose banjo bolt (arrowed) – ZR750-L/M

5.4c Brake hose banjo bolt (arrowed) – ZR1000-B/C

5.5a Slacken the cover screws

5.5b Undo the screw and remove the clamp

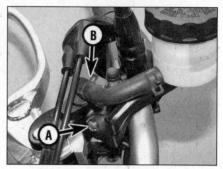

5.7a Undo the screw (A) then release the clip (B) and detach the hose

and lightly retighten the reservoir cover screws **(see illustration)**. On ZR750-L/M and ZR1000-B/C models remove the reservoir cap clamp screw and clamp, then slacken and lightly re-tighten the cap **(see illustration)**.
6 Unscrew the master cylinder clamp bolts and remove the back of the clamp, noting how it fits, then lift the master cylinder and reservoir away from the handlebar **(see illustration 5.2)**.
7 Remove the reservoir cover or cap, the diaphragm plate and the diaphragm. Drain the brake fluid from the master cylinder and reservoir into a suitable container. On ZR1000-B/C models undo the reservoir screw and detach it from the master cylinder, then release the hose clip and detach the hose **(see illustration)**. On ZR750-L/M models release the hose clip and detach the hose **(see illustration)**. Wipe any remaining fluid out of the reservoir with a clean rag.

8 If required, undo the screw securing the brake light switch to the bottom of the master cylinder and remove the switch **(see illustration 5.1)**.

Overhaul

9 On ZR750-L/M and ZR1000-B/C models lift the dust cap from the fluid reservoir hose union, then remove the circlip and detach the union from the master cylinder **(see illustration)**. Discard the O-ring as a new one must be fitted on reassembly. Inspect the reservoir hose for cracks or splits and replace it with a new one if necessary.
10 On Z750 models and ZR1000-A models carefully remove the rubber boot from the master cylinder. Depress the piston and use circlip pliers to remove the circlip, then slide out the piston assembly and the spring, noting how they fit. If they are difficult to

remove, apply low pressure compressed air to the brake fluid outlet. Lay the parts out in the proper order to prevent confusion during reassembly.
11 On ZR1000-B/C models carefully remove the rubber boot from the master cylinder, bringing the pushrod with it **(see illustration)**. Depress the piston and use circlip pliers to remove the circlip, then slide out the piston assembly, the spring, and the spring guide, noting how they fit **(see illustrations)**. If they are difficult to remove, apply low pressure compressed air to the brake fluid outlet. Lay the parts out in the proper order to prevent confusion during reassembly.
12 Clean the master cylinder with clean brake fluid. If compressed air is available, blow it through the fluid galleries to ensure they are clear (make sure the air is filtered and unlubricated).

5.7b Release the clip (arrowed) and detach the hose

5.9 Lift the cap off to access the circlip

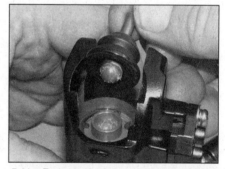

5.11a Remove the boot and pushrod from the end of the master cylinder piston . . .

5.11b . . . then depress the piston and remove the circlip . . .

5.11c . . . then draw out the piston . . .

5.11d . . . and the spring

5.14 Make sure the cup and seal are correctly installed on the piston – ZR1000-B/C type shown

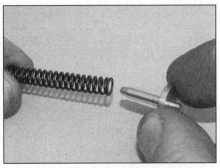

5.16a Fit the guide into the end of the spring

5.16b Push the piston into the bore . . .

5.16c . . . and hold it there while fitting the circlip

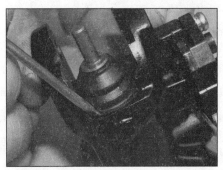

5.16d Feed the rim of the boot into the bore

Caution: Do not, under any circumstances, use a petroleum-based solvent to clean brake parts.

13 Check the master cylinder bore for corrosion, scratches, nicks and score marks. If damage or wear is evident, the master cylinder must be replaced with a new one. If the master cylinder is in poor condition, then the calipers should be checked as well.

14 The dust boot, circlip, piston and its cup and seal, the spring, and on ZR1000-B/C models the pushrod and spring guide, should all be included in the master cylinder rebuild kit (check with your dealer). Use all of the new parts, regardless of the apparent condition of the old ones. Lubricate the master cylinder bore and the piston, cup and seal with new brake fluid, and assemble the components according to the layout of the old ones – the wider ends of the seal and cup fit into the master cylinder first **(see illustration)**.

15 On Z750 models and ZR1000-A models fit the spring and piston assembly into the master cylinder, wide end of the spring first, and making sure the lips on the cup and seal do not turn inside out. Push the piston all the way in, compressing the spring and fit the new circlip. Fit the boot onto the piston so its narrow outer end lips locate in the groove. Press the wider rim of the boot into the master cylinder against the circlip.

16 On ZR1000-B/C models fit the spring guide into the end of the spring **(see illustration)**. Fit the spring guide and spring into the master cylinder, locating the pin on the end of the guide in the hole **(see illustration 5.11d)**. Lubricate the piston with clean brake fluid and slide it into the master cylinder and up against the spring **(see illustration 5.11c)**. Make sure the lips on the cup and seal do not turn inside out. Push the piston in to compress the spring and install the new circlip **(see illustrations)**. Smear the inner end of the pushrod with silicone grease. Fit the boot onto the pushrod so its narrow outer end lips locate in the groove **(see illustration 5.11a)**. Locate the inner end of the pushrod in the end of the piston, then press the wider rim of the boot into the master cylinder against the circlip **(see illustration)**.

17 On ZR750-L/M and ZR1000-B/C models

fit a new O-ring smeared with silicone grease onto the fluid reservoir hose union, then press the union into the master cylinder and secure it with the circlip **(see illustration 5.9)**. Fit the dust cap over the circlip.

18 Inspect the fluid reservoir diaphragm and fit a new one if it is damaged or deteriorated.

Installation

19 If removed, fit the brake light switch onto the bottom of the master cylinder, making sure the pin locates in the hole, and tighten the screw **(see illustration 5.1)**.

20 Attach the master cylinder to the handlebar, aligning the clamp joint with the punch mark on the top of the handlebar, then fit the back of the clamp with its UP mark facing up **(see illustration 5.2)**. Tighten the upper bolt to the torque setting specified at the beginning of this Chapter, followed by the lower bolt.

21 On ZR1000-B/C models fit the reservoir bracket onto the master cylinder and tighten the screw **(see illustration 5.7a)**. On ZR750-L/M and ZR1000-B/C models connect the reservoir hose to the union on the master cylinder and secure it with the clip **(see illustration 5.7b or a)**.

22 Connect the brake hose to the master cylinder, using new sealing washers on each side of the banjo fitting. Align the hose as noted on removal **(see illustration 5.4a, b or c)**. Tighten the banjo bolt to the torque setting specified at the beginning of this Chapter.

23 Install the brake lever (see Chapter 5), and the mirror (see Chapter 7).

24 Connect the brake light switch wiring connector **(see illustration 5.1)**.

25 Fill the fluid reservoir with new DOT 4 brake fluid (see *Pre-ride checks*). Refer to Section 11 and bleed the air from the system.

26 Check the operation of the brake before riding the motorcycle.

6 Rear brake pads

Warning: The dust created by the brake system may contain asbestos, which is harmful to your health. Never blow it out with compressed air and don't inhale any of it. An approved filtering mask should be worn when working on the brakes.

1 On ZR750-J and ZR1000-A models unscrew the caliper mounting bolts and slide the caliper off the disc **(see illustration)**. **Note:** *Do not*

6.1a Unscrew the bolts (arrowed) . . .

6.1b ... and slide the caliper off the disc

6.1c Remove the clip ...

6.1d ... then withdraw the pin

6.1e Pivot the inner pad up and slide it off the bracket ...

6.1f ... then remove the outer pad, noting how it locates

6.1g Slide the bracket out of the caliper

operate the brake pedal while the caliper is off the disc. Remove the clip from the pad pin, then withdraw the pin and remove the pads, noting how they fit **(see illustrations)**. Slide the caliper off its bracket **(see illustration)**.

2 On ZR750-L/M and ZR1000-B/C models, unscrew the pad pin plug, then slacken the pad pin **(see illustrations)**. Unscrew the caliper mounting bolt **(see illustration)**. Unscrew the pad pin, then pivot the back

of the caliper up and remove the pads **(see illustration)**. Pivot the caliper up further and slide it out of the bracket **(see illustration)**.

3 Note the pad spring in the top of caliper and the pad guide on the caliper bracket and remove them if required for cleaning or replacement, noting how they fit **(see illustrations 6.11a and b or c and d)**. Remove all traces of corrosion from the pad pin and check it for wear and damage.

4 Inspect the surface of each pad for contamination and check that the friction material has not worn beyond its service limit (see Chapter 1, Section 2). If either pad is worn down to, or beyond, the service limit wear indicator (i.e. the wear indicator is no longer visible), is fouled with oil or grease, or heavily scored or damaged, fit a set of new pads. **Note:** *It is not possible to degrease the friction material; if the pads are contaminated*

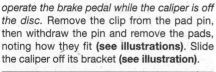

6.2a Unscrew the plug ...

6.2b ... then slacken the pin

6.2c Unscrew the mounting bolt ...

6.2d ... then unscrew the pad pin and remove the pads

6.2e Pivot the caliper up then slide it out of the bracket

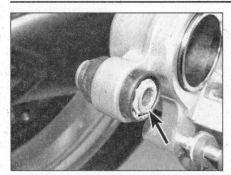
6.8 Withdraw the collar (arrowed)

6.9a You can push the piston in using your fingers . . .

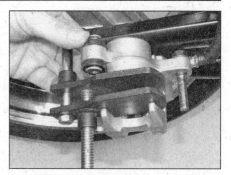
6.9b . . . or using the proper tool

in any way they must be replaced with new ones.
5 If the pads are in good condition clean them carefully, using a fine wire brush which is completely free of oil and grease to remove all traces of road dirt and corrosion. Using a pointed instrument, dig out any embedded particles of foreign matter. If required, spray with a dedicated brake cleaner to remove any dust.
6 Check the condition of the brake disc (see Section 8).
7 On ZR750-J and ZR1000-A models clean off all traces of corrosion and hardened grease from the slider pins on the bracket and from the rubber boots **(see illustration 6.1g)**. Check the boots for cracks and splits and replace them with new ones if necessary, making sure they locate correctly.
8 On ZR750-L/M and ZR1000-B/C models withdraw the collar from the rubber boot on the caliper **(see illustration)**. Clean off all traces

of corrosion and hardened grease from the slider pin, collar, mounting bolt and the boots – the boot for the slider is in the bracket **(see illustration 6.2e)**. Check the boots for cracks and splits and replace them with new ones if necessary, making sure they locate correctly.
9 Clean around the exposed section of the piston to remove any dirt or debris that could cause the seals to be damaged. If new pads are being fitted, now push the piston all the way back into the caliper to create room for them; if the old pads are still serviceable push the piston in a little way. To push the piston back use finger pressure or a piece of wood as leverage, or place the old pads back in the caliper and use a metal bar or a screwdriver inserted between them, or use grips and a piece of wood, with rag or card to protect the caliper body **(see illustration)**. Alternatively obtain a proper piston-pushing tool from a good tool supplier **(see illustration)**. Depending on the

level of fluid in the reservoir it may be necessary to remove the cap, plate and diaphragm and siphon out some fluid (see *Pre-ride checks*). If the piston is difficult to push back, remove the bleed valve cap, then attach a length of clear hose to the bleed valve and place the open end in a suitable container, then open the valve and try again (see Section 11). Take great care not to draw any air into the system. If in doubt, bleed the brake afterwards.
10 If the piston appears seized, apply the brake pedal and check whether the piston moves at all. If it moves out but can't be pushed back in, it is likely there is some hidden corrosion stopping it. If it doesn't move at all, or to fully clean and inspect the piston, disassemble the caliper and overhaul it (see Section 7).
11 If removed fit the pad spring into the caliper and the guide onto the bracket **(see illustrations)**. Apply some silicone grease to the slider pins/bolt and inside the boots. On ZR750-L/M and ZR1000-B/C models also grease the collar, then fit it into the boot on the caliper, making sure the outer rims of the boot locate in the grooves **(see illustration 6.8)**.
12 Lightly smear the back of the pad backing material and the edges of the backing material where it contacts the caliper body or bracket with copper-based grease, making sure that none gets on the friction material. Also smear the pad pin.
13 On ZR750-J and ZR1000-A models slide the caliper onto the bracket **(see illustration 6.1g)**, making sure the boots locate correctly to provide a seal **(see illustration)**. Fit the

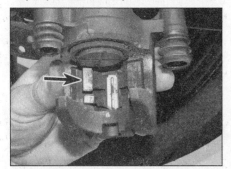
6.11a Pad spring (arrowed) . . .

6.11b . . . and guide (arrowed) – ZR750-J and ZR1000-A

6.11c Pad spring (arrowed) . . .

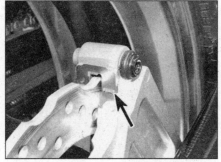
6.11d . . . and guide (arrowed) – ZR750-L/M and ZR1000-B/C

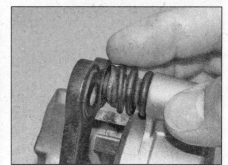
6.13a Make sure the boots locate correctly

6.13b Slide the caliper onto the disc and fit the bolts

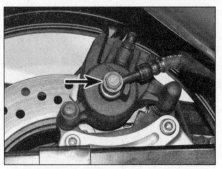

7.1a Brake hose banjo bolt (arrowed) – ZR750-J and ZR1000-A

7.1b Brake hose banjo bolt (arrowed) – ZR750-L/M and ZR1000-B/C

outer pad into the caliper, making sure it locates correctly against the guide (see illustration 6.1f). Fit the eye on the inner pad over the post on the bracket then pivot the pad into the caliper and onto the spring – make sure the friction material of each pad faces the other (see illustration 6.1e). Press the inner pad against the spring to align the holes and slide the pin through, aligning it so the hole is at the bottom (see illustration 6.1d). Fit the clip into the hole to secure the pin (see illustration 6.1c). Slide the caliper onto the disc, then fit the bolts and tighten them to the torque setting specified at the beginning of the Chapter (see illustration).

14 On ZR750-L/M and ZR1000-B/C models slide the caliper onto the bracket, making sure the boot locates correctly to provide a seal (see illustration 6.2e). Fit the pads into the caliper and insert the pad pin, tightening it finger-tight (see illustration 6.2d). Pivot the caliper down onto the disc, making sure the pads locate correctly on each side and against the guide on the bracket. Press down to align the mounting holes then fit the mounting bolt and tighten it to the torque setting specified at the beginning of the Chapter (see illustration 6.2c). Tighten the pad pin to the specified torque, then fit the blanking plug (see illustrations 6.2b and a).

15 Operate the brake pedal until the pads contact with the disc. Check the level of fluid in the hydraulic reservoir and top-up if necessary (see Pre-ride checks).

16 Check the operation of the rear brake before riding the motorcycle.

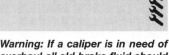

7 Rear brake caliper

⚠️ **Warning: If a caliper is in need of overhaul all old brake fluid should be flushed from the system. Also, the dust created by the brake system may contain asbestos, which is harmful to your health. Never blow it out with compressed air and do not inhale any of it. An approved filtering mask should be worn when working on the brakes. Overhaul must be done in a spotlessly clean work area to avoid contamination and possible failure of the brake hydraulic system components. Do not, under any circumstances, use petroleum-based solvents to clean brake parts. Use clean DOT 4 brake fluid, dedicated brake cleaner or denatured alcohol only, as described. To prevent damage from spilled brake fluid, always cover paintwork when working on the braking system.**

Removal

Note: *If the caliper is being overhauled (usually due to a sticking piston or fluid leak) read through the entire procedure first and make sure that you have obtained all the new parts*

required, including some new DOT 4 brake fluid.

1 If the caliper is being completely removed or overhauled, unscrew the brake hose banjo bolt and detach the hose, noting its alignment with the caliper (see illustrations). Wrap clingfilm around the banjo union and secure the hose in an upright position to minimise fluid loss, and place some rag or tissue around the caliper to catch the fluid inside. Discard the sealing washers as new ones must be fitted on reassembly.

2 If the caliper is being overhauled remove the brake pads (see Section 6, Steps 1 to 8).

3 If the caliper is just being displaced, on ZR750-J and ZR1000-A models unscrew the caliper mounting bolts and slide the caliper off the disc (see illustrations 6.1a and b). On ZR750-L/M and ZR1000-B/C models unscrew the caliper mounting bolt (see illustration 6.2c), then pivot the back of the caliper up, hold the pads clear of the disc, and slide caliper out of the bracket (see illustration).

Overhaul

4 Clean the exterior of the caliper with denatured alcohol or brake system cleaner. Have some clean rag ready to catch any spilled brake fluid.

5 On ZR750-J and ZR1000-A models withdraw the insert from the piston (see illustration). Stuff thick rag or place a piece of wood between the pistons and the caliper body – it should be just thick enough to stop the pistons leaving the bores entirely. Insert

7.3 Hold the pads clear and slide the caliper off the bracket

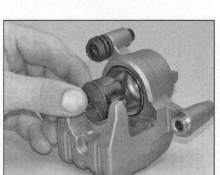

7.5a Withdraw the insert from the piston

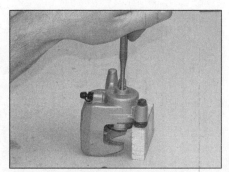

7.5b Push the piston out as shown

7.6 Using compressed air to force the piston out

7.8 Remove the seals and discard them

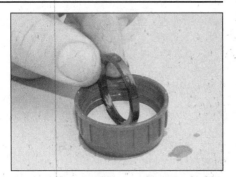

7.13a Lubricate the new piston seal with brake fluid . . .

a suitable drift into the fluid inlet passage and locate it against the piston, then press the piston out – do not strike the drift with a hammer **(see illustration)**.

6 On ZR750-L/M and ZR1000-B/C models, stuff thick rag or place a piece of wood between the pistons and the caliper body – it should be just thick enough to stop the piston leaving the bore entirely. Apply compressed air gradually and progressively, starting with a fairly low pressure, to the fluid inlet on the caliper and allow the piston to ease out of the bore **(see illustration)**.

7 If the piston is stuck in its bore due to corrosion the caliper should be replaced with a new one. Do not try to remove a piston by driving or levering it out or by using pliers or other grips.

8 Remove the dust seal and the piston seal

from the piston bore using a soft wooden or plastic tool to avoid scratching the bores **(see illustration)**. Discard the seals as new ones must be fitted on reassembly.

9 Clean the piston and bore with clean brake fluid. If compressed air is available, blow it through the fluid passages in the caliper to ensure they are clear (make sure it is filtered and unlubricated).

Caution: Do not, under any circumstances, use a petroleum-based solvent to clean brake parts.

10 Inspect the caliper bore and piston for signs of corrosion, nicks and burrs and loss of plating. If surface defects are present, the piston and/or the caliper assembly must be replaced with new ones. If the caliper is in poor condition, the master cylinder should also be checked.

11 On ZR750-J and ZR1000-A models clean off all traces of corrosion and hardened grease from the slider pins on the bracket and from the rubber boots **(see illustration 6.1g)**. Check the boots for cracks and splits and replace them with new ones if necessary, making sure they locate correctly.

12 On ZR750-L/M and ZR1000-B/C models withdraw the collar from the rubber boot on the caliper **(see illustration 6.8)**. Clean off all traces of corrosion and hardened grease from the slider pin, collar, mounting bolt and the boots – the boot for the slider is in the bracket **(see illustration 6.2e)**. Check the boots for cracks and splits and replace them with new ones if necessary, making sure they locate correctly.

13 Lubricate the new piston seal with clean brake fluid and fit it into its groove in the caliper bore **(see illustrations)**.

14 Lubricate the new dust seal with silicone grease and fit it into its groove in the caliper bore **(see illustration)**.

15 Lubricate the piston with clean brake fluid and fit it, closed-end first, into the caliper bore, taking care not to displace the seals **(see illustration)**. Using your thumbs, push the piston all the way in, making sure it enters the bore squarely. On ZR750-J and ZR1000-A models, fit the insert into the piston **(see illustration 7.5a)**.

Installation

16 If the caliper has been overhauled install the brake pads (see Section 6, Steps 11 to 16).

17 If the caliper was just displaced, on ZR750-J and ZR1000-A models slide the caliper onto the disc, then fit the bolts and tighten them to the torque setting specified at the beginning of the Chapter **(see illustration 6.13b)**. On ZR750-L/M and ZR1000-B/C models slide the caliper into the bracket, then pivot it down, making sure the pads locate over each side of the disc and against the guide on the bracket **(see illustration)**. Press down to align the mounting holes, then fit the mounting bolt and tighten it to the torque setting specified at the beginning of the Chapter **(see illustration 6.2c)**.

18 If detached, connect the brake hose to the

7.13b . . . then fit it into its groove . . .

7.14 . . . followed by the new dust seal

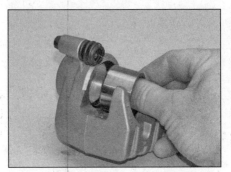

7.15 Fit the piston and push it all the way in

7.17 Make sure the pads sit on each side of the disc

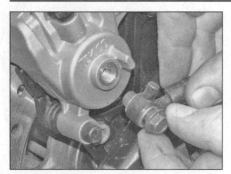

7.18 Always use new sealing washers

8.3 The disc is secured by four bolts (arrowed)

caliper, using new sealing washers on each side of the fitting **(see illustration)**. Make sure the hose is correctly aligned and tighten the banjo bolt to the torque setting specified at the beginning of the Chapter **(see illustration 7.1a or b)**.

19 Top up the hydraulic reservoir with DOT 4 brake fluid (see *Pre-ride checks*) and bleed the system as described in Section 11.

20 Check that there are no fluid leaks and test the operation of the brake before riding the motorcycle.

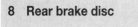

8 Rear brake disc

Inspection

1 Refer to Section 4 of this Chapter, noting that the dial gauge should be attached to the swingarm.

Removal

2 Remove the rear wheel (see Section 16).
Caution: Don't lay the wheel down and allow it to rest on the disc or sprocket – they could become warped. Set the wheel on wood blocks so the wheel rim supports the weight of the wheel.

3 If you are not replacing the disc with a new one, mark the relationship of the disc to the wheel so it can be installed in the same position. Unscrew the disc retaining bolts, loosening them evenly and a little at a time in a criss-cross pattern to avoid distorting the disc, then remove the disc – on ABS equipped models note the sensor rotor fitted on the outside of the disc **(see illustration)**. On ZR1000-A1 remove the gasket and discard it – a new one must be used.

Installation

4 Before installing the disc, make sure there is no dirt or corrosion where the disc seats on the hub. If the disc does not sit flat when it is bolted down, it will appear to be warped when checked or when the rear brake is used. On ABS models do the same where the sensor rotor seats on the disc.

5 On ZR1000-A1 up to frame No. -005854 fit a new gasket onto the wheel, aligning the holes. Fit the disc on the wheel with its marked side facing out, aligning the previously applied matchmarks (if you're reinstalling the original disc), and making sure the arrow pints in the direction of normal rotation. On ABS models fit the sensor rotor onto the disc with marked side facing out, again aligning the holes.

6 Clean the threads of the disc mounting bolts, then apply a suitable non-permanent thread locking compound. Install the bolts and tighten them evenly and a little at a time in a criss-cross pattern to the torque setting specified at the beginning of this Chapter. Clean the disc using acetone or brake system cleaner. If a new disc has been installed, remove any protective coating from its working surfaces and fit new brake pads.

7 Install the rear wheel (see Section 16).

8 Operate the brake pedal several times to bring the pads into contact with the disc. Check the operation of the brake before riding the motorcycle.

9 Rear brake master cylinder

⚠ *Warning: If the brake master cylinder is in need of overhaul all old brake fluid should be flushed from the system. Overhaul must be done in a spotlessly clean work area to avoid contamination and possible failure of the brake hydraulic system components. Do not, under any circumstances, use petroleum-based solvents to clean brake parts. Use clean DOT 4 brake fluid, dedicated brake cleaner or denatured alcohol only, as described. To prevent damage from spilled brake fluid, always cover paintwork when working on the braking system.*

Removal

Note: *If the master cylinder is being overhauled (usually due to sticking or poor action, or fluid leaks) read through the entire procedure first and make sure that you have obtained all the new parts required, including some new DOT 4 brake fluid.*

1 On ZR750-L/M and ZR1000-B/C remove the heel guard – there are nuts on the inner ends of the three bolts, and collars fit into the grommets from the inside **(see illustrations)**.

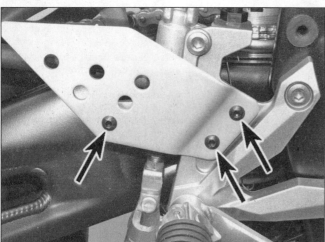

9.1a Unscrew the bolts (arrowed) . . .

9.1b . . . retrieving the nuts as you do

9.2 Remove the split pin (arrowed) then withdraw the clevis pin

9.3a Reservoir hose clip (arrowed) – ZR750-J and ZR1000-A

9.3b Reservoir hose clip (arrowed) – ZR750-L/M and ZR1000-B/C

2 Remove the split pin from the inner end of the clevis pin, then withdraw the clevis pin **(see illustration)**. Discard the split pin as a new one must be fitted on reassembly.
3 Prepare a container to drain the reservoir into. Release the clip securing the reservoir hose to the union on the master cylinder and detach the hose, and allow the fluid to drain **(see illustrations)**. Afterward wrap some rag around the end of the hose to catch residual drops. Undo the reservoir cap (slacken the screw to release the clamp first on ZR750-L/M and ZR1000-B/C models and remove the diaphragm plate and diaphragm **(see illustration)**. Wipe any remaining fluid out of the reservoir with a clean rag.
4 Undo the brake hose banjo bolt and detach the banjo union, noting its alignment with the master cylinder **(see illustration)**. Once disconnected, wrap clingfilm around the banjo union and secure the hose in an upright position to minimise fluid loss, and wrap some rag or tissue around it. Discard the sealing washers as new ones must be fitted on reassembly.
5 Undo the bolts securing the master cylinder to the footrest bracket and remove the master cylinder **(see illustration)**.

Overhaul

6 If required, remove the circlip securing the fluid reservoir hose union and detach it from the master cylinder. Discard the O-ring as a new one must be used. Inspect the reservoir hose for cracks or splits and replace it with a new one if necessary.

7 Dislodge the rubber dust boot from the base of the master cylinder. Push the pushrod in and, using circlip pliers, remove the circlip from its groove in the master cylinder and slide out the pushrod, piston and spring, noting how they fit. Lay the parts out in order as you remove them to prevent confusion during reassembly.
8 Clean the master cylinder with fresh brake fluid. If compressed air is available, blow it through the fluid galleries to ensure they are clear (make sure the air is filtered and unlubricated).
Caution: Do not, under any circumstances, use a petroleum-based solvent to clean brake parts.
9 Check the master cylinder bore for corrosion, scratches, nicks and score marks. If damage or wear is evident, the master cylinder must be replaced with a new one. If the master cylinder is in poor condition, then the caliper should be checked as well.
10 The piston, seal, cup and spring must be replaced with new ones and are available as a set – use all of the new parts, regardless of the apparent condition of the old ones. The pushrod assembly and rubber boot are also available as a set if required, and the circlip is available on its own.
11 Smear the piston, cup and seal with new brake fluid. If they are not already on the piston, fit them into their grooves, matching the layout of the originals, so the wider ends will fit into the master cylinder first. Lubricate the master cylinder bore with new brake fluid.
12 fit the spring and piston assembly into the

master cylinder, wide end of the spring first, and making sure the lips on the cup and seal do not turn inside out.
13 Smear some silicone grease onto the rounded end of the pushrod and locate it against the end of the piston. Fit the new circlip around the pushrod. Push the piston in using the pushrod until the washer is beyond the circlip groove, then locate the circlip in the groove.
14 Fit the rubber boot into the master cylinder and press the rim against the circlip. Make sure the outer lips are seated correctly around the pushrod.
15 Fit a new fluid reservoir hose union O-ring smeared with brake fluid, then press the union into the master cylinder and secure it with the circlip.

Installation

16 Locate the master cylinder on the inside of the footrest bracket and tighten the bolts to the torque setting specified at the beginning of this Chapter **(see illustration 9.5)**.
17 Lubricate the clevis pin with grease. Align the clevis with the brake pedal, then insert the pin and secure it with a new split pin **(see illustration 9.2)**. Bend the ends of the pin up to lock it. Check the brake pedal height (see Chapter 1, Section 2).
18 Connect the brake hose to the master cylinder, using new sealing washers on each side of the fitting, and making sure it is correctly aligned **(see illustration 9.4)**. Tighten the banjo bolt to the torque setting specified at the beginning of this Chapter.

9.3c Remove the cap, plate and diaphragm and wipe the reservoir out

9.4 Brake hose banjo bolt (arrowed)

9.5 Master cylinder bolts (arrowed)

19 Connect the reservoir hose to its union on the master cylinder and secure it with the clip **(see illustration 9.3a or b)**. Check that the hose is secured with a clip at the reservoir end as well. If the clips have weakened, use new ones.

20 Fill the fluid reservoir with new DOT 4 brake fluid (see *Pre-ride checks*). Refer to Section 11 and bleed the air from the system.

21 Check the operation of the brake carefully before riding the motorcycle.

10 Anti-lock brake system (ABS)

General information

⚠️ **Warning: The ABS system works by comparing the relative speed of the wheels, and is programmed using the wheel and tyre sizes specified and fitted as standard. If non-specified wheels or tyres are fitted the control unit may become confused and the system will not function correctly.**

1 The ABS system prevents the wheels from locking under heavy braking or on rough road surfaces. A sensor on each wheel transmits information about the speed of wheel rotation to the control unit. If the unit senses a difference in speed between the wheels it momentarily releases brake pressure to the relevant wheel. Pressure is controlled by the ABS hydraulic unit.

2 The ABS system is self checking, and assesses the electrical system as well as the function of the hydraulic unit. In the event of a problem the fault can be located via a fault code system.

3 When the ignition is switched on the ABS indicator light in the instrument cluster should come on. When the engine has been started and a speed of 4 mph (6 km/h) is reached the light should go off, which indicates the self-diagnosis is complete and the system is functioning normally. If the light does not come on when the ignition is turned on check the ABS indicator light circuit (Steps 45 to 47).

4 If a problem is detected the indicator light comes on, and a fault code will be stored – follow the fault code retrieval procedure to diagnose the problem.

5 Note that under certain conditions, the indicator light could come on and a fault code could be registered, even though there is no actual problem with the system. This can occur if the machine is ridden continuously on very bumpy roads, or if the rider does a wheelie, or if the air pressure on one tyre is extremely low, or if the machine is placed on an auxiliary stand with the engine running and the rear wheel is turning when the front is not. If this happens stop the bike and turn the engine off, then restart and ride the bike – the light may not come on again when the system realises everything is OK, but if it does the

fault code must be retrieved and then erased before the indicator light will go out.

Fault code retrieval and erasure

6 In the event of a problem the fault code must be retrieved, and it will then be displayed by the ABS indicator light. The code is deciphered by the way in which the light flashes.

7 The control unit can store up to 14 fault codes, and in the event of there being more than one it will indicate the codes sequentially in ascending numerical order, and will then repeat them. Write the fault code(s) down so no errors can be made, and to avoid having to repeat the retrieval procedure.

8 The ABS indicator light emits flashes to give out the fault code. The first flash or flashes are used to indicate the first digit of the fault code, then there is a gap of 1.5 seconds, then the second set of flashes indicate the second digit of the code. For example, two flashes followed by four flashes indicates the fault code number 24. If there is more than one fault code, there will be a 3.5 second gap before the other codes are revealed. The fault codes are shown in the table.

9 After retrieval the codes must be erased. After erasure perform the normal start-up routine so the system performs its own self-diagnosis to check that the codes have been erased, then ride the bike to check the light does not come on, and if you want to, check the function of the system by braking hard.

Retrieval

10 Make sure the ignition switch is OFF. Remove the seats (see Chapter 8).

11 Locate the self-diagnosis terminals, which are two open-ended bullet connectors, one with a grey wire and the other with a black/yellow wire. Using an auxiliary lead with connectors to fit the terminals, join between the grey and black/yellow wire terminals **(see illustration)**.

12 Turn the ignition switch ON. The ABS indicator light should come on for 2 seconds and then go out for 3.5 seconds, and then will begin to flash the fault codes as described in Step 8.

13 If no fault code is stored, and when stored codes have been erased, after the 2 second start signal the light will go out for 3.5 seconds, then come on and stay on with no flashing.

Erasure

14 After the code(s) have been displayed and recorded, disconnect the auxiliary wire from the black/yellow wire terminal, then reconnect and disconnect it three times within 12.5 seconds, each time keeping it connected for more than 1 second. The ABS light remains lit when doing this.

15 When the fault code has been erased the ABS indicator light will blink then come back on and stay on. If there is more than one code all codes will be erased at the same time. Now enter self-diagnosis mode again to check that

10.11 ABS self-diagnosis terminals (arrowed)

all codes have been erased, in which case the light comes on and stays on as in Step 13. Now perform the normal start-up routine as in Step 9.

Fault diagnosis

Fault code	Problem
13	Rear inlet solenoid valve – faulty solenoid or seized valve
14	Rear outlet solenoid valve – faulty solenoid or seized valve
17	Front inlet solenoid valve – faulty solenoid or seized valve
18	Front outlet solenoid valve – faulty solenoid or seized valve
19	ABS solenoid valve relay – faulty wiring or faulty relay
25	Tyre or wheel problem – wrong size tyre, warped wheel, sensor rotor damaged
35	ABS pump motor relay – faulty wiring or faulty relay
42	Front wheel sensor signal abnormal – missing sensor or sensor rotor, incorrect air gap, or sensor rotor damaged
43	Front wheel sensor – faulty wiring
44	Rear wheel sensor signal abnormal – missing sensor or sensor rotor, incorrect air gap, or sensor rotor damaged
45	Rear wheel sensor – faulty wiring
52	Power supply voltage too low
53	Power supply voltage too high
55	Faulty ABS electronic control unit (ECU)

16 Before checking the individual components according to the fault code table above, first check the system fuses, and the wiring and all connectors between the components (see *Wiring Diagrams* at the end of Chapter 9). A continuity test of all wires will locate a break or short in any circuit. Inspect the terminals inside the wiring connectors and ensure they are not broken, loose or corroded. Spray the inside of the connectors with an electrical terminal cleaner before reconnection. Repair or replace the wiring and/or connectors with new ones as necessary. Also check for dirt on the wheel sensors and the sensor rotors, which could affect the signal being transmitted.

17 If all the wiring and connectors and sensors are good refer to the fault code table above and check the system according to the fault code shown. If no problems can be found, see Step 5.

Fault codes 13, 14, 17 and 18 – solenoid valve

18 First check the brake fluid levels, signs of fluid leakage, the action of the brake lever and pedal, the brake pads and discs, that the wheels turn smoothly with no brake drag, the wheel bearings, and the wheels and discs for runout. Refer to Chapter 1 for further details.

19 If no problems are found, erase the service code, then start and ride the bike and check if the light comes on again and the same service code is shown (Steps 14, 15 and 9). If so, the hydraulic unit is faulty and must be replaced with a new one (see below). If the indicator light does not come back on assume the system is normal and that any fault was temporary.

Fault code 19 – solenoid valve relay

20 First check the solenoid valve relay 20A fuse in the ABS fusebox (see Chapter 8).

21 If the fuse has blown, disconnect the hydraulic unit wiring connector (see below for access), and check for continuity between the light green and black/yellow wire terminals on the hydraulic unit. If there is continuity replace the hydraulic unit with a new one. If there is no continuity, check for continuity in the light green wire between the wiring connector and the fusebox. If there is no continuity in the wire locate and repair the fault. Replace the fuse with a new one.

22 If the fuse is good, check for battery voltage at the light green wire terminal in the fusebox connector. If there is no voltage check for continuity between the battery positive (+) terminal and the light green wire terminal. If there is no continuity in the wire locate and repair the fault. If the voltage was good, erase the service code, then start and ride the bike and check if the light comes on again and the same service code is shown (Steps 14, 15 and 9). If so, the relay inside the hydraulic unit is faulty and the unit must be replaced with a new one (see below). If the indicator light does not come back on assume the system is normal and that any fault was temporary.

Fault code 25 – tyres and wheels

23 First check the tyre pressures (see *Pre-ride checks*), then check that the correct tyres are fitted (see Specifications at the beginning of this Chapter), then check the wheels, wheel bearings and tyres for damage, deformation and runout (see Chapter 1).

24 If no problems are found, erase the service code, then start and ride the bike and check if the light comes on again and the same service code is shown (Steps 14, 15 and 9). If so, the

ECU inside the hydraulic unit is faulty and the hydraulic unit must be replaced with a new one (see below). If the indicator light does not come back on assume the system is normal and that any fault was temporary.

Fault code 35 – pump motor relay

25 First check the 30A ABS motor fuse in the ABS fusebox (see Chapter 8).

26 If the fuse has blown, disconnect the hydraulic unit wiring connector (see below for access), and check for continuity between the red and light blue wire terminals on the hydraulic unit. If there is continuity replace the hydraulic unit with a new one. If there is no continuity, check for continuity in the red wire between the wiring connector and the fusebox. If there is no continuity in the wire locate and repair the fault. Replace the fuse with a new one.

27 If the fuse is good, check for battery voltage at the red wire terminal in the fusebox connector. If there is no voltage check for continuity between the battery positive (+) terminal and the light green wire terminal. If there is no continuity in the wire locate and repair the fault. If the voltage was good, erase the service code, then start and ride the bike and check if the light comes on again and the same service code is shown (Steps 14, 15 and 9). If so, the relay inside the hydraulic unit is faulty and the unit must be replaced with a new one (see below). If the indicator light does not come back on assume the system is normal and that any fault was temporary.

Fault code 42 – front wheel sensor

28 Using a feeler gauge check that the air gap between the sensor and the rotor is as specified at the beginning of the Chapter (see illustration 10.50). Check the gap at several points by turning the wheel. If the gap is incorrect check that the sensor and rotor mounting bolts are tight, and that neither component is distorted on its mount. The gap is not adjustable.

29 Make sure the sensor tip is clean and free of debris and corrosion – remove the sensor for cleaning if required (see below). If the sensor tip is damaged, replace the sensor with a new one.

30 Check the rotor for a build-up of dirt or debris or for broken or distorted segments and clean or replace the rotor with a new one as required (see below).

31 If no problems are found, erase the service code, then start and ride the bike and check if the light comes on again and the same service code is shown (Steps 14, 15 and 9). If so, the ECU inside the hydraulic unit is faulty and the hydraulic unit must be replaced with a new one (see below). If the indicator light does not come back on assume the system is normal and that any fault was temporary.

Fault code 43 – front wheel sensor wiring

32 Disconnect the ABS hydraulic unit and wheel sensor wiring connectors (see below for access).

33 Check for continuity in the black/red and green wires between the loom side of the connectors. If there is no continuity in either wire, locate and repair the fault.

34 Check for continuity between each terminal in the sensor wiring connector (sensor side) and earth (ground). There should be no continuity. If there is, replace the sensor with a new one (see below).

35 If no problems are found, erase the service code, then start and ride the bike and check if the light comes on again and the same service code is shown (Steps 14, 15 and 9). If so, the ECU inside the hydraulic unit is faulty and the hydraulic unit must be replaced with a new one (see below). If the indicator light does not come back on assume the system is normal and that any fault was temporary.

Fault code 44 – rear wheel sensor

36 The procedure is the same as fault code 42 for the front wheel sensor – see Steps 28 to 31 (see illustration 10.54).

Fault code 45 – rear wheel sensor wiring

37 The procedure is the same as fault code 43 for the front wheel sensor, except you are checking the black and brown/black wires for continuity between the hydraulic unit and sensor wiring connectors – see Steps 32 to 35.

Fault code 52 – power supply voltage low or non-existent

38 First check the 10A ABS system fuse in the ABS fusebox (see Chapter 8).

39 If the fuse is good disconnect the ABS hydraulic unit wiring connector (see below for access), and the ignition switch wiring connector (remove the fuel tank (Chapter 4) for access). Check for continuity in the yellow wire between the hydraulic unit connector and the fusebox, then in the brown wire between the loom side of the ignition switch wiring connector and the fusebox. If there is no continuity in either wire, locate and repair the fault.

40 If all is good so far, next check the battery, the ignition switch, the main fuse and if necessary the wiring between them (see Chapter 8) – if the voltage is low the problem is likely to be in the battery and its state of charge, and possibly in the charging system. If the voltage is non-existent the problem is likely to be a blown fuse or a broken ignition switch or a broken wire or wiring connector. You can check whether the voltage is low or non-existent at the supply to the ignition switch (white wire) or at the supply from the ignition switch to the hydraulic unit (brown wire in the ignition switch connector, with the ignition ON).

41 If no problems are found, erase the service code, then start and ride the bike and check if the light comes on again and the same service code is shown (Steps 14, 15 and 9). If so, the ECU inside the hydraulic unit is faulty and the hydraulic unit must be replaced with a new one (see below). If the indicator light does not

10.46 Disconnect the instrument wiring connector

10.49 Note the routing of the wiring and how it is held

10.50 Front wheel sensor mounting bolts (arrowed)

come back on assume the system is normal and that any fault was temporary.

Fault code 53 – power supply voltage high

42 The problem is likely to be that the regulator is allowing too much voltage from the alternator to reach the battery. Check the charging system (see Chapter 8).

43 If no problems are found, erase the service code, then start and ride the bike and check if the light comes on again and the same service code is shown (Steps 14, 15 and 9). If so, the ECU inside the hydraulic unit is faulty and the hydraulic unit must be replaced with a new one (see below). If the indicator light does not come back on assume the system is normal and that any fault was temporary.

Fault code 55 – ABS ECU

44 Erase the service code, then start and ride the bike and check if the light comes on again and the same service code is shown (Steps 14, 15 and 9). If so, the ECU inside the hydraulic unit is faulty and the hydraulic unit must be replaced with a new one (see below). If the indicator light does not come back on assume the system is normal and that any fault was temporary.

ABS indicator light circuit check

45 On Z750 models remove the fairing (see Chapter 7). On Z1000 models remove the windshield (see Chapter 7).

46 Disconnect the instrument cluster wiring connector **(see illustration)**. Connect the

positive (+) lead of a voltmeter to the black/white wire terminal in the connector and the negative (-) lead to earth (ground). Turn the ignition on – there should be about 10 volts. If the voltage is good, check the instrument cluster (see Chapter 8). If there is no voltage check the black/white wire for continuity between the instrument cluster and the ABS hydraulic unit wiring connector (see below for access), and repair the wiring if necessary. If the wiring is good the hydraulic unit could be faulty.

47 If the indicator light comes on and there is no fault code stored, and the cause is not one of those given in Step 5, the black/white wire between the instrument cluster and the hydraulic unit could be shorted to earth – check for continuity in the wire and if necessary trace the short and repair it.

Component removal and installation

Front wheel sensor

48 Remove the fairing (see Chapter 7). The sensor is mounted in the bottom of the left-hand fork.

49 Trace the wiring from the sensor and disconnect it at the connector. Free the wiring from any ties or guides and feed it down to the sensor, noting its routing **(see illustration)**.

50 Unscrew the two bolts securing the sensor and withdraw it from the fork **(see illustration)**.

51 Installation is the reverse of removal. Make sure the sensor tip is clean and undamaged,

and that the mounting lugs are not distorted. Check the air gap (see Step 28).

Rear wheel sensor

52 Remove the right-hand side panel (see Chapter 7). The sensor is mounted in the bottom of the rear brake caliper bracket.

53 Trace the wiring from the sensor and disconnect it at the connector. Free the wiring from any ties or guides and feed it down to the sensor, noting its routing **(see illustrations)**.

54 Unscrew the two bolts securing the sensor and withdraw it from the bracket **(see illustration)**.

55 Installation is the reverse of removal. Make sure the sensor tip is clean and undamaged, and that the mounting lugs are not distorted. Check the air gap (see Step 28).

Wheel sensor rotors

56 Refer to Section 4 for the front wheel rotor and Section 8 for the rear wheel rotor – each rotor is secured to the wheel by the brake disc bolts. Before installing the ring, make sure there is no dirt or corrosion where it seats on the disc, as this will not allow the ring to sit flat when it is bolted down and it will be warped and could cause the ABS system to indicate a fault. Follow the correct bolt installation and tightening procedure as directed in those Sections.

Hydraulic unit

57 Have some clean rag to hand to catch any spilled brake fluid and some clingfilm to wrap around the end of each pipe as it is disconnected. If required drain the brake fluid from the system (see Section 12). Remove

10.53a Note the routing of the wiring and how it is held around the back of the swingarm . . .

10.53b . . . and along the top

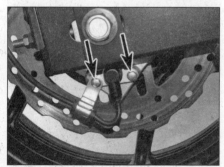

10.54 Rear wheel sensor mounting bolts (arrowed)

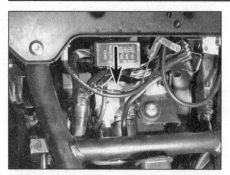

10.58 ABS system hydraulic unit (arrowed)

the seats and the seat cowling (see Chapter 7). Remove the tool kit. Remove the taillight and the battery (Chapter 8). Remove the ECU (see Chapter 4). Now displace or remove (as preferred) all the electrical components from the top of the rear fender, noting how they fit and how the wiring is routed. Unscrew the rear fender bolts, two at the back and one on each side at the front, and draw the fender out to the back, noting how it fits.

58 Release the security clip and disconnect the wiring connector from the unit **(see illustration)**.

59 Unscrew the bolt securing the hose/pipe joint blocks on the right-hand side to give them freedom of movement. Unscrew the input and output pipe nuts on the front and top of the unit and detach the pipes, being prepared with some rag to catch any residual fluid. Wrap the end of each pipe in clingfilm to prevent fluid loss and dirt getting in.

60 Unscrew the bolts on the top, left-hand side and the underside that hold the unit in its bracket. Draw the unit out to the rear and remove it.

61 Installation is the reverse of removal. The front brake system pipes connect to the left-hand side of the unit, with the input pipe from the master cylinder at the front and the output pipe to the caliper on the top. The rear brake system pipes connect to the right-hand side in the same layout. If the correct tools are available tighten the pipe joint nuts to the specified torque.

62 Bleed the hydraulic system following the procedure in Section 12. Check the operation of both brakes carefully before riding the motorcycle.

11 Brake hoses, pipes (ABS models) and fittings

Inspection

1 Brake hose condition should be checked regularly and the hoses replaced with new ones at the specified interval (see Chapter 1). Twist and flex the hoses while looking for cracks, bulges and seeping hydraulic fluid. Check extra carefully around the areas where the hoses connect with the banjo fittings, as these are common areas for hose failure.

2 On models with ABS remove the fuel tank (see Chapter 4) and check the brake pipes, the pipe joints and the ABS hydraulic unit for signs of fluid leakage and for any dents or cracks in the pipes.

3 Inspect the banjo fittings connected to the brake hoses and the pipe joints on ABS models. If the fittings are rusted, scratched or cracked, fit new ones.

Removal and installation

4 The brake hoses have banjo fittings on each end. Cover the surrounding area with plenty of rags and unscrew the banjo bolt at each end of the hose, noting the alignment of the fitting with the master cylinder or brake caliper **(see illustrations 3.1a or b, 5.4a, b or c, 7.1a or b, and 9.4)**. Free the hose from any clips or guides and remove it, noting its routing. Discard the sealing washers. **Note:** *Do not operate the brake lever or pedal while a brake hose is disconnected.*

5 Position the new hose, making sure it isn't twisted or otherwise strained, and ensure that it is correctly routed through any clips or guides and is clear of all moving components.

6 Check that the fittings align correctly, then install the banjo bolts, using new sealing washers on both sides of the fittings **(see illustration 7.18)**. Tighten the banjo bolts to the torque setting specified at the beginning of this Chapter.

7 On models with ABS the hoses join to pipes that connect the system components to the ABS hydraulic unit. The joints between the hoses and pipes, and where the pipes connect to the hydraulic unit are held by

nuts **(see illustrations)**. There are no sealing washers. Unscrew the nuts to separates the hoses from the pipes and to detach the pipes from the hydraulic unit. When refitting them tighten the nuts to the specified torque setting if the correct tools are available.

8 Flush the old brake fluid from the system, refill with new DOT 4 brake fluid (see *Pre-ride checks*) and bleed the air from the system (see Section 12).

9 Check the operation of the brakes before riding the motorcycle.

12 Brake system bleeding and fluid change

Note: *If bleeding the system using the conventional method (or one-man kit) described does not work sufficiently well, it is advisable to obtain a vacuum-type brake bleeding tool (see illustration 12.17).*

Bleeding

1 Bleeding the brakes is simply the process of removing air from the brake fluid reservoir, the hose and the brake caliper. Bleeding is necessary whenever a brake system hydraulic connection is loosened, after a component or hose is replaced with a new one, or when the master cylinder or caliper is overhauled. Leaks in the system may also allow air to enter, but leaking brake fluid will reveal their presence and warn you of the need for repair.

2 To bleed the brakes, you will need some new DOT 4 brake fluid, a length of clear vinyl or plastic hose, a small container partially filled with clean brake fluid, some rags, a spanner to fit the brake caliper bleed valve, and help from an assistant **(see illustration)**. On ZR1000-B/C models the front master cylinder is fitted with a bleed valve – when bleeding the front brakes, start with the master cylinder, then do the right-hand caliper then the left-hand caliper.

3 Cover painted components to prevent damage in the event that brake fluid is spilled.

4 Refer to 'Pre-ride checks' at the beginning of the manual and remove the reservoir cover or cap, diaphragm plate and diaphragm, and slowly pump the brake lever (front brake) or pedal (rear brake) a few times, until no air

11.7a Hose to pipe joint nuts ...

11.7b ... on ABS-equipped models

12.2 Set-up for bleeding the brakes

bubbles can be seen floating up from the holes in the bottom of the reservoir. This bleeds the air from the master cylinder end of the line (but on ZR1000-B/C models bleed via the valve as well – Step 5). Temporarily refit the reservoir cap or cover.

5 Pull the dust cap off the bleed valve **(see illustrations)**. Attach one end of the clear vinyl or plastic hose to the bleed valve and submerge the other end in the clean brake fluid in the container **(see illustration 12.2)**. If you're using a one-man type brake bleeder, there is no need for fluid in the container. **Note:** *To avoid damaging the bleed valve during the procedure, loosen it and then tighten it temporarily with a ring spanner before attaching the hose. With the hose attached, the valve can then be opened and closed either with an open-ended spanner, or by leaving the ring spanner located on the valve and fitting the hose above it.*

6 Check the fluid level in the reservoir. Do not allow the fluid level to drop below the lower mark during the procedure.

7 Carefully pump the brake lever or pedal three or four times, then hold it in (front) or down (rear) and open the bleed valve. When the valve is opened, brake fluid will flow out of the caliper into the clear tubing, and the lever will move toward the handlebar, or the pedal will move down. If there is air in the system there will be air bubbles in the brake fluid coming out of the caliper.

8 Tighten the bleed valve, then release the brake lever or pedal gradually. Top-up the reservoir and repeat the process until no air bubbles are visible in the brake fluid leaving the caliper, and the lever or pedal is firm when applied. On completion, disconnect the hose, then tighten the bleed valve to the torque setting specified at the beginning of this Chapter and install the dust cap.

9 Top-up the reservoir, then install the diaphragm, diaphragm plate, and cap (see *Pre-ride checks*). Wipe up any spilled brake fluid. Check the entire system for fluid leaks.

10 Check the operation of the brakes before riding the motorcycle.

> **HAYNES HiNT** *If it is not possible to produce a firm feel to the lever or pedal, the fluid may be aerated. Let the brake fluid in the system stabilise for a few hours and then repeat the procedure when the tiny bubbles in the system have settled out.*

Fluid change

11 Changing the brake fluid is a similar process to bleeding the brakes and requires the same materials plus a suitable tool for siphoning the fluid out of the reservoir. Also ensure that the container is large enough to take all the old fluid when it is flushed out of the system.

12 Follow Steps 3 and 5, then remove the reservoir cap, diaphragm plate and diaphragm and siphon the old fluid out of the reservoir. Fill the reservoir with new brake fluid, then carefully pump the brake lever or pedal three or four times and hold it in (front) or down (rear) while opening the caliper bleed valve. When the valve is opened, brake fluid will flow out of the caliper into the clear tubing, and the lever will move toward the handlebar, or the pedal will move down.

13 Tighten the bleed valve, then release the brake lever or pedal gradually. Keep the reservoir topped-up with new fluid to above the LOWER level at all times or air may enter the system and greatly increase the length of the task. Repeat the process until new fluid can be seen emerging from the caliper bleed valve.

> **HAYNES HiNT** *Old brake fluid is invariably much darker in colour than new fluid, making it easy to see when all old fluid has been expelled from the system.*

14 Disconnect the hose, then make sure the bleed valve is tightened to the specified torque setting and install the dust cap.

15 Top-up the reservoir, then install the diaphragm, diaphragm plate, and cap (see *Pre-ride checks*). Wipe up any spilled brake fluid. Check the entire system for fluid leaks.

16 Check the operation of the brakes before riding the motorcycle.

Draining the system for overhaul

17 Draining the brake fluid is again a similar process to bleeding the brakes. The quickest and easiest way is to use a commercially available vacuum-type brake bleeding tool **(see illustration)** – follow the manufacturer's instructions. Otherwise follow the procedure described above for changing the fluid, but quite simply do not put any new fluid into the reservoir – the system fills itself with air instead.

13 Wheel inspection and repair

1 In order to carry out a proper inspection of the wheels, it is necessary to support the bike upright so that the wheel being inspected is raised off the ground. Position the motorcycle on an auxiliary stand. Clean the wheels

12.5a Front master cylinder bleed valve (arrowed) – ZR1000-B/C

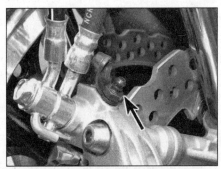
12.5b Front brake caliper bleed valve (arrowed) – ZR1000-B/C

12.5c Front brake caliper bleed valve (arrowed) – ZR750-J

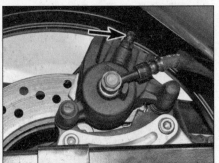
12.5d Rear brake caliper bleed valve (arrowed) – ZR750-J and ZR1000-A

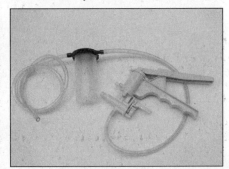
12.17 A vacuum-operated brake bleeding tool

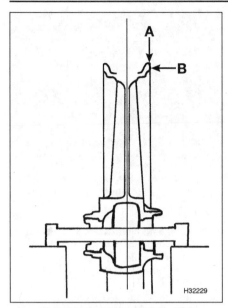

**13.2 Check the wheel for radial
(out-of-round) runout (A) and axial
(side-to-side) runout (B)**

thoroughly to remove mud and dirt that may interfere with the inspection procedure or mask defects. Make a general check of the wheels (see Chapter 1) and tyres (see *Pre-ride checks*).

2 Attach a dial gauge to the fork or the swingarm and position its tip against the side of the wheel rim. Spin the wheel slowly and check the axial (side-to-side) runout of the rim **(see illustration)**.

3 In order to accurately check radial (out of round) runout with the dial gauge, remove the wheel from the machine, and the tyre from the wheel. With the axle clamped in a vice and the dial gauge positioned on the top of the rim, the wheel can be rotated to check the runout **(see illustration 13.2)**.

4 An easier, though slightly less accurate, method is to attach a stiff wire pointer to the fork or the swingarm and position the end a fraction of an inch from the wheel rim where the wheel and tyre join. If the wheel is true, the distance from the pointer to the rim will be constant as the wheel is rotated. **Note:** *If wheel runout is excessive, check the wheel bearings very carefully before renewing the wheel.*

5 The wheels should also be inspected for cracks, flat spots on the rim and other damage. Look very closely for dents in the area where the tyre bead contacts the rim. Dents in this area may prevent complete sealing of the tyre against the rim, which leads to deflation of the tyre over a period of time. If damage is evident, or if runout in either direction is excessive, the wheel will have to be renewed. Never attempt to repair a damaged cast alloy wheel.

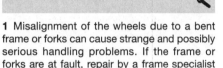

14 Wheel alignment check

1 Misalignment of the wheels due to a bent frame or forks can cause strange and possibly serious handling problems. If the frame or forks are at fault, repair by a frame specialist or renewal are the only options.

2 To check wheel alignment you will need an assistant, a length of string or a perfectly straight piece of wood and a ruler. A plumb bob or spirit level for checking that the wheels are vertical will also be required.

3 In order to make a proper check of the wheels it is necessary to support the bike in an upright position, using an auxiliary stand. First ensure that the chain adjuster markings coincide on each side of the swingarm (see Chapter 1, Section 1). Next, measure the width of both tyres at their widest points. Subtract the smaller measurement from the larger measurement, then divide the difference by two. The result is the amount of offset that should exist between the front and rear tyres on both sides of the machine.

4 If a string is used, have your assistant hold one end of it about halfway between the floor and the rear axle, with the string touching the back edge of the rear tyre sidewall.

5 Run the other end of the string forward and pull it tight so that it is roughly parallel to the floor **(see illustration)**. Slowly bring the string into contact with the front edge of the rear tyre sidewall, then turn the front wheel until it is parallel with the string. Measure the distance from the front tyre sidewall to the string.

6 Repeat the procedure on the other side of the motorcycle. The distance from the front tyre sidewall to the string should be equal on both sides.

7 As previously mentioned, a perfectly

straight length of wood or metal bar may be substituted for the string **(see illustration)**.

8 If the distance between the string and tyre is greater on one side, or if the rear wheel appears to be out of alignment, have your machine checked by a Kawasaki dealer or frame specialist.

9 If the front-to-back alignment is correct, the wheels still may be out of alignment vertically.

10 Using a plumb bob or spirit level, check the rear wheel to make sure it is vertical. To do this, hold the string of the plumb bob against the tyre upper sidewall and allow the weight to settle just off the floor. If the string touches both the upper and lower tyre sidewalls and is perfectly straight, the wheel is vertical. If it is not, adjust the stand until it is.

11 Once the rear wheel is vertical, check the front wheel in the same manner. If both wheels are not perfectly vertical, the frame and/or major suspension components are bent.

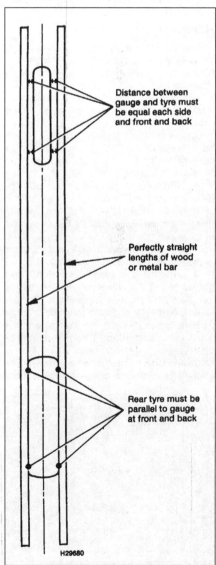

Distance between gauge and tyre must be equal each side and front and back

Perfectly straight lengths of wood or metal bar

Rear tyre must be parallel to gauge at front and back

14.7 Wheel alignment check using a straight-edge

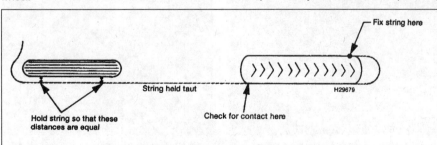

Fix string here

String held taut

Check for contact here

Hold string so that these distances are equal

14.5 Wheel alignment check using string

15.4 Slacken the axle clamp bolt (arrowed)

15.5a Unscrew the axle using a large hex bit – tool shown was made using two nuts welded together around a rod

15.5b Withdraw the axle and remove the wheel

15 Front wheel

Removal

1 Position the motorcycle on an auxiliary stand so that the front wheel is off the ground. Always make sure the motorcycle is properly supported.

2 Displace the front brake calipers (see Section 3). Support the calipers with a cable-tie or a bungee cord so that no strain is placed on the hydraulic hoses. There is no need to disconnect the hoses from the calipers. **Note:** *Do not operate the front brake lever with the calipers removed.*

3 On ABS equipped models displace the wheel sensor from the bottom of the left-hand fork (see Section 10) – there is no need to disconnect the wiring, just tie the sensor out of the way.

4 Slacken the axle clamp bolt on the bottom of the right-hand fork **(see illustration)**.

5 Unscrew the axle **(see illustration)**. Take the weight of the wheel, then withdraw the axle from the right **(see illustration)**. Carefully lower the wheel and draw it forwards.

6 Remove the spacer from each side of the wheel **(see illustration)**. Clean all old grease off the spacers, axle and seals.

Caution: Don't lay the wheel down and allow it to rest on a disc – the disc could

become warped. Set the wheel on wood blocks so the disc doesn't support the weight of the wheel.

7 Check the axle is straight by rolling it on a flat surface such as a piece of plate glass (first remove any corrosion using wire wool). If the equipment is available, place the axle in V-blocks and measure the runout using a dial gauge. If the axle is bent or the runout exceeds the limit specified, replace it with a new one.

8 Check the condition of the grease seals and wheel bearings (see Section 17).

Installation

9 Apply a smear of grease to the inside of the wheel spacers, and also to the outside where they fit into the wheel. Fit the spacers into each side of the wheel **(see illustration 15.6)**.

10 Manoeuvre the wheel into position between the forks, making sure the directional arrows on the tyre and wheel are pointing the same way and in the normal direction of rotation **(see illustration)**. Apply a thin coat of grease to the axle.

11 Lift the wheel into place, making sure the spacers remain in position. Slide the axle in from the right-hand side and locate it in the fork **(see illustration 15.5b)**.

12 Tighten the axle to the torque setting specified at the beginning of the Chapter **(see illustration)**.

13 Lower the front wheel to the ground, then install the brake calipers (see Section 3).

14 Apply the front brake a few times to bring the pads back into contact with the discs, then with the brake applied pump the front forks a few times to settle all components in position.

15 Now tighten the axle clamp bolt on the bottom of the right-hand fork to the specified torque **(see illustration 15.4)**.

16 Check for correct operation of the brakes before riding the motorcycle.

16 Rear wheel

Removal

1 Position the motorcycle on an auxiliary stand so that the rear wheel is off the ground. Always make sure the motorcycle is properly supported. Create some slack in the chain (see Chapter 1).

2 Displace the rear brake caliper (see Section 7).

3 On ABS equipped models displace the wheel sensor from the bottom of the brake caliper bracket (see Section 10) – there is no need to disconnect the wiring, just tie the sensor out of the way.

4 Straighten and remove the split pin on the left-hand end of the axle on Z750 models, and from the right-hand end on Z1000 **(see**

15.6 Remove the spacer from each side of the wheel

15.10 Make sure the directional arrows correspond to each other and to the way you are fitting the wheel

15.12 Tighten the axle to the specified torque

16.4a Remove the split pin . . .

16.4b . . . then unscrew the axle nut and remove the washer and the adjustment marker (arrowed)

16.5a Withdraw the axle . . .

16.5b . . . and remove the caliper bracket

16.6 Disengage the chain and draw the wheel back

illustration). Discard it as a new one must be used. Unscrew the axle nut and remove the washer (see illustration). Remove the chain adjustment marker.

5 Take the weight of the wheel, then withdraw the axle, bringing the chain adjustment marker with it, and lower the wheel to the ground (see illustration). Remove the rear brake caliper bracket, noting how it locates (see illustration). If the axle is difficult to withdraw, drive it through, making sure you don't damage the threads.

6 Disengage the chain from the sprocket and remove the wheel from the swingarm (see illustration).

Caution: Do not lay the wheel down and allow it to rest on the disc or the sprocket – they could become warped. Set the wheel on wood blocks so the disc or the sprocket doesn't support the weight of the wheel. Do not operate the brake pedal with the wheel removed.

7 Remove the spacer from each side of the wheel, noting which fits where and which way round (see illustration). Clean all old grease off the spacers, axle and seals. Slide the spacers onto the axle in the correct position so they cannot get muddled up, then lightly thread the nut onto the axle so they do not slide off.

8 Check the axle is straight by rolling it on a flat surface such as a piece of plate glass (first remove any corrosion with wire wool). If the equipment is available, place the axle in V-blocks and check the runout using a dial gauge. If the axle is bent or the runout

exceeds the limit specified at the beginning of the Chapter, replace it with a new one.

9 Check the condition of the grease seals and wheel bearings (see Section 17).

Installation

10 Take the wheel spacers off the axle, keeping them the correct way round. Apply a smear of grease to the inside of the wheel spacers, and also to the outside where they fit into the wheel. On ZR750-J models fit the larger spacer into the right-hand side of the wheel and the smaller one into the left-hand side. On ZR750-L/M models fit the shouldered spacer into the left-hand side of the wheel and the plain spacer into the right-hand side. On ZR1000-A models fit the shouldered spacer into the right-hand side of the wheel and the plain spacer into the left-hand side. On ZR1000-B/C models fit the narrow spacer into the right-hand side of the wheel and

the wider one into the left-hand side with its wider internal diameter end facing in (see illustration). Apply a thin coat of grease to the axle.

11 Manoeuvre the wheel into position between the ends of the swingarm with the brake disc on the right-hand side – if a new tyre has been fitted check that its directional arrow is pointing in the normal direction of rotation. Engage the drive chain with the sprocket (see illustration 16.6). Slide the brake caliper bracket between the wheel and the swingarm (see illustration 16.5b) – make sure the slot locates on its guide (see illustration).

12 On Z750 models slide the right-hand chain adjustment marker onto the axle with the angled ends at top and bottom and facing in and with the index mark at the top. On Z1000 models slide the left-hand chain adjustment marker onto the axle with the raised sections vertical and facing the axle head.

16.7 Remove the spacer from each side of the wheel

16.10 Fit the left-hand spacer with its wider end facing in

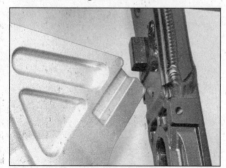

16.11 Slide the bracket into place locating the slot on the guide on the swingarm

16.13a Locate the axle head and adjustment marker as shown

16.13b Slide the adjustment marker onto the axle

16.15 Fit a new split pin and bend its ends round as shown

13 Lift the wheel into position and slide the axle in from the right on Z750 models and from the left on Z1000 models **(see illustration 16.5a)**, making sure the spacers and caliper bracket remain correctly installed. Locate the flat edges of the axle head between the raised sections of the adjustment marker **(see illustration)**. Check that everything is correctly aligned. Fit the other adjustment marker onto the end of the axle with its index line at the top **(see illustration)**. Fit the washer and axle nut but leave it loose **(see illustration 16.4b)**.

14 Check and adjust the drive chain slack (see Chapter 1). On completion tighten the axle nut to the torque setting specified at the beginning of the Chapter.

15 Check the alignment of the hole in the end of the axle with the slots in the nut – they must align to allow the split pin to be fitted.

17.2 Lever out the bearing seals

17.4a Push the spacer aside to reveal the inner race (arrowed) . . .

If necessary tighten the nut further until the nearest slots align with the hole. If you go too far slacken the nut and tighten it again, do not tighten further to the second nearest slot. Fit a new split pin and bend it around the nut as shown **(see illustration)**.

16 Install the brake caliper (see Section 7). Operate the brake pedal several times to bring the pads into contact with the disc. Check the operation of the rear brake carefully before riding the bike.

17 Wheel bearings

Caution: Don't lay the wheel down and allow it to rest on either disc (front) or the disc/sprocket (rear) – they could become warped. Set the wheel on wood blocks so the wheel rim supports the weight of the wheel.

Note: *Always renew the wheel bearings in sets, never individually. Avoid using a high pressure cleaner on the wheel bearing area.*

Front wheel bearings

1 Remove the wheel (see Section 15).

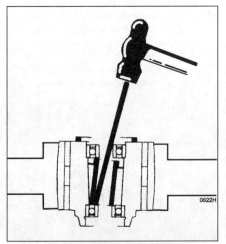

17.4b . . . then locate the drift on it as shown . . .

2 Lever out the bearing seal from each side of the hub using a flat-bladed screwdriver or a seal hook **(see illustration)**. Take care not to damage the hub. Discard the seals as new ones must be fitted on reassembly.

3 Inspect the bearings – check that the inner race turns smoothly and that the outer race is a tight fit in the hub (see *Tools and Workshop Tips* in the Reference Section). **Note:** *Do not remove the bearings unless they are going to be replaced with new ones.*

4 If the bearings are worn, remove them preferably using an internal expanding puller with slide-hammer attachment, which can be obtained commercially. Alternatively they can be driven out using a suitable punch inserted from the opposite side of the bearing being removed – move the bearing spacer to one side to reveal the inner race on which the drift can be located **(see illustrations)**. Use a drift with a shaped end for better purchase if necessary, and move the spacer and drift round to drive the bearing out evenly and squarely. After removing the first bearing the spacer which fits between the bearings will drop out.

5 Turn the wheel over and remove the other bearing using the same procedure.

6 Thoroughly clean the hub area of the wheel and inspect the bearing seats for scoring and wear. If the seats are damaged, consult a Kawasaki dealer or wheel specialist before reassembling the wheel.

7 Drive the new bearings, marked side facing out, into the hub until they seat using a bearing driver or suitable socket (see *Tools and*

17.4c . . . and drive the bearing out

17.7 Using a socket to drive the bearing in

17.9 Press the seal into place setting it flush with the rim

17.11a Lift the sprocket coupling off the wheel . . .

17.11b . . . and remove the spacer if it is loose

17.12 Lever out the bearing seal

17.14a Remove the circlip (arrowed)

Workshop Tips) **(see illustration)**. Ensure that the driver or socket bears only on the outer race. Ensure the bearing is fitted squarely and all the way onto its seat.

8 Turn the wheel over then install the bearing spacer and the other new bearing.

9 Apply a smear of grease to the new seals, then press them into the hub **(see illustration)**. Level the seals with the rim of the hub with a small block of wood if necessary **(see illustration 17.29b)**.

10 Clean the brake discs using acetone or brake system cleaner, then install the wheel (see Section 15).

Rear wheel bearings

11 Remove the wheel (see Section 16). Lift the sprocket coupling out of the hub, noting the spacer **(see illustrations)**.

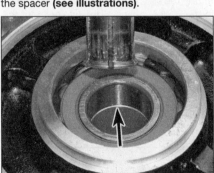

17.14b Locate the curved bottom edge of the puller in the gap between the bearing and the spacer (arrowed) then expand the ends to lock it in place . . .

12 Lever out the bearing seal from the right-hand side of the hub using a flat-bladed screwdriver or a seal hook **(see illustration)**. Take care not to damage the hub. Discard the seal as a new one should be fitted on reassembly.

13 Inspect the bearings in both sides of the hub – check that the inner race turns smoothly and that the outer race is a tight fit in the hub (see *Tools and Workshop Tips* in the Reference section). **Note:** *Do not remove the bearings unless they are going to be replaced with new ones.*

14 If the bearings are worn, on Z1000 models remove the circlip securing the right-hand bearing **(see illustration)** – a new one should be used on installation. Remove the bearing on one side using an internal expanding puller with slide-hammer attachment, which can be obtained commercially (see *Tools and Workshop Tips*) **(see illustrations)**. Having

17.14c . . . then use the slide-hammer to jar the bearing out

removed the first bearing remove the spacer which fits between the bearings.

15 Either turn the wheel over and remove the remaining bearing using the same procedure, or leave the wheel as it is and drive the bearing out from the top using a suitable drift.

16 Thoroughly clean the hub area of the wheel and inspect the bearing seats for scoring and wear. If the seats are damaged, consult a Kawasaki dealer or wheel specialist before reassembling the wheel.

17 Drive the new bearings into the hub with the marked side facing outwards using a bearing driver or suitable socket (see *Tools and Workshop Tips*) **(see illustration)**. Ensure that the driver or socket bears only on the outer race. Ensure each bearing is fitted squarely and all the way onto its seat.

18 Turn the wheel over then install the bearing spacer and the other new bearing. On Z1000 models fit a new circlip into its

17.17 Using a socket to drive the bearing in

17.19 Press the seal into place and set it flush

17.21 Fit a new O-ring if necessary

17.24 Lever out the bearing seal

groove outside the right-hand bearing **(see illustration 17.14a)**.

19 Apply a smear of grease to the new seal, then press it into the right-hand side of the hub **(see illustration)**. Level the seal with the rim of the hub with a small block of wood **(see illustration 17.29b)**.

20 Check the sprocket coupling/rubber dampers (see Section 21).

21 On Z750 models check the condition of the hub O-ring and clean it or replace it with a new one if necessary **(see illustration)**. Smear the O-ring with grease.

22 Make sure the spacer is in place then fit the sprocket coupling into the wheel **(see illustrations 17.11b and a)**. Clean the brake disc using acetone or brake system cleaner, then install the wheel (see Section 16).

Sprocket coupling bearing

23 Remove the wheel (see Section 16). Lift the sprocket coupling out of the hub, and remove the spacer **(see illustrations 17.11a and b)**.

24 Lever out the bearing seal on the outside of the coupling using a flat-bladed screwdriver or a seal hook **(see illustration)**. Take care not to damage the rim of the coupling. Discard the seal as a new one should be fitted on reassembly.

25 Inspect the bearing – check that the inner races turn smoothly and that the outer race is a tight fit in the coupling (see *Tools and Workshop Tips* (Section 5) in the Reference Section). **Note:** *Do not remove the bearing unless it is going to be replaced with a new one.*

26 If the bearing is worn, remove the circlip **(see illustration)**. Support the coupling on blocks of wood, sprocket side down, and drive the bearing out from the inside using a bearing driver or socket **(see illustration)**.

27 Thoroughly clean the bearing seat and inspect it for scoring and wear. If the seat is damaged, consult a Kawasaki dealer or wheel specialist before reassembling the wheel.

28 Drive the bearing, with its marked side facing out, into the coupling from the outside until it seats using a bearing driver or suitable socket (see *Tools and Workshop Tips*) **(see illustration)**. Ensure that the driver or socket bears only on the outer race. Ensure the bearing is fitted squarely and all the way into the seat.

29 Apply a smear of grease to the new seal, then press it into the coupling **(see illustration)**. Level the seal with the rim of the coupling using a small block of wood **(see illustration)**.

30 Check the sprocket coupling/rubber dampers (see Section 21).

31 On Z750 models check the condition of the hub O-ring and replace it with a new one if necessary **(see illustration 17.21)**. Smear the O-ring with grease.

32 Fit the spacer into the bearing then fit the sprocket coupling into the wheel **(see illustrations 17.11b and a)**. Install the wheel (see Section 16).

18 Tyres

General information

1 The wheels fitted to all models are designed to take tubeless tyres only. Tyre sizes are given in the Specifications at the beginning of this chapter.

17.26a Remove the circlip (arrowed) . . .

17.26b . . . then drive the bearing out from the inside

17.28 Using a socket to drive the bearings in

17.29a Fit the grease seal and set it flush . . .

17.29b . . . using a piece of wood as shown helps to do this

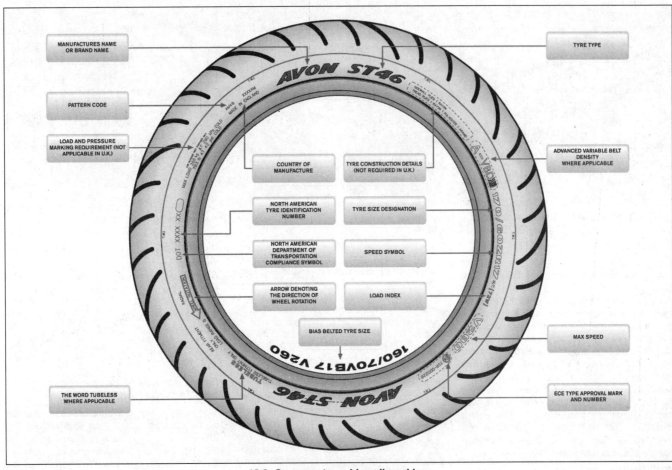

18.3 Common tyre sidewall markings

2 Refer to the *Pre-ride checks* listed at the beginning of this manual for tyre maintenance.

Fitting new tyres

3 When selecting new tyres, refer to the tyre information in the Owner's Handbook. Ensure that front and rear tyre types are compatible, the correct size and correct speed rating; if necessary seek advice from a Kawasaki dealer or tyre fitting specialist **(see illustration)**.

4 It is recommended that tyres are fitted by a motorcycle tyre specialist rather than

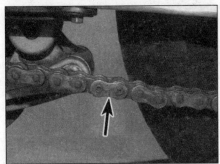

19.2 The joining link is identified by the different pin ends (arrowed)

attempted in the home workshop. This is particularly relevant in the case of tubeless tyres because the force required to break the seal between the wheel rim and tyre bead is substantial, and is usually beyond the capabilities of an individual working with normal tyre levers. Additionally, the specialist will be able to balance the wheels after tyre fitting.

5 Note that punctured tubeless tyres can in some cases be repaired. Repairs must be carried out by a motorcycle tyre fitting specialist. Kawasaki advise that a repaired tyre should not be used at speeds above 50 mph (80 kmh) for the first 24 hours, and not above 80 mph (130 kmh) thereafter.

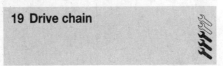

Note: *If the chain and sprockets are being replaced, slacken the sprocket nut before either removing the swingarm or splitting the chain – refer to Section 20.*

1 Inspect the chain for a joining link, recognisable by its different sideplate identification marks (and usually its different

colour), as well as by the staked ends of the link's two pins which look as if they have been deeply centre-punched, instead of peened over as with all the other pins. This type of chain can be separated at the joining link using a chain splitting/riveting tool. If no joining link can be found, the chain is endless and can only be removed by removing the rear wheel and swingarm.

Riveted link chain

Removal

2 Support the motorcycle on an auxiliary stand so that the rear wheel is off the ground. Locate the joining link in a suitable position to work on by rotating the back wheel **(see illustration)**. Slacken the drive chain as described in Chapter 1.

3 If required, remove the chainguard (Chapter 5, Section 14).

4 Remove the front sprocket cover (see Section 20).

5 Split the chain at the joining link using the chain tool, following carefully the manufacturer's operating instructions (see also *Tools and Workshop Tips* (Section 8) in the Reference Section). Remove the chain from the bike, noting its routing around the swingarm.

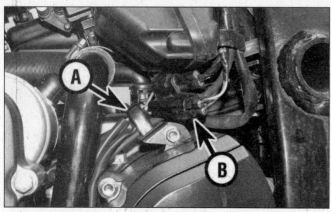

20.1 Free the wiring from the clamp (A). Speed sensor wiring connector (B) – ZR750-J and ZR1000-A

20.2a Unscrew the bolts (arrowed) . . .

Cleaning

6 Refer to Chapter 1, Section 1, for details of routine cleaning with the chain installed on the sprockets.

7 If the chain is extremely dirty remove it from the motorcycle and soak it in paraffin (kerosene) for approximately five or six minutes, then clean it using a soft brush. *Caution: Don't use gasoline (petrol), solvent or other cleaning fluids which might damage its internal sealing properties. Don't use high-pressure water. Remove the chain, wipe it off, then blow dry it with compressed air immediately. The entire process shouldn't take longer than ten minutes – if it does, the O-rings in the chain rollers could be damaged.*

Installation

8 Fit the drive chain through the swingarm and around the sprockets, leaving the two ends mid-way between the sprockets along the bottom run.

9 Refer again to *Tools and Workshop Tips* in the Reference Section. Install the new joining link from the inside with the four O-rings correctly located between the link plate and sideplate. Install the new side plate with its identification marks facing out, using the tool to press it into place. Stake the new link using the tool, following carefully the instructions of both the chain manufacturer and the tool manufacturer. DO NOT reuse old joining link components.

10 After staking, check the joining link and staking for any signs of cracking. If there is any evidence of cracking, the joining link, O-rings and sideplate must be replaced. Measure the diameter of the staked ends in two directions and check that it is evenly staked and within the measurements specified at the beginning of the Chapter. Also measure the thickness of the link, from the outside of each plate, and check it is as specified. Check that the link pivots freely.

11 Install the sprocket cover (see Section 20).

12 Install the chainguard if removed.

13 On completion, adjust and lubricate the chain following the procedures described in Chapter 1.

⚠ *Warning: NEVER install a drive chain which uses a clip-type master (split) link. Use ONLY the correct service tools to secure the joining link – if you do not have access to such tools, have the chain replaced by a dealer to be sure of having it securely installed.*

Endless chain

Removal

14 Remove the front sprocket cover (see Section 20).

15 Remove the swingarm (see Chapter 5).

16 Slip the chain off the front sprocket and remove it.

Cleaning

17 See Steps 6 and 7.

Installation

18 Installation is the reverse of removal. On completion adjust and lubricate the chain following the procedures described in Chapter 1.

20 Sprockets

Front sprocket cover removal and installation

1 Free the wiring from the clamp on the top of the sprocket cover **(see illustration)**. On ZR750-J and ZR1000-A models disconnect the speed sensor wiring connector – remove the frame cover if required to improve access (see Chapter 7).

2 Unscrew the bolts and remove the cover, noting how the wiring clamp fits **(see illustrations)**. Remove the dowels for safekeeping if they are loose. On ZR750-J and ZR1000-A models remove the speed sensor from the cover if required (see Chapter 8).

3 Installation is the reverse of removal. Make sure the dowels are fitted.

Sprocket check

4 Check the wear pattern on both sprockets (see Chapter 1, Section 1). If the sprocket teeth are worn excessively, replace the chain and both sprockets as a set. Whenever the sprockets are inspected, the drive chain should be inspected also (see Chapter 1). Always renew the chain and sprockets as a set – worn sprockets can ruin a new drive chain and vice versa.

5 Adjust and lubricate the chain following the procedures described in Chapter 1.

Sprocket removal and installation

Front sprocket

6 Remove the front sprocket cover (see Steps 1 to 3).

7 Bend back the locking tab on the sprocket nut washer using a suitable tool **(see illustration)**.

20.2b . . . and remove the cover, noting the dowels (arrowed)

20.7 Bend back the tab . . .

20.8a . . . then unscrew the nut . . .

20.8b . . . and remove the washer

20.10 Disengage the chain and draw the sprocket off the shaft

8 Have an assistant apply the rear brake, then unscrew the sprocket nut and remove the washer **(see illustrations)**. Fit a new washer on installation.

9 Fully slacken the drive chain as described in Chapter 1. If the rear sprocket is being removed as well, remove the rear wheel now to give full slack (see Section 16). Otherwise disengage the chain from the rear sprocket.

10 Slip the chain off the sprocket and slide the sprocket off the shaft **(see illustration)**.

11 Engage the new sprocket with the chain, making sure the side marked OUT SIDE is facing out, and slide it on the shaft **(see illustration 20.10)**.

12 If the rear wheel was removed, change the rear sprocket now then install the wheel (see Section 16). If the chain was merely disengaged, fit it back onto the rear sprocket. Take up the slack in the chain.

13 Install the sprocket nut with a new washer **(see illustrations 20.8b and a)**. Tighten the nut to the torque setting specified at the beginning of the Chapter, using the rear brake to prevent the sprocket turning. Bend up one side of the washer against a flat on the nut to lock it **(see illustration)**.

14 Fit the sprocket cover (see above).

Adjust and lubricate the chain following the procedures described in Chapter 1.

Rear sprocket

15 Remove the rear wheel (see Section 16).

16 Unscrew the nuts securing the sprocket to the hub assembly **(see illustration)**. Remove the sprocket, noting which way round it fits. Check the condition of the sprocket studs and replace them all if any are damaged. Make sure they are all tight – if any are loose, remove them, clean their threads and apply a suitable non-permanent thread locking compound before tightening them using two nuts locked together.

17 Fit the sprocket onto the hub with the stamped mark (denoting No. of teeth) facing out. Fit the nuts and tighten them evenly and in a criss-cross sequence to the torque setting specified at the beginning of the Chapter.

18 Install the rear wheel (see Section 16).

21 Rear sprocket coupling/ rubber dampers

1 Remove the rear wheel (see Section 16). Check for play between the sprocket coupling and the wheel hub by turning the sprocket. Any play indicates worn rubber damper segments.

Caution: Do not lay the wheel down on the disc as it could become warped. Lay the wheel on wooden blocks so that the disc is off the ground.

2 Lift the sprocket coupling away from the wheel leaving the rubber dampers in position **(see illustration 17.11a)**. Note the spacer inside the coupling and remove it if it is loose **(see illustration 17.11b)**. Check the coupling for cracks or any obvious signs of damage.

3 Lift the rubber damper segments from the wheel and check them for cracks, hardening and general deterioration **(see illustration)**. Replace them with a new set if necessary.

4 On Z750 models check the condition of the hub O-ring – if it is damaged, deformed or deteriorated replace it with a new one and smear it with grease **(see illustration 17.21)**. Otherwise clean it and smear it with grease.

5 Checking and replacement procedures for the sprocket coupling bearings are in Section 17.

6 Installation is the reverse of removal. Make sure the spacer is correctly installed in the coupling.

7 Install the rear wheel (see Section 16).

20.13 Bend the rim of the washer against the side of the nut

20.16 Rear sprocket nuts

21.3 Check the rubber dampers as described

Chapter 7
Bodywork

Contents

Degrees of difficulty

Easy, suitable for novice with little experience	**Fairly easy,** suitable for beginner with some experience	**Fairly difficult,** suitable for competent DIY mechanic	**Difficult,** suitable for experienced DIY mechanic	**Very difficult,** suitable for expert DIY or professional

1 General information

This Chapter covers the procedures necessary to remove and install the bodywork. Since many service and repair operations on these motorcycles require the removal of the body panels, the procedures are grouped here and referred to from other Chapters.

In the case of damage to the bodywork, it is usually necessary to remove the broken component and replace it with a new (or used) one. The material that the body panels are composed of doesn't lend itself to conventional repair techniques. Note that there are however some companies that specialize in 'plastic welding' and there are a number of bodywork repair kits now available for motorcycles.

When attempting to remove any body panel, first study it closely, noting any fasteners and associated fittings, to be sure of returning everything to its correct place on installation. In some cases the aid of an assistant will be required when removing panels, to help avoid the risk of damage to paintwork. Once the evident fasteners have been removed, try to withdraw the panel as described but DO NOT FORCE IT – if it will not release, check that all fasteners have been removed and try again.

When installing a body panel, first study it closely, noting any fasteners and associated fittings removed with it, to be sure of returning everything to its correct place. Check that all fasteners are in good condition, including the trim clips and damping/rubber mounts; replace any faulty fasteners with new ones before the panel is reassembled. Check also that all mounting brackets are straight and repair them or replace them with new ones if necessary before attempting to install the panel.

Tighten the fasteners securely, but be careful not to overtighten any of them or the panel may break (not always immediately) due to the uneven stress.

Trim clips

1 Three types of plastic trim clip are commonly used, so carefully note which type it may be before attempting to remove it.

2 The most commonly used type has a centre pin which you push into the body of the clip to allow the clip to be drawn out of the panel **(see illustrations)**. To install the clip, first expand the pawls of the clip body and push the centre pin back out **(see illustration)**. Now fit the clip body into its hole, then push the centre pin in so that it is flush with the clip head **(see illustration)**. The clip should now be locked in place.

3 Another type has a Phillips screw head. To

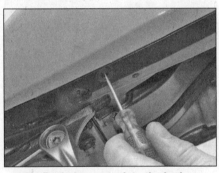

1.2a Push the centre into the body . . .

1.2b . . . then draw the body out

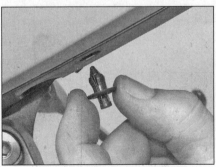

1.2c Reset the clip by drawing the centre out, then fit the body into the hole . . .

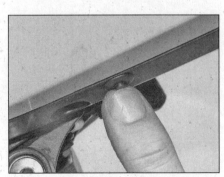

1.2d . . . and push the centre in flush to secure it

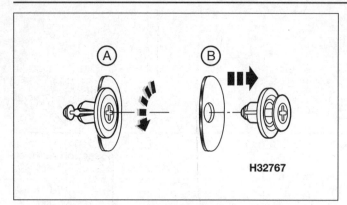

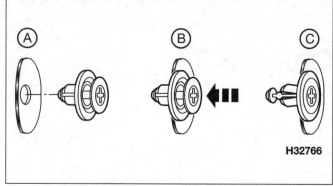

1.3a Unscrew the centre of the clip (A) then pull the clip body out (B)

1.3b Fit the clip body into its hole (A), then push the centre into the body (B) so that its head is flush (C)

release it unscrew the centre of the clip, then pull the body of the clip out of the panel (see illustration). When installing them, unscrew the centre of the clip and insert it in the panel then push the centre fully into the body (see illustration). As they are made of plastic, the threads easily become worn in which case the centres may not unscrew. If this happens, lever the centre out of the body using a small screwdriver and replace the trim clip with a new one.

4 Another has a protruding centre pin which you pull out of the body of the clip to allow the clip to be drawn out of the panel. To install

the clip, fit the clip body into its hole, then push the centre pin in. The clip should now be locked in place.

2 Seats

Removal

Passenger seat

1 Insert the ignition key into the seat lock on the left-hand side and turn it anti-clockwise to unlock the seat (see illustrations). Remove the seat, noting how it locates.

Rider's seat

2 Remove the passenger seat (Step 1).
3 On ZR750-J and ZR1000-A models unscrew the seat bracket bolt and remove the bracket, noting how it locates (see illustration). Lift the back of the seat and draw it back, noting how the tab at the front locates (see illustration).
4 On ZR750-L/M and ZR1000-B/C models pull the latch release cable, then lift the back

2.1a Removing the seat on ZR750-J and ZR1000-A models . . .

2.1b . . . note how the hooks locate

2.1c Removing the seat on ZR750-L/M and ZR1000-B/C models . . .

2.1d . . . note how the tab locates

2.3a Unscrew the bolt (arrowed) . . .

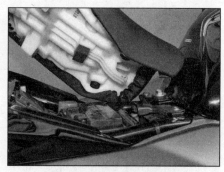

2.3b . . . and remove the seat

of the seat and draw it back, noting how the tab at the front locates **(see illustrations)**.

Installation

5 Installation is the reverse of removal. Make sure the seat locates correctly. Push down on the seat(s) to engage the latch.

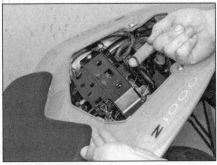
2.4a Pull the release cable . . .

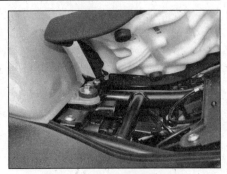
2.4b . . . and remove the seat

3 Seat cowling

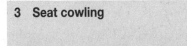

ZR750-J and ZR1000-A

1 Remove both seats (see Section 2).
2 Undo the two screws on the top at the back **(see illustration)**.
3 Remove the six trim clips on the underside (see Section 1 for information on trim clip removal and refitting) **(see illustration)**.
4 Pull the front away on each side to release the peg from the grommet, then draw the cowling up and back and remove it **(see illustrations)**.
5 Installation is the reverse of removal.

ZR750-L/M and ZR1000-B/C

6 Remove both seats (see Section 2), and the side panels (Section 7). Each side of the seat cowling is removed individually.
7 Remove the two trim clips on the underside (see Section 1 for information on trim clip removal and refitting) **(see illustration)**.
8 Undo the two screws securing the centre section, then release it from each

side and remove it, noting how it fits **(see illustration)**.
9 Undo the screw at the back **(see illustration)**.

10 Pull the cowling away to release the pegs at the front and back from the grommets **(see illustrations)**.
11 Installation is the reverse of removal.

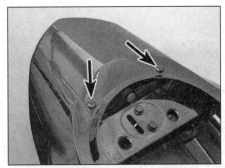
3.2 Undo the screws (arrowed) . . .

3.3 . . . release the trim clips (arrowed) on each side . . .

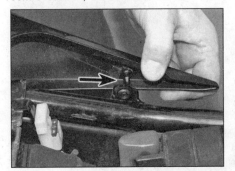
3.4a . . . and the peg (arrowed) on each side . . .

3.4b . . . then remove the cowling

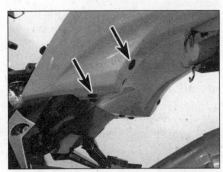
3.7 Release the trim clips (arrowed) . . .

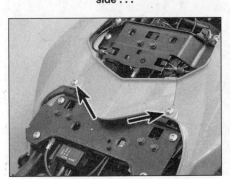
3.8 . . . then undo the screws and remove the centre section

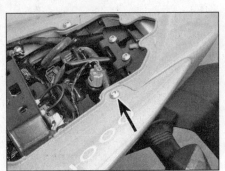
3.9 Undo the screw (arrowed) . . .

3.10 . . . then pull the cowling away and remove it

4.1a Undo the screws (arrowed) . . .

4.1b . . . and remove the windshield

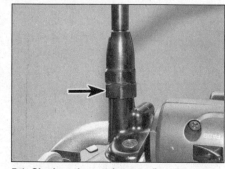

5.1 Slacken the nut (arrowed) and unscrew the mirror

4 Windshield (Z1000 models)

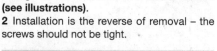

1 Undo the screws securing the windshield, noting the washers, then lift it off the bracket **(see illustrations)**.
2 Installation is the reverse of removal – the screws should not be tight.

5 Mirrors

Removal

1 Slacken the locknut on the bottom of the stem so the mirror is free of the holder **(see illustration)**.
2 Unscrew the complete mirror from the holder – on ZR750-L/M when removing the right-hand mirror note how the brake fluid reservoir bracket locates, and wrap the reservoir in rag and support it upright.

Installation

3 Installation is the reverse of removal –

thread the mirror into the holder until the locknut almost contacts it, then position the mirror as required and tighten the locknut onto the holder. On ZR750-L/M models secure the brake fluid reservoir bracket with the right-hand mirror.

6 Fairing

Z750

1 On ZR750-J models undo the two screws

6.1a Undo the screws (arrowed) . . .

securing each trim panel, noting the washers **(see illustration)**. Release and remove the panels, noting how they engage **(see illustration)**.
2 On ZR750-L/M models undo the two screws and remove the four trim clips securing the trim panel **(see illustration)**. Release and remove the panel, noting how it engages.
3 Unscrew the bolt on each side **(see illustration)**.
4 Carefully lift the fairing/headlight assembly to release the grommets on the bottom from the pegs on the bracket, then disconnect the headlight and sidelight wiring connectors and

6.1b . . . then release the tab on the front

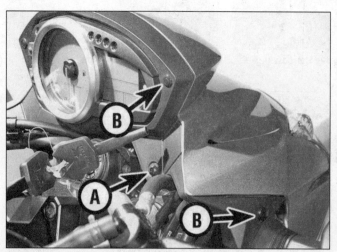

6.2 Undo the screw (A) and release the trim clips (B) on each side

6.3 Unscrew the bolt (arrowed) on each side . . .

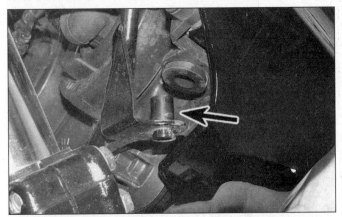

6.4a ... then lift the fairing to release the peg (arrowed) ...

6.4b ... and disconnect the headlight and sidelight (arrow) wiring connectors – ZR750-J shown

remove the fairing with the headlight **(see illustrations)**.

5 If required remove the headlight assembly (see Chapter 8).

6 Installation is the reverse of removal.

ZR1000-A

7 Remove the trim clip securing each side of the trim panel, then lift the panel to release the pegs from the grommets and remove it.

8 Remove the windshield (Section 4). Unscrew the windshield bracket nuts and remove the bracket, retrieving the washers between it and the fairing.

9 Unscrew the bolt on each side.

10 Carefully lift the fairing/headlight assembly off the windshield bracket studs and to release the grommets on the bottom from the pegs on the bracket, then disconnect the headlight and sidelight wiring connectors and remove the fairing with the headlight. Retrieve the washers from the studs if required.

11 If required remove the headlight assembly (see Chapter 8).

12 Installation is the reverse of removal. Make sure the washers are fitted between the fairing and the bracket, and between the windshield bracket and the fairing.

ZR1000-B/C

13 Remove the windshield (Section 4).

14 Remove the trim clip and the screw securing each trim panel, then release and remove the panels, noting how they engage with the fairing **(see illustrations)**.

15 Cut the cable-tie securing the wiring to the windshield bracket **(see illustration)**.

16 Unscrew the bolt on each side **(see illustration)**.

17 Carefully lift the fairing/headlight assembly to release the grommets on the bottom from the pegs on the bracket, then disconnect the headlight and sidelight wiring connectors, and

6.14a Release the trim clip (arrowed) ...

6.14c ... and remove the panel

6.14b ... then undo the screw (arrowed) ...

6.15 Cut the cable-tie (arrowed)

6.16 Unscrew the bolt (arrowed) on each side ...

6.17a . . . then lift the fairing to release the peg (arrowed) . . .

6.17b . . . and disconnect the headlight . . .

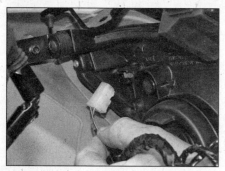

6.17c . . . and sidelight wiring connectors . . .

6.17d . . . and where fitted the immobiliser wiring connector

where fitted the immobiliser wiring connector, and remove the fairing with the headlight **(see illustrations)**.

18 If required remove the headlight assembly (see Chapter 8).

19 Installation is the reverse of removal. Make sure the washers are fitted between the fairing and the bracket, and between the windshield bracket and the fairing.

7 Body panels

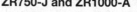

Side panels

ZR750-J and ZR1000-A

1 Undo the screw **(see illustration)**.
2 Pull the top edge of the panel away evenly to release the two pegs from the grommets **(see illustration)**.
3 Installation is the reverse of removal.

ZR750-L/M and ZR1000-B/C

4 Undo the screw securing the side trim panel **(see illustration)**. Pull the top edge of the panel away and the bottom up to release the two pegs from the grommets **(see illustrations)**.

7.1 Undo the screw (arrowed) . . .

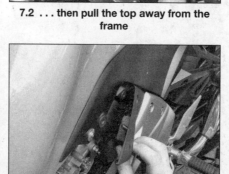

7.2 . . . then pull the top away from the frame

7.4a Undo the screw (arrowed) . . .

. . . then release the front peg . . .

7.4c . . . and the bottom peg

7.5a Undo the screw (arrowed) . . .

7.5b . . . then pull the panel away from the frame to release the pegs (arrowed)

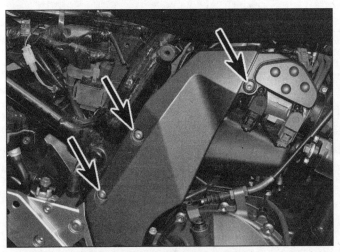

7.7a Undo the screws (arrowed) . . .

7.7b . . . and remove the cover

5 Undo the screw securing the front of the side panel (see illustration). Pull the panel away evenly to release the three pegs from the grommets (see illustration).

6 Installation is the reverse of removal.

Frame covers

ZR750-J and ZR1000-A

7 Undo the three screws and remove the cover (see illustrations).

8 Installation is the reverse of removal.

ZR750-L/M and ZR1000-B/C

9 Undo the screw securing the side trim panel (see illustration 7.4a). Pull the top edge of the panel away and the bottom up to release the two pegs from the grommets (see illustrations 7.4b and c).

10 Undo the two screws (see illustrations). Pull the panel away to release the peg from the grommet (see illustration).

11 Installation is the reverse of removal.

7.10a Undo the screws (arrowed) . . .

7.10b . . . noting the collar and grommet with the bottom one . . .

7.10c . . . then pull the panel away from the frame to release the peg (arrowed)

7.12a Undo the screws (arrowed) . . .

7.12b . . . then pull the cowl away to release the peg

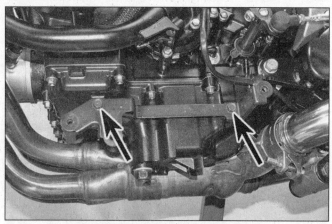

7.13 Sump cowl bracket bolts (arrowed)

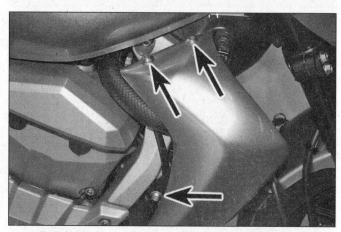

7.15 Undo the screws (arrowed) and remove the cowl

Sump cowls – ZR1000-B/C

12 Undo the two screws, noting the collars (see illustration). Pull the cowl away to release the peg from the grommet (see illustration).

13 If required undo the two bolts and remove the cowl bracket (see illustration).

14 Installation is the reverse of removal.

Radiator cowls

ZR750-L/M

15 Undo the three screws and remove the cowl (see illustration).

16 Installation is the reverse of removal.

ZR1000-A

17 Undo the three screws and remove the cowl.

18 Installation is the reverse of removal.

ZR1000-B/C

19 On the right-hand side undo the three screws, then pull the cowl away to release the peg from the grommet and disconnect the turn signal wiring connector (see illustrations).

20 On the left-hand side undo the four

7.19a Undo the screws (arrowed) . . .

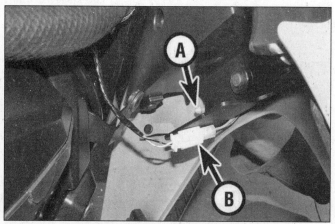

7.19b . . . then pull the cowl away to release the peg (A) and disconnect the wiring connector (B)

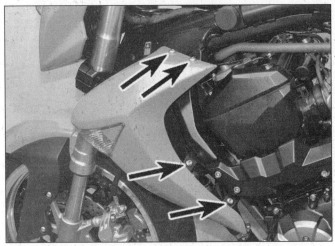

7.20a Radiator cowl screws (arrowed) – left-hand cowl

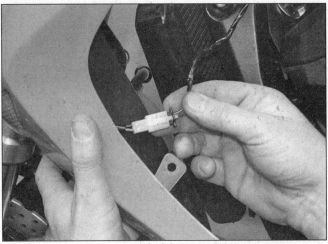

7.20b Displace the cowl then disconnect the wiring connector

screws and displace the cowl, then disconnect the turn signal wiring connector **(see illustrations)**.

21 Installation is the reverse of removal.

8 Front mudguard

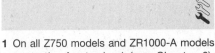

1 On all Z750 models and ZR1000-A models remove the front wheel (see Chapter 6). Release the brake hose holders from the mudguard by pinching their ends together on the underside and pulling them out. Unscrew the bolts securing each side of the mudguard, noting the washers. Draw the mudguard forwards, twisting the fork inwards so the brackets are clear **(see illustration)**.

2 On ZR1000-B/C models release the brake hose holders from the mudguard by pinching their sides together at the bottom and pulling them out **(see illustration)**. Unscrew the two bolts on each side, noting the washers, and draw the mudguard forwards **(see illustrations)**.

3 Installation is the reverse of removal.

8.1 Twist the forks in so the brackets are clear of the mudguard

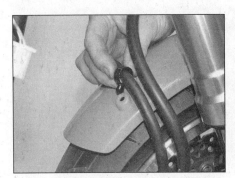

8.2a Pull the holders out as described

8.2b Unscrew the bolts (arrowed) . . .

8.2c . . . and remove the mudguard

Chapter 8
Electrical system

Contents

Degrees of difficulty

| **Easy,** suitable for novice with little experience | | **Fairly easy,** suitable for beginner with some experience | | **Fairly difficult,** suitable for competent DIY mechanic | | **Difficult,** suitable for experienced DIY mechanic | | **Very difficult,** suitable for expert DIY or professional | |

Specifications

Battery

Type	YTX9-BS, sealed
Capacity	12 V, 8 Ah
Voltage	
Fully-charged	13.0 to 13.2 V, min 12.8 V
Uncharged	below 12.3 V
Charging rate	
Normal	0.9 A for 5 to 10 hrs
Quick	4.0 A for 1 hr

Charging system

Alternator stator coil resistance	0.3 to 0.4 ohms
Alternator output	min 42 V @ 4000 rpm
Regulated voltage output	14.2 to 15.2 V @ 5000 rpm
Current leakage	2 mA (max)

Starter motor

Brush length	
Standard	12 mm
Service limit (min)	8.5 mm
Commutator diameter	
Standard	28 mm
Service limit (min)	27 mm

Fuses

ZR750-J and ZR1000-A

Main fuse	30 A
ECU fuse.	15 A
Cooling fan fuse	15 A
Headlight relay fuse	10 A
Tail light fuse.	10 A
Ignition fuse	10 A
Horn fuse	10 A
Turn signal relay fuse	10 A
ACC (instruments) fuse.	10 A

ZR750-L/M and ZR1000-B/C

Main fuse	30 A

Fusebox 1

Oxygen sensor heater fuse.	10 A
Horn fuse	10 A
Tail light fuse.	10 A
ABS motor relay fuse (ZR750-M and ZR1000-C).	30 A
ABS solenoid valve relay fuse (ZR750-M and ZR1000-C)	20 A
ABS ECU fuse (ZR750-M and ZR1000-C)	10 A

Fusebox 2

Cooling fan fuse	15 A
Instrument cluster fuse	10 A
ECU fuse.	10 A
Turn signal relay fuse	10 A
Ignition fuse	10 A
Headlight relay fuse	10 A

Bulbs

Headlights	55 W x 2 quartz halogen
Brake/tail light	LED
Licence plate light	5 W
Side light(s) (where fitted).	5 W

Turn signal lights

ZR750-J and ZR1000-A

European spec	21 W x 4

US and Canada spec

Front.	21/5 W x 2
Rear.	21 W x 2

ZR750-L/M

European spec	10 W x 4

US and Canada spec

Front.	21/5 W x 2
Rear.	21 W x 2

ZR1000-B/C

Front.	21 W x 2
Rear	10 W x 2
Instrument and warning lights	LED

Torque settings

Alternator cover bolts.	11 Nm

Alternator rotor bolt

Initial torque	70 Nm

Final torque

ZR750-J	110 Nm
ZR1000-A	108 Nm
ZR750-L/M and ZR1000-B/C	155 Nm
Alternator stator bolts.	12 Nm

Fork clamp bolts (top yoke)

ZR1000-A1 and A2.	9 Nm
ZR1000-A3 and A6.	13 Nm
All other models	20 Nm
Neutral switch.	15 Nm
Oil pressure switch.	15 Nm
Sidestand switch bolt.	9 Nm

Speed sensor bolt

ZR750-J	7 Nm
ZR1000-A.	7 Nm
ZR750-L/M and ZR1000-B/C.	12 Nm
Speed sensor cover bolts	7 Nm
Starter motor mounting bolts.	11 Nm
Steering stem bolt	108 Nm

1 General information

All models have a 12 volt electrical system charged by a three-phase alternator with a separate regulator/rectifier.

The regulator maintains the charging system output within the specified range to prevent overcharging, and the rectifier converts the ac (alternating current) output of the alternator to dc (direct current) to power the lights and other components and to charge the battery. The alternator rotor is mounted on the left-hand end of the crankshaft.

The starter motor is mounted on the top of the crankcase behind the cylinders. The starting system includes the motor, the battery, the relay and the various wires and switches. Some of the switches are part of a starter interlock system – see Chapter 1 for further information.

Note: *Keep in mind that electrical parts, once purchased, often cannot be returned. To avoid unnecessary expense, make very sure the faulty component has been positively identified before buying a replacement part.*

2 Electrical system fault finding

1 A typical electrical circuit consists of an electrical component, the switches, relays, etc, related to that component and the wiring and connectors that link the component to the battery and the frame.

2 Before tackling any troublesome electrical circuit, first study the wiring diagram thoroughly to get a complete picture of what makes up that individual circuit. Trouble spots, for instance, can often be narrowed down by noting if other components related to that circuit are operating properly or not. If several components or circuits fail at one time, chances are the fault lies either in the fuse or in the common earth (ground) connection, as several circuits are often routed through the same fuse and earth (ground) connections.

3 Electrical problems often stem from simple causes, such as loose or corroded connections or a blown fuse. Prior to any electrical fault finding, always visually check the condition of the fuse, wires and connections in the problem circuit. Intermittent failures can be especially frustrating, since you can't always duplicate the failure when it's convenient to test. In such situations, a good practice is to clean all connections in the affected circuit, whether or not they appear to be good – where possible use a dedicated electrical cleaning spray along with sandpaper, wire wool or other abrasive material to remove corrosion, and a dedicated electrical protection spray to prevent further problems. All of the connections and wires

should also be wiggled to check for looseness which can cause intermittent failure.

4 If you don't have a multimeter it is highly advisable to obtain one – they are not expensive and will enable a full range of electrical tests to be made. Go for a modern digital one with LCD display as they are easier to use. A continuity tester and/or test light are useful for certain electrical checks as an alternative, though are limited in their usefulness compared to a multimeter **(see illustrations)**.

Continuity checks

5 The term continuity describes the uninterrupted flow of electricity through an electrical circuit. Continuity can be checked with a multimeter set either to its continuity function (a beep is emitted when continuity is found), or to the resistance (ohms / Ω) function, or with a dedicated continuity tester. Both instruments are powered by an internal battery, therefore the checks are made with the ignition OFF. As a safety precaution, always disconnect the battery negative (-) lead before making continuity checks, particularly if ignition switch checks are being made.

6 If using a multimeter, select the continuity function if it has one, or the resistance (ohms) function. Touch the meter probes together and check that a beep is emitted or the meter reads zero, which indicates continuity. If there is no continuity there will be no beep or the meter will show infinite resistance. After using the meter, always switch it OFF to conserve its battery.

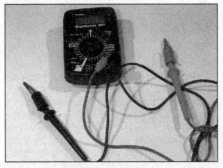

2.4a A digital multimeter can be used for all electrical tests

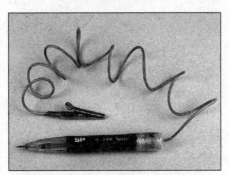

2.4c A simple test light is useful for voltage tests

7 A continuity tester can be used in the same way – its light should come on or it should beep to indicate continuity in the switch ON position, but should be off or silent in the OFF position.

8 Note that the polarity of the test probes doesn't matter for continuity checks, although care should be taken to follow specific test procedures if a diode or solid-state component is being checked.

Switch continuity checks

9 If a switch is at fault, trace its wiring to the wiring connectors. Separate the connectors and inspect them for security and condition. A build-up of dirt or corrosion here will most likely be the cause of the problem – clean up and apply a water dispersant such as WD40, or alternatively use a dedicated contact cleaner and protection spray.

10 If using a multimeter, select the continuity function if it has one, or the resistance (ohms) function, and connect its probes to the terminals in the connector **(see illustration)**. Simple ON/OFF type switches, such as brake light switches, only have two wires whereas combination switches, like the handlebar switches, have many wires. Study the wiring diagram to ensure that you are connecting to the correct pair of wires. Continuity should be indicated with the switch ON and no continuity with it OFF.

Wiring continuity checks

11 Many electrical faults are caused by damaged wiring, often due to incorrect routing or chaffing on frame components. Loose, wet

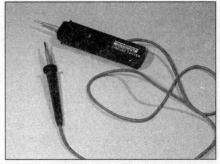

2.4b A battery-powered continuity tester

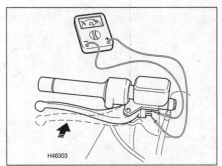

2.10 Continuity should be indicated across switch terminals when the lever is operated

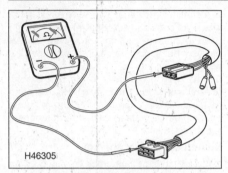

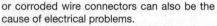

2.12 Wiring continuity check. Connect the meter probes across each end of the same wire

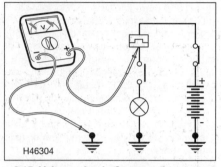

2.15 Voltage check. Connect the meter positive probe to the component and the negative probe to earth

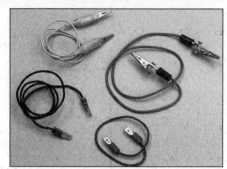

2.23 A selection of insulated jumper wires

or corroded wire connectors can also be the cause of electrical problems.

12 A continuity check can be made on a single length of wire by disconnecting it at each end and connecting the meter or continuity tester probes to each end of the wire **(see illustration)**. Continuity (low or no resistance – 0 ohms) should be indicated if the wire is good. If no continuity (high resistance) is shown, suspect a broken wire.

13 To check for continuity to earth in any earth wire connect one probe of your meter or tester to the earth wire terminal in the connector and the other to the frame, engine, or battery earth (-) terminal. Continuity (low or no resistance – 0 ohms) should be indicated if the wire is good. If no continuity (high resistance) is shown, suspect a broken wire or corroded or loose earth point (see below).

Voltage checks

14 A voltage check can determine whether power is reaching a component. Use a multimeter set to the dc voltage scale, or a test light. The test light is the cheaper component, but the meter has the advantage of being able to give a voltage reading.

15 Connect the meter or test light in parallel, i.e. across the load **(see illustration)**.

16 First identify the relevant wiring circuit by referring to the wiring diagram at the end of this manual. If other electrical components share the same power supply (i.e. are fed from the same fuse), take note whether they are working correctly – this is useful information in deciding where to start checking the circuit.

17 If using a meter, check first that the meter leads are plugged into the correct terminals on the meter (red to positive (+), black to negative (-). Set the meter to the dc volts function, where necessary at a range suitable for the battery voltage – 0 to 20 vdc. Connect the meter red probe (+) to the power supply wire and the black probe to a good metal earth (ground) on the motorcycle's frame or directly to the battery negative terminal. Battery voltage should be shown on the meter with the ignition switch, and if necessary any other relevant switch, ON.

18 If using a test light, connect its positive (+) probe to the power supply terminal and its negative (-) probe to a good earth (ground) on the motorcycle's frame. With the switch, and if necessary any other relevant switch, ON, the test light should illuminate.

19 If no voltage is indicated, work back towards the fuse continuing to check for voltage. When you reach a point where there is voltage, you know the problem lies between that point and your last check point.

Earth (ground) checks

20 Earth connections are made either directly to the engine or frame (such as neutral switch, oil pressure switch etc. which only have a positive feed) or by a separate wire into the earth circuit of the wiring harness. Alternatively a short earth wire is sometimes run from the component directly to the motorcycle's frame.

21 Corrosion is a common cause of a poor earth connection, as is a loose earth terminal fastener.

22 If total or multiple component failure is experienced, check the security of the main earth lead from the negative (-) terminal of the battery, the earth lead bolted to the engine, and the main earth point(s) on the frame. If corroded, dismantle the connection and clean all surfaces back to bare metal. Remake the connection and prevent further corrosion from forming by smearing battery terminal grease over the connection.

23 To check the earth of a component, use an insulated jumper wire to temporarily bypass its earth connection **(see illustration)** – connect one end of the jumper wire to the earth terminal or metal body of the component and the other end to the motorcycle's frame. If the circuit works with the jumper wire installed, the earth circuit is faulty.

24 To check an earth wire first check for corroded or loose connections, then check the wiring for continuity (Step 13) between each connector in the circuit in turn, and then to its earth point, to locate the break.

3 Battery removal, installation, inspection and maintenance

Caution: Be extremely careful when handling or working around the battery. The electrolyte is very caustic and an explosive gas (hydrogen) is given off when the battery is charging. Always disconnect the battery negative (-) lead first, and reconnect it last.

Removal and installation

1 Make sure the ignition is switched OFF. Remove the seats (see Chapter 7).

2 On ZR750-J and ZR1000-A models first lift up the black insulating cover, then unscrew the negative (–) terminal bolt and disconnect the lead from the battery **(see illustration)**. Next lift up the red insulating cover, then unscrew the positive (+) terminal bolt and disconnect the lead.

3 On ZR750-L/M and ZR1000-B/C models undo the two screws securing the centre section of the seat cowling, then release it from each side section and remove it, noting how it fits **(see illustration)**. Unscrew the front

3.2 Disconnect the negative lead (A) first, then disconnect the positive lead (B)

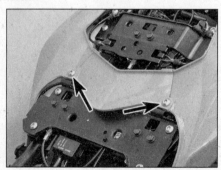

3.3a Undo the screws and remove the centre section

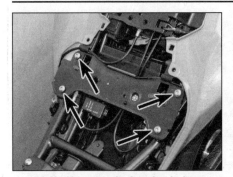

3.3b Unscrew the bracket bolts (arrowed) . . .

3.3c . . . then free the fusebox and place the bracket aside

3.3d Lift the battery out . . .

3.3e . . . then disconnect the negative lead, followed by the positive lead (arrowed) . . .

3.4 . . . and remove the battery

seat bracket bolts and displace the bracket, then release the fusebox from its bracket and lay it aside, then place the bracket clear of the battery on some rag **(see illustration)**. Lift the battery out of its holder **(see illustration)**. Unscrew the negative (–) terminal bolt first and disconnect the lead from the battery **(see illustration)**. Lift up the red insulating cover then unscrew the positive (+) terminal bolt and disconnect the lead.

4 Lift the battery from the bike **(see illustration)**.

5 On installation, clean the battery terminals and lead ends with a wire brush, fine sandpaper or steel wool. Reconnect the leads, connecting the positive (+) terminal first.

 Battery corrosion can be kept to a minimum by applying a layer of battery terminal grease or petroleum jelly (Vaseline) to the terminals after the leads have been connected. DO NOT use a mineral based grease.

Inspection and maintenance

6 The battery fitted to all models covered in this manual is of the maintenance free (sealed) type, therefore requiring no regular maintenance. However, the following checks should still be performed.

7 Check the battery terminals and leads are tight and free of corrosion. If corrosion is evident, clean the terminals as described in Step 5, then protect them from further corrosion **(see Haynes Hint)**.

8 Keep the battery case clean to prevent current leakage, which can discharge the battery over a period of time (especially when it sits unused). Wash the outside of the case with a solution of baking soda and water. Rinse the battery thoroughly, then dry it.

9 Look for cracks in the case and replace the battery with a new one if any are found. If acid has been spilled on the frame or battery box, neutralise it with a baking soda and water solution, dry it thoroughly, then touch up any damaged paint.

10 If the motorcycle sits unused for long periods of time, disconnect the cables from the battery terminals, negative (–) terminal

first. Refer to Section 4 and charge the battery once every month to six weeks.

11 Check the condition of the battery by measuring the voltage present at the battery terminals. Connect the voltmeter positive (+) probe to the battery positive (+) terminal, and the negative (–) probe to the battery negative (–) terminal. When fully-charged there should be 13.0 to 13.2 volts present. If the voltage falls below 12.3 volts remove the battery (see above), and recharge it as described below in Section 4.

4 Battery charging

Caution: Be extremely careful when handling or working around the battery. The electrolyte is very caustic and an

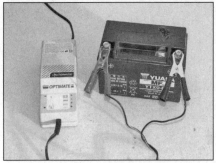

4.1 Battery connected to a charger

explosive gas (hydrogen) is given off when the battery is charging.

1 Remove the battery (see Section 3). Connect the charger to the battery, making sure that the positive (+) lead on the charger is connected to the positive (+) terminal on the battery, and the negative (–) lead is connected to the negative (–) terminal **(see illustration)**.

2 Kawasaki recommend that the battery is charged at the normal rate specified at the beginning of the Chapter. Exceeding this figure can cause the battery to overheat, buckling the plates and rendering it useless. Few owners will have access to an expensive current controlled charger, so if a normal domestic charger is used check that after a possible initial peak, the charge rate falls to a safe level **(see illustration)**. If the battery becomes hot during charging stop. Further charging

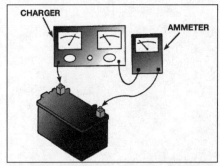

4.2 If the charger doesn't have an ammeter built in, connect one in series as shown. DO NOT connect the ammeter between the battery terminals or it will be ruined

5.2 Disconnect the relay wiring connector (arrowed) to access the fuse

5.3 ECU fuse and its spare (arrowed)

will cause damage. **Note:** *In emergencies the battery can be charged at the quick rate specified. However, this is not recommended and the normal charging rate is by far the safer method of charging the battery.*

3 If the recharged battery discharges rapidly if left disconnected it is likely that an internal short caused by physical damage or sulphation has occurred. A new battery will be required. A sound item will tend to lose its charge at about 1% per day.

4 Install the battery (see Section 3).

5 If the motorcycle sits unused for long periods of time, charge the battery once every month to six weeks and leave it disconnected.

An old battery that has become heavily discharged may require charging for longer than the 10 hours specified.

5 Fuses

1 The electrical system components and wiring are protected from overload by fuses, which have different ratings for different circuits (see Specifications). If all circuits fail simultaneously it is likely the main fuse has blown (but check the battery and its terminals as well).

Access

ZR750-J and ZR1000-A

2 The main fuse is housed in the starter motor relay, which is located behind the right-hand side panel – remove the panel to access it (see Chapter 7). To access the fuse, disconnect the relay wiring connector **(see illustration)**.

3 The ECU (engine management system) fuse is located in its own housing under the rider's seat **(see illustration)** – remove the seat to access it (see Chapter 7). To access the fuse unclip the fuseholder cap.

4 All other fuses are housed in the junction box, which is located under the rider's seat behind the battery **(see illustration)** – remove the seat to access it (see Chapter 7). To access the fuses unclip the junction box lid **(see illustration)**. The identity and location of each fuse and its rating is marked on the inside of the lid.

ZR750-L/M and ZR1000-B/C

5 The main fuse is housed in the starter motor relay, which is under the passenger seat bracket – to access the relay remove the left-hand side of the seat cowling (see Chapter 7). Unscrew the passenger seat bracket bolts and displace the bracket **(see illustration)**. To access the fuse, displace the relay from its mount then disconnect the relay wiring connector **(see illustration)**.

5.4a Junction box (arrowed)

5.4b Unclip the lid to access the fuses

5.5a Unscrew the bolts (arrowed) and displace the bracket

5.5b Displace the relay . . .

5.5c . . . then disconnect the wiring connector to access the fuse (arrowed)

5.6a Fusebox 1 (arrowed)

5.6b Fusebox 2 (arrowed)

6 All other fuses are housed in one of two fuseboxes – refer to the Specifications at the beginning of the Chapter. To access fusebox 1 remove the rider's seat (see Chapter 7) **(see illustration)**. To access fusebox 2 remove the passenger seat (see Chapter 7) **(see illustration)**.
7 To access the fuses unclip the fusebox lid **(see illustration)**. The identity and location of each fuse and its rating are marked on the top of the lid. On ABS models the arrangement of the fuses and spares is slightly different – see Specifications **(see illustration)**.

Check and replacement

8 The fuses can be removed and checked visually. If you can't pull the fuse out with your fingertips, use a pair of suitable pliers. A blown fuse is easily identified by a break in the element **(see illustration)**. Each fuse is clearly marked with its rating and must only be replaced by a fuse of the correct rating.
9 On ZR750-J and ZR1000-A models a spare 30 A (main) fuse and a spare 10 A fuse are housed in the junction box **(see illustration 5.4b)**, and a spare 15 A fuse is housed in the ECU fuse holder **(see illustration 5.3)**.
10 On ZR750-L/M and ZR1000-B/C models a spare 30 A (main) fuse is housed in the starter motor relay holder **(see illustration 5.5c)**, and a spare fuse of each other rating is housed in one

of the fuseboxes **(see illustration 5.6a and b)**.
11 If a spare fuse is used, always replace it with a new one so that a spare of each rating is carried on the bike at all times.

⚠ *Warning: Never put in a fuse of a higher rating or bridge the terminals with any other substitute, however temporary it may be. Serious damage may be done to the circuit, or a fire may start.*
12 If the new fuse blows immediately check the wiring circuit very carefully for evidence of a short-circuit. Look for bare wires and chafed, melted or burned insulation.
13 Occasionally a fuse will blow or cause an open-circuit for no obvious reason. Corrosion of the fuse ends and fusebox terminals may occur and cause poor fuse contact. If this happens, remove the corrosion with a wire brush or emery paper, and/or use a dedicated electrical contact cleaner, then spray the fuse end and terminals with a protection spray.

6 Lighting system check

1 The battery provides power for operation of the lights. If a light fails first check the bulb (see relevant Section), and the bulb terminals

in the holder. If none of the lights work, always check battery voltage before proceeding. Low battery voltage indicates either a faulty battery or a defective charging system. Refer to Section 3 for battery checks and Section 28 for charging system tests. Also, check the condition of the fuses – if there is more than one problem at the same time, it is likely to be a fault relating to a multi-function component, such as one of the fuses governing more than one circuit, or the ignition switch. When checking for a blown filament in a bulb, it is advisable to back up a visual check with a continuity test of the filament as it is not always apparent that a bulb has blown. When testing for continuity, remember that on single terminal bulbs it is the metal body of the bulb that is the earth (ground).

Headlight

2 All models have two single filament bulbs – the left-hand bulb works on LO beam and both bulbs work on HI beam. If one of the two bulbs in the headlight fails to work, check the bulb first (see Section 7). If both bulbs fail to work check the headlight fuse (Section 5), and then the relay (Step 6). If the HI beam bulbs fail to work check the dimmer switch (Section 19).
3 Next disconnect the relevant headlight bulb wiring connector (Section 7, Step 2),

5.7a Unclip the lid to access the fuses

5.7b Fusebox 1 on ABS models

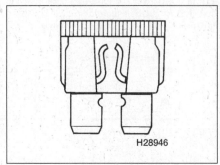

5.8 A blown fuse can be identified by a break in its element

6.6a Lift the junction box and disconnect the wiring connectors

6.6b Draw the relay box out of its holder

and check for battery voltage on the supply side of the wiring connector with a test light or multimeter – connect the negative probe of the multimeter to the black/yellow wire (earth), and the positive probe to the red/black wire for the high beam bulb connector and the blue/yellow wire for the low beam bulb connector, with the ignition switch ON. Don't forget to select either high or low beam as appropriate at the handlebar switch while conducting this test.

4 If no voltage is indicated, check for continuity between the black/yellow wire connector terminal and earth (ground). If there is no continuity, check the earth (ground) circuit for an open or poor connection.

5 If the earth circuit is good, check the wiring between the headlight connector, dimmer switch, relay (housed in the junction box on ZR750-J and ZR1000-A models and in the relay box on ZR750-L/M and ZR1000-B/C models – see Step 6), and the ignition switch, referring to *Wiring Diagrams* at the end of the chapter, then check the switches themselves.

6 To check the headlight relay, on ZR750-J and ZR1000-A models remove the rider's seat (see Chapter 7), then lift the junction box off its holder and disconnect the wiring connectors **(see illustration)**. On ZR750-L/M and ZR1000-B/C models remove the left-hand side of the seat cowling (see Chapter 7). Unscrew the passenger seat bracket bolts and displace the bracket **(see illustration 5.5a)**, then draw the relay box from its holder and disconnect the wiring connectors **(see illustration)**.

7 On ZR750-J and ZR1000-A models set a multimeter to the ohms x 1 scale and connect its probes to terminals 7 and 8 on the junction box, then to terminals 7 and

13 **(see illustration)**. There should be no continuity (infinite resistance) in each case. Using a fully-charged 12 volt battery and two insulated jumper wires, connect the positive (+) terminal of the battery to terminal 9 on the junction box, and the negative (–) terminal to terminal 13. There should now be continuity on the multimeter between terminals 7 and 8. If this is the case the relay is proven good. If the relay still indicates no continuity (infinite resistance) across terminals 7 and 8, it is faulty and the junction box must be replaced with a new one – individual components are not available. If the relay is good now check the diodes in the circuit using an ohmmeter. First connect the positive (+) probe to terminal 9 and the negative (–) to terminal 13 – the diode should show continuity. Now reverse the probes. The diode should show no continuity. Repeat the tests between terminals 8 and 13. The same results should be achieved. If the diodes don't behave as stated, replace the junction box with a new one.

8 On ZR750-L/M and ZR1000-B/C models set a multimeter to the ohms x 1 scale and connect its probes to terminals 1 and 3 on the relay box **(see illustration)**. There should be no continuity (infinite resistance). Using a fully-charged 12 volt battery and two insulated jumper wires, connect the positive (+) terminal of the battery to terminal 2, and the negative (–) terminal to terminal 11. At this point the multimeter should read 0 ohms (continuity). If this is the case the relay is proven good. If the relay still indicates no continuity (infinite resistance), it is faulty and the relay box must be replaced with a new one – individual relays are not available. If the relay is good now check the diodes in the circuit using

an ohmmeter. First connect the positive (+) probe to terminal 1 and the negative (–) probe to terminal 11 – the diode should show continuity. Now reverse the probes. The diode should show no continuity. Repeat the tests between terminals 2 and 11. The same results should be achieved. If the diodes don't behave as stated, replace the relay box with a new one.

Tail light

9 The tail light consists of a number of LEDs in a sealed unit. When a single LED fails it cannot be replaced with a new one, however the failure of one LED will not affect the function of the others. If enough LEDs have failed so as to impair the safe operation of the motorcycle, replace the tail light unit with a new one (Section 10).

10 If the tail light fails to work completely, first check the fuse, then the wiring connector (see Section 10 for access). Next check for battery voltage at the red wire terminal on the supply side of the tail light wiring connector, with the ignition switch ON.

11 If no voltage is indicated, check the wiring between the tail light and the ignition switch, then check the switch itself.

12 If voltage is indicated, check for continuity between the black/yellow wire terminal and earth (ground). If there is no continuity, check the earth (ground) circuit for a broken or poor connection.

Sidelight

13 If the sidelight(s) fail(s) to work with the ignition switch either in the ON position or in the P position check the fuse, then check the bulb(s) and the bulb terminals and wiring connector(s) (see Section 7). Next check for battery voltage at the red wire terminal on the supply side of the wiring connector, with the ignition switch first in the ON position, then in the P position.

14 If no voltage is indicated in either position, check the wiring between the sidelight and the ignition switch, then check the switch (Section 18).

15 If voltage is indicated, check for continuity between the wiring connector terminals on the bulb side of the wiring connector and the corresponding terminals in the bulbholder; no continuity indicates a break in the circuit.

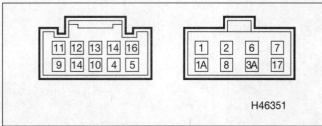

6.7 Junction box terminal identification

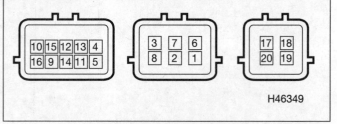

6.8 Relay box terminal identification

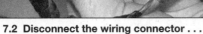

7.2 Disconnect the wiring connector . . .

7.3 . . . then remove the dust cover . . .

If continuity is present, check for continuity between the black/yellow wire terminal and earth (ground). If there is no continuity, check the earth (ground) circuit for a broken or poor connection.

16 If the sidelight bulbs work with the ignition switch in one position (ON or P) but not the other then the switch is faulty.

Brake light

17 The brake light consists of a number of LEDs in a sealed unit. When a single LED fails it cannot be replaced with a new one, however the failure of one LED will not affect the function of the others. If enough LEDs have failed so as to impair the safe operation of the motorcycle, replace the tail light unit with a new one (Section 10).

18 If the brake light fails to work completely, first check the fuse, then the wiring connector (see Section 10 for access). Next check for battery voltage at the blue/red wire terminal on the supply side of the tail light wiring connector, with the ignition switch ON and the brake lever or pedal applied.

19 If no voltage is indicated, check the brake light switches (see Section 14), then the wiring between the tail light and the switches.

20 If voltage is indicated, check for continuity

between the black/yellow wire terminal and earth (ground). If there is no continuity, check the earth (ground) circuit for a broken or poor connection.

Licence plate light

21 If the light fails to work, first check the bulb and the bulb terminals (Section 9), then the fuse (Section 5), then the wiring connector (see Section 10 for access). Next check for battery voltage at the red wire terminal on the supply side of the wiring connector, with the ignition switch ON.

22 If no voltage is indicated, check the wiring between the tail light and the ignition switch, then check the switch itself.

23 If voltage is indicated, check for continuity between the black/yellow wire terminal and earth (ground). If there is no continuity, check the earth (ground) circuit for a broken or poor connection.

Turn signal lights

24 If one light fails to work, check the bulb and the bulb terminals (see Section 12), then the wiring connector. If none of the turn signals work, check the turn signal relay fuse (Section 5).

25 If the fuse is good, check the turn signal relay (see Section 11).

7 Headlight bulbs and sidelight bulbs

Note: *The headlight bulbs are of the quartz-halogen type. Do not touch the bulb glass as skin acids will shorten the bulb's service life. If the bulb is accidentally touched, it should be wiped carefully when cold with a rag soaked in methylated spirit and dried before fitting. Use a paper towel or dry cloth when handling new bulbs to prevent injury if the bulb should break and to increase bulb life.*

Headlight

1 For best access remove the fairing (see Chapter 7).

2 If the fairing was not removed disconnect the wiring connector **(see illustration)**.

3 Remove the rubber cover **(see illustration)**.

4 Release the bulb retaining clip, noting how it fits, then remove the bulb **(see illustration)**.

5 Pull the old bulb out of the holder and fit the new one into it, bearing in mind the information in the Note above **(see illustrations)**.

6 Fit the bulb into the headlight, making sure it locates correctly, and secure it in position with the retaining clip.

7.4a . . . release the clip . . .

7.4b . . . and remove the bulbholder

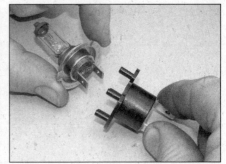

7.5 Pull the bulb out of the holder

7.10a Sidelight bulbholder – ZR750-J, ZR1000-A

7.10b Sidelight bulbholder – ZR750-L/M, ZR1000-B/C

7.10c Pull the bulb out of the holder

7 Connect the wiring connector. Check the operation of the headlight.
8 Fit the rubber cover.

Sidelight

9 Remove the fairing (see Chapter 7).
10 Release the bulbholder from the headlight **(see illustrations)**. Carefully pull the bulb out of the holder **(see illustration)**.
11 Fit the new bulb into the bulbholder then fit the holder into the headlight.
12 Check the operation of the sidelight.

8 Headlight

Removal

1 Remove the fairing (see Chapter 7).
2 On ZR750-J and ZR1000-A models unscrew the bolts securing the headlight assembly to the fairing and lift it out **(see illustration)**. Remove the collars from the rubber dampers if

required. Check the condition of the dampers and replace them with new ones if necessary. Make sure none of the clip nuts on the fairing drop off.
3 On ZR750-L/M and ZR1000-B/C models, if fitted unscrew the immobiliser amplifier bolts and remove the amplifier **(see illustration)**. Unscrew the bolts securing the headlight mounting brackets to the fairing then lift the headlight assembly out **(see illustrations)**. If required undo the headlight mounting screws, noting the washers, and remove the brackets,

8.2 Unscrew the bolts (arrowed) and remove the headlight

8.3a Unscrew the bolts (arrowed) and remove the amplifier

8.3b Unscrew the bracket bolts (arrowed) on each side . . .

8.3c . . . and lift the headlight out

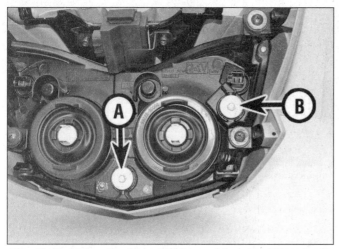

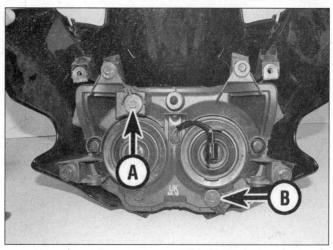

8.7a Vertical (A) and horizontal (B) beam adjusters – ZR1000-B/C

8.7b Vertical (A) and horizontal (B) beam adjusters – Z750, ZR1000-A

noting which fits where. Check the condition of the rubber dampers and replace them with new ones if necessary.

4 If required remove the headlight bulbs and the sidelight bulbholders (see Section 7).

Installation

5 Installation is the reverse of removal. Make sure all the wiring is correctly routed, connected and secured. Check the operation of the headlight and sidelight. Check the headlight aim.

Headlight aim

Note: *An improperly adjusted headlight may cause problems for oncoming traffic or provide poor, unsafe illumination of the road ahead. Before adjusting the headlight aim, be sure to consult with local traffic laws and regulations – for UK models refer to MOT Test Checks in the Reference section.*

6 The headlight beam can adjusted both horizontally and vertically. Adjustment is made either using a spanner on the adjuster hex, or using a suitable cross-head screwdriver under the notched rim of the adjuster. Before making any adjustment, check that the tyre pressures are correct and the suspension is adjusted as required. Make any adjustments

to the headlight aim with the machine on level ground, with the fuel tank half full and with an assistant sitting on the seat. If the bike is usually ridden with a passenger on the back, have a second assistant to do this.

7 On ZR1000-B/C models vertical adjustment is made by turning the adjuster screw in the middle of the headlight at the bottom **(see illustration)**. On all other models vertical adjustment is made by turning the adjuster screw on the left-hand side of the headlight **(see illustration)**.

8 Horizontal adjustment is made by turning the adjuster knob on the right-hand side of the headlight **(see illustration 8.7a or b)**.

9 Brake/tail light LEDs and licence plate bulb

Brake/tail light LEDs

1 The failure of one LED in the tail light will not affect the function of the others. If enough LEDs have failed so as to impair the safe operation of the motorcycle, replace the tail light unit with a new one (Section 10).

Licence plate light bulb

2 Undo the lens housing screws and remove the housing **(see illustration)**.

3 Push the bulb into the holder and twist it anti-clockwise to remove it **(see illustration)**. Check the socket terminals for corrosion and clean them if necessary.

4 Line up the pins of the new bulb with the slots in the socket, then push the bulb in and turn it clockwise until it locks into place. **Note:** *It is a good idea to use a paper towel or dry cloth when handling the new bulb to prevent injury if the bulb should break and to increase bulb life.*

5 Fit the lens housing and tighten the screws.

10 Tail light

Removal

ZR750-J and ZR1000-A

1 Remove the seat cowling (see Chapter 7).
2 Release the wiring clip **(see illustration)**. Disconnect the tail light, licence plate light

9.2 Undo the screws and remove the housing . . .

9.3 . . . then remove the bulb

10.2a Release the clip (arrowed) . . .

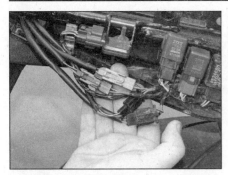

10.2b . . . and disconnect the wiring
connectors

10.3 Displace the three relays

10.4a Unscrew the bolts (arrowed) on the
top . . .

10.4b . . . and the bolt (arrowed) on each
side . . .

10.4c . . . and remove the holder

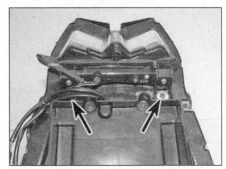

10.5a Undo the screws (arrowed) . . .

10.5b . . . then free the peg and remove
the tail light

and rear turn signal wiring connectors **(see
illustration)**. Note the routing of the wiring.
3 Displace the relays from their mounts **(see
illustration)**.
4 Undo the four bolts and remove the turn
signal/licence plate/tail light holder assembly,
noting how it fits **(see illustrations)**.
5 Undo the tail light screws, then free the peg
from the grommet and remove the tail light
(see illustrations).

ZR750-L/M and ZR1000-B/C

6 Remove the side sections of the seat
cowling (see Chapter 7).

7 Unscrew the passenger seat bracket bolts
and displace the bracket **(see illustration
5.5a)**. Disconnect the tail light, licence plate
light and rear turn signal wiring connectors
(see illustration). Note the routing of the
wiring.
8 Release the trim clips on the underside of
the centre section of the seat cowling **(see
illustration)**. Undo the two bolts and the
two nuts and displace the centre section,
then release the seat lock cable and
disconnect the tail light wiring connector **(see
illustrations)**.

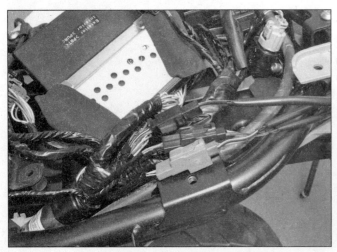

10.7 Disconnect the wiring connectors

10.8a Release the trim clip on each side

10.8b Unscrew the bolts (A) and nuts (B) and draw the cowling off . . .

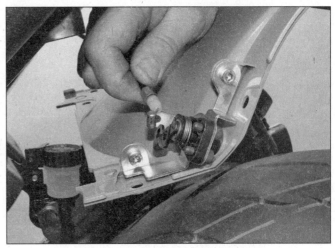

10.8c . . . then detach the seat lock cable . . .

9 Undo the tail light screws and remove the tail light (see illustration).

Installation

10 Installation is the reverse of removal. Check the operation of the tail and brake lights, the rear turn signals and the licence plate light.

11 Turn signal circuit check

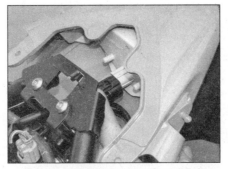

10.8d . . . and disconnect the tail light wiring connector

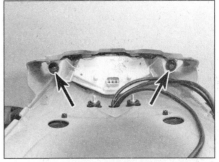

10.9 Undo the screws (arrowed) and remove the tail light

1 Most turn signal problems are the result of a burned out bulb or corroded socket. This is especially true when the turn signals function properly in one direction, but fail to flash in the other direction. If this is the case, first check the bulbs, the sockets and the wiring connectors. If all the turn signals fail to work, first check the turn signal relay fuse (see Section 5), and then the relay (see below). If they are good, the problem lies in the wiring or connectors, or the switch. Refer to Section 20 for the switch testing procedures, and also to the wiring diagrams at the end of this Chapter.
2 To check the relay, on ZR750-J and ZR1000-A models remove the seat cowling,

and on ZR750-L/M and ZR1000-B/C models remove the passenger seat (see Chapter 7), then unscrew the passenger seat bracket bolts and displace the bracket (see illustration 5.5a).
3 Displace the relay and disconnect the wiring connector (see illustrations). Check for battery voltage at the brown/yellow wire terminal on the loom side of the connector with the ignition ON. If no voltage is present, check the wiring from the relay to the ignition switch (via the fuse) for continuity.
4 If voltage was present, short between the

wire terminals on the connector using a jumper wire. Turn the ignition ON and operate the turn signal switch. If the lights come on (they will not flash), the relay is confirmed faulty and must be replaced with a new one.
5 If the lights do not come on, check the orange wire for continuity to the left-hand switch housing, and repair or renew the wiring or connectors as required.
6 If all is good so far, or if the lights work on one side but not the other, check the wiring between the left-hand switch housing and the turn signals themselves. Repair or renew the wiring or connectors as necessary.

11.3a Turn signal relay (arrowed) – ZR750-J, ZR1000-A

11.3b Turn signal relay (arrowed) – ZR750-L/M, ZR1000-B/C

11.3c Displace the relay and disconnect the wiring connector

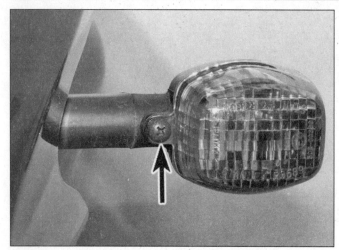

12.1 Undo the screw (arrowed) and remove the lens . . .

12.2 . . . then remove the bulb

12 Turn signal bulbs

ZR750-J and ZR1000-A – Europe models

1 Undo the screw securing the lens and detach it from the housing, noting how it fits **(see illustration)**. Remove the rubber seal if it is loose, and discard it if it is damaged, deformed or deteriorated.

2 Push the bulb into the holder and turn it anti-clockwise to remove it **(see illustration)**. Check the socket terminals for corrosion and clean them if necessary.

3 Line up the pins of the new bulb with the slots in the socket, then push the bulb in and turn it clockwise until it locks into place. **Note:** *It is a good idea to use a paper towel or dry cloth when handling the new bulb to prevent injury if the bulb should break and to increase bulb life.*

4 Fit a new rubber seal if required, and make sure it is properly seated and does not get pinched. Fit the lens onto the housing, locating the cut-out in the outer end onto the tab on the housing, and secure it with the screw **(see illustration)**. Do not overtighten the screw as it is easy to strip the threads or crack the lens.

ZR750-J and ZR1000-A – US and Canada models

5 Undo the screw on the back of the turn signal housing and withdraw the bulb housing. Undo the screws securing the lens and detach it from the bulb housing. Remove the rubber seal if it is loose, and discard it if it is damaged, deformed or deteriorated.

6 Push the bulb into the holder and turn it anti-clockwise to remove it. Check the socket terminals for corrosion and clean them if necessary.

7 Line up the pins of the new bulb with the slots in the socket (the pin depths differ), then push the bulb in and turn it clockwise until it locks into place. **Note:** *It is a good idea to use a paper towel or dry cloth when handling the new bulb to prevent injury if the bulb should break and to increase bulb life.*

8 Fit a new rubber seal if required, and make sure it is properly seated and does not get pinched. Fit the lens onto the bulb housing and secure it with the screws – do not overtighten them as it is easy to strip the threads or crack the lens. Fit the bulb housing into the turn signal housing and secure it with the screw.

ZR750-L/M

9 Undo the screw on the underside of the housing and detach the lens, noting how it fits **(see illustration)**.

10 Push the bulb into the holder and turn it anti-clockwise to remove it **(see illustration)**. Check the socket terminals for corrosion and clean them if necessary.

11 Line up the pins of the new bulb with the slots in the socket, then push the bulb in and turn it clockwise until it locks into place. **Note:** *It is a good idea to use a paper towel or dry cloth when handling the new bulb to prevent injury if the bulb should break and to increase bulb life.*

12 Fit the lens onto the housing and secure it with the screw. Do not overtighten the screw as it is easy to strip the threads or crack the lens.

13 Fit the turn signal and its mounting plate onto the cowl and secure them with the screw.

ZR1000-B/C

Front

14 Remove the fairing side panel (see Chapter 7).

15 Undo the inner panel screws and remove

12.4 Make sure the outer end of the lens locates correctly over the tab (arrowed)

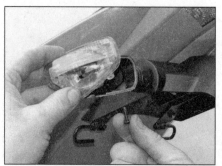

12.9 Undo the screw and remove the lens . . .

12.10 . . . then remove the bulb

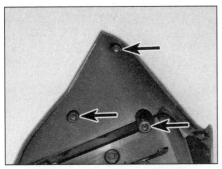

12.15a Undo the screws (arrowed) . . .

12.15b . . . then remove the inner panel . . .

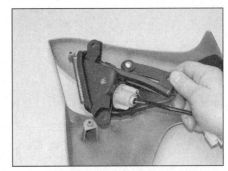

12.15c . . . and the turn signal

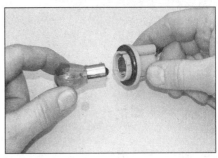

the panel, then remove the turn signal from the fairing **(see illustrations)**.

16 Turn the bulbholder anti-clockwise and remove it from the lens housing **(see illustration)**.

17 Push the bulb into the holder and turn it anti-clockwise to remove it **(see illustration)**. Check the socket terminals for corrosion and clean them if necessary.

18 Line up the pins of the new bulb with the slots in the socket, then push the bulb in and turn it clockwise until it locks into place. **Note:** *It is a good idea to use a paper towel or dry cloth when handling the new bulb to prevent injury if the bulb should break and to increase bulb life.*

19 Fit the bulbholder into the lens housing and turn it clockwise to lock it.

20 Fit the turn signal and inner panel onto the fairing side panel and secure them with the screws.

21 Install the fairing side panel (see Chapter 7).

Rear

22 See Steps 9 to 13.

13 Turn signal assemblies

Front turn signals

ZR1000-B/C

1 Remove the fairing side panel (see Chapter 7). Undo the inner panel screws and remove the panel, then remove the turn signal from the fairing.

All other models

2 Remove the fairing (see Chapter 7). Trace the wiring from the turn signal and disconnect it at the connector **(see illustrations)**. Free the wiring from any ties and feed it through to the turn signal, noting its routing.

3 On ZR750-J and ZR1000-A models unscrew the nut and remove the mounting plate, then remove the turn signal, taking care as you draw the wiring through **(see illustration)**.

4 On ZR750-L/M models undo the screw, remove the retainer plate and displace the wiring guide, then remove the turn signal, taking care as you draw the wiring through.

12.16 Release the bulbholder . . .

12.17 . . . then remove the bulb

Rear turn signals

5 On ZR750-J and ZR1000-A models remove the seat cowling (see Chapter 7).

6 On ZR750-L/M and ZR1000-B/C models remove the left-hand side of the seat cowling (see Chapter 7). Unscrew the passenger seat bracket bolts and displace the bracket **(see illustration 5.5a)**.

7 Disconnect the turn signal wiring connector **(see illustration 10.2b or 10.7)**. Free the wiring from any clips and feed it through to the turn signal, noting its routing.

8 On ZR750-J and ZR1000-A models unscrew the nut and remove the mounting plate, then remove the turn signal, taking care as you draw the wiring through **(see illustration)**.

13.2a Release the rubber cover where fitted

13.2b Disconnect the relevant wiring connector

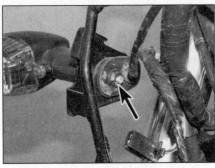

13.3 Unscrew the nut (arrowed) and remove the turn signal

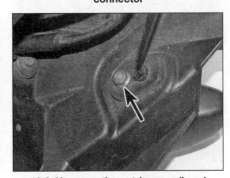

13.8 Unscrew the nut (arrowed) and remove the turn signal

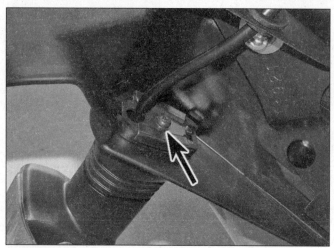

13.9 Undo the screw (arrowed) and remove the turn signal

14.2 Front brake switch wiring connector (arrowed)

9 On ZR750-L/M and ZR1000-B/C models undo the screw, remove the retainer plate and displace the wiring guide, then remove the turn signal, taking care as you draw the wiring through **(see illustration)**.

Installation

10 Installation is the reverse of removal. Check the operation of the turn signals.

14 Brake light switches

Circuit check

1 Before checking the switches, and if not already done, check the brake light circuit (see Section 6).
2 The front brake light switch is mounted on

the underside of the brake master cylinder. Disconnect the wiring connector(s) from the switch **(see illustration)**. Using a continuity tester, connect the probes to the terminals of the switch **(see illustration 2.10)**. With the brake lever at rest, there should be no continuity. With the brake lever applied, there should be continuity. If the switch does not behave as described, replace it with a new one.
3 The rear brake light switch is mounted on the inside of the rider's right-hand footrest bracket, above the brake pedal **(see illustrations)**. Remove the left-hand side panel (see Chapter 7) to access the wiring connector and disconnect it. Using a continuity tester, connect the probes to the terminals on the switch side of the wiring connector. With the brake pedal at rest, there should be no continuity. With the brake pedal applied, there should be continuity.

If the switch does not behave as described, replace it with a new one, although check first that switch is adjusted correctly (see Step 11).
4 If the switches are good, check for voltage at the red/blue wire on the loom side of the connector with the ignition switch ON – there should be battery voltage. If there's no voltage present, check the wiring between the connector and the ignition switch via the fuse (see the wiring diagrams at the end of this Chapter). If voltage is present, check the blue/red wire for continuity to the brake light bulb wiring connector, referring to the relevant wiring diagram. Repair or renew the wiring as necessary.

Switch replacement

Front brake lever switch

5 The switch is mounted on the underside of the brake master cylinder. Disconnect

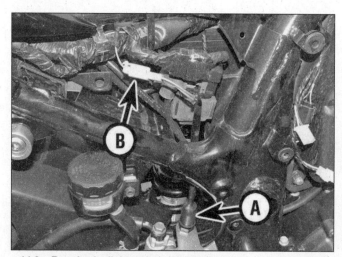

14.3a Rear brake light switch (A) and its wiring connector (B) – ZR750-J, ZR1000-A

14.3b Rear brake light switch (A) and its wiring connector (B) – ZR750-L/M, ZR1000-B/C

14.6 Undo the screw (arrowed) and remove the switch

14.9a Unhook the spring (arrowed) from the pedal return spring . . .

14.9b . . . then hold the nut (arrowed) and unscrew the switch

the wiring connector(s) from the switch **(see illustration 14.2).**

6 Remove the single screw securing the switch to the master cylinder and remove the switch **(see illustration).**

7 Installation is the reverse of removal. Make sure the switch is correctly located before tightening its screw. The switch isn't adjustable.

Rear brake pedal switch

8 The rear brake light switch is mounted on the inside of the rider's right-hand footrest bracket, above the brake pedal **(see illustration 14.3a or b).** Remove the left-hand side panel (see Chapter 7) to access the wiring connector and disconnect it. Feed the wiring down to the switch, noting its routing and releasing it from any ties.

9 Detach the bottom end of the switch spring **(see illustration).** Thread the switch out of its adjustment nut, then if required release the nut from the mounting **(see illustration).**

10 Installation is the reverse of removal. Make sure the brake light is activated just before the rear brake pedal takes effect. If adjustment is

necessary, hold the switch body and turn the adjustment nut as required until the brake light is activated correctly – if the brake light comes on too late or not at all, turn the nut clockwise (when looked at from the top) so the switch threads out of the bracket. If the brake light comes on too soon or is permanently on, turn the ring anti-clockwise so the switch threads into the bracket.

15 Instrument cluster removal and installation

Removal

1 Remove the fairing (see Chapter 7).
2 Pull the rubber boot off the wiring connector and disconnect it from the instrument cluster **(see illustrations).**

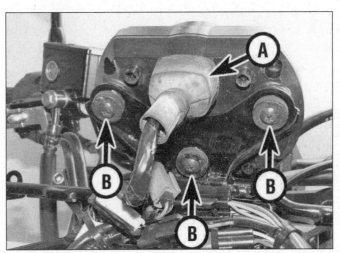

15.2a Instrument cluster wiring connector (A) and mounting screws (B) – ZR750-J, ZR1000-A

15.2b Disconnect the wiring connector . . .

15.3a ... then undo the screws (arrowed) ...

15.3b ... and remove the instrument cluster on ZR750-L/M, ZR1000-B/C

3 Undo the screws and remove the washers, then lift the instrument cluster off the bracket, noting how it locates **(see illustrations)**. Note the rubber grommets fitted in the mounts.

Installation

4 Installation is the reverse of removal. Check the rubber grommets in the bracket for damage, deformation and deterioration and replace them with new ones if necessary. Make sure the pegs locate correctly in the grommets. Make sure that the wiring connector is secure.

---

16 Instrument and speed sensor check

Instrument cluster

Power check

1 If none of the instruments or displays are working, first check the ignition fuse and the instrument (ACC) fuse on ZR750-J and ZR1000-A models or the instrument cluster fuse on ZR750-L/M and ZR1000-B/C models (see Section 5).
2 If the fuse is good, remove the fairing (see Chapter 7) and check the instrument cluster and front loom wiring connectors for loose or broken connections **(see illustration 15.2a or b)**.
3 To check the power input wire, connect the positive (+) probe of a voltmeter to the brown/white wire terminal on the loom side of the wiring connector, and the negative (-) probe to a good earth (ground). There should be battery voltage with the ignition switch ON. If there is no voltage, refer to the wiring diagrams and check the wire between the instrument cluster, the ignition fuse and the ignition switch for loose or broken connections or a damaged wire, then check the white wire from the switch to the main fuse and battery..
4 To check the back-up power wire, connect the positive (+) probe of a voltmeter to the white/green wire terminal on the loom side of the wiring connector, and the negative (-) probe to a good earth (ground). Check for battery voltage with the ignition switch OFF. There should be battery voltage. If there is no voltage, refer to the wiring diagrams and check the wire between the instrument cluster and the ACC fuse or instrument cluster fuse (according to model) for loose or broken connections or a damaged wire, then check the white wire from the fuse to the main fuse and battery.
5 If there is voltage, and to check the earth (ground) wire, check for continuity between the black/yellow wire terminal on the loom side of the wiring connector and earth (ground).

If there is no continuity, check the circuit for loose or broken connections or a damaged wire and repair as necessary.
6 If all power input and earth wires are good, but there is no display or instrument function, then the printed circuit board (PCB), which contains the LCD display, is faulty. Disassemble the instrument cluster and replace the PCB with a new one (see Steps 9 to 12).

Instrument check

7 To check the individual functions of the instrument cluster special electrical testing equipment and a harness adapter are needed. Take the cluster to a Kawasaki dealer for assessment.
8 Before doing this check the relevant wiring between the instrument cluster wiring connector and its sensor or switch for continuity, and check the sensor or switch itself, referring to the wiring diagrams, and the relevant Section of this Chapter, or to Chapter 3 for the temperature display and Chapter 4 for the fuel display.

Disassembly and PCB replacement

9 Remove the instrument cluster (see Section 15).
10 Undo the rear cover screws and lift the cover off **(see illustrations)**. Lift the PCB out of the front cover, noting how it locates **(see illustration)**.

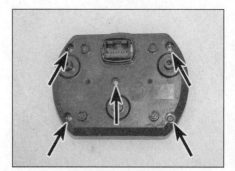

16.10a On ZR750-J and ZR1000-A models undo the screws (arrowed) ...

16.10b ... remove the cover ...

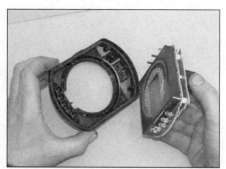

16.10c ... and lift the PCB out, noting how it locates

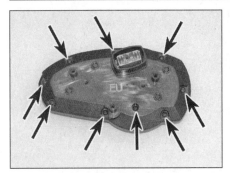

16.10d On ZR750-L/M and ZR1000-B/C models undo the screws (arrowed) . . .

11 All instrument and warning lights are LEDs, which are part of the instrument cluster printed circuit board and are not available individually.

12 Installation is the reverse of removal. On ZR750-J and ZR1000-A models make sure the sealing ring is correctly seated **(see illustration)**. Make sure the PCB locates correctly. Do not over-tighten the screws.

Speed sensor

Check

13 On ZR750-J and ZR1000-A models trace the wiring from the speed sensor, which is mounted in the front sprocket cover, and disconnect it at the 3-pin connector **(see illustration)** – remove the frame cover if required to improve access (see Chapter 7). On ZR750-L/M and ZR1000-B/C models disconnect the wiring connector from the sensor, which is mounted on the crankcase behind the starter motor **(see illustration)**. Check the connector for loose terminals.

14 To check the sensor you need either needle probes for your meter that can be inserted into the back of the connector to contact the terminals with the connector connected, or the Kawasaki test harness (Pt. No. 57001-1400 for ZR750-J and ZR1000-A models, and 57001-1667 for ZR750-L/M and ZR1000-B/C models) that fits between the sensor wiring connector sections.

15 To check the input voltage connect the positive (+) probe of a voltmeter to the pink wire terminal on ZR750-J and ZR1000-A models or the blue wire terminal on ZR750-L/M and

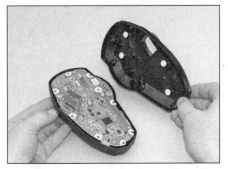

16.10e . . . remove the cover . . .

ZR1000-B/C models, then connect the negative (–) lead to the black wire terminal on ZR750-J and ZR1000-A models or brown/black wire terminal on ZR750-L/M and ZR1000-B/C models. Turn the ignition switch ON and check that a voltage of around 9 to 11 volts is present.

16 To check the output voltage connect the positive (+) probe of a voltmeter to the yellow wire terminal on ZR750-J and ZR1000-A models or the pink wire terminal on ZR750-L/M and ZR1000-B/C models, then connect the negative (–) lead to the black wire terminal on ZR750-J and ZR1000-A models or brown/black wire terminal on ZR750-L/M and ZR1000-B/C models. Turn the ignition switch ON and check that a voltage of around 0.05 to 0.07 volts is present. Turn the rear wheel and check that the voltage rises to around 5 volts.

17 If no voltage is obtained, on ZR750-J and ZR1000-A models check for continuity in the wiring between the speed sensor wiring connector and the instrument cluster and the ECU, and check for continuity to earth in the black/yellow wire, referring to the wiring diagrams. On ZR750-L/M and ZR1000-B/C models check for continuity in the wiring between the speed sensor wiring connector and the ECU. If there is an input voltage but no output voltage the sensor is faulty.

18 If the wiring is all good and the sensor is good, the printed circuit board (PCB), which contains the LCD display, is faulty. Disassemble the instrument cluster and replace the PCB with a new one (see Steps 9 to 12).

16.13b On ZR750-L/M and ZR1000-B/C models the speed sensor is behind the coolant pipe (arrowed) – disconnect the wiring connector from it

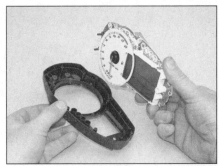

16.10f . . . and lift the PCB out, noting how it locates

16.12 Make sure the sealing ring is not kinked or twisted

Removal and installation

19 On ZR750-J and ZR1000-A models trace the wiring from the speed sensor, which is mounted in the front sprocket cover, and disconnect it at the 3-pin connector **(see illustration 16.13a)** – remove the frame cover if required to improve access (see Chapter 7). Remove the front sprocket cover (see Chapter 6). Undo the speed sensor cover bolts and remove the cover **(see illustration)**. Unscrew the sensor mounting bolt and remove the sensor.

20 On ZR750-L/M and ZR1000-B/C models drain the cooling system (see Chapter 1). Refer to Chapter 3 and remove the coolant outlet pipe from the top of the water pump. Disconnect the wiring connector from the sensor, which is mounted on the crankcase behind the starter motor **(see illustration 16.13b)**. Unscrew the sensor mounting bolt

16.13a Speed sensor wiring connector – ZR750-J, ZR1000-A

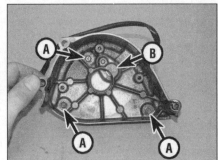

16.19 Undo the bolts (A) and remove the cover to access the sensor (B)

16.20 Unscrew the bolt (arrowed) and remove the sensor

17.2 Pull back the rubber then undo the terminal screw and detach the wiring

and remove the sensor **(see illustration)**. Check the condition of its O-ring and replace it with a new one if it is damaged. Plug the sensor orifice with clean rag to prevent anything falling into the engine.

21 Installation is the reverse of removal. On ZR750-J and ZR1000-A models, apply a suitable non-permanent thread locking compound to both the speed sensor bolt and the sensor cover bolts and tighten them to the torque setting specified at the beginning of the Chapter. On ZR750-L/M and ZR1000-B/C models smear the sensor O-ring with grease and tighten the bolt to the torque setting specified at the beginning of the Chapter. Refer to Chapters 3 and 1 for installation of the coolant pipe and to refill the system.

17 Oil pressure switch

Check

1 The oil pressure switch is screwed into the front of the crankcase on the right-hand side. The oil pressure warning display should come on when the ignition switch is turned ON and go out a few seconds after the engine is started. If the oil pressure warning light does not go out or comes on whilst the engine is running, stop the engine immediately and carry out an oil level check (see *Pre-ride checks*), and if the level is correct, an oil pressure check (see Chapter 2).

2 If the oil pressure warning light does not come on when the ignition is turned ON, but the LCD display and LEDs otherwise appear to be functioning, pull the rubber cover off the switch and undo the screw securing the wiring connector **(see illustration)**. With the ignition switched ON, earth (ground) the wire on the crankcase and check that the warning light comes on. If it does, the switch is defective and must be replaced with a new one.

3 If the light still does not come on, check for voltage at the wiring connector. If there is no voltage present, check the wire between the switch and the instrument cluster for continuity (see the wiring diagrams at the end of this Chapter). If all is good, the LED in the instrument cluster could be faulty.

4 If the warning light does not go out when the engine is started or comes on whilst the engine is running, yet the oil pressure is satisfactory, detach the wire from the oil pressure switch (see above). With the wire detached and the ignition switched ON the light should be out. If it is illuminated, the wire between the switch and instrument cluster is earthed (grounded) at some point. If the wiring is good, the switch must be assumed faulty and replaced with a new one.

Removal

5 The oil pressure switch is screwed into the front of the crankcase on the right-hand side. If required drain the engine oil (see Chapter 1), but note that if the bike is on its sidestand you should get away with just having a pan under the switch to catch any oil that comes out.

6 Pull the rubber cover off the switch, then undo the screw securing the wiring connector **(see illustration 17.2)**.

7 Unscrew and remove the switch **(see illustration)**.

17.7 Unscrew and remove the switch

Installation

8 Apply a suitable silicone sealant to the upper portion of the switch threads near the switch body, leaving the bottom 3 to 4 mm of thread clean. Install the switch and tighten it to the torque setting specified at the beginning of the Chapter. Attach the wiring connector and secure it with the screw, then smear it with grease. Fit the rubber cover **(see illustration 17.2)**.

9 Run the engine and check that the switch operates correctly without leakage.

10 Top the engine up with oil as required (see Chapter 1 and/or *Pre-ride checks*).

18 Ignition switch

⚠ **Warning: To prevent the risk of short circuits, disconnect the battery negative (–) lead before making any ignition switch checks.**

Check

1 Remove the fuel tank (see Chapter 4). Trace the wiring from the ignition switch and disconnect it at the connector **(see illustration)**. On ZR750-L/M and ZR1000-B/C

18.1a Ignition switch wiring connector (arrowed) – ZR750-J, ZR1000-A

18.1b On ZR750-L/M and ZR1000-B/C models detach the reservoir hose and place it aside . . .

18.1c . . . then lift and pull back the rubber boot (arrowed) . . .

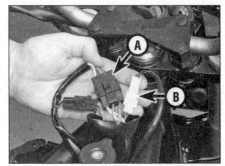
18.1d . . . to access the wiring connectors – ignition switch (A), immobiliser receiver (B)

models detach the reservoir hose from the filler neck to access the wiring boot below it – keep the hose above the level of the reservoir or it will drain.

2 Using an ohmmeter or a continuity tester, check the continuity of the connector terminal pairs (see the wiring diagrams at the end of this Chapter). Continuity should exist between the terminals connected by a solid line on the diagram when the switch is in the indicated position.

3 If the switch fails any of the tests, replace it with a new one.

Removal

Note: *For security the ignition switch is held by two shear-head bolts, which means they cannot be unscrewed using conventional*

tools (see Step 9). New bolts of the same type should be obtained before starting work.

4 Remove the fairing (see Chapter 7), the fuel tank (see Chapter 4), and the instrument cluster (see Chapter 8). Unscrew the bolts securing the fairing bracket to the top yoke **(see illustration)**.

5 Trace the wiring from the ignition switch, and where fitted the immobiliser receiver, and disconnect it/them at the connector **(see illustrations 18.1a or b, c and d)**. Feed the wiring back to the switch, freeing it from any clips and ties and noting its routing.

6 Displace the handlebars from the top yoke (see Chapter 5). Slacken the fork clamp bolts in the top yoke **(see illustration)**.

7 Remove the plug from the steering stem bolt **(see illustration)**. Unscrew the bolt and remove the washer **(see illustration)**.

8 Gently ease the top yoke up off the forks and remove it **(see illustration)**.

9 Secure the yoke in a soft-jawed vice with plenty of rag to protect it, then tap the bolt heads around using a suitable chisel or punch until loose **(see illustration)**. Unscrew the bolts and withdraw the switch from the top yoke.

10 Where fitted remove the immobiliser receiver (see Chapter 4).

Installation

11 Installation is the reverse of removal. Tighten the new ignition switch bolts until their heads shear off. Make sure the wiring connector is correctly routed and securely connected.

12 Fit the top yoke onto the steering stem **(see illustration 18.8)**. Install the steering

18.4 Unscrew the bracket bolts (arrowed)

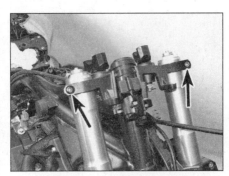
18.6 Slacken the fork clamp bolts (arrowed)

18.7a Remove the plug . . .

18.7b . . . then unscrew the bolt and remove the washer

18.8 Ease the yoke up off the forks

18.9 Ignition switch security screws (arrowed)

18.12a Fit the bolt with its washer . . .

18.12b . . . and tighten it to the specified torque

stem bolt with its washer and tighten it to the torque setting specified at the beginning of the Chapter (see illustrations). Fit the plug into the bolt (see illustration 18.7a). Tighten the fork clamp bolts to the specified torque (see illustration 18.6).
13 Bolt the fairing bracket to the top yoke (see illustration 18.4). Install the handlebars (see Chapter 5).
14 Install the fuel tank (see Chapter 4), the instrument cluster (see Chapter 8), and the fairing (see Chapter 7).

19 Handlebar switches

Check

1 Generally speaking, the switches are

19.3c . . . to access the wiring connectors

reliable and trouble-free. Most troubles, when they do occur, are caused by dirty or corroded contacts, but wear and breakage of internal parts is a possibility that should not be overlooked. If breakage does occur, the entire switch and related wiring harness will have to be replaced with a new one, as individual parts are not available.
2 The switches can be checked for continuity using a multimeter or continuity tester.
3 On ZR1000-B/C models remove the windshield, and on all other models remove the fairing, to access the switch wiring connectors (see Chapter 7). Trace the wiring from the relevant switch and disconnect it at the connector(s) (see illustrations).
4 Check for continuity between the terminals of the switch connector with the switch in the various positions (i.e. switch off – no continuity, switch on – continuity) – see the

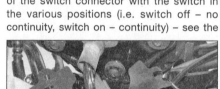

19.3a Switch wiring connectors (arrowed) – ZR1000-B/C

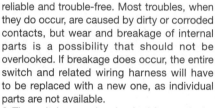

19.3b On ZR750-J and ZR1000-A models displace the rubber cover . . .

19.8a Right-hand switch housing screws (arrowed) – ZR1000-B/C

wiring diagrams at the end of this Chapter. Continuity should exist between the terminals connected by a solid line on the diagram when the switch is in the indicated position.
5 If the continuity check indicates a problem exists, displace the switch housing (step 10) and spray the switch contacts with electrical contact cleaner (there is no need to remove the switch completely). If they are accessible, the contacts can be scraped clean and polished with crocus cloth. If switch components are damaged or broken, it will be obvious when the switch is disassembled.

Removal

6 On ZR1000-B/C models remove the windshield, and on all other models remove the fairing, to access the switch wiring connectors (see Chapter 7). Trace the wiring from the relevant switch and disconnect it at the connector(s) (see illustrations 19.3a, b and c). Feed the wiring back to the switch, freeing it from any clips and ties and noting its routing.
7 If removing the right-hand switch disconnect the wiring connector(s) from the brake light switch (see illustration 14.2). If removing the left-hand switch disconnect the wiring connector from the clutch switch (see illustration 22.2).
8 On all Z750 models and the ZR1000-A, refer to Chapter 4 for the right-hand switch housing, which involves detaching the throttle cables. On ZR750-J and ZR1000-A models refer to Chapter 4 for the left-hand switch housing, which involves detaching the fast idle cable and lever. Otherwise unscrew the two handlebar switch screws and free the switch from the handlebar by separating the halves (see illustrations).

Installation

9 Installation is the reverse of removal. Make sure the locating pin in the switch housing locates in the hole in the handlebar. Where applicable refer to Chapter 4 for installation of the throttle cables, fast idle cable and lever if required.

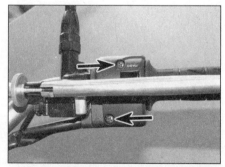

19.8b Left-hand switch housing screws (arrowed) – ZR750-L/M, ZR1000-B/C

20 Neutral switch

Check

1 The switch is located in the left-hand side of the transmission casing below the front sprocket cover. The switch is part of the starter interlock safety circuit which prevents or stops the engine running if the transmission is in gear whilst the sidestand is down, and prevents the engine from starting if the transmission is in gear unless the sidestand is up, and unless the clutch is pulled in.
2 Detach the wiring connector from the switch **(see illustration)**. Make sure the transmission is in neutral.
3 With the connector disconnected and the ignition switch ON, the neutral light should be out. If not, the wire between the connector and instrument cluster must be earthed (grounded) at some point.
4 Check for continuity between the switch terminal and the crankcase. With the transmission in neutral, there should be continuity. With the transmission in gear, there should be no continuity. If the tests prove otherwise, then remove the switch (see below) and check whether the plunger is bent or damaged, or just stuck **(see illustration)**. Replace the switch with a new one if necessary.
5 If the continuity tests prove the switch is good, check for voltage at the wire terminal with the ignition ON. If there's no voltage present, check the wire between the switch and the instrument cluster (see the wiring diagrams at the end of this Chapter). If all is good, the LED in the instrument cluster could be faulty.
6 If necessary also check the other components and the wiring and connectors between them in the starter circuit, namely the sidestand switch (Section 21), clutch switch (Section 22), and the starter circuit relay and diodes (Section 23) – see the wiring diagrams at the end of this Chapter.

Removal and installation

7 The switch is located in the left-hand side

20.2 Pull the wiring connector off the switch

of the transmission casing below the front sprocket cover.
8 Detach the wiring connector from the switch **(see illustration 20.2)**. Make sure the transmission is in neutral.
9 Clean the area around the switch, then unscrew it from the crankcase. Discard the sealing washer as a new one should be used.
10 Install the switch using a new washer and tighten it to the torque setting specified at the beginning of the Chapter.
11 Connect the wiring connector and check the operation of the neutral light **(see illustration 20.2)**.

21 Sidestand switch

Check

1 The sidestand switch is mounted on the stand pivot. The switch is part of the starter interlock safety circuit which prevents or stops the engine running if the transmission is in gear whilst the sidestand is down, and prevents the engine from starting if the transmission is in gear unless the sidestand is up, and unless the clutch is pulled in.
2 Trace the wiring back from the switch and disconnect at the wiring connector **(see illustrations)** – remove the frame cover if required to improve access (see Chapter 7).
3 Check the operation of the switch using an ohmmeter or continuity test light. Connect the

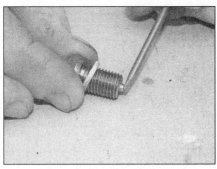

20.4 Make sure the plunger moves in and out smoothly and freely

meter between the terminals on the switch side of the connector. With the sidestand up there should be continuity (zero resistance) between the terminals, and with the stand down there should be no continuity (infinite resistance).
4 If the switch does not perform as expected, it is faulty and must be replaced with a new one.
5 If the switch is good, check for voltage at the green/white wire terminal on the loom side of the connector with the ignition ON – there should be battery voltage. Check for continuity to earth in the black/yellow wire on the loom side of the connector – there should be continuity. Also check the other components and the wiring and connectors between them in the starter circuit, namely the neutral switch (Section 20), clutch switch (Section 22), and the starter circuit relay and diodes (Section 23) – see the wiring diagrams at the end of this Chapter.

Replacement

6 The sidestand switch is mounted on the stand bracket. Trace the wiring back from the switch and disconnect at the wiring connector **(see illustration 21.2a or b)** – remove the frame cover if required to improve access (see Chapter 7). Feed the wiring back to the switch, freeing it from any clips and ties and noting its routing.
7 Undo the switch bolt and remove the switch, noting how it fits **(see illustration)**.
8 Fit the new switch, making sure the arm locates correctly under the post on the stand

21.2a Sidestand switch wiring connector (arrowed) – ZR750-J, ZR1000-A

21.2b Sidestand switch wiring connector – ZR750-L/M, ZR1000-B/C

21.7 Sidestand switch mounting bolt (arrowed)

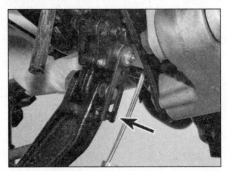

21.8 Make sure the arm locates correctly (arrowed)

(see illustration). Clean the threads on the bolt and apply a suitable non-permanent thread locking compound, and tighten it to the torque setting specified at the beginning of the Chapter (see illustration 21.7).
9 Feed the wiring up to its connector, making sure it is correctly routed and secured by any clips.
10 Reconnect the wiring connector and check the operation of the sidestand switch (see illustration 21.2a or b).

22 Clutch switch

Check

1 The clutch switch is mounted under the clutch lever bracket. The switch is part of the starter interlock safety circuit which prevents or stops the engine running if the transmission is in gear whilst the sidestand is down, and prevents the engine from starting if the transmission is in gear unless the sidestand is up and the clutch lever is pulled in. The switch isn't adjustable.
2 To check the switch, disconnect the wiring connector from it (see illustration). Connect the probes of an ohmmeter or a continuity tester to the two switch terminals. With the clutch lever pulled in, continuity should be indicated. With the clutch lever out, no continuity (infinite resistance) should be indicated.
3 If the switch is good, check for voltage at the red/green wire on the connector with the ignition switch ON – there should be battery voltage. If there's no voltage present, check the wiring between the connector and the ECU (see the wiring diagrams at the end of this Chapter). If voltage is present, check the green/white wire for continuity to the sidestand switch, referring to the relevant wiring diagram. Repair or renew the wiring as necessary.
4 If the switch and wiring good, check the other components and the wiring and connectors between them in the starter circuit, namely the neutral switch (Section 20), sidestand switch (Section 21), and the starter circuit relay and diodes (Section 23) – see the wiring diagrams at the end of this Chapter.

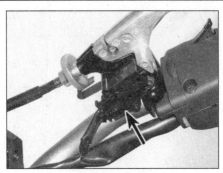

22.2 Clutch switch (arrowed)

Removal and installation

5 The clutch switch is mounted under the clutch lever bracket.
6 Disconnect the wiring connector from the switch (see illustration 22.2).
7 Undo the screws securing the switch and remove it, noting how it fits.
8 Installation is the reverse of removal. Make sure the switch is correctly located.

23 Starter interlock circuit relay and diodes

1 The relay and diodes are housed in the junction box on ZR750-J and ZR1000-A models and in the relay box on ZR750-L/M and ZR1000-B/C models. The diodes are part of the starter interlock safety circuit that prevents or stops the engine running if the transmission is in gear whilst the sidestand is down, and prevents the engine from starting if the transmission is in gear unless the sidestand is up and the clutch lever is pulled in.
2 To check the relay and diodes, on ZR750-J and ZR1000-A models remove the rider's seat (see Chapter 7), then lift the junction box off its holder and disconnect the wiring connectors (see illustration 6.6a). On ZR750-L/M and ZR1000-B/C models remove the left-hand side of the seat cowling (see Chapter 7). Unscrew the passenger seat bracket bolts and displace the bracket, then draw the relay box from its holder and disconnect the wiring connectors (see illustrations 5.5a and 6.6b).

ZR750-J and ZR1000-A

3 Set a multimeter to the ohms x 1 scale and connect its probes to terminals 9 and 11 on the relay box, then to terminals 12 and 13 (see illustration 6.7). There should be no continuity (infinite resistance) in each case. Using a fully-charged 12 volt battery and two insulated jumper wires, connect the positive (+) terminal of the battery to terminal 11 on the relay box, and the negative (–) terminal to terminal 12. There should now be continuity on the multimeter between terminals 11 and 13. If this is the case the relay is proven good.

4 If the relay still indicates no continuity (infinite resistance) across terminals 11 and 13, it is faulty and the junction box must be replaced with a new one – individual components are not available.
5 If the relay is good now check the diodes in the circuit using an ohmmeter. First connect the positive (+) probe to terminal 11 and the negative (–) to terminal 12 – the diode should show continuity. Now reverse the probes. The diode should show no continuity. Repeat the tests between terminals 14 and 12, then between 14 and 15, then between 14 and 16. The same results should be achieved. If the diodes don't behave as stated, replace the junction box with a new one.
6 There is another diode for the neutral switch circuit taped in the loom behind the fairing – remove the fairing (see Chapter 7), then cut the insulating tape covering the diode and unplug it from its connector (see illustrations 19.3b and c). First connect the positive (+) probe to one terminal and the negative (–) to the other, then reverse the probes. The diode should show continuity in one direction and no continuity in the other. If not, replace it with a new one. If the diode is good check for voltage at the red/green wire terminal in the diode connector with the ignition ON – there should be battery voltage. If there's no voltage present, check the wiring between the connector and the ECU (see the wiring diagrams at the end of this Chapter). If voltage is present, check the light green wire for continuity to the neutral switch, referring to the relevant wiring diagram. Repair or renew the wiring as necessary.

ZR750-L/M and ZR1000-B/C

7 Set a multimeter to the ohms x 1 scale and connect its probes to terminals 16 and 11 (see illustration 6.8). There should be no continuity (infinite resistance). Now connect to terminals 11 and 12. There should be no continuity. Using a fully-charged 12 volt battery and two insulated jumper wires, connect the positive (+) terminal of the battery to terminal 16, and the negative (–) terminal to terminal 12. At this point the multimeter should read 0 ohms (continuity) between terminals 11 and 12. If this is the case the relay is proven good.
8 If the relay still indicates no continuity (infinite resistance), it is faulty and the relay box must be replaced with a new one – individual relays are not available.
9 If the relay is good, now check the diodes in the circuit using an ohmmeter. First connect the positive (+) probe to terminal 12 and the negative (–) to terminal 15 – the diode should show continuity. Now reverse the probes. The diode should show no continuity. Repeat the tests between the terminals 13 and 15, then between 13 and 14, 13 and 12, and 16 and 12. The same results should be achieved. If the diodes don't behave as stated, replace the relay box with a new one.

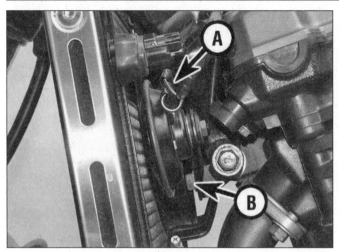

24.2a Horn wiring connectors (A) and mounting bolt (B) – ZR750-J

24.2b Horn wiring connectors (arrowed) . . .

24 Horn

Check

1 The horn is behind or below the radiator, depending on the model. First check the horn circuit fuse (see Section 5).
2 Disconnect the wiring connectors from the horn (see illustrations). Check them for loose wires. Using two jumper wires, apply voltage from a fully-charged 12V battery directly to the terminals on the horn. If the horn doesn't sound, replace it with a new one.
3 If the horn works when connected directly to a battery check for voltage at the brown/black wire connector with the ignition ON and the horn button pressed.
4 If no voltage was present, check the brown/black wire from the switch to the fusebox, and then to the ignition switch, and the black/white wire for continuity between the horn and the horn button (see the wiring diagrams at the end of this Chapter and Section 19 for access to the horn button). If all is good check the black/yellow wire from the horn button to earth.
5 If all the wiring and connectors are good, check the button contacts in the switch housing.

25.4a Displace the starter relay . . .

Replacement

6 The horn is behind or below the radiator, depending on the model.
7 Disconnect the wiring connectors from the horn (see illustration 24.2a or b). Unscrew the horn bracket bolt and remove the horn, noting how the bracket locates (see illustration 24.2c).
8 Fit the horn and tighten the bolt. Connect the wiring. Check that it works.

25 Starter motor relay

Check

1 On ZR750-J and ZR1000-A models the starter motor relay is located behind the right-hand side panel (see illustration 5.2) – remove the panel to access it (see Chapter 7).
2 On ZR750-L/M and ZR1000-B/C models the starter motor relay is located under the passenger seat bracket – to access the relay remove the left-hand side of the seat cowling (see Chapter 7). Unscrew the passenger seat bracket bolts and displace the bracket (see illustration 5.5a).
3 If the starter circuit is faulty, first check the main fuse (see Section 5).

25.4b . . . and lift the cover to access the terminals

24.2c . . . and mounting bolt (arrowed) – ZR1000-B/C

4 Displace the relay from its mount (see illustration). Lift the rubber terminal cover and unscrew the bolt securing the starter motor lead (see illustration); position the lead away from the relay terminal. With the ignition switch ON, the engine kill switch in the RUN position, and the transmission in neutral, press the starter switch. The relay should be heard to click.
5 If the relay doesn't click, switch off the ignition and remove the relay as described below; test it as follows.
6 Set a multimeter to the ohms x 1 scale and connect it across the relay's starter motor and battery lead terminals. There should be no continuity. Using a fully-charged 12 volt battery and two insulated jumper wires, connect the positive (+) terminal of the battery to the yellow/red wire terminal of the relay, and the negative (–) terminal to the black/yellow wire terminal of the relay. At this point the relay should be heard to click and the multimeter read 0 ohms (continuity). If this is the case the relay is proved good. If the relay does not click when battery voltage is applied and indicates no continuity (infinite resistance) across its terminals, it is faulty and must be replaced with a new one.
7 If the relay is good, check the heavy gauge cable from the battery to the relay, and from

25.13 Disconnect the wiring connector and unscrew the terminal bolts (arrowed)

26.3 Pull back the terminal cover then undo the screw and detach the lead

the relay to the starter motor, particularly that their terminals are tight and corrosion-free.

8 Next check for battery voltage at the yellow/red wire terminal on the relay wiring connector with the ignition ON, the kill switch in the RUN position, gearbox in neutral, and the starter button pressed. If there is no voltage, check the wiring to the junction or relay box (according to model), then check the starter circuit relay (Section 23).

9 If voltage is present, check that there is continuity to earth in the black/yellow wire. If not check the wiring and connectors.

Replacement

10 On ZR750-J and ZR1000-A models the starter motor relay is located behind the right-hand side panel **(see illustration 5.2)** – remove the panel to access it (see Chapter 7).

11 On ZR750-L/M and ZR1000-B/C models the starter motor relay is located under the passenger seat bracket – to access the relay remove the left-hand side of the seat cowling (see Chapter 7). Unscrew the passenger seat bracket bolts and displace the bracket **(see illustration 5.5a)**.

12 Disconnect the battery terminals, remembering to disconnect the negative (–) terminal first.

13 Displace the relay from its mount **(see illustration 25.4a)**. Disconnect the relay wiring connector, then lift the insulating cover and unscrew the bolts securing the starter motor and battery leads to the relay and detach the leads **(see illustration)**. Remove the relay from its rubber sleeve. If the relay is being replaced with a new one, remove the main fuse, and its spare where fitted, from the relay.

14 Installation is the reverse of removal. Make sure the terminal bolts are securely tightened. Do not forget to fit the main fuse and its spare into the relay. Connect the negative (–) lead last when reconnecting the battery.

26 Starter motor removal and installation

Removal

1 Remove the rider's seat (see Chapter 7).

Disconnect the battery negative (–) lead. The starter motor is mounted on the crankcase behind the cylinders.

2 On ZR750-L/M and ZR1000-B/C models drain the cooling system (see Chapter 1). Refer to Chapter 3 and detach the coolant outlet pipe from the top of the water pump and the hose it connects to from the cylinder block and remove the hose/pipe as one. On ZR750-J and ZR1000-A models you should be able to remove the starter motor with the hose and pipe in place, but remove them if required for improved access.

3 Peel back the rubber terminal cover on the starter motor. Undo the nut securing the starter lead to the motor and detach the lead **(see illustration)**.

4 Unscrew the two bolts securing the starter motor to the crankcase **(see illustration)**. Slide the starter motor out and remove it **(see illustration)** – if it is tight apply gentle leverage with a screwdriver.

5 Remove the O-ring on the end of the starter motor and discard it as a new one must be used.

26.4a Unscrew the two bolts (arrowed) . . .

26.4b . . . and remove the starter motor

26.6 Fit a new O-ring and lubricate it

27.4 Note the alignment marks between the housing and the covers or make your own

27.5a Unscrew and remove the two bolts . . .

Installation

6 Fit a new O-ring onto the end of the starter motor, making sure it is seated in its groove (see illustration). Apply a smear of engine oil to the O-ring. Make sure the bottom of the mounting lugs on the motor and tops of the mounts on the engine are clean.
7 Manoeuvre the motor into position and slide it into the crankcase (see illustration 26.4b). Ensure that the starter motor teeth mesh correctly with those of the starter idle/reduction gear. Install the mounting bolts and tighten them to the torque setting specified at the beginning of the Chapter (see illustration 26.4a).
8 Connect the starter lead to the motor and secure it with the screw (see illustration 26.3). Fit the rubber cover over the terminal.
9 Refer to Chapters 3 and 1 for installation of the coolant pipe and hose and to refill the system.
10 Connect the battery negative (–) lead and install the rider's seat (see Chapter 7).

27 Starter motor overhaul

Check

1 Remove the starter motor (see Section 26).

Cover the body in some rag and clamp the motor in a soft-jawed vice – do not overtighten it.
2 Using a fully-charged 12 volt battery and two insulated jumper wires, connect the positive (+) terminal of the battery to the protruding terminal on the rear cover of the starter motor, and the negative (–) terminal to one of the motor's mounting lugs. At this point the starter motor should spin. If this is the case the motor is proved good, though it is worth disassembling it and checking it if you suspect it of not working properly under load.

Disassembly

3 Remove the starter motor (see Section 26).
4 Note any alignment marks between the main housing and the front and rear covers, or make your own if they aren't clear (see illustration).
5 Unscrew the two long bolts, noting the O-rings, then remove the front cover from the motor along with its sealing ring (see illustrations). If fitted remove the tabbed washer (from the cover or the armature shaft) and slide the shim(s) off the shaft.
6 Draw the main housing off the armature – it is held in by the attraction of the magnets, so hold the armature in place while you remove the housing (see illustration).
7 Draw the armature out of the rear cover,

noting how the brushes locate on the commutator (see illustration). Remove any shims.
8 Slide the terminal bolt brush out of its housing.
9 At this stage check for continuity between the (terminal bolt) and the positive brush – there should be continuity (zero resistance). Check for continuity between the terminal bolt and the cover – there should be no continuity (infinite resistance). Similarly check for continuity between the terminal bolt and the brushplate – there should be no continuity (infinite resistance). Also check for continuity between the negative brush and the brushplate – there should be continuity (zero resistance). If there is no continuity when there should be or vice versa, replace the brushplate assembly and/or terminal bolt assembly with a new one.
10 Remove the brushplate from the rear cover noting how it locates (see illustration 27.19a). Unscrew the nut on the terminal bolt then remove the outer insulator and the O-ring (see illustrations 27.18d and c). Withdraw the bolt and remove the inner insulator (see illustrations 27.18b and a).

Inspection

11 The parts of the starter motor that are most likely to require attention are the brushes. Measure the length of each brush and compare

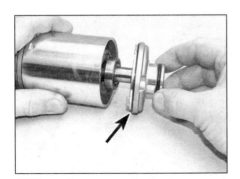

27.5b . . . then remove the front cover and sealing ring (arrowed)

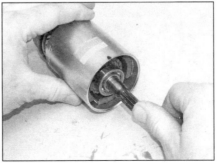

27.6 Draw the housing off the armature . . .

27.7 . . . then draw the armature out of the rear cover

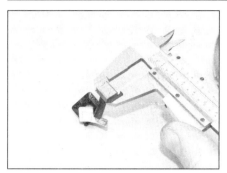

27.11 Measure the length of each brush

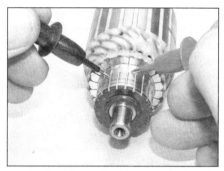

27.13a There should be continuity between the bars . . .

27.13b . . . and no continuity between the bars and the shaft

27.15a Check the seal in the front cover and the bearing (arrowed) on the shaft . . .

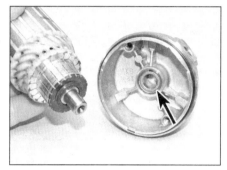

27.15b . . . and the bush (arrowed) in the rear cover

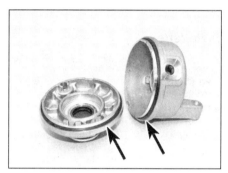

27.17 Fit new cover sealing rings (arrowed) if necessary

the results to the length listed in this Chapter's Specifications **(see illustration)**. If any of the brushes are worn beyond the service limit, replace the rear brushplate and terminal bolt assemblies with new ones – individual components (with the exception of the brush springs) are not available. If the brushes are not worn excessively, nor cracked, chipped, or otherwise damaged, they may be reused.

12 Inspect the commutator bars on the armature for scoring, scratches and discoloration. The commutator can be cleaned and polished with crocus cloth, but do not use sandpaper or emery paper. After cleaning, wipe away any residue with a cloth soaked in electrical system cleaner or denatured alcohol.

13 Using an ohmmeter or a continuity test light, check for continuity between the commutator bars **(see illustration)**. Continuity should exist between each bar and all of the

others. Also, check for continuity between the commutator bars and the armature shaft **(see illustration)**. There should be no continuity (infinite resistance) between the commutator and the shaft. If the checks indicate otherwise, the armature is defective and a new starter motor must be obtained – the armature is not available separately.

14 Check the front end of the armature shaft for worn, cracked, chipped and broken teeth. If the shaft is damaged or worn, a new starter motor must be obtained – the armature is not available separately.

15 Inspect the front and rear covers for signs of cracks or wear. Check the oil seal in the front cover, the bearing on the armature shaft, and the bush in the rear cover for wear and damage **(see illustrations)** – the seal, bearing, front cover, rear cover and bush are not listed as being available separately, so if necessary a new starter motor must be fitted,

but note that aftermarket seals and bearings are readily available from good suppliers, you just need to remove the old ones and note the size markings.

16 Inspect the magnets in the main housing and the housing itself for cracks.

17 Inspect the O-rings and sealing rings for signs of damage, deformation and deterioration and replace them with new ones if necessary **(see illustration)** – Kawasaki specify that new ones should be used as a matter of course.

Reassembly

18 Fit the sealing ring onto the rear cover **(see illustration 27.17)**. Fit the inner insulator piece into the rear cover **(see illustration)**. Insert the terminal bolt, then carefully feed the O-ring down bolt so it sits around its base between it and the rear cover **(see illustrations)**. Fit the

27.18a Fit the inner insulator . . .

27.18b . . . the terminal bolt . . .

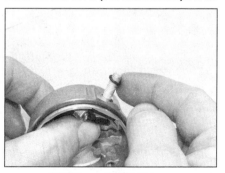

27.18c . . . the O-ring . . .

27.18d . . . the outer insulator (arrowed) and the nut

27.19a Fit the brush into its housing . . .

27.19b . . . then fit the brushplate onto the rear cover, aligning the notches (arrowed)

outer insulator then fit and tighten the nut **(see illustration)**. Make sure the brush springs are correctly fitted. Slide the negative brush into its housing if necessary.

19 Fit the brushplate onto the rear cover, locating the positive brush into its housing as you do, and aligning the notches between plate and cover **(see illustrations)**.

20 Apply a smear of grease to the end of the shaft. Fit any shims that were removed **(see illustration)**. Insert the armature into the rear cover at an angle so the brushes locate against the commutator, then push the brushes back into their housings and the end of the shaft in the bush **(see illustration)**.

21 Grasp both the armature and the rear cover in one hand and hold them together – this will prevent the armature being drawn out by the magnets in the housing **(see illustration)**. Note however that you should take care not to let the housing be drawn forcibly onto the armature by the magnets. Carefully allow the housing to be drawn onto the armature, making sure the end with the indent faces the rear cover and aligns with the raised tabs – aligning the marks between the cover and housing (Step 4) will help.

22 Apply a smear of grease to the front cover oil seal lip. Where fitted locate the tabbed washer into the cover so that its teeth are correctly engaged with the cover ribs and slide the shim(s) onto the front end of the armature shaft. Fit the sealing ring onto the front cover **(see illustration 27.17)**.

23 Slide the front cover into position, aligning the marks made on removal **(see illustration)**.

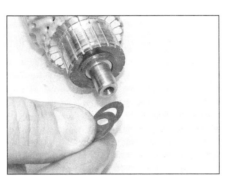

27.20a Fit the shims onto the shaft . . .

27.20b . . . then fit the armature into the rear cover making sure the brushes locate correctly onto the commutator

24 Check the marks made on removal are correctly aligned then fit the long bolts, not forgetting the O-rings (using new ones if necessary) and tighten them **(see illustration)**.

25 Install the starter motor (see Section 26).

28 Charging system testing

1 If the performance of the charging system is suspect, the system as a whole should be checked first, followed by testing of the individual components. **Note:** *Before beginning the checks, make sure the battery is fully charged and that all system connections are clean and tight.*

2 Checking the output of the charging

system and the performance of the various components within the charging system requires the use of a multimeter (with voltage, current, resistance checking facilities). If a multimeter is not available, the job of checking the charging system should be left to a Kawasaki dealer.

3 When making the checks, follow the procedures carefully to prevent incorrect connections or short circuits resulting in irreparable damage to electrical system components.

Leakage test

Caution: Always connect an ammeter in series, never in parallel with the battery, otherwise it will be damaged. Do not turn the ignition ON or operate the starter motor when the ammeter is connected – a sudden surge in current will blow the meter's fuse.

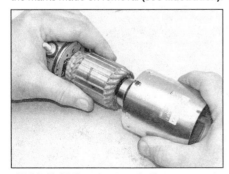

27.21 Hold the armature in the rear cover when fitting the housing

27.23 Fit the front cover . . .

27.24 . . . then fit the long bolts with their O-rings

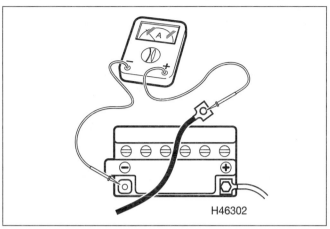

28.5 Checking the charging system leakage rate – connect the meter as shown

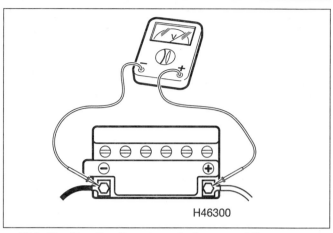

28.9 Checking the alternator output – connect the meter as shown

4 Ensure the ignition is OFF, then disconnect the battery negative (-) lead (see Section 3).

5 Set the multimeter to the Amps function and connect its negative (-) probe to the battery negative (-) terminal, and positive (+) probe to the disconnected negative (-) lead **(see illustration)**. Always set the meter to a high amps range initially and then bring it down to the mA (milli Amps) range; if there is a high current flow in the circuit it may blow the meter's fuse.

6 Battery current leakage should not exceed the maximum limit (see Specifications). If a higher leakage rate is shown there is a short circuit in the wiring, although if an alarm is fitted its current draw should be taken into account. Disconnect the meter and reconnect the battery negative (-) lead.

7 If leakage is indicated, refer to the wiring diagrams at the end of this Chapter to systematically disconnect individual electrical components and repeat the test until the source is identified.

Output test

8 Refer to Section 3 for access to the battery terminals. Start the engine and warm it up.

9 To check the regulated (DC) voltage output, allow the engine to idle. Connect a multimeter set to the 0 – 20 volts DC scale across the terminals of the battery with the positive (+) meter probe to battery positive (+) terminal and the negative (-) meter probe to battery negative (-) terminal **(see illustration)**.

10 Slowly increase the engine speed and note the reading obtained – it should rise from normal battery voltage as engine speed increases, reaching a maximum as specified at the beginning of this Chapter. If the regulated voltage output is outside the specification, check the alternator and the regulator (see Sections 29 and 30).

 HAYNES HiNT *Clues to a faulty regulator are constantly blowing bulbs, with brightness varying considerably with engine speed, and battery overheating.*

29 Alternator

Check

1 Remove the left-hand frame cover (see Chapter 7).

2 Trace the wiring from the alternator and disconnect it at the connector **(see illustrations)**. Check the connector terminals for corrosion and security.

3 Using a multimeter set to the ohms x 1 (ohmmeter) scale measure the resistance between each of the wires on the alternator side of the connector, taking a total of three readings, then check for continuity between each terminal and ground (earth). If the stator coil windings are in good condition the three readings should be within the range shown in the Specifications at the start of this Chapter, and there should be no continuity (infinite resistance) between any of the terminals and

29.2a Alternator wiring connector (arrowed) – ZR750-J, ZR1000-A

29.2b Alternator wiring connector (arrowed) – ZR750-L/M, ZR1000-B/C

29.7 Alternator cover bolts (arrowed)

29.8 Remove the idle/reduction gear and its shaft

ground (earth). If not, the alternator stator coil assembly is at fault and should be replaced with a new one. **Note:** *Before condemning the stator coils, check the fault is not due to damaged wiring between the connector and the coils.*

Removal

4 Remove the left-hand frame cover (see Chapter 7).
5 Either drain the engine oil (see Chapter 1), or place a container under the engine to catch the oil that will come out when the alternator cover is removed. If you have an auxiliary stand, place the bike on it so that it is level – this minimises oil loss. If you do not have an auxiliary stand it is best to drain the oil.
6 Trace the wiring from the alternator and disconnect it at the connector **(see illustration 29.2a or b)**. Feed the wiring down to the alternator, freeing it from any clips and noting its routing – on ZR750-L/M and ZR1000-B/C models due to the size and position of the connector, removal of the coolant outlet pipe from the water pump could well be necessary (according to Kawasaki). Refer to Chapter 1 to

drain the coolant, and to Chapter 3 to remove the pipe.
7 Working in a criss-cross pattern, evenly slacken the alternator cover bolts **(see illustration)**. Draw the cover off the engine, noting that it will be restrained by the force of the rotor magnets, and be prepared to catch any residual oil. Discard the gasket – a new one must be used. Remove the dowels from either the cover or the crankcase if they are loose.
8 Withdraw the idle/reduction gear shaft and remove the gear **(see illustration)**.
9 To remove the rotor bolt it is necessary to stop the rotor from turning. The best way is to use a commercially available rotor strap – make sure the rotor is free of oil and grease by cleaning it with solvent **(see illustration)**. If a rotor strap is not available, try placing the transmission in gear and having an assistant apply the rear brake hard. Unscrew the bolt. Note the washer fitted with the bolt and keep them together so the washer is installed the same way round.
10 To remove the rotor from the shaft it is necessary to use a rotor puller (Kawasaki part No. 57001-1405 or equivalent). Thread

29.9 Using a rotor strap to hold the rotor while unscrewing the bolt

the body of the rotor puller onto the hub of the rotor, then turn the bolt in its centre until the rotor is displaced from the shaft, holding the rotor to prevent the engine turning **(see illustration)**. Remove the Woodruff key from its slot **(see illustration 29.14)**.
11 To remove the stator from the cover, unscrew its bolts, and the bolt securing the wiring clamp, then remove the assembly, noting how the rubber wiring grommet fits **(see illustration)**.

29.10 Thread the puller onto the rotor then hold the rotor and turn the puller bolt

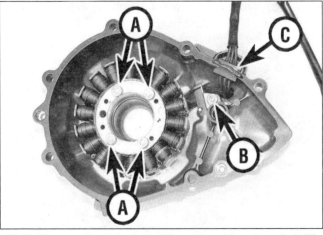

29.11 Unscrew the stator bolts (A) and the wiring clamp bolt (B) and free the grommet (C)

29.13 Clean the tapered section of the shaft

29.14 Fit the key into its slot (arrowed)

29.15 Slide the rotor onto the shaft and onto the gear hub – turn the gear clockwise to help the rotor fit

29.16a Fit the bolt with its washer . . .

29.16b . . . and tighten it as described

29.18a Apply sealant . . .

Installation

12 Clean all traces of old gasket and sealant from the cover and crankcase mating surfaces. Clean the threads of the stator and clamp bolts. Fit the stator into the cover, aligning the rubber wiring grommet with the groove **(see illustration 29.11)**. Apply a suitable non-permanent thread locking compound to the stator and wiring clamp bolts and tighten them to the torque setting specified at the beginning of the Chapter. Apply a suitable sealant to the wiring grommet, then press it into the cut-out in the cover.

13 Clean the tapered end of the crankshaft and the corresponding mating surface on the inside of the rotor thoroughly with a suitable solvent and a clean cloth **(see illustration)**.

14 Fit the Woodruff key into its slot in the crankshaft **(see illustration)**.
15 Make sure that no metal objects have attached themselves to the magnet on the inside of the rotor. Slide the rotor onto the shaft and the starter driven gear, turning the gear clockwise as you do **(see illustration)**.
16 Install the rotor bolt with its washer and tighten it to the initial torque setting specified at the beginning of the Chapter, using the method employed on removal to prevent the rotor from turning **(see illustrations)**. Now loosen and remove the bolt and its washer, then fit the rotor puller and check that its bolt can be tightened to 20 Nm without the rotor being displaced – if so the rotor is correctly installed. If not, remove the rotor, clean up the crankshaft and rotor bore and start again. With

the rotor correctly installed, fit the bolt with its washer and tighten it to the final torque setting specified.
17 Apply some clean oil to the idle/reduction gear shaft, then locate gear with its smaller pinion innermost and fit the shaft **(see illustration 29.8)**.
18 Apply a smear of suitable sealant to the crankcase joints and the wiring grommet **(see illustration)**. Fit the dowels into the crankcase if removed, then fit a new gasket onto them **(see illustration)**. Install the alternator cover, noting that the rotor magnets will forcibly draw the cover/stator on, making sure it locates onto the dowels **(see illustration)**. Tighten the cover bolts evenly in a criss-cross sequence to the specified torque setting.

29.18b . . . then fit the new gasket onto the dowels (arrowed) . . .

29.18c . . . and fit the cover

30.1a **Regulator/rectifier wiring connector (A) and mounting bolts (B) – ZR750-J, ZR1000-A**

30.1b **Regulator/rectifier wiring connector (arrowed) – ZR750-L/M, ZR1000-B/C**

19 Reconnect the wiring at the connector **(see illustration 29.2a or b)**.

20 Replenish the engine oil and check the level (see *Pre-ride checks*). On ZR750-L/M and ZR1000-B/C models refer to Chapters 3 and 1 for installation of the coolant pipe and hose and to refill the system.

30 Regulator/rectifier

Check

1 Disconnect the regulator/rectifier wiring connector **(see illustrations)**. Check the connector terminals for corrosion and security.

2 Set the multimeter to the 0 to 20 dc volts setting. Connect the meter positive (+) probe to the white wire terminal on the loom side of the connector and the negative (–) probe to a suitable ground (earth) and check for voltage. Full battery voltage should be present at all times (i.e. with the ignition OFF). Repeat the check at the brown wire terminal there should be voltage with the ignition switch ON. Also check for continuity to earth in the black/yellow wire.

3 If the above checks do not produce the expected results check the wiring and connectors between the battery, ignition switch and regulator/rectifier for shorts, breaks, and loose or corroded terminals (see the wiring diagrams at the end of this chapter).

4 Refer to Section 29, Step 3 and perform the same test between each of the black wire terminals on the loom side of the regulator/rectifier wiring connector. If the results are not as expected check the wiring between the regulator/rectifier connector and the alternator connector for continuity, and check for loose wires or terminals. If the wiring is good the stator could be faulty.

5 Switch the multimeter to the resistance (ohms) scale (x10 or x100). Connect the negative (-) probe to the white wire terminal on the regulator/rectifier, then connect the positive (+) probe to each of the three black wire terminals in turn – there should be no continuity (infinite resistance) in each case. Now reverse the probes and take three readings again – some resistance should be shown. Now repeat the checks between the black/yellow wire terminal and the three black wire terminals – the results should be the same values but the other way round (i.e. infinite resistance with the positive probe connected to the black/yellow wire, and a small resistance when connected to the negative).

6 If the results are not as specified, the regulator/rectifier unit is faulty.

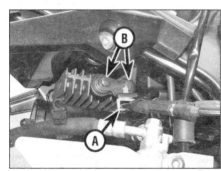

30.8 **On ZR750-L/M and ZR1000-B/C models free the guide (A) from the bracket then unscrew the bracket bolts (B)**

Removal and installation

7 Disconnect the regulator/rectifier wiring connector **(see illustrations 30.1a or b)**.

8 Unscrew the bolts securing the regulator/rectifier to its bracket and remove it. On ZR750-L/M and ZR1000-B/C models if access is restricted by the shock absorber for the tools you have available unscrew the bracket bolts and remove the regulator/rectifier with the bracket **(see illustration)** – first free the exhaust valve cable guide from the bracket, then unscrew the bolts and detach the regulator/rectifier from the bracket.

9 Installation is the reverse of removal.

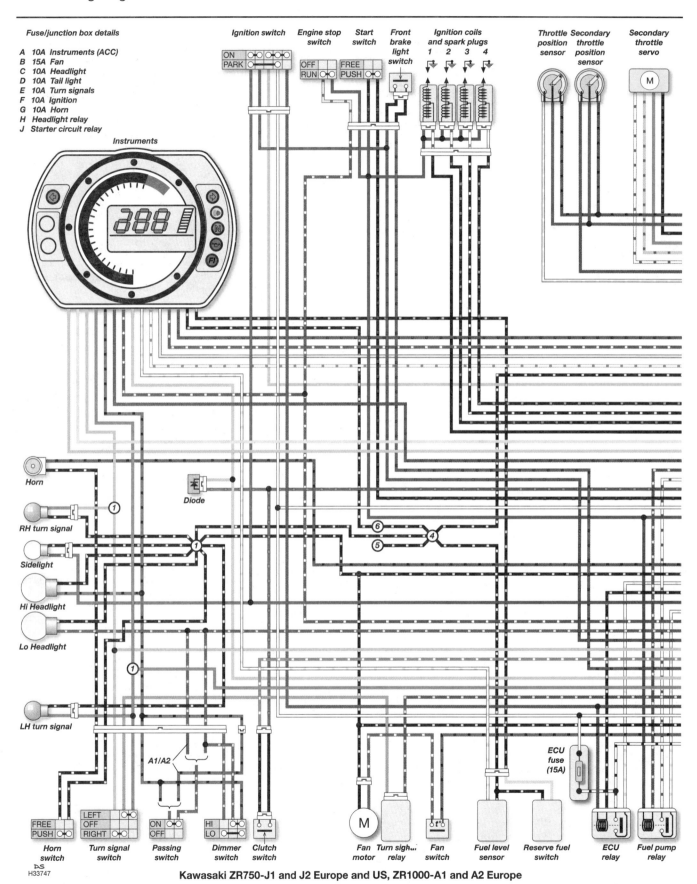

Kawasaki ZR750-J1 and J2 Europe and US, ZR1000-A1 and A2 Europe

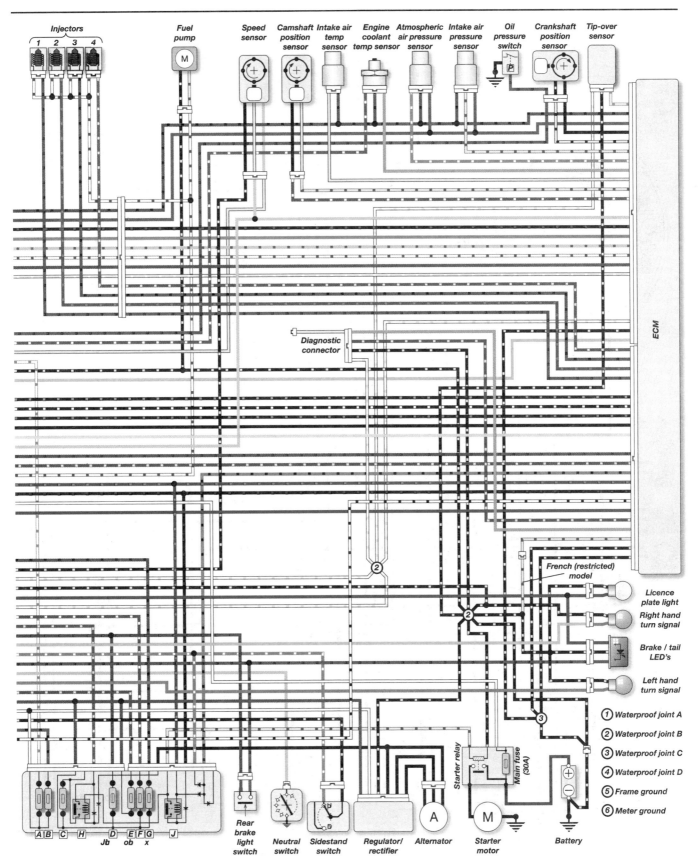

Kawasaki ZR750-J1 and J2 Europe and US, ZR1000-A1 and A2 Europe

H33747

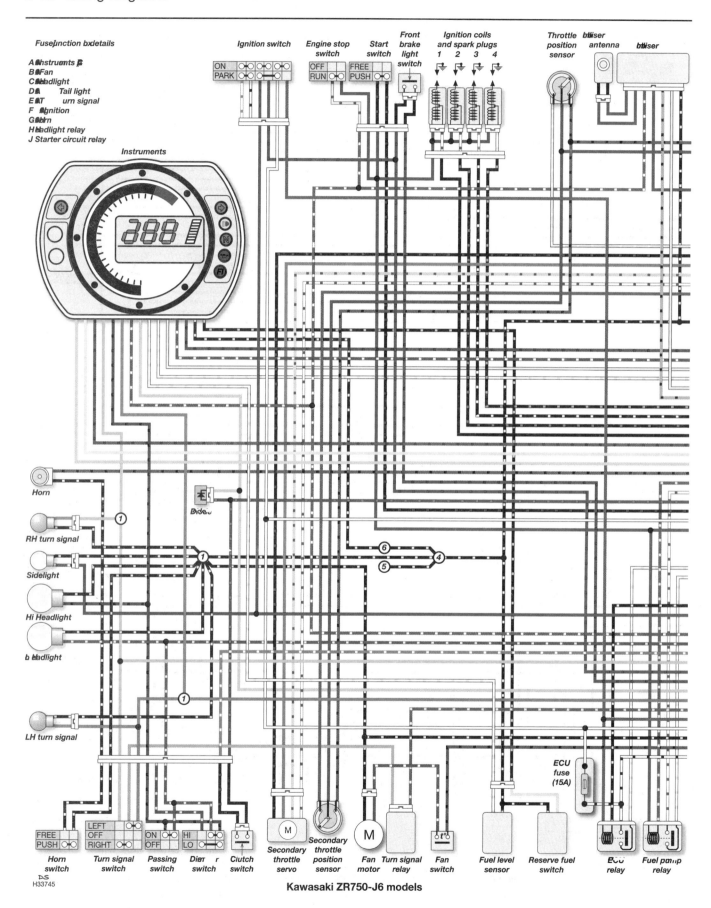

Kawasaki ZR750-J6 models

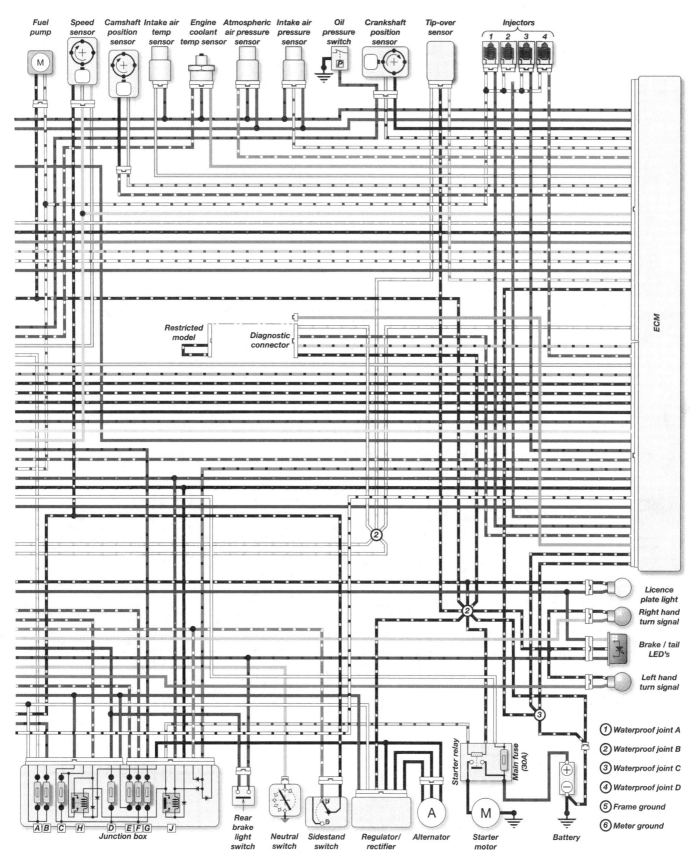

Kawasaki ZR750-J6 models

H33745

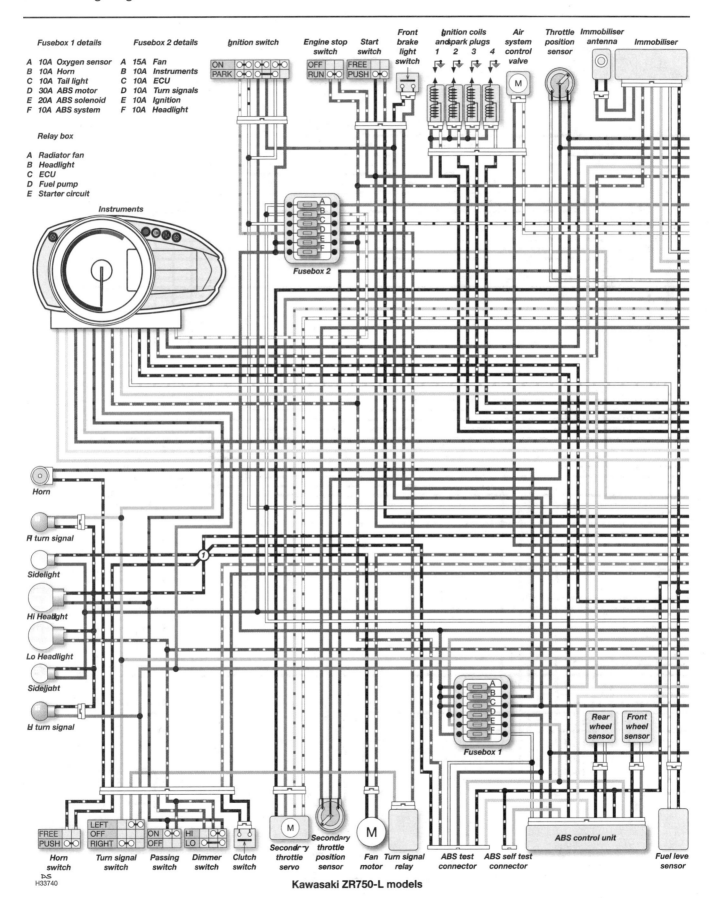

Fusebox 1 details

A 10A Oxygen sensor
B 10A Horn
C 10A Tail light
D 30A ABS motor
E 20A ABS solenoid
F 10A ABS system

Relay box

A Radiator fan
B Headlight
C ECU
D Fuel pump
E Starter circuit

Fusebox 2 details

A 15A Fan
B 10A Instruments
C 10A ECU
D 10A Turn signals
E 10A Ignition
F 10A Headlight

Ignition switch

Engine stop switch

Start switch

Front brake light switch

Ignition coils and spark plugs
1 2 3 4

Air system control valve

Throttle position sensor

Immobiliser antenna

Immobiliser

Instruments

Fusebox 2

Horn

R turn signal

Sidelight

Hi Headlight

Lo Headlight

Sidelight

R turn signal

Fusebox 1

Rear wheel sensor

Front wheel sensor

Horn switch

Turn signal switch

Passing switch

Dimmer switch

Clutch switch

Secondary throttle servo

Secondary throttle position sensor

Fan motor

Turn signal relay

ABS test connector

ABS self test connector

ABS control unit

Fuel level sensor

Kawasaki ZR750-L models

H33740

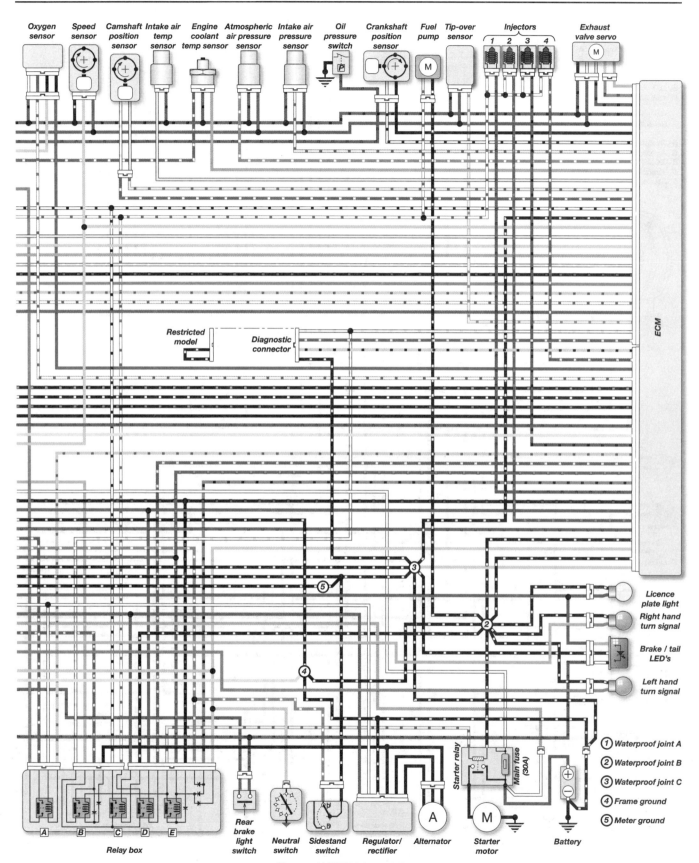

Kawasaki ZR750-L models

H33740

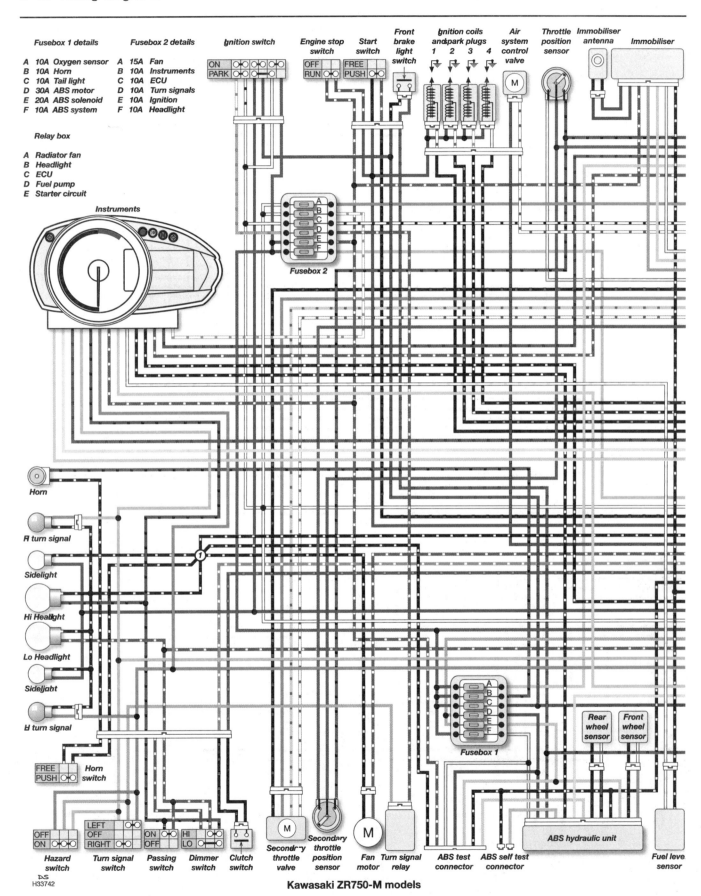

Kawasaki ZR750-M models

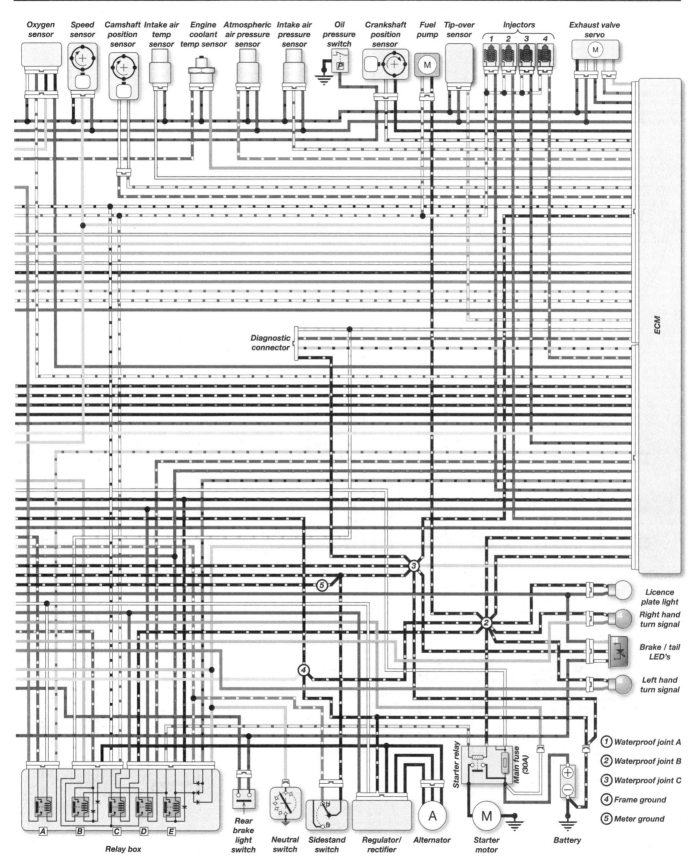

Oxygen sensor | Speed sensor | Camshaft position sensor | Intake air temp sensor | Engine coolant temp sensor | Atmospheric air pressure sensor | Intake air pressure sensor | Oil pressure switch | Crankshaft position sensor | Fuel pump | Tip-over sensor | Injectors 1 2 3 4 | Exhaust valve servo

ECM

Diagnostic connector

Licence plate light
Right hand turn signal
Brake / tail LED's
Left hand turn signal

① Waterproof joint A
② Waterproof joint B
③ Waterproof joint C
④ Frame ground
⑤ Meter ground

Relay box A B C D E

Rear brake light switch | Neutral switch | Sidestand switch | Regulator/ rectifier | Alternator | Starter motor | Battery

Starter relay
Main fuse (30A)

Kawasaki ZR750-M models

H33742

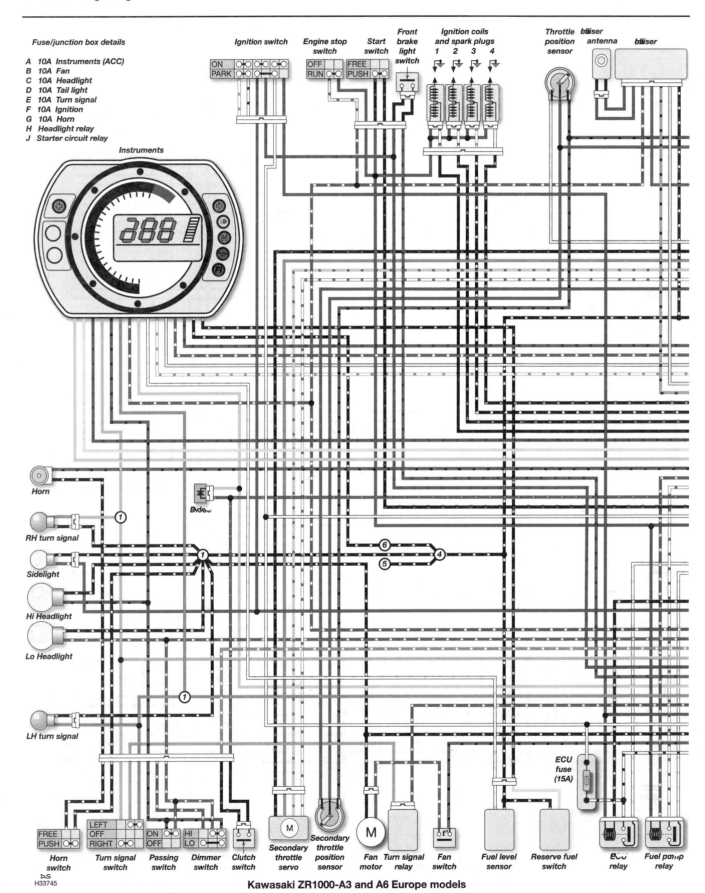

Fuse/junction box details

A 10A Instruments (ACC)
B 10A Fan
C 10A Headlight
D 10A Tail light
E 10A Turn signal
F 10A Ignition
G 10A Horn
H Headlight relay
J Starter circuit relay

Instruments

Ignition switch

Engine stop switch

Start switch

Front brake light switch

Ignition coils and spark plugs
1 2 3 4

Throttle position sensor

Immobiliser antenna

Immobiliser

Horn

RH turn signal

Sidelight

Hi Headlight

Lo Headlight

LH turn signal

ECU fuse (15A)

Horn switch

Turn signal switch

Passing switch

Dimmer switch

Clutch switch

Secondary throttle servo

Secondary throttle position sensor

Fan motor

Turn signal relay

Fan switch

Fuel level sensor

Reserve fuel switch

ECU relay

Fuel pump relay

H33745

Kawasaki ZR1000-A3 and A6 Europe models

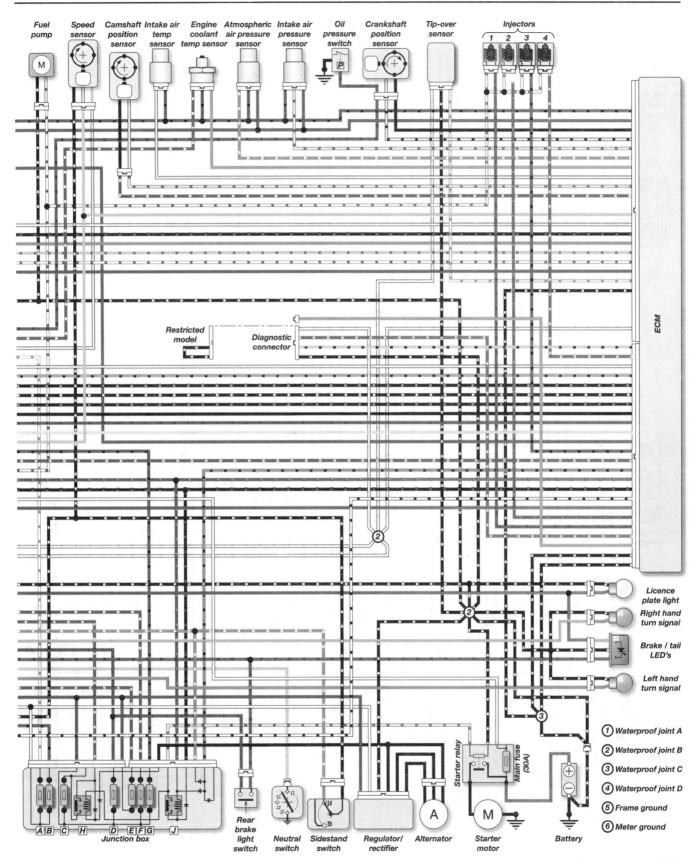

Fuel pump

Speed sensor

Camshaft position sensor

Intake air temp sensor

Engine coolant temp sensor

Atmospheric air pressure sensor

Intake air pressure sensor

Oil pressure switch

Crankshaft position sensor

Tip-over sensor

Injectors
1 2 3 4

ECM

Restricted model

Diagnostic connector

Licence plate light

Right hand turn signal

Brake / tail LED's

Left hand turn signal

1 **Waterproof joint A**
2 **Waterproof joint B**
3 **Waterproof joint C**
4 **Waterproof joint D**
5 **Frame ground**
6 **Meter ground**

Starter relay

Main fuse (30A)

A B C H D E F G J

Junction box

Rear brake light switch

Neutral switch

Sidestand switch

Regulator/ rectifier

Alternator

Starter motor

Battery

Kawasaki ZR1000-A3 and A6 Europe models

H33745

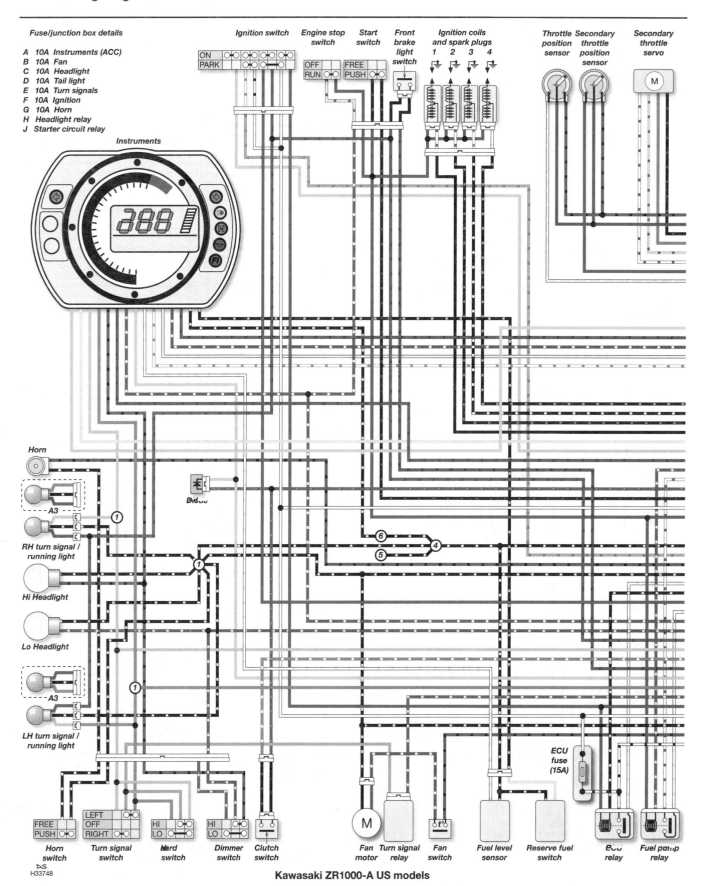

Fuse/junction box details

A 10A Instruments (ACC)
B 10A Fan
C 10A Headlight
D 10A Tail light
E 10A Turn signals
F 10A Ignition
G 10A Horn
H Headlight relay
J Starter circuit relay

Ignition switch
Engine stop switch
Start switch
Front brake light switch
Ignition coils and spark plugs
1 2 3 4
Throttle position sensor
Secondary throttle position sensor
Secondary throttle servo

ON
PARK
OFF
RUN
FREE
PUSH

Instruments

Horn

RH turn signal / running light

Hi Headlight

Lo Headlight

LH turn signal / running light

ECU fuse (15A)

Horn switch
Turn signal switch
Hazard switch
Dimmer switch
Clutch switch
Fan motor
Turn signal relay
Fan switch
Fuel level sensor
Reserve fuel switch
ECU relay
Fuel pump relay

FREE
PUSH
LEFT
OFF
RIGHT
HI
LO
HI
LO

H33748

Kawasaki ZR1000-A US models

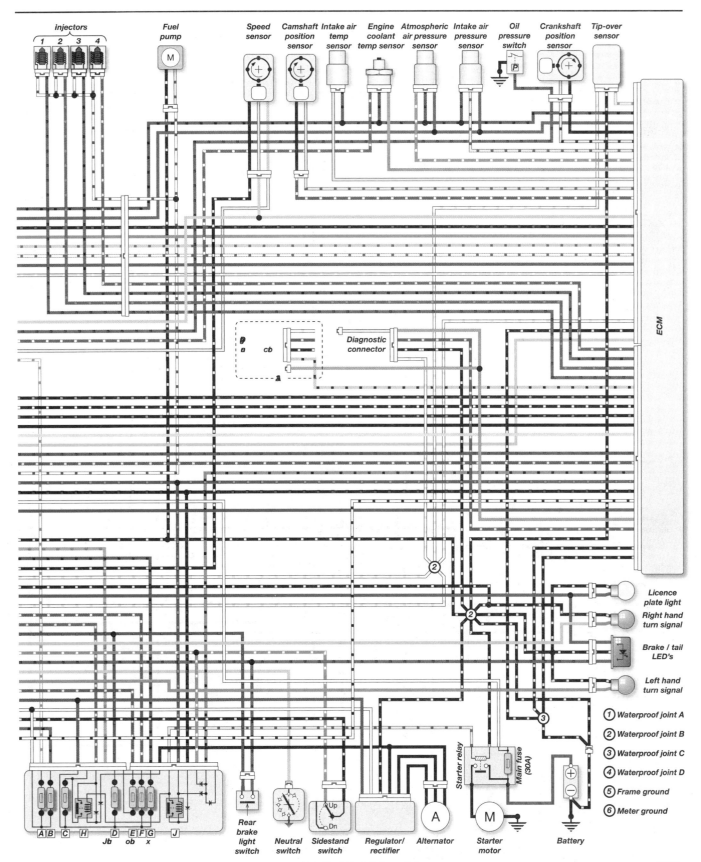

Kawasaki ZR1000-A US models

H33748

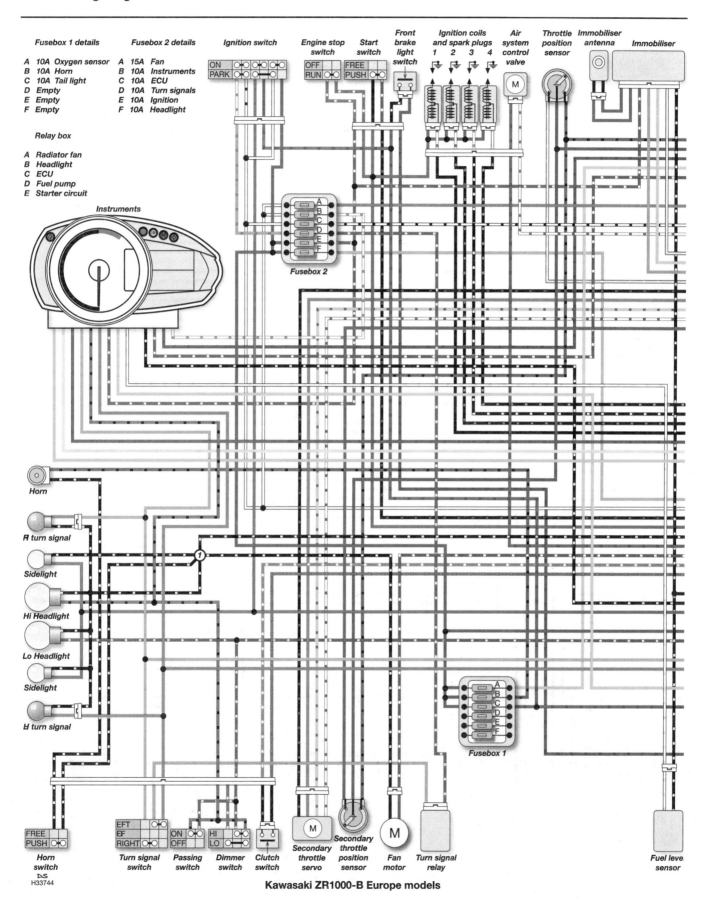

Fusebox 1 details

A 10A Oxygen sensor
B 10A Horn
C 10A Tail light
D Empty
E Empty
F Empty

Relay box

A Radiator fan
B Headlight
C ECU
D Fuel pump
E Starter circuit

Fusebox 2 details

A 15A Fan
B 10A Instruments
C 10A ECU
D 10A Turn signals
E 10A Ignition
F 10A Headlight

Ignition switch

Engine stop switch

Start switch

Front brake light switch

Ignition coils and spark plugs
1 2 3 4

Air system control valve

Throttle position sensor

Immobiliser antenna

Immobiliser

Instruments

Fusebox 2

Horn

R turn signal

Sidelight

Hi Headlight

Lo Headlight

Sidelight

H turn signal

Fusebox 1

FREE
PUSH

Horn switch

Turn signal switch

Passing switch

Dimmer switch

Clutch switch

Secondary throttle servo

Secondary throttle position sensor

Fan motor

Turn signal relay

Fuel level sensor

Kawasaki ZR1000-B Europe models

H33744

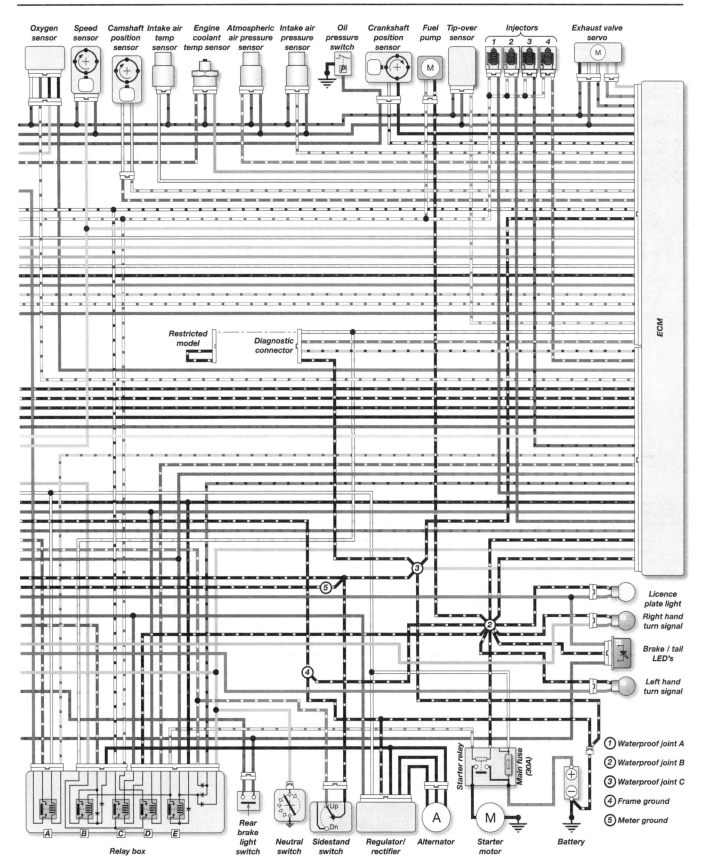

Kawasaki ZR1000-B Europe models

H33744

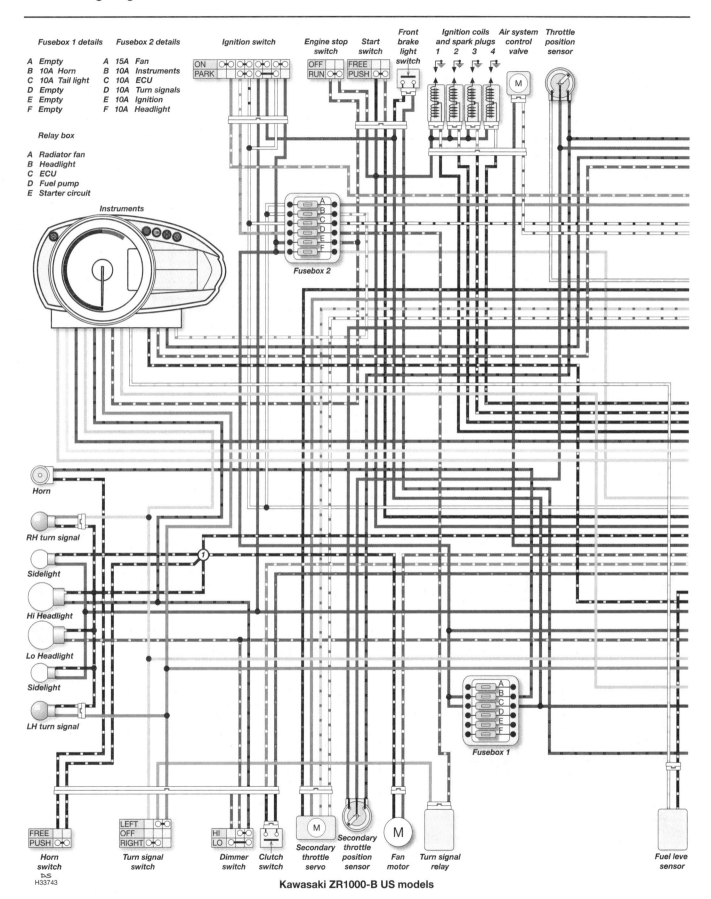

Fusebox 1 details

A Empty
B 10A Horn
C 10A Tail light
D Empty
E Empty
F Empty

Fusebox 2 details

A 15A Fan
B 10A Instruments
C 10A ECU
D 10A Turn signals
E 10A Ignition
F 10A Headlight

Relay box

A Radiator fan
B Headlight
C ECU
D Fuel pump
E Starter circuit

Instruments

Ignition switch

Engine stop switch

Start switch

Front brake light switch

Ignition coils and spark plugs
1 2 3 4

Air system control valve

Throttle position sensor

ON
PARK

OFF
RUN

FREE
PUSH

Fusebox 2

Fusebox 1

Horn

RH turn signal

Sidelight

Hi Headlight

Lo Headlight

Sidelight

LH turn signal

FREE
PUSH
Horn switch

LEFT
OFF
RIGHT
Turn signal switch

HI
LO
Dimmer switch

Clutch switch

Secondary throttle servo

Secondary throttle position sensor

Fan motor

Turn signal relay

Fuel leve sensor

H33743

Kawasaki ZR1000-B US models

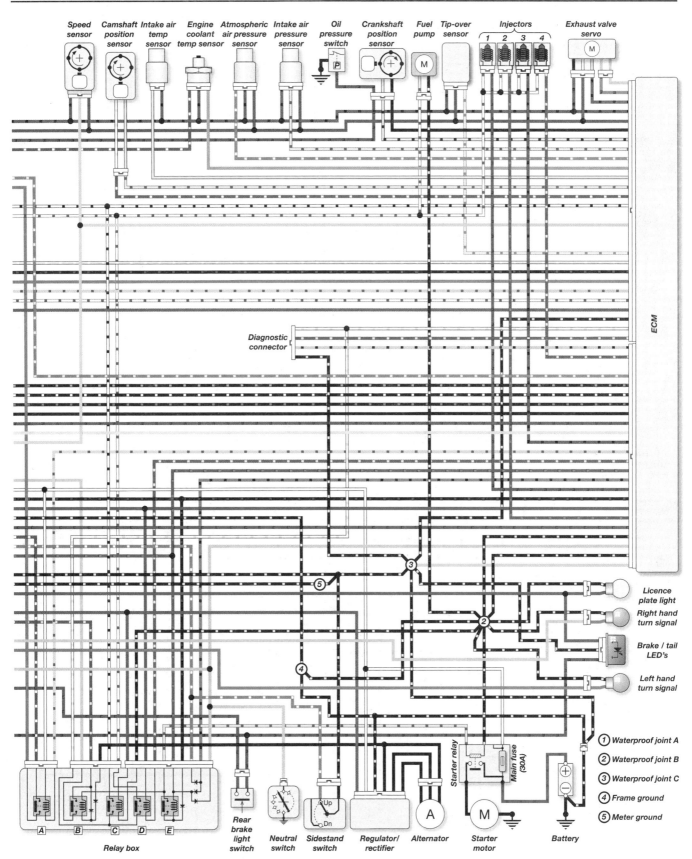

Speed sensor | Camshaft position sensor | Intake air temp sensor | Engine coolant temp sensor | Atmospheric air pressure sensor | Intake air pressure sensor | Oil pressure switch | Crankshaft position sensor | Fuel pump | Tip-over sensor | Injectors 1 2 3 4 | Exhaust valve servo

ECM

Diagnostic connector

Licence plate light

Right hand turn signal

Brake / tail LED's

Left hand turn signal

1 Waterproof joint A
2 Waterproof joint B
3 Waterproof joint C
4 Frame ground
5 Meter ground

Relay box | Rear brake light switch | Neutral switch | Sidestand switch | Regulator/ rectifier | Alternator | Starter motor | Battery

Starter relay

Main fuse (30A)

Up / Dn

Kawasaki ZR1000-B US models

H33743

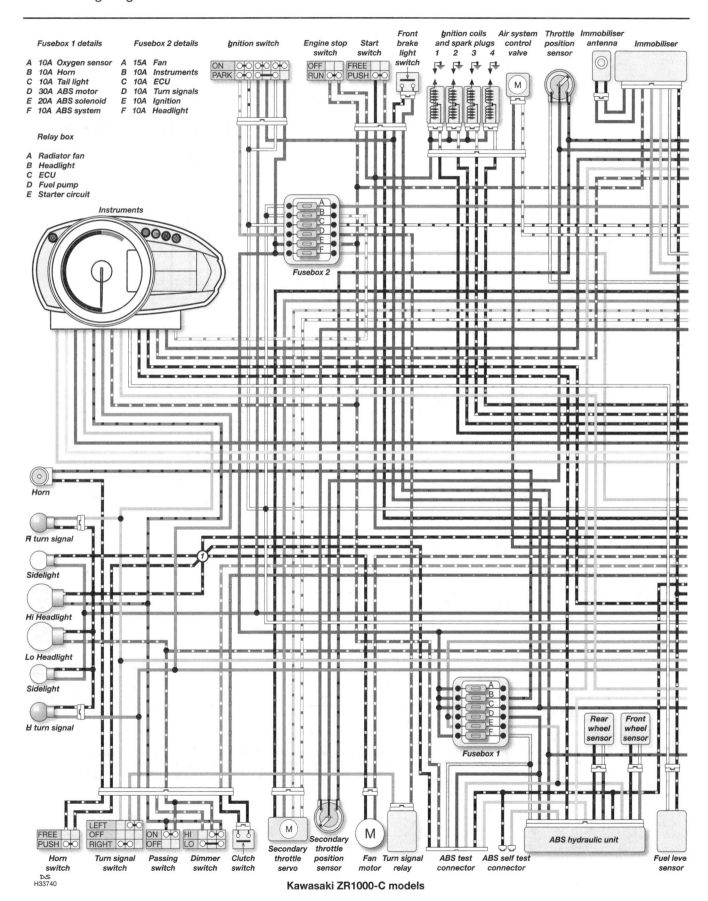

Fusebox 1 details

A 10A Oxygen sensor
B 10A Horn
C 10A Tail light
D 30A ABS motor
E 20A ABS solenoid
F 10A ABS system

Fusebox 2 details

A 15A Fan
B 10A Instruments
C 10A ECU
D 10A Turn signals
E 10A Ignition
F 10A Headlight

Relay box

A Radiator fan
B Headlight
C ECU
D Fuel pump
E Starter circuit

Instruments

Ignition switch

Engine stop switch

Start switch

Front brake light switch

Ignition coils and spark plugs
1 2 3 4

Air system control valve

Throttle position sensor

Immobiliser antenna

Immobiliser

Fusebox 2

Horn

R turn signal

Sidelight

Hi Headlight

Lo Headlight

Sidelight

H turn signal

Fusebox 1

Rear wheel sensor

Front wheel sensor

Horn switch

Turn signal switch

Passing switch

Dimmer switch

Clutch switch

Secondary throttle servo

Secondary throttle position sensor

Fan motor

Turn signal relay

ABS test connector

ABS self test connector

ABS hydraulic unit

Fuel level sensor

FREE / PUSH

LEFT / OFF / RIGHT

ON / OFF

HI / LO

ON / PARK

OFF / RUN

FREE / PUSH

H33740

Kawasaki ZR1000-C models

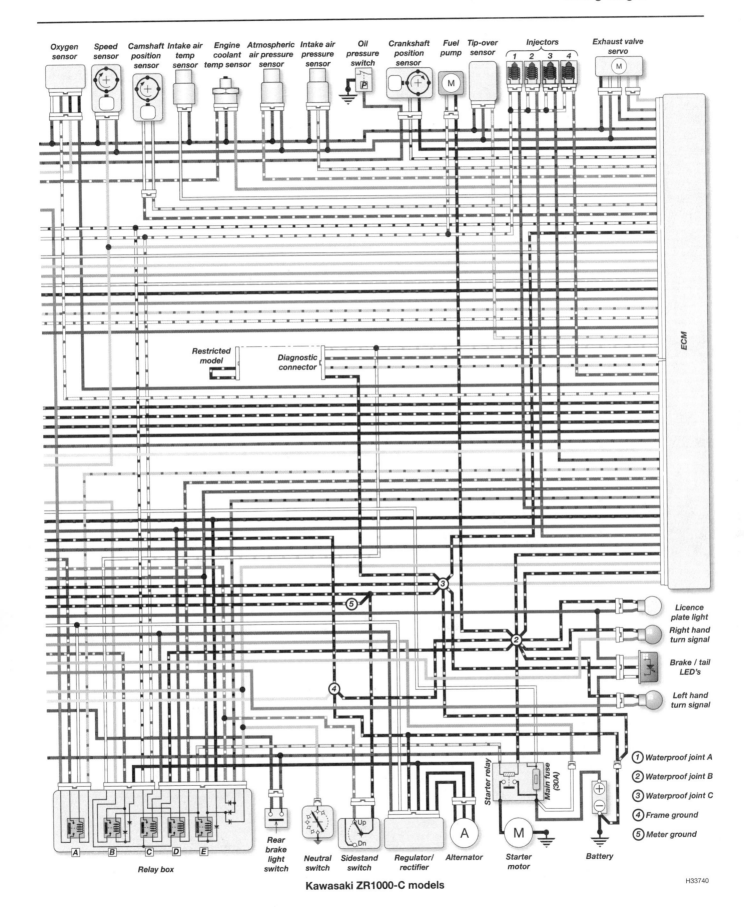

Oxygen sensor • Speed sensor • Camshaft position sensor • Intake air temp sensor • Engine coolant temp sensor • Atmospheric air pressure sensor • Intake air pressure sensor • Oil pressure switch • Crankshaft position sensor • Fuel pump • Tip-over sensor • Injectors 1 2 3 4 • Exhaust valve servo • ECM

Restricted model • Diagnostic connector

Licence plate light
Right hand turn signal
Brake / tail LED's
Left hand turn signal

① Waterproof joint A
② Waterproof joint B
③ Waterproof joint C
④ Frame ground
⑤ Meter ground

Relay box — A B C D E • Rear brake light switch • Neutral switch • Sidestand switch Up Dn • Regulator/ rectifier • Alternator A • Starter relay • Main fuse (30A) • Starter motor M • Battery

Kawasaki ZR1000-C models

H33740

Notes

Reference

Tools and Workshop Tips   REF•2

- Building up a tool kit and equipping your workshop ● Using tools ● Understanding bearing, seal, fastener and chain sizes and markings ● Repair techniques

Security   REF•20

- Locks and chains
- U-locks ● Disc locks
- Alarms and immobilisers
- Security marking systems ● Tips on how to prevent bike theft

Lubricants and fluids   REF•23

- Engine oils
- Transmission (gear) oils
- Coolant/anti-freeze
- Fork oils and suspension fluids ● Brake/clutch fluids
- Spray lubes, degreasers and solvents

Conversion Factors   REF•26

$$34\ Nm \times 0.738$$
$$= 25\ lbf\ ft$$

- Formulae for conversion of the metric (SI) units used throughout the manual into Imperial measures

MOT Test Checks   REF•27

- A guide to the UK MOT test ● Which items are tested ● How to prepare your motorcycle for the test and perform a pre-test check

Storage   REF•32

- How to prepare your motorcycle for going into storage and protect essential systems ● How to get the motorcycle back on the road

Fault Finding   REF•35

- Common faults and their likely causes ● Links to main chapters for testing or repair procedures

Technical Terms Explained   REF•46

- Component names, technical terms and common abbreviations explained

Index   REF•50

Buying tools

A toolkit is a fundamental requirement for servicing and repairing a motorcycle. Although there will be an initial expense in building up enough tools for servicing, this will soon be offset by the savings made by doing the job yourself. As experience and confidence grow, additional tools can be added to enable the repair and overhaul of the motorcycle. Many of the specialist tools are expensive and not often used so it may be preferable to hire them, or for a group of friends or motorcycle club to join in the purchase.

As a rule, it is better to buy more expensive, good quality tools. Cheaper tools are likely to wear out faster and need to be renewed more often, nullifying the original saving.

> **Warning: To avoid the risk of a poor quality tool breaking in use, causing injury or damage to the component being worked on, always aim to purchase tools which meet the relevant national safety standards.**

The following lists of tools do not represent the manufacturer's service tools, but serve as a guide to help the owner decide which tools are needed for this level of work. In addition, items such as an electric drill, hacksaw, files, soldering iron and a workbench equipped with a vice, may be needed. Although not classed as tools, a selection of bolts, screws, nuts, washers and pieces of tubing always come in useful.

For more information about tools, refer to the Haynes *Motorcycle Workshop Practice Techbook* (Bk. No. 3470).

Manufacturer's service tools

Inevitably certain tasks require the use of a service tool. Where possible an alternative tool or method of approach is recommended, but sometimes there is no option if personal injury or damage to the component is to be avoided. Where required, service tools are referred to in the relevant procedure.

Service tools can usually only be purchased from a motorcycle dealer and are identified by a part number. Some of the commonly-used tools, such as rotor pullers, are available in aftermarket form from mail-order motorcycle tool and accessory suppliers.

Maintenance and minor repair tools

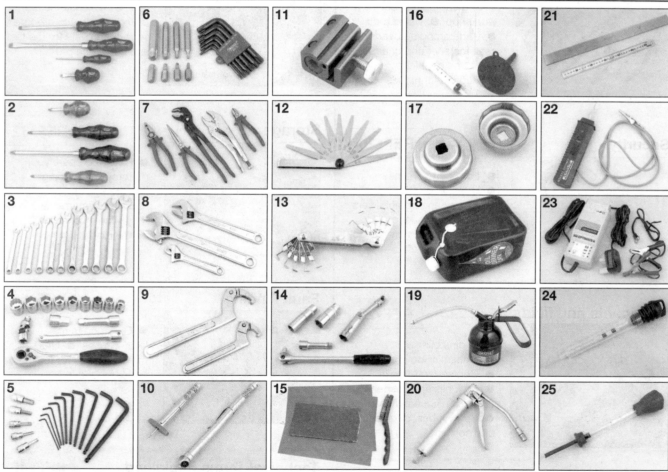

1 Set of flat-bladed screwdrivers
2 Set of Phillips head screwdrivers
3 Combination open-end and ring spanners
4 Socket set (3/8 inch or 1/2 inch drive)
5 Set of Allen keys or bits
6 Set of Torx keys or bits
7 Pliers, cutters and self-locking grips (Mole grips)
8 Adjustable spanners
9 C-spanners
10 Tread depth gauge and tyre pressure gauge
11 Cable oiler clamp
12 Feeler gauges
13 Spark plug gap measuring tool
14 Spark plug spanner or deep plug sockets
15 Wire brush and emery paper
16 Calibrated syringe, measuring vessel and funnel
17 Oil filter adapters
18 Oil drainer can or tray
19 Pump type oil can
20 Grease gun
21 Straight-edge and steel rule
22 Continuity tester
23 Battery charger
24 Hydrometer (for battery specific gravity check)
25 Anti-freeze tester (for liquid-cooled engines)

Repair and overhaul tools

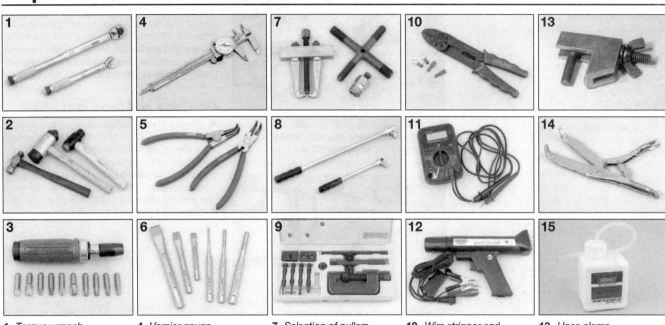

1 Torque wrench
(small and mid-ranges)
2 Conventional, plastic or
soft-faced hammers
3 Impact driver set

4 Vernier gauge
5 Circlip pliers (internal and
external, or combination)
6 Set of cold chisels
and punches

7 Selection of pullers
8 Breaker bars
9 Chain breaking/
riveting tool set

10 Wire stripper and
crimper tool
11 Multimeter (measures
amps, volts and ohms)
12 Stroboscope (for
dynamic timing checks)

13 Hose clamp
(wingnut type shown)
14 Clutch holding tool
15 One-man brake/clutch
bleeder kit

Specialist tools

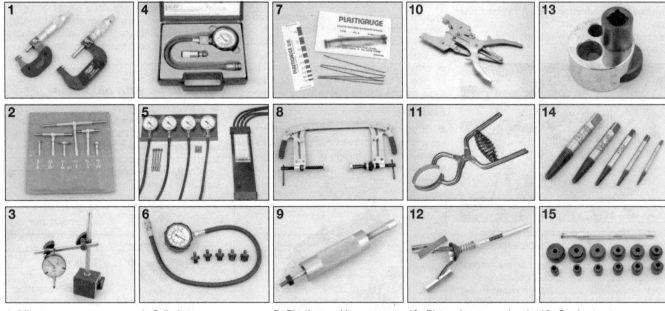

1 Micrometers
(external type)
2 Telescoping gauges
3 Dial gauge

4 Cylinder
compression gauge
5 Vacuum gauges (left) or
manometer (right)
6 Oil pressure gauge

7 Plastigauge kit
8 Valve spring compressor
(4-stroke engines)
9 Piston pin drawbolt tool

10 Piston ring removal and
installation tool
11 Piston ring clamp
12 Cylinder bore hone
(stone type shown)

13 Stud extractor
14 Screw extractor set
15 Bearing driver set

1 Workshop equipment and facilities

The workbench

● Work is made much easier by raising the bike up on a ramp - components are much more accessible if raised to waist level. The hydraulic or pneumatic types seen in the dealer's workshop are a sound investment if you undertake a lot of repairs or overhauls **(see illustration 1.1)**.

1.1 Hydraulic motorcycle ramp

● If raised off ground level, the bike must be supported on the ramp to avoid it falling. Most ramps incorporate a front wheel locating clamp which can be adjusted to suit different diameter wheels. When tightening the clamp, take care not to mark the wheel rim or damage the tyre - use wood blocks on each side to prevent this.
● Secure the bike to the ramp using tie-downs **(see illustration 1.2)**. If the bike has only a sidestand, and hence leans at a dangerous angle when raised, support the bike on an auxiliary stand.

1.2 Tie-downs are used around the passenger footrests to secure the bike

● Auxiliary (paddock) stands are widely available from mail order companies or motorcycle dealers and attach either to the wheel axle or swingarm pivot **(see illustration 1.3)**. If the motorcycle has a centrestand, you can support it under the crankcase to prevent it toppling whilst either wheel is removed **(see illustration 1.4)**.

1.3 This auxiliary stand attaches to the swingarm pivot

1.4 Always use a block of wood between the engine and jack head when supporting the engine in this way

Fumes and fire

● Refer to the Safety first! page at the beginning of the manual for full details. Make sure your workshop is equipped with a fire extinguisher suitable for fuel-related fires (Class B fire - flammable liquids) - it is not sufficient to have a water-filled extinguisher.
● Always ensure adequate ventilation is available. Unless an exhaust gas extraction system is available for use, ensure that the engine is run outside of the workshop.
● If working on the fuel system, make sure the workshop is ventilated to avoid a build-up of fumes. This applies equally to fume build-up when charging a battery. Do not smoke or allow anyone else to smoke in the workshop.

Fluids

● If you need to drain fuel from the tank, store it in an approved container marked as suitable for the storage of petrol (gasoline) **(see illustration 1.5)**. Do not store fuel in glass jars or bottles.

1.5 Use an approved can only for storing petrol (gasoline)

● Use proprietary engine degreasers or solvents which have a high flash-point, such as paraffin (kerosene), for cleaning off oil, grease and dirt - never use petrol (gasoline) for cleaning. Wear rubber gloves when handling solvent and engine degreaser. The fumes from certain solvents can be dangerous - always work in a well-ventilated area.

Dust, eye and hand protection

● Protect your lungs from inhalation of dust particles by wearing a filtering mask over the nose and mouth. Many frictional materials still contain asbestos which is dangerous to your health. Protect your eyes from spouts of liquid and sprung components by wearing a pair of protective goggles **(see illustration 1.6)**.

1.6 A fire extinguisher, goggles, mask and protective gloves should be at hand in the workshop

● Protect your hands from contact with solvents, fuel and oils by wearing rubber gloves. Alternatively apply a barrier cream to your hands before starting work. If handling hot components or fluids, wear suitable gloves to protect your hands from scalding and burns.

What to do with old fluids

● Old cleaning solvent, fuel, coolant and oils should not be poured down domestic drains or onto the ground. Package the fluid up in old oil containers, label it accordingly, and take it to a garage or disposal facility. Contact your local authority for location of such sites or ring the oil care hotline.

OIL CARE
FOLLOW THE CODE
OIL BANK LINE
0800 66 33 66
www.oilbankline.org.uk

Note: It is antisocial and illegal to dump oil down the drain. To find the location of your local oil recycling bank, call this number free.

In the USA, note that any oil supplier must accept used oil for recycling.

Fastener types and applications

Bolts and screws

● Fastener head types are either of hexagonal, Torx or splined design, with internal and external versions of each type (see illustrations 2.1 and 2.2); splined head fasteners are not in common use on motorcycles. The conventional slotted or Phillips head design is used for certain screws. Bolt or screw length is always measured from the underside of the head to the end of the item (see illustration 2.11).

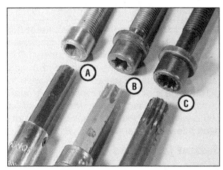

2.1 Internal hexagon/Allen (A), Torx (B) and splined (C) fasteners, with corresponding bits

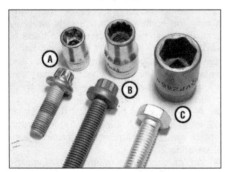

2.2 External Torx (A), splined (B) and hexagon (C) fasteners, with corresponding sockets

● Certain fasteners on the motorcycle have a tensile marking on their heads, the higher the marking the stronger the fastener. High tensile fasteners generally carry a 10 or higher marking. Never replace a high tensile fastener with one of a lower tensile strength.

Washers (see illustration 2.3)

● Plain washers are used between a fastener head and a component to prevent damage to the component or to spread the load when torque is applied. Plain washers can also be used as spacers or shims in certain assemblies. Copper or aluminium plain washers are often used as sealing washers on drain plugs.

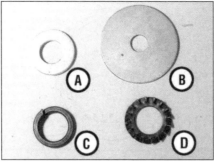

2.3 Plain washer (A), penny washer (B), spring washer (C) and serrated washer (D)

● The split-ring spring washer works by applying axial tension between the fastener head and component. If flattened, it is fatigued and must be renewed. If a plain (flat) washer is used on the fastener, position the spring washer between the fastener and the plain washer.
● Serrated star type washers dig into the fastener and component faces, preventing loosening. They are often used on electrical earth (ground) connections to the frame.
● Cone type washers (sometimes called Belleville) are conical and when tightened apply axial tension between the fastener head and component. They must be installed with the dished side against the component and often carry an OUTSIDE marking on their outer face. If flattened, they are fatigued and must be renewed.
● Tab washers are used to lock plain nuts or bolts on a shaft. A portion of the tab washer is bent up hard against one flat of the nut or bolt to prevent it loosening. Due to the tab washer being deformed in use, a new tab washer should be used every time it is disturbed.
● Wave washers are used to take up endfloat on a shaft. They provide light springing and prevent excessive side-to-side play of a component. Can be found on rocker arm shafts.

Nuts and split pins

● Conventional plain nuts are usually six-sided (see illustration 2.4). They are sized by thread diameter and pitch. High tensile nuts carry a number on one end to denote their tensile strength.

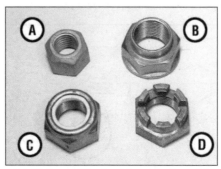

2.4 Plain nut (A), shouldered locknut (B), nylon insert nut (C) and castellated nut (D)

● Self-locking nuts either have a nylon insert, or two spring metal tabs, or a shoulder which is staked into a groove in the shaft - their advantage over conventional plain nuts is a resistance to loosening due to vibration. The nylon insert type can be used a number of times, but must be renewed when the friction of the nylon insert is reduced, ie when the nut spins freely on the shaft. The spring tab type can be reused unless the tabs are damaged. The shouldered type must be renewed every time it is disturbed.
● Split pins (cotter pins) are used to lock a castellated nut to a shaft or to prevent slackening of a plain nut. Common applications are wheel axles and brake torque arms. Because the split pin arms are deformed to lock around the nut a new split pin must always be used on installation - always fit the correct size split pin which will fit snugly in the shaft hole. Make sure the split pin arms are correctly located around the nut (see illustrations 2.5 and 2.6).

2.5 Bend split pin (cotter pin) arms as shown (arrows) to secure a castellated nut

2.6 Bend split pin (cotter pin) arms as shown to secure a plain nut

Caution: If the castellated nut slots do not align with the shaft hole after tightening to the torque setting, tighten the nut until the next slot aligns with the hole - never slacken the nut to align its slot.

● R-pins (shaped like the letter R), or slip pins as they are sometimes called, are sprung and can be reused if they are otherwise in good condition. Always install R-pins with their closed end facing forwards (see illustration 2.7).

**2.7 Correct fitting of R-pin.
Arrow indicates forward direction**

Circlips (see illustration 2.8)

● Circlips (sometimes called snap-rings) are used to retain components on a shaft or in a housing and have corresponding external or internal ears to permit removal. Parallel-sided (machined) circlips can be installed either way round in their groove, whereas stamped circlips (which have a chamfered edge on one face) must be installed with the chamfer facing away from the direction of thrust load **(see illustration 2.9)**.

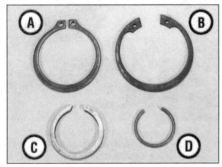

2.8 External stamped circlip (A), internal stamped circlip (B), machined circlip (C) and wire circlip (D)

● Always use circlip pliers to remove and install circlips; expand or compress them just enough to remove them. After installation, rotate the circlip in its groove to ensure it is securely seated. If installing a circlip on a splined shaft, always align its opening with a shaft channel to ensure the circlip ends are well supported and unlikely to catch **(see illustration 2.10)**.

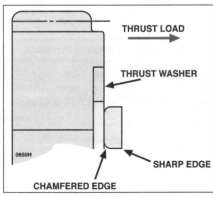

2.9 Correct fitting of a stamped circlip

THRUST LOAD
THRUST WASHER
SHARP EDGE
CHAMFERED EDGE
0650H

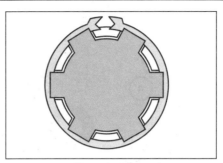

**2.10 Align circlip opening
with shaft channel**

● Circlips can wear due to the thrust of components and become loose in their grooves, with the subsequent danger of becoming dislodged in operation. For this reason, renewal is advised every time a circlip is disturbed.
● Wire circlips are commonly used as piston pin retaining clips. If a removal tang is provided, long-nosed pliers can be used to dislodge them, otherwise careful use of a small flat-bladed screwdriver is necessary. Wire circlips should be renewed every time they are disturbed.

Thread diameter and pitch

● Diameter of a male thread (screw, bolt or stud) is the outside diameter of the threaded portion **(see illustration 2.11)**. Most motorcycle manufacturers use the ISO (International Standards Organisation) metric system expressed in millimetres, eg M6 refers to a 6 mm diameter thread. Sizing is the same for nuts, except that the thread diameter is measured across the valleys of the nut.
● Pitch is the distance between the peaks of the thread **(see illustration 2.11)**. It is expressed in millimetres, thus a common bolt size may be expressed as 6.0 x 1.0 mm (6 mm thread diameter and 1 mm pitch). Generally pitch increases in proportion to thread diameter, although there are always exceptions.
● Thread diameter and pitch are related for conventional fastener applications and the accompanying table can be used as a guide. Additionally, the AF (Across Flats), spanner or socket size dimension of the bolt or nut **(see illustration 2.11)** is linked to thread and pitch specification. Thread pitch can be measured with a thread gauge **(see illustration 2.12)**.

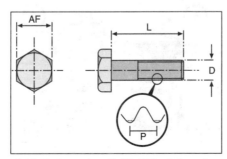

AF
L
D
P

2.11 Fastener length (L), thread diameter (D), thread pitch (P) and head size (AF)

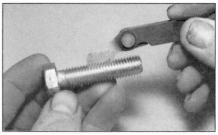

**2.12 Using a thread gauge
to measure pitch**

AF size	Thread diameter x pitch (mm)
8 mm	M5 x 0.8
8 mm	M6 x 1.0
10 mm	M6 x 1.0
12 mm	M8 x 1.25
14 mm	M10 x 1.25
17 mm	M12 x 1.25

● The threads of most fasteners are of the right-hand type, ie they are turned clockwise to tighten and anti-clockwise to loosen. The reverse situation applies to left-hand thread fasteners, which are turned anti-clockwise to tighten and clockwise to loosen. Left-hand threads are used where rotation of a component might loosen a conventional right-hand thread fastener.

Seized fasteners

● Corrosion of external fasteners due to water or reaction between two dissimilar metals can occur over a period of time. It will build up sooner in wet conditions or in countries where salt is used on the roads during the winter. If a fastener is severely corroded it is likely that normal methods of removal will fail and result in its head being ruined. When you attempt removal, the fastener thread should be heard to crack free and unscrew easily - if it doesn't, stop there before damaging something.
● A smart tap on the head of the fastener will often succeed in breaking free corrosion which has occurred in the threads **(see illustration 2.13)**.
● An aerosol penetrating fluid (such as WD-40) applied the night beforehand may work its way down into the thread and ease removal. Depending on the location, you may be able to make up a Plasticine well around the fastener head and fill it with penetrating fluid.

2.13 A sharp tap on the head of a fastener will often break free a corroded thread

● If you are working on an engine internal component, corrosion will most likely not be a problem due to the well lubricated environment. However, components can be very tight and an impact driver is a useful tool in freeing them **(see illustration 2.14)**.

2.14 Using an impact driver to free a fastener

● Where corrosion has occurred between dissimilar metals (eg steel and aluminium alloy), the application of heat to the fastener head will create a disproportionate expansion rate between the two metals and break the seizure caused by the corrosion. Whether heat can be applied depends on the location of the fastener - any surrounding components likely to be damaged must first be removed **(see illustration 2.15)**. Heat can be applied using a paint stripper heat gun or clothes iron, or by immersing the component in boiling water - wear protective gloves to prevent scalding or burns to the hands.

2.15 Using heat to free a seized fastener

● As a last resort, it is possible to use a hammer and cold chisel to work the fastener head unscrewed **(see illustration 2.16)**. This will damage the fastener, but more importantly extreme care must be taken not to damage the surrounding component.

Caution: Remember that the component being secured is generally of more value than the bolt, nut or screw - when the fastener is freed, do not unscrew it with force, instead work the fastener back and forth when resistance is felt to prevent thread damage.

2.16 Using a hammer and chisel to free a seized fastener

Broken fasteners and damaged heads

● If the shank of a broken bolt or screw is accessible you can grip it with self-locking grips. The knurled wheel type stud extractor tool or self-gripping stud puller tool is particularly useful for removing the long studs which screw into the cylinder mouth surface of the crankcase or bolts and screws from which the head has broken off **(see illustration 2.17)**. Studs can also be removed by locking two nuts together on the threaded end of the stud and using a spanner on the lower nut **(see illustration 2.18)**.

2.17 Using a stud extractor tool to remove a broken crankcase stud

2.18 Two nuts can be locked together to unscrew a stud from a component

● A bolt or screw which has broken off below or level with the casing must be extracted using a screw extractor set. Centre punch the fastener to centralise the drill bit, then drill a hole in the fastener **(see illustration 2.19)**. Select a drill bit which is approximately half to three-quarters the

2.19 When using a screw extractor, first drill a hole in the fastener . . .

diameter of the fastener and drill to a depth which will accommodate the extractor. Use the largest size extractor possible, but avoid leaving too small a wall thickness otherwise the extractor will merely force the fastener walls outwards wedging it in the casing thread.

● If a spiral type extractor is used, thread it anti-clockwise into the fastener. As it is screwed in, it will grip the fastener and unscrew it from the casing **(see illustration 2.20)**.

2.20 . . . then thread the extractor anti-clockwise into the fastener

● If a taper type extractor is used, tap it into the fastener so that it is firmly wedged in place. Unscrew the extractor (anti-clockwise) to draw the fastener out.

⚠ *Warning: Stud extractors are very hard and may break off in the fastener if care is not taken - ask an engineer about spark erosion if this happens.*

● Alternatively, the broken bolt/screw can be drilled out and the hole retapped for an oversize bolt/screw or a diamond-section thread insert. It is essential that the drilling is carried out squarely and to the correct depth, otherwise the casing may be ruined - if in doubt, entrust the work to an engineer.

● Bolts and nuts with rounded corners cause the correct size spanner or socket to slip when force is applied. Of the types of spanner/socket available always use a six-point type rather than an eight or twelve-point type - better grip

2.21 Comparison of surface drive ring spanner (left) with 12-point type (right)

is obtained. Surface drive spanners grip the middle of the hex flats, rather than the corners, and are thus good in cases of damaged heads **(see illustration 2.21)**.

● Slotted-head or Phillips-head screws are often damaged by the use of the wrong size screwdriver. Allen-head and Torx-head screws are much less likely to sustain damage. If enough of the screw head is exposed you can use a hacksaw to cut a slot in its head and then use a conventional flat-bladed screwdriver to remove it. Alternatively use a hammer and cold chisel to tap the head of the fastener around to slacken it. Always replace damaged fasteners with new ones, preferably Torx or Allen-head type.

HAYNES HINT

A dab of valve grinding compound between the screw head and screwdriver tip will often give a good grip.

Thread repair

● Threads (particularly those in aluminium alloy components) can be damaged by overtightening, being assembled with dirt in the threads, or from a component working loose and vibrating. Eventually the thread will fail completely, and it will be impossible to tighten the fastener.

● If a thread is damaged or clogged with old locking compound it can be renovated with a thread repair tool (thread chaser) **(see illustrations 2.22 and 2.23)**; special thread

2.22 A thread repair tool being used to correct an internal thread

2.23 A thread repair tool being used to correct an external thread

chasers are available for spark plug hole threads. The tool will not cut a new thread, but clean and true the original thread. Make sure that you use the correct diameter and pitch tool. Similarly, external threads can be cleaned up with a die or a thread restorer file **(see illustration 2.24)**.

2.24 Using a thread restorer file

● It is possible to drill out the old thread and retap the component to the next thread size. This will work where there is enough surrounding material and a new bolt or screw can be obtained. Sometimes, however, this is not possible - such as where the bolt/screw passes through another component which must also be suitably modified, also in cases where a spark plug or oil drain plug cannot be obtained in a larger diameter thread size.

● The diamond-section thread insert (often known by its popular trade name of Heli-Coil) is a simple and effective method of renewing the thread and retaining the original size. A kit can be purchased which contains the tap, insert and installing tool **(see illustration 2.25)**. Drill out the damaged thread with the size drill specified **(see illustration 2.26)**. Carefully retap the thread **(see illustration 2.27)**. Install the

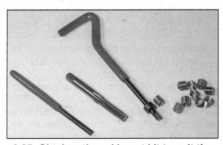

2.25 Obtain a thread insert kit to suit the thread diameter and pitch required

2.26 To install a thread insert, first drill out the original thread . . .

2.27 . . . tap a new thread . . .

2.28 . . . fit insert on the installing tool . . .

2.29 . . . and thread into the component . . .

2.30 . . . break off the tang when complete

insert on the installing tool and thread it slowly into place using a light downward pressure **(see illustrations 2.28 and 2.29)**. When positioned between a 1/4 and 1/2 turn below the surface withdraw the installing tool and use the break-off tool to press down on the tang, breaking it off **(see illustration 2.30)**.

● There are epoxy thread repair kits on the market which can rebuild stripped internal threads, although this repair should not be used on high load-bearing components.

Thread locking and sealing compounds

● Locking compounds are used in locations where the fastener is prone to loosening due to vibration or on important safety-related items which might cause loss of control of the motorcycle if they fail. It is also used where important fasteners cannot be secured by other means such as lockwashers or split pins.

● Before applying locking compound, make sure that the threads (internal and external) are clean and dry with all old compound removed. Select a compound to suit the component being secured - a non-permanent general locking and sealing type is suitable for most applications, but a high strength type is needed for permanent fixing of studs in castings. Apply a drop or two of the compound to the first few threads of the fastener, then thread it into place and tighten to the specified torque. Do not apply excessive thread locking compound otherwise the thread may be damaged on subsequent removal.

● Certain fasteners are impregnated with a dry film type coating of locking compound on their threads. Always renew this type of fastener if disturbed.

● Anti-seize compounds, such as copper-based greases, can be applied to protect threads from seizure due to extreme heat and corrosion. A common instance is spark plug threads and exhaust system fasteners.

3 Measuring tools and gauges

Feeler gauges

● Feeler gauges (or blades) are used for measuring small gaps and clearances **(see illustration 3.1)**. They can also be used to measure endfloat (sideplay) of a component on a shaft where access is not possible with a dial gauge.

● Feeler gauge sets should be treated with care and not bent or damaged. They are etched with their size on one face. Keep them clean and very lightly oiled to prevent corrosion build-up.

3.1 Feeler gauges are used for measuring small gaps and clearances - thickness is marked on one face of gauge

● When measuring a clearance, select a gauge which is a light sliding fit between the two components. You may need to use two gauges together to measure the clearance accurately.

Micrometers

● A micrometer is a precision tool capable of measuring to 0.01 or 0.001 of a millimetre. It should always be stored in its case and not in the general toolbox. It must be kept clean and never dropped, otherwise its frame or measuring anvils could be distorted resulting in inaccurate readings.

● External micrometers are used for measuring outside diameters of components and have many more applications than internal micrometers. Micrometers are available in different size ranges, eg 0 to 25 mm, 25 to 50 mm, and upwards in 25 mm steps; some large micrometers have interchangeable anvils to allow a range of measurements to be taken. Generally the largest precision measurement you are likely to take on a motorcycle is the piston diameter.

● Internal micrometers (or bore micrometers) are used for measuring inside diameters, such as valve guides and cylinder bores. Telescoping gauges and small hole gauges are used in conjunction with an external micrometer, whereas the more expensive internal micrometers have their own measuring device.

External micrometer

Note: *The conventional analogue type instrument is described. Although much easier to read, digital micrometers are considerably more expensive.*

● Always check the calibration of the micrometer before use. With the anvils closed (0 to 25 mm type) or set over a test gauge (for

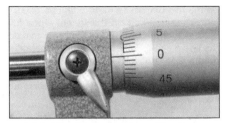

3.2 Check micrometer calibration before use

the larger types) the scale should read zero **(see illustration 3.2)**; make sure that the anvils (and test piece) are clean first. Any discrepancy can be adjusted by referring to the instructions supplied with the tool. Remember that the micrometer is a precision measuring tool - don't force the anvils closed, use the ratchet (4) on the end of the micrometer to close it. In this way, a measured force is always applied.

● To use, first make sure that the item being measured is clean. Place the anvil of the micrometer (1) against the item and use the thimble (2) to bring the spindle (3) lightly into contact with the other side of the item **(see illustration 3.3)**. Don't tighten the thimble down because this will damage the micrometer - instead use the ratchet (4) on the end of the micrometer. The ratchet mechanism applies a measured force preventing damage to the instrument.

● The micrometer is read by referring to the linear scale on the sleeve and the annular scale on the thimble. Read off the sleeve first to obtain the base measurement, then add the fine measurement from the thimble to obtain the overall reading. The linear scale on the sleeve represents the measuring range of the micrometer (eg 0 to 25 mm). The annular scale

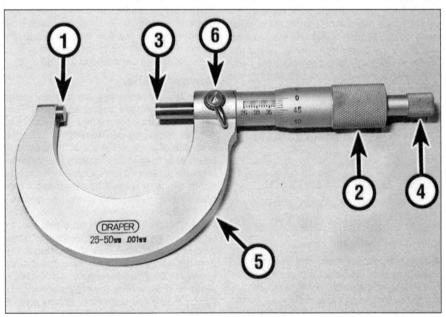

3.3 Micrometer component parts

1 Anvil	3 Spindle	5 Frame
2 Thimble	4 Ratchet	6 Locking lever

on the thimble will be in graduations of 0.01 mm (or as marked on the frame) - one full revolution of the thimble will move 0.5 mm on the linear scale. Take the reading where the datum line on the sleeve intersects the thimble's scale. Always position the eye directly above the scale otherwise an inaccurate reading will result.

In the example shown the item measures 2.95 mm **(see illustration 3.4)**:

Linear scale	2.00 mm
Linear scale	0.50 mm
Annular scale	0.45 mm
Total figure	**2.95 mm**

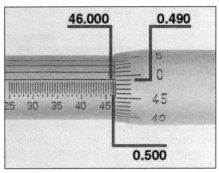

3.5 Micrometer reading of 46.99 mm on linear and annular scales . . .

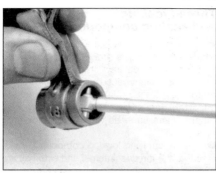

3.7 Expand the telescoping gauge in the bore, lock its position . . .

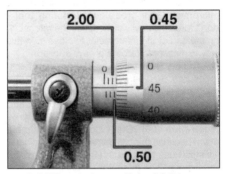

3.4 Micrometer reading of 2.95 mm

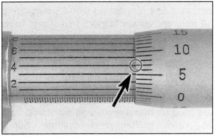

3.6 . . . and 0.004 mm on vernier scale

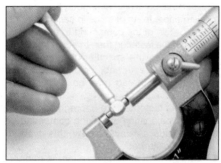

3.8 . . . then measure the gauge with a micrometer

Most micrometers have a locking lever (6) on the frame to hold the setting in place, allowing the item to be removed from the micrometer.

● Some micrometers have a vernier scale on their sleeve, providing an even finer measurement to be taken, in 0.001 increments of a millimetre. Take the sleeve and thimble measurement as described above, then check which graduation on the vernier scale aligns with that of the annular scale on the thimble **Note:** *The eye must be perpendicular to the scale when taking the vernier reading - if necessary rotate the body of the micrometer to ensure this.* Multiply the vernier scale figure by 0.001 and add it to the base and fine measurement figures.

In the example shown the item measures 46.994 mm **(see illustrations 3.5 and 3.6)**:

Linear scale (base)	46.000 mm
Linear scale (base)	00.500 mm
Annular scale (fine)	00.490 mm
Vernier scale	00.004 mm
Total figure	**46.994 mm**

Internal micrometer

● Internal micrometers are available for measuring bore diameters, but are expensive and unlikely to be available for home use. It is suggested that a set of telescoping gauges and small hole gauges, both of which must be used with an external micrometer, will suffice for taking internal measurements on a motorcycle.

● Telescoping gauges can be used to

measure internal diameters of components. Select a gauge with the correct size range, make sure its ends are clean and insert it into the bore. Expand the gauge, then lock its position and withdraw it from the bore **(see illustration 3.7)**. Measure across the gauge ends with a micrometer **(see illustration 3.8)**.

● Very small diameter bores (such as valve guides) are measured with a small hole gauge. Once adjusted to a slip-fit inside the component, its position is locked and the gauge withdrawn for measurement with a micrometer **(see illustrations 3.9 and 3.10)**.

Vernier caliper

Note: *The conventional linear and dial gauge type instruments are described. Digital types are easier to read, but are far more expensive.*

● The vernier caliper does not provide the precision of a micrometer, but is versatile in being able to measure internal and external diameters. Some types also incorporate a depth gauge. It is ideal for measuring clutch plate friction material and spring free lengths.

● To use the conventional linear scale vernier, slacken off the vernier clamp screws (1) and set its jaws over (2), or inside (3), the item to be measured **(see illustration 3.11)**. Slide the jaw into contact, using the thumbwheel (4) for fine movement of the sliding scale (5) then tighten the clamp screws (1). Read off the main scale (6) where the zero on the sliding scale (5) intersects it, taking the whole number to the left of the zero; this provides the base measurement. View along the sliding scale and select the division which

3.9 Expand the small hole gauge in the bore, lock its position . . .

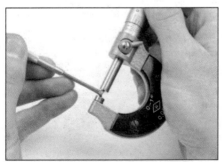

3.10 . . . then measure the gauge with a micrometer

lines up exactly with any of the divisions on the main scale, noting that the divisions usually represents 0.02 of a millimetre. Add this fine measurement to the base measurement to obtain the total reading.

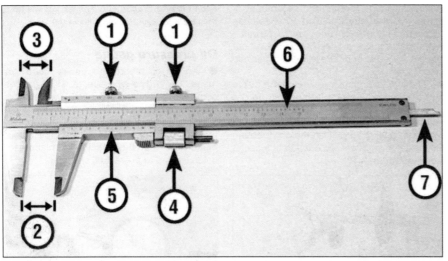

3.11 Vernier component parts (linear gauge)

1 Clamp screws	3 Internal jaws	5 Sliding scale	7 Depth gauge
2 External jaws	4 Thumbwheel	6 Main scale	

In the example shown the item measures 55.92 mm **(see illustration 3.12)**:

Base measurement	55.00 mm
Fine measurement	00.92 mm
Total figure	**55.92 mm**

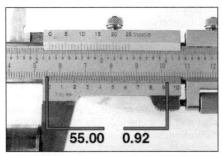

3.12 Vernier gauge reading of 55.92 mm

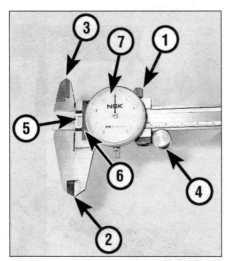

3.13 Vernier component parts (dial gauge)

1 Clamp screw	5 Main scale
2 External jaws	6 Sliding scale
3 Internal jaws	7 Dial gauge
4 Thumbwheel	

● Some vernier calipers are equipped with a dial gauge for fine measurement. Before use, check that the jaws are clean, then close them fully and check that the dial gauge reads zero. If necessary adjust the gauge ring accordingly. Slacken the vernier clamp screw (1) and set its jaws over (2), or inside (3), the item to be measured **(see illustration 3.13)**. Slide the jaws into contact, using the thumbwheel (4) for fine movement. Read off the main scale (5) where the edge of the sliding scale (6) intersects it, taking the whole number to the left of the zero; this provides the base measurement. Read off the needle position on the dial gauge (7) scale to provide the fine measurement; each division represents 0.05 of a millimetre. Add this fine measurement to the base measurement to obtain the total reading.

In the example shown the item measures 55.95 mm **(see illustration 3.14)**:

Base measurement	55.00 mm
Fine measurement	00.95 mm
Total figure	**55.95 mm**

3.14 Vernier gauge reading of 55.95 mm

Plastigauge

● Plastigauge is a plastic material which can be compressed between two surfaces to measure the oil clearance between them. The width of the compressed Plastigauge is measured against a calibrated scale to determine the clearance.

● Common uses of Plastigauge are for measuring the clearance between crankshaft journal and main bearing inserts, between crankshaft journal and big-end bearing inserts, and between camshaft and bearing surfaces. The following example describes big-end oil clearance measurement.

● Handle the Plastigauge material carefully to prevent distortion. Using a sharp knife, cut a length which corresponds with the width of the bearing being measured and place it carefully across the journal so that it is parallel with the shaft **(see illustration 3.15)**. Carefully install both bearing shells and the connecting rod. Without rotating the rod on the journal tighten its bolts or nuts (as applicable) to the specified torque. The connecting rod and bearings are then disassembled and the crushed Plastigauge examined.

3.15 Plastigauge placed across shaft journal

● Using the scale provided in the Plastigauge kit, measure the width of the material to determine the oil clearance **(see illustration 3.16)**. Always remove all traces of Plastigauge after use using your fingernails.

Caution: Arriving at the correct clearance demands that the assembly is torqued correctly, according to the settings and sequence (where applicable) provided by the motorcycle manufacturer.

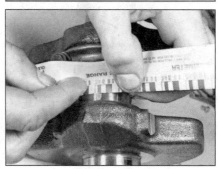

3.16 Measuring the width of the crushed Plastigauge

Dial gauge or DTI (Dial Test Indicator)

● A dial gauge can be used to accurately measure small amounts of movement. Typical uses are measuring shaft runout or shaft endfloat (sideplay) and setting piston position for ignition timing on two-strokes. A dial gauge set usually comes with a range of different probes and adapters and mounting equipment.

● The gauge needle must point to zero when at rest. Rotate the ring around its periphery to zero the gauge.

● Check that the gauge is capable of reading the extent of movement in the work. Most gauges have a small dial set in the face which records whole millimetres of movement as well as the fine scale around the face periphery which is calibrated in 0.01 mm divisions. Read off the small dial first to obtain the base measurement, then add the measurement from the fine scale to obtain the total reading.

In the example shown the gauge reads 1.48 mm (see illustration 3.17):

Base measurement	1.00 mm
Fine measurement	0.48 mm
Total figure	**1.48 mm**

3.17 Dial gauge reading of 1.48 mm

● If measuring shaft runout, the shaft must be supported in vee-blocks and the gauge mounted on a stand perpendicular to the shaft. Rest the tip of the gauge against the centre of the shaft and rotate the shaft slowly whilst watching the gauge reading (see illustration 3.18). Take several measurements along the length of the shaft and record the

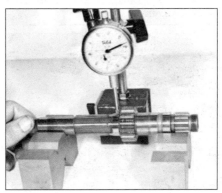

3.18 Using a dial gauge to measure shaft runout

maximum gauge reading as the amount of runout in the shaft. **Note:** *The reading obtained will be total runout at that point - some manufacturers specify that the runout figure is halved to compare with their specified runout limit.*

● Endfloat (sideplay) measurement requires that the gauge is mounted securely to the surrounding component with its probe touching the end of the shaft. Using hand pressure, push and pull on the shaft noting the maximum endfloat recorded on the gauge (see illustration 3.19).

3.19 Using a dial gauge to measure shaft endfloat

● A dial gauge with suitable adapters can be used to determine piston position BTDC on two-stroke engines for the purposes of ignition timing. The gauge, adapter and suitable length probe are installed in the place of the spark plug and the gauge zeroed at TDC. If the piston position is specified as 1.14 mm BTDC, rotate the engine back to 2.00 mm BTDC, then slowly forwards to 1.14 mm BTDC.

Cylinder compression gauges

● A compression gauge is used for measuring cylinder compression. Either the rubber-cone type or the threaded adapter type can be used. The latter is preferred to ensure a perfect seal against the cylinder head. A 0 to 300 psi (0 to 20 Bar) type gauge (for petrol/gasoline engines) will be suitable for motorcycles.

● The spark plug is removed and the gauge either held hard against the cylinder head (cone type) or the gauge adapter screwed into the cylinder head (threaded type) (see illustration 3.20). Cylinder compression is measured with the engine turning over, but not running - carry out the compression test as described in

3.20 Using a rubber-cone type cylinder compression gauge

Fault Finding Equipment. The gauge will hold the reading until manually released.

Oil pressure gauge

● An oil pressure gauge is used for measuring engine oil pressure. Most gauges come with a set of adapters to fit the thread of the take-off point (see illustration 3.21). If the take-off point specified by the motorcycle manufacturer is an external oil pipe union, make sure that the specified replacement union is used to prevent oil starvation.

3.21 Oil pressure gauge and take-off point adapter (arrow)

● Oil pressure is measured with the engine running (at a specific rpm) and often the manufacturer will specify pressure limits for a cold and hot engine.

Straight-edge and surface plate

● If checking the gasket face of a component for warpage, place a steel rule or precision straight-edge across the gasket face and measure any gap between the straight-edge and component with feeler gauges (see illustration 3.22). Check diagonally across the component and between mounting holes (see illustration 3.23).

3.22 Use a straight-edge and feeler gauges to check for warpage

3.23 Check for warpage in these directions

4 Torque and leverage

What is torque?

● Torque describes the twisting force about a shaft. The amount of torque applied is determined by the distance from the centre of the shaft to the end of the lever and the amount of force being applied to the end of the lever; distance multiplied by force equals torque.

● The manufacturer applies a measured torque to a bolt or nut to ensure that it will not slacken in use and to hold two components securely together without movement in the joint. The actual torque setting depends on the thread size, bolt or nut material and the composition of the components being held.

● Too little torque may cause the fastener to loosen due to vibration, whereas too much torque will distort the joint faces of the component or cause the fastener to shear off. Always stick to the specified torque setting.

Using a torque wrench

● Check the calibration of the torque wrench and make sure it has a suitable range for the job. Torque wrenches are available in Nm (Newton-metres), kgf m (kilograms-force metre), lbf ft (pounds-feet), lbf in (inch-pounds). Do not confuse lbf ft with lbf in.

● Adjust the tool to the desired torque on the scale (see illustration 4.1). If your torque wrench is not calibrated in the units specified, carefully convert the figure (see *Conversion Factors*). A manufacturer sometimes gives a torque setting as a range (8 to 10 Nm) rather than a single figure - in this case set the tool midway between the two settings. The same torque may be expressed as 9 Nm ± 1 Nm. Some torque wrenches have a method of locking the setting so that it isn't inadvertently altered during use.

4.1 Set the torque wrench index mark to the setting required, in this case 12 Nm

● Install the bolts/nuts in their correct location and secure them lightly. Their threads must be clean and free of any old locking compound. Unless specified the threads and flange should be dry - oiled threads are necessary in certain circumstances and the manufacturer will take this into account in the specified torque figure. Similarly, the manufacturer may also specify the application of thread-locking compound.

● Tighten the fasteners in the specified sequence until the torque wrench clicks, indicating that the torque setting has been reached. Apply the torque again to double-check the setting. Where different thread diameter fasteners secure the component, as a rule tighten the larger diameter ones first.

● When the torque wrench has been finished with, release the lock (where applicable) and fully back off its setting to zero - do not leave the torque wrench tensioned. Also, do not use a torque wrench for slackening a fastener.

Angle-tightening

● Manufacturers often specify a figure in degrees for final tightening of a fastener. This usually follows tightening to a specific torque setting.

● A degree disc can be set and attached to the socket (see illustration 4.2) or a protractor can be used to mark the angle of movement on the bolt/nut head and the surrounding casting (see illustration 4.3).

4.2 Angle tightening can be accomplished with a torque-angle gauge . . .

4.3 . . . or by marking the angle on the surrounding component

Loosening sequences

● Where more than one bolt/nut secures a component, loosen each fastener evenly a little at a time. In this way, not all the stress of the joint is held by one fastener and the components are not likely to distort.

● If a tightening sequence is provided, work in the REVERSE of this, but if not, work from the outside in, in a criss-cross sequence (see illustration 4.4).

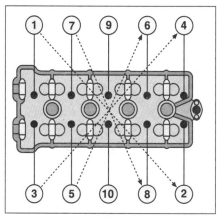

4.4 When slackening, work from the outside inwards

Tightening sequences

● If a component is held by more than one fastener it is important that the retaining bolts/nuts are tightened evenly to prevent uneven stress build-up and distortion of sealing faces. This is especially important on high-compression joints such as the cylinder head.

● A sequence is usually provided by the manufacturer, either in a diagram or actually marked in the casting. If not, always start in the centre and work outwards in a criss-cross pattern (see illustration 4.5). Start off by securing all bolts/nuts finger-tight, then set the torque wrench and tighten each fastener by a small amount in sequence until the final torque is reached. By following this practice,

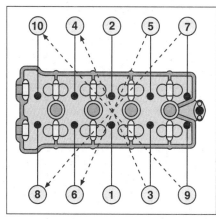

4.5 When tightening, work from the inside outwards

the joint will be held evenly and will not be distorted. Important joints, such as the cylinder head and big-end fasteners often have two- or three-stage torque settings.

Applying leverage

● Use tools at the correct angle. Position a socket wrench or spanner on the bolt/nut so that you pull it towards you when loosening. If this can't be done, push the spanner without curling your fingers around it (see illustration 4.6) - the spanner may slip or the fastener loosen suddenly, resulting in your fingers being crushed against a component.

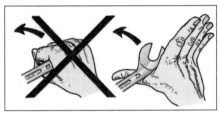

4.6 If you can't pull on the spanner to loosen a fastener, push with your hand open

● Additional leverage is gained by extending the length of the lever. The best way to do this is to use a breaker bar instead of the regular length tool, or to slip a length of tubing over the end of the spanner or socket wrench.
● If additional leverage will not work, the fastener head is either damaged or firmly corroded in place (see *Fasteners*).

5 Bearings

Bearing removal and installation

Drivers and sockets

● Before removing a bearing, always inspect the casing to see which way it must be driven out - some casings will have retaining plates or a cast step. Also check for any identifying markings on the bearing and if installed to a certain depth, measure this at this stage. Some roller bearings are sealed on one side - take note of the original fitted position.
● Bearings can be driven out of a casing using a bearing driver tool (with the correct size head) or a socket of the correct diameter. Select the driver head or socket so that it contacts the outer race of the bearing, not the balls/rollers or inner race. Always support the casing around the bearing housing with wood blocks, otherwise there is a risk of fracture. The bearing is driven out with a few blows on the driver or socket from a heavy mallet. Unless access is severely restricted (as with wheel bearings), a pin-punch is not recommended unless it is moved around the bearing to keep it square in its housing.

● The same equipment can be used to install bearings. Make sure the bearing housing is supported on wood blocks and line up the bearing in its housing. Fit the bearing as noted on removal - generally they are installed with their marked side facing outwards. Tap the bearing squarely into its housing using a driver or socket which bears only on the bearing's outer race - contact with the bearing balls/rollers or inner race will destroy it (see illustrations 5.1 and 5.2).
● Check that the bearing inner race and balls/rollers rotate freely.

5.1 Using a bearing driver against the bearing's outer race

5.2 Using a large socket against the bearing's outer race

Pullers and slide-hammers

● Where a bearing is pressed on a shaft a puller will be required to extract it (see illustration 5.3). Make sure that the puller clamp or legs fit securely behind the bearing and are unlikely to slip out. If pulling a bearing

5.3 This bearing puller clamps behind the bearing and pressure is applied to the shaft end to draw the bearing off

off a gear shaft for example, you may have to locate the puller behind a gear pinion if there is no access to the race and draw the gear pinion off the shaft as well (see illustration 5.4).

> **Caution: Ensure that the puller's centre bolt locates securely against the end of the shaft and will not slip when pressure is applied. Also ensure that puller does not damage the shaft end.**

5.4 Where no access is available to the rear of the bearing, it is sometimes possible to draw off the adjacent component

● Operate the puller so that its centre bolt exerts pressure on the shaft end and draws the bearing off the shaft.
● When installing the bearing on the shaft, tap only on the bearing's inner race - contact with the balls/rollers or outer race with destroy the bearing. Use a socket or length of tubing as a drift which fits over the shaft end (see illustration 5.5).

5.5 When installing a bearing on a shaft use a piece of tubing which bears only on the bearing's inner race

● Where a bearing locates in a blind hole in a casing, it cannot be driven or pulled out as described above. A slide-hammer with knife-edged bearing puller attachment will be required. The puller attachment passes through the bearing and when tightened expands to fit firmly behind the bearing (see illustration 5.6). By operating the slide-hammer part of the tool the bearing is jarred out of its housing (see illustration 5.7).
● It is possible, if the bearing is of reasonable weight, for it to drop out of its housing if the casing is heated as described opposite. If this

5.6 Expand the bearing puller so that it locks behind the bearing . . .

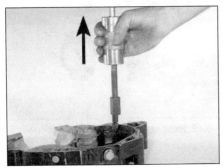

5.7 . . . attach the slide hammer to the bearing puller

method is attempted, first prepare a work surface which will enable the casing to be tapped face down to help dislodge the bearing - a wood surface is ideal since it will not damage the casing's gasket surface. Wearing protective gloves, tap the heated casing several times against the work surface to dislodge the bearing under its own weight **(see illustration 5.8)**.

5.8 Tapping a casing face down on wood blocks can often dislodge a bearing

● Bearings can be installed in blind holes using the driver or socket method described above.

Drawbolts

● Where a bearing or bush is set in the eye of a component, such as a suspension linkage arm or connecting rod small-end, removal by drift may damage the component. Furthermore, a rubber bushing in a shock absorber eye cannot successfully be driven out of position. If access is available to a engineering press, the task is straightforward. If not, a drawbolt can be fabricated to extract the bearing or bush.

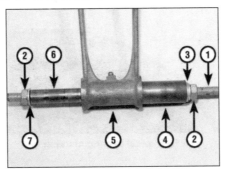

5.9 Drawbolt component parts assembled on a suspension arm

1   Bolt or length of threaded bar
2   Nuts
3   Washer (external diameter greater than tubing internal diameter)
4   Tubing (internal diameter sufficient to accommodate bearing)
5   Suspension arm with bearing
6   Tubing (external diameter slightly smaller than bearing)
7   Washer (external diameter slightly smaller than bearing)

5.10 Drawing the bearing out of the suspension arm

● To extract the bearing/bush you will need a long bolt with nut (or piece of threaded bar with two nuts), a piece of tubing which has an internal diameter larger than the bearing/bush, another piece of tubing which has an external diameter slightly smaller than the bearing/ bush, and a selection of washers **(see illustrations 5.9 and 5.10)**. Note that the pieces of tubing must be of the same length, or longer, than the bearing/bush.
● The same kit (without the pieces of tubing) can be used to draw the new bearing/bush back into place **(see illustration 5.11)**.

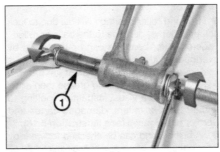

5.11 Installing a new bearing (1) in the suspension arm

Temperature change

● If the bearing's outer race is a tight fit in the casing, the aluminium casing can be heated to release its grip on the bearing. Aluminium will expand at a greater rate than the steel bearing outer race. There are several ways to do this, but avoid any localised extreme heat (such as a blow torch) - aluminium alloy has a low melting point.
● Approved methods of heating a casing are using a domestic oven (heated to 100°C) or immersing the casing in boiling water **(see illustration 5.12)**. Low temperature range localised heat sources such as a paint stripper heat gun or clothes iron can also be used **(see illustration 5.13)**. Alternatively, soak a rag in boiling water, wring it out and wrap it around the bearing housing.

> ⚠ **Warning: All of these methods require care in use to prevent scalding and burns to the hands. Wear protective gloves when handling hot components.**

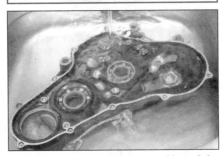

5.12 A casing can be immersed in a sink of boiling water to aid bearing removal

5.13 Using a localised heat source to aid bearing removal

● If heating the whole casing note that plastic components, such as the neutral switch, may suffer - remove them beforehand.
● After heating, remove the bearing as described above. You may find that the expansion is sufficient for the bearing to fall out of the casing under its own weight or with a light tap on the driver or socket.
● If necessary, the casing can be heated to aid bearing installation, and this is sometimes the recommended procedure if the motorcycle manufacturer has designed the housing and bearing fit with this intention.

● Installation of bearings can be eased by placing them in a freezer the night before installation. The steel bearing will contract slightly, allowing easy insertion in its housing. This is often useful when installing steering head outer races in the frame.

Bearing types and markings

● Plain shell bearings, ball bearings, needle roller bearings and tapered roller bearings will all be found on motorcycles (see illustrations 5.14 and 5.15). The ball and roller types are usually caged between an inner and outer race, but uncaged variations may be found.

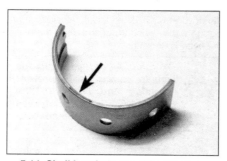

5.14 Shell bearings are either plain or grooved. They are usually identified by colour code (arrow)

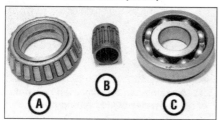

5.15 Tapered roller bearing (A), needle roller bearing (B) and ball journal bearing (C)

● Shell bearings (often called inserts) are usually found at the crankshaft main and connecting rod big-end where they are good at coping with high loads. They are made of a phosphor-bronze material and are impregnated with self-lubricating properties.

● Ball bearings and needle roller bearings consist of a steel inner and outer race with the balls or rollers between the races. They require constant lubrication by oil or grease and are good at coping with axial loads. Taper roller bearings consist of rollers set in a tapered cage set on the inner race; the outer race is separate. They are good at coping with axial loads and prevent movement along the shaft - a typical application is in the steering head.

● Bearing manufacturers produce bearings to ISO size standards and stamp one face of the bearing to indicate its internal and external diameter, load capacity and type (see illustration 5.16).

● Metal bushes are usually of phosphor-bronze material. Rubber bushes are used in suspension mounting eyes. Fibre bushes have also been used in suspension pivots.

5.16 Typical bearing marking

Bearing fault finding

● If a bearing outer race has spun in its housing, the housing material will be damaged. You can use a bearing locking compound to bond the outer race in place if damage is not too severe.

● Shell bearings will fail due to damage of their working surface, as a result of lack of lubrication, corrosion or abrasive particles in the oil (see illustration 5.17). Small particles of dirt in the oil may embed in the bearing material whereas larger particles will score the bearing and shaft journal. If a number of short journeys are made, insufficient heat will be generated to drive off condensation which has built up on the bearings.

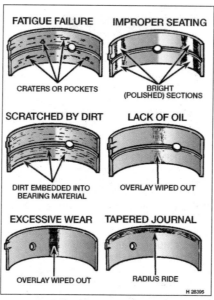

5.17 Typical bearing failures

● Ball and roller bearings will fail due to lack of lubrication or damage to the balls or rollers. Tapered-roller bearings can be damaged by overloading them. Unless the bearing is sealed on both sides, wash it in paraffin (kerosene) to remove all old grease then allow it to dry. Make a visual inspection looking to dented balls or rollers, damaged cages and worn or pitted races (see illustration 5.18).

● A ball bearing can be checked for wear by listening to it when spun. Apply a film of light oil to the bearing and hold it close to the ear - hold the outer race with one hand and spin the inner

5.18 Example of ball journal bearing with damaged balls and cages

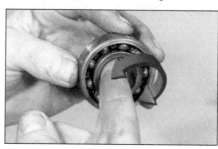

5.19 Hold outer race and listen to inner race when spun

race with the other hand (see illustration 5.19). The bearing should be almost silent when spun; if it grates or rattles it is worn.

6 Oil seals

Oil seal removal and installation

● Oil seals should be renewed every time a component is dismantled. This is because the seal lips will become set to the sealing surface and will not necessarily reseal.

● Oil seals can be prised out of position using a large flat-bladed screwdriver (see illustration 6.1). In the case of crankcase seals, check first that the seal is not lipped on the inside, preventing its removal with the crankcases joined.

6.1 Prise out oil seals with a large flat-bladed screwdriver

● New seals are usually installed with their marked face (containing the seal reference code) outwards and the spring side towards the fluid being retained. In certain cases, such as a two-stroke engine crankshaft seal, a double lipped seal may be used due to there being fluid or gas on each side of the joint.

● Use a bearing driver or socket which bears only on the outer hard edge of the seal to install it in the casing - tapping on the inner edge will damage the sealing lip.

Oil seal types and markings

● Oil seals are usually of the single-lipped type. Double-lipped seals are found where a liquid or gas is on both sides of the joint.
● Oil seals can harden and lose their sealing ability if the motorcycle has been in storage for a long period - renewal is the only solution.
● Oil seal manufacturers also conform to the ISO markings for seal size - these are moulded into the outer face of the seal **(see illustration 6.2)**.

6.2 These oil seal markings indicate inside diameter, outside diameter and seal thickness

7 Gaskets and sealants

Types of gasket and sealant

● Gaskets are used to seal the mating surfaces between components and keep lubricants, fluids, vacuum or pressure contained within the assembly. Aluminium gaskets are sometimes found at the cylinder joints, but most gaskets are paper-based. If the mating surfaces of the components being joined are undamaged the gasket can be installed dry, although a dab of sealant or grease will be useful to hold it in place during assembly.
● RTV (Room Temperature Vulcanising) silicone rubber sealants cure when exposed to moisture in the atmosphere. These sealants are good at filling pits or irregular gasket faces, but will tend to be forced out of the joint under very high torque. They can be used to replace a paper gasket, but first make sure that the width of the paper gasket is not essential to the shimming of internal components. RTV sealants should not be used on components containing petrol (gasoline).
● Non-hardening, semi-hardening and hard setting liquid gasket compounds can be used with a gasket or between a metal-to-metal joint. Select the sealant to suit the application: universal non-hardening sealant can be used on virtually all joints; semi-hardening on joint faces which are rough or damaged; hard setting sealant on joints which require a permanent bond and are subjected to high temperature and pressure. **Note:** *Check first if the paper gasket has a bead of sealant*

impregnated in its surface before applying additional sealant.
● When choosing a sealant, make sure it is suitable for the application, particularly if being applied in a high-temperature area or in the vicinity of fuel. Certain manufacturers produce sealants in either clear, silver or black colours to match the finish of the engine. This has a particular application on motorcycles where much of the engine is exposed.
● Do not over-apply sealant. That which is squeezed out on the outside of the joint can be wiped off, whereas an excess of sealant on the inside can break off and clog oilways.

Breaking a sealed joint

● Age, heat, pressure and the use of hard setting sealant can cause two components to stick together so tightly that they are difficult to separate using finger pressure alone. Do not resort to using levers unless there is a pry point provided for this purpose **(see illustration 7.1)** or else the gasket surfaces will be damaged.
● Use a soft-faced hammer **(see illustration 7.2)** or a wood block and conventional hammer to strike the component near the mating surface. Avoid hammering against cast extremities since they may break off. If this method fails, try using a wood wedge between the two components.

Caution: If the joint will not separate, double-check that you have removed all the fasteners.

7.1 If a pry point is provided, apply gently pressure with a flat-bladed screwdriver

7.2 Tap around the joint with a soft-faced mallet if necessary - don't strike cooling fins

Removal of old gasket and sealant

● Paper gaskets will most likely come away complete, leaving only a few traces stuck on

HAYNES HiNT

Most components have one or two hollow locating dowels between the two gasket faces. If a dowel cannot be removed, do not resort to gripping it with pliers - it will almost certainly be distorted. Install a close-fitting socket or Phillips screwdriver into the dowel and then grip the outer edge of the dowel to free it.

the sealing faces of the components. It is imperative that all traces are removed to ensure correct sealing of the new gasket.
● Very carefully scrape all traces of gasket away making sure that the sealing surfaces are not gouged or scored by the scraper **(see illustrations 7.3, 7.4 and 7.5)**. Stubborn deposits can be removed by spraying with an aerosol gasket remover. Final preparation of

7.3 Paper gaskets can be scraped off with a gasket scraper tool . . .

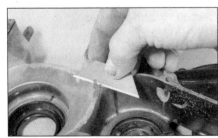

7.4 . . . a knife blade . . .

7.5 . . . or a household scraper

7.6 Fine abrasive paper is wrapped around a flat file to clean up the gasket face

7.7 A kitchen scourer can be used on stubborn deposits

the gasket surface can be made with very fine abrasive paper or a plastic kitchen scourer **(see illustrations 7.6 and 7.7)**.

● Old sealant can be scraped or peeled off components, depending on the type originally used. Note that gasket removal compounds are available to avoid scraping the components clean; make sure the gasket remover suits the type of sealant used.

8 Chains

Breaking and joining final drive chains

● Drive chains for all but small bikes are continuous and do not have a clip-type connecting link. The chain must be broken using a chain breaker tool and the new chain securely riveted together using a new soft rivet-type link. Never use a clip-type connecting link instead of a rivet-type link, except in an emergency. Various chain breaking and riveting tools are available, either as separate tools or combined as illustrated in the accompanying photographs - read the instructions supplied with the tool carefully.

> ⚠ **Warning: The need to rivet the new link pins correctly cannot be overstressed - loss of control of the motorcycle is very likely to result if the chain breaks in use.**

● Rotate the chain and look for the soft link. The soft link pins look like they have been

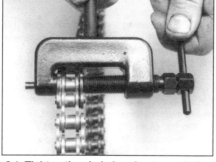

8.1 Tighten the chain breaker to push the pin out of the link . . .

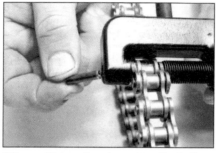

8.2 . . . withdraw the pin, remove the tool . . .

8.3 . . . and separate the chain link

deeply centre-punched instead of peened over like all the other pins **(see illustration 8.9)** and its sideplate may be a different colour. Position the soft link midway between the sprockets and assemble the chain breaker tool over one of the soft link pins **(see illustration 8.1)**. Operate the tool to push the pin out through the chain **(see illustration 8.2)**. On an O-ring chain, remove the O-rings **(see illustration 8.3)**. Carry out the same procedure on the other soft link pin.

> **Caution: Certain soft link pins (particularly on the larger chains) may require their ends to be filed or ground off before they can be pressed out using the tool.**

● Check that you have the correct size and strength (standard or heavy duty) new soft link - do not reuse the old link. Look for the size marking on the chain sideplates **(see illustration 8.10)**.

● Position the chain ends so that they are engaged over the rear sprocket. On an O-ring

8.4 Insert the new soft link, with O-rings, through the chain ends . . .

8.5 . . . install the O-rings over the pin ends . . .

8.6 . . . followed by the sideplate

chain, install a new O-ring over each pin of the link and insert the link through the two chain ends **(see illustration 8.4)**. Install a new O-ring over the end of each pin, followed by the sideplate (with the chain manufacturer's marking facing outwards) **(see illustrations 8.5 and 8.6)**. On an unsealed chain, insert the link through the two chain ends, then install the sideplate with the chain manufacturer's marking facing outwards.

● Note that it may not be possible to install the sideplate using finger pressure alone. If using a joining tool, assemble it so that the plates of the tool clamp the link and press the sideplate over the pins **(see illustration 8.7)**. Otherwise, use two small sockets placed over

8.7 Push the sideplate into position using a clamp

8.8 Assemble the chain riveting tool over one pin at a time and tighten it fully

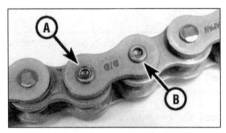

8.9 Pin end correctly riveted (A), pin end unriveted (B)

 the rivet ends and two pieces of the wood between a G-clamp. Operate the clamp to press the sideplate over the pins.

● Assemble the joining tool over one pin (following the maker's instructions) and tighten the tool down to spread the pin end securely **(see illustrations 8.8 and 8.9)**. Do the same on the other pin.

> ⚠ **Warning: Check that the pin ends are secure and that there is no danger of the sideplate coming loose. If the pin ends are cracked the soft link must be renewed.**

Final drive chain sizing

● Chains are sized using a three digit number, followed by a suffix to denote the chain type **(see illustration 8.10)**. Chain type is either standard or heavy duty (thicker sideplates), and also unsealed or O-ring/X-ring type.

● The first digit of the number relates to the pitch of the chain, ie the distance from the centre of one pin to the centre of the next pin **(see illustration 8.11)**. Pitch is expressed in eighths of an inch, as follows:

8.10 Typical chain size and type marking

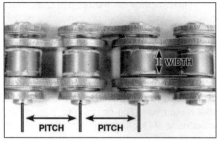

8.11 Chain dimensions

Sizes commencing with a 4 (eg 428) have a pitch of 1/2 inch (12.7 mm)
Sizes commencing with a 5 (eg 520) have a pitch of 5/8 inch (15.9 mm)
Sizes commencing with a 6 (eg 630) have a pitch of 3/4 inch (19.1 mm)

● The second and third digits of the chain size relate to the width of the rollers, again in imperial units, eg the 525 shown has 5/16 inch (7.94 mm) rollers **(see illustration 8.11)**.

9 Hoses

Clamping to prevent flow

● Small-bore flexible hoses can be clamped to prevent fluid flow whilst a component is worked on. Whichever method is used, ensure that the hose material is not permanently distorted or damaged by the clamp.

a) A brake hose clamp available from auto accessory shops **(see illustration 9.1)**.
b) A wingnut type hose clamp **(see illustration 9.2)**.

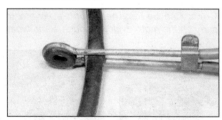

9.1 Hoses can be clamped with an automotive brake hose clamp . . .

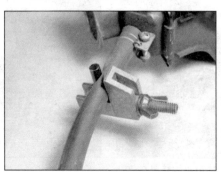

9.2 . . . a wingnut type hose clamp . . .

c) Two sockets placed each side of the hose and held with straight-jawed self-locking grips **(see illustration 9.3)**.
d) Thick card each side of the hose held between straight-jawed self-locking grips **(see illustration 9.4)**.

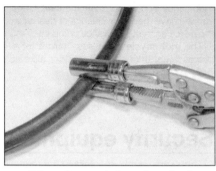

9.3 . . . two sockets and a pair of self-locking grips . . .

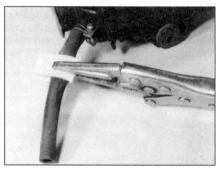

9.4 . . . or thick card and self-locking grips

Freeing and fitting hoses

● Always make sure the hose clamp is moved well clear of the hose end. Grip the hose with your hand and rotate it whilst pulling it off the union. If the hose has hardened due to age and will not move, slit it with a sharp knife and peel its ends off the union **(see illustration 9.5)**.

● Resist the temptation to use grease or soap on the unions to aid installation; although it helps the hose slip over the union it will equally aid the escape of fluid from the joint. It is preferable to soften the hose ends in hot water and wet the inside surface of the hose with water or a fluid which will evaporate.

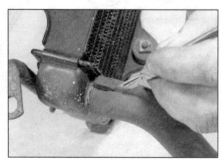

9.5 Cutting a coolant hose free with a sharp knife

Introduction

In less time than it takes to read this introduction, a thief could steal your motorcycle. Returning only to find your bike has gone is one of the worst feelings in the world. Even if the motorcycle is insured against theft, once you've got over the initial shock, you will have the inconvenience of dealing with the police and your insurance company.

The motorcycle is an easy target for the professional thief and the joyrider alike and the official figures on motorcycle theft make for depressing reading; on average a motorcycle is stolen every 16 minutes in the UK!

Motorcycle thefts fall into two categories, those stolen 'to order' and those taken by opportunists. The thief stealing to order will be on the look out for a specific make and model and will go to extraordinary lengths to obtain that motorcycle. The opportunist thief on the other hand will look for easy targets which can be stolen with the minimum of effort and risk.

Whilst it is never going to be possible to make your machine 100% secure, it is estimated that around half of all stolen motorcycles are taken by opportunist thieves. Remember that the opportunist thief is always on the look out for the easy option: if there are two similar motorcycles parked side-by-side, they will target the one with the lowest level of security. By taking a few precautions, you can reduce the chances of your motorcycle being stolen.

Security equipment

There are many specialised motorcycle security devices available and the following text summarises their applications and their good and bad points.

Once you have decided on the type of security equipment which best suits your needs, we recommended that you read one of the many equipment tests regularly carried

Ensure the lock and chain you buy is of good quality and long enough to shackle your bike to a solid object

out by the motorcycle press. These tests compare the products from all the major manufacturers and give impartial ratings on their effectiveness, value-for-money and ease of use.

No one item of security equipment can provide complete protection. It is highly recommended that two or more of the items described below are combined to increase the security of your motorcycle (a lock and chain plus an alarm system is just about ideal). The more security measures fitted to the bike, the less likely it is to be stolen.

Lock and chain

Pros: *Very flexible to use; can be used to secure the motorcycle to almost any immovable object. On some locks and chains, the lock can be used on its own as a disc lock (see below).*

Cons: *Can be very heavy and awkward to carry on the motorcycle, although some types*

will be supplied with a carry bag which can be strapped to the pillion seat.

● Heavy-duty chains and locks are an excellent security measure **(see illustration 1)**. Whenever the motorcycle is parked, use the lock and chain to secure the machine to a solid, immovable object such as a post or railings. This will prevent the machine from being ridden away or being lifted into the back of a van.

● When fitting the chain, always ensure the chain is routed around the motorcycle frame or swingarm **(see illustrations 2 and 3)**. Never merely pass the chain around one of the wheel rims; a thief may unbolt the wheel and lift the rest of the machine into a van, leaving you with just the wheel! Try to avoid having excess chain free, thus making it difficult to use cutting tools, and keep the chain and lock off the ground to prevent thieves attacking it with a cold chisel. Position the lock so that its lock barrel is facing downwards; this will make it harder for the thief to attack the lock mechanism.

Pass the chain through the bike's frame, rather than just through a wheel . . .

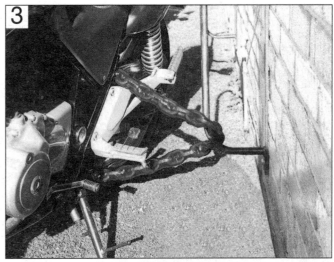

. . . and loop it around a solid object

U-locks

Pros: *Highly effective deterrent which can be used to secure the bike to a post or railings. Most U-locks come with a carrier which allows the lock to be easily carried on the bike.*

Cons: *Not as flexible to use as a lock and chain.*

● These are solid locks which are similar in use to a lock and chain. U-locks are lighter than a lock and chain but not so flexible to use. The length and shape of the lock shackle limit the objects to which the bike can be secured **(see illustration 4)**.

Disc locks

Pros: *Small, light and very easy to carry; most can be stored underneath the seat.*

Cons: *Does not prevent the motorcycle being lifted into a van. Can be very embarrassing if you*

U-locks can be used to secure the bike to a solid object – ensure you purchase one which is long enough

forget to remove the lock before attempting to ride off!

● Disc locks are designed to be attached to the front brake disc. The lock passes through one of the holes in the disc and prevents the wheel rotating by jamming against the fork/brake caliper **(see illustration 5)**. Some are equipped with an alarm siren which sounds if the disc lock is moved; this not only acts as a theft deterrent but also as a handy reminder if you try to move the bike with the lock still fitted.

● Combining the disc lock with a length of cable which can be looped around a post or railings provides an additional measure of security **(see illustration 6)**.

Alarms and immobilisers

Pros: *Once installed it is completely hassle-free to use. If the system is 'Thatcham' or 'Sold Secure-approved', insurance companies may give you a discount.*

Cons: *Can be expensive to buy and complex to install. No system will prevent the motorcycle from being lifted into a van and taken away.*

● Electronic alarms and immobilisers are available to suit a variety of budgets. There are three different types of system available: pure alarms, pure immobilisers, and the more expensive systems which are combined alarm/immobilisers **(see illustration 7)**.
● An alarm system is designed to emit an audible warning if the motorcycle is being tampered with.
● An immobiliser prevents the motorcycle being started and ridden away by disabling its electrical systems.
● When purchasing an alarm/immobiliser system, check the cost of installing the system unless you are able to do it yourself. If the motorcycle is not used regularly, another consideration is the current drain of the system. All alarm/immobiliser systems are powered by the motorcycle's battery; purchasing a system with a very low current drain could prevent the battery losing its charge whilst the motorcycle is not being used.

A typical disc lock attached through one of the holes in the disc

A disc lock combined with a security cable provides additional protection

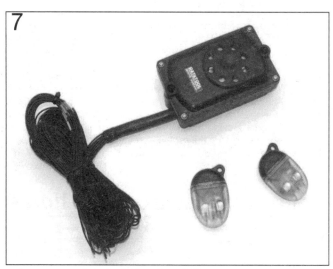

A typical alarm/immobiliser system

Indelible markings can be applied to most areas of the bike – always apply the manufacturer's sticker to warn off thieves

Chemically-etched code numbers can be applied to main body panels . . .

. . . again, always ensure that the kit manufacturer's sticker is applied in a prominent position

Security marking kits

Pros: *Very cheap and effective deterrent. Many insurance companies will give you a discount on your insurance premium if a recognised security marking kit is used on your motorcycle.*

Cons: *Does not prevent the motorcycle being stolen by joyriders.*

● There are many different types of security marking kits available. The idea is to mark as many parts of the motorcycle as possible with a unique security number **(see illustrations 8, 9 and 10)**. A form will be included with the kit to register your personal details and those of the motorcycle with the kit manufacturer. This register is made available to the police to help them trace the rightful owner of any motorcycle or components which they recover should all other forms of identification have been removed. Always apply the warning stickers provided with the kit to deter thieves.

Ground anchors, wheel clamps and security posts

Pros: *An excellent form of security which will deter all but the most determined of thieves.*

Cons: *Awkward to install and can be expensive.*

● Whilst the motorcycle is at home, it is a good idea to attach it securely to the floor or a solid wall, even if it is kept in a securely locked garage. Various types of ground anchors, security posts and wheel clamps are available for this purpose **(see illustration 11)**. These security devices are either bolted to a solid concrete or brick structure or can be cemented into the ground.

Permanent ground anchors provide an excellent level of security when the bike is at home

Security at home

A high percentage of motorcycle thefts are from the owner's home. Here are some things to consider whenever your motorcycle is at home:

✔ Where possible, always keep the motorcycle in a securely locked garage. Never rely solely on the standard lock on the garage door, these are usual hopelessly inadequate. Fit an additional locking mechanism to the door and consider having the garage alarmed. A security light, activated by a movement sensor, is also a good investment.

✔ Always secure the motorcycle to the ground or a wall, even if it is inside a securely locked garage.

✔ Do not regularly leave the motorcycle outside your home, try to keep it out of sight wherever possible. If a garage is not available, fit a motorcycle cover over the bike to disguise its true identity.

✔ It is not uncommon for thieves to follow a motorcyclist home to find out where the bike is kept. They will then return at a later date. Be aware of this whenever you are returning

home on your motorcycle. If you suspect you are being followed, do not return home, instead ride to a garage or shop and stop as a precaution.

✔ When selling a motorcycle, do not provide your home address or the location where the bike is normally kept. Arrange to meet the buyer at a location away from your home. Thieves have been known to pose as potential buyers to find out where motorcycles are kept and then return later to steal them.

Security away from the home

As well as fitting security equipment to your motorcycle here are a few general rules to follow whenever you park your motorcycle.

✔ Park in a busy, public place.

✔ Use car parks which incorporate security features, such as CCTV.

✔ At night, park in a well-lit area, preferably directly underneath a street light.

✔ Engage the steering lock.

✔ Secure the motorcycle to a solid, immovable object such as a post or railings with an additional lock. If this is not possible,

secure the bike to a friend's motorcycle. Some public parking places provide security loops for motorcycles.

✔ Never leave your helmet or luggage attached to the motorcycle. Take them with you at all times.

Lubricants and fluids

A wide range of lubricants, fluids and cleaning agents is available for motor-cycles. This is a guide as to what is available, its applications and properties.

Four-stroke engine oil

● Engine oil is without doubt the most important component of any four-stroke engine. Modern motorcycle engines place a lot of demands on their oil and choosing the right type is essential. Using an unsuitable oil will lead to an increased rate of engine wear and could result in serious engine damage. Before purchasing oil, always check the recommended oil specification given by the manufacturer. The manufacturer will state a recommended 'type or classification' and also a specific 'viscosity' range for engine oil.

● The oil 'type or classification' is identified by its API (American Petroleum Institute) rating. The API rating will be in the form of two letters, e.g. SG. The S identifies the oil as being suitable for use in a petrol (gasoline) engine (S stands for spark ignition) and the second letter, ranging from A to J, identifies the oil's performance rating. The later this letter, the higher the specification of the oil; for example API SG oil exceeds the requirements of API SF oil. **Note:** *On some oils there may also be a second rating consisting of another two letters, the first letter being C, e.g. API SF/CD. This rating indicates the oil is also suitable for use in a diesel engines (the C stands for compression ignition) and is thus of no relevance for motorcycle use.*

● The 'viscosity' of the oil is identified by its SAE (Society of Automotive Engineers) rating. All modern engines require multigrade oils and the SAE rating will consist of two numbers, the first followed by a W, e.g. 10W/40. The first number indicates the viscosity rating of the oil at low temperatures (W stands for winter – tested at –20°C) and the second number represents the viscosity of the oil at high temperatures (tested at 100ºC). The lower the number, the thinner the oil. For example an oil with an SAE 10W/40 rating will give better cold starting and running than an SAE 15W/40 oil.

● As well as ensuring the 'type' and 'viscosity' of the oil match the recommendations, another consideration to make when buying engine oil is whether to purchase a standard mineral-based oil, a semi-synthetic oil (also known as a synthetic blend or synthetic-based oil) or a fully-synthetic oil. Although all oils will have a similar rating and viscosity, their cost will vary considerably; mineral-based oils are the cheapest, the fully-synthetic oils the most expensive with the semi-synthetic oils falling somewhere in-between. This decision is very much up to the owner, but it should be noted that modern synthetic oils have far better lubricating and cleaning qualities than traditional mineral-based oils and tend to retain these properties for far longer. Bearing in mind the operating conditions inside a modern, high-revving motorcycle engine it is highly recommended that a fully synthetic oil is used. The extra expense at each service could save you money in the long term by preventing premature engine wear.

● As a final note always ensure that the oil is specifically designed for use in motorcycle engines. Engine oils designed primarily for use in car engines sometimes contain additives or friction modifiers which could cause clutch slip on a motorcycle fitted with a wet-clutch.

Two-stroke engine oil

● Modern two-stroke engines, with their high power outputs, place high demands on their oil. If engine seizure is to be avoided it is essential that a high-quality oil is used. Two-stroke oils differ hugely from four-stroke oils. The oil lubricates only the crankshaft and piston(s) (the transmission has its own lubricating oil) and is used on a total-loss basis where it is burnt completely during the combustion process.

● The Japanese have recently introduced a classification system for two-stroke oils, the JASO rating. This rating is in the form of two letters, either FA, FB or FC – FA is the lowest classification and FC the highest. Ensure the oil being used meets or exceeds the recommended rating specified by the manufacturer.

● As well as ensuring the oil rating matches the recommendation, another consideration to make when buying engine oil is whether to purchase a standard mineral-based oil, a semi-synthetic oil (also known as a synthetic blend or synthetic-based oil) or a fully-synthetic oil. The cost of each type of oil varies considerably; mineral-based oils are the cheapest, the fully-synthetic oils the most expensive with the semi-synthetic oils falling somewhere in-between. This decision is very much up to the owner, but it should be noted that modern synthetic oils have far better lubricating properties and burn cleaner than traditional mineral-based oils. It is therefore recommended that a fully synthetic oil is used. The extra expense could save you money in the long term by preventing premature engine wear, engine performance will be improved, carbon deposits and exhaust smoke will be reduced.

Always ensure that the oil is specifically designed for use in an injector system. Many high quality two-stroke oils are designed for competition use and need to be pre-mixed with fuel. These oils are of a much higher viscosity and are not designed to flow through the injector pumps used on road-going two-stroke motorcycles.

Transmission (gear) oil

On a two-stroke engine, the transmission and clutch are lubricated by their own separate oil bath which must be changed in accordance with the Maintenance Schedule.

Although the engine and transmission units of most four-strokes use a common lubrication supply, there are some exceptions where the engine and gearbox have separate oil reservoirs and a dry clutch is used.

Motorcycle manufacturers will either recommend a monograde transmission oil or a four-stroke multigrade engine oil to lubricate the transmission.

Transmission oils, or gear oils as they are often called, are designed specifically for use in transmission systems. The viscosity of these oils is represented by an SAE number, but the scale of measurement applied is different to that used to grade engine oils. As a rough guide a SAE90 gear oil will be of the same viscosity as an SAE50 engine oil.

Shaft drive oil

On models equipped with shaft final drive, the shaft drive gears are will have their own oil supply. The manufacturer will state a recommended 'type or classification' and also a specific 'viscosity' range in the same manner as for four-stroke engine oil.

Gear oil classification is given by the number which follows the API GL (GL standing for gear lubricant) rating, the higher the number, the higher the specification of the oil, e.g. API GL5 oil is a higher specification than API GL4 oil. Ensure the oil meets or

exceeds the classification specified and is of the correct viscosity. The viscosity of gear oils is also represented by an SAE number but the scale of measurement used is different to that used to grade engine oils. As a rough guide an SAE90 gear oil will be of the same viscosity as an SAE50 engine oil.

If the use of an EP (Extreme Pressure) gear oil is specified, ensure the oil purchased is suitable.

Fork oil and suspension fluid

Conventional telescopic front forks are hydraulic and require fork oil to work. To ensure the forks function correctly, the fork oil must be changed in accordance with the Maintenance Schedule.

Fork oil is available in a variety of viscosities, identified by their SAE rating; fork oil ratings vary from light (SAE 5) to heavy (SAE 30). When purchasing fork oil, ensure the viscosity rating matches that specified by the manufacturer.

Some lubricant manufacturers also produce a range of high-quality suspension fluids which are very similar to fork oil but are designed mainly for competition use. These fluids may have a different viscosity rating system which is not to be confused with the SAE rating of normal fork oil. Refer to the manufacturer's instructions if in any doubt.

Brake and clutch fluid

All disc brake systems and some clutch systems are hydraulically operated. To ensure correct operation, the hydraulic fluid must be changed in accordance with the Maintenance Schedule.

Brake and clutch fluid is classified by its DOT rating with most motorcycle manufacturers specifying DOT 3 or 4 fluid. Both fluid types are glycol-based and

can be mixed together without adverse effect; DOT 4 fluid exceeds the requirements of DOT 3

fluid. Although it is safe to use DOT 4 fluid in a system designed for use with DOT 3 fluid, never use DOT 3 fluid in a system which specifies the use of DOT 4 as this will adversely affect the system's performance. The type required for the system will be marked on the fluid reservoir cap.

Some manufacturers also produce a DOT 5 hydraulic fluid. DOT 5 hydraulic fluid is silicone-based and is not compatible with the glycol-based DOT 3 and 4 fluids. Never mix DOT 5 fluid with DOT 3 or 4 fluid as this will seriously affect the performance of the hydraulic system.

Coolant/antifreeze

When purchasing coolant/antifreeze, always ensure it is suitable for use in an aluminium engine and contains corrosion inhibitors to prevent possible blockages of the internal coolant passages of the system. As a general rule, most coolants are designed to be used neat and should not be diluted whereas antifreeze can be mixed with distilled water to

provide a coolant solution of the required strength. Refer to the manufacturer's instructions on the bottle.

Ensure the coolant is changed in accordance with the Maintenance Schedule.

Chain lube

Chain lube is an aerosol-type spray lubricant specifically designed for use on motorcycle final drive chains. Chain lube has two functions, to minimise friction between the final drive chain and sprockets and to prevent corrosion of the chain. Regular use of a good-quality chain lube will extend the life of the drive chain and sprockets and thus maximise the power being transmitted from the transmission to the rear wheel.

When using chain lube, always allow some time for the solvents in the lube to evaporate before riding the motorcycle. This will minimise the amount of lube which will 'fling' off from the chain when the motorcycle is used. If the motorcycle is equipped with an 'O-ring' chain, ensure the chain lube is labelled as being suitable for use on 'O-ring' chains.

Degreasers and solvents

● There are many different types of solvents and degreasers available to remove the grime and grease which accumulate around the motorcycle during normal use. Degreasers and solvents are usually available as an aerosol-type spray or as a liquid which you apply with a brush. Always closely follow the manufacturer's instructions and wear eye protection during use. Be aware that many solvents are flammable and may give off noxious fumes; take adequate precautions when using them (see Safety First!).

● For general cleaning, use one of the many solvents or degreasers available from most motorcycle accessory shops. These solvents are usually applied then left for a certain time before being washed off with water.

Brake cleaner is a solvent specifically designed to remove all traces of oil, grease and dust from braking system components. Brake cleaner is designed to evaporate quickly and leaves behind no residue.

Carburettor cleaner is an aerosol-type solvent specifically designed to clear carburettor blockages and break down the hard deposits and gum often found inside carburettors during overhaul.

Contact cleaner is an aerosol-type solvent designed for cleaning electrical components. The cleaner will remove all traces of oil and dirt from components such as switch contacts or fouled spark plugs and then dry, leaving behind no residue.

Gasket remover is an aerosol-type solvent designed for removing stubborn gaskets from engine components during overhaul. Gasket remover will minimise the amount of scraping required to remove the gasket and therefore reduce the risk of damage to the mating surface.

Spray lubricants

● Aerosol-based spray lubricants are widely available and are excellent for lubricating lever pivots and exposed cables and switches. Try to use a lubricant which is of the dry-film type as the fluid evaporates, leaving behind a dry-film of lubricant. Lubricants which leave behind an oily residue will attract dust and dirt which will increase the rate of wear of the cable/lever.

● Most lubricants also act as a moisture dispersant and a penetrating fluid. This means they can also be used to 'dry out' electrical components such as wiring connectors or switches as well as helping to free seized fasteners.

Greases

● Grease is used to lubricate many of the pivot-points. A good-quality multi-purpose grease is suitable for most applications but some manufacturers will specify the use of specialist greases for use on components such as swingarm and suspension linkage bushes. These specialist greases can be purchased from most motorcycle (or car) accessory shops; commonly specified types include molybdenum disulphide grease, lithium-based grease, graphite-based grease, silicone-based grease and high-temperature copper-based grease.

Gasket sealing compounds

● Gasket sealing compounds can be used in conjunction with gaskets, to improve their sealing capabilities, or on their own to seal metal-to-metal joints. Depending on their type, sealing compounds either set hard or stay relatively soft and pliable.

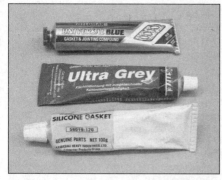

● When purchasing a gasket sealing compound, ensure that it is designed specifically for use on an internal combustion engine. General multi-purpose sealants available from DIY stores may appear visibly similar but they are not designed to withstand the extreme heat or contact with fuel and oil encountered when used on an engine (see 'Tools and Workshop Tips' for further information).

Thread locking compound

● Thread locking compounds are used to secure certain threaded fasteners in position to prevent them from loosening due to vibration. Thread locking compounds can be purchased from most motorcycle (and car) accessory shops. Ensure the threads of the both components are completely clean and dry before sparingly applying the locking compound (see 'Tools and Workshop Tips' for further information).

Fuel additives

● Fuel additives which protect and clean the fuel system components are widely available. These additives are designed to remove all traces of deposits that build up on the carburettors/injectors and prevent wear, helping the fuel system to operate more efficiently. If a fuel additive is being used, check that it is suitable for use with your motorcycle, especially if your motorcycle is equipped with a catalytic converter.

● Octane boosters are also available. These additives are designed to improve the performance of highly-tuned engines being run on normal pump-fuel and are of no real use on standard motorcycles.

Conversion factors

Length (distance)

Inches (in)	x 25.4	= Millimetres (mm)	x 0.0394	= Inches (in)
Feet (ft)	x 0.305	= Metres (m)	x 3.281	= Feet (ft)
Miles	x 1.609	= Kilometres (km)	x 0.621	= Miles

Volume (capacity)

Cubic inches (cu in; in³)	x 16.387	= Cubic centimetres (cc; cm³)	x 0.061	= Cubic inches (cu in; in³)
Imperial pints (Imp pt)	x 0.568	= Litres (l)	x 1.76	= Imperial pints (Imp pt)
Imperial quarts (Imp qt)	x 1.137	= Litres (l)	x 0.88	= Imperial quarts (Imp qt)
Imperial quarts (Imp qt)	x 1.201	= US quarts (US qt)	x 0.833	= Imperial quarts (Imp qt)
US quarts (US qt)	x 0.946	= Litres (l)	x 1.057	= US quarts (US qt)
Imperial gallons (Imp gal)	x 4.546	= Litres (l)	x 0.22	= Imperial gallons (Imp gal)
Imperial gallons (Imp gal)	x 1.201	= US gallons (US gal)	x 0.833	= Imperial gallons (Imp gal)
US gallons (US gal)	x 3.785	= Litres (l)	x 0.264	= US gallons (US gal)

Mass (weight)

Ounces (oz)	x 28.35	= Grams (g)	x 0.035	= Ounces (oz)
Pounds (lb)	x 0.454	= Kilograms (kg)	x 2.205	= Pounds (lb)

Force

Ounces-force (ozf; oz)	x 0.278	= Newtons (N)	x 3.6	= Ounces-force (ozf; oz)
Pounds-force (lbf; lb)	x 4.448	= Newtons (N)	x 0.225	= Pounds-force (lbf; lb)
Newtons (N)	x 0.1	= Kilograms-force (kgf; kg)	x 9.81	= Newtons (N)

Pressure

Pounds-force per square inch (psi; lbf/in²; lb/in²)	x 0.070	= Kilograms-force per square centimetre (kgf/cm²; kg/cm²)	x 14.223	= Pounds-force per square inch (psi; lbf/in²; lb/in²)
Pounds-force per square inch (psi; lbf/in²; lb/in²)	x 0.068	= Atmospheres (atm)	x 14.696	= Pounds-force per square inch (psi; lbf/in²; lb/in²)
Pounds-force per square inch (psi; lbf/in²; lb/in²)	x 0.069	= Bars	x 14.5	= Pounds-force per square inch (psi; lbf/in²; lb/in²)
Pounds-force per square inch (psi; lbf/in²; lb/in²)	x 6.895	= Kilopascals (kPa)	x 0.145	= Pounds-force per square inch (psi; lbf/in²; lb/in²)
Kilopascals (kPa)	x 0.01	= Kilograms-force per square centimetre (kgf/cm²; kg/cm²)	x 98.1	= Kilopascals (kPa)
Millibar (mbar)	x 100	= Pascals (Pa)	x 0.01	= Millibar (mbar)
Millibar (mbar)	x 0.0145	= Pounds-force per square inch (psi; lbf/in²; lb/in²)	x 68.947	= Millibar (mbar)
Millibar (mbar)	x 0.75	= Millimetres of mercury (mmHg)	x 1.333	= Millibar (mbar)
Millibar (mbar)	x 0.401	= Inches of water (inH₂O)	x 2.491	= Millibar (mbar)
Millimetres of mercury (mmHg)	x 0.535	= Inches of water (inH₂O)	x 1.868	= Millimetres of mercury (mmHg)
Inches of water (inH₂O)	x 0.036	= Pounds-force per square inch (psi; lbf/in²; lb/in²)	x 27.68	= Inches of water (inH₂O)

Torque (moment of force)

Pounds-force inches (lbf in; lb in)	x 1.152	= Kilograms-force centimetre (kgf cm; kg cm)	x 0.868	= Pounds-force inches (lbf in; lb in)
Pounds-force inches (lbf in; lb in)	x 0.113	= Newton metres (Nm)	x 8.85	= Pounds-force inches (lbf in; lb in)
Pounds-force inches (lbf in; lb in)	x 0.083	= Pounds-force feet (lbf ft; lb ft)	x 12	= Pounds-force inches (lbf in; lb in)
Pounds-force feet (lbf ft; lb ft)	x 0.138	= Kilograms-force metres (kgf m; kg m)	x 7.233	= Pounds-force feet (lbf ft; lb ft)
Pounds-force feet (lbf ft; lb ft)	x 1.356	= Newton metres (Nm)	x 0.738	= Pounds-force feet (lbf ft; lb ft)
Newton metres (Nm)	x 0.102	= Kilograms-force metres (kgf m; kg m)	x 9.804	= Newton metres (Nm)

Power

Horsepower (hp)	x 745.7	= Watts (W)	x 0.0013	= Horsepower (hp)

Velocity (speed)

Miles per hour (miles/hr; mph)	x 1.609	= Kilometres per hour (km/hr; kph)	x 0.621	= Miles per hour (miles/hr; mph)

Fuel consumption*

Miles per gallon (mpg)	x 0.354	= Kilometres per litre (km/l)	x 2.825	= Miles per gallon (mpg)

Temperature

Degrees Fahrenheit = (°C x 1.8) + 32   Degrees Celsius (Degrees Centigrade; °C) = (°F - 32) x 0.56

It is common practice to convert from miles per gallon (mpg) to litres/100 kilometres (l/100km), where mpg x l/100 km = 282

About the MOT Test

In the UK, all vehicles more than three years old are subject to an annual test to ensure that they meet minimum safety requirements. A current test certificate must be issued before a machine can be used on public roads, and is required before a road fund licence can be issued. Riding without a current test certificate will also invalidate your insurance.

For most owners, the MOT test is an annual cause for anxiety, and this is largely due to owners not being sure what needs to be checked prior to submitting the motorcycle for testing. The simple answer is that a fully roadworthy motorcycle will have no difficulty in passing the test.

This is a guide to getting your motorcycle through the MOT test. Obviously it will not be possible to examine the motorcycle to the same standard as the professional MOT tester, particularly in view of the equipment required for some of the checks. However, working through the following procedures will enable you to identify any problem areas before submitting the motorcycle for the test.

It has only been possible to summarise the test requirements here, based on the regulations in force at the time of printing. Test standards are becoming increasingly stringent, although there are some exemptions for older vehicles. More information about the MOT test can be obtained from the TSO publications, *How Safe is your Motorcycle* and *The MOT Inspection Manual for Motorcycle Testing.*

Many of the checks require that one of the wheels is raised off the ground. If the motorcycle doesn't have a centre stand, note that an auxiliary stand will be required. Additionally, the help of an assistant may prove useful.

Certain exceptions apply to machines under 50 cc, machines without a lighting system, and Classic bikes - if in doubt about any of the requirements listed below seek confirmation from an MOT tester prior to submitting the motorcycle for the test.

Check that the frame number is clearly visible.

Electrical System

Lights, turn signals, horn and reflector

✔ With the ignition on, check the operation of the following electrical components. **Note:** *The electrical components on certain small-capacity machines are powered by the generator, requiring that the engine is run for this check.*

a) *Headlight and tail light. Check that both illuminate in the low and high beam switch positions.*

b) *Position lights. Check that the front position (or sidelight) and tail light illuminate in this switch position.*

c) *Turn signals. Check that all flash at the correct rate, and that the warning light(s) function correctly. Check that the turn signal switch works correctly.*

d) *Hazard warning system (where fitted). Check that all four turn signals flash in this switch position.*

e) *Brake stop light. Check that the light comes on when the front and rear brakes are independently applied. Models first used on or after 1st April 1986 must have a brake light switch on each brake.*

f) *Horn. Check that the sound is continuous and of reasonable volume.*

✔ Check that there is a red reflector on the rear of the machine, either mounted separately or as part of the tail light lens.

✔ Check the condition of the headlight, tail light and turn signal lenses.

Headlight beam height

✔ The MOT tester will perform a headlight beam height check using specialised beam setting equipment **(see illustration 1)**. This equipment will not be available to the home mechanic, but if you suspect that the headlight is incorrectly set or may have been maladjusted in the past, you can perform a rough test as follows.

✔ Position the bike in a straight line facing a brick wall. The bike must be off its stand, upright and with a rider seated. Measure the height from the ground to the centre of the headlight and mark a horizontal line on the wall at this height. Position the motorcycle 3.8 metres from the wall and draw a vertical

Headlight beam height checking equipment

line up the wall central to the centreline of the motorcycle. Switch to dipped beam and check that the beam pattern falls slightly lower than the horizontal line and to the left of the vertical line **(see illustration 2)**.

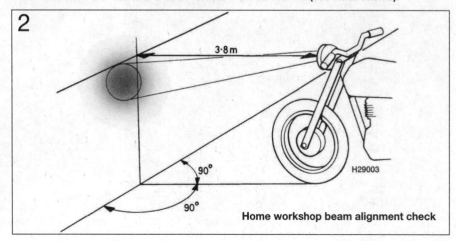

3·8 m

90°

90°

H29003

Home workshop beam alignment check

Exhaust System and Final Drive

Exhaust

✔ Check that the exhaust mountings are secure and that the system does not foul any of the rear suspension components.
✔ Start the motorcycle. When the revs are increased, check that the exhaust is neither holed nor leaking from any of its joints. On a linked system, check that the collector box is not leaking due to corrosion.

✔ Note that the exhaust decibel level ("loudness" of the exhaust) is assessed at the discretion of the tester. If the motorcycle was first used on or after 1st January 1985 the silencer must carry the BSAU 193 stamp, or a marking relating to its make and model, or be of OE (original equipment) manufacture. If the silencer is marked NOT FOR ROAD USE, RACING USE ONLY or similar, it will fail the MOT.

Final drive

✔ On chain or belt drive machines, check that the chain/belt is in good condition and does not have excessive slack. Also check that the sprocket is securely mounted on the rear wheel hub. Check that the chain/belt guard is in place.
✔ On shaft drive bikes, check for oil leaking from the drive unit and fouling the rear tyre.

Steering and Suspension

Steering

✔ With the front wheel raised off the ground, rotate the steering from lock to lock. The handlebar or switches must not contact the fuel tank or be close enough to trap the rider's hand. Problems can be caused by damaged lock stops on the lower yoke and frame, or by the fitting of non-standard handlebars.
✔ When performing the lock to lock check, also ensure that the steering moves freely without drag or notchiness. Steering movement can be impaired by poorly routed cables, or by overtight head bearings or worn bearings. The tester will perform a check of the steering head bearing lower race by mounting the front wheel on a surface plate, then performing a lock to lock check with the weight of the machine on the lower bearing (see illustration 3).
✔ Grasp the fork sliders (lower legs) and attempt to push and pull on the forks (see

Front wheel mounted on a surface plate for steering head bearing lower race check

illustration 4). Any play in the steering head bearings will be felt. Note that in extreme cases, wear of the front fork bushes can be misinterpreted for head bearing play.
✔ Check that the handlebars are securely mounted.
✔ Check that the handlebar grip rubbers are secure. They should by bonded to the bar left end and to the throttle cable pulley on the right end.

Front suspension

✔ With the motorcycle off the stand, hold the front brake on and pump the front forks up and down (see illustration 5). Check that they are adequately damped.

Checking the steering head bearings for freeplay

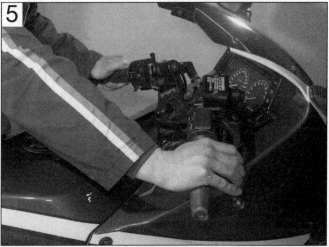
Hold the front brake on and pump the front forks up and down to check operation

6

Inspect the area around the fork dust seal for oil leakage (arrow)

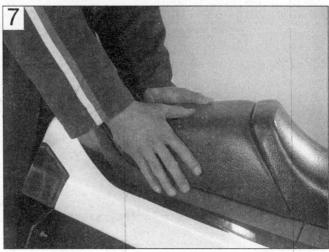

7

Bounce the rear of the motorcycle to check rear suspension operation

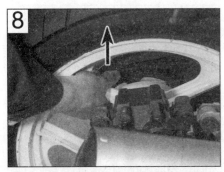

8

Checking for rear suspension linkage play

✔ Inspect the area above and around the front fork oil seals **(see illustration 6)**. There should be no sign of oil on the fork tube (stanchion) nor leaking down the slider (lower leg). On models so equipped, check that there is no oil leaking from the anti-dive units.

✔ On models with swingarm front suspension, check that there is no freeplay in the linkage when moved from side to side.

Rear suspension

✔ With the motorcycle off the stand and an assistant supporting the motorcycle by its handlebars, bounce the rear suspension **(see illustration 7)**. Check that the suspension components do not foul on any of the cycle parts and check that the shock absorber(s) provide adequate damping.

✔ Visually inspect the shock absorber(s) and check that there is no sign of oil leakage from its damper. This is somewhat restricted on certain single shock models due to the location of the shock absorber.

✔ With the rear wheel raised off the ground, grasp the wheel at the highest point and attempt to pull it up **(see illustration 8)**. Any play in the swingarm pivot or suspension linkage bearings will be felt as movement. **Note:** *Do not confuse play with actual suspension movement.* Failure to lubricate suspension linkage bearings can lead to bearing failure **(see illustration 9)**.

✔ With the rear wheel raised off the ground, grasp the swingarm ends and attempt to move the swingarm from side to side and forwards and backwards - any play indicates wear of the swingarm pivot bearings **(see illustration 10)**.

9

Worn suspension linkage pivots (arrows) are usually the cause of play in the rear suspension

10

Grasp the swingarm at the ends to check for play in its pivot bearings

Brake pad wear can usually be viewed without removing the caliper. Most pads have wear indicator grooves (1) and some also have indicator tangs (2)

On drum brakes, check the angle of the operating lever with the brake fully applied. Most drum brakes have a wear indicator pointer and scale.

Brakes, Wheels and Tyres

Brakes

✔ With the wheel raised off the ground, apply the brake then free it off, and check that the wheel is about to revolve freely without brake drag.

✔ On disc brakes, examine the disc itself. Check that it is securely mounted and not cracked.

✔ On disc brakes, view the pad material through the caliper mouth and check that the pads are not worn down beyond the limit **(see illustration 11)**.

✔ On drum brakes, check that when the brake is applied the angle between the operating lever and cable or rod is not too great **(see illustration 12)**. Check also that the operating lever doesn't foul any other components.

✔ On disc brakes, examine the flexible hoses from top to bottom. Have an assistant hold the brake on so that the fluid in the hose is under pressure, and check that there is no sign of fluid leakage, bulges or cracking. If there are any metal brake pipes or unions, check that these are free from corrosion and damage. Where a brake-linked anti-dive system is fitted, check the hoses to the anti-dive in a similar manner.

✔ Check that the rear brake torque arm is secure and that its fasteners are secured by self-locking nuts or castellated nuts with split-pins or R-pins **(see illustration 13)**.

✔ On models with ABS, check that the self-check warning light in the instrument panel works.

✔ The MOT tester will perform a test of the motorcycle's braking efficiency based on a calculation of rider and motorcycle weight. Although this cannot be carried out at home, you can at least ensure that the braking systems are properly maintained. For hydraulic disc brakes, check the fluid level, lever/pedal feel (bleed of air if its spongy) and pad material. For drum brakes, check adjustment, cable or rod operation and shoe lining thickness.

Wheels and tyres

✔ Check the wheel condition. Cast wheels should be free from cracks and if of the built-up design, all fasteners should be secure. Spoked wheels should be checked for broken, corroded, loose or bent spokes.

✔ With the wheel raised off the ground, spin the wheel and visually check that the tyre and wheel run true. Check that the tyre does not foul the suspension or mudguards.

✔ With the wheel raised off the ground, grasp the wheel and attempt to move it about the axle (spindle) **(see illustration 14)**. Any play felt here indicates wheel bearing failure.

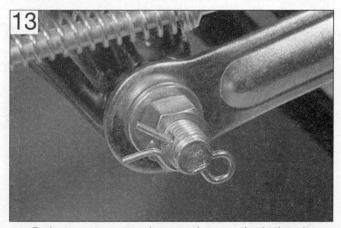

Brake torque arm must be properly secured at both ends

Check for wheel bearing play by trying to move the wheel about the axle (spindle)

Checking the tyre tread depth

Tyre direction of rotation arrow can be found on tyre sidewall

Castellated type wheel axle (spindle) nut must be secured by a split pin or R-pin

Two straightedges are used to check wheel alignment

✔ Check the tyre tread depth, tread condition and sidewall condition **(see illustration 15)**.
✔ Check the tyre type. Front and rear tyre types must be compatible and be suitable for road use. Tyres marked NOT FOR ROAD USE, COMPETITION USE ONLY or similar, will fail the MOT.

✔ If the tyre sidewall carries a direction of rotation arrow, this must be pointing in the direction of normal wheel rotation **(see illustration 16)**.
✔ Check that the wheel axle (spindle) nuts (where applicable) are properly secured. A self-locking nut or castellated nut with a split-pin or R-pin can be used **(see illustration 17)**.
✔ Wheel alignment is checked with the motorcycle off the stand and a rider seated. With the front wheel pointing straight ahead, two perfectly straight lengths of metal or wood and placed against the sidewalls of both tyres **(see illustration 18)**. The gap each side of the front tyre must be equidistant on both sides. Incorrect wheel alignment may be due to a cocked rear wheel (often as the result of poor chain adjustment) or in extreme cases, a bent frame.

General checks and condition

✔ Check the security of all major fasteners, bodypanels, seat, fairings (where fitted) and mudguards.

✔ Check that the rider and pillion footrests, handlebar levers and brake pedal are securely mounted.

✔ Check for corrosion on the frame or any load-bearing components. If severe, this may affect the structure, particularly under stress.

Sidecars

A motorcycle fitted with a sidecar requires additional checks relating to the stability of the machine and security of attachment and swivel joints, plus specific wheel alignment (toe-in) requirements. Additionally, tyre and lighting requirements differ from conventional motorcycle use. Owners are advised to check MOT test requirements with an official test centre.

Preparing for storage

Before you start

If repairs or an overhaul is needed, see that this is carried out now rather than left until you want to ride the bike again.

Give the bike a good wash and scrub all dirt from its underside. Make sure the bike dries completely before preparing for storage.

Engine

● Remove the spark plug(s) and lubricate the cylinder bores with approximately a teaspoon of motor oil using a spout-type oil can **(see illustration 1)**. Reinstall the spark plug(s). Crank the engine over a couple of times to coat the piston rings and bores with oil. If the bike has a kickstart, use this to turn the engine over. If not, flick the kill switch to the OFF position and crank the engine over on the starter **(see illustration 2)**. If the nature on the ignition system prevents the starter operating with the kill switch in the OFF position,

remove the spark plugs and fit them back in their caps; ensure that the plugs are earthed (grounded) against the cylinder head when the starter is operated **(see illustration 3)**.

⚠️ *Warning: It is important that the plugs are earthed (grounded) away from the spark plug holes otherwise there is a risk of atomised fuel from the cylinders igniting.*

HAYNES HINT *On a single cylinder four-stroke engine, you can seal the combustion chamber completely by positioning the piston at TDC on the compression stroke.*

● Drain the carburettor(s) otherwise there is a risk of jets becoming blocked by gum deposits from the fuel **(see illustration 4)**.

● If the bike is going into long-term storage, consider adding a fuel stabiliser to the fuel in the tank. If the tank is drained completely, corrosion of its internal surfaces may occur if left unprotected for a long period. The tank can be treated with a rust preventative especially for this purpose. Alternatively, remove the tank and pour half a litre of motor oil into it, install the filler cap and shake the tank to coat its internals with oil before draining off the excess. The same effect can also be achieved by spraying WD40 or a similar water-dispersant around the inside of the tank via its flexible nozzle.

● Make sure the cooling system contains the correct mix of antifreeze. Antifreeze also contains important corrosion inhibitors.

● The air intakes and exhaust can be sealed off by covering or plugging the openings. Ensure that you do not seal in any condensation; run the engine until it is hot,

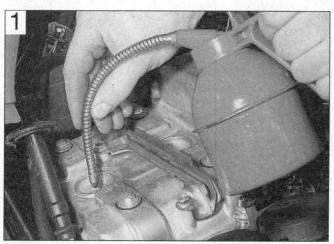
Squirt a drop of motor oil into each cylinder

Flick the kill switch to OFF . . .

. . . and ensure that the metal bodies of the plugs (arrows) are earthed against the cylinder head

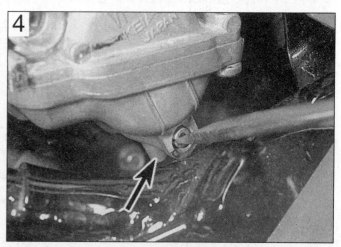
Connect a hose to the carburettor float chamber drain stub (arrow) and unscrew the drain screw

Exhausts can be sealed off with a plastic bag

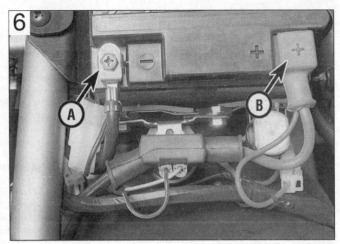

Disconnect the negative lead (A) first, followed by the positive lead (B)

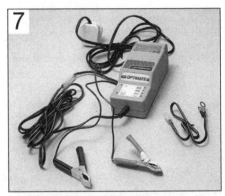

Use a suitable battery charger - this kit also assess battery condition

then switch off and allow to cool. Tape a piece of thick plastic over the silencer end(s) **(see illustration 5)**. Note that some advocate pouring a tablespoon of motor oil into the silencer(s) before sealing them off.

Battery

● Remove it from the bike - in extreme cases of cold the battery may freeze and crack its case **(see illustration 6)**.

● Check the electrolyte level and top up if necessary (conventional refillable batteries). Clean the terminals.
● Store the battery off the motorcycle and away from any sources of fire. Position a wooden block under the battery if it is to sit on the ground.
● Give the battery a trickle charge for a few hours every month **(see illustration 7)**.

Tyres

● Place the bike on its centrestand or an auxiliary stand which will support the motorcycle in an upright position. Position wood blocks under the tyres to keep them off the ground and to provide insulation from damp. If the bike is being put into long-term storage, ideally both tyres should be off the ground; not only will this protect the tyres, but will also ensure that no load is placed on the steering head or wheel bearings.
● Deflate each tyre by 5 to 10 psi, no more or the beads may unseat from the rim, making subsequent inflation difficult on tubeless tyres.

Pivots and controls

● Lubricate all lever, pedal, stand and

footrest pivot points. If grease nipples are fitted to the rear suspension components, apply lubricant to the pivots.
● Lubricate all control cables.

Cycle components

● Apply a wax protectant to all painted and plastic components. Wipe off any excess, but don't polish to a shine. Where fitted, clean the screen with soap and water.
● Coat metal parts with Vaseline (petroleum jelly). When applying this to the fork tubes, do not compress the forks otherwise the seals will rot from contact with the Vaseline.
● Apply a vinyl cleaner to the seat.

Storage conditions

● Aim to store the bike in a shed or garage which does not leak and is free from damp.
● Drape an old blanket or bedspread over the bike to protect it from dust and direct contact with sunlight (which will fade paint). This also hides the bike from prying eyes. Beware of tight-fitting plastic covers which may allow condensation to form and settle on the bike.

Getting back on the road

Engine and transmission

● Change the oil and replace the oil filter. If this was done prior to storage, check that the oil hasn't emulsified - a thick whitish substance which occurs through condensation.
● Remove the spark plugs. Using a spout-type oil can, squirt a few drops of oil into the cylinder(s). This will provide initial lubrication as the piston rings and bores comes back into contact. Service the spark plugs, or fit new ones, and install them in the engine.

● Check that the clutch isn't stuck on. The plates can stick together if left standing for some time, preventing clutch operation. Engage a gear and try rocking the bike back and forth with the clutch lever held against the handlebar. If this doesn't work on cable-operated clutches, hold the clutch lever back against the handlebar with a strong elastic band or cable tie for a couple of hours **(see illustration 8)**.
● If the air intakes or silencer end(s) were blocked off, remove the bung or cover used.
● If the fuel tank was coated with a rust

Hold clutch lever back against the handlebar with elastic bands or a cable tie

preventative, oil or a stabiliser added to the fuel, drain and flush the tank and dispose of the fuel sensibly. If no action was taken with the fuel tank prior to storage, it is advised that the old fuel is disposed of since it will go off over a period of time. Refill the fuel tank with fresh fuel.

Frame and running gear

● Oil all pivot points and cables.
● Check the tyre pressures. They will definitely need inflating if pressures were reduced for storage.
● Lubricate the final drive chain (where applicable).
● Remove any protective coating applied to the fork tubes (stanchions) since this may well destroy the fork seals. If the fork tubes weren't protected and have picked up rust spots, remove them with very fine abrasive paper and refinish with metal polish.
● Check that both brakes operate correctly. Apply each brake hard and check that it's not possible to move the motorcycle forwards, then check that the brake frees off again once released. Brake caliper pistons can stick due to corrosion around the piston head, or on the sliding caliper types, due to corrosion of the slider pins. If the brake doesn't free after repeated operation, take the caliper off for examination. Similarly drum brakes can stick

due to a seized operating cam, cable or rod linkage.
● If the motorcycle has been in long-term storage, renew the brake fluid and clutch fluid (where applicable).
● Depending on where the bike has been stored, the wiring, cables and hoses may have been nibbled by rodents. Make a visual check and investigate disturbed wiring loom tape.

Battery

● If the battery has been previously removal and given top up charges it can simply be reconnected. Remember to connect the positive cable first and the negative cable last.
● On conventional refillable batteries, if the battery has not received any attention, remove it from the motorcycle and check its electrolyte level. Top up if necessary then charge the battery. If the battery fails to hold a charge and a visual checks show heavy white sulphation of the plates, the battery is probably defective and must be renewed. This is particularly likely if the battery is old. Confirm battery condition with a specific gravity check.
● On sealed (MF) batteries, if the battery has not received any attention, remove it from the motorcycle and charge it according to the information on the battery case - if the battery fails to hold a charge it must be renewed.

Starting procedure

● If a kickstart is fitted, turn the engine over a couple of times with the ignition OFF to distribute oil around the engine. If no kickstart is fitted, flick the engine kill switch OFF and the ignition ON and crank the engine over a couple of times to work oil around the upper cylinder components. If the nature of the ignition system is such that the starter won't work with the kill switch OFF, remove the spark plugs, fit them back into their caps and earth (ground) their bodies on the cylinder head. Reinstall the spark plugs afterwards.
● Switch the kill switch to RUN, operate the choke and start the engine. If the engine won't start don't continue cranking the engine - not only will this flatten the battery, but the starter motor will overheat. Switch the ignition off and try again later. If the engine refuses to start, go through the fault finding procedures in this manual. **Note:** *If the bike has been in storage for a long time, old fuel or a carburettor blockage may be the problem. Gum deposits in carburettors can block jets - if a carburettor cleaner doesn't prove successful the carburettors must be dismantled for cleaning.*

● Once the engine has started, check that the lights, turn signals and horn work properly.

● Treat the bike gently for the first ride and check all fluid levels on completion. Settle the bike back into the maintenance schedule.

This Section provides an easy reference-guide to the more common faults that are likely to afflict your machine. Obviously, the opportunities are almost limitless for faults to occur as a result of obscure failures, and to try and cover all eventualities would require a book. Indeed, a number have been written on the subject.

Successful troubleshooting is not a mysterious 'black art' but the application of a bit of knowledge combined with a systematic and logical approach to the problem. Approach any troubleshooting by first accurately identifying the symptom and then checking through the list of possible causes, starting with the simplest or most obvious and progressing in stages to the most complex.

Take nothing for granted, but above all apply liberal quantities of common sense.

The main symptom of a fault is given in the text as a major heading below which are listed the various systems or areas which may contain the fault. Details of each possible cause for a fault and the remedial action to be taken are given, in brief, in the paragraphs below each heading. Further information should be sought in the relevant Chapter.

1 Engine doesn't start or is difficult to start

- ☐ Starter motor doesn't rotate
- ☐ Starter motor rotates but engine does not turn over
- ☐ Starter works but engine won't turn over (seized)
- ☐ No fuel flow
- ☐ Engine flooded
- ☐ No spark or weak spark
- ☐ Compression low
- ☐ Stalls after starting
- ☐ Rough idle

2 Poor running at low speed

- ☐ Spark weak
- ☐ Fuel/air mixture incorrect
- ☐ Compression low
- ☐ Poor acceleration

3 Poor running or no power at high speed

- ☐ Firing incorrect
- ☐ Fuel/air mixture incorrect
- ☐ Compression low
- ☐ Knocking or pinking
- ☐ Miscellaneous causes

4 Overheating

- ☐ Engine overheats
- ☐ Firing incorrect
- ☐ Fuel/air mixture incorrect
- ☐ Compression too high
- ☐ Engine load excessive
- ☐ Lubrication inadequate
- ☐ Miscellaneous causes

5 Clutch problems

- ☐ Clutch slipping
- ☐ Clutch not disengaging completely

6 Gearchanging problems

- ☐ Doesn't go into gear, or lever doesn't return
- ☐ Jumps out of gear
- ☐ Overselects

7 Abnormal engine noise

- ☐ Knocking or pinking
- ☐ Piston slap or rattling
- ☐ Valve noise
- ☐ Other noise

8 Abnormal driveline noise

- ☐ Clutch noise
- ☐ Transmission noise
- ☐ Final drive noise

9 Abnormal frame and suspension noise

- ☐ Front end noise
- ☐ Shock absorber noise
- ☐ Brake noise

10 Oil pressure warning light comes on

- ☐ Engine lubrication system
- ☐ Electrical system

11 Excessive exhaust smoke

- ☐ White smoke
- ☐ Black smoke
- ☐ Brown smoke

12 Poor handling or stability

- ☐ Handlebar hard to turn
- ☐ Handlebar shakes or vibrates excessively
- ☐ Handlebar pulls to one side
- ☐ Poor shock absorbing qualities

13 Braking problems

- ☐ Brakes are spongy, don't hold
- ☐ Brake lever or pedal pulsates
- ☐ Brakes drag

14 Electrical problems

- ☐ Battery dead or weak
- ☐ Battery overcharged

1 Engine doesn't start or is difficult to start

Starter motor doesn't rotate

☐ Engine kill switch OFF.
☐ Fuse blown. Check main fuse (Chapter 8).
☐ Battery voltage low. Check and recharge battery (Chapter 8).
☐ Starter motor defective. Make sure the wiring to the starter is secure. Make sure the starter relay clicks when the start button is pushed. If the relay clicks, then the fault is in the wiring or motor (see Chapter 8).
☐ Starter switch not contacting. The contacts could be wet, corroded or dirty. Disassemble and clean the switch (Chapter 8).
☐ Wiring open or shorted. Check all wiring connections and harnesses to make sure that they are dry, tight and not corroded. Also check for broken or frayed wires that can cause a short to ground (earth) (see *Wiring diagrams*, Chapter 8).
☐ Ignition switch defective. Check the switch and replace with a new one if it is defective (see Chapter 8).
☐ Engine kill switch defective. Check for wet, dirty or corroded contacts. Clean or replace the switch with a new one as necessary (see Chapter 8).
☐ Faulty neutral switch, sidestand switch or clutch switch. Check the wiring to each switch and the switch itself (see Chapter 8).
☐ Faulty starter circuit relay or diode (Chapter 8).
☐ Fuel injection system shutdown due to system fault (Chapter 4).

Starter motor rotates but engine does not turn over

☐ Starter clutch defective. Inspect and repair or replace with a new one (see Chapter 2).
☐ Damaged idler or starter gears. Inspect and replace the damaged parts (see Chapter 2).

Starter works but engine won't turn over (seized)

☐ Seized engine caused by one or more internally damaged components. Failure due to wear, abuse or lack of lubrication. Damage can include seized valves, followers, camshafts, pistons, crankshaft, connecting rod bearings, or transmission gears or bearings. Refer to Chapter 2 for engine disassembly.

No fuel flow

☐ No fuel in tank.
☐ Fuel tank breather hose obstructed.
☐ Faulty fuel pump relay. Check the relay (see Chapter 4).
☐ Fuel pump faulty, or the fuel filter is blocked (see Chapter 4).
☐ Fuel hose clogged. Remove the fuel hose and carefully blow through it.
☐ Fuel rail or injector clogged. For all of the injectors to be clogged, either a very bad batch of fuel with an unusual additive has been used, or some other foreign material has entered the tank. In some cases, if a machine has been unused for several months, the fuel turns to a varnish-like liquid which can cause an injector needle to stick to its seat. Drain the tank and fuel system (Chapter 4).

Engine flooded

☐ Injector needle valve worn or stuck open. A piece of dirt, rust or other debris can cause the needle to seat improperly, causing excess fuel to be admitted to the throttle body. In this case, the injector should be cleaned and the needle and seat inspected (see Chapter 4). If the needle and seat are worn, then the leaking will persist and the parts should be renewed.
☐ Starting technique incorrect. Under normal circumstances (i.e. if all the components of the fuel injection system are good) the machine should start with the throttle closed.

No spark or weak spark

☐ Ignition switch OFF.
☐ Engine kill switch turned to the OFF position.

☐ Faulty immobilizer system or damaged key (where fitted) – (Chapter 5).
☐ Ignition or kill switch shorted. This is usually caused by water, corrosion, damage or excessive wear. The switches can be disassembled and cleaned with electrical contact cleaner. If cleaning does not help, replace the switches (see Chapter 8).
☐ Battery voltage low. Check and recharge the battery as necessary (Chapter 8).
☐ Ignition coil not making good contact. Make sure that the coils fit snugly over the plug ends.
☐ Spark plugs dirty, defective or worn out. Locate reason for fouled plugs using spark plug condition chart on the inside back cover and follow the plug maintenance procedures (see Chapter 1).
☐ Incorrect spark plugs. Wrong type or heat range. Check and install correct plugs (see Chapter 1).
☐ Ignition coil defective. Test and renew if necessary (Chapter 4).
☐ Fuel injection system shutdown due to system fault (Chapter 4).
☐ Camshaft position (CMP) sensor defective (see Chapter 4).
☐ Crankshaft position (CKP) sensor defective (see Chapter 4).
☐ Engine control unit (ECU) defective (see Chapter 4).
☐ Wiring shorted or broken between:
    a) Ignition switch and engine kill switch (or blown fuse)
    b) ECU and engine kill switch
    c) ECU and ignition coils
    d) ECU and CKP
☐ Make sure that all wiring connections are clean, dry and tight. Look for chafed and broken wires (see Chapters 4 and 8).

Compression low

☐ Spark plugs loose. Remove the plugs and inspect their threads. Reinstall and tighten securely (see Chapter 1).
☐ Cylinder head not sufficiently tightened down. If the cylinder head is suspected of being loose, then there's a chance that the gasket or head is damaged if the problem has persisted for any length of time. The head bolts should be tightened to the proper torque and in the correct sequence (Chapter 2).
☐ Improper valve clearance. This means that the valve is not closing completely and compression pressure is leaking past the valve. Check and adjust the valve clearances (Chapter 1).
☐ Cylinder and/or piston worn. Excessive wear will cause compression pressure to leak past the rings. This is usually accompanied by worn rings as well. A top-end overhaul is necessary (Chapter 2).
☐ Piston rings worn, weak, broken, or sticking. Broken or sticking piston rings usually indicate a lubrication or fuelling problem that causes excess carbon deposits to form on the pistons and rings. Top-end overhaul is necessary (Chapter 2).
☐ Piston ring-to-groove clearance excessive. This is caused by excessive wear of the piston ring lands. Piston renewal is necessary (Chapter 2).
☐ Cylinder head gasket damaged. If a head is allowed to become loose, or if excessive carbon build-up on the piston crown and combustion chamber causes extremely high compression, the head gasket may leak. Retorquing the head is not always sufficient to restore the seal, so a new gasket is necessary (Chapter 2).
☐ Cylinder head warped. This is caused by overheating or improperly tightened head bolts. Machine shop resurfacing or head renewal is necessary (Chapter 2).
☐ Valve spring broken or weak. Caused by component failure or wear; the springs must be renewed (Chapter 2).
☐ Valve not seating properly. This is caused by a bent valve (from over-revving or improper valve adjustment), burned valve or seat (improper fuelling) or an accumulation of carbon deposits on the seat. The valves must be cleaned and/or renewed and the seats serviced (Chapter 2).

1 Engine doesn't start or is difficult to start (continued)

Stalls after starting

- [ ] Engine idle speed incorrect. Turn idle adjusting screw until the engine idles at the specified rpm (Chapter 1).
- [ ] Ignition malfunction (see Chapter 4).
- [ ] Fuel injection system malfunction (see Chapter 4).
- [ ] Fuel contaminated. The fuel can be contaminated with either dirt or water, or can change chemically if the machine has been unused for several months. Drain the tank and fuel system (Chapter 4).
- [ ] Intake air leak. Check for loose throttle body-to-intake manifold connections, loose or damaged air system vacuum hose or missing vacuum gauge blanking caps (Chapter 4).

Rough idle

- [ ] Idle speed incorrect (see Chapter 1).
- [ ] Ignition fault (see Chapter 4).
- [ ] Throttle bodies not synchronised. Adjust them as described in Chapter 1.
- [ ] Fuel injection system malfunction (see Chapter 4).
- [ ] Fuel contaminated. The fuel can be contaminated with either dirt or water, or can change chemically if the machine has been unused for several months. Drain the tank and the fuel system (Chapter 4).
- [ ] Intake air leak. Check for loose throttle body-to-intake manifold connections, loose or damaged air system vacuum hose or missing vacuum gauge blanking caps (Chapter 4).
- [ ] Air filter clogged. Clean the air filter element or replace it with a new one (Chapter 1).

2 Poor running at low speeds

Spark weak

- [ ] Battery voltage low. Check and recharge battery (see Chapter 8).
- [ ] Ignition coils not making good contact. Make sure that the coils fit snugly over the plug ends.
- [ ] Spark plugs dirty, defective or worn out. Locate reason for fouled plugs using spark plug condition chart on the inside back cover and follow the plug maintenance procedures (see Chapter 1).
- [ ] Incorrect spark plugs. Wrong type or heat range. Check and install correct plugs (see Chapter 1).
- [ ] Ignition coil defective. Test and renew if necessary (see Chapter 4).

Fuel/air mixture incorrect

- [ ] Fuel tank breather hose obstructed.
- [ ] Fuel pump faulty, or the fuel filter is blocked (see Chapter 4).
- [ ] Fuel hose clogged. Remove the fuel hose and carefully blow through it.
- [ ] Fuel rail or injector clogged. For all of the injectors to be clogged, either a very bad batch of fuel with an unusual additive has been used, or some other foreign material has entered the tank. In some cases, if a machine has been unused for several months, the fuel turns to a varnish-like liquid which can cause an injector needle to stick to its seat. Drain the tank and fuel system (Chapter 4).
- [ ] Intake air leak. Check for loose throttle body-to-intake manifold connections, loose or damaged vacuum hose or missing vacuum gauge blanking caps (Chapter 4).
- [ ] Air filter clogged. Clean the air filter element or replace it with a new one (Chapter 1).

Compression low

- [ ] Spark plugs loose. Remove the plugs and inspect their threads. Reinstall and tighten securely (see Chapter 1).
- [ ] Cylinder head not sufficiently tightened down. If the cylinder head is suspected of being loose, then there's a chance that the gasket or head is damaged if the problem has persisted for any length of time. The head bolts should be tightened to the proper torque and in the correct sequence (Chapter 2).
- [ ] Improper valve clearance. This means that the valve is not closing completely and compression pressure is leaking past the valve. Check and adjust the valve clearances (Chapter 1).
- [ ] Cylinder and/or piston worn. Excessive wear will cause compression pressure to leak past the rings. This is usually accompanied by worn rings as well. A top-end overhaul is necessary (Chapter 2).
- [ ] Piston rings worn, weak, broken, or sticking. Broken or sticking piston rings usually indicate a lubrication or fuelling problem that causes excess carbon deposits to form on the pistons and rings. Top-end overhaul is necessary (Chapter 2).
- [ ] Piston ring-to-groove clearance excessive. This is caused by excessive wear of the piston ring lands. Piston renewal is necessary (Chapter 2).
- [ ] Cylinder head gasket damaged. If the head is allowed to become loose, or if excessive carbon build-up on the piston crown and combustion chamber causes extremely high compression, the head gasket may leak. Retorquing the head is not always sufficient to restore the seal, so a new gasket is necessary (Chapter 2).
- [ ] Cylinder head warped. This is caused by overheating or improperly tightened head bolts. Machine shop resurfacing or head renewal is necessary (Chapter 2).
- [ ] Valve spring broken or weak. Caused by component failure or wear; the springs must be renewed (Chapter 2).
- [ ] Valve not seating properly. This is caused by a bent valve (from over-revving or improper valve adjustment), burned valve or seat (improper fuelling) or an accumulation of carbon deposits on the seat (from fuelling or lubrication problems). The valves must be cleaned and/or renewed and the seats serviced (Chapter 2).

Poor acceleration

- [ ] Timing not advancing. The crankshaft position sensor (CKP) or the engine control unit (ECU) may be defective (see Chapter 4). If so, they must be renewed.
- [ ] Engine oil viscosity too high. Using a heavier oil than that recommended in Pre-ride checks can damage the oil pump or lubrication system and cause drag on the engine.
- [ ] Brakes dragging. Usually caused by debris which has entered the brake caliper piston seals, or from a warped disc or bent axle (see Chapter 6).

3 Poor running or no power at high speed

Firing incorrect

- [ ] Ignition coil not making good contact. Make sure that the coils fit snugly over the plug ends and that the wiring is secure.
- [ ] Spark plugs dirty, defective or worn out. Locate reason for fouled plugs using spark plug condition chart on the inside back cover and follow the plug maintenance procedures (see Chapter 1).
- [ ] Incorrect spark plugs. Wrong type or heat range. Check and install correct plugs (see Chapter 1).
- [ ] Ignition coil defective. Test and renew if necessary (see Chapter 4).
- [ ] Faulty ECU (engine control unit) (see Chapter 4.

Fuel/air mixture incorrect

- [ ] Fuel tank breather hose obstructed.
- [ ] Fuel pump faulty, or the fuel filter is blocked (see Chapter 4).
- [ ] Fuel hose clogged. Remove the fuel hose and carefully blow through it.
- [ ] Fuel rail or injector clogged. For all of the injectors to be clogged, either a very bad batch of fuel with an unusual additive has been used, or some other foreign material has entered the tank. In some cases, if a machine has been unused for several months, the fuel turns to a varnish-like liquid which can cause an injector needle to stick to its seat. Drain the tank and fuel system (Chapter 4).
- [ ] Intake air leak. Check for loose throttle body-to-intake manifold connections, loose or damaged vacuum hose or missing vacuum gauge blanking caps (Chapter 4).
- [ ] Air filter clogged. Clean the air filter element or replace it with a new one (Chapter 1).

Compression low

- [ ] Spark plugs loose. Remove the plugs and inspect their threads. Reinstall and tighten securely (see Chapter 1).
- [ ] Cylinder head not sufficiently tightened down. If the cylinder head is suspected of being loose, then there's a chance that the gasket or head is damaged if the problem has persisted for any length of time. The head bolts should be tightened to the proper torque and in the correct sequence (Chapter 2).
- [ ] Improper valve clearance. This means that the valve is not closing completely and compression pressure is leaking past the valve. Check and adjust the valve clearances (Chapter 1).
- [ ] Cylinder and/or piston worn. Excessive wear will cause compression pressure to leak past the rings. This is usually accompanied by worn rings as well. A top-end overhaul is necessary (Chapter 2).
- [ ] Piston rings worn, weak, broken, or sticking. Broken or sticking piston rings usually indicate a lubrication or fuelling problem that causes excess carbon deposits to form on the pistons and rings. Top-end overhaul is necessary (Chapter 2).
- [ ] Piston ring-to-groove clearance excessive. This is caused by excessive wear of the piston ring lands. Piston renewal is necessary (Chapter 2).
- [ ] Cylinder head gasket damaged. If a head is allowed to become loose, or if excessive carbon build-up on the piston crown and combustion chamber causes extremely high compression, the head gasket may leak. Retorquing the head is not always sufficient to restore the seal, so a new gasket is necessary (Chapter 2).
- [ ] Cylinder head warped. This is caused by overheating or improperly tightened head bolts. Machine shop resurfacing or head renewal is necessary (Chapter 2).
- [ ] Valve spring broken or weak. Caused by component failure or wear; the springs must be replaced with new ones (Chapter 2).
- [ ] Valve not seating properly. This is caused by a bent valve (from over-revving or improper valve adjustment), burned valve or seat (improper fuelling) or an accumulation of carbon deposits on the seat (from fuelling or lubrication problems). The valves must be cleaned and/or renewed and the seats serviced (Chapter 2).

Knocking or pinking

- [ ] Carbon build-up in combustion chamber. Use of a fuel additive that will dissolve the adhesive bonding the carbon particles to the piston crown and chamber is the easiest way to remove the build-up. Otherwise, the cylinder head will have to be removed and decarbonised (Chapter 2).
- [ ] Incorrect or poor quality fuel. Old or improper grades of fuel can cause detonation. This causes the piston to rattle, thus the knocking or pinking sound. Drain old fuel and always use the recommended fuel grade.
- [ ] Spark plug heat range incorrect. Uncontrolled detonation indicates the plug heat range is too hot. The plug in effect becomes a glow plug, raising cylinder temperatures. Install the proper heat range plug (Chapter 1).
- [ ] Improper air/fuel mixture. This will cause the cylinders to run hot, which leads to detonation. A blockage in the fuel system or an air leak can cause this imbalance (see Chapter 4).

Miscellaneous causes

- [ ] Throttle valve doesn't open fully. Adjust the throttle twistgrip freeplay (see Chapter 1).
- [ ] Clutch slipping due loose or worn clutch components (see Chapter 2).
- [ ] Timing not advancing. The crankshaft position sensor (CKP) or the engine control unit (ECU) may be defective (see Chapter 4). If so, they must be replaced with new ones.
- [ ] Engine oil viscosity too high. Using a heavier oil than the one recommended in Chapter 1 can damage the oil pump or lubrication system and cause drag on the engine.
- [ ] Brakes dragging. Usually caused by debris which has entered the brake caliper piston seals, or from a warped disc or bent axle (see Chapter 6).

4 Overheating

Engine overheats

- ☐ Coolant level low. Check and add coolant (see *Pre-ride checks*).
- ☐ Leak in cooling system. Check cooling system hoses and radiator for leaks and other damage. Repair system or renew parts as necessary (see Chapter 3).
- ☐ Faulty thermostat. Check and renew as described in Chapter 3.
- ☐ Faulty radiator cap. Remove the cap and have it pressure tested.
- ☐ Coolant passages clogged. Have the entire system drained and flushed, then refill with fresh coolant.
- ☐ Water pump defective. Remove the pump and check the components (see Chapter 3).
- ☐ Clogged or damaged radiator fins (see Chapter 3).
- ☐ Faulty cooling fan, ECT sensor or relay (see Chapter 3).

Firing incorrect

- ☐ Wrongly connected ignition coil wiring.
- ☐ Spark plugs dirty, defective or worn out. Locate reason for fouled plugs using spark plug condition chart on the inside back cover and follow the plug maintenance procedures (see Chapter 1).
- ☐ Incorrect spark plugs. Wrong type or heat range. Check and install correct plugs (see Chapter 1).
- ☐ Ignition coil defective. Test and replace with a new one if necessary (see Chapter 5).
- ☐ Faulty ECU (engine control unit) (see Chapter 4).

Fuel/air mixture incorrect

- ☐ Fuel tank breather hose obstructed.
- ☐ Fuel pump faulty, or the fuel filter is blocked (see Chapter 4).
- ☐ Fuel hose clogged. Remove the fuel hose and carefully blow through it.
- ☐ Fuel rail or injector clogged. For all of the injectors to be clogged, either a very bad batch of fuel with an unusual additive has been used, or some other foreign material has entered the tank. In some cases, if a machine has been unused for several months, the fuel turns to a varnish-like liquid which can cause an injector needle to stick to its seat. Drain the tank and fuel system (Chapter 4).
- ☐ Intake air leak. Check for loose throttle body-to-intake manifold connections, loose or damaged air system vacuum hose or missing vacuum gauge blanking caps (Chapter 4).
- ☐ Air filter clogged. Clean the air filter element or replace it with a new one (Chapter 1).

Compression too high

- ☐ Carbon build-up in combustion chamber. Use of a fuel additive that will dissolve the adhesive bonding the carbon particles to the piston crown and chamber is the easiest way to remove the build-up. Otherwise, the cylinder head will have to be removed and decarbonised (Chapter 2).
- ☐ Improperly machined head surface or installation of incorrect gasket during engine assembly.

Engine load excessive

- ☐ Clutch slipping due loose or worn clutch components (see Chapter 2).
- ☐ Engine oil level too high. Too much oil will cause pressurisation of the crankcase and inefficient engine operation. Check the level (see *Pre-ride checks*).
- ☐ Engine oil viscosity too high. Using a heavier oil than the one recommended in Chapter 1 can damage the oil pump or lubrication system as well as cause drag on the engine.
- ☐ Brakes dragging. Usually caused by debris which has entered the brake caliper piston seals, or from a warped disc or bent axle (see Chapter 6).

Lubrication inadequate

- ☐ Engine oil level too low. Friction caused by intermittent lack of lubrication or from oil that is overworked can cause overheating. The oil provides a definite cooling function in the engine. Check the oil level (see *Pre-ride checks*).
- ☐ Low engine oil pressure. Check the pressure (see Chapter 1).
- ☐ Blocked oil filter or oil cooler (see Chapter 2).
- ☐ Poor quality engine oil or incorrect viscosity or type. Oil is rated not only according to viscosity but also according to type. Some oils are not rated high enough for use in this engine. Check the Specifications section and change to the correct oil (see *Pre-ride checks*).

Miscellaneous causes

- ☐ Modification to exhaust system. Most aftermarket exhaust systems cause the engine to run leaner, which make them run hotter. When installing an accessory exhaust system, always check with the manufacturer/supplier as to whether the ECU requires re-mapping.

5 Clutch problems

Clutch slipping

- [ ] Insufficient clutch cable freeplay. Check and adjust (see Chapter 1).
- [ ] Clutch plates worn or warped. Overhaul the clutch assembly (see Chapter 2).
- [ ] Clutch springs broken or weak. Old or heat-damaged (from slipping clutch) springs should be renewed (Chapter 2).
- [ ] Faulty clutch release mechanism. Replace any defective parts with new ones (see Chapter 2).
- [ ] Clutch centre or housing unevenly worn. This causes improper engagement of the plates. Replace the damaged or worn parts (see Chapter 2).
- [ ] Use of a motor oil designed for car engines.

Clutch not disengaging completely

- [ ] Excessive clutch cable freeplay. Check and adjust (see Chapter 1).
- [ ] Clutch plates warped or damaged. This will cause clutch drag, which in turn will cause the machine to creep. Overhaul the clutch assembly (see Chapter 2).

- [ ] Clutch springs fatigued or broken. Check and renew the springs (see Chapter 2).
- [ ] Engine oil deteriorated. Old, thin oil will not provide proper lubrication for the plates, causing the clutch to drag. Renew the oil and filter (see Chapter 1).
- [ ] Engine oil viscosity too high. Using a heavier oil than recommended in Chapter 1 can cause the plates to stick together. Change to the correct weight oil.
- [ ] Clutch housing bearing seized on the transmission input shaft. Lack of lubrication, severe wear or damage can cause the bearing to seize. Overhaul of the clutch, and perhaps transmission, may be necessary to repair system the damage (see Chapter 2).
- [ ] Faulty clutch release mechanism. Renew any defective parts (see Chapter 2).
- [ ] Loose clutch centre nut. Causes housing and centre misalignment putting a drag on the engine. Engagement adjustment continually varies. Overhaul the clutch assembly (see Chapter 2).

6 Gearchanging problems

Doesn't go into gear or lever doesn't return

- [ ] Clutch not disengaging (see above).
- [ ] Gearchange mechanism stopper arm spring weak or broken, or arm roller broken or worn. Replace the spring or arm with a new one (see Chapter 2).
- [ ] Selector fork(s) bent, worn or seized. Overhaul the transmission (see Chapter 2).
- [ ] Gear(s) stuck on shaft. Most often caused by a lack of lubrication or excessive wear in transmission bearings and bushes. Overhaul the transmission (see Chapter 2).
- [ ] Selector drum binding. Caused by lubrication failure or excessive wear. Replace the drum and/or its bearing with a new one (see Chapter 2).
- [ ] Gearchange mechanism return spring weak or broken (see Chapter 2).

- [ ] Gearchange linkage arm broken. Splines stripped out of arm or shaft, caused by a loose linkage arm pinch bolt or from dropping the machine (see Chapter 2).

Jumps out of gear

- [ ] Selector fork(s) worn (see Chapter 2).
- [ ] Selector fork groove(s) in selector drum worn (see Chapter 2).
- [ ] Gear pinion dogs or dog slots worn or damaged. The gear pinions should be inspected and renewed. No attempt should be made to repair the worn parts.

Overselects

- [ ] Gearchange mechanism stopper arm spring weak or broken, or arm roller broken or worn. Renew the spring or arm (see Chapter 2).
- [ ] Gearchange mechanism return spring weak or broken (see Chapter 2).

7 Abnormal engine noise

Knocking or pinking

☐ Carbon build-up in combustion chamber. Use of a fuel additive that will dissolve the adhesive bonding the carbon particles to the piston crown and chamber is the easiest way to remove the build-up. Otherwise, the cylinder head will have to be removed and decarbonised (Chapter 2).

☐ Incorrect or poor quality fuel. Old or improper grades of fuel can cause detonation. This causes the piston to rattle, thus the knocking or pinking sound. Drain old fuel and always use the recommended fuel grade.

☐ Spark plug heat range incorrect. Uncontrolled detonation indicates the plug heat range is too hot. The plug in effect becomes a glow plug, raising cylinder temperatures. Install the proper heat range plug (Chapter 1).

☐ Improper air/fuel mixture. This will cause the cylinders to run hot, which leads to detonation. A blockage in the fuel system or an air leak can cause this imbalance (see Chapter 4).

Piston slap or rattling

☐ Cylinder-to-piston clearance excessive. Cylinder and/or piston worn, usually accompanied by worn rings as well. A top-end overhaul is necessary (see Chapter 2).

☐ Piston ring(s) worn, broken or sticking. Overhaul the top-end (see Chapter 2).

☐ Piston pin, piston pin bore or connecting rod small-end worn from high mileage or seized due to lack of lubrication (see Chapter 2).

☐ Piston seizure damage. Usually from lack of lubrication or overheating. Replace the pistons and upper crankcase, as necessary (see Chapter 2).

☐ Connecting rod big-end clearance excessive. Caused by excessive wear or lack of lubrication. Replace worn parts.

☐ Connecting rod bent. Caused by over-revving, trying to start a badly flooded engine or from ingesting a foreign object into the combustion chamber. Replace the damaged parts (Chapter 2).

Valve noise

☐ Incorrect valve clearances – check and adjust (see Chapter 1).

☐ Valve spring broken or weak. Check and replace weak valve springs with new ones (see Chapter 2).

☐ Camshaft or camshaft journals in the cylinder head worn or damaged. Lubrication failure at high rpm is usually the cause of damage due to insufficient oil or failure to change the oil at the recommended intervals. Since there are no replaceable bearings in the head, the head itself will have to be replaced with a new one (see Chapter 2).

Other noise

☐ Cylinder head gasket leaking. Check around the joint for blowing with the engine running.

☐ Exhaust pipe leaking at cylinder head connection. Caused by incorrect fit of pipe(s), loose exhaust flange or damaged gasket. All exhaust system fasteners should be tightened evenly and carefully to avoid leaks (see Chapter 4).

☐ Crankshaft runout excessive. Caused by a bent crankshaft (from over-revving) or damage from an upper cylinder component failure. Can also be attributed to dropping the machine on either of the crankshaft ends.

☐ Engine mounting bolts loose – ensure all the bolts are tightened to the specified torque settings (see Chapter 2).

☐ Crankshaft bearings worn (see Chapter 2).

☐ Cam chain rattle, due to worn chain or defective tensioner. Also worn chain tensioner/guide blades (see Chapter 2).

8 Abnormal driveline noise

Clutch noise

☐ Clutch housing/friction plate clearance excessive (Chapter 2).
☐ Wear between the clutch housing splines and input shaft splines (Chapter 2).
☐ Worn release bearing (Chapter 2).

Transmission noise

☐ Bearings worn. Also includes the possibility that the shafts are worn. Overhaul the transmission (Chapter 2).
☐ Gears worn or chipped (Chapter 2).
☐ Metal chips jammed in gear teeth. Probably pieces from a broken clutch, gear or selector mechanism that were picked up by the gears. This will cause early bearing failure (Chapter 2).
☐ Engine oil level too low. Causes a howl from transmission. Also affects engine power and clutch operation (see *Pre-ride checks*).

Final drive noise

☐ Chain not adjusted properly (Chapter 1).
☐ Front or rear sprocket loose. Tighten fasteners (Chapter 6).
☐ Sprockets and/or chain worn. Fit new sprockets and chain (Chapter 6).
☐ Rear sprocket warped. Fit a new sprocket (Chapter 6).
☐ Rubber dampers in rear wheel worn (Chapter 6).

9 Abnormal frame and suspension noise

Front end noise

☐ Low fluid level or improper viscosity oil in forks. This can sound like spurting and is usually accompanied by irregular fork action (Chapter 5).
☐ Spring weak or broken. Makes a clicking or scraping sound. Fork oil, when drained, will have a lot of metal particles in it (Chapter 5).
☐ Steering head bearings loose or damaged. Clicks when braking. Check and adjust or replace with new ones as necessary (Chapters 1 and 5).
☐ Fork yoke clamp bolts loose – ensure all the bolts are tightened to the specified torque (Chapter 6).
☐ Forks bent. Good possibility if machine has been dropped. Replace the inner tubes with new ones as required (Chapter 5).
☐ Front axle or axle pinch bolts loose. Tighten them to the specified torque (Chapter 6).
☐ Loose or worn wheel bearings. Check and replace with new ones as needed (Chapters 1 and 6).

Shock absorber noise

☐ Fluid level incorrect. Indicates a leak caused by defective seal. Shock will be covered with oil. Replace shock with a new one or seek advice on repair from a suspension specialist (Chapter 5).
☐ Defective shock absorber with internal damage. This is in the body of the shock and can't be remedied. The shock must be replaced with a new one or rebuilt (Chapter 5).

☐ Bent or damaged shock body. Replace the shock with a new one (Chapter 5).
☐ Loose or worn suspension linkage components. Check and replace with new ones as necessary (Chapter 5).

Brake noise

☐ Squeal caused by dust on brake pads. Usually found in combination with glazed pads. Clean using brake cleaning solvent (Chapter 6).
☐ Pads glazed. Caused by excessive heat from prolonged hard use or from contamination. DO NOT use sandpaper, emery cloth, carborundum cloth or any other abrasive to roughen the pad surfaces as abrasives will stay in the pad material and damage the disc. A very fine flat file can be used, but new pads is the best remedy (Chapter 6).
☐ Contamination of brake pads. Oil or brake fluid can cause the brake pads to chatter or squeal. Fit new pads. Identify the cause of the contamination, especially check the caliper piston seals for leaking fluid. Clean disc thoroughly with brake system cleaner (Chapter 6).
☐ Disc warped. Can cause a chattering, clicking or intermittent squeal. Usually accompanied by a pulsating lever and uneven braking. Replace the disc with new one (Chapter 6).
☐ Loose or worn wheel bearings. Check and replace with new ones as needed (Chapters 1 and 6).

10 Oil pressure warning light comes on

Engine lubrication system

- ☐ Engine oil level low. Inspect for leak or other problem causing low oil level and add recommended oil (see *Pre-ride checks*).
- ☐ Engine oil pump defective, blocked oil strainer gauze or failed pressure regulator. Carry out an oil pressure check (Chapter 2).
- ☐ Engine oil viscosity too low. Very old, thin oil or an improper weight of oil used in the engine. Change to correct oil (see *Pre-ride checks*).
- ☐ Camshaft or crankshaft journals worn. Excessive wear causing drop in oil pressure. Abnormal wear could be caused by oil starvation at high rpm from low oil level or improper weight or type of oil (Chapter 1).

Electrical system

- ☐ Oil pressure switch defective. Check the switch according to the procedure in Chapter 8. Replace it with a new one it if it is defective.
- ☐ Oil pressure warning LED or circuit defective. Check for pinched, shorted, disconnected or damaged wiring (Chapter 8).

11 Excessive exhaust smoke

White smoke

- ☐ Piston rings worn or broken, causing oil from the crankcase to be pulled past the piston into the combustion chamber. Replace the rings with new ones (Chapter 2).
- ☐ Cylinders worn or scored. Caused by overheating or oil starvation. Install a new cylinder block (Chapter 2).
- ☐ Valve stem oil seal damaged or worn. Replace the oil seals with new ones (Chapter 2).
- ☐ Valve guide worn. Perform a complete valve job (Chapter 2).
- ☐ Engine oil level too high, which causes the oil to be forced past the rings. Drain oil to the proper level (see *Pre-ride checks*).
- ☐ Head gasket broken between oil return and cylinder. Causes oil to be pulled into the combustion chamber. Replace the head gasket with a new one and check the head for warpage (Chapter 2).
- ☐ Abnormal crankcase pressurisation which forces oil past the rings, usually caused by a clogged breather.

Black smoke

- ☐ Air filter clogged. Clean the air filter element or replace it with a new one (Chapter 1).
- ☐ Fuel injection system malfunction (Chapter 4).

Brown smoke

- ☐ Air filter poorly sealed or not installed (Chapter 1).
- ☐ Fuel injection system malfunction (Chapter 4).

12 Poor handling or stability

Handlebars hard to turn

- ☐ Steering head bearing adjuster nut too tight. Check adjustment as described in Chapter 1.
- ☐ Bearings damaged. Roughness can be felt as the bars are turned from side-to-side. Replace the bearings with new ones (Chapter 5).
- ☐ Races dented or worn. Denting results from wear in only one position (e.g., straight ahead), from a collision or hitting a pothole or from dropping the machine. Replace the bearings with new ones (Chapter 5).
- ☐ Steering stem lubrication inadequate. Causes are grease getting hard from age or being washed out by high pressure car washes. Disassemble steering head and repack bearings (Chapter 5).
- ☐ Steering stem bent. Caused by a collision, hitting a pothole or by dropping the machine. Replace damaged part. Don't try to straighten the steering stem (Chapter 5).
- ☐ Front tyre air pressure too low (see *Pre-ride checks*).

Handlebar shakes or vibrates excessively

- ☐ Tyres worn or out of balance (Chapter 6).
- ☐ Swingarm bearings worn. Replace the bearings with new ones (Chapter 5).
- ☐ Wheel rim(s) warped or damaged. Inspect wheels for runout (Chapter 6).
- ☐ Wheel bearings worn. Worn front or rear wheel bearings can cause poor tracking. Worn front bearings will cause wobble (Chapters 1 and 6).
- ☐ Fork yoke clamp bolts or handlebar clamp bolts loose. Tighten them to the specified torque (Chapter 5).
- ☐ Engine mounting bolts loose. Will cause excessive vibration with increased engine rpm – ensure all the bolts are tightened to the specified torque settings (see Chapter 2).

Machine pulls to one side

- ☐ Frame bent. Definitely suspect this if the machine has been dropped. May or may not be accompanied by cracking near the steering head, swingarm mountings or engine mountings. Replace the frame with a new one (Chapter 5).
- ☐ Wheels out of alignment. Caused by improper location of axle spacers or from bent steering stem or frame (Chapter 5).
- ☐ Forks bent. Disassemble the forks and replace the damaged parts (Chapter 5).
- ☐ Swingarm bent or twisted. Replace the arm with a new one (Chapter 5).
- ☐ Fork oil level uneven. Check and add or drain as necessary (Chapter 5).

Poor shock absorbing qualities

- ☐ Too hard:
  - a) Suspension settings incorrect.
  - b) Fork oil level excessive (Chapter 5).
  - c) Fork oil viscosity too high. Use a lighter oil (see the Specifications in Chapter 5).
  - d) Fork inner tube bent. Causes a harsh, sticking feeling (Chapter 5).
  - e) Fork internal damage (Chapter 5).
  - f) Shock shaft or body bent or damaged (Chapter 5).
  - g) Shock internal damage.
  - h) Tyre pressure too high (see Pre-ride checks).
- ☐ Too soft:
  - a) Suspension settings incorrect.
  - b) Fork oil level too low (Chapter 5).
  - c) Fork oil viscosity too light (Chapter 5).
  - d) Fork springs weak or broken (Chapter 5).
  - e) Fork or shock oil leaking (Chapter 5).
  - f) Shock internal damage (Chapter 5).

13 Braking problems

Brakes are spongy, don't hold

☐ Low brake fluid level (see *Pre-ride checks*).
☐ Air in hydraulic system. Caused by inattention to master cylinder fluid level or by leakage. Locate problem and bleed brakes (Chapter 6).
☐ Pad or disc worn (Chapters 1 and 6).
☐ Contaminated pads. Caused by contamination with oil, grease, brake fluid, etc. Fit new pads. Identify the cause of the contamination, especially check the caliper piston seals for leaking fluid. Clean disc thoroughly with brake system cleaner (Chapter 6).
☐ Brake fluid deteriorated. Fluid is old or contaminated. Drain system, replenish with new fluid and bleed the system (Chapter 6).
☐ Master cylinder internal seals worn or damaged causing fluid to bypass (Chapter 6).
☐ Master cylinder bore scratched by foreign material or broken spring. Fit a new master cylinder (Chapter 6).
☐ Disc warped. Replace disc with new one (Chapter 6).

Brake lever or pedal pulsates

☐ Disc warped. Replace disc with new one (Chapter 6).
☐ Axle bent. Replace axle with new one (Chapter 6).

☐ Brake caliper bolts loose – tighten the bolts to the specified torque (Chapter 6).
☐ Wheel warped or otherwise damaged (Chapter 6).
☐ Wheel bearings damaged or worn (Chapters 1 and 6).

Brakes drag

☐ Master cylinder piston seized. Caused by wear or damage to piston or cylinder bore (Chapter 6).
☐ Lever balky or stuck. Check pivot and lubricate (Chapter 6).
☐ Brake caliper piston seized in bore. Caused by corrosion or ingestion of dirt past deteriorated seal (Chapter 6).
☐ Caliper sticking on slider pins due to corrosion (front calipers on Z750 models, rear caliper on all models). Clean and lubricate pins and check dust boots (Chapter 6).
☐ Brake pad damaged. Pad material separated from backing plate. Usually caused by faulty manufacturing process or from contact with chemicals. Fit new pads (Chapter 6).
☐ Pads improperly installed (Chapter 6).
☐ Brake caliper incorrectly installed (Chapter 6).

ABS indicator light comes on – ZR750-M and ZR1000-C

☐ If the light remains on after start-up or comes on while riding, investigate the fault as described in Chapter 6, Section 10.

14 Electrical problems

Battery dead or weak

☐ Battery faulty. Caused by sulphated plates which are shorted through sedimentation. Confirm with battery condition check (Chapter 8).
☐ Broken battery terminal making only occasional contact.
☐ Battery leads making poor contact (Chapter 8).
☐ Load excessive. Caused by addition of high wattage lights or other electrical accessories.
☐ Ignition switch defective. Switch either grounds (earths) internally or fails to shut off system. Renew the switch (Chapter 8).
☐ Regulator/rectifier defective (Chapter 8).
☐ Alternator stator coil open or shorted (Chapter 8).

☐ Charging system fault. Check for excessive current leakage (Chapter 8).
☐ Wiring faulty. Wiring grounded (earthed) or connections loose in ignition, charging or lighting circuits (Chapter 8).

Battery overcharged

☐ Regulator/rectifier defective. Overcharging is noticed when battery gets excessively warm (Chapter 8).
☐ Battery faulty. Confirm with battery condition check (Chapter 8).
☐ Battery amperage too low, wrong type or size of battery. Install manufacturer's specified amp-hour battery to handle charging load (Chapter 8).

A

ABS (Anti-lock braking system) A system, usually electronically controlled, that senses incipient wheel lockup during braking and relieves hydraulic pressure at wheel which is about to skid.

Aftermarket Components suitable for the motorcycle, but not produced by the motorcycle manufacturer.

Allen key A hexagonal wrench which fits into a recessed hexagonal hole.

Alternating current (ac) Current produced by an alternator. Requires converting to direct current by a rectifier for charging purposes.

Alternator Converts mechanical energy from the engine into electrical energy to charge the battery and power the electrical system.

Ampere (amp) A unit of measurement for the flow of electrical current. Current = Volts ÷ Ohms.

Ampere-hour (Ah) Measure of battery capacity.

Angle-tightening A torque expressed in degrees. Often follows a conventional tightening torque for cylinder head or main bearing fasteners **(see illustration)**.

Angle-tightening cylinder head bolts

Antifreeze A substance (usually ethylene glycol) mixed with water, and added to the cooling system, to prevent freezing of the coolant in winter. Antifreeze also contains chemicals to inhibit corrosion and the formation of rust and other deposits that would tend to clog the radiator and coolant passages and reduce cooling efficiency.

Anti-dive System attached to the fork lower leg (slider) to prevent fork dive when braking hard.

Anti-seize compound A coating that reduces the risk of seizing on fasteners that are subjected to high temperatures, such as exhaust clamp bolts and nuts.

API American Petroleum Institute. A quality standard for 4-stroke motor oils.

Asbestos A natural fibrous mineral with great heat resistance, commonly used in the composition of brake friction materials. Asbestos is a health hazard and the dust created by brake systems should never be inhaled or ingested.

ATF Automatic Transmission Fluid. Often used in front forks.

ATU Automatic Timing Unit. Mechanical device for advancing the ignition timing on early engines.

ATV All Terrain Vehicle. Often called a Quad.

Axial play Side-to-side movement.

Axle A shaft on which a wheel revolves. Also known as a spindle.

B

Backlash The amount of movement between meshed components when one component is held still. Usually applies to gear teeth.

Ball bearing A bearing consisting of a hardened inner and outer race with hardened steel balls between the two races.

Bearings Used between two working surfaces to prevent wear of the components and a build-up of heat. Four types of bearing are commonly used on motorcycles: plain shell bearings, ball bearings, tapered roller bearings and needle roller bearings.

Bevel gears Used to turn the drive through 90°. Typical applications are shaft final drive and camshaft drive **(see illustration)**.

Bevel gears are used to turn the drive through 90°

BHP Brake Horsepower. The British measurement for engine power output. Power output is now usually expressed in kilowatts (kW).

Bias-belted tyre Similar construction to radial tyre, but with outer belt running at an angle to the wheel rim.

Big-end bearing The bearing in the end of the connecting rod that's attached to the crankshaft.

Bleeding The process of removing air from an hydraulic system via a bleed nipple or bleed screw.

Bottom-end A description of an engine's crankcase components and all components contained there-in.

BTDC Before Top Dead Centre in terms of piston position. Ignition timing is often expressed in terms of degrees or millimetres BTDC.

Bush A cylindrical metal or rubber component used between two moving parts.

Burr Rough edge left on a component after machining or as a result of excessive wear.

C

Cam chain The chain which takes drive from the crankshaft to the camshaft(s).

Canister The main component in an evaporative emission control system (California market only); contains activated charcoal granules to trap vapours from the fuel system rather than allowing them to vent to the atmosphere.

Castellated Resembling the parapets along the top of a castle wall. For example, a castellated wheel axle or spindle nut.

Catalytic converter A device in the exhaust system of some machines which converts certain pollutants in the exhaust gases into less harmful substances.

Charging system Description of the components which charge the battery, ie the alternator, rectifier and regulator.

Circlip A ring-shaped clip used to prevent endwise movement of cylindrical parts and shafts. An internal circlip is installed in a groove in a housing; an external circlip fits into a groove on the outside of a cylindrical piece such as a shaft. Also known as a snap-ring.

Clearance The amount of space between two parts. For example, between a piston and a cylinder, between a bearing and a journal, etc.

Coil spring A spiral of elastic steel found in various sizes throughout a vehicle, for example as a springing medium in the suspension and in the valve train.

Compression Reduction in volume, and increase in pressure and temperature, of a gas, caused by squeezing it into a smaller space.

Compression damping Controls the speed the suspension compresses when hitting a bump.

Compression ratio The relationship between cylinder volume when the piston is at top dead centre and cylinder volume when the piston is at bottom dead centre.

Continuity The uninterrupted path in the flow of electricity. Little or no measurable resistance.

Continuity tester Self-powered bleeper or test light which indicates continuity.

Cp Candlepower. Bulb rating commonly found on US motorcycles.

Crossply tyre Tyre plies arranged in a criss-cross pattern. Usually four or six plies used, hence 4PR or 6PR in tyre size codes.

Cush drive Rubber damper segments fitted between the rear wheel and final drive sprocket to absorb transmission shocks **(see illustration)**.

Cush drive rubbers dampen out transmission shocks

D

Degree disc Calibrated disc for measuring piston position. Expressed in degrees.

Dial gauge Clock-type gauge with adapters for measuring runout and piston position. Expressed in mm or inches.

Diaphragm The rubber membrane in a master cylinder or carburettor which seals the upper chamber.

Diaphragm spring A single sprung plate often used in clutches.

Direct current (dc) Current produced by a dc generator.

Decarbonisation The process of removing carbon deposits - typically from the combustion chamber, valves and exhaust port/system.

Detonation Destructive and damaging explosion of fuel/air mixture in combustion chamber instead of controlled burning.

Diode An electrical valve which only allows current to flow in one direction. Commonly used in rectifiers and starter interlock systems.

Disc valve (or rotary valve) A induction system used on some two-stroke engines.

Double-overhead camshaft (DOHC) An engine that uses two overhead camshafts, one for the intake valves and one for the exhaust valves.

Drivebelt A toothed belt used to transmit drive to the rear wheel on some motorcycles. A drivebelt has also been used to drive the camshafts. Drivebelts are usually made of Kevlar.

Driveshaft Any shaft used to transmit motion. Commonly used when referring to the final driveshaft on shaft drive motorcycles.

E

Earth return The return path of an electrical circuit, utilising the motorcycle's frame.

ECU (Electronic Control Unit) A computer which controls (for instance) an ignition system, or an anti-lock braking system.

EGO Exhaust Gas Oxygen sensor. Sometimes called a Lambda sensor.

Electrolyte The fluid in a lead-acid battery.

EMS (Engine Management System) A computer controlled system which manages the fuel injection and the ignition systems in an integrated fashion.

Endfloat The amount of lengthways movement between two parts. As applied to a crankshaft, the distance that the crankshaft can move side-to-side in the crankcase.

Endless chain A chain having no joining link. Common use for cam chains and final drive chains.

EP (Extreme Pressure) Oil type used in locations where high loads are applied, such as between gear teeth.

Evaporative emission control system Describes a charcoal filled canister which stores fuel vapours from the tank rather than allowing them to vent to the atmosphere. Usually only fitted to California models and referred to as an EVAP system.

Expansion chamber Section of two-stroke engine exhaust system so designed to improve engine efficiency and boost power.

F

Feeler blade or gauge A thin strip or blade of hardened steel, ground to an exact thickness, used to check or measure clearances between parts.

Final drive Description of the drive from the transmission to the rear wheel. Usually by chain or shaft, but sometimes by belt.

Firing order The order in which the engine cylinders fire, or deliver their power strokes, beginning with the number one cylinder.

Flooding Term used to describe a high fuel level in the carburettor float chambers, leading to fuel overflow. Also refers to excess fuel in the combustion chamber due to incorrect starting technique.

Free length The no-load state of a component when measured. Clutch, valve and fork spring lengths are measured at rest, without any preload.

Freeplay The amount of travel before any action takes place. The looseness in a linkage, or an assembly of parts, between the initial application of force and actual movement. For example, the distance the rear brake pedal moves before the rear brake is actuated.

Fuel injection The fuel/air mixture is metered electronically and directed into the engine intake ports (indirect injection) or into the cylinders (direct injection). Sensors supply information on engine speed and conditions.

Fuel/air mixture The charge of fuel and air going into the engine. See **Stoichiometric ratio**.

Fuse An electrical device which protects a circuit against accidental overload. The typical fuse contains a soft piece of metal which is calibrated to melt at a predetermined current flow (expressed as amps) and break the circuit.

G

Gap The distance the spark must travel in jumping from the centre electrode to the side electrode in a spark plug. Also refers to the distance between the ignition rotor and the pickup coil in an electronic ignition system.

Gasket Any thin, soft material - usually cork, cardboard, asbestos or soft metal - installed between two metal surfaces to ensure a good seal. For instance, the cylinder head gasket seals the joint between the block and the cylinder head.

Gauge An instrument panel display used to monitor engine conditions. A gauge with a movable pointer on a dial or a fixed scale is an analogue gauge. A gauge with a numerical readout is called a digital gauge.

Gear ratios The drive ratio of a pair of gears in a gearbox, calculated on their number of teeth.

Glaze-busting see **Honing**

Grinding Process for renovating the valve face and valve seat contact area in the cylinder head.

Gudgeon pin The shaft which connects the connecting rod small-end with the piston. Often called a piston pin or wrist pin.

H

Helical gears Gear teeth are slightly curved and produce less gear noise that straight-cut gears. Often used for primary drives.

Installing a Helicoil thread insert in a cylinder head

Helicoil A thread insert repair system. Commonly used as a repair for stripped spark plug threads **(see illustration)**.

Honing A process used to break down the glaze on a cylinder bore (also called glaze-busting). Can also be carried out to roughen a rebored cylinder to aid ring bedding-in.

HT (High Tension) Description of the electrical circuit from the secondary winding of the ignition coil to the spark plug.

Hydraulic A liquid filled system used to transmit pressure from one component to another. Common uses on motorcycles are brakes and clutches.

Hydrometer An instrument for measuring the specific gravity of a lead-acid battery.

Hygroscopic Water absorbing. In motorcycle applications, braking efficiency will be reduced if DOT 3 or 4 hydraulic fluid absorbs water from the air - care must be taken to keep new brake fluid in tightly sealed containers.

I

lbf ft Pounds-force feet. An imperial unit of torque. Sometimes written as ft-lbs.

lbf in Pound-force inch. An imperial unit of torque, applied to components where a very low torque is required. Sometimes written as in-lbs.

IC Abbreviation for Integrated Circuit.

Ignition advance Means of increasing the timing of the spark at higher engine speeds. Done by mechanical means (ATU) on early engines or electronically by the ignition control unit on later engines.

Ignition timing The moment at which the spark plug fires, expressed in the number of crankshaft degrees before the piston reaches the top of its stroke, or in the number of millimetres before the piston reaches the top of its stroke.

Infinity (∞) Description of an open-circuit electrical state, where no continuity exists.

Inverted forks (upside down forks) The sliders or lower legs are held in the yokes and the fork tubes or stanchions are connected to the wheel axle (spindle). Less unsprung weight and stiffer construction than conventional forks.

J

JASO Quality standard for 2-stroke oils.

Joule The unit of electrical energy.

Journal The bearing surface of a shaft.

K

Kickstart Mechanical means of turning the engine over for starting purposes. Only usually fitted to mopeds, small capacity motorcycles and off-road motorcycles.

Kill switch Handebar-mounted switch for emergency ignition cut-out. Cuts the ignition circuit on all models, and additionally prevent starter motor operation on others.

km Symbol for kilometre.

kmh Abbreviation for kilometres per hour.

L

Lambda (λ) sensor A sensor fitted in the exhaust system to measure the exhaust gas oxygen content (excess air factor).

Lapping see **Grinding**.
LCD Abbreviation for Liquid Crystal Display.
LED Abbreviation for Light Emitting Diode.
Liner A steel cylinder liner inserted in a aluminium alloy cylinder block.
Locknut A nut used to lock an adjustment nut, or other threaded component, in place.
Lockstops The lugs on the lower triple clamp (yoke) which abut those on the frame, preventing handlebar-to-fuel tank contact.
Lockwasher A form of washer designed to prevent an attaching nut from working loose.
LT Low Tension Description of the electrical circuit from the power supply to the primary winding of the ignition coil.

M

Main bearings The bearings between the crankshaft and crankcase.
Maintenance-free (MF) battery A sealed battery which cannot be topped up.
Manometer Mercury-filled calibrated tubes used to measure intake tract vacuum. Used to synchronise carburettors on multi-cylinder engines.
Micrometer A precision measuring instrument that measures component outside diameters **(see illustration)**.

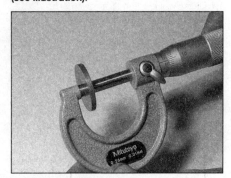

Tappet shims are measured with a micrometer

MON (Motor Octane Number) A measure of a fuel's resistance to knock.
Monograde oil An oil with a single viscosity, eg SAE80W.
Monoshock A single suspension unit linking the swingarm or suspension linkage to the frame.
mph Abbreviation for miles per hour.
Multigrade oil Having a wide viscosity range (eg 10W40). The W stands for Winter, thus the viscosity ranges from SAE10 when cold to SAE40 when hot.
Multimeter An electrical test instrument with the capability to measure voltage, current and resistance. Some meters also incorporate a continuity tester and buzzer.

N

Needle roller bearing Inner race of caged needle rollers and hardened outer race. Examples of uncaged needle rollers can be found on some engines. Commonly used in rear suspension applications and in two-stroke engines.
Nm Newton metres.
NOx Oxides of Nitrogen. A common toxic pollutant emitted by petrol engines at higher temperatures.

O

Octane The measure of a fuel's resistance to knock.
OE (Original Equipment) Relates to components fitted to a motorcycle as standard or replacement parts supplied by the motorcycle manufacturer.
Ohm The unit of electrical resistance. Ohms = Volts ÷ Current.
Ohmmeter An instrument for measuring electrical resistance.
Oil cooler System for diverting engine oil outside of the engine to a radiator for cooling purposes.
Oil injection A system of two-stroke engine lubrication where oil is pump-fed to the engine in accordance with throttle position.
Open-circuit An electrical condition where there is a break in the flow of electricity - no continuity (high resistance).
O-ring A type of sealing ring made of a special rubber-like material; in use, the O-ring is compressed into a groove to provide the sealing action.
Oversize (OS) Term used for piston and ring size options fitted to a rebored cylinder.
Overhead cam (sohc) engine An engine with single camshaft located on top of the cylinder head.
Overhead valve (ohv) engine An engine with the valves located in the cylinder head, but with the camshaft located in the engine block or crankcase.
Oxygen sensor A device installed in the exhaust system which senses the oxygen content in the exhaust and converts this information into an electric current. Also called a Lambda sensor.

P

Plastigauge A thin strip of plastic thread, available in different sizes, used for measuring clearances. For example, a strip of Plastigauge is laid across a bearing journal. The parts are assembled and dismantled; the width of the crushed strip indicates the clearance between journal and bearing.
Polarity Either negative or positive earth (ground), determined by which battery lead is connected to the frame (earth return). Modern motorcycles are usually negative earth.
Pre-ignition A situation where the fuel/air mixture ignites before the spark plug fires. Often due to a hot spot in the combustion chamber caused by carbon build-up. Engine has a tendency to 'run-on'.
Pre-load (suspension) The amount a spring is compressed when in the unloaded state. Preload can be applied by gas, spacer or mechanical adjuster.
Premix The method of engine lubrication on older two-stroke engines. Engine oil is mixed with the petrol in the fuel tank in a specific ratio. The fuel/oil mix is sometimes referred to as "petroil".
Primary drive Description of the drive from the crankshaft to the clutch. Usually by gear or chain.
PS Pfedestärke - a German interpretation of BHP.
PSI Pounds-force per square inch. Imperial measurement of tyre pressure and cylinder pressure measurement.
PTFE Polytetrafluroethylene. A low friction substance.

Pulse secondary air injection system A process of promoting the burning of excess fuel present in the exhaust gases by routing fresh air into the exhaust ports.

Q

Quartz halogen bulb Tungsten filament surrounded by a halogen gas. Typically used for the headlight **(see illustration)**.

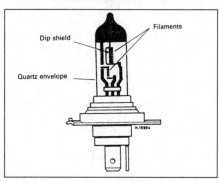

Quartz halogen headlight bulb construction

R

Rack-and-pinion A pinion gear on the end of a shaft that mates with a rack (think of a geared wheel opened up and laid flat). Sometimes used in clutch operating systems.
Radial play Up and down movement about a shaft.
Radial ply tyres Tyre plies run across the tyre (from bead to bead) and around the circumference of the tyre. Less resistant to tread distortion than other tyre types.
Radiator A liquid-to-air heat transfer device designed to reduce the temperature of the coolant in a liquid cooled engine.
Rake A feature of steering geometry - the angle of the steering head in relation to the vertical **(see illustration)**.

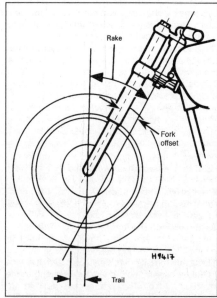

Steering geometry

Rebore Providing a new working surface to the cylinder bore by boring out the old surface. Necessitates the use of oversize piston and rings.

Rebound damping A means of controlling the oscillation of a suspension unit spring after it has been compressed. Resists the spring's natural tendency to bounce back after being compressed.

Rectifier Device for converting the ac output of an alternator into dc for battery charging.

Reed valve An induction system commonly used on two-stroke engines.

Regulator Device for maintaining the charging voltage from the generator or alternator within a specified range.

Relay A electrical device used to switch heavy current on and off by using a low current auxiliary circuit.

Resistance Measured in ohms. An electrical component's ability to pass electrical current.

RON (Research Octane Number) A measure of a fuel's resistance to knock.

rpm revolutions per minute.

Runout The amount of wobble (in-and-out movement) of a wheel or shaft as it's rotated. The amount a shaft rotates 'out-of-true'. The out-of-round condition of a rotating part.

S

SAE (Society of Automotive Engineers) A standard for the viscosity of a fluid.

Sealant A liquid or paste used to prevent leakage at a joint. Sometimes used in conjunction with a gasket.

Service limit Term for the point where a component is no longer useable and must be renewed.

Shaft drive A method of transmitting drive from the transmission to the rear wheel.

Shell bearings Plain bearings consisting of two shell halves. Most often used as big-end and main bearings in a four-stroke engine. Often called bearing inserts.

Shim Thin spacer, commonly used to adjust the clearance or relative positions between two parts. For example, shims inserted into or under tappets or followers to control valve clearances. Clearance is adjusted by changing the thickness of the shim.

Short-circuit An electrical condition where current shorts to earth (ground) bypassing the circuit components.

Skimming Process to correct warpage or repair a damaged surface, eg on brake discs or drums.

Slide-hammer A special puller that screws into or hooks onto a component such as a shaft or bearing; a heavy sliding handle on the shaft bottoms against the end of the shaft to knock the component free.

Small-end bearing The bearing in the upper end of the connecting rod at its joint with the gudgeon pin.

Spalling Damage to camshaft lobes or bearing journals shown as pitting of the working surface.

Specific gravity (SG) The state of charge of the electrolyte in a lead-acid battery. A measure of the electrolyte's density compared with water.

Straight-cut gears Common type gear used on gearbox shafts and for oil pump and water pump drives.

Stanchion The inner sliding part of the front forks, held by the yokes. Often called a fork tube.

Stoichiometric ratio The optimum chemical air/fuel ratio for a petrol engine, said to be 14.7 parts of air to 1 part of fuel.

Sulphuric acid The liquid (electrolyte) used in a lead-acid battery. Poisonous and extremely corrosive.

Surface grinding (lapping) Process to correct a warped gasket face, commonly used on cylinder heads.

T

Tapered-roller bearing Tapered inner race of caged needle rollers and separate tapered outer race. Examples of taper roller bearings can be found on steering heads.

Tappet A cylindrical component which transmits motion from the cam to the valve stem, either directly or via a pushrod and rocker arm. Also called a cam follower.

TCS Traction Control System. An electronically-controlled system which senses wheel spin and reduces engine speed accordingly.

TDC Top Dead Centre denotes that the piston is at its highest point in the cylinder.

Thread-locking compound Solution applied to fastener threads to prevent slackening. Select type to suit application.

Thrust washer A washer positioned between two moving components on a shaft. For example, between gear pinions on gearshaft.

Timing chain See **Cam Chain.**

Timing light Stroboscopic lamp for carrying out ignition timing checks with the engine running.

Top-end A description of an engine's cylinder block, head and valve gear components.

Torque Turning or twisting force about a shaft.

Torque setting A prescribed tightness specified by the motorcycle manufacturer to ensure that the bolt or nut is secured correctly. Undertightening can result in the bolt or nut coming loose or a surface not being sealed. Overtightening can result in stripped threads, distortion or damage to the component being retained.

Torx key A six-point wrench.

Tracer A stripe of a second colour applied to a wire insulator to distinguish that wire from another one with the same colour insulator. For example, Br/W is often used to denote a brown insulator with a white tracer.

Trail A feature of steering geometry. Distance from the steering head axis to the tyre's central contact point.

Triple clamps The cast components which extend from the steering head and support the fork stanchions or tubes. Often called fork yokes.

Turbocharger A centrifugal device, driven by exhaust gases, that pressurises the intake air. Normally used to increase the power output from a given engine displacement.

TWI Abbreviation for Tyre Wear Indicator. Indicates the location of the tread depth indicator bars on tyres.

U

Universal joint or U-joint (UJ) A double-pivoted connection for transmitting power from a driving to a driven shaft through an angle. Typically found in shaft drive assemblies.

Unsprung weight Anything not supported by the bike's suspension (ie the wheel, tyres, brakes, final drive and bottom (moving) part of the suspension).

V

Vacuum gauges Clock-type gauges for measuring intake tract vacuum. Used for carburettor synchronisation on multi-cylinder engines.

Valve A device through which the flow of liquid, gas or vacuum may be stopped, started or regulated by a moveable part that opens, shuts or partially obstructs one or more ports or passageways. The intake and exhaust valves in the cylinder head are of the poppet type.

Valve clearance The clearance between the valve tip (the end of the valve stem) and the rocker arm or tappet/follower. The valve clearance is measured when the valve is closed. The correct clearance is important - if too small the valve won't close fully and will burn out, whereas if too large noisy operation will result.

Valve lift The amount a valve is lifted off its seat by the camshaft lobe.

Valve timing The exact setting for the opening and closing of the valves in relation to piston position.

Vernier caliper A precision measuring instrument that measures inside and outside dimensions. Not quite as accurate as a micrometer, but more convenient.

VIN Vehicle Identification Number. Term for the bike's engine and frame numbers.

Viscosity The thickness of a liquid or its resistance to flow.

Volt A unit for expressing electrical "pressure" in a circuit. Volts = current x ohms.

W

Water pump A mechanically-driven device for moving coolant around the engine.

Watt A unit for expressing electrical power. Watts = volts x current.

Wear limit see **Service limit**

Wet liner A liquid-cooled engine design where the pistons run in liners which are directly surrounded by coolant **(see illustration).**

Wet liner arrangement

Wheelbase Distance from the centre of the front wheel to the centre of the rear wheel.

Wiring harness or loom Describes the electrical wires running the length of the motorcycle and enclosed in tape or plastic sheathing. Wiring coming off the main harness is usually referred to as a sub harness.

Woodruff key A key of semi-circular or square section used to locate a gear to a shaft. Often used to locate the alternator rotor on the crankshaft.

Wrist pin Another name for gudgeon or piston pin.

Note: *References throughout this index are in the form - "Chapter number" • "Page number"*

Haynes Motorcycle Manuals – The Complete List

Title	Book No
APRILIA RS50 (99 - 06) & RS125 (93 - 06)	4298
Aprilia RSV1000 Mille (98 - 03)	◆ 4255
BMW 2-valve Twins (70 - 96)	◆ 0249
BMW K100 & 75 2-valve Models (83 - 96)	◆ 1373
BMW R850, 1100 & 1150 4-valve Twins (93 - 04)	◆ 3466
BMW R1200 (04 - 06)	◆ 4598
BSA Bantam (48 - 71)	0117
BSA Unit Singles (58 - 72)	0127
BSA Pre-unit Singles (54 - 61)	0326
BSA A7 & A10 Twins (47 - 62)	0121
BSA A50 & A65 Twins (62 - 73)	0155
DUCATI 600, 620, 750 and 900 2-valve V-Twins (91 - 05)	◆ 3290
Ducati MK III & Desmo Singles (69 - 76)	◇ 0445
Ducati 748, 916 & 996 4-valve V-Twins (94 - 01)	◆ 3756
GILERA Runner, DNA, Ice & SKP/Stalker (97 - 07)	4163
HARLEY-DAVIDSON Sportsters (70 - 03)	◆ 2534
Harley-Davidson Shovelhead and Evolution Big Twins (70 - 99)	◆ 2536
Harley-Davidson Twin Cam 88 (99 - 03)	◆ 2478
HONDA NB, ND, NP & NS50 Melody (81 - 85)	◇ 0622
Honda NE/NB50 Vision & SA50 Vision Met-in (85 - 95)	◇ 1278
Honda MB, MBX, MT & MTX50 (80 - 93)	0731
Honda C50, C70 & C90 (67 - 03)	0324
Honda XR80/100R & CRF80/100F (85 - 04)	2218
Honda XL/XR 80, 100, 125, 185 & 200 2-valve Models (78 - 87)	0566
Honda H100 & H100S Singles (80 - 92)	◇ 0734
Honda CB/CD125T & CM125C Twins (77 - 88)	◇ 0571
Honda CG125 (76 - 07)	◇ 0433
Honda NS125 (86 - 93)	◇ 3056
Honda CBR125R (04 - 07)	4620
Honda MBX/MTX125 & MTX200 (83 - 93)	◇ 1132
Honda CD/CM185 200T & CM250C 2-valve Twins (77 - 85)	0572
Honda XL/XR 250 & 500 (78 - 84)	0567
Honda XR250L, XR250R & XR400R (86 - 03)	2219
Honda CB250 & CB400N Super Dreams (78 - 84)	◇ 0540
Honda CR Motocross Bikes (86 - 01)	2222
Honda CRF250 & CRF450 (02 - 06)	2630
Honda CBR400RR Fours (88 - 99)	◇ ◆ 3552
Honda VFR400 (NC30) & RVF400 (NC35) V-Fours (89 - 98)	◇ ◆ 3496
Honda CB500 (93 - 01)	3753
Honda CB400 & CB550 Fours (73 - 77)	0262
Honda CX/GL500 & 650 V-Twins (78 - 86)	0442
Honda CBX550 Four (82 - 86)	◇ 0940
Honda XL600R & XR600R (83 - 00)	2183
Honda XL600/650V Transalp & XRV750 Africa Twin (87 to 07)	◆ 3919
Honda CBR600F1 & 1000F Fours (87 - 96)	◆ 1730
Honda CBR600F2 & F3 Fours (91 - 98)	◆ 2070
Honda CBR600F4 (99 - 06)	◆ 3911
Honda CB600F Hornet & CBF600 (98 - 06)	◇ ◆ 3915
Honda CBR600RR (03 - 06)	◆ 4590
Honda CB650 sohc Fours (78 - 84)	0665
Honda NTV600 Revere, NTV650 and NT650V Deauville (88 - 05)	◇ ◆ 3243
Honda Shadow VT600 & 750 (USA) (88 - 03)	2312
Honda CB750 sohc Four (69 - 79)	0131
Honda V45/65 Sabre & Magna (82 - 88)	0820
Honda VFR750 & 700 V-Fours (86 - 97)	◆ 2101
Honda VFR800 V-Fours (97 - 01)	◆ 3703
Honda VFR800 V-Tec V-Fours (02 - 05)	◆ 4196
Honda CB750 & CB900 dohc Fours (78 - 84)	0535
Honda VTR1000 (FireStorm, Super Hawk) & XL1000V (Varadero) (97 - 00)	◆ 3744
Honda CBR900RR FireBlade (92 - 99)	◆ 2161
Honda CBR900RR FireBlade (00 - 03)	◆ 4060
Honda CBR1000RR Fireblade (04 - 07)	◆ 4604
Honda CBR1100XX Super Blackbird (97 - 07)	◆ 3901
Honda ST1100 Pan European V-Fours (90 - 02)	◆ 3384
Honda Shadow VT1100 (USA) (85 - 98)	2313
Honda GL1000 Gold Wing (75 - 79)	0309
Honda GL1100 Gold Wing (79 - 81)	0669
Honda Gold Wing 1200 (USA) (84 - 87)	2199
Honda Gold Wing 1500 (USA) (88 - 00)	2225
KAWASAKI AE/AR 50 & 80 (81 - 95)	1007
Kawasaki KC, KE & KH100 (75 - 99)	1371
Kawasaki KMX125 & 200 (86 - 02)	◇ 3046
Kawasaki 250, 350 & 400 Triples (72 - 79)	0134
Kawasaki 400 & 440 Twins (74 - 81)	0281
Kawasaki 400, 500 & 550 Fours (79 - 91)	0910
Kawasaki EN450 & 500 Twins (Ltd/Vulcan) (85 - 04)	2053
Kawasaki EX500 (GPZ500S) & ER500 (ER-5) (87 - 05)	◆ 2052
Kawasaki ZX600 (ZZ-R600 & Ninja ZX-6) (90 - 06)	◆ 2146
Kawasaki ZX-6R Ninja Fours (95 - 02)	◆ 3541
Kawasaki ZX-6R (03 - 06)	◆ 4742
Kawasaki ZX600 (GPZ600R, GPX600R, Ninja 600R & RX) & ZX750 (GPX750R, Ninja 750R)	◆ 1780
Kawasaki 650 Four (76 - 78)	0373
Kawasaki Vulcan 700/750 & 800 (85 - 04)	◆ 2457
Kawasaki 750 Air-cooled Fours (80 - 91)	0574
Kawasaki ZR550 & 750 Zephyr Fours (90 - 97)	◆ 3382
Kawasaki Z750 & Z1000 (03 - 08)	◆ 4762
Kawasaki ZX750 (Ninja ZX-7 & ZXR750) Fours (89 - 96)	◆ 2054
Kawasaki Ninja ZX-7R & ZX-9R (94 - 04)	◆ 3721
Kawasaki 900 & 1000 Fours (73 - 77)	0222
Kawasaki ZX900, 1000 & 1100 Liquid-cooled Fours (83 - 97)	◆ 1681
KTM EXC Enduro & SX Motocross (00 - 07)	◆ 4629
MOTO GUZZI 750, 850 & 1000 V-Twins (74 - 78)	0339
MZ ETZ Models (81 - 95)	◇ 1680
NORTON 500, 600, 650 & 750 Twins (57 - 70)	0187
Norton Commando (68 - 77)	0125
PEUGEOT Speedfight, Trekker & Vivacity Scooters (96 - 05)	◇ 3920
PIAGGIO (Vespa) Scooters (91 - 06)	◆ 3492
SUZUKI GT, ZR & TS50 (77 - 90)	◇ 0799
Suzuki TS50X (84 - 00)	◇ 1599
Suzuki 100, 125, 185 & 250 Air-cooled Trail bikes (79 - 89)	0797
Suzuki GP100 & 125 Singles (78 - 93)	◇ 0576
Suzuki GS, GN, GZ & DR125 Singles (82 - 05)	◇ 0888
Suzuki 250 & 350 Twins (68 - 78)	0120
Suzuki GT250X7, GT200X5 & SB200 Twins (78 - 83)	◇ 0469
Suzuki GS/GSX250, 400 & 450 Twins (79 - 85)	0736
Suzuki GS500 Twin (89 - 06)	◆ 3238
Suzuki GS550 (77 - 82) & GS750 Fours (76 - 79)	0363
Suzuki GS/GSX550 4-valve Fours (83 - 88)	1133
Suzuki SV650 & SV650S (99 - 05)	◆ 3912
Suzuki GSX-R600 & 750 (96 - 00)	◆ 3553
Suzuki GSX-R600 (01 - 03), GSX-R750 (00 - 03) & GSX-R1000 (01 - 02)	◆ 3986
Suzuki GSX-R600/750 (04 - 05) & GSX-R1000 (03 - 06)	◆ 4382
Suzuki GSF600, 650 & 1200 Bandit Fours (95 - 06)	◆ 3367
Suzuki Intruder, Marauder, Volusia & Boulevard (85 - 06)	◆ 2618
Suzuki GS850 Fours (78 - 88)	0536
Suzuki GS1000 Four (77 - 79)	0484
Suzuki GSX-R750, GSX-R1100 (85 - 92), GSX600F, GSX750F, GSX1100F (Katana) Fours	◆ 2055
Suzuki GSX600/750F & GSX750 (98 - 06)	◆ 3987
Suzuki GS/GSX1000, 1100 & 1150 4-valve Fours (79 - 88)	0737
Suzuki TL1000S/R & DL1000 V-Strom (97 - 04)	◆ 4083
Suzuki GSX1300R Hayabusa (99 - 04)	◆ 4184
Suzuki GSX1400 (02 - 07)	◆ 4758
TRIUMPH Tiger Cub & Terrier (52 - 68)	0414
Triumph 350 & 500 Unit Twins (58 - 73)	0137
Triumph Pre-Unit Twins (47 - 62)	0251
Triumph 650 & 750 2-valve Unit Twins (63 - 83)	0122
Triumph Trident & BSA Rocket 3 (69 - 75)	0136
Triumph Bonneville (01 - 07)	◆ 4364
Triumph Daytona, Speed Triple, Sprint & Tiger (97 - 05)	◆ 3755
Triumph Triples and Fours (carburettor engines) (91 - 04)	◆ 2162
VESPA P/PX125, 150 & 200 Scooters (78 - 06)	0707
Vespa Scooters (59 - 78)	0126
YAMAHA DT50 & 80 Trail Bikes (78 - 95)	◇ 0800
Yamaha T50 & 80 Townmate (83 - 95)	◇ 1247
Yamaha YB100 Singles (73 - 91)	◇ 0474
Yamaha RS/RXS100 & 125 Singles (74 - 95)	0331
Yamaha RD & DT125LC (82 - 87)	◇ 0887
Yamaha TZR125 (87 - 93) & DT125R (88 - 02)	◇ 1655
Yamaha TY50, 80, 125 & 175 (74 - 84)	◇ 0464
Yamaha XT & SR125 (82 - 03)	◇ 1021
Yamaha Trail Bikes (81 - 00)	2350
Yamaha 2-stroke Motocross Bikes 1986 - 2006	2662
Yamaha YZ & WR 4-stroke Motocross Bikes (98 - 07)	2689
Yamaha 250 & 350 Twins (70 - 79)	0040
Yamaha XS250, 360 & 400 sohc Twins (75 - 84)	0378
Yamaha RD250 & 350LC Twins (80 - 82)	0803
Yamaha RD350 YPVS Twins (83 - 95)	1158
Yamaha RD400 Twin (75 - 79)	0333
Yamaha XT, TT & SR500 Singles (75 - 83)	0342
Yamaha XZ550 Vision V-Twins (82 - 85)	0821
Yamaha FJ, FZ, XJ & YX600 Radian (84 - 92)	2100
Yamaha XJ600S (Diversion, Seca II) & XJ600N Fours (92 - 03)	◆ 2145
Yamaha YZF600R Thundercat & FZS600 Fazer (96 - 03)	◆ 3702
Yamaha FZ-6 Fazer (04 - 07)	◆ 4751
Yamaha YZF-R6 (99 - 02)	◆ 3900
Yamaha YZF-R6 (03 - 05)	◆ 4601
Yamaha 650 Twins (70 - 83)	0341
Yamaha XJ650 & 750 Fours (80 - 84)	0738
Yamaha XS750 & 850 Triples (76 - 85)	0340
Yamaha TDM850, TRX850 & XTZ750 (89 - 99)	◇ ◆ 3540
Yamaha YZF750R & YZF1000R Thunderace (93 - 00)	◆ 3720
Yamaha FZR600, 750 & 1000 Fours (87 - 96)	◆ 2056
Yamaha XV (Virago) V-Twins (81 - 03)	◆ 0802
Yamaha XVS650 & 1100 Drag Star/V-Star (97 - 05)	◆ 4195
Yamaha XJ900F Fours (83 - 94)	◆ 3239
Yamaha XJ900S Diversion (94 - 01)	◆ 3739
Yamaha YZF-R1 (98 - 03)	◆ 3754
Yamaha YZF-R1 (04 - 06)	◆ 4605
Yamaha FZS1000 Fazer (01 - 05)	◆ 4287
Yamaha FJ1100 & 1200 Fours (84 - 96)	◆ 2057
Yamaha XJR1200 & 1300 (95 - 06)	◆ 3981
Yamaha V-Max (85 - 03)	◆ 4072

ATVs

Title	Book No
Honda ATC70, 90, 110, 185 & 200 (71 - 85)	0565
Honda Rancher, Recon & TRX250EX ATVs	2553
Honda TRX300 Shaft Drive ATVs (88 - 00)	2125
Honda TRX300EX, TRX400EX & TRX450R/ER ATVs (93 - 06)	2318
Kawasaki Bayou 220/250/300 & Prairie 300 ATVs (86 - 03)	2351
Polaris ATVs (85 - 97)	2302
Polaris ATVs (98 - 06)	2508
Yamaha YFS200 Blaster ATV (88 - 02)	2317
Yamaha YFB250 Timberwolf ATVs (92 - 00)	2217
Yamaha YFM350 & YFM400 (ER and Big Bear) ATVs (87 - 03)	2126
Yamaha Banshee and Warrior ATVs (87 - 03)	2314
Yamaha Kodiak and Grizzly ATVs (93 - 05)	2567
ATV Basics	10450

TECHBOOK SERIES

Title	Book No
Twist and Go (automatic transmission) Scooters Service and Repair Manual	4082
Motorcycle Basics TechBook (2nd Edition)	3515
Motorcycle Electrical TechBook (3rd Edition)	3471
Motorcycle Fuel Systems TechBook	3514
Motorcycle Maintenance TechBook	4071
Motorcycle Modifying	4272
Motorcycle Workshop Practice TechBook (2nd Edition)	3470

◇ = not available in the USA   ◆ = Superbike

The manuals on this page are available through good motorcycle dealers and accessory shops.
In case of difficulty, contact: **Haynes Publishing**
(UK) +44 1963 442030   (USA) +1 805 498 6703
(SV) +46 18 124016
(Australia/New Zealand) +61 3 9763 8100

MCL23.12/07

Preserving Our Motoring Heritage

< *The Model J Duesenberg Derham Tourster. Only eight of these magnificent cars were ever built – this is the only example to be found outside the United States of America*

Almost every car you've ever loved, loathed or desired is gathered under one roof at the Haynes Motor Museum. Over 300 immaculately presented cars and motorbikes represent every aspect of our motoring heritage, from elegant reminders of bygone days, such as the superb Model J Duesenberg to curiosities like the bug-eyed BMW Isetta. There are also many old friends and flames. Perhaps you remember the 1959 Ford Popular that you did your courting in? The magnificent 'Red Collection' is a spectacle of classic sports cars including AC, Alfa Romeo, Austin Healey, Ferrari, Lamborghini, Maserati, MG, Riley, Porsche and Triumph.

A Perfect Day Out

Each and every vehicle at the Haynes Motor Museum has played its part in the history and culture of Motoring. Today, they make a wonderful spectacle and a great day out for all the family. Bring the kids, bring Mum and Dad, but above all bring your camera to capture those golden memories for ever. You will also find an impressive array of motoring memorabilia, a comfortable 70 seat video cinema and one of the most extensive transport book shops in Britain. The Pit Stop Cafe serves everything from a cup of tea to wholesome, home-made meals or, if you prefer, you can enjoy the large picnic area nestled in the beautiful rural surroundings of Somerset.

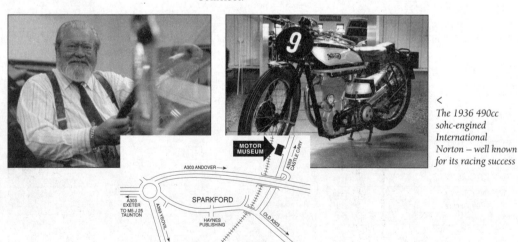

> *John Haynes O.B.E., Founder and Chairman of the museum at the wheel of a Haynes Light 12.*

< *The 1936 490cc sohc-engined International Norton – well known for its racing success*

The Museum is situated on the A359 Yeovil to Frome road at Sparkford, just off the A303 in Somerset. It is about 40 miles south of Bristol, and 25 minutes drive from the M5 intersection at Taunton.

Open 9.30am - 5.30pm (10.00am - 4.00pm Winter) 7 days a week, *except Christmas Day, Boxing Day and New Years Day*

Special rates available for schools, coach parties and outings Charitable Trust No. 292048